NEW YORK FAMILY LAW
for Legal Assistants

Sara P. Schechter

Judge, New York Family Court
Adjunct Professor, New York City Technical College, CUNY

D0074039

West
I(T)P® An International Thomson Publishing Company

Minneapolis/St. Paul • Albany • Bonn • Boston • Cincinnati • Detroit • London
• Madrid • Melbourne • Mexico City • New York • Pacific Grove • Paris
• San Francisco • Singapore • Tokyo • Toronto • Washington

Cover Image: From the collection of the Staten Island Institute of Arts and Sciences, NY.

Cover Design: Eric Mueller, Eric Mueller Design, NY.

Permission to reprint the form in Figure 3-2 has been granted by the copyright holder, Lawyers Cooperative Publishing, a division of Thomson Legal Publishing Inc.

WEST'S COMMITMENT TO THE ENVIRONMENT

In 1906, West Publishing Company began recycling materials left over from the production of books. This began a tradition of efficient and responsible use of resources. Today, 100% of our legal bound volumes are printed on acid-free, recycled paper consisting of 50% new fibers. West recycles nearly 27,700,000 pounds of scrap paper annually—the equivalent of 229,300 trees. Since the 1960s, West has devised ways to capture and recycle waste inks, solvents, oils, and vapors created in the printing process. We also recycle plastics of all kinds, wood, glass, corrugated cardboard, and batteries, and have eliminated the use of polystyrene book packaging. We at West are proud of the longevity and the scope of our commitment to the environment.

West pocket parts and advance sheets are printed on recyclable paper and can be collected and recycled with newspapers. Staples do not have to be removed. Bound volumes can be recycled after removing the cover.

Production, Prepress, Printing and Binding by West Publishing Company.

 TEXT IS PRINTED ON 10% POST CONSUMER RECYCLED PAPER   ∞

British Library Calaloguiing-in-Publication Data. A catalogue for this book is available from the Britich Library.

ISBN 0–314–20622–1

CONTENTS IN BRIEF

CONTENTS

TABLE OF CASES

Excerpted cases are in bold type. Cases cited in excerpted cases and within other quoted materials are not included.

PREFACE

No textbook can replace the interaction between a good teacher and a conscientious student. The primary aim of this New York-specific textbook is to facilitate that interaction by liberating instructor and student from the tedium of lecturing and note taking, freeing class time for all the other pedagogic strategies that bring the law to life.

Since state-specific textbooks are still a rarity, this may be the only one the students use in their entire course of study. Thus, the book seeks to review and consolidate the student's knowledge of New York's court system, procedure, terminology, and citation form, as well as to provide a solid foundation in Family Law. The focus on New York is not myopic, however. Where New York is significantly out of step with the rest of the world, whether it is in the vanguard of a new trend or steadfastly upholding tradition, that fact is noted. Issues of current nationwide debate are presented in their national context, and federal legislation is discussed.

Legal Assistant Studies programs vary in their length, curricula and admission requirements. Legal Assistant students also vary in their educational backgrounds, their aspirations for future employment and further education, and in the life experiences they bring to the classroom. The instructors, too, have various professional backgrounds and a healthy range of opinions about the relative emphasis that should be accorded to drafting, research, discussion, practical applications, and role-playing in the Family Law course. This textbook strives to be a flexible tool that can be adapted to the teaching and learning styles of instructors and students across this spectrum.

While it is assumed that most students will have had introductory courses in Paralegalism, Civil Procedure, and Legal Research before taking Family Law, basic concepts and key terms are reviewed as they naturally arise. Statutory and case citations within the text serve not only as authority for the propositions they support, but also as keys for further research. The Practice Tips provide guidance for the practical application of the law, while the Discussion Topics raise theoretical and philosophical issues. Since New York forms and excerpts of New York cases are integrated into the text, the learning experience should be one of natural absorption rather than force feeding.

The Family Law course offers an unparalleled opportunity for students to be drawn into the law. We are all members of a family, and each of us brings a natural interest and intuitive understanding to this area of law. Ironically, it is also the area where the law seeks to regulate that which is most ungovernable, the primal passions at the very core of our humanity. Above all, this textbook endeavors to capture the tension, comedy, violence, tenderness, and sheer inspiration of that drama.

ACKNOWLEDGMENTS

Without the encouragement and support of friends, colleagues, and children who unceasingly champion their mother's cause, this textbook would have remained a pipedream. The author gratefully acknowledges the contributions of Rachael Adams, Frank Argano, Curt Arnel, Samaad Bishop, Ivy Cook, Charles Coleman, Mary Kay Conwell, John Eyerman, Jill Hyman, Marcia Jones, Arlene Kayatt, George Kelly, Pat Maniscalco, Concetta Mennella, Michael Milsap, Eric Mueller, Douglas Reiniger, Laura Scott, Sharon Scott, Gerald Sheindlin, Kim Susser, Valerie Wolfman, and the reviewers, whose guidance and generous suggestions are reflected throughout the book:

Raymond Canals
Bronx Community College

Gregory Dalton
Corning Community College

Catherine R. Johns
Genesee Community College

Helene Kulczycki
Briarcliffe College

Leslie S. Lowenstein
Baruch College

Scott F. Myers
Marist College

Lillian O'Reilly
Berkeley College

Susan Sadinsky
Bryant & Stratton Business College

Robert A. Sarachan
Tompkins Cortland Community College

Heather A. Scher
Bryant & Stratton Business College

Roger Stone
Hilbert College

Mary A. Whiting
Brooklyn College

1 INTRODUCTION

"Several distinctly different types of families already coexisted in Colonial times: On the East Coast, the Iroquois lived in longhouses with large extended families. Small families were more common among the nomadic Indian groups... African American slaves, whose nuclear families had been torn apart, built extended family networks through ritual coparenting, the adoption of orphans, and complex naming patterns designed to preserve links among families across space and time. White Colonial families were also diverse: High death rates meant that a majority spent some time in a stepfamily." Coontz, Stephanie (1996) "Where Are the Good Old Days?" *Modern Maturity*, 39.3 (May/June 1996): 38.

WHAT IS A FAMILY?

TRADITIONAL FAMILIES

Families come in so many sizes and shapes that the law is not always sure it recognizes one when it sees it. The traditional definition of a family is persons related by **consanguinity** or **affinity**. Consanguinity is blood relationship, while affinity is relationship established by law, through marriage or adoption. When two people marry, they form a legal relationship not only with each other as spouses, but with their in-laws and step-children. Similarly, the law gives an adoptive child not only new parents, but an entire set of kin -- grandparents, aunts and uncles, cousins, and perhaps siblings.

Even using the traditional definition of family, the field is crowded with players, and balancing the needs and rights of so many individuals has always been challenging for the law. Think of planning a large family gathering such as a wedding. There are many tough decisions: If you invite the bride's second cousins, with whom she has been close from childhood, do you also have to invite the groom's first cousins, to whom he barely speaks but who are great favorites of the groom's grandmother? Should you be influenced by the anticipated size of the wedding gift when you decide whom to invite, and if you do not invite the groom's cousins, might his grandmother cut him out of her will?

These are the headaches of family life and ultimately, of family law, deciding who is included and who should have pride of place. How do we even begin to sort it all out? Is it relevant that the bride's cousins are only second cousins, while the groom's cousins are first cousins, or should all cousins go into the same tier on the invitation list? Does the bride's affection for her cousins outweigh the groom's grandmother's fondness for his cousins? The wedding is the bride's special day, but the groom's grandmother's age and senior position in the family entitle her to respect. Should you take a short-term or a long-term view? At the moment, the young couple are adamant that they want only the bride's cousins at the wedding, but will they be sorry later that they missed out on a substantial wedding gift or got left out of Grandma's will?

Family Law deals with issues like these on a broader scale, and sometimes its rules may surprise you. In Chapter 13 you will learn, for example, that although a biological parent has no right to visitation with the child after adoption, the biological grandparents are allowed to sue for visitation even after the child has been adopted. Would you have arranged your "guest list" in this fashion? You will also learn that the rights of a parent cannot be terminated on the ground of abandonment if the parent has regularly contributed a reasonable amount towards the child's support, even though the parent has had no personal contact with the child for a long time. Would you give preference to a parent who writes a regular support check over a step-parent who helps the child with homework and makes peanut butter and jelly sandwiches for the child's lunch box?

In New York the concept of "family" is like an amoeba, expanding in some directions even as it is contracting in others. At present in New York, a Family Offense (domestic violence) petition can be filed against anyone related to the petitioner by consanguinity or affinity, a former spouse, or a person with whom the petitioner has a child in common, regardless of whether these persons reside in the same household. Former spouses and persons who have a child in common are fairly recent additions to the list, and the legislature is debating whether the statute should be amended to include domestic partners who do not have a child in common. During the same period, however, the number of family members to whom a duty of support is owed has shrunk. Prior to 1966, the spouse, father, mother, grandparents, and children of a public assistance recipient were obligated to contribute towards the public assistance recipient's support. Now only a spouse or parent of the recipient owes a duty of support, and that obligation continues only until the child reaches the age of 21 years. What concerns do you think the legislature is addressing in each of these situations?

All who work in the law -- lawyers, legislators, law professors, judges, and legal assistants -- must think deeply about such fundamental questions. Even as we master the law's many rules and sometimes tedious details, we must remain attuned to its rich melodies. Reflecting on the law's fundamental purposes helps us to carry out our individual responsibilities with honor and commitment.

Legal Presumptions

One of the most important tools the law employs to express broad policies and preferences is the **legal presumption**. A presumption is a statement or allegation or averment that a court will accept as true without proof. Presumptions are not unique to Family Law; you may have encountered them in other courses. In Family Law, however, they are especially numerous and meaningful. Often they convey what the legal system considers core values, and they serve as the guidelines for drawing up the Family Law guest list and seating chart. Some presumptions are created by statute, like the presumption you will learn about in Chapter 8 which holds that property acquired during a marriage is marital property subject to equitable distribution upon dissolution of the marriage. This presumption embodies the concept that marriage is an economic partnership in which the contributions of both partners are entitled to recognition.

Other presumptions arise from case law, and these are usually ancient presumptions embedded deep in the fiber of our common law tradition. Some case law presumptions are later codified in statutes. Examples of case law presumptions include the presumption of legitimacy, which holds that a child born during marriage is the legitimate child of the husband of the mother, and the presumption that a child should be in the custody of a fit biological parent. These presumptions are so fundamental to Family Law that they are discussed in several chapters throughout this textbook. When you encounter these terms in later chapters, you may want to refresh your recollection concerning their meaning. It will not be necessary to search for them in the text, as all terms that appear in bold face type in the text are also defined in the Glossary at the end of the book.

Most presumptions are **rebuttable**, meaning that the other party is allowed to present evidence to disprove the presumption. A few are **irrebuttable**; they are the law's way of saying, "Don't bother me with facts, my mind is made up." The presumption of legitimacy is normally rebuttable, for example, but if a child is named in a divorce judgment as a child of the marriage, the presumption becomes irrebuttable. Even a rebuttable presumption puts a heavy thumb on the scales of justice, because it shifts the burden of proof to the party who does not wish to be bound by the presumption.

NON-TRADITIONAL FAMILIES

As if ordering the priorities among members of a traditional family was not complicated enough, the law has also had to grapple with the fact that many families in this last decade of the twentieth century are far from traditional. Some non-traditional families are relatives by consanguinity or affinity who live in groupings that do not fit the stereotypical picture of a **nuclear family.** Instead of Mom, Dad, and 2.5 children, the family may consist of a grandmother raising her grandchildren or a step-mother raising one child she had before the marriage along with a child of the marriage and a child of the husband from a previous relationship. Other non-traditional families consist of individuals who live together in combinations falling entirely outside the traditional definition of family, but who nevertheless consider themselves families and are demanding that the law recognize them as such. When it decides which combinations of individuals to recognize as a family and under what circumstances to recognize them, the law struggles to keep its footing on shifting sands.

A chronically difficult first question is whether the legislature or the judiciary should be the engineer of social change. Sometimes this process proceeds something like a tennis match. In recognizing the rights of out-of-wedlock fathers, as Chapter 13 discusses, the courts spoke first, saying that out-of-wedlock fathers could not as a class be disregarded. The legislature then promulgated certain criteria defining which out-of-wedlock fathers were entitled to legal recognition. The courts then ruled that some of the criteria in the statute were unconstitutional. The ball is now back in the legislature's court to reformulate the criteria in a manner consistent with the United States and New York Constitutions. As you encounter each of the many complicated social issues that lie just below the surface of Family Law, ask yourself: who should decide this question?

Whether change occurs as a result of statutory revision or judicial decision, it usually comes about in a piecemeal fashion. Even a comprehensive piece of legislation, such as the Civil Rights Act of 1964, does not make a clean sweep of all the problems. Over 30 years later we are still trying to decide, for example, whether certain forms of affirmative action are a violation of the Act or an implementation of it. Particularly when courts decide an issue, because judicial decision is narrowly focused on the case at hand, it is often hard to predict whether the opinion is a signpost guiding us to a new kingdom or a small detour from the well-trod path of tradition. As you read the cases excerpted in this textbook, ask yourself: where are we headed and what are the social implications of this decision? The Discussion Questions throughout the book are intended to stimulate your thinking about these issues.

Families enjoy a special status in the eyes of the law. Not only do the members of a family acquire certain rights with regard to each other, such as a child's right to be supported by its parents, for example, but they also enjoy certain rights with regard to the outside world. These **extrafamilial** rights include privileges, such as a spouse's right to refuse to testify concerning confidences revealed within the marriage, and benefits, such as the right to cover one's spouse and children under a health insurance plan. Most significantly, families are protected from governmental intrusion except when the government has an important State interest at stake. In *Moore v. City of East Cleveland, Ohio* (Case 1-1) the United States Supreme Court discusses the protected status of families. Notice the interplay between the legislative and judicial branches of government when the court says that in a case such as this "the usual judicial deference to the legislature is inappropriate."

📖 **CASE 1-1**

MOORE v. CITY OF EAST CLEVELAND, OHIO
431 U.S. 494, 97 S.Ct. 1932 (1977)

Mr. Justice POWELL announced the judgment of the Court, and delivered an opinion in which Mr. Justice BRENNAN, Mr. Justice MARSHALL, and Mr. Justice BLACKMUN joined.

East Cleveland's housing ordinance, like many throughout the country, limits occupancy of a dwelling unit to members of a single family. But the ordinance contains an unusual and complicated definitional section that recognizes as a "family" only a few categories of related individuals. Because her family, living together in her home, fits none of those categories, appellant stands convicted of a criminal offense. The question in this case is whether the ordinance violates the Due Process Clause of the Fourteenth Amendment.

Appellant, Mrs. Inez Moore, lives in her East Cleveland home together with her son, Dale Moore Sr., and her two grandsons, Dale, Jr., and John Moore, Jr. The two boys are first cousins rather than brothers; we are told that John came to live with his grandmother and with the elder and younger Dale Moores after his mother's death.

In early 1973, Mrs. Moore received a notice of violation from the city, stating that John was an "illegal occupant" and directing her to comply with the ordinance. When she failed to remove him from her home, the city filed a criminal charge. Mrs. Moore moved to dismiss, claiming that the ordinance was constitutionally invalid on its face. Her motion was overruled, and upon conviction she was sentenced to five days in jail and a $25 fine. The Ohio Court of Appeals affirmed after giving full consideration to her constitutional claims, and the Ohio Supreme Court denied review.

***

When a city undertakes such intrusive regulation of the family...the usual judicial deference to the legislature is inappropriate. "This Court has long recognized that marriage and family life is one of the liberties protected by the Due Process Clause of the Fourteenth Amendment." ...Of course, the family is not beyond regulation....But

📖 **CASE 1-1 continued**

when the government intrudes on choices concerning family living arrangements, this Court must examine carefully the importance of the governmental interests advanced and the extent to which they are served by the challenged regulation....

When thus examined, this ordinance cannot survive. The city seeks to justify it as a means of preventing overcrowding, minimizing traffic and parking congestion, and avoiding an undue financial burden on East Cleveland's school system. Although these are legitimate goals, the ordinance before us serves them marginally, at best. For example, the ordinance permits any family consisting only of husband, wife, and unmarried children to live together, even if the family contains a half dozen licensed drivers, each with his or her own car. At the same time it forbids an adult brother and sister to share a household, even if both faithfully use public transportation. The ordinance would permit a grandmother to live with a single dependent son and children, even if his school-age children number a dozen, yet it forces Mrs. Moore to find another dwelling for her grandson John, simply because of the presence of his uncle and cousin in the same household. We need not labor the point. Section 1341.08 [the ordinance] has but a tenuous relation to alleviation of the conditions mentioned by the city.

***

Ours is by no means a tradition limited to respect for the bonds uniting the members of the nuclear family. The tradition of uncles, aunts, cousins, and especially grandparents sharing a household along with parents and children has roots equally venerable and equally deserving of constitutional recognition. Over the years millions of our citizens have grown up in just such an environment, and most, surely, have profited from it. Even if conditions of modern society have brought about a decline in extended family households, they have not erased the accumulated wisdom of civilization, gained over the centuries and honored throughout our history, that supports a larger conception of the family. Out of choice, necessity, or a sense of family responsibility, it has been common for close relatives to draw together and participate in the duties and the satisfactions of a common home. Decisions concerning child rearing, which *Yoder, Meyer, Pierce* and other cases have recognized as entitled to constitutional protection, long have been shared with grandparents or other relatives who occupy the same household -- indeed who may take on major responsibility for the rearing of the children. Especially in times of adversity, such as the death of a spouse or economic need, the broader family has tended to come together for mutual sustenance and to maintain or rebuild a secure home life. This is apparently what happened here.

Whether or not such a household is established because of personal tragedy, the choice of relatives in this degree of kinship to live together may not lightly be denied by the State. *Pierce* struck down an Oregon law requiring all children to attend the State's public schools,

📖 **CASE 1-1 continued**

holding that the Constitution "excludes any general power of the State to standardize its children by forcing them to accept instruction from public teachers only."...By the same token the Constitution prevents East Cleveland from standardizing its children -- and its adults -- by forcing all to live in certain narrowly defined family patterns.
Reversed.

***

Although the law accords the family as a unit protection from intrusion by the outside world, its approach to resolving conflicts within a family is to view the family as a collection of individuals each of whom has certain "rights." Family Law is ever concerned with determining which rights take precedence, an awkward and artificial process, since families actually function in a much more subtle and complicated dynamic of give and take. The concept that family harmony might be more important than any individual family member's rights does not fare well in our adversarial legal system.

An interesting example is the case of *Commissioner of Social Services of the City of New York v. Hector S.*, 216 A.D.2d 81, 628 N.Y.S.2d 270 (1 Dept. 1995). The Commissioner brought a paternity proceeding seeking an order establishing that Hector S. was the father of fraternal twins born to a woman receiving public assistance. The ultimate purpose of the proceeding was to collect child support from Hector S. to offset the public funds being expended for the support of the children. Blood tests were ordered which revealed that Hector S. was the father of only one of the twins. After reviewing the medical testimony, the court concluded that it was entirely possible that if the mother had ovulated at two different times during a 48-72 hour period and had sexual relations with two men within that span of time, each of the eggs could have been fertilized by sperm from a different man. The Appellate Division, First Department, reversed the Family Court and entered an order adjudicating Hector S. to be the father of "Baby C." The court then noted, "We further reject Family Court's rationale that the petition should be dismissed because of the disparity which might be created between developing twin siblings, one of whom has an identifiable father and the other who does not. However compassionately motivated, this rationale is jurisprudentially unsound. We cannot right every peripheral wrong, but are limited to the parties and issues before us."

The realization that the law is not adept at fine tuning family life is probably the most significant reason that the law intrudes on families as seldom as possible. Another explanation lies in our belief that a democratic society thrives on diversity. Since each family is unique, every home becomes a mini-laboratory for social experimentation. Unless the family crumbles or the welfare of a family member is endangered, the law maintains a hands-off policy. In Family Law, the goal is to have more family and less law.

Another constraint on the law's intervention in family life is the major role religion has historically played in the regulation of family matters. Long before secular law got into the business, religious authorities regulated marriage and promulgated the rules governing child-rearing and family life. Indeed, many people in today's world still look first to their clergy for guidance in family matters. Since the United States and New York Constitutions prohibit the courts both from preferring one religion to another and from interfering with an individual's right to practice his or her religion, the courts often walk a tightrope in family matters.

A famous example of this conflict is the case of *Reynolds v. United States*, 98 U.S. 145 (1878) involving a prosecution for the crime of bigamy. **Bigamy**, having more than one spouse at a time, was a crime in all the states that had been admitted to the Union at that time. Utah was still a territory and, in hopes of getting admitted to the Union as a state, had outlawed bigamy. Utah was populated almost entirely by Mormons, however, and the Mormon religion at that time encouraged **polygamy**, that is, marrying more than one wife at a time. The first man to be prosecuted under the new statute was a Mormon who claimed a constitutional right to practice polygamy, as it was a "duty" of male members of the Church of Jesus Christ of Latter Day Saints, as the Mormon Church is formally known. The defendant believed that the penalty for refusal to practice polygamy would be "damnation in the life to come."

This old decision may be hard to find in your school library, but if you have access to WESTLAW or another on-line legal research service, you might enjoy reading it. It is entertaining for its account of the prosecution's difficulties in finding an unbiased jury pool and in securing the testimony of the second wife, who was a most unwilling witness. The decision's real value, however, is in its discussion of the uneasy relationship between religion and the law in the regulation of family life. That portion of the decision opens with a historical analysis of the separation of church and state, from which the court concluded that the framers of the constitution did not intend to surrender the power of the government to regulate marriage. "Marriage, while from its very nature a sacred obligation, is nevertheless, in most civilized nations, a civil contract, and usually regulated by law. Upon it society may be said to be built, and out of its fruits spring social relations and social obligations and duties, with which government is necessarily required to deal. In fact, according as monogamous or polygamous marriages are allowed, do we find the principles on which the government of the people, to a greater or less extent, rests," the court wrote.

The *Reynolds* court was aware of the cultural associations of monogamy. The decision states, "Polygamy has always been odious among the northern and western nations of Europe, and, until the establishment of the Mormon Church, was almost exclusively a feature of the life of Asiatic and African people. At common law, the second marriage was always void and from the earliest history of England polygamy has been treated as an offense against society." In the minds of present day readers, the cultural specificity of monogamy might be reason to delve deeper into its social implications, but to the court at that time it had the opposite effect. Having reassured itself that monogamy was the rule in the places where Western notions of democracy developed, the court moved swiftly to the conclusion that polygamy "fetters the people in stationary despotism." Since "despotism" threatens to undermine the foundations of democracy, the government's right to suppress polygamy was held to outweigh the defendant's right to practice his religion, and his conviction was affirmed.

Modern Family Law presents many opportunities to reconsider the delicate relationship between religion and the law, and you will encounter the issue throughout this textbook. Should a man be punished by the courts for refusing to grant his wife a religious divorce that his religion allows him to withhold? Should a parent be found to have neglected or abused a child by refusing to authorize medical care that is contrary to the parent's religious beliefs? Should a birth parent be allowed to block or delay the adoption of a child by an adoptive parent who is of a religion not approved by the birth parent? As you study the ways courts have answered these questions, ask yourself whether our solutions will appear sound to students of the law a century from now.

Reproductive Technologies

Children are being born through reproductive technologies that did not exist a generation ago. These miracles of modern science have confronted the courts with issues of which our forbears never dreamed. **Artificial insemination**, although by now scientifically old hat, continues to pose challenges for the legal system, as discussed in Chapter 9. Is the child so conceived legitimate, and what are the rights of the sperm donor? If the husband's sperm has been frozen for later use, can it be used after the couple divorce?

When a woman is impregnated by artificial insemination, at least it is clear who the mother is. The technique of *in vitro* **fertilization**, on the other hand, has cast the courts in an altogether novel role as determiners of maternity. *In vitro* fertilization involves the mixing of egg and sperm "in glass" in a laboratory. The fertilized egg is then implanted into the body of a woman, who carries the child through the pregnancy and ultimately gives birth to the child. The legally simplest version of this procedure occurs when the egg and sperm of a married couple are mixed and the wife then carries the fetus to term and gives birth, but, scientifically, the possibilities are endless. The sperm might come from a man who is not the husband, the egg might come from a woman other than the wife, and the woman who carries the child through the pregnancy might be a woman other than the woman from whom the egg came and might be a woman other than the wife.

In *McDonald v. McDonald*, 196 A.D.2d 7, 608 N.Y.S.2d 477 (2 Dept. 1994) the court faced a situation where the husband's sperm had been mixed with the egg of an egg donor, and the embryo had then been implanted in the wife, who carried the child to term. The court concluded that the wife, called the "gestational mother," was the mother of the child. The decision quoted with approval the language of a similar California case that "she who intended to procreate the child -- that is, she who intended to bring about the birth of a child that she intended to raise as her own -- is the natural mother."

Alternative Families

When the law is confronted with a "family" made up of individuals who are not related by consanguinity or affinity, the tennis match between the legislature and the court sometimes turns into a free-for-all. Currently there is much public discussion about whether same-sex couples should be allowed to marry. A court in Hawaii has ruled that same-sex couples presumptively have the same right to marry as opposite-sex couples [*Baehr v. Lewin*, 74 Haw. 530, 852 P.2d 44 (1993)], and the issue is now before Hawaii's highest appellate court. While no other state has allowed such marriages, the debate has prompted several states to consider legislation which would ban or deny recognition to same-sex marriages. Georgia, South Carolina, Tennessee, Oklahoma, Arizona, Utah, and South Dakota have already passed such legislation.

In 1996, the United States Congress enacted the "Defense of Marriage Act," which states that "No State, territory, or possession of the United States, or Indian tribe, shall be required to give effect to any public act, record, or judicial proceeding of any other State, territory, possession, or tribe respecting a relationship between persons of the same sex that is treated as a marriage under the laws of such other State, territory, possession, or tribe, or a right or claim arising from such relationship." Accordingly, each state will be allowed to decide for itself whether to recognize same-sex marriages performed in other states. The legislation also provides that for the purposes of Federal law "marriage" is defined as "only a legal union between one man and one woman as husband and wife." Thus, partners in same-sex marriages will be precluded from receiving Federal spousal benefits such as Social Security.

The same-sex marriage debate raises basic questions concerning marriage's social purposes and what State interests are advanced by the regulation of marriage. Is the primary purpose of marriage procreation? If so, should we deny a marriage license to anyone who is sterile or past the age to bear children? Is marriage basically an economic partnership? If so, why do we have divorce laws instead of treating marriage like any other business or professional partnership, which the partners can dissolve at will? Is marriage intended to regulate sexual conduct and prevent promiscuity? If so, should we permit marriage by any two people who are willing to commit themselves to being sexually faithful to each other? In fact, does marriage serve any secular purpose at all, or should it be considered strictly a religious rite? This is an enormously complicated and emotionally-charged issue, on which the United States Supreme Court is likely to have the final word. People of intelligence and good will stand on both sides of the question, and the ongoing debate should prove fascinating for students of Family Law.

While we do not permit same sex-couples to marry in New York, a recent Court of Appeals decision, *Matter of Dana*, discussed in Chapter 13, does permit the domestic partner in a same-sex couple to adopt the biological child of the other person in the relationship. Several years before the Court of Appeals issued this decision, it had held in *Ronald FF. v. Cindy GG.* (Case 6-4) that an unmarried partner in a relationship does not have the legal right to visitation with the partner's child after the relationship has broken up. *Alison D. v. Virginia M.* (Case 1-2), with its vigorous dissent, takes up the questions raised above of who is included within the ambit of Family Law and whether the legislature or the court should decide. As you read it, ask yourself whose rights the decision is protecting.

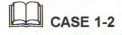 **CASE 1-2**

ALISON D. v. VIRGINIA M.
77 N.Y.2d 651, 569 N.Y.S.2d 586 (1991)

At issue in this case is whether petitioner, a biological stranger to a child who is properly in the custody of his biological mother, has standing to seek visitation with the child under Domestic Relations Law § 70. Petitioner relies on both her established relationship with the child and her alleged agreement with the biological mother to support her claim that she has standing. We agree with the Appellate Division that, although petitioner apparently nurtured a close and loving relationship with the child, she is not a parent within the meaning of Domestic Relations Law § 70. Accordingly, we affirm.

Petitioner Alison D. and respondent Virginia M. established a relationship in September 1977 and began living together in March 1978. In March 1980, they decided to have a child and agreed that respondent would be artificially inseminated. Together, they planned for the conception and birth of the child and agreed to share jointly all rights and responsibilities of child-rearing. In July 1981, respondent gave birth to a baby boy, A.D.M., who was given petitioner's last name as his middle name and respondent's last name became his last name. Petitioner shared in all birthing expenses and, after A.D.M.'s birth, continued to provide for his support. During A.D.M.'s first two years, petitioner and respondent jointly cared for and made decisions regarding the child.

In November 1983, when the child was 2 years and 4 months old, petitioner and respondent terminated their relationship and petitioner moved out of the home they jointly owned. Petitioner and respondent agreed to a visitation schedule whereby petitioner continued to see the child a few times a week. Petitioner also agreed to continue to pay one half of the mortgage and major household expenses. By this time, the child had referred to both respondent and petitioner as "mommy." Petitioner's visitation with the child continued until 1986, at which time respondent bought out petitioner's interest in the house and then began to restrict petitioner's visitation with the

📖 CASE 1-2 continued

child.   In 1987 petitioner moved to Ireland to pursue career opportunities, but continued her attempts to communicate with the child. Thereafter, respondent terminated all contact between petitioner and the child, returning all of petitioner's gifts and letters. No dispute exists that respondent is a fit parent. Petitioner commenced this proceeding seeking visitation rights pursuant to Domestic Relations Law § 70.

***

Petitioner concedes that she is not the child's "parent"; that is, she is not the biological mother of the child nor is she a legal parent by virtue of an adoption. Rather she claims she has acted as a "de facto" parent or that she should be viewed as a parent "by estoppel". Therefore, she claims she has standing to seek visitation rights.

***

Section 70 gives *parents* the right to bring proceedings to ensure their proper exercise of their care, custody and control.... Where the Legislature deemed it appropriate, it gave other categories of persons standing to seek visitation and it gave the courts the power to determine whether an award of visitation would be in the child's best interests.... We decline petitioner's invitation to read the term parent in section 70 to include categories of nonparents who have developed a relationship with a child or who have had prior relationships with a child's parents and who wish to continue visitation with the child.... While one may dispute in an individual case whether it would be beneficial to a child to have continued contact with a nonparent, the Legislature did not in section 70 give such nonparent the opportunity to compel a fit parent to allow them to do so....

Accordingly, the order of the Appellate Division should be affirmed, with costs.

KAYE, J. (dissenting). The Court's decision, fixing biology as the key to visitation rights, has impact far beyond this particular controversy, one that may affect a wide spectrum of relationships -- including those of longtime heterosexual stepparents, "common-law" and nonheterosexual partners such as involved here, and even participants in scientific reproduction procedures. Estimates that more than 15.5 million children do not live with two biological parents, and that as many as 8 to 10 million children are born into families with a gay or lesbian parent, suggest just how widespread the impact may be....

But the impact of today's decision falls hardest on the children of those relationships, limiting their opportunity to maintain bonds that may be crucial to their development. The majority's retreat from the courts' proper role -- its tightening of rules that in visitation petitions, above all, retain the capacity to take the children's interests into account -- compels this dissent.

***

📖 **CASE 1-2 continued**

Of course, there must be some limitation on who can petition for visitation. Domestic Relations Law § 70 specifies that the person must be the child's "parent," and the law additionally recognizes certain rights of biological and legal parents. Arguments that every dedicated caretaker could sue for visitation if the term "parent" were broadened, or that such action would necessarily effect sweeping change throughout the law, overlook and misportray the Court's role in defining otherwise undefined statutory terms to effect particular statutory purposes, and to do so narrowly, for those purposes only.

Countless examples of that process may be found in our case law, the Court looking to modern-day realities in giving definition to statutory concepts.... Only recently, we defined the term "family" in the eviction provisions of the rent stabilization laws so as to advance the legislative objective, making abundantly clear that the definition was limited to the statute in issue and did not effect a wholesale change in the law (*see, Braschi v. Stahl Assocs. Co.*, 74 NY2d 201, 211-213).

***

It is not my intention to spell out a definition but only to point out that it is surely within our competence to do so. It is indeed regrettable that we decline to exercise that authority in this visitation matter, given the explicit statutory objectives, the courts' power, and the fact that all consideration of the child's interest is, for the future, otherwise absolutely foreclosed.

***

The *Braschi* case mentioned in Judge Kaye's dissent dealt with the question whether the surviving partner of a ten-year relationship had the right to continue to occupy a rent-controlled apartment after the death of the partner who was the lease holder. The regulation in question, 9 NYCRR 2204.6(d), provided that the landlord could not dispossess "either the surviving spouse of the deceased tenant or some other member of the deceased tenant's family who has been living with the tenant." The Court of Appeals held that the partner could not be evicted, stating: "Contrary to all of these arguments, we conclude that the term family, as used in 9 NYCRR 2204.6(d), should not be rigidly restricted to those people who have formalized their relationship by obtaining, for instance, a marriage certificate or an adoption order. The intended protection against sudden eviction should not rest on fictitious legal distinctions or genetic history, but instead should find its foundation in the reality of family life. In the context of eviction, a more realistic, and certainly equally valid, view of a family includes two adult lifetime partners whose relationship is long term and characterized by an emotional and financial commitment and interdependence."

Foster Families

Nowhere is the gap between a family's perception of itself and the law's conception of it wider than in the case of foster families. Foster parents are licensed by the state to care for children, and the children usually are supported by public funds while in foster care. Foster parents sign an agreement with the agency from which they receive children, promising to abide by the agency's regulations and to comply with all efforts to reunify the children with their natural parents. That done, the foster family then proceeds to function just like any other family. The foster parents kiss scraped knees, attend open school night, and keep peace in the sand box. Naturally the foster children perceive the foster parents as Mommy and Daddy and view the other foster children in the home with the same mixture of attachment and rivalry as any other siblings. As the United States Supreme Court noted, "The New York [foster care] system divides parental functions among agency, foster parents, and natural parents, and the definitions of the respective roles are often complex and often unclear." *Smith v. Organization of Foster Families*, 431 U.S. 816, 97 S.Ct. 2094 (1977).

Recognizing that foster parents have a special right to be heard in court cases concerning their foster children, New York accords them the right to participate in any proceeding concerning a child in their care. Foster parents also have the right, pursuant to Social Services Law section 400, to an **administrative hearing** before a child is removed from the foster home, except in an emergency, but may not petition for custody of a foster child in their care. Once a child is removed from the foster home, usually to be returned to the care of a natural parent or biological relative, the foster parents have no right to further contact with the child. Neither is there a legal right nor an existing mechanism for the child to maintain contact with the other foster children that the child perceived as siblings. In *Bessette v. Buitrago-Falcon*, 209 A.D.2d 838, 619 N.Y.S.2d 359 (3 Dept. 1994) the Appellate Division, Third Department, denied visitation to former foster parents, citing *Alison D. v. Virginia M.* (Case 1-2). The court concluded by saying, "Our holding should not be viewed as disparaging either petitioners' interest in the emotional well-being of their former foster children or the concerns expressed by Family Court. We hold only that, in the absence of any statutory grant of standing to former foster parents, petitioners have no right to seek visitation which would limit or diminish the right of the biological parent, who has not been found to be unfit, to choose with whom her children associate."

THE CHANGING LEGAL STATUS OF WOMEN

The legal profile of today's woman is as different from that of her Colonial counterpart as her fashion profile. While some of the topics discussed below, such as women's suffrage, employment rights, and educational opportunities, are not strictly speaking Family Law issues, they make up the social backdrop for the dramatic relocation of women within the family circle.

THE MARRIED WOMEN'S PROPERTY ACTS

Married women have the same rights with respect to property as single women. DRL § 50; General Obligations Law § 3-301. Today, it might seem unnecessary to have laws declaring the equality of married and single women, but married women have not always enjoyed the same rights as unmarried women. At common law, a married woman was her husband's property. She had no legal existence or rights apart from her husband's, a fiction known as the merger or unity of identities. This merger of identities meant that married women could not do many of the things women take for granted today. Married women were prohibited from making contracts, owning or transferring property, suing or being sued, and keeping their own earnings. Husbands had absolute rights to their wives' real and personal property, while wives had no parallel interests in their husbands' property.

Beginning in 1848, married women's situations improved in New York when a series of Married Women's Property Acts (MWPA) were passed. These acts provided that property owned by a wife at the time of marriage or acquired by her after marriage remained her own separate property. The modern sections of the Domestic Relations Law and the General Obligations Law mentioned above are derived from these acts. (As you will learn in Chapter 8, the adoption in New York of equitable distribution of property upon dissolution of marriage restricted the rule of the MWPA with regard to property acquired after marriage.) These acts did not, however, create a complete revolution in married women's rights. The MWPA did not give wives the right to wages from their husbands for the work they did in the family home. Even today courts are unlikely to uphold contracts between spouses for domestic services, although they will consider homemaking contributions in the division of property upon dissolution of marriage.

An interesting example is the case of *Coleman v. Burr*, 93 N.Y. 17 (1883). Isaac Burr agreed to pay his wife, Ellen Burr, five dollars per week for caring for his elderly and sick mother in their home. Mrs. Burr cared for her mother-in-law for over eight years, a task that the court described as "onerous, exacting and disagreeable." Still, the Court of Appeals set aside the conveyance of land from Mr. Burr to Mrs. Burr that was to have served as payment for this care. The court recognized that, according to Chapter 90 of Laws of 1860 (one of the Married Women's Property Acts), a married woman could work "on her sole and separate account" and that she could keep any earnings from such work. The court reasoned, however, that caring for a family member in the home could not be on a woman's sole and separate account and thus was not covered by the Married Women's Property Acts. Instead, this care was part of a wife's duty to her husband. According to the court, allowing a woman to contract with her husband for domestic services would "degrade the wife by making her a menial servant in the home where she should discharge marital duties in loving and devoted ministrations" and would defraud creditors.

PROPERTY DISTRIBUTION UPON DISSOLUTION OF MARRIAGE

Two major areas of change in the laws relating to divorce are the gender-neutralization of spousal support statutes and the replacement of the title system of property distribution with equitable distribution.

Gender and Spousal Support

Historically, husbands had duties toward their wives. In New York, a husband's common law duty to support his wife financially during marriage was codified in the Domestic Relations Law and Family Court Act. Until 1980, a wife had a duty to support her husband only if he was a recipient of public assistance or likely to become one. In 1980, section 412 of the Family Court Act, pertaining to spousal support during marriage, and sections of the Domestic Relations Law relating to post-dissolution support were made gender-neutral as a result of the United States Supreme Court case, *Orr v. Orr,* 440 U.S. 268, 99 S.Ct. 1102 (1979). *Orr* held an Alabama statute that permitted alimony to be granted only to wives to be unconstitutional on equal protection grounds. In New York, some of the statutes could be construed in a gender-neutral manner, while others had to be rewritten. For example, in *Childs v. Childs,* 69 A.D.2d 406, 419 N.Y.S.2d 533 (2 Dept. 1979), the, Appellate Division, Second Department, construed two sections of the Domestic Relations Law which awarded counsel fees in divorce and custody proceedings to wives in a gender-neutral way by substituting the word "spouse" for the word "wife," rather than declaring the sections unconstitutional. In contrast, in *Kane v. Kane,* 101 Misc.2d 143, 420 N.Y.S.2d 627 (N.Y. Sup. Ct. 1979), the Supreme Court dealt with section 5-311 of the General Obligations Law, which prohibited absolutely a husband from contracting to relieve himself from supporting his wife, but prohibited a wife from making the same sort of contract only where the wife had sufficient means to support her husband and the husband was incapable of supporting himself and was likely to become a public charge. The court decided that it could not read the statute in a gender-neutral fashion because of the explicit differentiation between husband and wife. This provision was repealed and replaced with language that does not distinguish between a husband's obligations and a wife's.

Equitable Distribution

When people use the term "divorce reform," they are often referring to the concept of equitable distribution of property upon dissolution of marriage. Traditionally, property was distributed according to the "title" system. Under the title system, property acquired during marriage was awarded to the spouse named in the deed or certificate of title. In practice, this often meant that husbands, who frequently held title in their own names only, were awarded the property when marriages were dissolved. In awarding property, this system did not take account of the contributions of the non-title holding spouses. As the use of the term "equitable distribution" implies, systems of equitable distribution are intended to award property in a more fair and flexible way than the title system.

Equitable distribution became law in New York in 1980, when the so-called "Equitable Distribution Law" (Chapter 281 of the Laws of 1980) reformed many of New York's laws relating to dissolution of marriage. One of the laws reformed was section 236 of the Domestic Relations Law, which pertains to distribution of property and spousal support after dissolution of marriage. In awarding property, the revised section 236 takes into account the non-monetary contributions of a spouse in parenting and homemaking. DRL § 236 Part B(5). It also replaces alimony with "maintenance." DRL § 236 Part B(6). Maintenance was intended to help economically dependent spouses, often wives, only until they could provide for themselves, rather than to be permanent support, as alimony was. As you will learn in Chapter 8, there is criticism of the actual effect of divorce reform on the economic conditions of women after divorce. In 1986, section 236 was amended to address some of the problems with the new system. The amendment added new factors the court should consider in determining the amount and duration of maintenance, including the "ability of the party seeking maintenance to become self-supporting" and the "reduced or lost lifetime earning capacity of the party seeking maintenance as a result of having foregone or delayed education, training, employment, or career opportunities during the marriage." DRL § 236 Part B(6).

DOMESTIC VIOLENCE

Historical Perspectives

Although domestic violence is a modern term, it represents an old and, unfortunately, ongoing problem. At both common law and religious law, husbands were allowed and even encouraged to discipline their wives using physical force, if necessary. The popularly used expression, "a rule of thumb," came from a husband's common law right to beat his wife using a stick no thicker in diameter than his thumb. The justification for condoning the use of physical violence lay in the fact that wives were considered their husbands' property and that husbands were held legally responsible for their wives' behavior. At common law, before the Married Women's Property Acts, a wife could not sue on her own behalf. Her husband had to sue (or be sued) in her place. This incapacity meant that a wife could not sue her husband for injuries he inflicted on her because the resulting suit would be both for and against him.

While major reforms in domestic violence laws have come about only recently, there were three historical eras of public outcry in America against domestic violence. The public sentiment against domestic violence during these eras reflected more general societal concerns and beliefs. First, in the Colonial era, the Puritans believed that domestic violence interfered with the "orderliness and stability" of their settlements. Accordingly, some laws against wife abuse were passed in New England, but the larger concern was with more public threats to societal order, such as vagrancy, and prosecutions of domestic violence cases (and other "private" crimes) declined over the Colonial period. Second, women activists in the nineteenth century identified domestic violence, along with temperance, suffrage, and social purity, as a reform issue. Their activism in other reform issues often informed their beliefs about the reasons for domestic violence. For example, the temperance advocates believed that husbands' use of alcohol was the root of domestic violence, while the social purists believed that husbands' ownership of wives was the cause. Finally, for women and African-Americans, the 1960's were a time of changing societal and self-perceptions. The feminist movement, which had its roots in the civil rights and anti-war movements of the 1960's, gave rise to advocacy for battered women in the 1970's and 1980's. The feminists' work against rape influenced the battered women's movement in ideology and methodology.

Legislative Reform

Despite these historic periods of public disapproval of domestic violence, legislative reforms and judicial intervention have been slow in coming. One reason for this lag is the reluctance of judges, legislators, and law enforcement officials to intrude in issues that implicate the privacy of family and home. The Family Violence and Services Act (42 U.S.C. § 10401), the first federal legislation relating to domestic violence, was passed in 1984. This legislation provided aid to abuse victims. In 1987, New York's Domestic Violence Protection Act (Article 6-A of the Social Services Law) was passed to provide funding for programs for domestic violence victims, such as residential programs, which provide services and shelter, and non-residential programs, which provide referrals to emergency shelters, medical services, and counseling. SSL § 459-a.

Changing beliefs about the proper response to domestic violence have led the legislature to give jurisdiction over domestic violence cases to different courts in New York over the years. When Article 8 of the Family Court Act (the Family Offenses article) was passed in 1962, treatment and reconciliation, rather than prosecution, were believed to be the appropriate response to domestic violence. The legislature gave original jurisdiction over family offenses to the Family Court, and the Family Court judge could determine whether a domestic violence case should be transferred to Criminal Court. The decriminalizing focus on treatment and reconciliation was not always effective in protecting victims of domestic violence. As a result, today the Family Court and the Criminal Court have concurrent jurisdiction over family offenses cases. FCA § 812(1).

Despite these legislative efforts, domestic violence remains a highly controversial issue. A constant criticism by advocates of battered women is that police and prosecutors have not actively prosecuted domestic violence cases and that judges do not take the cases seriously enough. The officials respond that battered women too often drop the charges against their batterers (if they bring them at all) and that they are uncooperative in helping to convict batterers. This interchange leads to debate about "no drop" policies and laws, that is, whether all domestic violence cases should be prosecuted in the same way as assaults by strangers and whether victims should be compelled to testify against their batterers.

If "family violence" should be treated differently from violence perpetrated by acquaintances or strangers, then who should be treated as "family" for these purposes? Domestic violence is clearly not a problem limited to married couples. There are differences in the classes of unmarried persons protected by New York's domestic violence laws, however, and some classes are not protected at all. For example, both the Domestic Violence Prevention Act and Article 8 of the Family Court Act cover persons related by consanguinity or affinity, persons legally married to one another, persons formerly married to one another, and persons who have a child in common regardless whether such persons have been married or have lived together at any time. FCA § 812(1)(a)-(d); SSL § 459-a(2)(a)-(d). The Domestic Violence Prevention Act, however, also includes "unrelated persons who are continually or at regular intervals living in the same household or who have in the past continually or at regular intervals lived in the same household" and "any other category of individuals deemed to be a victim of domestic violence as defined by the department in regulation." SSL § 459-a(2)(e),(f). Neither of these provisions explicitly protects teenagers and others who are involved in battering situations, but who have never lived with their batterers.

SEXUAL OFFENSES

The law's changing perception of women has resulted in, and been reflected in, three major changes in the laws relating to rape and sexual misconduct. First, there have been changes in the evidentiary requirements for prosecution. Second, most statutes having to do with rape and sexual misconduct have been gender-neutralized. Third, women can now prosecute their husbands for rape.

Evidentiary Requirements

The evidentiary requirements of corroboration and resistance illustrate the societal tendency to blame and disbelieve rape victims. Under the Penal Law until 1974, each element of a sexual offense had to be corroborated in order for there to be a conviction. The testimony of the victim was not enough to convict the rapist. The problem with this requirement is that rapes do not usually take place in the presence of witnesses. As one observer noted, "If it didn't happen in Macy's window, you didn't have a case." This section was later repealed and replaced with Penal Law section 130.16, which requires corroboration only in cases of sex offenses in which the victim is deemed incapable of consent because of a mental defect or mental incapacity.

The resistance requirement in sex offense statutes has also evolved. For a rape victim, resistance requirements created a catch 22. If the victim did not resist her rapist, he would not be convicted, but if she did resist she might be injured even more severely or killed. Until 1977, the New York rape statute's requirement of forcible compulsion was interpreted to require proof of "utmost resistance" by the victim in order for there to be a conviction. In 1977, the Legislature changed this requirement to "earnest resistance." In 1982, the requirement of earnest resistance was repealed, but the burden remained on the victim. The revised statute required force or threat which placed the victim in fear of death, serious physical injury, or kidnaping of herself or another to establish a rape. In addition, the revision still suggested that the use of physical force in itself might be insufficient to constitute forcible compulsion and that a victim's general fear of the entire situation (rather than fear specifically of death, serious injury, or kidnaping) might constitute a defense. Finally, in 1983, the definition of rape was changed again to make it clear that physical force *or* fear of physical injury (rather than of serious physical injury) were sufficient to constitute forcible compulsion.

Gender-Neutralization of Statutes

Until the case of *People v. Liberta,* 64 N.Y.2d 152, 485 N.Y.S.2d 207 (1984), *cert. denied,* 471 U.S. 1020, 105 S.Ct. 2029, New York's sex offense statutes provided that only men could commit rape. Women could not rape men, according to the statute, creating a so-called "gender exemption" for women. In *Liberta,* the Court of Appeals struck the gender exemption from section 130.35 of the Penal Law (forcible rape) as a violation of the Equal Protection Clause of the Fourteenth Amendment to the United States Constitution because the distinction between men and women was not substantially related to an important governmental objective. In 1987, the Legislature removed the gender exemption from the other rape statutes. The gender exemption has not been legislatively removed from the sexual misconduct statute, but the Fourth Department Appellate Division has struck the gender exemption from that statute. *Matter of Jessie C.,* 164 A.D.2d 731, 565 N.Y.S.2d 941(4 Dept. 1991), *appeal dismissed* 78 N.Y.2d 907, 573 N.Y.S.2d 467. Like the Court of Appeals in *Liberta*, the Appellate Division in *Jessie C.* found no substantial relation to the achievement of an important governmental objective in the gender distinction, thus creating a violation of equal protection. The court reasoned that the statute's gender-based classification did not serve the stated governmental purpose of prevention of teenage pregnancies better than would a gender-neutral statute.

Marital Rape

The "marital exemption" to rape has both a statutory and historical basis. The marital exemption in New York's rape and sodomy statutes arises from section 130.00 of the Penal Law, which defines "female" as "any female person who is not married to the actor." In addition, the definition of "deviate sexual intercourse" specifies that the parties not be married to each other. Penal Law § 130.00(2).

Historically, several arguments have been advanced in favor of the marital exemption. The traditional justifications for an exemption for marital rape are that there is an implied consent to sexual intercourse in marriage and that a woman is her husband's property. More modern justifications are that the exemption protects against governmental intrusion into marital privacy and promotes reconciliation of the spouses. Other proponents of the exemption point out the difficulty of proving marital rape and argue that marital rape is not as serious a crime as rape by others and can be prosecuted under statutes that provide for less serious punishment. As you will see in Case 1-3, the Court of Appeals did not find any of these arguments persuasive. The court found no rational basis for the marital exemption and thus held it to be a violation of the Equal Protection Clauses of the New York and United States Constitutions. Since *Liberta*, other courts have held that the scope of its analysis is not limited to rape and sodomy statutes, but rather that "the *Liberta* protections extend to all sexual offenses in which a victim's lack of consent is the result of forcible compulsion." *People v. Prudent,* 143 Misc.2d 50, 539 N.Y.S.2d 651 (N.Y. City Crim. Ct. 1989). Interestingly, although the gender exemption was removed from the text of most of the rape statutes shortly after the *Liberta* decision, the marital exemption remains on the books, although it is, of course, disregarded.

 **CASE 1-3**

PEOPLE v. LIBERTA
64 N.Y.2d 152, 485 N.Y.S.2d 207 (1984)

WACHTLER, J.

The defendant, while living apart from his wife pursuant to a Family Court order, forcibly raped and sodomized her in the presence of their 2½ year old son. Under the New York Penal Law a married man ordinarily cannot be prosecuted for raping or sodomizing his wife. The defendant, however, though married at the time of the incident, is treated as an unmarried man under the Penal Law because of the Family Court order. On this appeal, he contends that because of the exemption for married men, the statutes for rape in the first degree (Penal Law, § 130.35) and sodomy in the first degree (Penal Law, § 130.50), violate the equal protection clause of the Federal Constitution (US Const, 14th Amdt)....

I

Defendant Mario Liberta and Denise Liberta were married in 1978. Shortly after the birth of their son, in October of that year, Mario began to beat Denise. In early 1980 Denise brought a proceeding in the Family Court in Erie County seeking protection from the defendant. On April 30, 1980 a temporary order of protection was issued to her by the Family Court. Under this order, the defendant was to move out and remain away from the family home, and stay away from Denise. The order provided that the defendant could visit with his son once each weekend.

On the weekend of March 21, 1981, Mario, who was then living in a motel, did not visit his son. On Tuesday, March 24, 1981 he called Denise to ask if he could visit his son on that day. Denise would not allow the defendant to come to her house, but she did agree to allow him to pick up their son and her and take them both back to his motel after being assured that a friend of his would be with them at all times. The defendant and his friend picked up Denise and their son and the

📖 **CASE 1-3 continued**

four of them drove to defendant's motel.

When they arrived at the motel the friend left. As soon as only Mario, Denise, and their son were alone in the motel room, Mario attacked Denise, threatened to kill her, and forced her to perform fellatio on him and to engage in sexual intercourse with him. The son was in the room during the entire episode, and the defendant forced Denise to tell their son to watch what the defendant was doing to her.

The defendant allowed Denise and their son to leave shortly after the incident. Denise, after going to her parents' home, went to a hospital to be treated for scratches on her neck and bruises on her head and back, all inflicted by her husband. She also went to the police station, and on the next day she swore out a felony complaint against the defendant. On July 15, 1981 the defendant was indicted for rape in the first degree and sodomy in the first degree.

A. THE MARITAL EXEMPTION

As noted above, under the Penal Law a married man ordinarily cannot be convicted of forcibly raping or sodomizing his wife. This is the so-called marital exemption for rape.... Although a marital exemption was not explicit in earlier rape statutes..., an 1852 treatise stated that a man could not be guilty of raping his wife....The assumption, even before the marital exemption was codified, that a man could not be guilty of raping his wife, is traceable to a statement made by the 17th century English jurist Lord Hale, who wrote: "[T]he husband cannot be guilty of a rape committed by himself upon his lawful wife, for by their mutual matrimonial consent and contract the wife hath given up herself in this kind unto her husband, which she cannot retract."...Although Hale cited no authority for his statement it was relied on by State Legislatures which enacted rape statutes with a marital exemption and by courts which established a common-law exemption for husbands.

***

Presently, over 40 States still retain some form of marital exemption for rape. While the marital exemption is subject to an equal protection challenge, because it classifies unmarried men differently that married men, the equal protection clause does not prohibit a State from making classifications, provided the statute does not arbitrarily burden a particular group of individuals.... Where a statute draws a distinction based upon marital status, the classification must be reasonable and must be based upon "some ground of difference that rationally explains the different treatment."...

We find that there is no rational basis for distinguishing between marital rape and nonmarital rape. The various rationales which have been asserted in defense of the exemption are either based upon archaic notions about the consent and property rights incident to marriage or are simply unable to withstand even the slightest scrutiny. We therefore declare the marital exemption for rape

📖 **CASE 1-3 continued**

in the New York statute to be unconstitutional.

Lord Hale's notion of an irrevocable implied consent by a married woman to sexual intercourse has been cited most frequently in support of the marital exemption.... Any argument based on a supposed consent, however, is untenable. Rape is not simply a sexual act to which one party does not consent. Rather, it is a degrading, violent act which violates the bodily integrity of the victim and frequently causes severe, long-lasting physical and psychic harm.... To ever imply consent to such an act is irrational and absurd. Other than in the context of rape statutes, marriage has never been viewed as giving a husband the right to coerced intercourse on demand.... Certainly, then, a marriage license should not be viewed as a license for a husband to forcibly rape his wife with impunity. A married woman has the same right to control her own body as does an unmarried woman.... If a husband feels "aggrieved" by his wife's refusal to engage in sexual intercourse, he should seek relief in the courts governing domestic relations, not in "violent or forceful self-help."...

The other traditional justifications for the marital exemption were the common-law doctrines that a woman was the property of her husband and that the legal existence of the woman was "incorporated and consolidated into that of the husband."...Both theses doctrines, of course, have long been rejected in this State. Indeed, "[n]owhere in the common-law world -- [or] in any modern society -- is a woman regarded as chattel or demeaned by denial of a separate legal identity and the dignity associated with recognition as a whole human being."...

Because the traditional justifications for the marital exemption no longer have any validity, other arguments have been advanced in its defense. The first of these rationales, which is stressed by the People in this case, is that the marital exemption protects against governmental intrusion into marital privacy and promotes reconciliation of the spouses, and thus that elimination of the exemption would be disruptive to marriages. While protecting marital privacy and encouraging reconciliation are legitimate State interests, there is no rational relation between allowing a husband to forcibly rape his wife and these interests. The marital exemption simply does not further marital privacy because this right of privacy protects consensual acts, not violent sexual assaults.... Just as a husband cannot invoke a right of privacy to escape liability for beating his wife, he cannot justifiably rape his wife under the guise of a right to privacy.

Similarly, it is not tenable to argue that elimination of the marital exemption would disrupt marriages because it would discourage reconciliation. Clearly, it is the violent act of rape and not the subsequent attempt of the wife to seek protection through the criminal justice system which "disrupts" a marriage.... Moreover, if the marriage has already reached the point where intercourse is accomplished by violent assault it is doubtful that there is anything left to reconcile.... This, of course, is particularly true if the wife is willing to bring criminal

CASE 1-3 continued

charges against her husband which could result in a lengthy jail sentence.

Another rationale sometimes advanced in support of the marital exemption is that marital rape would be a difficult crime to prove. A related argument is that allowing such prosecutions could lead to fabricated complaints by "vindictive" wives. The difficulty of proof argument is based on the problem of showing lack of consent. Proving lack of consent, however, is often the most difficult part of any rape prosecution, particularly where the rapist and the victim had a prior relationship.... Similarly, the possibility that married women will fabricate complaints would seem to be no greater than the possibility of unmarried women doing so.... The criminal justice system, with all of its built-in safeguards, is presumed to be capable of handling any false complaints. Indeed, if the possibility of fabricated complaints were a basis for not criminalizing behavior which would otherwise be sanctioned, virtually all crimes other than homicides would go unpunished.

The final argument in defense of the marital exemption is that marital rape is not as serious an offense as other rape and is thus adequately dealt with by the possibility of prosecution under criminal statutes, such as assault statutes, which provide for less severe punishment. The fact that rape statutes exist, however, is a recognition that the harm caused by a forcible rape is different, and more severe than the harm caused by an ordinary assault.... "Short of homicide, [rape] is the 'ultimate violation of self'"...

Moreover, there is no evidence to support the argument that marital rape has less severe consequences than other rape. On the contrary, numerous studies have shown that marital rape is frequently quite violent and generally has *more* severe, traumatic effects on the victim than other rape....

Among the recent decisions in this country addressing the marital exemption, only one court has concluded that there is a rational basis for it [Colorado]. We agree with the other courts which have analyzed the exemption, which have been unable to find any present justification for it.... Justice Holmes wrote: "It is revolting to have no better reason for a rule of law than that so it was laid down in the time of Henry IV. It is still more revolting if the grounds upon which it was laid down have vanished long since, and the rule simply persists from blind imitation of the past."... This statement is an apt characterization of the marital exemption; it lacks a rational basis, and therefore violates the equal protection clauses of both the Federal and State Constitutions.

***

EMPLOYMENT

Historical Perspectives

The primary forms of paying work for women in the United States before industrialization were domestic service and sewing piece work at home (known as "home work"). Industrialization in the nineteenth century brought factory work for men and women. Women (and children) often found work in the textile industry. While this work brought a certain measure of independence for many women, it also often involved long hours and dangerous working conditions. Women were often given the factory jobs that required the least skill and the lowest pay.

Protective Statutes

From 1908 to 1911 Congress studied the working conditions of women in industry. The congressional report quoted an 1845 newspaper investigation of the same topic in New York, which described "a most deplorable degree of servitude, privation, and misery among this helpless and dependent class of people, including hundreds and thousands of shoe binders, type rubbers, artificial-flower makers, matchbox makers, straw braiders, etc., who drudge[d] away, heartbroken in want, disease and wretchedness."

While this observation was made in dramatic terms, it highlighted the need for legislation correcting the working conditions of all factory workers, male and female. During the late nineteenth century and early twentieth century, female reformers began organizing laborers and advocating improved working conditions. The result of their efforts was legislation that created special protections for women and children, including a minimum wage and limits on the number of hours worked. These protections, however, were used by the unions of the time as a way to exclude women from factory work, rather than as a catalyst to improve working conditions for men. Union leaders argued that women physically could not handle the working conditions involved in some jobs, preventing women from taking part in higher paying work. This "protective" discrimination became an issue once again after World War II, when it was used to remove women from the industrial jobs they had taken as part of the war effort. In New York, many of the protective laws were repealed in 1973.

Discrimination

In the 1960's, federal legislation was enacted to prevent discrimination against women in employment. The Equal Pay Act of 1963 requires that employers provide equal pay for equal work. 29 U.S.C. § 206(d). The Civil Rights Act of 1964 (Title VII) banned discrimination in employment based on sex, race, ethnicity, religion, and national origin. 42 U.S.C. § 2000e. In New York, the

Labor Law has prohibited discrimination in pay on the basis of sex since 1944. Labor Law § 194. Interestingly, this section does not apply to domestic service. The Human Rights Law (Article 15 of the Executive Law) declares equality of opportunity to obtain employment without discrimination on the basis of age, race, creed, color, and national origin to be a civil right. Executive Law § 291(1). In 1964, sex was added to this list, and in 1975 marital status was added. Executive Law § 291(1). Another section of the Human Rights Law enumerates unlawful discriminatory practices, which include discrimination on the basis of sex or marital status in hiring, employment, firing, union membership, advertising for employment, apprenticeship, and job training. Executive Law § 296. Employer rules requiring pregnant women to leave employment for a fixed period of time have been held to be discriminatory in violation of Article 15. *Board of Education of Union Free School District v. New York State Div. of Human Rights*, 42 A.D.2d 600, 345 N.Y.S. 101 (2 Dept. 1973).

VOTING AND PUBLIC OFFICE

Women's suffrage was one of several issues addressed by women's rights activists in the middle of the nineteenth century, along with temperance, married women's property rights, and the abolition of slavery. After abolition, the suffragists were divided as to whether they should support the ratification of the Fifteenth Amendment, which gave black men the right to vote, if it did not also enfranchise women. There was also debate over whether women's suffrage should be pursued at the Federal constitutional level or at the State level. Western states were the first to allow women to vote, granting suffrage in 1910 and 1911. The Nineteenth Amendment to the United States Constitution, which gives women the right to vote, was passed by the House of Representatives in 1918 and was finally ratified in 1920. In New York, women's right to vote had already been guaranteed by the Suffrage Article of the New York Constitution, since the word "male" was removed from the qualifications of voters in 1917.

The fight for women's suffrage also led to questions about the proper role of women in public office. The case of *Burton v. Schmidt*, 128 Misc. 270, 218 N.Y.S. 416 (1926) provides an interesting contemporary judicial response to women's suffrage and to an attempt to help women gain public office. It seems that the Republican State Committee had tried to provide that of the two members elected from each assembly district, at least one should be a woman. The court held this provision to be in violation of the New York Election Law, the Public Officers Law, and the United States and New York Constitutions. The court noted that as a result of the Nineteenth Amendment, "All invidious distinction between the sexes was done away with when it came to voting. It has taken many years to bring about such equality, but it has come at last, and men and women now stand on the same footing when it comes to the right of franchise. The federal Constitution goes so far as to provide that the right of a citizen shall not be abridged or denied on account of sex either by the United States or any other state." From this premise the court reasoned that "Any law or rule which restricts the free choice of a voter in expressing his or her choice for an official to represent him is contrary to the spirit of the Constitution."

Women can now hold any public office in New York for which they are qualified. Since 1975 there has been no automatic exemption from jury duty for women. Section 13 of the Civil Rights Law provides that women cannot be disqualified from jury membership on the basis of sex.

EQUAL RIGHTS

Equal Protection

The case of *Reed v. Reed,* 404 U.S. 71, 92 S.Ct. 251 (1971) was the first time the United States Supreme Court held that statutes which distinguish between men and women might violate the constitution. In that case, a woman wanted to administer the estate of her deceased son. An Idaho statute preferred male administrators, and Mrs. Reed's husband, from whom she was separated, was appointed instead. The Supreme Court stated the test of whether a classification based on gender could withstand judicial scrutiny: classifications based on gender must serve important governmental objectives and must be substantially related to the achievement of those objectives. Since the preference for male administrators did not serve any governmental objective, Mrs. Reed was allowed to administer her son's estate.

Equal Rights

The Equal Rights Amendment (ERA) was first introduced in Congress in 1923. The ERA had the support of Eleanor Roosevelt and was nearly passed in 1941, but it was put aside because of World War II. It was finally passed by Congress in 1972, but it was ratified by only 35 of the requisite 38 state legislatures and did not become part of the Constitution. In New York, a state ERA was proposed and passed by the Legislature in 1974 and 1975, but it was defeated in a public referendum. The issue was raised again in 1984 and was passed by the Assembly, but it was not passed in the Senate.

Despite the difficulties with passage of the ERA, there are several statutory protections for women in New York. In addition to the jury membership and employment provisions discussed above, section 40-c of the Civil Rights Law, which provides equal rights in places of public accommodation and amusement, was amended in 1982 to include "sex, marital status or disability." It now provides that "No person shall, because of race, creed, color, national origin, sex, marital status or disability...be subjected to any discrimination in his civil rights, or to any harassment...in the exercise thereof, by any other person or by any firm, corporation or institution, or by the state or any agency or subdivision of the state." Civil Rights Law§ 40-c(2).

EDUCATION

Historical Perspectives

The separation of men's and women's "natures," duties, and spheres has often been advanced as a reason to educate women differently from men. In the Colonial period, few women were educated formally, although in New England girls were often apprenticed. After the Revolutionary War, education for women was advocated as a way to strengthen the new republic that had been formed. Women were seen as the mothers of the new nation's citizen-leaders and, as such, should be educated enough to instill in them the proper virtues. Other advocates of education for women argued that an educated woman would be a better wife. Literacy among women improved rapidly in the nineteenth century, and women began teaching in greater numbers. Women soon outnumbered men in the teaching profession, although they taught at lower wages than the male teachers. In addition, women founded female academies and seminaries, which had curricula similar to those in male seminaries, except that female seminaries did not teach classical languages. At the same time, however, it was feared that too much education would make women masculine. Before the Civil War, Oberlin College was the only institution of higher learning to admit women. Mount Holyoke, the nation's first women's college, was founded in 1837, with others being formed in the years after the Civil War. Land grant colleges and universities in the West were opened to men and women. Despite these advances, discrimination against women persisted in graduate education and university administration into the second half of the twentieth century.

Equal Access

At the federal level, the equal protection clause of Fourteenth Amendment to the United States Constitution and Title IX of the Education Amendments of 1972 (20 U.S.C. §§ 1681 et seq.) prohibit sex discrimination in public schools and colleges. In New York, § 3201-a of the Education Law prohibits girls being refused admission or excluded from any course of instruction offered in state public schools. It also generally prohibits the exclusion of girls from school athletic teams, "except pursuant to regulations promulgated by the state commissioner of education." Education Law § 3201-a.

Perhaps the last frontier for women in access to education was the publicly funded, single-sex military institution. Although the military service academies are now all coeducational, military colleges like the Virginia Military Institute and the Citadel in South Carolina still admit only male students. The Supreme Court has recently ruled in *United States v. Virginia*, -- U.S. --, 116 S.Ct. 2264 (1996) that the male-only admission policies of Virginia Military Institute violate the equal protection clause of the Constitution. Writing for the majority, Justice Ruth Bader Ginsberg stated that "generalizations about 'the way women are,' estimates of what is appropriate for most women, no longer justify denying opportunity to women whose talent and capacity place them outside the average description." Justice Scalia, on the other hand, scathingly dissented that the matter should have been left to the legislature. He noted, "The virtue of a democratic system with a First Amendment is that it readily enables the people, over time, to be persuaded that what they took for granted is not so, and to change their laws accordingly. That system is destroyed if the smug assurances of each age are removed from the democratic process and written into the Constitution."

THE CHANGING LEGAL STATUS OF CHILDREN

Students of Family Law at the end of the twentieth century may be amazed to learn that not long ago children were considered valuable financial assets. Most of us today would consider them our dearest (in both senses of the word) liabilities. While women have become more economically productive, and concomitantly legally independent, children often linger in financial dependence while they complete the protracted education required by the current job market. Paradoxically, these modern "children" appear more sophisticated and assertive than their nineteenth century counterparts. The legal system is kept busy tailoring rights and remedies to fit the changing image of the child.

PARENT AND CHILD

The rights and obligations of children are bound up with those of their parents, and the state historically has been reluctant to intervene in the parent-child relationship. At common law, parents had a duty to support their children. The children were left with little financial security, however, in the absence of effective enforcement mechanisms. The common law put children born out of wedlock in an even more tenuous situation; they had no right to parental support, nor could they inherit from their parents in the absence of a will.

The corollary of the parents' duty to support their children financially was the parents' (especially the father's) right to the services of their children. As one prominent nineteenth century legal commentator put it, "[I]n consequence of the obligation of the father to provide for the maintenance, and, in some qualified degree, for the education of his infant children, he is entitled to the custody of their persons, and to the value of their labor and services." James Kent, *Commentaries on American Law*, excerpted in Grace Abbott, *The Child and the State* 51 (1938). In custody disputes between parents, fathers were usually awarded custody. An example of the strength of the presumption in favor of fathers was the case of *Mercien v. People ex rel. Barry*, 25 Wendell (N.Y.) 64 (1840). In that case Mrs. Barry, who lived in New York, refused to move with her husband and their children to Nova Scotia. The court saw the case as one of "desertion" by Mrs. Barry of Mr. Barry and stated that even if there was some marital misconduct on Mr. Barry's part, he still might get custody. The court explained the presumption in favor of the father: "[I]n these unhappy controversies between husband and wife, the former, if he chooses to assert his right, has the better title to the custody of their minor children. The law regards him as the head of the family; obliges him to provide for its wants; and commits the children to his charge, in preference to the claims of the mother or any other person."

Today, the tradition of limited state intervention into the parent-child relationship is qualified. Both parents in New York are now required by statute to support their children, whether born in or out of wedlock, until age 21. FCA §§ 413, 513; SSL § 101. In addition, by law there is no longer a presumption of a right to custody in favor of either parent. Instead, in making custody decisions, the court must consider "the circumstances of the case and of the respective parties and...the best interests of the child." DRL § 240. Still, there has not been a complete reversal of the common law. Parents today still have no legal obligation to provide for their minor children in their wills. In addition, in custody disputes, the state, through its courts, retains its hands-off approach by respecting parents' rights to the custody of their children as superior to those of all others. Courts will not award custody to someone other than a natural parent unless the parent is proved to be unfit.

FROM PROPERTY TO PERSON

Legal historians identify four eras in the history of children and the law in the United States. The legal treatment of children during these periods reflected and institutionalized society's views of the nature, roles, and rights of children. The first era identified is the early 1600's to the early 1800's. During this time, which included the colonization and founding of the United States, hard work and strict religious and moral standards were emphasized. Childhood was seen as a time of sin, and idle children were believed to be especially susceptible to corruption. The Puritans and the Quakers saw work as an element of the training of children. Accordingly, children were often apprenticed, and parents were encouraged to keep their children occupied through work.

The second era, the first half of the nineteenth century, was a time of increased immigration and industrialization. Children worked in factories, instead of being apprenticed. The combination of factory work and the increased numbers of children living in crowded cities gave rise to concern among social reformers about the well-being of children. This concern led to the enactment of child labor and compulsory education laws. Homes for poor, wayward, and abandoned children were established, with a focus on rehabilitation, rather than punishment.

Historians attribute the rise of the state as *parens patriae* to the third period, which encompassed the late 1800's to 1967. During this era, the first statewide juvenile courts were formed, beginning in Illinois in 1899. These courts continued to emphasize protection, rehabilitation, treatment, and benevolence. The involvement of lawyers in juvenile courts was discouraged, and children were not considered to have the same constitutional rights as adults.

The beginning of the final period, 1967 to the present, was marked by a United

States Supreme Court case, *In re Gault*, 387 U.S. 1, 87 S.Ct. 1428 (1967), in which the Supreme Court began to recognize the Constitutional rights of juveniles. Since *Gault*, children have been held to have most of the constitutional rights afforded to adults in juvenile delinquency proceedings, and children have the right to independent counsel in most types of cases affecting their welfare. Some commentators believe that we are in the early stages of another era, as states, including New York, impose adult criminal liability on younger and younger children. A child as young as 13 can be tried as an adult for murder in New York.

Children Born Out of Wedlock

One group of children whose rights have expanded dramatically in the latter half of the twentieth century are those who used to be called "illegitimate." At common law, children born out of wedlock were seen either as the child of no one, or the child of the public. They did not have a right to support or inheritance from their fathers. One justification for limiting the rights of these children was the difficulty of proving paternity. Modern courts have settled on a compromise: the United States Supreme Court has held unconstitutional State laws that deny inheritance rights to out-of-wedlock children that are available to marital children, but it has allowed to stand additional procedural requirements for children born out of wedlock, such as a court order of filiation before a child can inherit from his or her father. *Trimble v. Gordon*, 430 U.S. 762, 97 S.Ct. 1459 (1977); *Lalli v. Lalli*, 439 U.S. 259, 99 S.Ct. 518 (1978).

WHEN IS A CHILD NOT A CHILD?

Should children have all of the rights of adults? When we categorize someone as a child, we must consider what we mean by "child" and what rights we believe it is appropriate for that child to have. While children's rights have expanded over the years, being classified as a child or minor still limits the child's rights, but also affords special protections. A child cannot bring a lawsuit in his or her own name, for example, but statutes of limitations are tolled for causes of action that arise during the time a person is classified as a minor.

Ages of Majority

There are several possible ways to approach setting an age of majority. One way would be to set the age of majority uniformly for all issues. Under such an approach, a person would become an adult for all purposes upon reaching a certain age, such as 18, for example. Another possibility is to have the age of majority vary, depending on the issue at hand. Under this method, a person might be allowed to vote at age 18, but be entitled to parental support until age 21. Another technique would be to have the age of majority be simply a presumption that is rebuttable, depending on the circumstance and maturity of the child.

While legislatures have generally chosen to set ages of majority that depend on the issue, today there is a movement toward adoption of 18 as the uniform age of majority. The age of majority in New York was 21 until 1974, when it was reduced to 18. Today, for example, the Social Services Law, the Civil Rights Law, the Domestic Relations Law, and the Real Property Law all generally define "infant" or "minor" as a person who has not attained the age of 18 years. SSL § 2(31); Civil Rights Law § 1-a; DRL § 2; Real Property Law § 2(2). One exception is that the child support obligation continues until the child reaches age 21. SSL § 101; FCA § 413; DRL § 32.

Besides the major exception for child support, New York's laws contain other inconsistencies that cause confusion for parents, practitioners of family law, and probably for the young people as well. Although a 19-year-old can vote and serve in the military, he or she cannot legally buy an alcoholic drink in a bar in New York. Moreover, while children are not generally considered adults until age 18 and parents are responsible for supporting their children to age 21, the statute that defines "Persons in Need of Supervision" (PINS) has been read by courts to apply to children of both sexes only to age 16. FCA § 712(a). PINS petitions are most often brought by parents who feel they can no longer control their child's behavior. Thus, if the child over the age of 16 runs away or refuses to obey the parent's lawful commands, the parent has no legal recourse.

Emancipation

An **emancipated minor** is one who is no longer subject to the care and control of the parents. Emancipation has been defined as "the renunciation of legal duties by a parent and the surrender of parental rights to a child." *Matter of Bates v. Bates,*, 62 Misc.2d 498, 310 N.Y.S.2d 26 (Fam. Ct. Westchester County 1970). Emancipation may occur in several ways; at common law the traditional avenues to emancipation were for the child to get married, to join the military, to refuse to live with the parents, or to become economically self-supporting. As you will see in Chapter 7, today courts are reluctant to find a child emancipated unless adequate support for the child is assured. An emancipated minor may be treated legally as an adult for many purposes, among others, the choice of where to live, the right to wages, the forfeiture of the right to parental support, and the right to sue and be sued.

New York's law regarding emancipation is unusual in that emancipation has been litigated almost exclusively in the context of terminating a parent's obligation to support the child. In other words, the issue arises as a defense to a parental obligation, and not by virtue of the child's having initiated a legal proceeding to have him or herself declared emancipated.

CHILD LABOR

During the Colonial period, children were apprenticed to masters in order to learn a trade. There were both charitable and practical reasons for the growth of apprenticeship in the colonies. During the seventeenth century, sending children from London to be apprenticed in the colonies was seen as a way to rescue poor children from the trials of life in London. It was also a way to teach children a valuable skilled trade. Practically, apprentices provided inexpensive, much-needed labor. Apprenticeship was also a way to keep poor children from becoming dependent on community resources for their support.

There were, of course, abuses of this system. Masters did not always instruct apprentices properly, and some did not provide adequate food or lodging. Sometimes children were apprenticed for excessive amounts of time. Others were hired simply to provide additional labor, and then later laid off when demand for the master's product declined. As a result of these abuses, in New York, the Apprenticeship Law of 1871 made masters liable for not teaching the art or craft agreed upon or for not providing proper board, lodging, or medical attention to their apprentices. It also required masters to certify in writing at the end of the apprenticeship that the apprentice had been taught a particular trade or craft over the course of only three to five years.

The Apprenticeship Law came too late, however, to be of assistance to most apprentices. With industrialization in the nineteenth century, there was less need for skilled workers. By the time the Apprenticeship Law was passed, most child workers were no longer apprentices, but factory workers, and the Apprenticeship Law did not apply to them.

The factory system brought its own exploitation of children. Children once again provided inexpensive labor. Since factory work was unskilled, the children worked long hours at often dangerous tasks for low wages, and they learned nothing that would be of further value to them. By the end of the nineteenth century, activists were already trying to improve the working conditions of children through protective statutes. Once again, there were both altruistic and self-serving reasons for this activism. On the charitable side, the reformers recognized the neglect of education as a result of the long hours children worked. The need for literacy in a democratic nation was one of the reasons advanced for legislation limiting the hours that children could work. The danger to children's health from machinery was also deplored. On the less altruistic side, trade unions were concerned about the competition that children created for their members. They also recognized that children made up so large a part of the work force that reducing working hours for children would have the same result for adult workers.

Beginning in 1876, a series of "wrongs to children" laws were passed in New York. These laws limited the number of hours and the industries in which children could work, prohibited night work, raised the minimum age for factory work, and developed a system of inspection for enforcement. Such laws were not, however, without their opponents. The child's wages were often an important source of income for poor families. In states where manufacturers were politically powerful, it was hard to enforce the compulsory education laws that accompanied the child labor laws. In addition, industrialists argued that laws mandating shorter working hours for children would put them at a comparative disadvantage to manufacturers in states whose legislatures were not concerned with child labor.

The first federal legislation regulating child labor was the Owen-Keating Bill which was passed in 1916. The United States Supreme Court soon held this "Act to Prevent Interstate Commerce in the Products of Child Labor" to be an unconstitutional use of Congress' powers to regulate interstate commerce. *Hammer v. Dagenhart*, 247 U.S. 251, 38 S.Ct. 529 (1918). A law that taxed profits of industries which improperly employed children was also held unconstitutional. *Bailey v. Drexel Furniture Co.*, 259 U.S. 20, 42 S.Ct. 449 (1922). Reformers then tried in 1924 to amend the Constitution in order to allow Congress to pass laws relating to child labor, but those efforts met with an effective campaign of resistance from manufacturers' associations. They argued that the amendment was sponsored by communists and that, "If adopted, this amendment would be the greatest thing ever done in America in behalf of the activities of Hell. It would make millions of young people under 18 years of age idlers in brain and body, and thus make them the devil's best workshop. It would destroy the initiative and self-reliance and manhood and womanhood of all the coming generations." "What the Child Labor Amendment Means," *Manufacturers' Record* (Baltimore, MD), Sept. 4, 1924, excerpted in Grace Abbott, *The Child and the State* 546-547 (1938).

The amendment was never ratified, but in 1940, *Hammer* was finally overturned, and the constitutionality of the 1938 Fair Labor Standards Act (29 U.S.C. §§ 201 et seq.) was sustained. *U.S. v. Darby Lumber Co.*, 312 U.S. 100, 61 S.Ct. 451 (1941). The Fair Labor Standards Act prohibits and punishes "oppressive child labor practices" among employers engaged in interstate commerce. State child labor laws protect children in employment not covered by the federal law. In New York, for example, Article 4 of the Labor Law regulates the employment of minors. Section 130 of that statute prohibits the employment of children under age 14, with exceptions for child performers, models, and newspaper carriers. The Article also prohibits employment of children during school hours, depending on their age. Labor Law § 131.

THE RIGHT TO EDUCATION

Historical Perspectives

The state's interest in an educated citizenry has long been recognized, and education is now considered a basic function of government. There have been attempts at "universal" education in New York since the days when it was still New Netherlands. The Revolutionary War interfered with efforts to establish public schools, but the Regents of the University of the State of New York was founded shortly after independence was achieved. In 1795, a bill was enacted to provide public elementary schools, known as "common schools," on an experimental basis, and permanent funding was granted in 1805.

While education has not been recognized as a fundamental constitutional right, whatever education a state provides must be available to all resident children on an equal basis. Access may not be denied on the basis of race, wealth, sex, or national origin. Equal access has only recently become the law. Until 1954 the United States Supreme Court upheld the so-called "separate but equal" doctrine, which allowed schools to be segregated on the basis of race. *Plessy v. Ferguson*, 163 U.S. 537, 16 S.Ct. 1138 (1896). In 1954, the Supreme Court desegregated American schools in *Brown v. Board of Education*, 347 U.S. 483, 74 S.Ct. 686 (1954).

Compulsory Education

All states now have compulsory education laws. In fact, under New York law, a parent's failure to encourage and facilitate his or her child's attendance at school is a form of neglect. FCA § 1012(f)(i)(A); SSL § 371(a)(i)(A). The constitutionality of general compulsory education laws has been upheld. The Supreme Court did hold that an Oregon statute that required all school-aged children to attend *public* school impermissibly interfered with the parent's liberty to direct the rearing and education of their children. *Pierce v. Society of Sisters*, 268 U.S. 510, 45 S.Ct. 571 (1925). Today, acceptable alternatives to public schools are private schools, parochial schools, and "adequate" home schooling. There are exceptions to compulsory education laws in situations where they infringe a protected constitutional right. The United States Supreme Court held in *Wisconsin v. Yoder*, 406 U.S. 205, 92 S.Ct. 1526 (1972) that Amish religious beliefs outweighed the state's interest in compulsory education. The Court allowed parents not to send their son to school after the eighth grade, since to force the child to go to school until age 16 (in accordance with the state statute) would violate the parents' religious beliefs. This exception is, however, a very narrow one. Federal courts have denied a similar argument based on Native American beliefs. *Duro v. District Attorney of the Second Judicial District of North Carolina*, 712 F.2d 96 (4 Cir. 1983).

CORPORAL PUNISHMENT

Corporal Punishment at Home

At common law, the same duty to support children that entitled parents to the services of their children also entitled parents to use reasonable physical punishment against their children. A nineteenth century commentator recognized the potential for misuse of this privilege: "As [parents] are bound to maintain and educate their children, the law has given them a right to such authority; and in support of that authority, a right to the exercise of such discipline as may be requisite for the discharge of their sacred trust. This is the true foundation of parental power; and yet the ancients generally carried the power of the parent to a most atrocious extent over the person and liberty of the child." James Kent, *Commentaries on American Law*, excerpted in Grace Abbott, *The Child and the State* 51 (1938). Today, parents are still allowed to use reasonable corporal punishment. The parental privilege does not, however, extend to use of "excessive" corporal punishment. What is "excessive"?

Factors that courts have considered in deciding what constitutes excessive corporal punishment include the child's age, sex, and mental capacity to understand the punishment; the means, severity, nature, and purpose of the punishment; and the parent's conduct. See *In the Matter of Rodney C.*, 91 Misc.2d 677, 398 N.Y.S.2d 511 (Fam. Ct. Onondaga County 1977).

Corporal Punishment at School

At common law, teachers, standing in the place of parents during school hours, were allowed to use physical punishment against their students to an extent deemed reasonably necessary for the students' education and discipline. The United States Supreme Court upheld the constitutionality of the use of corporal punishment in public schools for disciplinary purposes in *Ingraham v. Wright*, 430 U.S. 651, 97 S.Ct. 1401 (1977). In *Ingraham*, the Court held that paddling did not constitute cruel and unusual punishment and that prior notice and a hearing were not required before a student could be disciplined physically. In New York, a teacher is justified in using physical force against a student "when and to the extent that he reasonably believes it necessary to maintain discipline or to promote the welfare of such person." Penal Law § 35.10(1).

The justification for using physical force is not unlimited. The punishment must not be excessive. According to the statute, teachers cannot use "deadly" physical force. Penal Law § 35.10(1). In addition, even if a teacher's use of corporal punishment would be justified under the criminal law, it may still be grounds for disciplinary action against the teacher by a local school board, since New York state educational policy delegates the power to regulate the use of corporal punishment to local school districts. *Bott v. Board of Ed., Deposit Cent. Sch. Dist.*, 41 N.Y.2d 265, 392 N.Y.S.2d 274 (1977). The New York City Board of Education has banned corporal punishment and "punishment of any kind tending to cause excessive fear or physical or mental distress" in New York City public schools. Violation of this rule constitutes grounds for a teacher's dismissal. Bylaws of the Board of Education, City School District of the City of New York, § 10.4.

CONCLUSION

The mythical "typical" American family has never existed. No two families, happy or unhappy, are alike. What has changed in the latter half of this century is not the diversity of families but the law's perhaps belated recognition that there is more to "family" than blood ties or legal documents. Within the context of Family Law, legislatures and courts have struggled and continue to struggle with fundamental questions about the law itself: What is "private" and, thus, entirely beyond the reach of the law? What societal expectations is the legal system entitled to impose on families? What rights do family members have within the family and within our society as a whole? How much deference should the law give to the role of religion in family life? Are legislatures or courts better suited to attempt to regulate familial relationships?

With each change in the law, the legal system both acknowledges shifting social norms and sets the stage for further evolution. When the legislators of the past century gave women the right to own property in their own names, they may not have anticipated that women would one day be required to pay alimony or that they would compete with men for the privilege of piloting jet planes, but in retrospect the progression appears inevitable. Family Law challenges us to define who we are and in what direction we are moving.

CHAPTER REVIEW QUESTIONS

1. State whether each of the following persons whose names are underlined are related by consanguinity or affinity:
   - Laura and Amy are first cousins. Their mothers are twin sisters.
   - June is Laura's sister-in-law. June's brother is Laura's husband.
   - Daquan is Laura's step-brother. Laura's mother is married to Daquan's father.
   - Earnest is Laura's grandfather. Earnest adopted Laura's father when he was a baby.
   - Laura is Alexander's aunt. June is Alexander's mother.

2. Martha files a petition seeking custody of her neighbor Mimi's four-month-old baby. Mimi works full time and leaves the baby in a licensed day care facility during the day. Martha alleges that the baby would be better off with a custodian who is a full-time homemaker. The judge dismisses Martha's petition on a summary judgment motion without conducting a trial. Why?

3. List four legal rights women have gained during the twentieth century and the year in which they acquired each right in New York.

4. How do rights like the right to own property, to receive equal pay for equal work, to hold public office and to vote affect women's roles in their families?

5. What is the age of majority in New York for most purposes? What is the most significant exception?

6. Andy is a 17-year-old computer whiz who has just sold the patent on a new type of software for a million dollars. If Andy's father no longer wishes to contribute to his support, what might he argue that Andy is?

CHAPTER ASSIGNMENT

Read one of the cases cited (but not excerpted) in this chapter and, without quoting headnotes, prepare a synopsis of the case, using interoffice memorandum format.

FOR FURTHER READING

Sara M. Evans, *Born For Liberty* (1989).

The Female Experience: An American Documentary (Gerda Lerner, ed. 1992).

Bernadette Dunn Sewell, Note: "History of Abuse: Societal, Judicial, and Legislative Responses to the Problem of Wife Beating," 23 *Suffolk Univ. Law Rev.* 983 (1989).

New York City Commission on the Status of Women, *Legislative Achievements for Women in New York State: A 20-Year Retrospective, 1965-1985* (1985).

Susan Cary Nicholas et al., *Rights and Wrongs: Women's Struggle for Legal Equality* (2d ed. 1986).

Women's Rights in the United States: A Documentary History (Winston E. Langley and Vivian C. Fox, eds., 1994).

2 WORKING IN FAMILY LAW

PARALEGAL

Busy midtown law firm seeks bright & responsible indv. for entry level position. Applicant must be detail oriented & possess strong writing skills. Send resume.

The legal assistant who chooses to work in the field of Family Law must be ready for the challenges of finding a job and performing the paralegal tasks effectively. This chapter, a compendium of practical information, discusses how to search for a job in Family Law and how to approach the work in an organized and efficient manner. Working in New York Family Law requires a firm grasp of several fundamental concepts, as well as an understanding of the structure of the New York child welfare and court systems, which are explained in this chapter. The legal assistant must also be familiar with the research tools and peculiarities of citation form used in New York Family Law.

EMPLOYMENT OPPORTUNITIES

Family Law offers a rich variety of employment opportunities for legal assistants. In both the public and private sectors, legal assistants are essential for the provision of quality legal services at affordable rates. Probably no other legal specialty offers a wider choice of work settings in which a legal assistant's talents can be utilized. In the private sector, New York has an abundance of law firms that specialize in Family Law. Some are glamorously appointed offices handling the matrimonial problems of the rich and famous, while many others are more modest small or medium sized firms or solo practitioners who include a substantial amount of Family Law work along with other cases in a general practice.

In the public sector, the office of the Corporation Counsel within the City of New York and the County Attorneys elsewhere throughout the state provide legal representation to the child welfare components of the local Social Services districts, and they are responsible for prosecuting child protective proceedings, termination of parental rights cases, and agency adoptions. Paralegals in these offices are employed under a variety of titles such as legal assistant, trial preparation assistant, and investigator. In the Erie County District Attorney's office, for example, legal assistants are used to monitor child abuse and neglect cases that might result in criminal prosecutions.

The Unified Court System is also a major employer of legal assistants under titles such as Court Assistant and Court Clerk. In the Family Court, legal assistants serve in a variety of capacities in addition to the traditional court clerk jobs with which you may be familiar. Because Family Court is designed to be accessible to unrepresented (*pro se*) litigants, legal assistants work directly with litigants, drafting petitions and giving instructions and explanations about the legal process. Of course, they cannot give legal advice. If a litigant needs the help of a lawyer, but cannot afford to retain an attorney, the court may assign an attorney from the Assigned Indigent Counsel Panel. The Panel attorneys, called **"18-b" attorneys** after the section of the County Law that authorizes payment for their services, are private practitioners who are paid with public money for their work on assigned cases. They often serve as defense counsel to adult defendants or law guardians for the children in the cases brought by the attorneys for the child care agencies.

Not-for-profit agencies also play a prominent role in Family Law. The not-for-profit sector consists of agencies incorporated as charitable or public interest corporations that are funded through a combination of private contributions and public funds. The voluntary child care agencies, discussed below, are a large component of the not-for-profit sector, along with agencies devoted to such specialized concerns as representation of victims of domestic violence and collection of child support. These not-for-profit organizations usually have some in-house paralegals who draft documents and interview litigants, and they also often retain outside counsel for some portion of their legal work. Some law firms devote a significant proportion of their practice to such agencies. The Legal Aid Society and other similar organizations that provide legal assistance to indigent litigants also comprise an important part of the not-for-profit sector.

In organizing your job search within the Family Law arena, you should begin by asking yourself some preliminary questions. Would you be more comfortable in a large organization or a small office? Are you more concerned about the starting salary or prospects for promotion or job security? Are you a "people person," or are you more comfortable in a back office? Do you have strong pro-prosecution or pro-defense leanings, or will you be comfortable working on whatever case comes through the door? Are you especially committed to a particular issue, such as domestic violence or child abuse? Usually, trade-offs must be made. Particularly in your first job, you may not get a big salary and job security and the chance to do personally satisfying work all together in one glorious package. Taking stock of yourself will help you sell yourself convincingly to a prospective employer and will increase the likelihood that you will be happy with the job offer you decide to accept.

The search for a Family Law job does not begin and end with the classified section of your local newspaper. The *New York Law Journal* and *National Law Journal* contain advertisements for paralegal jobs, and local paralegal associations also usually maintain job placement banks. Entry level public sector jobs are generally filled from a list of those who have passed open competitive exams. Advance planning is required, as timing can be tricky. Applications to sit for civil service exams must be filed by a specified date in advance of the test, and the list of successful candidates appears months later. Those who passed the test are offered jobs in the order of their test scores, so that those in the middle of the list may get hired months after the list appears. To make sure that "your job" is ready for you when you are ready for it, begin the process about a year in advance of your anticipated graduation date. Start by looking at the postings in the nearest City, County, and State public employment offices and in the *Chief,* a newspaper devoted to public employment that is sold at newsstands around civic centers. In addition, notices for upcoming examinations and for jobs that do not require examination in the Unified Court System are posted in courthouses and are available for public inspection. The court system also maintains two telephone hotlines that provide up-to-date information regarding examinations and job announcements. For examination information call (212) 417-4738, and to learn about other available jobs call 1-800-654-5578.

Carefully scrutinize the minimum qualifications required for the jobs that interest you. Sometimes the postings say a particular educational degree is required "or equivalent experience." Once you have identified the jobs for which you are qualified to compete, check the dates of the next exams and file applications for the exams you think you have a reasonable chance of passing. Since there is usually an application fee, you will want to be realistic, but do not sell yourself short. Consider investing in a preparation book, from which you can glean an idea of the type of questions that usually appear on the exam and the general level of difficulty of the test. Bookstores around civic centers (the section of town where the courts and government offices are) often stock preparation books for civil service examinations.

Networking is particularly important in the private and not-for-profit areas, since many jobs are filled almost as soon as they open up. Not-for-profit agencies, such as the Erie County Citizens Committee on Rape and Sexual Assault and the Volunteer Lawyers Project, Inc. in Buffalo, often draw on a pool of applicants who have demonstrated a commitment to the issues with which the organization is particularly concerned. Internships are an excellent way to get a foot in the door, and an unpaid internship or volunteer service may be well worth the sacrifice in the long term. Even if you do not obtain a paying job in the agency in which you performed your internship, the experience will help you qualify for other positions that may require previous paralegal work history. Use the resources of your school placement office fully, and by all means discuss your plans with your Family Law professor.

LEGAL ASSISTANT TASKS AND SKILLS

In public, private, and not-for-profit settings, legal assistants perform the same tasks in Family Law matters as they do in other areas of law: interviewing clients; gathering information; drafting simple pleadings and legal documents; conducting preliminary research; and providing litigation support. The Chapter Assignments at the end of each chapter of this textbook provide an opportunity to strengthen each of these skills by applying them to the types of Family Law cases in which they are most needed.

Getting Oriented

Legal cases do not begin as contracts or law suits. They start with a client who has a problem and a raw, sometimes *very* raw, set of facts. The first step in building a legal case, therefore, is not to answer the legal question but to ask it. To find the legal issues in the thicket of facts, think of yourself as a reporter asking the questions every good news story must answer – who, what, where, when, and why. In law, these questions translate into the issues of standing, grounds and defenses, subject matter jurisdiction, venue, statutes of limitations and client's goals. Whether you are interviewing a client, gathering information, or drafting pleadings, you need to keep these concepts in mind. They are the trail markers all legal practitioners use to avoid wandering in a wilderness of information. The Basics Box preceding each subject area covered in this textbook summarizes standing, grounds, subject matter jurisdiction, venue, statutes of limitations, and applicable statutes as each type of Family Law case is introduced.

STANDING

The "*who*" question in law is, "Does this person have **standing** to raise this legal issue in court?" In its simplest form the question may be phrased, "Does this client have the right to sue for the relief or remedy he or she wants?" Who has the right to sue for divorce? Either spouse. Can a child sue to get his parents divorced? Of course not. Can a mother-in-law file suit to end her son's marriage to the daughter-in-law she thinks unworthy of her son? Obviously not, otherwise the courts would be even more overcrowded than they are now. Can a child petition to terminate her mother's parental rights? Ah, now you have to go and look it up. Flip to the Basics Box preceding Termination Of Parental Rights in Chapter 12, and you will see that under certain circumstances a Law Guardian for the child can initiate proceedings to terminate parental rights. You may have heard about a sensational case in Florida where a child, "Gregory K.," sued to "divorce" his parents. The term "divorce" was a misnomer in the popular press for the child's suit to terminate his biological parents' rights to him so that he could be adopted by his foster parents. Are you surprised to learn that such a suit could be entertained here in New York?

Standing in Family Law matters is almost always statutorily determined. If you need to answer a standing question at a time when you do not have your textbook handy, or if you want to make sure (as you should) the statute has not been amended since this book was published, go directly to the statute book that deals with the type of case you are working on. The index may not be helpful, so find the Article that pertains to your case type and scan the headings. Near the beginning of the Article, usually in a group of sections called "Preliminary Procedure," you will find a section headed something like "Who may file petition," which should answer the standing question.

GROUNDS AND DEFENSES

What must a plaintiff or petitioner prove in order to establish his or her right to the relief requested from the court? The elements a plaintiff must establish to be entitled to the relief requested are the **grounds** for a law suit. Does your firm's client complain that his wife is unsympathetic to his career goals or that she refuses to cook his favorite dinner? Unhappy as he may be, this client does not have grounds for divorce unless there is much more to the story. What if he alleges that the wife walked out on him last night and went to stay at her parents' house? Abandonment, you say; now we are getting someplace. Not so fast. In Family Law, some grounds for suit specify not only that certain conduct must have occurred, but also that it must have persisted for a certain length of time. To sue for divorce based on abandonment, for example, the abandonment must have lasted for a year. These **durational requirements** must not be confused with statutes of limitation, discussed below. Durational requirements are time periods *before* which suit cannot be brought, whereas statutes of limitation are time periods *after* which suit cannot be filed.

Defenses are the flip side of the grounds coin. They are facts that defeat the plaintiff's or petitioner's right to judicial relief. In a divorce case based on abandonment, for example, it might be a defense that the spouses reconciled during the period of alleged abandonment and resumed living together as husband and wife. Whether the client is a potential plaintiff or has already been sued, the legal assistant must note facts supporting both grounds and possible defenses with equal care.

SUBJECT MATTER JURISDICTION

The issue of subject matter jurisdiction is the first, and most crucial, part of the two-part *"where"* question, the other part being venue. **Subject matter jurisdiction** means that a particular court has the power to decide certain types of cases. New York's court system, although administratively unified, is highly fragmented in subject matter jurisdiction. Several trial-level courts share jurisdiction over closely related issues, and there are three levels of appellate courts. One family's problems may be divided among several different courts, therefore, and they may not be the courts you would first guess. The Family Court does *not* have jurisdiction to hear divorce cases, for example, although most people would certainly think of divorce as a family problem. The New York State constitution determines the structure of the court system, and amending the constitution is a complex and time-consuming process. Even though many commentators and jurists believe that the existing structure could benefit from some streamlining, it is unlikely to be changed in the near future. Learn to live with it as it is, even if you cannot love it, because mistakes in subject matter jurisdiction are disastrous.

Subject matter jurisdiction is an entirely separate principle from **personal jurisdiction** over the defendant in a law suit. Personal jurisdiction is usually acquired by service of process, such as a summons or a citation, upon the defendant or respondent in the manner specified by statute. Objections to defects in service are waivable, however. If a defendant has been improperly served, or never even served at all, he or she may nevertheless choose to appear in the proceeding and litigate the merits of the case.

Objections to subject matter jurisdiction, on the other hand, are *not* waivable. If a case has been brought in a court that does not have jurisdiction over that type of case, the resulting order is void, even if the defendant appeared, raised no objection, and fully litigated the matter. Objections to subject matter jurisdiction may be raised for the first time on appeal, even if they were not preserved before the trial court, and may even be raised months or years later when one party attempts to enforce the void order. They may even be raised by persons who were not involved in the lawsuit. An heir claiming under a will, for example, might assert that the "wife" of the deceased is not entitled to the spousal election because the marriage was bigamous, since the "wife's" divorce from her first husband (granted by a court that lacked subject matter jurisdiction) was void. Needless to say, the client who finds him or herself in possession of an "order" that is not worth the paper it is written on will start to think of a malpractice suit, at the very least. When it comes to subject matter jurisdiction, do not play your hunches. Get it right!

Trial Courts

Trial courts have **original jurisdiction**, that is the case begins there. Trial courts are also called *nisi prius* courts or **IAS** courts. IAS stands for Individual Assignment System, the Unified Court System's method of distributing cases to trial judges.

Trial courts may have general or limited jurisdiction. The New York Supreme Court is the only court of **general jurisdiction**. Under the New York constitution the Supreme Court may hear any case that is filed there. As the volume of litigation increased, however, several courts of limited jurisdiction were created with statutorily defined areas of responsibility. Courts of **limited jurisdiction** can hear only the types of cases authorized by the constitution and the applicable court act. Family Court, Surrogate's Court, County Court, Civil Court, District Court, and Criminal Court are all courts of limited jurisdiction. Even though the Supreme Court can constitutionally hear any case the courts of limited jurisdiction can hear, as a practical matter it will not.

Only in the rarest circumstances will the Supreme Court entertain a case that is within the jurisdiction of the courts of limited jurisdiction. In *Schneider v. Schneider*, 127 A.D.2d 491, 511 N.Y.S.2d 847 (1 Dept. 1987), *aff'd sub nom. Paul B.S. v. Pamela J.S.*, 70 N.Y.2d 739, 519 N.Y.S.2d 962 (1987), for example, the dispositional phase of a Family Court child abuse proceeding was consolidated with a custody case pending in Supreme Court. The court noted that the unusual procedure was necessary in that case "to deter the parents from racing between courts to maneuver for custody of and visitation with [the child]." Normally, however, the resources of the Unified Court System, including the number of judges sitting in each court, are allocated in expectation that each court will do its own work, and if you try to file a Family Court case in Supreme Court, you will be politely directed to the nearest Family Court. The Basics Box for each case type covered in this textbook specifies which courts have jurisdiction of that kind of case.

For each court of limited jurisdiction, there is a statute setting forth exactly what cases that court is authorized to hear. The two that are most relevant to Family Law are the Family Court Act and the Surrogate's Court Procedure Act. Often these statutes not only specify what sort of cases the court is allowed to entertain, but also what procedures should be followed. If a court act specifies a procedure for a particular type of case, such as a special method for service of process or a specific statute of limitations, that procedure takes precedence over the general procedure in the CPLR. If the court act is silent concerning the procedure to be followed in a certain situation, use the CPLR. Remember that a court of limited jurisdiction has *only* the powers the statute says it has, and you cannot read into the statute anything that is not there. Since divorce is a family problem, for example, you might reasonably expect the Family Court to have jurisdiction over divorce cases. Searching all three McKinney's volumes of the Family Court Act cover to cover, however, you will find no section authorizing the Family Court to hear divorce cases. Thus, you would correctly conclude that the Family Court *cannot* entertain divorce proceedings.

Trial courts may have exclusive original jurisdiction, concurrent original jurisdiction, ancillary jurisdiction, or referral jurisdiction. When a court has **exclusive original jurisdiction** over a particular type of case, it is the only court in which a petition or complaint can be filed for that relief. Supreme Court has exclusive original jurisdiction over divorce cases, for example. When a petitioner or plaintiff is allowed to choose among two or more courts in which to proceed, those courts have **concurrent jurisdiction** of that type of case. Supreme Court and Family Court have concurrent original jurisdiction over custody and visitation cases, and Family Court and Surrogate's Court have concurrent original jurisdiction over adoptions. The petitioner may chose whichever court is more convenient.

Some courts are authorized to deal with certain issues only when they arise in connection with other types of cases. This is called **ancillary jurisdiction**, meaning that the power to decide the issue is attached to the power the court has over the primary case. Family Court has exclusive original jurisdiction over paternity proceedings, for example, but the Surrogate's Court has ancillary jurisdiction to decide who is the father of an out-of-wedlock child when the issue arises in the context of an adoption or probate proceeding over which the Surrogate's Court has jurisdiction. A petitioner could not file a paternity case in Surrogate's Court, but once the issue has been decided there in connection with a pending adoption or probate case, the decision is binding on the parties. Think of ancillary jurisdiction as a case riding piggy-back on another case. The primary case must carry in the "rider" case, which would not otherwise be allowed through the door.

Referral jurisdiction is the power a court has to hear a certain type of case when another court sends it. In addition to its own original jurisdiction, Family Court also has jurisdiction to hear custody cases referred by the Supreme Court, and the Supreme Court can also refer the support and property division aspects of a divorce case to the Family Court. The following table shows the jurisdiction of the Supreme, Family, and Surrogate's courts in Family Law matters:

TABLE 2-1

A=Ancillary; CO=Concurrent Original; EO=Exclusive Original; R=Referral

CASE	SUPREME	FAMILY	SURROGATE'S
Adopt./Guard.		CO	CO
Annulment	EO		
Custody	CO	CO & R	
Divorce	EO	R (Equit. Dist.)	
Family Offenses	A (matrimonial)	CO (criminal)	
Foster Care		EO	
Neglect/Abuse		EO	
Paternity		EO	A
Separation	EO		
Support	A (matrimonial)	EO	
Term. Par. Rts.		CO	CO

Appellate Courts

Appellate courts have **appellate jurisdiction**. Our highest court, the Court of Appeals, sits in Albany and has seven judges. There are four Appellate Divisions, one for each of the four judicial departments, each of which has many judges. In deciding an appeal, Justices of the Appellate Division sit in panels, which usually consist of five justices, although sometimes the panels are smaller. The Appellate Term also consists of several specially designated Supreme Court Justices, and their panels normally consist of three justices. The following map shows which counties are in each of New York's four judicial departments:

Figure 2-1

NEW YORK JUDICIAL DEPARTMENTS AND DISTRICTS

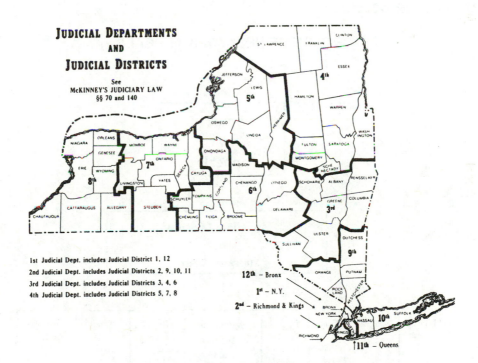

JUDICIAL DEPARTMENTS AND JUDICIAL DISTRICTS
See McKINNEY'S JUDICIARY LAW §§ 70 and 140

1st Judicial Dept. includes Judicial District 1, 12
2nd Judicial Dept. includes Judicial Districts 2, 9, 10, 11
3rd Judicial Dept. includes Judicial Districts 3, 4, 6
4th Judicial Dept. includes Judicial Districts 5, 7, 8

12th – Bronx
1st – N.Y.
2nd – Richmond & Kings
11th – Queens

Appellate courts do not take testimony or receive evidence. Rather, they review the record, consisting of transcripts of the court reporter's minutes and exhibits, and decide whether the trial court properly weighed the facts and applied the law. Generally, appellate courts either **reverse, affirm,** or **modify** the trial court's order or judgment. Occasionally the Appellate Division substitutes its own findings of facts for those of the trial court, as it is empowered to do, and enters an order or judgment accordingly. If an appellate court feels that the record below is incomplete, it may **remand** the case back to the next lowest court for further proceedings.

Appeals from trial courts follow two different routes. Some go directly to the Appellate Division, while others must go first to the Appellate Term. The chart below will help you identify where to take an appeal. As you see, appeals from the Family Court, Surrogate's Court, and trial terms of the Supreme Court go directly to the Appellate Division.

FIGURE 2-2

ROUTE OF NEW YORK APPEALS

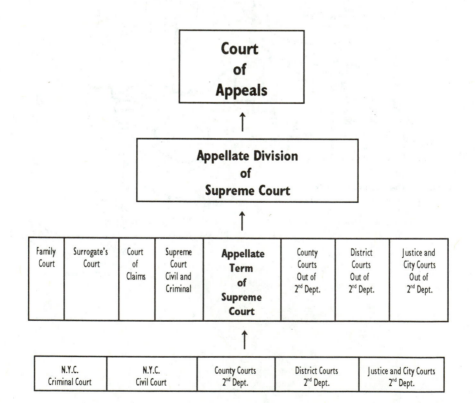

VENUE

Venue is the geographic location, the county, in which a particular case should be brought. For most case types, venue is based on the residence of at least one of the parties, but sometimes it is determined by where the acts complained of occurred. Objections to venue are waivable, and venue is less legally significant than subject matter jurisdiction. Venue provisions exist primarily to prevent "forum shopping," that is to keep a party from putting a case before a judge one party thinks might be sympathetic to that side, and to discourage the parties from deliberately inconveniencing each other by choosing a geographically remote location.

Venue is worthy of attention, because if the case is in the wrong venue the court may dismiss it **without prejudice**, which means that the petitioner or plaintiff will have to incur the expense and delay of refiling in the appropriate county. Practitioners in New York City should remember that the county names are not the same as the borough names: Queens is Queens and Bronx is Bronx, but Staten Island is Richmond County, Brooklyn is Kings County, and Manhattan is New York County. You can find the appropriate venue for each case type listed in the Basics Boxes and in the applicable statutes, usually at the beginning of the Article with the other preliminary topics.

STATUTES OF LIMITATIONS

Statutes of limitations are time periods at the expiration of which a legal case can no longer be brought based upon particular incidents or events. Regardless of how meritorious the plaintiff's grounds for relief may have been, the courthouse door will be shut if the statute of limitations has run. Thus, it is always essential to nail down precisely *when* the events at the heart of the case occurred. If the expiration is near, be sure to highlight that fact for the attorney in charge of the case.

Statutes of limitations play an important role in due process by preventing a potential defendant from having to respond to charges long after the event, when witnesses may no longer be available and memories have faded. Their enormous variation in length, from one year to upwards of 21 years, reflects legislative assessment of what is a reasonable time for a plaintiff to initiate legal proceedings, the difficulties a defendant might face in countering such charges, and the public importance of the issue that would be litigated. Generally the time runs from the occurrence of the event, but in some cases it is measured from the discovery of the event by the plaintiff. The time in which to file for divorce based on adultery, for example, is five years from the innocent spouse's discovery of the adultery. Most of the statutes of limitations are set out in Article 2 of the CPLR, but some are in the various court acts and in the Domestic Relations Law. Check the Article of the statute pertaining to the specific case type first; if no statute of limitation is specified, use the CPLR.

WHY IS THE CLIENT IN YOUR OFFICE?

Although neither the paralegal nor the attorney in charge may ever fully understand the clients' reasons for living as they have, you do need to understand enough to know whether they need a lawyer. Sometimes people come to an attorney's office when they really want a mediator or a psychotherapist or a member of the clergy. In your preliminary interview with a potential client, therefore, you will need to take the time to ascertain what outcome the potential client seeks concerning the problems at hand. Does the potential client want to divorce his wife, for example, or does he want to persuade her to reconcile with him? If he seeks reconciliation, it is the attorney's ethical duty to respect that wish and, if possible, to refer the client for marriage counseling. Of course, the legal assistant will not so advise the potential client, because the advice that one does not need legal advice is in itself a form of legal advice. The legal assistant should communicate the client's ultimate objectives to the attorney handling the case, along with other information obtained in the preliminary interview.

WHERE TO FIND NEW YORK FAMILY LAW

Before taking the Family Law course, most students have already taken a basic legal research course, which covered the fundamentals of legal research and citation form. Those ground rules apply to Family Law and need not be repeated here. Beyond the basics, however, are materials and techniques that will make your research in the field of Family Law more productive. Most of us do not have the luxury of performing research at a leisurely pace. We need a correct answer, fast. The quickest route to the result depends upon what materials you have at hand. Most offices do not have a perfectly equipped legal library, and traveling to one may take longer than the boss or the client is willing to wait. The improvisational aspect of legal research makes it more of an art than a science.

PRIMARY SOURCES

The definitive answer to any legal question must come from the **primary sources** of law, which are statutes and case law. All other sources are useful only to help you find the primary sources and to interpret or apply them.

Statutes

Since most of Family Law, except custody, is now codified in statutes, your research should begin there. Finding the applicable statutes can be complicated, as the same case types are often covered in more than one statute. The primary statutes dealing with Family Law issues are:

- **Domestic Relations Law (DRL)** ☞ Matrimonial Actions (Annulment, Separation, Divorce); Support; Property Division; Custody; Adoption.

- **Family Court Act (FCA)** ☞ Support; Paternity; Custody; Child Protective Proceedings; Termination of Parental Rights; Adoption; Family Offenses (Domestic Violence).

- **Social Services Law (SSL)** ☞ Termination of Parental Rights; Adoption; Approval of Voluntary Foster Care Agreements; Surrenders for Adoption; Authority and Duties of Child Care and Child Protective Agencies; Putative Fathers Register; Statewide Central Register of Child Abuse and Maltreatment.

- **Surrogate's Court Procedure Act (SCPA)** ☞ Termination of Parental Rights; Adoption; Guardainship; Paternity.

Since these statutes are ubiquitous in Family Law, this textbook will refer to them by their abbreviations. Other less frequently cited statutes will be referred to by their full names. Since all New York legal practitioners are on a first-name basis with the Civil Practice Law and Rules, this textbook follows custom and calls it the CPLR.

In addition to these four primary statutes, Family Law practitioners will have more than a passing acquaintance with several other statutes. The Internal Revenue Code, a Federal statute, plays a big role in support and property division. Also, the Family Court Act is cross-referenced to the Penal Law for the definitions of family offenses and sex offenses. The New York State constitution contains a number of provisions specifically relevant to Family Law, particularly concerning religion as a factor in foster care and adoption. The United States Constitution is the supreme law of the land to which all other laws must conform.

The statutes of New York are available in several versions. The words of the statutes are the same in all versions, of course, but the formatting varies. The official edition, to which citation must be made in all court papers, briefs and memoranda, is *McKinney's Consolidated Laws of New York Annotated,* published by West Publishing Company. In addition to the text of the statutes, *McKinney's* contains a treasure trove of useful information: 1) Practice Commentaries, in which specialists discuss the practical application of each statute and its interface with other related statutes; 2) Notes of Decisions, which are brief synopses of important cases interpreting or applying the statute; 3) Historical Notes, brief legislative histories indicating when and how a statute has been amended; and 4) Library References, which point the reader to treatises and other secondary sources pertaining to the topic the statute addresses. The books are updated with annual pocket parts inserted into the back cover of each book. An alternative hardcover edition of the New York statutes is *New York Consolidated Laws Service Annotated Statutes with Forms,* published by Lawyers Cooperative Publishing Company. A useful feature of the CLS statutes is that forms are included in the same volumes as the statutes, following the sections of the statutes to which they are relevant.

Standing in front of a full set of McKinney's statutes, which takes up about 22 feet of bookshelf space, you will quickly notice that the statutes are in alphabetical order. The Domestic Relations Law is Book 14, actually two volumes plus a soft-cover supplementary pamphlet. Naturally, your eyes then travel to "f" to find the Family Court Act, but it is not there. Fight through the moment of panic and move down to the "j's," where you will find it under Judiciary -- Court Acts. It is in three volumes, all, rather confusingly, numbered 29A. The Social Services Law and the Surrogate's Procedure Act are where they belong alphabetically. The Social Services Law is two volumes numbered 52A, while the Surrogate's Court Procedure Act is in three volumes as 58A.

If you need portability more than comprehensiveness, you may choose to use another version of the statutes. Looseleaf Law Publications, Inc. produces *Family Law of the State of New York*, a ring binder containing the Family Court Act, Family Court Rules, the Domestic Relations Law and Extracts of the Social Services Law. Although this version contains only the statutes and lacks the useful information that adds bulk to McKinney's, it has the advantage of compactness and updates after each session of the legislature. The updates are looseleaf pages that slip right into their proper place in the ring binder. Another looseleaf version is the *Family Law Handbook*, published by Gould, which contains the complete Family Court Act and Domestic Relations Law and Uniform Court Rules a well as Articles 5 and 6 of the Social Services Law. This book is also available in a bound version.

A word of caution about statutory citation is in order. Some of the statutes that are important in Family Law, particularly the Child Support Standards Act (in the Family Court Act and the Domestic Relations Law) and Article 10 of the Family Court Act and section 384-b of the Social Services Law, are heavily subdivided. Statute subdivisions differ from one statute to another. In some, the first "bite" is a letter and in others a number. The subdivisions may be demarcated with a combination of upper and lower case letters, Roman numerals and regular numbers. What matters is getting the letters or numbers in the right sequence in the citation and not skipping a larger subdivision to get to the smaller one. Each subdivision goes into its own parentheses, and there should be as many parentheses as it takes to reach the specific material you are referring to. The process is similar to the connect-the-dots games we all loved as children. Just go with the flow, but do not leave out any steps.

Another tip to bear in mind in researching statutes is that some section numbers have letters attached that are part of the section number, rather than subdivisions. For example, section 384-b of the Social Services Law, which deals with termination of parental rights, is a free-standing section, separate from section 384 of that statute, which concerns voluntary surrenders for adoption, and also distinct from sections 384-a and 384-c. As new sections are added to an existing statute, they are inserted near existing sections that pertain to related topics, rather than being tacked on to the end of the Article.

Published Judicial Opinions

The introductory research course covers the basics of finding and citing case law, and decisions pertaining to Family Law are mixed in with the myriad of other decisions. To protect the privacy of the litigants, Family Law cases are often published with the family names of the litigants reduced to initials, or as "Anonymous" or under pseudonyms. To further confuse things, the name of a case occasionally changes form from one level court to the next, as you may have noticed in the *Schneider* case discussed on page 45. Cite the case as it appears in the decision you are referring to, and do not worry about the discrepancy. Family Law practitioners are used to this problem. If, by chance, you know the full names of the litigants in a case that has been published anonymously or with initials, do *not* put the real names in your citation. When you Shepardize a Family Law case using the volume and page number of the decision, you will turn up any higher appellate decisions. Incidentally, decisions published in New York's official reporter -- New York Reports 2d, Appellate Division Reports 2d, and Miscellaneous Reports 2d -- do not follow Blue Book citation form. If you want to cite in a brief or memorandum a case you have come across in a published judicial opinion, use Blue Book form, not the citation as it appears in the published opinion.

Although all appellate decisions are published, only selected trial court opinions are published. If you come into possession of an unpublished trial court decision you think might be useful in the future, keep it in your office's files. If you decide to refer to it in a memorandum, you should attach the entire opinion as an exhibit to the memorandum, after having redacted the names of the litigants to preserve their privacy. Decisions published in the *New York Law Journal* are not always published in the reporters, but you are allowed to cite such cases by their WESTLAW citation or by their page and column numbers in the *Law Journal*. Check first, however, to make sure there is no official citation.

SECONDARY SOURCES

Secondary sources include all materials about law other than the actual statutes and published judicial opinions. Treatises, commentaries, textbooks, law review articles, law journal articles, and form books are all secondary sources. Some are national in scope, while others focus specifically on New York law. Works of national scope are useful if the problem you are working on is novel in New York, or if you are urging the court to adopt an approach that has been accepted in other jurisdictions. Generally, however, New York specific materials are a faster route to the answer. Family Law practitioners in New York are blessed with an abundant selection of secondary sources. One of the most respected is *Law and the Family New York*, a multi-volume set published by Lawyers Cooperative Publishing. *New York Matrimonial Law and Practice* and *Family Court Law and Practice in New York* are also useful general references, as are the Domestic Relations volumes of *New York Jurisprudence 2d*, all from the same publisher. Some treatises cover one area of Family Law in great depth. *Lindey on Separation Agreements and Antenuptial Contracts*, published by

Matthew Bender, is considered by many the bible on the subject, while *Spouse and Child Support in New York*, published by Lawyers Cooperative in a ring binder format, is a comprehensive but concise treatment of that topic.

Useful source materials that should not be overlooked are the handouts prepared for continuing legal education seminars and workshops. Often these outlines and course books save hours of tedium. PLI and the National Federation of Paralegal Associations sponsor such workshops specifically for legal assistants. Bar associations regularly produce them for attorneys, and usually legal assistants are welcome to attend. The four departments of the Appellate Division also sponsor training programs, and some produce books as well as outlines. The *Lawyer's Manual on Domestic Violence: Representing the Victim*, published by the Appellate Division, First Department, for example, is chock full of valuable information, including a directory of service providers.

Never cite a case or statute from a secondary source without looking it up first. Mistakes and typos occur, and even works in an updatable format usually lag weeks or months behind the primary sources. Besides, when you actually read the case, you may decide it does not hit your issue right on the head the way you hoped it would.

Form Books

Most law offices maintain an in-house data bank, in hard copy or on disks, of the forms they use most often. Once in a while, however, you will need to turn to a form book for help. *McKinney's New York Forms*, published by West, and *New York Lawyer's Formbook*, published by the New York State Bar Association, are both excellent sources. *Family Practice in N.Y.S. A Practical Approach*, published by Looseleaf Law Publications, Inc., contains both text and forms. Drafting Libraries and MatLaw are companies that make Family Law software with which you can generate tailored Family Law documents directly through your computer. MatLaw also contains a library of annotations in a context-sensitive format, which you can also use to obtain statutory references, court rules, and digests of court decisions for guidance in completing the forms.

Computerized Legal Research

If you are fortunate enough to work in a law office that subscribes to a computer-assisted legal research data base, such as WESTLAW or Lexis, you have a magic carpet for legal research. Once you master the basics, all the statutes and published opinions are at your fingertips, along with an astounding quantity of secondary material. The *New York Law Journal*, with its hot-off-the-press decisions and up-to-the minute commentaries on topics of current interest, is just a click away. Law reviews, compendiums of scholarly articles published at most major law schools, are also available, a great boon since the hardcopy versions are usually stocked only at law schools, which may allow admittance only to students and faculty of the university.

One tool you always have with you is your memory. Cases and statutes you have read in the course of your education or your work will stick with you if you read them with real comprehension. What does not always stick, unfortunately, is the name of the case or the section number of the statute. If you can remember anything at all about the subject, you are ahead of the game using an on-line or CD-ROM research base, such as West CD-ROM Jurisdictional Libraries. You will be able to make good use of any fragmentary memory you can dredge up, because you can search by a description of the issue, or by the name of the judge who wrote the opinion, or even by the date, if you happen to remember that you read the opinion in the *Law Journal* on your birthday. You can also combine these bits of information to narrow down the focus of your search.

If your computer can access the Internet, you can obtain a great deal of law-related material. For example the *Law Journal* has a web page, www.ljx.com, as do many bar associations, such as the American Bar Association, www.abanet.org, and the United States Federal Judiciary, www.uscourts.gov. Use your favorite web browser, searching a topic such as "United States Supreme Court."

LIBRARIES

For the student, gaining access to a library with a reasonable selection of primary or secondary materials about law can be a challenge. Although some paralegal programs are associated with universities that also have a law school, many are not. If the available school library is not as extensive as you may need or if it is not open at hours convenient to you, other options may be available. First, inquire whether your school has a courtesy admission arrangement with the library of a law school. If not, call the local bar associations to ask whether they will allow non-members to use the association's library. Many do permit such access, although most charge a fee to non-members. The law library of the Fourth Department Appellate Division in Buffalo is open to the public, although users are not allowed to remove materials. The SUNY Buffalo Law School also permits public access, and it has generous hours: Saturdays 9 a.m. to 6 p.m.; Sundays noon to 11 p.m.; Mondays through Thursdays 8 a.m. to 11 p.m. and Fridays 8 a.m. to 9 p.m.

Public libraries also often contain more law materials than you might expect. In New York City, for example, Mid-Manhattan Library contains many books and treatises in various areas of law, *Corpus Juris Secundum*, and a small collection of law journals indexed in the *Index to Legal Periodicals* and Legaltrac on CD-ROM. They also have the United States Code Annotated, United States Reports and Supreme Court Slip Opinions (those which have not yet been published in the reporters). U.S. Supreme Court Digest and the oral arguments presented to the Supreme Court are available on microfiche. New York materials include *McKinney's Consolidated Laws of New York Annotated* and the *New York State Register*, while New York City is covered in the New York City Charter and Code and the *City Record*. The Bronx Reference Center and St. George (Staten Island) Reference Center also have Federal, New York State and New

York City laws. Some of the larger reference rooms in the branch libraries also have New York State and New York City statutes. When using legal materials in public libraries, inquire whether the materials are updated on a regular basis. Some no longer are, due to budgetary constraints.

Some law libraries are open to the public on a limited basis through the New York Public Library's METRO (New York Metropolitan Reference and Research Library Agency) Referral card. There are two types of METRO referral cards. The first allows library users access to another member library to consult a specific title not available in the New York Public Library. Such cards are issued for the one-time use of a specific title. The second type permits access to a subject portion of the host library for a specific period. METRO referral cards are issued by Mid-Manhattan Library, the Bronx and St. George Reference Centers, and all major units of the Research Libraries. The Donnell Reference Library does not issue METRO referral cards. The number in New York City to call for general information is (212) 237-8225, and for reference questions (212) 237-8246.

ETHICS

Although the fundamental rules of ethics are covered in introductory courses that are prerequisites to the Family Law course in most curriculums, their importance warrants a brief review. In 1995, the Association of the Bar of the City of New York issued Formal Opinion 1995-11 updating its position on the ethical responsibilities of attorneys with regard to legal assistants and other non-lawyer employees. Because of the prestige of the organization, Opinion 1995-11 merits serious attention, and its salient points are summarized here:

- Disciplinary Rule 1-104(A) makes an attorney who employs another attorney or non-lawyer responsible for the ethical conduct of those employees. Because many paralegals do not have legal training and are not subject to discipline as attorneys are, the attorney employing a paralegal has a heightened duty of supervision with regard to the non-lawyer employee. Thus, as questions inevitably arise in the course of a legal assistant's work, the legal assistant should turn first to the attorney-employer for guidance. To receive meaningful guidance, the legal assistant must ask questions forthrightly as they arise. Do not act first and ask later, and do not bury the question in a long conversation about other issues.

- N.Y. Judiciary Law §§ 478 and 484 prohibit the unauthorized practice of law, and the non-lawyer who violates this rule is subject to punishment along with the attorney-employer. Precisely what constitutes the unauthorized practice of law, however, is less clear than the legal assistant might wish. Definitely prohibited are appearance in court, holding oneself out to be a lawyer, and rendering legal advice to a particular client. Tasks that may be performed *under the close supervision of an attorney* include: 1) investigating the facts of a case; 2) conducting legal research to identify relevant laws, judicial opinions, and legal articles; 3) organizing and analyzing information; 4) preparing reports for the attorney's use; 5) helping to prepare legal arguments; 6) drafting pleadings to be filed with the court; 7) obtaining affidavits; 8) assisting the attorney during trial; 9) keeping files of all documents and correspondence important to a case; 10) helping to draft documents such as contracts, mortgages, separation agreements, and trust instruments; 11) helping to prepare tax returns; 12) helping to plan estates; 13) coordinating the activities of the other law office employees; 14) keeping financial records for the office.

- A legal assistant is to maintain the confidentiality of clients' confidences and secrets. A **confidence** is information revealed by a client to an attorney in the course of the professional relationship. Confidences are protected by the attorney-client privilege and may not be revealed except as required by law or court order or upon the consent of the client. A **secret** is other information gained in the professional relationship that the client has requested be held inviolate or the disclosure of which would be embarrassing or detrimental to the client.

- A lawyer may not list paralegals on letterhead or business cards without clearly identifying their non-lawyer status. In communicating, either orally or in writing, with a client, another lawyer or member of the public, the legal assistant must make known his or her lay status. Thus, a legal assistant who goes to court to request an adjournment or to file documents should state that he or she is a paralegal employed by the attorney of record for the case, rather than saying, "I am from the office of Mr. Lawyer," which might create the misunderstanding that he or she is an associate of the firm.

- A non-lawyer may not share fees with an attorney, but may receive a bonus tied to the net profits of the firm rather than to the volume of business brought or referred by the non-lawyer to the firm. A non-lawyer may also be included in a retirement plan based on a profit-sharing arrangement.

Beyond these general guidelines, Family Law presents many special ethical considerations, which are discussed in the relevant chapters of this textbook. Family Court records enjoy a confidential status conferred by sections 166, 351.1, 381.2, 435, 625, 783, 835, 915, and 1047 of the Family Court Act and by Rule 205.5 of the Uniform Rules of Court.

THE FAMILY COURT

The Family Court was established in 1962 as a statewide court with uniform procedures, eliminating the separate systems that had existed with the Children's

Court upstate and the Domestic Relations Court in New York City. In addition to its jurisdiction over support, paternity, custody, adoption, guardianship, family offenses, child abuse and neglect proceedings, foster care approval and review, and termination of parental rights cases, the Family Court also has exclusive original jurisdiction over juvenile delinquency and PINS (Persons In Need Of Supervision) cases. Juvenile Delinquency and PINS proceedings are not covered in this textbook because their quasi-criminal nature makes them conceptually distinct from the rest of Family Law. If you visit or work in a Family Court, however, you will see that juvenile delinquency cases consume a large portion of the court's working day.

DOCKET NUMBERS

Docket numbers for Family Court cases begin with a letter prefix that tells what type of case the number belongs to. The prefix is an integral part of the docket number, and is essential for the record room to be able to find the case. The prefixes applicable to each case type are governed by Rule 205.7 of the Uniform Rules. The prefixes applicable to the types of cases discussed in this textbook are set out for reference (not memorization) in the following table:

TABLE 2-2

PREFIX	CASE TYPE
A	Adoption
B	Termination of Parental Rights
F	Support
G	Guardianship
K	Foster Care Review
L	Approval of Foster Care Placement
M	Court Consent to Marry
N	Neglect or Abuse
O	Family Offense
P	Paternity
R	Referral from Supreme Court
U	Uniform Support of Dependents Law
V	Custody or Visitation

TERMINOLOGY

Supreme Court and Family Court often use different terminology, which can be confusing for the beginner. Some of the important words in each "language" appear in the following table:

TABLE 2-3

SUPREME COURT	FAMILY COURT
Plaintiff	Petitioner
Defendant	Respondent
Complaint	Petition
Trial	Hearing
Action	Proceeding
Verdict	Disposition

In addition to its formal terminology, the newcomer to Family Court will hear what may seem to be a secret code made up of letters. These are acronyms and abbreviations for commonly-used Family Court terms. These shorthand terms are explained more fully in the relevant chapters of this textbook.

TABLE 2-4

SHORTHAND	TERM
ACD	Adjournment in Contemplation of Dismissal
COI	Court Ordered Investigation
18-B	Court Appointed Attorney
I&R	Investigation and Report
MGM/PGM	Maternal/Paternal Grandmother
MHS	Mental Health Study
NYSID	N.Y. State Identification (for prisoners)
O/B/O	On behalf of
RM/RF	Respondent mother/respondent father
SCR	State Central Register of Child Abuse
TPR	Termination of Parental Rights

STRUCTURE OF THE NEW YORK CHILD WELFARE SYSTEM

The various agencies of the New York child welfare system are perennial litigants in Family Court, as their duties require them to bring many proceedings. In addition, individuals seeking to obtain custody of a child in foster care must name the child care agency as a respondent. The system is multi-layered and complex, with many patches and make-shift mechanics. The child welfare system is almost entirely publicly funded, with monies being contributed by the Federal, State, and local governments in proportions varying according to the type of service involved.

The non-governmental agencies, called private or voluntary agencies, are mostly religiously affiliated. They are paid per child or per service with public funds for the cases they accept under contract with the Department of Social Services. Although they have the right to refuse to provide service to an individual or family that does not meet the criteria of their programs, they are forbidden by law to discriminate in favor of members of any religion or against anyone based on religion, race or ethnic origin. Figure 2-3 illustrates the basic arrangement.

FIGURE 2-3

STRUCTURE OF THE CHILD WELFARE SYSTEM

STATE DEPARTMENT OF SOCIAL SERVICES
Regulatory and Fiscal Responsibility
Accounts to Federal Government for Federal $$ received;
Audits local DSS's for compliance with regulations and use of State $$;
Administers the Interstate Compact on the Placement of Children;
Maintains the State Central Register of Child Abuse and Maltreatment.

↓

LOCAL DISTRICT DEPARTMENTS OF SOCIAL SERVICES
Investigate reports of suspected child abuse and maltreatment;
Provide some foster care and adoption services directly;
Provide some preventive services directly;
Oversee voluntary child care agencies under contract to DSS.

↓

SPCC's
(Not-for-Profit Corporations)
Investigate reports of child abuse;
May provide other services, such as supervised visitation programs.

VOLUNTARY AGENCIES
(Not-for-Profit Corporations)
Provide foster care, adoption and preventive services under contract with DSS.

CONCLUSION

Family Law provides an exciting variety of work settings in which legal assistants may utilize their talents for their own professional development and for the good of the community. Whatever the task at hand, the legal assistant must be scrupulous about ethics and attentive to the fundamental issues of standing, grounds, subject matter jurisdiction, venue, and statutes of limitations.

CHAPTER REVIEW QUESTIONS

For each of the following, state whether the issue you would research first is one of standing, grounds, subject matter jurisdiction, venue, or statute of limitations:

1.   Your firm's client states that after the death of her son, her daughter-in-law remarried and now refuses to permit her to see her grandchildren. The client would like to petition the court for visitation rights.

2.   Your firm's client is the unmarried mother of a 15-year-old daughter. The client wishes to initiate paternity proceedings so that the daughter will be eligible to inherit from the father, who is now suffering from a terminal illness.

3.   Your firm's clients, who reside in Nassau County, are the prospective adoptive parents of a child born in Syracuse. The clients received the child from an agency whose principle place of business is in Manhattan. The attorney in charge of the case asks you to get a set of adoption forms from the Family Court in the county where the petition should be filed.

4.   Your firm's client is being sued in Family Court for an increase in the amount of child support that was awarded in the Supreme Court judgment of divorce. Since the matter is already in the Family Court, the client would like to cross-petition in that court for increased visitation with his son.

5.   Your firm's client wants to file for divorce from his wife who left him for another man eight months ago.

CHAPTER ASSIGNMENT

You are the paralegal in question 3 above, who has been instructed to obtain the adoption forms for your firm's clients. In what county should the adoption be filed? Cite the statute that gave you the answer.

3 MARRIAGE

"It is not surprising that the decision to marry has been placed on the same level of importance as decisions relating to procreation, childbirth, child rearing, and family relationships....[I]t would make little sense to recognize a right of privacy with respect to other matters of family life and not with respect to the decision to enter the relationship that is the foundation of the family in our society...." *Zablocki v. Redhail*, 434 U.S. 374, 98 S.Ct. 673 (1978)

Marriage is a word with two meanings. On one hand, it means the wedding ceremony or the act of getting married. In another sense it indicates the ongoing legal relation between husband and wife, which carries many rights and obligations. Although legal writers often use the term, "the marriage contract," marriage as a legal relationship is only partially contractual in nature. In many respects it constitutes a **status**. A legal status is a constellation of legal consequences associated with a particular fact or condition. Minority, for example, is the legal status accorded to persons under the age of 18, and it imposes numerous restrictions upon the minor, as well as offering various protections. One does not choose to be a minor, nor can one overcome minority except by living long enough to outgrow it. Seen in this light, it might be more accurate to describe marriage as a legal status voluntarily assumed. Marriage is like a contract in that it must be freely and voluntarily entered into without fraud or duress, but it is unlike a contract in that it cannot be rescinded at the mutual will of the parties, but rather can be dissolved only upon grounds promulgated by the legislature. In addition, the obligations of marriage do not remain fixed as they were at the time of the wedding, but rather change over time as the law changes. The wife who is ordered to pay maintenance to her husband cannot evade that obligation by saying, "At the time of my marriage only men had to pay alimony; therefore, this obligation is not part of my contract."

While the obligations of marriage may be changed by the legislature over time, the marriage relation itself is protected by a constitutional "zone of privacy" that the government may not intrude upon without good reason. *Griswold v. State of Connecticut*, 381 U.S. 479, 85 S.Ct. 1678 (1965). As Justice Douglas wrote in the majority opinion in that famous case establishing the right of married couples to use birth control, "We deal with a right of privacy older than the Bill of Rights, older than our political parties, older than our school system. Marriage is a coming together for better or for worse, hopefully enduring, and intimate to the degree of being sacred."

DISCUSSION TOPIC

What rights and obligations toward each other do a husband and wife incur by virtue of their marriage? How many **extrafamilial** privileges and duties can you think of which arise out of the status of marriage?

ENTERING INTO MARRIAGE

Those who find the many rapid developments in Family Law somewhat disorienting will be relieved to learn that the New York requirements for entering into a valid marriage have remained essentially unchanged since 1933, when New York abolished common-law marriage. Often, however, New York courts are required to determine the validity of marriages alleged to have taken place in other jurisdictions. A plaintiff and defendant in a divorce case pending in New York, for example, may have been married in Rome, Georgia, or in Rome, Italy. If the defendant in the divorce case asserts that plaintiff was never his or her lawful spouse, the New York court must rule on the issue in the context of the divorce case. In so doing, the New York court will apply the law in effect *at the time and place of the purported marriage*. New York will recognize the validity of the marriage if it was valid under the then existing law of the jurisdiction where it was entered into, unless the marriage was **polygamous** or involved a degree of **incest** generally regarded as within the prohibitions of natural law.

The case of *In re May's Estate*, 305 N.Y. 486, 114 N.E.2d 4 (1953), for example, posed the question of whether the marriage of an uncle and niece, which was valid under the laws of the state of Rhode Island where it was performed, would be recognized by New York, where marriage between an uncle and niece is prohibited as incestuous. In 1913, when the marriage was performed, Rhode Island also generally prohibited such marriages, but the Rhode Island statute contained an exception for Jewish people marrying within a degree of consanguinity permitted by their religion. Mr. and Mrs. May came within the scope of this exception. The Court of Appeals held that New York would recognize the marriage, even though it would have been void if performed in New York.

DISCUSSION TOPIC

What do courts mean when they speak about the prohibitions of "Natural Law"? Do all cultures agree that having more than one wife or husband is wrong? Do all agree that marriage between relatives is wrong? Should exceptions be made for individuals whose religion permits or encourages them to have more than one spouse? You might want to read *Reynolds v. United States*, 98 U.S. 145 (1878), which held that the government's right to prohibit polygamy outweighs a Mormon's right to practice that aspect of his religion.

COMMON-LAW MARRIAGE

Contrary to popular belief, common-law marriage is not the original form of marriage. Ceremonial marriage, which was an **ecclesiastical** function, was the only valid form of marriage until the twelfth century in England. The doctrine was well established at the time our country was founded, however, and became a part of our jurisprudence along with the entire body of English common law at the time the United States gained its independence. The instability of frontier life and difficulties in record-keeping gave the doctrine a vitality and importance here which it never had in England.

Common-law marriage has always presented problems of proof, and ultimately, most states abandoned it. New York abolished common-law marriage effective April 29, 1933, although it recognizes those which were contracted in New York prior to that date. Thirteen states and the District of Columbia still permit common-law marriage, however, and since New York recognizes any marriage which was valid at the time and place when it occurred, New York practitioners must be alert to the possibility that a common-law marriage may exist in a case where a ceremonial marriage cannot be proved or never occurred.

The core element of a common-law marriage is the agreement between a man and a woman in words of the present tense that they take each other as husband and wife. The requirement that the vow be in the present tense serves to distinguish a common-law marriage from a betrothal, or engagement to be married, which is of no legal significance, as New York does not permit breach of promise or "heart balm" suits. Civil Rights Law § 80-a. Neither a witness nor an officiant is required for a common-law marriage. To alleviate the inherent problems of proof, the various common law jurisdictions added probative requirements, either through case law or by statute. These extra elements include **cohabitation** for a specified period, reputation as husband and wife, acknowledgments, declarations, and other forms of conduct evincing marital status. Since these requirements vary from state to state, both the law as well as the underlying facts of the alleged marriage must be proved in a New York proceeding in which the existence of a valid common-law marriage is contested. Particularly in the case of a marriage alleged to have occurred years ago, this may require expert testimony.

NON-MARITAL PARTNERS

Not only does New York not permit common-law marriages, but it has also been unwilling to recognize an **implied contract** of marriage such as the California court found in the highly publicized case of *Marvin v. Marvin*, 18 Cal.3d 660, 557 P.2d 106 (1976). The New York courts reasoned that to imply a marital contract where a man and woman are living together would be too close to reinstituting common-law marriage, which the legislature had already abolished. In *Morone v. Morone*, 50 N.Y. 2d 481, 429 N.Y.S.2d 592 (1980) the Court of Appeals held, however, that an **express contract** for personal services in exchange for property and financial rights is enforceable, so long as the personal services do not include illicit sexual relations. Between themselves, therefore, non-marital partners have the option of contractually making some of the same provisions which would occur by operation of law if they were married.

With regard to receiving the sort of benefits to which spouses are generally entitled from employers and government agencies, non-marital partners are at a considerable disadvantage compared to married couples, but they have made some important gains in recent years. In addition to the right to take over the lease of a rent-controlled or rent-stabilized apartment upon the death of the lessee, discussed in Chapter 1, non-marital partners have achieved recognition from the City and State of New York. The first breakthrough for non-marital partners came in 1989, when Mayor Edward I. Koch issued an Executive Order allowing New York City employees to take bereavement leave upon the death of their "**domestic partners**." This was followed in 1993 by two Executive Orders of Mayor David N. Dinkins, which extended domestic partner benefits to all residents of New York City, whether or not they are City employees.

In Executive Order 48, domestic partners are defined as two people, 1) both of whom are 18 or older, 2) neither of whom is married, 3) who are not related in a manner that would bar their marriage in New York State, 4) who have a "close and committed personal relationship," 5) who live together and have been living together on a continuous basis at the time of registration, and 6) who have registered as domestic partners and have not terminated the registration. Domestic partners may be of the same or opposite sex. Registration is accomplished by executing a domestic partnership registration certificate and submitting it to the City Clerk.

Executive Order 49, issued at the same time, spells out the benefits to which domestic partners are entitled. In addition to the bereavement leave for City employees previously granted, domestic partner benefits include child care leave for New York City employees when the domestic partner becomes a parent, visitation rights in New York City correctional and juvenile detention facilities and hospitals with the domestic partner and members of the partner's family, occupancy rights as a family member entitled to be added to an existing tenancy in New York City Housing Authority buildings, and the right to succeed to the tenancy or occupancy of a building supervised by the New York City

Department of Housing Preservation and Development.

As of 1995, by Executive Order of Governor George Pataki, New York State employees are allowed to cover their domestic partners on their health insurance plans, and several private employers have followed the State's lead in extending health coverage to domestic partners.

DISCUSSION TOPIC
Do you think Executive Orders 48 and 49 give domestic partners all the benefits they should have, too many benefits, or not enough? What benefits would you add or take away? Would you be in favor of extending the provisions of these orders to residents of other parts of New York outside of New York City? Would you like to change the definition of "domestic partners" in any way? Why do you suppose the first recognition of domestic partnership came in the form of bereavement leave?

CEREMONIAL MARRIAGE

Ceremonial marriage not only provides a clear, documentary record of the existence of the marriage, but it also offers states the opportunity to regulate the conditions under which a couple will be allowed to enter into marriage. New York is typical of most states in the matters which it regulates, which include the requirement for a marriage license, a period of validity of the license, age of consent, degree of consanguinity, blood tests, witnesses, and a proper officiant.

In New York a marriage license is required, but failure to obtain a license does not render a marriage void. DRL § 25. The ceremony must occur at least 24 hours but no more than 60 days after the issuance of the license. DRL § 13-b. The waiting period is a "cooling off period," which deters the parties from acting impulsively. The primary purpose of the 60 day expiration period is to insure that the information upon which the license was based is current at the time the wedding is performed. Although New York has abolished the requirement of blood tests to detect venereal diseases, a test for sickle cell anemia is required for African-American license applicants, except where the religious beliefs of the applicants would be violated by such a test. An application may not be denied solely on the grounds that the test proved positive, nor does the absence of such a test invalidate a marriage. DRL § 13-aa.

A ceremonial marriage must be performed by an **authorized officiant**, among which are clergy, mayors, justices, judges, the city clerk of a city with over a million inhabitants, and marriage officers appointed by the governing body of a village, town or city. DRL § 11. Although the statute specifically states that no marriage is valid unless performed by one of the specified officiants, it is highly questionable whether a marriage would be ruled void because of a technical defect in the qualifications of an officiant, assuming that all concerned acted in good faith. No particular form or ceremony is required so long as the parties solemnly declare in the presence of at least one witness that they take each other as husband and wife. DRL § 12.

A person may marry without parental consent at age 18 [DRL §7(1)], with parental consent between the ages of 16 and 18, and with the consent of a family court judge or justice of the supreme court between 14 and 16. DRL § 15-a.

Marriages between blood relatives are prohibited when the relationship between them is that of ancestor/descendent (parent/child or grandparent/grandchild), brother/sister of whole or half blood, uncle/niece or aunt/nephew DRL § 5. Although there is lower court authority for the proposition that these prohibitions pertain only to blood relatives, and not to those related by adoption or marriage, this issue must be regarded as unsettled. As our society has become more aware of the dynamics of **intrafamilial** sex abuse, there is greater understanding that the virtually certain psychological damage associated with the exploitation of vulnerable family members is a type of harm at least as worthy of prevention as the speculative risk of passing on genetic diseases.

Although no statute in New York specifies that a marriage license may be issued only to persons of the opposite sex, various New York cases in which the issue has been **collaterally** raised assume that marriage can only occur between a man and a woman. *Matter of Cooper*, 187 A.D.2d 128, 592 N.Y.S.2d 797 (2 Dept. 1993) held that the survivor of a homosexual relationship was not a "surviving spouse" entitled to elect against decedent's will. The decision cited with approval a Minnesota case, *Baker v. Nelson*, 291 Minn. 310, 191 N.W.2d 185 (1971), which, relying upon Webster's Dictionary and the book of Genesis, had ruled that a Minnesota statute prohibiting same-sex marriages was not unconstitutional. In 1996, the refusal by the City Clerk of Ithaca to issue a marriage license to a same sex couple was challenged in the Supreme Court of Tompkins County. The Supreme Court Justice, in *Storrs v. Holcomb*,--Misc. 2d--, 645 N.Y.S.2d 286 (N.Y. Sup.Ct. 1996), upheld the denial of the license, relying on *Matter of Cooper*. The decision stated that marriage in New York "is limited to opposite sex couples and that the gender classification serves a valid public purpose." The court noted, however, that the appellant's arguments had merit and looked to possible legislative change when "a new consensus may emerge."

Although states have broad power to enact marriage regulations which serve a legitimate state purpose, the Constitution limits the states' power to promulgate regulations which have a discriminatory impact, as *Loving v. Virginia* (Case 3-1) illustrates.

📖 **CASE 3-1**

LOVING v. COMMONWEALTH OF VIRGINIA
388 U.S. 1, 87 S.Ct. 1817 (1967)

Mr. Justice STEWART delivered the opinion of the Court.

This case presents a constitutional question never addressed by this Court: whether a statutory scheme adopted by the State of Virginia to prevent marriages between persons solely on the basis of racial classifications violates the Equal Protection and Due Process Clauses of the Fourteenth Amendment. For reasons which seem to us to reflect the central meaning of those constitutional commands, we conclude that these statutes cannot stand consistently with the Fourteenth Amendment.

In June 1958, two residents of Virginia, Mildred Jeter, a Negro woman, and Richard Loving, a white man, were married in the District of Columbia pursuant to its laws. Shortly after their marriage, the Lovings returned to Virginia and established their marital abode in Caroline County. At the October Term, 1958, of the Circuit Court of Caroline County, a grand jury issued an indictment charging the Lovings with violating Virginia's ban on interracial marriages. On January 6, 1959, the Lovings pleaded guilty to the charge and were sentenced to one year in jail; however, the trial judge suspended the sentence for a period of 25 years on the condition that the Lovings leave the State and not return to Virginia together for 25 years. He stated in an opinion that:

> "Almighty God created the races white, black, yellow, malay and red, and he placed them on separate continents. And but for the interference with his arrangement there would be no cause for such marriages. The fact that he separated the races shows that he did not intend for the races to mix."

***

The Supreme Court of Appeals upheld the constitutionality of the antimiscegenation statutes and, after modifying the sentence, affirmed the convictions.

***

There can be no question but that Virginia's miscegenation statutes rest solely upon distinctions drawn according to race. The statutes proscribe generally accepted conduct if engaged in by members of different races. Over the years, this Court has consistently repudiated "[d]istinctions between citizens solely because of their ancestry" as being "odious to a free people whose institutions are founded upon the doctrine of equality."... At the very least, the Equal Protection Clause demands that racial classifications, especially suspect in criminal statutes, be subjected to the "most rigid scrutiny,"...and, if they are ever to be upheld, they must be shown to

📖 **CASE 3-1 continued**

be necessary to the accomplishment of some permissible state objective, independent of the racial discrimination which it was the object of the Fourteenth Amendment to eliminate....

There is patently no legitimate overriding purpose independent of invidious racial discrimination which justifies this classification. The fact that Virginia prohibits only interracial marriages involving white persons demonstrates that the racial classifications must stand on their own justification, as measures designed to maintain White Supremacy.

***

These convictions must be reversed. It is so ordered.

VOID AND VOIDABLE MARRIAGES

Although there are many requirements pertaining to how the act of marriage should be performed, the requirements are not of equal significance. Violations of certain requirements render a marriage **void**, while others make it **voidable**, and still others do not affect the validity of the marriage at all. Since all the regulations concerning ceremonial marriage are in derogation of the common law, they are to be strictly construed, and the courts will not read into the law a provision that failure to comply with a regulation constitutes grounds to invalidate a marriage unless the statute specifically so states. Thus, rules such as time limitations connected with the marriage license, blood tests, and the issuance of the license itself do not render a marriage either void or voidable. They do have very real practical impact, however, because the town and city clerks have the authority to refuse to issue a marriage license until satisfied that legal mandates have been met [DRL § 15], and no authorized officiant will knowingly perform a wedding without a valid license.

The distinction between a void marriage and a voidable marriage is of enormous legal import. With narrow exceptions, a *void* marriage is accorded no legal effect whatsoever. It is as if the marriage never occurred. The validity of a void marriage can be challenged at any point when the issue arises, by any person who has a legal interest in the resolution of the issue. Such challenges often arise in probate proceedings, when a relative of the deceased who would inherit were there no surviving spouse, disputes the spouse's claim on the grounds that the marriage was void. They may also arise when an insurance company or government agency contests the spouse's claim to spousal benefits. Such disputes may be litigated whenever they arise, even though the couple may have lived together as man and wife for 50 years or more. The only defects which render a marriage *void* in New York are that the marriage is either bigamous (polygamous) [DRL § 6] or incestuous [DRL § 5].

An important exception to the rule of the absolute nullity of a void marriage is the statute which preserves the legitimacy of any child born of a ceremonial marriage or of a common-law marriage which was valid where it occurred. Such a child is the legitimate child of both natural parents notwithstanding that the marriage is void or voidable or has been judicially declared void. DRL § 24.

Since incest and bigamy render a marriage void, a spouse may simply walk away from such a marriage without judicial intervention. Any of the three parties involved in the triangle of a bigamous marriage may prefer, however, to clear the legal record by bringing an action for a declaration of nullity. DRL § 140(1). As a practical matter, this form of relief is available only to an "innocent spouse," since incest is an offense punishable by fine and imprisonment [DRL § 5][PL § 255.25], and bigamy is a Class E felony [PL § 255.15]. Although a declaration of nullity renders the marriage void from the inception, the legislature, with more compassion than logic, has included declarations of nullity in the category of matrimonial actions in which maintenance and equitable distribution may be sought as ancillary relief.

A *voidable* marriage, on the other hand, can be challenged only through an annulment proceeding, which is subject to the statute of limitations and restrictions on standing discussed below. If the statute of limitations has expired without the commencement of an annulment proceeding, the validity of the marriage cannot later be challenged by anyone, even though grounds for annulment may have existed. In addition, a decree of annulment terminates the marriage only as of the date of the decree, and the marriage status is recognized as having existed until that date. All rights and obligations of the marital status which accrued prior to the annulment are, therefore, enforceable.

ANNULMENT

BASICS BOX

Subject matter jurisdiction: Supreme Court has exclusive original jurisdiction.

Venue: County of residence of either party.

Standing: Either spouse, except that spouse who was of age may not sue for annulment based on nonage of other spouse and non-afflicted spouse may not sue on the basis of spouse's mental retardation. Additional persons are accorded standing for specified grounds.

Grounds: Nonage, mental defect, physical incapacity, force, duress, fraud, five years incurable mental illness.

Statute of Limitations: Varies according to grounds; if no other statute of limitations is specified by DRL § 140, then 6 years. CPLR § 213(1).

Applicable statutes: DRL Art. IX; DRL Art. XIII; DRL § 7.

Although annulment and divorce both dissolve a marriage, the two types of proceedings are conceptually different. **Annulment** is the judicial declaration of the nullity of a marriage due to a defect in the inception of the marriage, whereas divorce ends a marriage due to one spouse's failure to fulfill spousal obligations during the course of a valid marriage. The grounds for annulment specified in DRL § 140 all render a marriage *voidable*. Thus, the marriage is void from the date of the decree and the parties may request maintenance and equitable distribution of property as ancillary relief in an annulment proceeding. The decision whether to grant an annulment always lies within the sound discretion of the court, and, if justice so requires, the court may refuse to grant an annulment even though the grounds have been established. Annulment is a **matrimonial action** subject to the special procedural rules governing all matrimonial actions, which are discussed in Chapter 5.

GROUNDS FOR ANNULMENT

Nonage

Where a person under 18 marries, annulment may be sought by either party to the marriage who was under the age of 18 at the time of the marriage. A parent of the infant spouse or a guardian or next friend of the infant may also bring suit. An infant who freely cohabits with the spouse as husband and wife after reaching the age of 18, however, loses the right to sue for annulment. DRL § 140(b). The parents may seek annulment even though they consented to the marriage. If a minor who is domiciled or resident in New York marries under the age of 18 in another jurisdiction which permits marriage at a younger age, the marriage is voidable even though it was valid where contracted. *Cunningham v. Cunningham*, 206 N.Y. 341, 99 N.E. 845 (1912). In such a situation, the court's *parens patriae* authority to protect children within its jurisdiction prevails over the general rule of recognizing the validity of a marriage which was lawful where it took place. The mere fact that one or both of the spouses was under the age of consent does not, in itself, guarantee an annulment. The court will consider the fundamental question of whether there is a reasonable likelihood that the parties could make a successful marriage, having regard for the maturity of the parties, the degree of affection between them and their conduct towards each other.

Mental Illness or Defect

An action for annulment on the grounds of mental illness may be maintained during the illness by any interested relative of the mentally ill person or by the spouse who is not ill, provided that he or she did not know of the illness at the time of the marriage. An action may also be maintained by the mentally ill spouse after he or she is restored to sound mind, provided that the parties did not cohabit as husband and wife after the recovery. An action based on the mental retardation of one spouse may be maintained at any time during the lifetime of either party by an interested relative or designated next friend. Note that the spouse of normal intelligence is not granted standing to sue on this ground. DRL § 140(c).

Physical Incapacity

The physical incapacities which provide grounds for annulment are the inability to have sexual intercourse and the inability to procreate *at the time of the marriage*. Subsequent loss of either capacity does not provide a basis for annulment. The non-afflicted spouse may maintain an action on this ground, and the incapacitated spouse may also sue, but only if he or she was unaware of the incapacity at the time of the marriage, or, if aware, did not know that it was incurable. If the incapacity is cured, an action may no longer be maintained, and in no case may the action be maintained after five years have expired since the marriage. DRL § 140(d).

Consent Obtained by Force, Duress, or Fraud

An action to annul a marriage based on allegations that a spouse's consent was obtained by force or duress may be brought by the person whose consent was so obtained at any time. However, it may not be brought if the parties voluntarily cohabited as husband and wife prior to the commencement of the action. An action on these grounds may also be maintained during the lifetime of the guilty party by a parent or interested relative of the coerced party. DRL § 140(e).

Fraud entails more than mere misrepresentation. The misrepresentation must pertain to something which goes to the heart of the decision to marry, and the misrepresentation must be intentional and calculated to deceive a reasonably prudent person. An annulment complaint based on fraud (Form 3-1) must contain factual allegations in support of each element. False promises to convert to the other spouse's religion, for example, have often been found to constitute **material misrepresentations**. Numerous cases hold, however, that because of the strong community interest in marriage, a higher degree of proof is required to establish fraud for annulment than is required with regard to an ordinary civil contract.

Sometimes silence is a form of misrepresentation. The intent to bear children is so essential to the marriage contract that failure to disclose a known inability or unwillingness to bear children has consistently been held to constitute fraud, even if no overt misrepresentation was made, as have failures to disclose other deeply shocking information such as the fact that one is addicted to drugs, [*Courreges v. Courreges*, 229 N.Y.S. 2d 73 (N.Y. Sup. Ct. 1961)], or the fact that one had been a member of the Nazi party and believed in the extermination of the Jewish people [*Kober v. Kober*, 16 N.Y.2d 191, 264 N.Y.S. 2d 364 (1965)]. Whether a misrepresentation is material to the decision to marry must be evaluated in light of the values of the particular parties in each case and the social norms of the time and place where the marriage occurred.

The statute of limitations for annulment on the grounds of fraud is three years from the date of the discovery of the fraud by the defrauded spouse. Even if the plaintiff is a parent, guardian or interested relative of the defrauded spouse who may have learned of the fraud later than the spouse, the time starts to run from the date of the defrauded spouse's discovery of the fraud. CPLR § 214(7).

📁 **FORM 3-1**

SUPREME COURT OF THE STATE OF NEW YORK
COUNTY OF OSWEGO
---X   Index No.

SAMUEL GOODMAN,

                                Plaintiff,   **VERIFIED COMPLAINT**
          against   ACTION FOR
                                                                         ANNULMENT
DOLLY DISH a/k/a DOLLY GOODMAN
               and
VENERABLE GOODMAN

                         Defendants.

---X

The plaintiff, by his attorney, Howard Hammar, Esq., complaining of Defendants, respectfully alleges:

1.   Plaintiff is a resident of Sweetwater Township, State of New York.

2.   At the time of the commencement of this action, Defendants, Dolly Dish and Venerable Goodman, were, and they still are, residents of the County of Oswego, State of New York,

3.   Plaintiff is the sole surviving child of defendant Venerable Goodman by his deceased wife Rachel Goodman, and as such is a potential distributee and next of kin of said Venerable Goodman.

4.   Upon information and belief, defendants participated in an alleged ceremonial marriage in the City of Bridal Falls, County of Oswego, State of New York on the third day of June, 1995.

5.   At the time of said purported marriage, and for upwards of five years prior thereto, defendant, Dolly Dish, had been employed by the defendant, Venerable Goodman, as a housekeeper.

6.   At the time of said purported marriage, said defendant was upwards of 70 years of age, was a widower with an adult son, the plaintiff herein, was in poor health, and was possessed of a substantial amount of personal property, and these facts were well known to defendant.

7.   At the time of the alleged marriage, defendant Dolly Dish was 35 years of age, and from 1990 until the present time, in addition to acting as housekeeper for defendant Venerable Goodman, defendant Dolly Dish performed the duties of nursing defendant and, upon information and belief, managed and controlled his personal and household financial affairs.

8.   Upon information and belief, during the course of the employment of defendant Dolly Dish by defendant Venerable Goodman, and prior to their purported marriage, defendant Dolly Dish falsely represented to Venerable Goodman that her child Delia Dish, born April 21, 1994, was the child of defendant, Venerable Goodman.

9.   Upon information and belief, the truth is that the child Delia Dish is not the biological child of Venerable Goodman, and the identity of the actual father of said child is unknown to plaintiff.

📁 FORM 3-1 continued

10.   Upon information and belief, when the aforesaid false representations were made, they were known by the said defendant Dolly Dish to be false and fraudulent and were made by her with the intent to deceive defendant Venerable Goodman and induce him to participate in a marriage ceremony with her.

11.   At the time the aforesaid false representations were made, defendant Venerable Goodman believed them to be true and was thereby induced to participate in the alleged marriage ceremony with defendant.

12.   That this action for annulment was commenced on November 17, 1995.

13.   That this action for annulment is commenced, pursuant to CPLR 214(7), within 3 years from the time when the cause of action herein alleged accrued.

WHEREFORE, plaintiff demands judgment as follows:

1.   That the purported marriage of defendant Dolly Dish to defendant Venerable Goodman be annulled and declared void;

2.   Awarding to Venerable Goodman title and possession to all of his separate property;

3.   Awarding to Venerable Goodman his just and equitable share of all marital property;

4.   Compelling defendant to pay to plaintiff or on plaintiff's behalf reasonable and suitable counsel, accountant, appraisal, actuarial and investigative fees and expenses incurred or to be incurred by plaintiff in the prosecution of this action;

5.   Granting to plaintiff such other and further relief as to the Court may seem just and proper, together with the costs and disbursements of this action.

Dated: January 6, 1996

> Howard Hammar, Esq.
> Attorney for Plaintiff
> 5 Court Street
> Sweetwater Township, New York
> Telephone number

(*Annex verification*)

Incurable Mental Illness

An action for annulment may be maintained when one spouse has been "incurably mentally ill" for five years or more, by the spouse who is not ill or by a person acting on behalf of either spouse. DRL § 140(f). The onset of the illness may have occurred subsequent to the marriage. This ground for annulment appears inconsistent with the theory of annulment as an attack on the original validity of a marriage. Like the statute which preserves the legitimacy of children after a declaration of nullity, it may be simply a triumph of compassion over logic, or perhaps it was based on a now-discredited notion that all mental illness is of genetic origin, in which case the "defect" would have existed at the time of the marriage. In any case, the section is rarely used, probably because few psychiatrists are willing to testify that a mental illness is "incurable," given the current availability of medicines to treat mental illness.

ANTENUPTIAL AGREEMENTS

Antenuptial agreements, which are also called **prenuptial agreements** or **premarital agreements**, are contracts entered into before marriage which set forth the rights and obligations of the parties during the marriage and in the event that the marriage is dissolved by death or through a matrimonial action. Once considered a tool of the rich and famous, these agreements have now come into common usage by ordinary people. The high divorce rate and the complexities of New York's equitable distribution law have undoubtedly spurred many people to attempt to forestall unhappy contingencies, even as they enter into marriage with hope in their hearts.

Agreements that serve the same purposes may also be executed after marriage, in which case they are called **postnuptial agreements**. Postnuptial agreements, which define the rights of the parties in an ongoing marriage, are different from **separation agreements**. Separation agreements, which are discussed in Chapter 4, are executed when the spouses plan to live apart. Thus, separation agreements deal with a different set of concerns and contain provisions inappropriate in a prenuptial or postnuptial agreement.

While antenuptial agreements are prudent for many couples, there are some for whom they are a virtual necessity. A person who has children from a prior marriage to whom he or she wishes to leave the bulk of an estate, or who owns a business or other substantial assets, or who is marrying someone considerably younger or less affluent than him or herself would be well advised to insist upon a prenuptial agreement. By entering into an antenuptial contract the parties can change the distribution of assets which would occur by operation of the Estates Powers and Trusts Law in the event of death or of the equitable distribution law in the event the marriage is terminated by annulment or divorce. Entering into a prenuptial agreement with a complete inventory of the assets each owns before marriage can also simplify problems of proof which may later arise concerning what property each owned at the time of the marriage.

Since the antenuptial agreement is a contract, the parties can negotiate whatever terms they like within certain broad bounds. Suppose that the wife has substantial assets which she would like to leave to her children from her first marriage. In that case the new husband-to-be might agree to waive his entire right of spousal election against the will or to accept a smaller percentage than is provided by the EPTL. Another possibility is that he might waive his right of election provided that the wife's will leaves him a specified sum. Alternatively, he might agree to any of those provisions contingent upon the children from the prior marriage being alive at the time of the wife's death. Form 3-2 is a sample antenuptial agreement, but it contains only some of the many perfectly legal terms a couple might negotiate.

📁 **FORM 3-2**

FORM 20-6   **NEW YORK MATRIMONIAL PRACTICE**

Prenuptial Agreement

AGREEMENT made as of this _____ day of _____, 19__, between _____ ("Laurie"), and _____ ("Peter"), both residing at _____, _____, New York

WITNESSETH:

Whereas, each of the parties has known the other for a period of time, is fully satisfied with the disclosure of the financial circumstances of the other and desires to make an agreement regarding his and her property rights in consideration of the marriage to each other, and

Whereas, each party acknowledges that the other may hereafter acquire by gift and inheritance, as well as through professional endeavor and from other sources, assets and income of value, and

Whereas, each of the parties has assets and earnings, or earnings potential, sufficient to provide for his or her own maintenance and support in a proper and acceptable standard of living without the necessity of financial contributions by the other, and each of the parties is aware of the hazards and risks of the continuance of earnings and of the changes in assets and liabilities of the other and of the possibility of substantially changed financial circumstances of the other with the result that the earnings and/or net worth of one party is or may be substantially different from those of the other party, and

Whereas, each of the parties desires to own, hold, acquire and dispose of property now and in the future and subsequent to their marriage to each other with the same freedom as though unmarried and to dispose of said property during their respective lifetimes or upon death or upon any other termination of the marriage without restriction or limitation in accordance with his and her own desires, and

Whereas, it is the intention of each of the parties by entering into this agreement to determine unilaterally what property, now and in the future, shall be his or her own separate property and that all of the property of each, however acquired or held, shall be free from any consideration as marital property, community property, quasi-community property or any other form of marital or community property, as those terms are used and understood in any jurisdiction, including but not limited to the State of New York,

NOW, THEREFORE, in consideration of the marriage of each party to the other and the mutual promises and covenants herein, the parties have mutually agreed as follows:

1. *Present property.* All of the property, real, personal and mixed, which each party has previously acquired and now holds in his or her name or possession shall be and continue to remain the sole and separate property of

📁 FORM 3-2 continued

NEGOTIATION AND AGREEMENT FORMS   **FORM 20-6**

that person, together with all future appreciation, increases and other changes in value of that property and irrespective of the contributions (if any) which either party might have made or may hereafter make to said property or to the marriage, directly or indirectly.

2. *Future property.* All of the property, real, personal or mixed, which each party may hereafter acquire in his or her own name or possession shall be and remain the sole and separate property of that person, together with all future appreciation, increases and other changes in value of that property and irrespective of the contributions (if any) which either party may make to said property or to the marriage, directly or indirectly.

3. *Joint property.* Any property, real, personal or mixed, which shall now or hereafter be held in the joint names of the parties shall be owned in accordance with the kind of joint ownership as title is held, and if there is no other designation, shall be presumed to be held equally by the parties with such survivorship rights (if any) as may be specifically designated by the title ownership or as may be implied or be derived by operation of law other than the operation of the so-called equitable distribution law or community property or any similar law of any jurisdiction involving marital property, community property, quasi-community property or any other form of marital or community property.

4. *Estate rights.* Each party hereby releases, waives and relinquishes any right or claim of any nature whatsoever in the property of the other or otherwise, now or hereafter acquired, and, without limitation, expressly forever waives any right or claim which he or she may have or hereafter acquire, whether as the spouse of the other or otherwise, under the present or future laws of any jurisdiction: (a) to share in the estate of the other party upon the death of the other party; and (b) to act as executor or administrator of the estate of the other or as trustee, personal representative or in any fiduciary capacity with respect to the estate of the other. All rights which either party may acquire in the other's estate by virtue of the marriage, including but not limited to rights of set-off in § 5-3.1, all distributive shares in § 4-1.1 and all rights of election in § 5-1.1-A of the Estates, Powers and Trusts Law of New York, as such laws may now exist or hereafter be changed, and any similar or other provision of law in this or any other jurisdiction and all causes of action and claims arising out of the wrongful death of a party are hereby waived by each party.

5. *Wills.* Nothing in this agreement shall prevent or limit either party from hereafter making provisions for the other by Last Will and Testament, in which event the provisions thus made shall control.

6. *Disclosure.* Each party has been apprised of the right to obtain further disclosure of the financial circumstances of the other party and is satisfied

FORM 3-2 continued

with the disclosure made. Each party expressly waives the right to any further financial disclosure and acknowledges that said waiver is made with the full benefit of legal counsel and knowledge of the legal consequences thereof and that neither party properly cannot, and shall not, subsequently assert that this agreement should be impaired or invalidated by reason of any lack of financial disclosure or lack of understanding or of fraud, duress or coercion. Without limiting the generality of the foregoing, Peter represents that his present net worth is in excess of $_____ and that his annual income is in excess of $_____; and Laurie represents that her assets are presently minimal and her present annual income is about $_____; which representations by both parties admittedly are not all-inclusive and which are not intended to be relied upon by either party. (See annexed financial statements.)

7. *General provisions.* This agreement shall be construed as an agreement made and to be performed in the State of New York and cannot be changed, or any of its terms waived, except by a writing signed and acknowledged by both parties. Each party hereby consents to the personal jurisdiction of the State of New York in the event of any dispute or question regarding the interpretation, validity and making of this agreement and the enforcement of its provisions. Each party acknowledges receipt of a fully executed copy of this agreement, has had an opportunity to read it and understands the same after consultation with independent counsel and is fully satisfied with the disclosure made of all of the financial circumstances of the other party. The paragraph captions in this agreement are for the purpose of convenience only and are not a part of this agreement.

8. Each party has been separately represented by an attorney of his or her own choice. Laurie has been represented by _____

_____ and Peter has been represented by _____
_____ in connection with the negotiation, making and execution of this agreement.

IN WITNESS WHEREOF the parties, for themselves, their heirs, next-of-kin, representatives and assigns have executed these presents prior to their marriage to each other on the day and year first above written.

_____ L.S.
_____ L.S.

STATE OF NEW YORK }
COUNTY OF   } ss.:

On the _____ day of _____, 19__, before me _____ personally came _____ to me known and known to be the individual described in and who

FORM 3-2 continued

NEGOTIATION AND AGREEMENT FORMS FORM 20-6

executed the foregoing instrument, and she did duly acknowledge to me that she executed the same.

_____
Notary Public, State of New York

STATE OF NEW YORK } ss.:
COUNTY OF

On the ____ day of _____, 19__, before me ____ personally came ____ to me known and known to be the individual described in and who executed the foregoing instrument, and he did duly acknowledge to me that he executed the same.

_____
Notary Public, State of New York

Editor's Note: The provision in Paragraph 4 regarding actions arising out of the wrongful death of a party has been added in light of a decision by the Alabama Supreme Court in Steele v Steele (1993, Ala) 623 So 2d 1140, which held that a prenuptial agreement did not waive claims arising out of the wrongful death of a spouse.

PRACTICE TIP: The sample agreement consists of three sections. The preliminary clauses, which begin with the word, "Whereas," make up the **recitals** section of the agreement. The recitals set the stage, in a legal sense, for the agreement. They explain the parties' motivations in entering into the agreement and tell what information each possessed when they executed the contract. The sample agreement recites that the parties are satisfied with the disclosure they have had about each other's assets. The approximate total net worth of each is stated, but the agreement does not include each party's net worth statement as an exhibit. If the parties have substantial assets, a net worth statement is preferable to a general recital of disclosure. The agreement also recites that the parties were represented by counsel, who are named. If one was represented, while the other was not, the agreement should recite that the unrepresented party was aware of his or her right to counsel and voluntarily waived that right. The "THEREFORE" clauses are the substance of the actual agreement. Note that they are in clearly organized, numbered paragraphs. The paragraph which begins "IN WITNESS WHEREOF" is the execution section of the instrument. The parties' signatures are acknowledged (not sworn to) before a notary.

In the past, courts were uneasy with antenuptial agreements because they seemed to make it too easy to get a divorce. As the divorce rate continued to skyrocket, however, courts came to recognize that many marriages would end, with or without an antenuptial agreement. They began to appreciate that in many cases the existence of an antenuptial agreement took some of the sting out of the divorce proceedings and shortened the litigation. Thus, when the equitable distribution statute was passed, the legislature specifically permitted couples to avoid equitable distribution through prenuptial agreements. "Opting out" is discussed in Chapters 7 and 8.

In recent years the courts have been more than willing to enforce prenuptial agreements, so long as they are fair and are not tainted by fraud, misrepresentation or overreaching. An antenuptial agreement is void as against public policy, however, if it contains an express provision requiring the dissolution of the marriage or provides for the procurement of grounds for divorce. General Obligations Law § 5-311. Similarly, although a prenuptial agreement may recite that the parties do not contemplate having children, thereby eliminating any threat of annulment on that grounds, they cannot waive the obligation to support a child who is nevertheless born of the marriage. Spousal support may be waived, but only as between the parties. If either spouse becomes a public charge (goes on welfare), the Commissioner of Social Services may seek support from the other spouse. General Obligations Law § 5-311.

REQUIREMENTS FOR ENFORCEABILITY

To satisfy the Statute of Frauds, an antenuptial agreement must be in writing, and to comply with the equitable distribution law, it must be subscribed and acknowledged in the manner required to record a deed, that is, it must be witnessed. (See Real Property Law §§ 304, 291.) However, the Appellate Division, First Department, recently upheld a prenuptial agreement that was not acknowledged in *Matisoff v. Dobi*, --- A. D.2d ---, 644 N.Y.S.2d 13 (1 Dept. 1996), holding that the statutory purpose of acknowledgment was to prevent fraud and overreaching, which were absent in that case. In addition the agreement must be fair and reasonable when made and not **unconscionable** at the time of trial. DRL § 236 (B)(3). Prenuptial agreements executed as part of a religious marriage ceremony, such as a Jewish Ketubah or Islamic Sadaq, are enforceable so long as they satisfy these requirements. Courts have refused to enforce religious marriage contracts which are too vague or too one-sided, or which otherwise fail to comport with civil law. See *Habibi-Fahnrich v. Fahnrich*, No. 46186/93, 1995 WL 507388 (N.Y. Sup. Ct.).

Parties who are about to enter into marriage are in a far different relationship from parties negotiating an ordinary commercial contract. Theirs is a state of mutual trust and affection, and they are in no mood to "kick the tires" of the impending marriage. Because of the trusting relationship which exists between the parties, the prenuptial agreement will be subjected to a higher standard of fairness. In deciding whether an agreement is unconscionable, the courts will look at the agreement as a whole, having regard for the circumstances of the parties. In scrutinizing the agreement, the court will be alert to the slightest whiff of overreaching, nondisclosure, undue advantage, and unethical behavior, as well as outright fraud, duress or coercion. Although full disclosure of financial matters is not a prerequisite for an enforceable antenuptial agreement, lack of disclosure will be considered by the court in deciding whether the agreement is unfair or unconscionable. Consider the following example:

Henry, 53 years of age, is about to marry Liza, age 21. Henry, who comes from a wealthy family, is a distinguished professor at a major university. Liza is an aspiring actress whom Henry met when she was working part-time in the coat check room of Henry's favorite restaurant. Liza is not on good terms with her parents, who disapproved of her dropping out of high school to pursue her acting career. Henry agrees to marry Liza only on condition that she execute a prenuptial agreement in which she waives all claims to his estate and agrees that during the course of the marriage all property held in the sole name of each spouse will be considered the separate property of each, not subject to equitable distribution. The agreement further provides that if the marriage is dissolved within the first five years, Henry will pay Liza $1000 per month for spousal support for 3 years. Liza knows that Henry is "rich," but has not been informed in any detail about his income and assets. The agreement recites that all questions each asked have been answered. The agreement is silent concerning representation by counsel. Henry and Liza are getting divorced after three years of marriage. They have no children. Liza moves to set aside the antenuptial agreement.

Will the prenuptial agreement between Henry and Liza be enforced? Probably it will not. Because he was older, more established in the world, and better educated, Henry was clearly in a superior position in negotiating the agreement. Liza was apparently unsophisticated and alone in the world. The rights Liza waived are potentially enormous, while the guarantee of support she got in exchange is a largely illusory benefit, since a court would probably award her at least that much maintenance. Had the agreement made full financial disclosure and had Liza been represented by an attorney, the agreement would have had a much greater chance of survival, since an agreement is not necessarily unconscionable merely because it is improvident. The outcome might be different, however, if Liza's acting career had flourished and she had made a very successful movie during the marriage. Remember, an agreement must be found not unconscionable *at the time of trial*.

CONCLUSION

Annulment proceedings have declined dramatically since New York broadened the grounds for divorce in 1966. Still, there are a number of couples who for religious or personal reasons would prefer to sue for annulment rather than divorce, if grounds for annulment exist. The issue of the validity of a marriage also arises in many other situations apart from annulment proceedings. Divorce cases, which have become more common as annulment has become rarer, always present the issue, although it is not often litigated. Since marriage is the still the most common way of forming a family in our society, it is essential to understand this fundamental building block of Family Law.

CHAPTER REVIEW QUESTIONS

1. In what ways is marriage like a contract and in what ways different?

2. What are the two defects which render a marriage *void* in New York?

3. What are two essential elements of a ceremonial marriage which a common law marriage does not have?

4. Joe and Joan, while living together in Pennsylvania, a state which allows common law marriage, considered themselves married. For ten years they were known in their community as a married couple. They later moved to New York, where they bought a house in Joe's sole name and continued to reside together. Both in Pennsylvania and New York, Joe carried

Joan on his health insurance, where she was listed as "wife." Joe died intestate, and his brother, who is his only surviving blood relative, has filed a claim to the house in a New York Surrogate's Court. If Joan was Joe's wife, she inherits the house. Who do you think will get the house? Why? What additional information would you need to be sure?

5. Exeter and Nina were married when he was 26 and she was 17. After six months of marriage, Exeter has grown bored with Nina, who spends all her after-school hours reading teen magazines and talking on the telephone. Does Exeter have standing to sue for annulment? If Nina's mother sues for annulment, do you think a court is likely to exercise its discretion to grant the annulment? Why or why not?

6. Melanie and Ashley (male) are first cousins. Can they get married in New York?

7. Briefly describe three couples for whom an antenuptial agreement would be particularly advisable.

8. Donald and Diana executed a prenuptial agreement in which both waived their rights of spousal support. Diana was, and still is, president of a flourishing design company, from which she is paid a six figure yearly salary. Donald was making a similar salary at the time of the marriage, but he was laid off in a downsizing. Now he makes $28,000 annually in a civil service job. They are divorcing, and Donald is asking for maintenance. Do you think the antenuptial agreement will block Donald's claim for maintenance? Why or why not?

CHAPTER ASSIGNMENT

Prepare an interview questionnaire for a client of your firm who wishes to have an antenuptial agreement prepared. Assume that the client will arrive at the interview with a net worth statement already prepared, so that your questionnaire need not delve into financial details. Also make up a fact pattern about such a client. During the next session of class, you and a fellow student will take turns interviewing each other, using the questionnaire you prepared to obtain the information in your fact patterns.

4 SEPARATION

"It has been repeatedly held that a separation agreement entered into after the parties had separated is valid, and that it neither contravenes public policy which seeks to keep the home and the marital relationship intact...nor violates the statute which prohibits contracts to alter the marriage or to relieve the husband from his liability to support his wife...." *In re Tierney's Estate*, 148 Misc. 378, 266 N.Y.S. 51 (Sur. Ct. Bronx County 1933).

If a husband and wife both wish to separate, they may do so by a written agreement. Later, if they decide to divorce, they may use the agreement as the basis for a **conversion divorce**, that is, a divorce based upon the grounds of living apart pursuant to a separation agreement for one year or more. If only one spouse wants the separation, however, he or she may bring an action for separation, but only upon the grounds specified in the Domestic Relations Law. Since the grounds for divorce and the grounds for **judicial separation** are similar, a spouse who is sure that he or she wants a divorce will usually sue for divorce without bringing a separation action first. There is no requirement that separation precede divorce.

Both separation by written agreement and judicial separation are entirely different from informal, physical separation. Informal separation, "splitting up," does not provide a basis for a conversion divorce later on. Nor does it provide any other grounds for divorce, unless the separation resulted from the abandonment of one spouse by the other. Informal separation leaves the spouses in a legal limbo, with none of their rights or responsibilities toward each other spelled out. As soon as a couple realizes that their physical separation is not the result of a passing quarrel, but rather that it signals the end of their marriage, they should promptly take steps to formalize their separation.

Of the two methods of formal separation, separation by agreement is preferable to judicial separation. It is less expensive, since litigation is not required, and it gives the parties more control over decisions affecting their lives. Most couples nowadays prefer to use separation agreements, and judicial separation actions have become quite rare. Spouses execute separation agreements when they have decided to live apart indefinitely. Often at the time they negotiate the separation agreement, they already contemplate divorce. The function of the separation agreement, therefore, is to define the rights and responsibilities of the spouses during the period of separation and in the event of divorce.

Although the parties may already know that they will divorce, the agreement cannot contain an express provision requiring divorce. General Obligations Law § 5-311. A provision in a separation agreement that the parties "shall proceed" with divorce on the grounds of abandonment has been held to violate GOL § 5-311. *Taft v. Taft*, 156 A.D.2d 444, 548 N.Y.S.2d 726 (2 Dept. 1989). If the parties reconcile and resume living together as husband and wife, the agreement is abrogated. Isolated acts of sexual intercourse between the parties do not nullify the agreement, however, without further proof that the parties intended to abandon the agreement. *Farkas v. Farkas*, 26 A.D.2d 919, 274 N.Y.S.2d 842 (1 Dept. 1966). If the spouses have carried out a property settlement in conjunction with the execution of the separation agreement, the property settlement is not undone by their later reconciliation, unless there is proof that they intended to do so. For example, if real property is conveyed to a spouse in conjunction with a separation agreement, a reconciliation of the parties does not have any effect upon the conveyance in the absence of proof that the spouses meant to cancel the conveyance.

SEPARATION AGREEMENTS

Like antenuptial agreements, discussed in Chapter 3, separation agreements are fully enforceable contracts. Also like antenuptial agreements, separation agreements must be in writing, subscribed by the parties and acknowledged in the manner required to entitle a deed to be recorded. DRL § 236(B)(3). They may be enforced in Supreme Court or any other court which has jurisdiction over contract actions, including Civil Court in New York City and the County Courts throughout the rest of the state. Family Court does *not* have jurisdiction over proceedings to enforce, set aside or modify separation agreements. *Kleila v. Kleila*, 50 N.Y.2d 277, 428 N.Y.S.2d 896 (1980). Within the same public policy bounds applicable to antenuptial agreements, the parties can include in the separation agreement any terms they please.

If the spouses do decide to proceed with divorce, the separation agreement can be **incorporated** into the divorce judgment. The terms of the separation agreement then become part of the Supreme Court order, which allows the parties to sue for enforcement in Supreme Court or in any court which has power to enforce an order of the Supreme Court. By settling in advance the custody, support, and property division aspects of the divorce, the parties shorten the divorce litigation and spare themselves considerable expense. The divorce proceeding will usually be placed on an uncontested matrimonial calendar when there are no disputed issues. Depending on how congested the court is, the uncontested calendar will be heard weeks or months faster than the calendar for contested proceedings.

The incorporation of the separation agreement can be handled in either of two ways: the agreement may be **incorporated and merged** into the divorce decree or **incorporated but not merged**. When the agreement is merged into the divorce decree, the agreement as a contract ceases to exist. All that remains is the divorce judgment. When the agreement is incorporated but *not* merged, the agreement "survives," that is, it continues in effect as a contract. The practical effect is that a party seeking to enforce an agreement which is not merged has a broader choice of courts in which to sue and a wider range of remedies to request. Suppose, for example, that one spouse has failed to pay for a major repair to the marital home as called for by the agreement. (See paragraph 18 of the sample separation agreement, Form 4-2.) The other spouse has paid the bill and now seeks to be reimbursed. If the agreement was not merged, the spouse to whom the money is owed can either sue in the Supreme Court where the divorce decree was issued for enforcement of the divorce decree, or may go to Civil or County Court to sue on the contract. In Supreme Court the plaintiff would sue for **contempt**, and the case would probably be assigned to Matrimonial Term, which may be backlogged. In the Civil or County Court the plaintiff could sue for **breach of contract** or **specific performance** or any other available contract remedy, and the case might be heard sooner.

The parties may also agree that any disputes which may arise about the provisions of the agreement will be submitted to **binding arbitration**. *Avitzur v. Avitzur*, 86 A.D.2d 133, 449 N.Y.S.2d 83 (3 Dept. 1982), *revd* 58 N.Y.2d 108, 459 N.Y.S.2d 572 (1983), *cert. denied* 464 U.S. 817, 104 S.Ct. 76. Custody issues are not subject to binding arbitration, however. *Sheets v. Sheets*, 22 A.D.2d 176, 254 N.Y.S.2d 320 (1 Dept. 1964); *Glauber v. Glauber*, 192 A.D.2d 94, 600 N.Y.S.2d 740 (2 Dept. 1993). The *Avitzur* case presented an interesting issue concerning the Constitutional separation of church and state. As was discussed in Chapter 1, the entanglement between church and state in family matters, which both attempt to regulate, is a pervasive concern in Family Law. In *Avitzur*, an Orthodox Jewish couple had signed a marriage contract, called a Ketubah, as part of their marriage ceremony. The Ketubah provided that the parties would submit themselves to a Beth Din, a Rabbinical court, if any disputes arose within the marriage. The Court of Appeals held that the Ketubah was a valid civil contract to submit disputes to a nonjudicial forum and the fact that the agreement was entered into as part of a religious ceremony did not render it unenforceable.

HIGH STANDARD OF FAIRNESS

Before incorporating a separation agreement into a matrimonial decree, the court will carefully scrutinize the agreement to see if there is any sign of fraud or overreaching. While courts will not redesign the parties' bargain, they will subject it to strict surveillance. Because spouses are in a **fiduciary relationship**, they must deal with each other in the utmost good faith, and courts will not enforce an agreement which is unconscionable. The Court of Appeals has described an "unconscionable bargain" as one "such as no person in his or her senses and not under delusion would make on the one hand, and as no honest and fair person would accept on the other." *Christian v. Christian*, 42 N.Y.2d 63, 396 N.Y.S.2d 817 (1977). Whether each spouse was represented by an attorney of his or her own choosing is one factor which the courts weigh in deciding whether an agreement is unconscionable. Although an agreement is not automatically invalid because one attorney represented both spouses, such an agreement is vulnerable to challenge, as Case 4-1 illustrates.

 **CASE 4-1**

LEVINE v. LEVINE
56 N.Y.2d 42, 451 N.Y.S.2d 26 (1982)

JASEN, J.

We are asked on this appeal to determine whether the fact that a separation agreement was prepared by one attorney representing both husband and wife is sufficient, in and of itself, to establish overreaching requiring a rescission of the agreement.

***

The separation agreement was prepared by an attorney related to the husband by marriage, who had previously represented the husband in connection with his business and who had known both parties for a number of years. The husband initially contacted the attorney and informed him that he had discussed the possibility of a separation agreement with his wife and that the couple had agreed on the essential terms. The attorney then arranged to meet with the wife at his office.

At this meeting, the attorney told the wife that he was involved in the matter only because the basic terms of the agreement had already been settled by the parties and that the wife was free to seek the advice of another attorney. Based on conversations with both parties, the attorney prepared a draft agreement. Further negotiations and consultations followed, after which a final agreement was drawn up, thoroughly reviewed by the plaintiff [wife], and then signed by her.

***

📖 **CASE 4-1 continued**

The wife...commenced this action seeking to have the separation agreement...set aside as "inequitable" and "unconscionable". In her complaint, the wife alleged that she "was not represented by counsel of her own choosing, but instead and without her consent was represented by the defendant's attorney" in the execution of the separation agreement....

***

For the most part, a separation agreement which is regular on its face will be recognized and enforced by the courts in much the same manner as an ordinary contract. However, because of the fiduciary relationship between husband and wife, separation agreements generally are closely scrutinized by the courts, and such agreements are more readily set aside in equity under circumstances that would be insufficient to nullify an ordinary contract.... Although courts may examine the terms of the agreement as well as the surrounding circumstances to ascertain whether there has been overreaching, the general rule is that "if the execution of the agreement...be fair, no further inquiry will be made."...

Nor does the fact that the same attorney represented both parties in the preparation to the agreement require an automatic nullification of the agreement. While the absence of independent representation is a significant factor to be taken into consideration when determining whether a separation agreement was freely and fairly entered into, the fact that each party retained the same attorney does not, in and of itself, provide a basis for rescission.... Of course, a claim of overreaching will be subject to a "far more searching scrutiny" and, as a result, is less likely to prevail where the party had the benefit of independent representation during the negotiation and execution of the agreement.... Nevertheless, as long as the attorney fairly advises the parties of both the salient issues and the consequences of joint representation, and the separation agreement arrived at was fair, rescission will not be granted. While the potential conflict of interests inherent in such joint representation suggests that the husband and wife should retain separate counsel, the parties have an absolute right to be represented by the same attorney provided "there has been full disclosure between the parties, not only of all relevant facts, but also of the contextual significance, and there has been an absence of inequitable conduct or other infirmity which might vitiate the execution of the agreement"....

Applying these principles to the case before us, we cannot conclude that it was error for the trial court, as a matter of law, to have found that the separation agreement in this case is fair, both on its face and when considered in light of the parties' circumstances at the time of execution. The husband undertook a variety of financial obligations, all of which were designed to maintain the wife and the two children in

📖 **CASE 4-1 continued**

the style to which they were accustomed to living. Although the wife has contended throughout this action that the husband earns a far greater income than the record reflects, she has not come forward with an evidentiary showing to support this claim. We agree with the trial court that the wife's bare allegations to the effect that the husband has been "living high on the hog" provide no basis for overturning the parties' agreement.

***

Accordingly, the order of the Appellate Division should be reversed, with costs, and the judgment of Supreme Court, Westchester County, reinstated.

***

SPOUSAL SUPPORT PROVISIONS

Prior to 1966 a husband's obligation to support his wife was not waivable. When the statutes were made gender neutral, however, that provision was eliminated. Now, either party may waive support unless he or she should become a public charge. Of course, if one spouse is unable to fully support him or herself at the time of the separation, that spouse will not be willing to waive support. In such a case, spousal support will be an important term of the separation agreement. If the parties are represented by counsel, their attorneys will advise them concerning the standards which courts apply in awarding spousal support, which are discussed in Chapter 7. Both spouses prepare net worth statements (Form 8-1), usually with the help of a paralegal. The net worth statements show how much the spouse who is asking for support needs to maintain the standard of living the couple enjoyed as a married couple and how much disposable income the other spouse has to contribute. Using all of this information, the couple then agree upon an amount, duration, and method of spousal support.

The spouse who will be the recipient of support may agree to accept less than a court might have awarded. Unless the agreement overall is unconscionable, courts will not set aside the agreement merely because the spousal support allowance seems inadequate. Rather, the court will assume that in the negotiation process the spouse accepted less support because he or she got something in exchange for that concession. Once the agreement is made, the spousal support provision is binding forever. If the agreement has subsequently been incorporated into a divorce judgment, the divorce judgment may be modified only if the recipient spouse is about to become a public charge. *McMains v. McMains*, 15 N.Y.2d 283, 258 N.Y.S.2d 93 (1965). Where the spousal support provisions in a divorce judgment have been set by the court, rather than by agreement, they are more easily modifiable, as is discussed in Chapter 7. Using an agreement to settle this issue, therefore, gives both parties the advantage of greater certainty, so they can plan their financial future with confidence. Obviously, when the agreement is being negotiated, however, careful consideration must be given not only to the parties' present circumstances but to their future prospects as well.

Sometimes the form of payment is an important issue in the negotiation of the separation agreement. If the payor is salaried, the support payments are usually made on the same schedule as the payor's paycheck. If the payor is freelance or otherwise receives income irregularly, the couple may agree upon some other increment for payment of the support. They might also agree upon a lump sum payment, but the payor runs the risk that the recipient will use up the lump sum and become a public charge. Even if the lump sum was dissipated by the waste and extravagance of the recipient spouse, the payor will still be liable for support if the recipient becomes a public charge. *De Robertis v. De Robertis*, 261 App.Div. 476, 25 N.Y.S.2d 929 (1941).

CHILD SUPPORT PROVISIONS

If there are children of the marriage, child support will be an important provision in the separation agreement. Child support is calculated by a different method from spousal support. As Chapter 7 discusses more fully, courts calculate child support upon a percentage of the parents' income specified by the Child Support Standards Act [DRL § 240]. If the parties decide to "opt out" of the CSSA formula, the separation agreement must recite that they have been advised of the amount of child support which would have been allowed under the CSSA and must state their reasons for departing from the formula.

While spousal support is modifiable only in cases of extreme hardship, child support provisions may be modified whenever a court determines that the child's best interests require a larger allowance. The courts base their authority to modify child support both on the premise that the child is not a party to its parents' agreement and on the courts' *parens patriae* responsibility to protect children within its jurisdiction. When child support has been set in the separation agreement, the courts will not modify it solely because the child's needs have increased and the non-custodial parent is financially able to pay more. The custodial parent must also prove that he or she is unable to meet the child's increased needs. In *Boden v. Boden*, 42 N.Y.2d 210, 397 N.Y.S.2d 701 (1977), for example, the separation agreement called for the non-custodial father to pay a specified amount for the child's college education. When the child reached college age and was admitted to Yale University, the mother sought an upward modification to meet the high cost of the Yale tuition. The court refused, because the mother herself was financially able to pay the difference between the father's contribution and the cost of the Yale tuition. The court declined to readjust the respective obligations of the parents to support their child. If, however, the child support award is so inadequate that the child is experiencing deprivation, the courts may award child support in excess of the amount provided for in the separation agreement. *Brescia v. Fitts*, 56 N.Y.2d 132, 451 N.Y.S.2d 68 (1982).

CUSTODY PROVISIONS

Because the spouses will be living apart following the execution of their separation agreement, they will need to provide for the custody of their children and for visitation with the non-custodial parent. In fact, the parties will not be able to negotiate the amount of child support until they have first determined which parent will have custody. Parents should always be encouraged to resolve these issues whenever possible without litigation. Although mediation of custody and visitation disputes is not mandatory in New York, as it is in some states, it is nevertheless highly advisable. Throughout New York State, programs are being developed and expanded to provide professional mediation services relating to custody and visitation issues. In New York City, for example, a mediation service has recently been launched which is a joint effort of the Association of the Bar of the City of New York, the New York Society for the Prevention of Cruelty to Children, and Victim Services.

Agreements concerning custody and visitation spare the parents the enormous expense of custody litigation and spare both the parents and the children stress and heartache. The parents' agreement is not binding on the court, however, and may be modified if it proves not to serve the best interest of the child. In such a situation, the court's *parens patriae* authority to protect the child overrides the parents' agreement. Even if the agreement has been incorporated into the decree of divorce, it may be modified without a showing of extraordinary circumstances, as Case 4-2 shows.

📖 **CASE 4-2**

FRIEDERWITZER v. FRIEDERWITZER
55 N.Y.2d 89, 447 N.Y.S.2d 893 (1982)

MEYER, J.

***

The parties were married in 1968. An uncontested divorce was awarded plaintiff wife after inquest, by judgment dated July 24, 1979. The separation agreement entered into by them provided that as to the two children of the marriage, Lisa and Nicole, the husband and wife would have joint custody with the children residing with the wife and reasonable visitation rights to the husband. It provided further that the terms of the agreement would survive a judgment of divorce "without merging, other than child support which shall merge in said decree." The judgment of divorce provided that the parties have joint custody of the children, the father to have visitation as provided in the separation

📖 **CASE 4-2 continued**

agreement, and that the agreement should survive and not merge in the judgment....

In September, 1979, the mother, who had been living with the children on Long Island close to the residence of the father, moved with the children to an apartment on East 93rd Street in Manhattan. Both parties and the children have been reared as Orthodox Jews, strictly observing both the Sabbath and the dietary laws. The children, who had attended a yeshiva on Long Island, were transferred to a yeshiva in Manhattan. Less than a year after the original judgment, in April, 1980, the father moved for modification of the judgment of divorce so as to award him sole custody of his daughters. The mother cross-moved for sole custody. After a trial during which the mother, father and both children testified, the Trial Judge found the father to be "a loving and caring person...well qualified as a fit parent." He found that the mother, while not unfit, was less fit to have custody than the father because her own best interests and social life appeared to be of "paramount concern to her, to the total exclusion of the best interest of her children." He predicated that conclusion on the mother having frequently left her then 11- and 8-year-old girls alone in the apartment until late at night, when she went out for the evening even though the children informed her that they were afraid to stay alone, and on the mother's profession of raising the children in the tenets of Orthodox Judaism while at the same time flagrantly violating those tenets by permitting a male friend to stay in the apartment and share her bed to the knowledge of the children, by failing except rarely, to take the children to Sabbath services, and by permitting the male friend to violate the Sabbath by turning on the television, all of which confused the children and was contrary to their religious beliefs and detrimental to their religious feeling. Noting the older daughter's strong desire to live with her father and the younger child's wish to continue living with her mother but not to be separated from her sister, the Trial Judge acknowledged that the wishes of the children was an element to be considered, but held it controlled in this instance by the overriding considerations above detailed. He therefore modified the judgment to award custody of both children to the father.

The Appellate Division by a divided court...affirmed Special Term's order....

The only absolute in the law governing custody of children is that there are no absolutes. The Legislature has so declared in directing that custody be determined by the circumstances of the case and of the parties and the best interests of the child, but then adding "In all cases there shall be no prima facie right to the custody of the child in either parent" (Domestic Relations Law § 240; see also § 70). Because the section speaks to modification as well as to an original matrimonial judgment, "all cases" must be read as including both. That, of course, does not mean that custody may be changed without regard to the circumstances considered by the court when the earlier

📖 **CASE 4-2 continued**

award was made but rather that no one factor, including the existence of the earlier decree or agreement, is determinative of whether there should, in the exercise of sound judicial discretion, be a change in custody.

***

The priority which is accorded the first award of custody, whether contained in court order or voluntary agreement, results not from the policy considerations involved in *res judicata* (which permits change in custody decrees when warranted by the circumstances...), so much as from the conceptions that stability in a child's life is in the child's best interests and that the prior determination reflects a considered and experienced judgment concerning all of the factors involved.... But the weight to be given the prior award necessarily depends upon whether it results from the Trial Judge's judgment after consideration of all relevant evidence introduced during a plenary trial or, as here, finds its way into the judgment through agreement of the parties proven as part of a proceeding in which custody was not contested and no evidence contradictory of the agreement's custody provision has been presented. No agreement of the parties can bind the court to a disposition other than that which a weighing of all of the factors involved shows to be in the child's best interest....

An additional reason for so holding in the instant case exists in rule 699.9 of the Appellate Division, Second Department, to which the decree in the instant case is subject.... Rule 699.9 expressly states that "as to support, custody and visitation, no such [separation] agreement or stipulation is binding" (22 NYCRR 699.9 [f] [4]) and requires, as earlier noted, that the judgment contain the provision that the court retains jurisdiction for the purpose of making such further custody decree "as it finds appropriate under the circumstances existing *at the time application for that purpose is made to it*" (italics supplied)....

It thus appears that the standard applied by the courts below was not legally incorrect. Moreover, the record supports the determination of the courts below that the change of custody was warranted by the lesser concern of the mother for the emotional well-being of her children than for her own life style demonstrated after the original award was made, particularly in light of the short period of time it had been in existence when the application for modification was made and the fact that the custody provisions of the divorce judgment were based on the agreement of the parties rather than plenary consideration by the trial court.

For the foregoing reasons, the order of the Appellate Division should be affirmed, without costs.

```
DISCUSSION TOPIC
How free should courts be to modify parents' agreements concerning custody
and visitation issues?  Is the "best interest of the child" standard too broad for
modification cases?   If so, would you substitute "substantial change of
circumstances," "extraordinary circumstances," or some other standard?  What
can courts do to prevent modification applications designed to harass the other
parent?   What is the effect on a child of constant custody and visitation
litigation?
```

Before commencing negotiations concerning the custody and visitation aspects of the separation agreement, the attorney in charge of the case will need a great deal of detailed information about the client's wishes with regard to these issues and about the present division of child care responsibilities between the parents. The attorney may ask the legal assistant to acquire this information in a preliminary interview. As Chapter 6 discusses in greater detail, the term "custody" is used to mean both "legal custody," the authority to make decisions concerning the child, and "physical custody," the right to have the child stay with a particular adult at specified times. Since lay people, and some attorneys, use terms like "custody" and "visitation" rather loosely, it is important to be specific and avoid legalistic language when interviewing a client. Form 4-1 is a sample of a questionnaire which may be used to obtain information pertinent to the issues of custody and visitation. Information must be obtained about each child of the marriage.

FORM 4-1

CUSTODY AND VISITATION QUESTIONNAIRE

- Child's Name:
- Child's Age:
- School child attends:
- With which parent is child now residing?
- Does child have any special physical, medical or emotional needs? If so, how are those needs now being met?
- Who picks child up from school and cares for child until parents come home from work?
- Child's after-school and extra curricular activities (sports, music lessons, etc.):
- Which parent prepares meals, supervises homework, bathes child, supervises bedtime, attends school meetings?
- Are important decisions concerning the child now made jointly or by one parent? If one, which parent? Ask for examples.
- How is child disciplined? Which parent usually disciplines child? Ask for examples.
- If child is living with one parent now, what contact is the other parent having with the child and how is that time spent?
- Does either parent have any physical, emotional, medical or

📁 **FORM 4-1 continued**

       other sort of problem which limits child caring ability or renders it unsafe for child to be alone with that parent? If so, are relatives available to assist or supervise that parent's time with the child?

- How does the client wish the child's time to be divided between the parents following the execution of the separation agreement?
- Is there any obstacle to the child's staying overnight with either parent? If so, what?
- How should decision-making be handled in the agreement? Will the parents reach joint decisions, or will one parent have the final say? If one parent will have final authority, will that parent be required to consult with the other parent? Are there particular issues (e.g., medical issues, choice of school) about which either parent would particularly wish to be consulted?
- If the child is to reside with one parent primarily, should the other parent receive copies of the child's report card, invitations to open school night, graduations, etc.? Obtain specifics if there is any information which the client does not want the other parent to have or events at which the presence of the other parent would be unwelcome.
- Is the child to participate in decision-making concerning him or herself? Should the child be permitted to decide whether to go for scheduled visitation with the non-custodial parent or to decide how much contact to have with each parent?
- Is the move of either parent from the current city of residence contemplated? If so, where? How would the move alter the custody and visitation arrangements?
- If relocation is not currently contemplated by either parent, should the agreement restrict a future move? Should such a move result in a change of custody? Should it have any impact on child support?
- Should the child's religious upbringing be addressed in the agreement? If so, what are the client's wishes on the subject?
- Will the contemplated custodial arrangements result in the child's being separated from siblings or half-siblings or step-siblings with whom the child has formed a relationship? If so, does the client want the agreement to provide for continued contact between the siblings?

PARTIAL INVALIDITY

Since separation agreements cover such a wide range of issues, it is not surprising that courts sometimes find one provision of the agreement invalid. In such a situation, what becomes of the rest of the agreement? If a provision has been found invalid due to fraud, coercion, or overreaching, the entire agreement is vitiated. Otherwise, if the invalid clause does not go to the heart of the agreement, the courts will usually permit the rest of the agreement to remain in effect. A provision for a penalty in case of default in making periodic support payments was ruled invalid, for example, but the court found that it was readily severable from the remainder of the agreement. *Kroll v. Kroll*, 4 Misc.2d 520, 158 N.Y.S.2d 930 (N.Y. Sup. Ct. 1956). The parties can enhance the likelihood of the agreement surviving by including in the agreement a **severability clause** specifying that the agreement survives if one or more individual clauses are ruled invalid.

BREACH

If one party **breaches** the agreement, that is, fails to fulfill one or more of its terms, the other spouse may either 1) affirm the agreement and bring an action on the agreement, or 2) treat the breach as a repudiation of the agreement, which terminates the agreement. If the spouse treats the breach as a repudiation of the agreement, he or she is then free to pursue statutory remedies, such as suing for maintenance or child support, but loses all the rights accruing under the agreement. If the spouse affirms the agreement and sues for its enforcement, the defendant may claim as a defense that the plaintiff has also failed to live up to the agreement. A typical example is that the plaintiff sues to collect past due child support, and the defendant claims that he or she has been denied the visitation called for in the agreement. As is discussed in Chapter 7, this defense is limited by DRL § 241 once the child support provisions have been incorporated into a court order. Courts are reluctant to suspend child support as a way of enforcing visitation, since the net effect may be to leave a child without adequate support. Occasionally, however, courts have found it the only method to insure visitation or to do justice between the parties. Such a defense has a greater likelihood of success if the agreement specifically conditions the child support obligation upon the continued enjoyment of the right of visitation. In *Vastola v. Vastola*, 23 Misc.2d 39, 200 N.Y.S.2d 512 (N.Y.Sup. Ct. 1960), for example, the court refused to suspend child support where the custodial parent had frustrated the father's visitation by moving with the children to Florida. The court noted that the child support provision of the agreement was not conditioned upon the right of visitation and was, therefore, an independent obligation.

PROVISIONS THAT PREVENT FUTURE LEGAL PROBLEMS

A well-drafted separation agreement not only makes provisions for the issues which are of immediate concern to the parties, such as custody, child support, and property division, but it also contains clauses designed to prevent problems in the future. For example, the parties may find that in the future they need to change some of the terms of the agreement. Thus, the agreement should contain a **modification clause** which spells out how the agreement may be altered. Also, one of the parties may move to another state. If litigation involving the agreement occurs in another jurisdiction, that jurisdiction may have laws about child support, spousal support or property division which differ substantially from New York law. Since the parties negotiated the agreement with New York law in mind, the agreement should contain a **governing law clause** which specifies whether they intend that New York law always be applied whenever and wherever the agreement is interpreted or enforced. Unfortunately, it is also possible that one party will not live up to the terms of the agreement. Thus, the agreement should contain a **default clause**, which requires the party who breaches the agreement to pay any legal fees which the other party incurs in enforcing it. The parties will also probably want to bind each other's estate to the terms of the agreement in the event that either should die before all the obligations under the agreement are fulfilled.

PREPARING THE AGREEMENT

Legal assistants should not be expected to draft separation agreements. They are expected, however, to be able to cull form books, computer software, and the firm's files for forms which the attorney may use as a model or guide for the case at hand. Thus, the paralegal should be comfortable in reading separation agreements and should learn to recognize certain standard clauses which are frequently utilized. The sample separation agreement (Form 4-2) might be negotiated by a couple who have few assets, are both able to support themselves without assistance from the other, and who have a child of the marriage.

FORM 4-2

SEPARATION AGREEMENT BETWEEN HERBERT BROWN AND EMILY COOK BROWN

THIS AGREEMENT, made August 31, 1996, by and between Emily Cook Brown, of the Town of Hempstead, County of Nassau, State of New York (hereinafter referred to as the "Wife"), and Herbert Brown, of the City of New York, County of New York, State of New York (hereinafter referred to as the "Husband"),

WHEREAS, the parties were duly married to each other in the Town of Great Neck, County of Nassau, State of New York on April 3, 1990; and

WHEREAS, there is one child of the marriage, namely Charles Cook Brown (hereinafter referred to as the "Child"), born on June 12, 1992; and there are no expected additional children of the marriage; and

WHEREAS, certain unhappy and irreconcilable differences have arisen between the parties as a result of which they have separated and are now living separate and apart from each other and intend to continue to live separate and apart from each other for the rest of their lives; and

WHEREAS, the parties are desirous of entering into this Agreement under which they may hereafter live separate and apart and which Agreement shall state their understanding with respect to their rights, privileges, duties, and obligations and the conduct of each to the other and which shall further provide for the support of the Child, and the custody, and control of such Child, and which Agreement further shall provide for the full and final determination of any and all rights which either of the parties now has or will claim to have against the other; and

📁 FORM 4-2 continued

WHEREAS, each party is being represented by separate and independent counsel of his or her own choosing with whom each has discussed his or her rights and obligations and the terms of this Agreement; and

WHEREAS, each party has received all disclosure as to the other's finances, assets, income, expectancies, and other economic matters that he or she has requested and each has received from the other a Net Worth Statement, annexed hereto as exhibits "A" and "B" respectively; and

WHEREAS, the parties hereto, through their respective counsel, have agreed upon all questions of custody, maintenance, support, inheritance, and property rights and all of the other rights of any kind or character that have accrued or may accrue to either by reason of their marital relations.

NOW, THEREFORE, in consideration of the promises and agreements hereinafter set forth, it is hereby stipulated, covenanted, and agreed by and between the parties, as follows:

ARTICLE I
LIVING SEPARATE AND APART

1. Wife and Husband may, for all time, live and continue to live separate and apart from each other and shall reside from time to time at such place or places as either may deem fit and may conduct themselves without interference, directly or indirectly, from the other, in all respects, as if each of said parties was single and unmarried.

ARTICLE II
NONMOLESTATION

2. Except as otherwise specifically set forth in this Agreement, neither of the parties shall interfere with the other in his or her respective liberty of action or conduct, and except as otherwise set forth in this Agreement, each agrees that the other may at any and all times reside and be in such places and with such relatives, friends, and acquaintances as he or she may choose, and each party agrees that he or she will not interfere with the other or compel or seek to compel the other to cohabit or dwell with him or her or institute any proceeding for the restoration of conjugal rights.

ARTICLE III
WAIVER OF RIGHTS IN ESTATES

3. (a) Each party hereby waives, releases, and relinquishes any and all rights that he or she may now have in the property of the other (such as right of election, dower, curtesy, and inheritance) and all rights he or she may now have or hereafter acquire under the laws of the State of New York and any other jurisdiction:

(i) To share, as a result of the marital relationship, in the other party's property or estate upon the latter's death; or

(ii) To act as executor or administrator of the other's estate, or to participate in the administration thereof.

This Agreement shall and does constitute a mutual waiver by the parties of their respective rights of election to take against each others's last will and testament now or hereafter in force under the laws of any jurisdiction.

FORM 4-2 continued

It is the intention of the parties that their respective estates shall be administered and distributed in all respects as though no marriage had been solemnized between them. The consideration for each party's waiver and release is the other party's reciprocal waiver and release.

(b) Nothing contained above in this Paragraph shall constitute:

(I) a release or discharge of either party or such party's estate or property of or from any of such party's covenants, agreements, promises, representations, warranties, or other undertakings or obligations set forth in this Agreement or a release, waiver, relinquishment, or renunciation by either party of his or her right, or the right of his or her respective heirs, legal representatives, executors, administrators, or assigns to require and enforce performance of the other party's covenants, agreements, promises, representations, warranties, and other undertakings and obligations set forth in this Agreement; or

(ii) a release, waiver, relinquishment, or renunciation by either party of any devise, bequest, or other provision for the benefit of such party which may be set forth in the Last Will and Testament (or any codicil thereto) of the other party. The parties specifically do not intend to imply that any such devise, bequest, or other provision will be made or has been promised by the other party or by any third person.

ARTICLE IV
WAIVER OF MAINTENANCE

4. Each party acknowledges that he or she is capable of being self supporting and is self supporting and is possessed of sufficient assets and income to support himself or herself, respectively; and each party hereby waives and renounces all right to make or assert any claim for maintenance, alimony, support, counsel fees, or any like claim, now or in the future.

ARTICLE V
CUSTODY

5. The Wife shall have exclusive custody of the Child. Notwithstanding the foregoing, the Wife agrees to consult with the Husband upon all major decisions affecting the children, but the final decision shall be the Wife's.

6. In the event of the death of either parent, the surviving parent shall, forthwith, have the sole and exclusive legal and physical custody of the Child.

ARTICLE VI
VISITATION

7. The Husband shall have the following visitation rights, at his option, with the Child as set out below:

(1) Every Wednesday evening from 6:00 p.m. until 9:00 p.m.;

(2) In alternating weeks from Friday at 6:00 p.m. until Sunday at 9:00 p.m.;

📁 FORM 4-2 continued

(3) The night before or after the Child's birthday;

(4) The month of July or the month of August, at the Father's option, to be exercised in writing on or before April 15 of each year. Should the Husband fail to timely exercise his option, the Wife may select the month;

(5) Alternating Memorial Day, Labor Day, Columbus Day, Veterans' Day, Thanksgiving, Christmas Eve (2:00 p.m. to 9:00 p.m.) and Christmas Day (10:00 a.m. until the next morning at 10:00 a.m.) holidays;

(6) The second week of the Child's Christmas school vacation;

(7) In alternating years, either the Child's Easter or February school vacation:

(8) Notwithstanding the foregoing, in each year, the Husband shall have visitation from 11:00 a.m. to 7:00 p.m. on Father's Day and on the Father's birthday.

ARTICLE VII
CHILD SUPPORT

8. Beginning upon the execution of this Agreement, and in conformity with the provision of DRL § 240(1)(b), the Husband shall pay to the Wife, as and for the support and maintenance of the parties' unemancipated child, by check or money order sent to her at her present place of residence, or at such other address as she may hereafter in writing designate to the Husband, the sum of $567 per month, said sum representing approximately 17% of the Husband's income as set forth in exhibit "A" annexed hereto.

9. The parties further agree that the sum of $567 per month in child support payable by the Husband to the Wife shall not be subject to reduction, even if the Husband's income should decrease below present levels prior to the emancipation of the Child, and that he shall pay at least this sum regardless of his income in the future.

10. The parties further agree that the amount of child support payable monthly by the Husband to the Wife shall increase 10% every three years on the anniversary of the execution of this Agreement until the Child reaches the age of 21 years or becomes emancipated, whichever comes sooner.

11. The parties further agree that the increases in the Husband's child support obligation provided for in paragraph 10 of this Agreement will satisfy all of the Child's reasonable anticipated needs and that the Wife shall not seek upward modification of the Husband's child support obligation beyond the amounts set forth in this Agreement.

12. The parties further agree that should the Child pursue an academic or vocational course of study after graduation from high-school, the Husband will contribute two-thirds (⅔) of the educational expenses thereof (including but not limited to tuition, books, transportation, housing and miscellaneous fees) at any accredited public, private or parochial institution of higher learning in which the Child is enrolled as a full-time matriculated student, until the Child reaches the age of 23 years or becomes emancipated, whichever occurs sooner, and the Wife shall pay the remaining one-third (⅓).

🗁 **FORM 4-2 continued**

13. The parties further agree that in addition to the child support set forth above, the Husband shall continue through the minority of the Child to maintain for the Child medical and dental insurance, if any, as provided by his employer or future employers, or its equivalent, and to pay one-half (½) of all unreimbursed medical and dental expenses, including orthodontia, of which the Wife shall pay the other one-half (½). In the event the Husband does not have medical insurance available to him through employment and the Wife does, she shall obtain insurance for the Child, for whose cost, if any, the Husband shall reimburse her.

14.	(a) The parties each acknowledge being informed of the provisions of the so-called Child Support Standards Act, DRL § 240(b-1), and having reviewed the application of the formula to their income as set forth in the Child Support Worksheet annexed hereto as Exhibit "C". They have taken this statute and Exhibit "C" into consideration in arriving at the child support provided for herein. The parties intend and agree that their respective child support obligations are to be governed by this Agreement, and they waive the right to fix the child support obligations under the Child Support Standards Act.

(b) The parties have been informed that the present amount of the Husband's child support obligation as set forth in this Agreement is approximately that which would be provided under the Child Support Standard Act. In possibly deviating from the Child Support Act with regard to the future level of support, the parties represent that they have considered the standard of living the Child has heretofore enjoyed and the historical level of each party's income. The parties further represent that they have possibly deviated from the child support standards in regard to the future level of support also in consideration of the fact that the Child's education to the fullest extent of his academic potential is of paramount concern to each of them.

ARTICLE VIII
EMANCIPATION

15. The Child shall be deemed to have become emancipated upon the happening of any of the following events:

(a) The Child's attainment of the age of twenty-one (21) years;

(b) The marriage of the Child;

(c) The Child's permanent residence away from the residence of the Wife. The following do not constitute permanent residence away from the residence of the Wife: residence at a boarding school, residence at camp or college, temporary active duty in the military service;

(d) The death of the Child;

(e) The Child's entry into the armed forces of the United States. However, if the Child is discharged prior to attaining the age of twenty-one (21) years, then he shall not be deemed to be emancipated, and the child support payments provided for in this Agreement shall recommence and continue until terminated under another provision of this Agreement.

(f) The Child's engagement in full-time employment, upon and after reaching age eighteen, except that engaging in full-time employment during any school vacation periods (including summer vacations), or while the Child is a full-time student, shall not be deemed adequate to establish the Child's emancipation. Further, emancipation based on the Child's full-time employment shall be

FORM 4-2 continued

deemed terminated and nullified upon the cessation by the Child, for any reason, of the full-time employment, and the child support payments provided for in this Agreement shall recommence and continue until terminated under another provision of the Agreement.

ARTICLE IX
MARITAL RESIDENCE

16. The parties acknowledge that the dwelling house and place where the parties resided as Husband and Wife with the Child at 3 Post Path, Hempstead, New York (the "Marital Residence"), is now owned by the parties as tenants by the entirety, with a mortgage and note held by the Best Bank in the present amount of $57,947.

17. The parties agree that the Wife shall have exclusive occupancy, use, and possession of the Marital Residence from the date of the execution of this Agreement until the earliest to occur of the events set forth in paragraph 19 of this Agreement.

18. During the period in which the Wife has exclusive occupancy, use, and possession of the Marital Residence, the expenses of the upkeep of the Marital residence shall be divided between the parties as follows:

    (a) The Wife will make all payments due on account of the Marital Residence, except as otherwise set forth herein, and will be entitled to all the tax deductions permissible on account of said payments;

    (b)   (i) The Wife shall pay for any nonmajor repairs to the Marital Residence; and

              (ii) The parties shall share equally any major repairs made in excess of $300 in any one calendar year; the Wife shall pay for all repairs up to $300 in any one calendar year.

              (iii) For the purpose of this Agreement, major repairs shall mean repairs to the heating, ventilation, air-conditioning, and/or electrical systems, the plumbing system, and/or the roof or other structural repairs, the cost of which exceeds $300.

    (c) The Wife may, at her sole and unreimbursable expense, decorate or remodel the Marital Residence as she sees fit; provided, however, that such decoration or remodeling does not impair or reduce the fair market value of the Marital Residence.

19. Upon the earliest to occur of:
    (a) The Wife's death; or

    (b) The Wife's remarriage; or

    (c) The eighteenth birthday of the parties' Child,

the parties agree to place the Marital Residence on the market for sale and to divide the proceeds of the sale as set forth in paragraph 22 of this Agreement.

20. Upon the commencement of proceedings to sell the Marital Residence pursuant to paragraph 19 above, the

📁 **FORM 4-2 continued**

parties will endeavor, in good faith, to arrive at a mutually acceptable selling price. Furthermore, both parties agree to cooperate in the sale of the Marital Residence.

21. If the parties are unable to agree upon a mutually acceptable selling price, then the parties shall agree upon a real estate appraiser, or failing such agreement, the parties shall request the American Arbitration Association to appoint a real estate appraiser, who will make an appraisal of the fair market value of the Marital Residence. The parties will share equally the expense of the real estate appraiser.

22. The proceeds of the sale of the Marital Residence shall be distributed in the following manner:

> (a) Brokerage fees and other customary costs attendant to the sale, if actually incurred, shall first be deducted from the gross sale price, as shall the then outstanding principal balance due on the present first mortgage.

> (b) The Wife shall then be reimbursed an amount equal to that amount by which the principal amount of the mortgage was reduced by payments by her during her period of exclusive occupancy.

> (c) The remaining net balance of the proceeds shall be distributed so that 50% thereof shall be paid to the Wife, and 50% thereof shall be paid to the Husband, provided, however, that any second mortgage or unsatisfied liens upon the Marital Residence shall be paid and satisfied solely out of the share otherwise belonging to whichever of the Husband or Wife caused the said lien or second mortgage to be placed upon the Marital Residence, and if his or her share is inadequate to do so, then the Husband or the Wife, as the case may be, will be indebted to the other party for such inadequacy; provided, however, that at any closing the Wife shall be paid, out of the Husband's share, any monies which the Husband was obligated to pay pursuant to this Agreement but which he has not previously paid to her.

23.   (a) In the event that either party elects to purchase the other's right, title, and interest in the Marital Residence, then the payment to the seller shall be calculated by first determining the fair market value in the manner set forth above and then deducting therefrom the then outstanding principal balance due on the present first mortgage as provided in paragraph 22 of this Agreement.

          (b) The fair market value of the premises as so reduced shall be divided in two and the result of that division shall be paid to the seller by the buyer and the seller shall execute a bargain and sale deed transferring all the right, title, and interest to the buyer; provided, however, that any second mortgage or unsatisfied liens upon the Marital Residence which were placed on account of any indebtedness of, or any action or omission by the seller, shall be paid and satisfied solely out of the share otherwise belonging to the seller; and provided, further, that the buyer may deduct from the seller's share as determined herein, any monies which the seller was obligated to pay pursuant to this Agreement but which he or she has not previously paid.

ARTICLE X
PERSONAL PROPERTY

24. The Wife is hereby granted sole and exclusive ownership of all of the household furniture, furnishings, appliances, and household effects presently in the Marital Residence; and the Husband is hereby divested of all right, title, and interest therein and saved harmless from any and all liability thereon.

📁 **FORM 4-2 continued**

25. Except as stated in paragraph 24 of this Agreement, all personal property now in the possession of either party shall, upon the execution of this Agreement, be deemed the separate property of the party having possession thereof, the parties having heretofore divided all of their personal property. By executing this Agreement, each party waives any and all claims, right, title, and interest therein.

ARTICLE XI
DEBTS

26. Each party represents and warrants to the other that each has not incurred any obligations for which the other shall or may be liable other than the first mortgage on the marital home payable to Best Bank with an approximate remaining balance of $57,947. Each further promises that each will not hereafter contract any such obligations, and each will hold the other and the other's personal representatives, heirs, and assigns, harmless from any and all debts, charges, and liabilities heretofore or hereafter contracted by each, and will indemnify the other for reasonable attorneys' fees incurred in connection with any claim made against the other or the other's estate as a result of any such debt, charge, or liability incurred by each. Each, or the estate of each, promises to notify the other if any claim is made against each or each's estate as a result of any debt, charge, or liability incurred by the other, to afford the other an opportunity to defend against any such claim.

ARTICLE XII
DEFAULT

27. If either party shall default in the performance of any of the material provisions of this agreement, including and without limitation, the financial provisions, and if the other party shall institute, and prevail in, legal proceedings to enforce the performance of such provisions by the defaulting party, then the defaulting party shall pay to the other party the necessary and reasonable costs and expenses incurred by the other party (including reasonable attorneys' fees) in connection with such proceedings. For purposes of this Agreement, the substantial performance by the defaulting party of the provisions after notification of a default shall be deemed to be the equivalent of the non-defaulting party's having prevailed in a legal proceeding.

ARTICLE XIII
MODIFICATION AND WAIVER

28. Neither this Agreement nor any provision hereof may be amended, waived, or modified or deemed amended, waived, or modified except by an agreement in writing, identifying each particular provision amended, waived, or modified and duly subscribed and acknowledged by both parties with the same formality as this Agreement. No oral representation or statement shall constitute an amendment, waiver, or modification even if substantially and detrimentally relied upon. Any waiver by either party of any provision of this Agreement or any right or option hereunder shall not prevent or estop such party from thereafter enforcing such provision, right, or option, and the failure of either party to insist in any one or more instances upon the strict performance of any of the terms and provisions of this Agreement by the other party shall not be construed as a waiver or relinquishment for the future of any such term or provision, but the same shall continue in full force and effect.

ARTICLE XIV
MATRIMONIAL DECREES

FORM 4-2 continued

30. This Agreement shall not be invalidated or otherwise affected by any decree or judgment of separation, annulment, or divorce made by any court in any action which may hereafter be instituted by either party against the other for a separation, annulment, or divorce. The obligations and covenants of this Agreement shall be incorporated in and shall survive any such decree or judgment and shall not merge therein.

ARTICLE XV
NONABROGATION BY TEMPORARY RECONCILIATION

31. In the event the parties reconcile and within six (6) months again separate, then this Agreement shall thereafter be deemed to be in full force and effect.

ARTICLE XVI
ENTIRE UNDERSTANDING

31. This Agreement contains the entire agreement of the parties, who acknowledge that there are no representations, warranties, promises, or undertakings not herein set forth. Except as otherwise specifically defined in this Agreement, the terms used in this Agreement have the same meaning as accorded to them when used in ordinary every day speech.

ARTICLE XVII
SEVERABILITY

32. If any provision of this Agreement shall be held invalid or unlawful by any court of competent jurisdiction, the remainder of this Agreement shall nevertheless remain valid and enforceable according to its terms.

ARTICLE XVIII
ARTICLE HEADINGS

33. The headings appearing throughout this Agreement are for reference purposes and shall not, in any manner, constitute terms or conditions of this Agreement, nor shall they be applicable to any interpretation of the intent or meaning of any part of this Agreement.

ARTICLE XIX
NOTICES AND NOTIFICATION OF CHANGE OF ADDRESS

34. Notice required by this Agreement is to be sent to the Wife by registered mail at 3 Post Path, Hempstead, New York. Notice required by this Agreement is to be sent to the Husband by registered mail at 606 East 96th Street, New York, New York. The parties agree that each will notify the other of any change of address and/or telephone number within five days of any such event.

ARTICLE XX
NOTIFICATION IN THE EVENT OF REMARRIAGE

35. In the event of the remarriage of the Wife, the Wife shall advise the Husband of such remarriage within five (5) days of any such event.

📁 **FORM 4-2 continued**

ARTICLE XXI
GOVERNING LAW

36. All matters relating to the execution, validity, interpretation, and performance of this Agreement shall be governed, construed, and determined in accordance with the laws of the State of New York.

ARTICLE XXII
ESTATE OBLIGATIONS

37. This Agreement shall bind and inure to the benefit of the parties hereto, their heirs, executors, administrators, representatives and assigns, and shall be enforceable by either party and/or his or her estate against the other.

         IN WITNESS WHEREOF, the parties hereto have hereunto set their hands and seals the day and year first above written.

                 _____
                 HERBERT BROWN

                 _____
                 EMILY COOK BROWN

STATE OF NEW YORK)
                    ss.:
COUNTY OF NASSAU)

On the _____ day of _____, 19_____, before me personally came_____ _____ to me known and known to be the individual described in and who executed the foregoing instrument, and he did duly acknowledge to me that he executed the same.

                             _____
                             Notary Public, State of New York

STATE OF NEW YORK)
                    ss.:
COUNTY OF NASSAU)

On the _____ day of _____, 19_____, before me personally came_____ _____ to me known and known to be the individual described in and who executed the foregoing instrument, and she did duly acknowledge to me that she executed the same.

                             _____
                             Notary Public, State of New York

PRACTICE TIP: The separation agreement is organized in the same manner as the prenuptial agreement in Chapter 3 (Form 3-2) with recitals, agreement clauses and an execution section. The recitals state the date and place of the marriage, the names and birth dates of all the children of the marriage, and that the parties are now living apart or are about to begin living apart. They also indicate which party or parties were represented by counsel and what financial disclosure has taken place. The THEREFORE clauses, which contain the substance of the agreement, are formatted differently in this agreement from the way they appeared in the sample prenuptial agreement. Because separation agreements cover so many issues and are typically much longer than prenuptial agreements, the paragraphs are not only numbered but are also preceded by Article Headings, which make it easier to find specific topics within the agreement. The Articles are usually numbered with Roman numerals. A Table of Contents is customarily prepared for ease of reference. While the sample agreement covers the standard issues in the customary degree of detail, it is important to remember that each separation agreement must cover what is important to that particular couple. If the religious upbringing of the children is a bone of contention, for example, the separation agreement would contain provisions on that subject. A separation agreement is executed in the same way as a prenuptial agreement; each party signs and acknowledges his or her signature before a notary public.

JUDICIAL SEPARATION

Since the grounds for divorce were liberalized in 1968, judicial separation actions have become less frequent. If one spouse knows at the time of the physical separation that he or she wishes to be divorced, usually that spouse will file for divorce without bringing a separation action first. Sometimes, for religious or personal reasons, however a spouse does not wish to actually terminate the marriage, but prefers merely to formalize the separation of the parties. If the other spouse is unwilling to negotiate a separation agreement or is unavailable to do so, the spouse who wishes to define the terms of the separation will be forced to bring an action for judicial separation. A separation decree does *not* terminate the marriage, and the parties are not free to remarry until they obtain a divorce. Since the marriage is on-going, equitable division of property cannot not occur in a separation action.

Like annulment and divorce, separation actions are matrimonial actions subject to the special procedures set forth in Article 13 of the Domestic Relations Law. These procedures are discussed in Chapter 5. One important provision unique to separation actions, however, is that a judgment for separation may be revoked at any time by the court which rendered it, upon the joint application of the parties, accompanied with satisfactory evidence of their reconciliation. DRL § 203.

BASICS BOX

Subject matter jurisdiction: Supreme Court has exclusive original jurisdiction.
Venue: Current county of residence of either of the parties.
Standing: Either "subsisting" (currently married) spouse may sue.
Grounds: Cruel and inhuman treatment; nonsupport; adultery; abandonment; confinement of defendant in prison for 3 or more consecutive years.
Statute of Limitations: 5 years from when the grounds arose, except adultery (5 years from discovery) and abandonment (no statute of limitations).
Applicable statutes: DRL Art. 11; DRL Art. 11-A; DRL Art. 13.

GROUNDS FOR SEPARATION

The grounds for separation are similar to divorce. Cruel and inhuman treatment, adultery, and confinement of the defendant to prison for three consecutive years are all grounds which are identical to their counterparts in divorce law, and these grounds are discussed fully in Chapter 5. The abandonment ground for separation differs from that for divorce in that for separation there is no requirement that the abandonment have persisted for a year. There is one additional ground available for separation, nonsupport, that is not a ground for divorce.

Nonsupport

Prior to 1981, the neglect or refusal of a husband to support his wife was a ground for separation. When the statutes were made gender-neutral to avoid challenges pursuant to the Equal Protection clauses of the New York and United States constitutions, this provision was amended to provide that an action for separation may be maintained upon the neglect or refusal of the defendant-spouse to provide for the support of the plaintiff-spouse, where the defendant-spouse is chargeable with such support under the provisions of the Domestic Relations Law or the Family Court Act. DRL § 200(3); FCA § 412. As is discussed in Chapter 7, a spouse is obligated to support the other spouse at the marital standard of living if possessed of sufficient means to do so and if the spouse requesting support is unable to support him or herself at that standard. Note that failure to provide adequate child support is not a ground for separation.

CONCLUSION

Formal separation, by written agreement or court decree, is the method by which spouses who intend to live apart define their rights and responsibilities during the period of separation. If they contemplate divorce, they may also use a separation agreement as the blueprint for the custody, support and property division terms of the divorce, by providing that the separation agreement will be incorporated into the judgment of divorce. Preparing a separation agreement which will withstand judicial scrutiny and will provide the basis for a peaceful period of separation between the parties requires detailed information from the parties. The agreement must be comprehensive; if any important terms are omitted, the court may find that the agreement is unconscionable. It must also be sufficiently detailed to address the pressing concerns of the individuals involved; if the parties cannot live with the agreement, they will wind up in court trying to modify or set aside the agreement. Acquiring the fund of information upon which the agreement will be based is often the responsibility of the legal assistant. Special listening skills are required for this task, as the legal assistant must note not only what the client says, but how he or she says it. Several interviews may be needed to sort through the many issues involved. While the legal assistant should not be expected to become the client's crisis therapist, a good rapport will improve the chances of obtaining reliable information. Since the agreement will be the end product of negotiation and compromise, the client will probably not get everything he or she wanted in the agreement. The support of a careful and caring legal assistant may enable the client to tolerate some disappointment without rancor and may make all the difference in the client's decision to use or recommend the law firm in the future.

CHAPTER REVIEW QUESTIONS

Referring to the sample separation agreement (Form 4-2), answer the following questions:

1. Three months after executing the separation agreement, Herbert and Emily decide to give their marriage one more try. Herbert moves back into the residence in Great Neck, but within a month they begin to argue about the same old issues. Six weeks later, Herbert moves back to his apartment in Manhattan. Is the separation agreement still in effect? Which paragraph of the agreement answers this question?

2. A year after executing the separation agreement, Herbert and Emily divorced in the Supreme Court, Nassau County. The agreement was dealt with in the divorce as provided in paragraph 30 of the agreement. Two years later, while still in occupancy in the marital residence, Emily failed to make three mortgage payments. After receiving a warning letter from Best Bank, Herbert made the payments. He now seeks to recover from Emily the amount he paid. Since the sale of the house is still many years in the future, he does not want to wait to recoup the sum from the sale price of the house, but prefers to initiate legal action now. In which court(s) could he sue?

3. Herbert brings suit for the money referred to in question 2, and the night before the case is to be heard in court Emily hands him a check for the amount he paid to Best Bank. Can Herbert nevertheless pursue a claim for the legal fees and costs he incurred in bringing suit? Which

paragraph of the agreement applies?

4. When Charles is 13, Emily remarries. Charles does not get along well with the new husband and resents the fact that there is a new "man of the house." Charles's academic performance slips, and his teachers report that he has become a behavior problem as well. Charles tells Herbert that his mother gives all her attention to her new husband and begs Herbert to let him come to live with him. Herbert has mixed feelings about this idea, since he is away from home on business much of the time. He doesn't want to let Charles down, however, so he promises to consult an attorney. Does the separation agreement, now incorporated into the divorce decree, make a change of custody impossible? Looking at the factors *Friederwitzer* (Case 4-2) stresses, do you think a court is likely to grant a change of custody in this situation? Do you think it is wise for Herbert to sue for custody of Charles under these circumstances? What alternatives might the parents consider?

5. Assume that instead of changing Charles's custody, the parents decide to send him to boarding school. Does Herbert still have to pay child support? What paragraphs of the agreement apply?

6. When Charles is 15, Herbert incurs some heavy personal expenses. In a telephone call, he tells Emily that he will be sending her only $400 per month for child support until he can get his finances sorted out. She replies, "Well, if that's the best you can do, I guess we'll have to see how it goes." By accepting the checks for $400, does Emily lose her right to sue on the agreement for the balance of the child support provided for in the agreement? Which paragraph of the agreement applies?

7. The day after Charles's 18th birthday, Herbert is tragically killed in a plane crash. Does Emily have to sell the house? If she decides to remain in the house, does she have to pay anything to Herbert's estate? What paragraphs of the agreement apply?

8. To Emily's surprise, Herbert's will leaves her a valuable painting of which she was always especially fond. Does the agreement prohibit her receiving the bequest? What paragraph of the agreement applies?

CHAPTER ASSIGNMENT

Using a standard treatise with forms, such as *Lindey on Separation Agreements and Antenuptial Contracts* or *Separation Agreements and Marital Contracts*, by Stephen W. Schlissel, find and copy a model separation agreement clause to cover each of the following situations:

1. Monies in joint savings account to be distributed to the wife.
2. Division of debt liabilities between the parties.
3. Transfer of jointly owned marital residence to one party.
4. Merger of separation agreement into matrimonial decree.
5. Joint or shared custody.
6. Restriction on physical custodian's right to relocate with child.

5 DIVORCE

"[J]urisdiction of the courts to grant a divorce exists only by virtue of statute." *Pajak v. Pajak*, 56 N.Y.2d 394, 452 N.Y.S.2d 381 (1982).

Depending on your point of view, the mushrooming divorce rate is either a sign of a corrupt or a liberated society. Even those who do not oppose divorce on religious or moral grounds cannot help wondering what the soaring divorce rate signals about our society and what it portends for the future. While this is a national trend, New York is certainly contributing its share to the national statistics. In 1995, almost 70,000 divorces were granted in New York State, and another 66,227 divorce cases were filed. This reflects an increase of approximately 2,000 filings over 1994.

For many years, the only basis for divorce in New York was adultery. In 1968, after impassioned public debate, the grounds for divorce were liberalized. New York remains among the more conservative states in its approach to divorce. Grounds such as "irremediable breakdown of the marriage," "incompatibility," and "irreconcilable differences" do not exist in this state. New York has only one "no-fault" ground for divorce, living apart pursuant to a written separation agreement. This ground for divorce, as discussed below, is consensual. Both spouses must execute the separation agreement that provides the basis for the subsequent divorce. The vast majority of divorces in New York continue to be based on fault grounds. In 1993, out of a total of 55,202 divorces granted, 29,696 were based on abandonment, while 16,384 were on the ground of cruel and inhuman treatment. Only 5,072 were based on the no-fault, separation agreement, ground. New York's conservative divorce policy seems to have little impact on the rate of divorce, however, as roughly 50,000 of the divorces granted in both 1994 and 1995 were uncontested.

BASICS BOX

> **Subject matter jurisdiction:** Supreme Court has exclusive original jurisdiction.
>
> **Venue:** County of residence of either party at the time of the commencement of the action.
>
> **Standing:** Either "subsisting" (currently married) spouse may sue.
>
> **Grounds:** Cruel and inhuman treatment; adultery; abandonment; confinement of defendant in prison for 3 or more consecutive years; living separate and apart pursuant to a written separation agreement or decree of separation for 1 year or more.
>
> **Statute of Limitations:** As to cruel and inhuman treatment and imprisonment, 5 years from when grounds arose; as to adultery, 5 years from discovery by plaintiff; as to abandonment and separation pursuant to a decree of separation or written agreement, no statute of limitations.
>
> **Applicable statutes:** DRL Art. 10; DRL Art. 11-A; DRL Art. 13.

SPECIAL ETHICAL CONSIDERATIONS

UNAUTHORIZED PRACTICE OF LAW

The burgeoning demand for divorce has created a market of litigants who seek to reduce the expense of a "simple" divorce by using do-it-yourself kits. The kits are not in themselves illegal, although they may prove penny-wise and pound-foolish. It is illegal, however, to accompany the sale of the kit with any advice concerning its use. One such company, Divorce Associated & Publishing, Ltd., was permanently enjoined from all activity except the sale of the kits, after one undercover investigator found that employees helped him select the proper grounds for divorce and gave advice concerning his liability for marital debts and the probability of having to pay alimony. Another employee actually drew up the papers, including a complaint for divorce on the grounds of cruel and inhuman treatment. *People v. Divorce Associated & Pub. Ltd.*, 95 Misc.2d 340, 407 N.Y.S.2d 142 (N.Y. Sup. Ct. 1978).

> DISCUSSION TOPIC
> Why are paralegals prohibited from giving legal advice? What is the difference between a paralegal's drafting a divorce complaint under the supervision of an attorney and assisting a *pro se* litigant in drafting a complaint?

DUAL REPRESENTATION

Even in an uncontested, "friendly" divorce where there has been full disclosure, a lawyer should not represent both spouses. Although as a general rule a fully informed client, able to understand all ramifications of a conflict, may consent to dual representation, this is not so in a matrimonial case. All the bar associations which have issued ethics opinions on this subject are in accord that the potential for conflict and overreaching are so great in a divorce case that an attorney should not undertake to represent both parties, even with consent. See, for example, New York State Bar Association Committee on Professional Ethics Opinion #258 (9/15/72).

CONTINGENT FEE AGREEMENTS

Contingent fee arrangements, whereby the attorney agrees to represent a client and collect a fee only if the client wins the case, are common and legal in some areas of law. The New York Disciplinary Rules, however, prohibit their use in Family Law cases. DR 2-106(C). The fear is that, in the domestic relations area, contingent fees would encourage divorce.

MILONAS COMMITTEE RULES

As a result of widespread criticism of the way domestic relations law was being practiced, a panel was formed under the chairmanship of Justice E. Leo Milonas to propose improvements. The recommendations of this body, known as the Milonas Committee, were enacted as Part 1400 of the Disciplinary Rules and became effective November 30, 1993. The new rules prohibit an attorney in a domestic relations matter from beginning a sexual relationship with a client during the course of the lawyer's representation of the client [DR 1-102(a)(7)], and require an attorney to provide the client at the initial conference, before any retainer agreement is signed, with a Statement of Client's Rights and Responsibilities, Form 5-1.

FORM 5-1

STATEMENT OF CLIENT'S RIGHT AND RESPONSIBILITIES

YOUR ATTORNEY is providing you with this document to inform you of what you, as a client, are entitled to by law or custom. To help prevent a misunderstanding between you and your attorney, please read this document carefully.

If you ever have any questions about these rights, or about the way your case is being handled, do not hesitate to ask your attorney. Your attorney should be readily available to represent your best interests and keep you informed about your case.

An attorney may not refuse to represent you on the basis of race, creed, color, sex, sexual orientation, national origin or disability.

You are entitled to an attorney who will be capable of handling your case; show you courtesy and consideration at all times; represent you zealously; and preserve your confidences and secrets that are revealed in the course of the relationship.

🗁 FORM 5-1 continued

You are entitled to a written retainer agreement which must set forth, in plain language, the nature of the relationship and the details of the fee arrangement.   At your request, and before you sign the agreement, you are entitled to have your attorney clarify in writing any of its terms, or include additional provisions.

You are entitled to fully understand the rates and retainer fee before you sign a retainer agreement, as in any other contract.

You may refuse to enter into any fee arrangement that you find unsatisfactory.

Your attorney may not request a fee that is contingent on the securing of a divorce or on the amount of money or property that may be obtained.

Your attorney may not request a retainer fee that is nonrefundable. That is, should you discharge your attorney, or should your attorney withdraw from the case before the retainer is used up, he or she is entitled to be paid commensurate with the work performed on your case, but must return the balance of the retainer to you. However, your attorney may enter into a minimum fee arrangement with you that provides for the payment of a specific amount below which the fee will not fall based upon the handling of the case to its conclusion.

You are entitled to know the approximate number of attorneys and other legal staff members who will be working on your case at any given time and what you will be charged for the services of each.

You are entitled to know in advance how you will be asked to pay legal fees and expenses and how the retainer, if any, will be spent.

At your request, and after your attorney has had a reasonable opportunity to investigate your case, you are entitled to be given an estimate of approximate future costs of your case, which estimate shall be made in good faith but may be subject to change due to facts and circumstances affecting the case.

You are entitled to receive a written, itemized bill on a regular basis, at least every 60 days.

You are expected to review the bills sent by counsel, and to raise any objections or errors in a timely manner.   Time spent in discussion of bills will not be charged to you.

You are expected to be truthful in all discussions with your attorney, and to provide all relevant information and documentation to enable him or her to competently prepare your case.

You are entitled to be kept informed of the status of your case, and to be provided with copies of correspondence and documents prepared on your behalf or received from the court or your adversary.

You have the right to be present in court at the time that conferences are held.

You are entitled to make the ultimate decision on the objectives to be pursued in your case, and to make the final decision regarding settlement of your case.

Your attorney's written retainer agreement must specify under what circumstances he or she might seek to withdraw as your attorney for nonpayment of legal fees. If an action or proceeding is pending, the court

📁 FORM 5-1 continued

may give your attorney a "charging lien," which entitles your attorney to payment for services already rendered at the end of the case out of the proceeds of the final order or judgment.

You are under no legal obligation to sign a confession of judgment or promissory note, or to agree to a lien or mortgage on your home to cover legal fees. Your attorney's written retainer agreement must specify whether, and under what circumstances, such security may be requested. In no event may such security interest be obtained by your attorney without prior court approval and notice to your adversary. An attorney's security interest in the marital residence cannot be foreclosed against you.

You are entitled to have your attorney's best efforts exerted on your behalf, but no particular results can be guaranteed.

If you entrust money with an attorney for an escrow deposit in your case, the attorney must safeguard the escrow in a special bank account. You are entitled to a written escrow agreement, and may request that one or more interest-bearing bank accounts be used. You also are entitled to a written receipt and a complete record concerning the escrow. When the terms of the escrow agreement have been performed, the attorney must promptly make payment of the escrow to all persons who are entitled to it.

In the event of a fee dispute, you may have the right to seek arbitration. Your attorney will provide you with the necessary information regarding arbitration in the event of a fee dispute, or upon your request.

Dated:

RECEIPT ACKNOWLEDGED:

_____
ATTORNEY

_____
CLIENT

As you see in the Statement of Client's Rights and Responsibilities, the new rules require that an attorney who undertakes to represent a client in a domestic relations matter execute with the client a retainer agreement written in plain language (Form 5-2). One trial court Justice has held this rule unconstitutional as an impairment of the right to contract. *Corletta v. Oliveri*, ---Misc.2d---, 641 N.Y.S.2d 498 (N.Y. Sup.Ct.. 1996). Until this issue is settled on an appellate level, the rule should be followed. In any matrimonial action in Supreme Court the retainer agreement must be filed with the court along with the net worth statement. DR 1-400.3.

□ **FORM 5-2**

RETAINER AGREEMENT

Agreement for legal services by and between (Attorney's Name), (Firm's Address), hereinafter referred to as "Law Firm," and (Client's Name), residing at (Client's address), hereinafter referred to as "client."

I. NATURE OF THE SERVICES TO BE RENDERED

    A. You have retained this firm as your attorneys to represent you in connection with

        a. [ ] the prosecution or defense of a divorce action, including the attempt to negotiate a resolution of the matter;

        b. [ ] the prosecution or defense of an uncontested divorce action, including negotiation of a settlement;

        c. [ ] the negotiation, preparation and/or renewal of a separation agreement or other marital settlement agreement;

        d. [ ] post-judgment of divorce enforcement proceeding;

        e. [ ] the prosecution or the defense of a Family Court proceeding concerning_____.

    B. It is further understood that:

        a. The retainer fee does not include any services rendered in appellate courts or any actions or proceedings other than the action for which this office has been retained.

        b. With respect to the matter which is specified above, the Retainer Agreement and any sums paid to this firm pursuant hereto, do not cover any services relative to any appeal or any other services which might be required following the entry of a Final Judgment or Order, including but not limited to such matters as enforcement or modification. Our representation shall terminate with the entry of Final Judgment or Order in your matter, unless extended by mutual agreement between us in writing.

        c. The client authorizes the Law Firm to take any steps which, in the sole discretion of the firm, are deemed necessary or appropriate to protect the client's interest in the matter.

2. RETAINER AND FEE

    A. In order for us to begin our representation, you have agreed to pay us and we have agreed to accept a Retainer payment of $_____ . We have agreed that the retainer fee shall be paid in the following manner:_____
_____

📁 FORM 5-2 continued

B. The Retainer payment does not necessarily represent the amount of the overall fee which the client may incur by virtue of our services.

C. The amount of our overall fee will be based upon our regular schedule of established hourly time charges, along with any out-of-pocket disbursements (such as court costs, messenger services, transcripts of proceedings, long distance telephone calls, faxes, process service fees, deposition and court transcripts, and excess postage) which are incurred on your behalf.

D. The client understands that the hourly rates apply to all time expended relative to the client's matter, including but not limited to, office meetings and conferences; telephone calls and conferences, either placed by or placed to the client, or otherwise made or had on the client's behalf or related to the client's matter; preparation, review and revision of correspondence; pleadings; motions; disclosure demands and responses; affidavits and affirmations, or any other documents, memoranda, research, financial statements of net worth, court preparation time, and any other time expended on behalf of or in connection with the client's matter.

E. In the event that we obtain a disposition of your matter, either by way of settlement agreement or judgment by the Court of the issues involved in your case, the aforementioned Retainer fee shall also be the minimum fee charged to you. There will be no refund of the Retainer fee. However, notwithstanding the above, if you discontinue our services prior to a final disposition of your matter by agreement or judgment of the Court, or if this firm is relieved as your attorneys by Court order, any unearned portion of the Retainer Fee you advanced to this firm shall be refunded to you.

F. You have the absolute right to cancel this Retainer Agreement at any time.

G. The Retainer Fee shall be credited towards an hourly rate of $_____ per hour for time I expend: $_____ per hour for time other partners expend; $_____ per hour for time expended by paralegals in this office.

H. Hours expended on your matter will be charged against the Retainer Fee and, in the event the Retainer Fee is depleted, the client agrees to replenish his or her account by payment of a further Retainer Fee in like amount, or at the option of the Law Firm, the fee shall be paid in accordance to the bills forwarded by the Law Firm. You agree to pay such additional fees and to reimburse us for our advances on your behalf no later than 30 days from the date that we shall submit a bill to you for service.

3. BILLING

You will be billed periodically, generally every 60 days. Included in the billing will be a detailed explanation of the services rendered, by whom rendered, and the disbursements incurred by our firm in connection with your matter. Upon receipt of our bill, you are expected to review the bill and promptly bring to our attention any objections you may have to the bill.

📁 **FORM 5-2 continued**

4. WITHDRAWAL AS ATTORNEYS

You are advised that if in the judgment of this firm, we decide that there has been an irretrievable breakdown in the attorney-client relationship or a material breach of the terms of this Retainer Agreement, we may decide to make application to the Court in which your action is pending to be relieved as your attorneys. In such event, you will be provided with notice of the application and an opportunity to be heard. Should any fees be due and owing to our firm at the time of our discharge, we shall have the right to seek a charging lien, i.e., a lien upon the property that is awarded to you as a result of equitable distribution in the final Order or Judgment in your case. No such lien may attach to maintenance or child support payments.

5. APPLICATION FOR FEES

While we seek to avoid any fee disputes with our clients, and rarely have such disputes, in the event such a dispute does arise, you are advised that you have the right, at your election, to seek arbitration to resolve the dispute. In such event, we shall advise you in writing by certified mail that you have 30 days from receipt of such notice in which to elect to resolve the dispute by arbitration, and we shall enclose a copy of the arbitration rules and a form requesting arbitration. The decision resulting from arbitration is binding upon both you and this firm.

6. RETENTION OF EXPERTS

You have been advised that in order for us to properly protect your interest it may be necessary to retain outside experts such as appraisers, actuaries and accountants. You will be responsible for the cost incurred for any such service, which in some cases may have to be paid in advance depending upon the requirements of the particular expert. No expert or appraiser shall be retained without your prior approval. If necessary and applicable, an application will be made to the Court to have your spouse pay all or part of the aforementioned fees for experts.

7. ACKNOWLEDGMENT AND UNDERSTANDING

The client acknowledges that her or she has read this agreement in its entirety, has had full opportunity to consider its terms and has had full and satisfactory explanation of same, and fully understands its terms and agrees to such terms.

8. CERTIFICATIONS

We have informed you that pursuant to Court rule, we are required, as your attorneys, to certify court papers submitted by you that contain statements of fact, and specifically to certify that we have no knowledge that the substance of the submission is false. Accordingly, you agree to provide us with complete and accurate information which forms the basis of court papers and to certify in writing to us, prior to the time the papers are actually submitted to the Court, the accuracy of the Court submissions that we prepare on your behalf, and which you shall review and sign.

9. CLOSING

You are aware of the hazards of litigation and acknowledge that we have made no guarantees in the disposition of any phase of the matter for which you have retained this office. If this fee arrangement meets with approval,

📁 **FORM 5-2 continued**

kindly sign your name where indicated on the copy of this letter and return same to me in the envelope enclosed for your convenience. You acknowledge that pursuant to court rule, a copy of this retainer letter is required to be filed with the court in which your action is pending.

_____
Attorney

_____
Client

CONFIDENTIALITY

Although courts are as a general rule open to the public, the Domestic Relations Law creates an exception for matrimonial proceedings and custody, visitation, and child support matters due to their sensitive and sometimes embarrassing nature. Access to pleadings, affidavits, findings of fact, conclusions of law, judgments of dissolution, and written separation agreements is restricted to the parties and their attorneys. In addition, the court may exclude spectators from the room during the testimony of witnesses and may order evidence sealed. This confidentiality endures for 100 years, after which all such materials become public records available for public inspection. DRL § 235. This provision expressly extends to court employees, including court clerks.

SPECIAL PROCEDURES APPLICABLE TO MATRIMONIAL ACTIONS

CASE MANAGEMENT PROCEDURES

In addition to concerns about the ethics of the matrimonial bar, the Milonas Committee also addressed itself to the cost and length of matrimonial litigation, which were widely perceived as excessive. Primarily the new rules pertain to the pre-trial stage of a contested divorce proceeding. The following Timetable (Form 5-3) should aid the legal assistant in tracking the many deadlines the new rules impose:

📁 **FORM 5-3**

TIMETABLE FOR CONTESTED DIVORCE ACTIONS

- Retainer Agreement --- Filed with affidavit of Net Worth

- Request for Judicial Intervention or Notice of No Necessity (for judicial intervention) --- within 45 days from Summons

📁 **FORM 5-2 continued**

- If Notice of No Necessity is filed within 45 days from Summons, Request for Judicial Intervention ---- 120 days from Summons

- Case assigned to a judge upon receipt of Request for Judicial Intervention

- Preliminary Conference --- Scheduled within 45 days after action has been assigned to a judge

- Affidavit of Net Worth --- At least 10 days prior to Preliminary Conference

- Preliminary Conference --- Written challenges to the Net Worth affidavit must be presented at this time or a presumption of its accuracy is created. A timetable for discovery is established at the Preliminary Conference. Both parties must be present in court at the time of the Preliminary Conference.

- Experts and Law Guardian Appointments --- List must be provided within 20 days of the Preliminary Conference

- Expert Witnesses' Reports --- Must be provided to opposing counsel and submitted to the court at least 60 days prior to trial

- Reply Reports of Experts --- Must be provided to opposing counsel and submitted to the court at least 30 days prior to trial. Failure to provide the reports on time without good cause may result in preclusion of the expert.

- Statement of Proposed Disposition --- With Notice of Issue

- Other side's Statement of Proposed Disposition --- 20 days after service of Notice of Issue

- Completion of Discovery --- Within 6 months after case assigned to judge

Even in an uncontested case, an enormous number of documents are required in a matrimonial proceeding. In addition to those required by statute and rules of statewide applicability, specific courts often have their own ways of doing things, which vary from county to county. Legal assistants are usually charged with the responsibility of keeping the firm up to date on the various courts' procedures. This is accomplished by obtaining current guidelines from the clerk of court or the clerk of the part in which the firm regularly has cases pending. Court clerks are goldmines of detailed information, and the paralegal would be well advised to establish pleasant professional relationships with them. Form 5-4 is an example of guidelines distributed by the Matrimonial Part of the New York County Supreme Court.

GROUNDS FOR DIVORCE

Because the overwhelming majority of divorces in New York are based on fault, the grounds for divorce assume an importance in New York that they lack in most states. While in many jurisdictions only the economic issues are likely to be disputed, in New York the grounds for divorce are also often contested. Domestic Relations Law § 170 provides six grounds for divorce:

CRUEL AND INHUMAN TREATMENT

To constitute grounds for divorce, the defendant's treatment of plaintiff must have been "such that the conduct of the defendant so endangers the physical or mental well being of the plaintiff as renders it unsafe or improper for the plaintiff to cohabit with the defendant." DRL § 170(1). In 1974, the Court of Appeals made it clear that this ground for divorce was not to be construed as permitting divorce due to incompatibility. In *Hessen v. Hessen*, 33 N.Y.2d 406, 353 N.Y.S.2d 421 (1974), the court stated that a divorce may not be granted merely because it is perceived that the marriage is "dead." The decision sets forth several factors that should be considered in deciding whether the defendant's conduct constitutes grounds for divorce, including the respective ages of the husband and wife, the duration of their marriage, and whether there is objective proof (such as medical records) of physical or mental injury to the complaining spouse. The court suggested that a higher degree of proof would be required to terminate a marriage of long standing.

While the courts have not freely granted divorces where the complaint was based solely on verbal abuse, they have generally been willing to terminate marriages in which verbal abuse was accompanied by physical violence. In *Domin v. Domin*, 188 A.D.2d 1026, 592 N.Y.S.2d 190 (4 Dept. 1992), for example, the husband was granted a divorce because of the wife's constant verbal abuse and unjustifiable accusation that plaintiff was lazy and because the wife's outbursts included instances in which she threatened the husband with a butcher knife, stabbed him in the cheek with a paring knife, and grabbed his genitals, threatening to rip them out, and threw things at him. Similarly, in *Zack v. Zack*, 183 A.D.2d 382, 590 N.Y.S.2d 632 (4 Dept. 1992), divorce was granted to a wife whose husband had "embarked upon an unrelenting campaign of physical and emotional terror against her," including grabbing and squeezing her breasts, punching her in the head, grabbing her hair and pushing her into a wall, and smashing her hand in a kitchen drawer.

 **FORM 5-4**

Effective July 22, 1996

NEW YORK COUNTY

PROCEDURE IN UNDEFENDED MATRIMONIAL CASES

Obtain Index # from County Clerk's Office, Room 141b [$170 fee] and file a copy of the summons the same day. Place the index number on two other copies of the summons along with the date of this filing and then cause the summons to be served. File a copy of the proof of this service no later than 120 days of the original filing.

AFTER DEFAULT IN APPEARING OR ANSWERING. OR A WAIVER

1. Personally present to the Matrimonial Clerk's Office, Room 311, the following documents with <u>proper notarization</u> where necessary, in the following order, to be approved.

   a. Note of Issue (3 copies) with proof of the index # attached.
   b. Summons. [Must have index # and the date it was filed with the County Clerk]
   c. Verified Complaint.
   d. Proof of service [affidavit of server, defendant's waiver or a notice of appearance with consent].
   e. Affidavit of Regularity.
   f. Affidavit as to military status of the defaulting party. [Not necessary with waiver by defendant or notice of appearance].
   g. Plaintiff's Affidavit establishing all elements to warrant the relief sought.
   h. If there are children of the marriage under 18 years of age and the defendant has not appeared, an affidavit pursuant to 75j must be submitted.
   i. If there are children of the marriage under 21 years of age, a child support worksheet or stipulation must be submitted to determine child support {DRL 240[1][b],[h] & [i]}.
   j. Conform with DRL 253 where applicable [Removal of Barriers to Remarriage].
   k. Proposed Findings of Fact & Conclusions of Law [Decision].
   l. Proposed Judgment.
   m. Certificate of Dissolution [VS-140] [Issued by Matrimonial Clerk].
   n. Unified Court System Divorce and Child Support Summary Form [UCS 113] [Issued by Matrimonial Clerk].
   o. A stamped, self addressed post card containing the title of the action as well as the calendar & index #s.

2. Have Note of Issue checked by the Trial Support Clerk's Office, Room 158.

3. Obtain Calendar # from the Cashier in Room 160 [$100 fee].

4. On a future date the papers will be submitted to a Justice or Special Referee for consideration. If the Court is satisfied as to the proof, the proposed Decision & Judgment will be signed. Otherwise, a hearing might be directed, the papers may be marked defective, or the complaint may be dismissed. If your papers are marked defective, you will be notified by post card to come in and correct your papers.

Suggestions for preparing proper papers.
1. If the cause of action is based on Cruelty, detail 2 acts of cruelty giving dates and places of said acts.
2. If cause of action is based on Abandonment, state date and place [address] of abandonment.
3. If the cause of action is based on a Separation Agreement, submit a photocopy of the signed and acknowledged agreement. Include in the Decision & Judgment "The Separation Agreement shall be incorporated by reference in the Judgment and shall survive."

• When you receive your postcard indicating that the Judgment had been granted, a copy of the Judgment may be obtained from the County Clerk's Office, room 103b.

COURT PERSONNEL ARE PROHIBITED FROM AIDING IN THE PREPARATION OF LEGAL DOCUMENTS.

Cruel and inhuman treatment involves a course of conduct. An isolated, rafter-shaking argument would be insufficient to make out a complaint for divorce. The five-year statute of limitations runs from the date of the *last* episode or event.

ADULTERY

Adultery, sexual intercourse or deviate sexual intercourse voluntarily performed with a person other than one's spouse, was for many years in New York the only ground for divorce. This ground for divorce is unique in that it is the only ground against which the defendant can raise the affirmative defense that plaintiff has committed the same misconduct. Defendant has to plead and prove this defense, however. If plaintiff's adultery is not plead by defendant, the court will not permit defendant to put in any proof of it at trial. Adultery, customarily a clandestine act, may be proved circumstantially. Plaintiff must prove opportunity, inclination, and intent. The sort of proof which will convince a court on these points changes over time. In the past, the mere fact that a man and a woman not his wife were alone in a hotel room would have gone far to persuade a court that they were up to no good. Nowadays, when men and women travel on business together, a court would likely find that such circumstances proved no more than opportunity, and the court would look carefully at the evidence of what the courts call "lascivious desire."

ABANDONMENT

It is hornbook law that abandonment requires proof of four elements: 1) a voluntary separation of one spouse from the other, 2) with intent not to resume cohabitation, 3) without the consent of the other spouse, and, 4) without justification. The actual published decisions do not always follow this textbook pattern, however, but tend to focus on the one or two elements which were apparently most fully litigated in the particular case. Focusing on the first element, voluntary departure, it is obvious that if the spouse's absence from the marital home results from military orders or from being held hostage in a foreign land, it does not constitute abandonment. The issue is less clear, however, when the spouse contends that he or she was forced to leave the home to escape the cruelty or misconduct of the other spouse. In *Phillips v. Phillips*, 70 A.D.2d 30, 419 N.Y.S.2d 573 (2 Dept. 1979), the court came to an odd result. The wife left the home and sued for divorce on the ground of cruel and inhuman treatment. The husband counterclaimed for divorce on the ground of abandonment. The court denied the wife's claim as unproved. It also denied the husband's counterclaim, however, holding that the wife's departure from the home as a result of what she believed to be the misconduct of the husband, *even though she was mistaken in her belief*, did not constitute abandonment. The parties thus remained married, a result neither had desired.

The issue of intent not to resume cohabitation is most often litigated after the spouse who has left the home offers to return. In *Bohmert v. Bohmert*, 241 N.Y.

446, 150 N.E. 511 (1926), the Court of Appeals said that in order to be considered bona fide, an offer to return must be made in good faith and within a reasonable time after departure. The court pointed out that an offer to return may not only come too late, but may also be made too soon to be considered reasonable, if the departing spouse is still in the throes of anger from the quarrel which precipitated the departure. What is reasonable depends on the circumstances of the case.

A parting of the spouses by mutual consent does not give rise to a cause of action for abandonment. If the initial separation is by mutual consent, neither party will be entitled to a divorce based on abandonment. "Mutual abandonment" is not a recognized ground for divorce under the Domestic Relations Law. *Henderson v. Henderson*, 63 A.D.2d 853, 405 N.Y.S.2d 857 (4 Dept. 1978).

Divorce on the ground of abandonment will not be granted if the spouse who left was justified in doing so. In determining what conduct constitutes justification, the courts are on the horns of a dilemma. If justification is construed as including only conduct which would constitute grounds for divorce, the spouse who wants to leave may feel compelled to remain, thus jeopardizing his or her safety or well-being. On the other hand, if justification is deemed to include misconduct which would not constitute grounds for divorce, then "abandonment" thus construed may become in effect an incompatibility ground for divorce. The New York courts have toed this line uneasily. They have rejected the "harsh" interpretation that justification lies only in conduct which would constitute grounds for divorce, but they have tried to limit it to situations where the departing spouse had genuine fear for his or her safety. *Del Galdo v. Del Galdo*, 51 A.D.2d 741, 379 N.Y.S.2d 479 (2 Dept. 1976). Incompatibility and extreme bickering have been held not to constitute justification. *Phoenix v. Phoenix*, 41 A.D.2d 683, 340 N.Y.S.2d 977 (3 Dept. 1973).

CONSTRUCTIVE ABANDONMENT

Even without leaving the marital home, a spouse may be guilty of abandonment by unjustifiably forcing the other spouse to leave the home. Thus, a spouse who without good cause locks the other spouse out of the marital home may be found to have abandoned the excluded spouse. If, however, the spouse changes the locks in genuine fear for his or her safety, the exclusion may be found justified. A spouse's willful, continued, and unjustified refusal to engage in sexual relations for one year or more may also constitute abandonment. Merely establishing that sexual relations did not occur is insufficient, however. Plaintiff must also show that he or she requested resumption of sexual relations. *Lyons v. Lyons*, 187 A.D.2d 415, 589 N.Y.S.2d 557 (2 Dept. 1992). A spouse's refusal to engage in sexual relations may be justified, as, for example, where sex is requested in an atmosphere of coercion or where one spouse demands forms of sexual activity which are painful or unpleasant for the other spouse. *George M. v. Mary Ann M.*, 171 A.D.2d 651, 567 N.Y.S.2d 132 (2 Dept. 1991).

Another variant of constructive abandonment occurs when a wife without good cause refuses to live in her husband's choice of domicile. At common law a husband had the right to choose the marital domicile. This element of common law was incorporated into New York law and has never been changed by statute. *Hunt v. Hunt*, 72 N.Y. 217 (1878). The rule was reiterated as recently as 1981 by the Appellate Division, Fourth Department, in *Bazant v. Bazant*, 80 A.D.2d 310, 439 N.Y.S.2d 521 (4 Dept. 1981). In that case, however, the court found good cause for the wife's refusal to move, as she had a good professional position, difficult to duplicate in the location to which the husband proposed to move. One Supreme Court justice has recently refused to grant a divorce on this ground, however, stating: "It is time the law viewed marital domicile in a gender neutral fashion. Partners in a marriage should be granted the same equality in decision making as is given to those in business." *Szumanski v. Szumanska*, 160 Misc.2d 861, 611 N.Y.S.2d 737 (N.Y. Sup. Ct. 1994).

To provide grounds for divorce, the abandonment must have persisted for one year or more. DRL § 170(2). Note that this durational requirement exists only for divorce and not for separation actions. The year starts to run when the abandonment first takes place and is supposed to be a continuous period. If the parties reconcile for a while, and then a later abandonment takes place, the two periods are added to make out the year if the alleged reconciliation was not in good faith. Isolated acts of sexual intercourse between the parties do not usually stop the running of the statutory period. The effect of a brief, good faith attempted reconciliation is less certain. As you see in Case 5-1, the Appellate Division, First Department, has held that such a resumption of cohabitation does not automatically preclude a finding of abandonment.

 **CASE 5-1**

HAYMES v. HAYMES
221 A.D.2d 73, 646 N.Y.S.2d 315, (1 Dept. 1996)

MAZZARELLI, J.

In this action for divorce, plaintiff Gail Lowe Haymes' complaint originally alleged four causes of action, the second and third of which were, respectively, for actual and constructive abandonment. The factual allegations in the plaintiff's complaint indisputably stated a prima facie cause of action of abandonment and constructive abandonment. Plaintiff alleged that defendant Stephen Denis Haymes had left the marital home to live apart from her and abstained from engaging in sexual relations with her for a period of one or more years. However, just prior to opening statements, the trial court granted an oral motion by defendant for partial summary judgment dismissing these two causes of action. It held that the parties' failed six-week attempt at reconciliation, which occurred after the maturation of plaintiff's claims, and after this lawsuit for divorce had been

📖 **CASE 5-1 continued**

commenced, barred plaintiff from succeeding on her abandonment claims as a matter of law. We now reverse the order dismissing the abandonment causes of action, reinstate the second and third causes of action, and remand for a trial on same.

Gail and Stephen Haymes were married in 1965 and lived together, without interruption, until 1987. They are the parents of two adult children, born in 1967 and 1975. According to plaintiff's allegations, beginning in December 1984, defendant refused to have sexual relations with her, rejecting her repeated overtures. In September 1987, defendant moved out of the couple's home, an act which plaintiff maintains was without her consent and without justification. The plaintiff claimed that defendant engaged in several adulterous relationships with women identified in the complaint. Defendant retained legal counsel, who wrote to plaintiff, suggesting that she retain her own matrimonial lawyer. This action for divorce and related relief was commenced in September of 1988, after defendant had remained out of the marital abode for more than one year.

The couple attempted a reconciliation between November 18, 1988 and January 4, 1989, during which time they resumed residing unhappily together. According to Ms. Haymes, her husband expressed neither remorse for his adultery nor any affection for her during this six-week period. Unable to resolve their problems, Gail and Stephen Haymes returned to living apart and pursuing their respective marital claims. Indeed, in January 1989, defendant asserted his counterclaim for divorce.

***

As recognized by the trial court, there is a dearth of current appellate authority in this state directly addressing the legal question presented by this dispute, whether a relatively brief attempt at a reconciliation, after otherwise valid claims of abandonment have matured and been alleged in an action, should require plaintiff to forfeit these otherwise facially valid causes of action for divorce. Contrary to the reading of the case law propounded by defendant, we find that none of the matters cited directly supports his proposition that a finding of abandonment cannot be sustained if the parties have attempted a reconciliation that involved their engaging in sexual relations on at least one occasion....

In our view, common sense teaches that it is consistent with the public policy of this state that couples enduring marital disharmony should be encouraged to attempt reconciliation, particularly when, as here, the marriage is one of long duration. That the courts should, when practicable, encourage the preservation of families, in all their permutations, is so painfully obvious, that the lack of appellate authority so declaring can only be explained by the failure heretofore of anyone to contest such a basic proposition.

***

...Today, we hold that an estranged couple's attempt at a

CASE 5-1 continued

reconciliation, even where it involves the brief and isolated resumption of cohabitation and/or sexual relations, after a matrimonial action has already been commenced, does not, as a matter of law, preclude an entry of judgment in favor of the spouse who originally had an otherwise valid claim for abandonment. Rather, the trial court should examine the totality of the circumstances surrounding the purported reconciliation, before determining its effect, if any, upon the pending marital proceeding. Among the many factors for the trial court to consider are whether the reconciliation and any cohabitation were entered into in good faith, whether it was at all successful, who initiated it and with what motivation. Although concededly more difficult to apply than a rule which automatically results in the forfeiture of abandonment claims upon the parties making even the most hollow attempt at reconciliation, we conclude that the approach we adopt is not only consonant with human experience and common sense, but with the public policy and law of our State as well.

***

IMPRISONMENT

A divorce may be granted where the defendant has been confined in prison for a period of three or more consecutive years after the marriage. DRL § 170(3). The spouse of the prisoner has the option whether or not to seek to terminate the marriage in such circumstances; a valid marriage is not automatically terminated by the imprisonment of one spouse for any number of years. Even a life sentence no longer terminates a marriage by operation of law. The imprisonment ground for divorce has not been extensively litigated, and questions spring to mind for which there are as yet no judicial answers. The most obvious question is whether an action for divorce on this ground can be maintained after the defendant has been released from prison. Moreover, the constitutionality of this provision may be subject to challenge in some circumstances. Some issues have been addressed by trial courts, however. The time the defendant was in custody prior to the commencement of his term in prison may be included in the statutory three years, [*Pergolizzi v. Pergolizzi*, 59 Misc.2d 1927, 301 N.Y.S.2d 366 (N.Y. Sup. Ct. 1969)] and the period a defendant spent in a state hospital operated by the State Department of Correctional Services after he was found incompetent to stand trial may also be included [*Cerami v. Cerami*, 95 Misc.2d 840, 408 N.Y.S.2d 591 (N.Y. Sup. Ct. 1978)]. A wife was also held entitled to a divorce notwithstanding that the husband's conviction was reversed after the initiation of the divorce action. *Colascione v. Colascione*, 57 Misc.2d 199, 291 N.Y.S.2d 559 (N.Y. Sup. Ct. 1968).

LIVING SEPARATE PURSUANT TO SEPARATION DECREE

When a couple has been living separate and apart for a year or more pursuant to a decree or judgment of separation, either spouse may sue for divorce if he or she has substantially performed all the terms and conditions of such decree. DRL § 170(5). This is commonly called "conversion divorce," meaning that the separation is converted into a divorce. It is important to remember that the divorce does not occur automatically, however. One spouse must file suit for divorce. This is not a pure "no-fault" ground for divorce, since the grounds for judicial separation, discussed in Chapter 4, are all based on fault. The plaintiff in the divorce case may be the spouse who was the defendant in the separation action, however, so the statute does permit the "guilty" spouse to divorce the "innocent" spouse. This has resulted in a drastic reduction of filings of separation actions since 1966, when this ground for divorce was added to the Domestic Relations Law. Spouses who had obtained separation decrees prior to the amendment were confronted with an entirely unexpected consequence of having prevailed in their separation actions. When Jackie Gleason sued for divorce from his wife, who had obtained a separation decree against him in 1954, the courts were required to rule upon the constitutionality of retroactive application of the new ground for divorce.

 CASE 5-2

GLEASON v. GLEASON
26 N.Y.2d 28, 308 N.Y.S.2d 347 (1970)

FULD, Chief Judge

In 1966, the Legislature repealed this State's ancient divorce laws -- which for almost 200 years had sanctioned divorce solely for adultery -- and enacted the Divorce Reform Law...authorizing divorce on other grounds.... In addition to four grounds based on "fault," new section 170 of the Domestic Relations Law specified two "nonfault" grounds predicated on a couple's living apart for a period of two years after the granting of a separation judgment or decree (subd. [5]) or the execution of a written separation agreement (sub.[6]). In the two cases before us, we are called upon to decide whether subdivision (5) is available where the decree was rendered prior to the enactment of the new statute and in favor of the spouse opposing the divorce.
***
We agree with the dissenter in the First Department...that the Legislature intended that subdivision (5) of section 170 of the Domestic Relations Law should be applied "retroactively", in the sense of encompassing pre-1966 decrees, and that, as so applied, it offends against neither due process, the equal protection of the law nor any other constitutional provision.
***
As we have already pointed out, implicit in the statutory scheme

📖 **CASE 5-2 continued**

is the recognition that it is socially and morally undesirable to compel a couple whose marriage is dead to remain subject to its bonds. If subdivision (5) were not to be applied retroactively, the legislative purpose would be seriously thwarted in the many cases in which spouses have been living separate and apart for more than two years pursuant to pre-1966 separation decrees, and the defendant in the separation action seeks a divorce. An insistence upon a fault-oriented ground of divorce, where the marriage, under the Legislature's present policy, ought to be dissolved, would for years perpetuate two of the chief evils the new divorce law was designed to eliminate -- collusive or fraud-ridden divorce actions in this State and the continued pursuit of out-of-state divorces based upon spurious residence and baseless claims. If, therefore, the legislative aims and purposes are to be achieved, the statute must be interpreted as making divorce available on living apart grounds pursuant to pre-1966 decrees just as it would be if the decree were obtained later and regardless of the "guilt" or "innocence" of the party seeking it.

This brings us to the constitutional arguments against retroactive application of subdivision (5). The principal contention is that a wife who prevailed in the separation action, having had no warning that the separation decree granted to her might later furnish basis or ground for divorce by the "guilty" husband, would be deprived of valuable rights without notice. More particularly, it is claimed that those rights -- social security and pension rights, inheritance rights and a right in the marital status itself -- are "vested" and, by that token, protected by the Due Process and Equal Protection Clauses of both the Federal and New York constitutions. These contentions lack substance.

A vested right, it has been said, is an "immediate, fixed right of present or future enjoyment."...Marital rights, however, have always been treated as inchoate or contingent and may be taken away by legislation before they vest.... [A] wife's prospective right of inheritance is inchoate and expectant, not becoming vested until the death of her husband.... Since, then, no vested rights of the [wife] have been adversely affected, there has been no denial of due process.

Likewise without merit is the defendant's equal protection argument that the Legislature, by making subdivision (5) retroactive and subdivision (6) prospective, unreasonably differentiated between a party to a pre-separation *decree* and a party to a pre-1966 separation *agreement*. The short answer is that there is no denial of equal protection of the laws if the differentiation made rests upon some rational consideration and is not palpably arbitrary....The differences between separation decrees and separation agreements are numerous and fully justify the distinction which has been made. We need but mention that one is imposed by judicial fiat, whereas the other is the product of a voluntary undertaking; that one requires the intervention of the State, the other does not; that one is subject to modification, the

📖 **CASE 5-2 continued**

other not; that the legal rights and remedies as to enforcement of the decree differ substantially from those available for breach of the agreement. Consequently, since there is reasonable basis for the legislative classification, the courts will uphold it even if they were to disagree with its wisdom.

Nor is there substance to the further contention that the statute unconstitutionally impairs contract rights. "Marriage is not a contract," we wrote in Fearon v. Treanor, 272 N.Y. 268, 172, 5 N.E.2d 815, 816, appl dsmd. 301 U.S. 6677, 57 S.Ct. 933, 81 L.Ed. 1332, "within the meaning of the provision of the Federal Constitution which prohibits the impairment by the States of the obligation of contracts." This being so, "Rights growing out of the [marriage] relationship may be modified or abolished by the Legislature without violating the provisions of the Federal or State Constitution which forbid the taking of life, liberty, or property without due process of law."...

***

It has been well said that "[a] giant step has been taken in the Divorce Reform Law to bring New York into the twentieth century."...The courts should not dilute its effectiveness by denying it the full scope intended for it. It applies retroactively, as we have declared, to permit divorce on the strength of a separation decree rendered before the new statute was enacted, and as so construed, it does not violate any constitutional provision.

***

DISCUSSION TOPIC

The debate concerning "no-fault" grounds for divorce is still being carried on with vigor in New York. An editorial in the *New York Times* on February 15, 1996 stated: "The nation should be concentrating on ways to reduce the economic stresses that experts say contribute both to the high divorce rate and to the rising number of children born to unmarried couples. Absent fathers should be required to live up to their child support obligations. But making it more difficult for people to escape a broken marriage seems cruel and counterproductive." *N.Y. Times*, 2/15/96, p. A26, col. 1. Do you agree or disagree with that opinion? What public policy considerations favor a liberal divorce law? What are the arguments in favor of keeping the grounds for divorce narrow? How does each position impact upon children?

LIVING SEPARATE AND APART PURSUANT TO AGREEMENT

An action for divorce may be maintained by either husband or wife when the parties have been living separate and apart pursuant to a written separation agreement, duly subscribed and acknowledged, for a period of one or more years after the execution of the agreement. (As you may have noticed in the *Gleason* case, the period was originally two years, but was shortened to one year effective

September 1, 1972.) The legislature did *not* make this ground for divorce applicable to *agreements* executed before the amendment. Plaintiff must present proof that he or she has substantially performed all the terms and conditions of the separation agreement.

Shortly after its enactment, several major questions arose concerning this new basis for divorce. A significant issue was resolved by the Court of Appeals in *Christian v. Christian*, 42 N.Y.2d 63, 396 N.Y.S.2d 817 (1977). In this case, one clause of the parties' separation agreement had been found unenforceable due to overreaching by the husband. The court had severed that clause, but had not invalidated the entire agreement. The issue, therefore, was whether the agreement, minus the invalid clause, could still provide the basis for a conversion divorce. The Court held that it could, but cautioned against using separation agreements inequitably to obtain unconscionable terms.

In a further retreat from the permissive philosophy of the *Gleason* case, the Court of Appeals held in 1982 that a conversion divorce may not be granted if the separation agreement is void *ab initio* [from the inception] due to fraud, duress or incapacity. *Angeloff v. Angeloff*, 56 N.Y.2d 982, 453 N.Y.S.2d 630 (1982). Thus, a husband was denied a conversion divorce based upon a "patently unconscionable" separation agreement, in which the wife in a 22-year marriage waived all rights with respect to equitable distribution of the husband's assets, which were estimated to be in excess of $2,000,000. Further, the agreement conditioned the wife's receipt of maintenance upon her employment, and she was required to transfer her share of the marital home to the husband and to grant to him an irrevocable power of attorney. *Weinstock v. Weinstock*, 167 A.D.2d 394, 561 N.Y.S.2d 807 (2 Dept. 1990).

JURISDICTION AND SERVICE

RESIDENCE AND DOMICILE

Understanding the restrictions on jurisdiction in matrimonial proceedings requires a mastery of two terms that are crucial to the issue: residence and domicile. **Residence** is where a person is actually living. There are no hard and fast rules about how long a person must stay in a particular place to establish residence, but the intent must be to live there, as opposed to taking a vacation. **Domicile** is a person's one, true abode, a place with which he or she has an enduring connection and to which he or she intends to return. In determining a person's place of domicile, courts look at factors such as the place of one's business, voter registration, and home ownership. For most of us, our residence is also our domicile, but this is not always the case. Consider the following example:

> Professor Jones owns a house in New York, is registered to
> vote in New York, and is employed by a university in New
> York. After seven years of faithful service to the university,

> Professor Jones is granted a one-year sabbatical leave, which she decides to use doing research at a library in London, England. She rents out her New York house and subleases a flat in London for the year. After six months in London, her research is going so well that she decides to reward herself with a two-week trip to Paris, after which she will return to London to complete the research. While in Paris, Professor Jones is a *visitor* to Paris, a *resident* of London, and a *domiciliary* of New York.

At common law a wife's residence was presumed to be that of her husband. Because of a 1976 statutory change, a wife in New York may now establish her own separate domicile, without regard to whose fault it was that the parties separated. DRL §§ 61 and 231.

Required Residence of Parties

A matrimonial action may be maintained in New York only when:

> 1. The parties were married in the state and either party is a resident when the action is commenced and has been a resident for a continuous period of one year immediately preceding;
>
> 2. The parties have resided in N.Y. as husband and wife and either party is a resident when the action is commenced and has been a resident for a continuous period of one year immediately preceding;
>
> 3. The cause (grounds) occurred in N.Y. and either party has been a resident for a continuous period of at least one year immediately preceding the commencement of the action;
>
> 4. The cause occurred in N.Y. and both parties are residents of N.Y. at the time of the commencement of the action;
>
> 5. Either party has been a resident of N.Y. for a continuous period of at least two years immediately preceding the comment of the action. DRL § 230.

Although meeting one of the above requirements will permit a plaintiff to file a divorce action, there are further hurdles to overcome to obtain all the relief the plaintiff may be seeking in the case. If the plaintiff meets one of the DRL § 230 requirements, a New York court will adjudicate the status of the marriage; that is, if the plaintiff proves that grounds exist, the court will grant a judgment of divorce dissolving the marriage. Power to adjudicate only the status of the marriage is called *in rem* **jurisdiction** (jurisdiction over the thing). Ancillary relief such as support and maintenance (formerly called alimony), will be granted only if the court has jurisdiction *over the person of the party adversely* *affected by the determination.* For example:

> Cornell and Rosalie were married in Montana in 1990. In 1992 Rosalie left Cornell due to his abusive conduct and moved with their child to New York. In 1995 she files for divorce in New York alleging cruel and inhuman conduct and in the alternative, constructive abandonment. Based on her two-year residence in New York, Rosalie may sue for divorce here, but the court may not make an award of maintenance or child support because Cornell has no connection with New York.

PERSONAL AND *IN REM* JURISDICTION

Personal jurisdiction over support and maintenance extends to nonresident parties only if the affected party is a New York domiciliary or has, or in the recent past had, some connection with New York, such as that New York was the **matrimonial domicile** of the parties before their separation or the defendant abandoned the plaintiff in the state. CPLR 302(b). The matrimonial domicile is the place where the parties when last together made their home.

In a situation where the defendant has no such connection, the plaintiff may choose either to obtain the divorce judgment in New York without any adjudication of child support and maintenance and later sue for alimony and maintenance in the defendant's state, or to sue for divorce and ancillary relief in the state that has jurisdiction over the defendant, so that all issues can be resolved in one proceeding. Jurisdiction in child custody matters is governed by entirely different principles, set forth in the Uniform Child Custody Jurisdiction statute, which will be discussed in Chapter 6.

Personal jurisdiction, also referred to by the Latin term *in personam jurisdiction,* may be acquired by a New York court in a divorce case in several ways:

1. By personal service of process within the jurisdiction;

2. By consent, express or implied, to such jurisdiction;

3. By substituted service or publication upon a resident of the state;

4. By service outside the state upon a New York domiciliary. CPLR § 308.

Thus, if a defendant who is not a New York resident is served in another state by substituted service or publication, the New York court generally acquires jurisdiction only to dissolve the marriage. Likewise, if a defendant who is not a New York domiciliary is personally served in another state, the court generally will have only *in rem* jurisdiction to adjudicate the status of the marriage. If, however, the defendant has recent substantial connections with this state or if New York was the matrimonial domicile or if the defendant abandoned the plaintiff in this state, then the court may acquire "long arm" personal jurisdiction pursuant to CPLR § 302(b) to deal with the ancillary matters of maintenance and property distribution as well.

Service of Summons

Even if the defendant is a New York resident, a divorce can only be rendered if the defendant has been properly served with process, which in the case of a matrimonial action is the summons. Although the summons and complaint may be served together, personal jurisdiction may be obtained by service of the summons by itself. If the summons is served alone, however, the summons must state legibly on its face both the primary relief requested, such as "ACTION FOR DIVORCE," and must also specify any ancillary relief demanded, such as "maintenance," "child support," or "counsel fees." DRL § 232. A summons containing such information is called a "**summons with notice**." In all matrimonial proceedings filed after January 1, 1993, the summons and complaint or summons with notice *must be filed with the court* prior to service. The court then issues an index number, which must appear on the summons at the time of service. CPLR § 305. The action is deemed commenced by the filing with the court rather than by service of the summons. DRL § 211. If the summons does not contain notice of ancillary relief requested, the court will not grant any such relief in the event of the defendant's default, but will merely adjudicate the status of the marriage. DRL § 232.

As with all civil proceedings, service in a matrimonial action by personal delivery within the state by a person over the age of 18 years who is not a party to the action is the best form of notice. In order to authorize or approve any other form of service, the court must be satisfied that personal delivery could not be accomplished and that the alternative form proposed is the next most likely to give actual notice to the defendant, so that the defendant will have the opportunity to contest the action if he or she so chooses. If the plaintiff knows from the outset that personal service will not be possible, plaintiff is not required to go through a futile exercise of attempting such service. In such a case, the plaintiff's attorney submits an affidavit to the court explaining why personal service cannot be accomplished, and if the court is satisfied that personal delivery cannot be made, it will authorize some other form of service.

Usually the second best form of service is substituted service, generally by "nail and mail" to the defendant's last known address within the state. Since all New York City apartment doors are metal (a fire code requirement), the "nailing" to the door of the defendant's abode is accomplished with tape, a less dramatic but equally effective method of affixing the summons. "Nail and mail" service is often utilized when the defendant actually resides at the address, but refuses to open the door to the process server. In support of the request for substituted service, the plaintiff's attorney submits to the court the process server's affidavits of attempted service. By custom and practice, three attempts on different days and different times of day are thought sufficient to support a request for substituted service, but this is a rule of thumb rather than a statutory mandate.

The least desirable form of service is by publication in a newspaper. In small towns and rural communities, reading the legal notices in the newspaper is a popular way of obtaining the local gossip. In urban areas, however, few people trouble to read so much fine print that is unlikely to have anything to do with anyone they know. Thus, publication is the least likely way of providing actual notice of the legal action to the defendant. It is also not desirable from the plaintiff's point of view because it is expensive and highly subject to later challenge. Sometimes, however, the defendant simply cannot be located, and publication is the only possible form of service. In such a case, the plaintiff's attorney submits a "**diligent search**" affidavit to the court outlining all the unsuccessful efforts that have been made to find the defendant. If the court is convinced that the defendant cannot be found, it will authorize service by publication. The components of a diligent search are discussed in Chapter 12.

Service outside New York State, referred to in the CPLR as "service without the state," may be made in the same manner as service within New York. CPLR § 314. Remember, however, that service without the state does not give the court personal jurisdiction over the defendant unless he or she is a domiciliary or is a nondomiciliary over whom the court may exercise jurisdiction because the long-arm statute applies.

THE COMPLAINT

VERIFICATION

The complaint in a divorce action must be **verified**. DRL § 211. It is not sufficient that the attorney for the plaintiff merely sign the complaint, but the plaintiff must swear to the truth of its contents. The answer must also be verified, unless adultery is alleged. Usually a plaintiff has **personal knowledge** of many of the facts alleged; he or she knows when and where the marriage took place, for example, because he or she was there. Other matters alleged, however, the plaintiff may know only by reliable report; plaintiff may not have ever been to the defendant's current residence, for example, but may believe that it is at a certain address because the defendant said so. When a plaintiff alleges facts without personal knowledge, those aspects of the complaint are sworn to **upon information and belief**. A plaintiff should never speculate wildly in a complaint, however. If scandalous allegations are made, such as adultery, the plaintiff must have a **good faith basis** for the allegation.

SPECIFIC PLEADING

New York requires **specific pleadings**, that is the complaint must spell out the defendant's misconduct complete with names, dates to the best of plaintiff's recollection, and sufficient detail to give the defendant notice of what he or she has allegedly done. This rule does nothing to calm the hostility between the parties, and many other jurisdictions permit **conclusory pleading**, tracking the language of the statute, in matrimonial proceedings. Our New York rule is probably rooted in this state's historical resistance to divorce generally, but there is no sign of its being changed. Thus, it is of the utmost importance that the paralegal conducting the preliminary interview with the client gather all the detail that will be required.

ALTERNATIVE PLEADING

In matrimonial proceedings, as in other proceedings, **alternative pleading** is allowed. Sometimes a plaintiff, or a defendant who is filing a counterclaim, has more than one ground for divorce. The defendant may have committed two separate wrongs, such as adultery and abandonment of the plaintiff. It is also possible that the defendant's conduct may lend itself to more than one legal theory upon which to sue for divorce. If a defendant has inflicted numerous acts of cruelty upon the plaintiff, as a result of which the plaintiff has been forced to leave the marital home, the plaintiff might allege both cruel and inhuman treatment and constructive abandonment grounds for divorce. Each ground for divorce is set forth in a separate **cause of action** so that the court can easily see which facts support each claim.

Why should a plaintiff allege more than one ground for divorce, since the result in any event will be one divorce? The answer is, to cover all bases. The defendant might have a successful defense to one of the grounds, of which the plaintiff was unaware at the time the complaint was drafted, or there might be a failure of proof in some portion of the plaintiff's case. A witness might become unavailable or experience a mysterious memory loss on the eve of trial. Drafting a complaint that includes every possible allegation depends upon copious fact-gathering, a task which is often delegated to the legal assistant. Be sure your checklist for the preliminary interview covers all conduct that might provide grounds for divorce, and ask all the questions, even if it seems that the response to the first question is more than sufficient. Since a spouse who has been sued for divorce may file a counterclaim for divorce, you will need to use the same checklist even when the client is a defendant in a pending divorce action.

REMOVAL OF BARRIERS TO REMARRIAGE

All complaints for dissolution of a marriage through annulment or divorce in New York are required to contain an allegation that to the best of plaintiff's knowledge he or she has taken, or will take prior to the entry of final judgment, all steps solely within his or her power to remove any barrier to the defendant's remarriage following the dissolution of the marriage. DRL § 253. Despite its neutral language, the legislative history of this provision reveals that it attempts to address the dilemma of Jewish women whose husbands refuse to give them a religious divorce, called a *Get*. In fact, since its passage in 1983, this statute has generally been called the "***Get law***." Under Jewish law, a man may divorce his wife, but she may divorce him only with his consent. Although a Jewish woman may, of course, obtain a civil divorce in Supreme Court without her husband's consent, she remains religiously married until he gives the *Get*. For Orthodox couples who cannot religiously remarry until they have been religiously divorced, this creates an enormous imbalance of power. If a husband, out of spite or for economic leverage, refuses the *Get*, the wife is a prisoner to his whim. The *Get* law was designed to prevent the inequity of a man being able to civilly divorce his wife while under religious law retaining his power over her. It is obvious that this statute is constitutionally questionable, and many scholars and commentators have stated their belief that it violates the freedom of religion clauses of the Federal and New York constitutions. The appellate courts have so far managed to avoid ruling on this issue. In 1992, the legislature went further and attempted to put economic teeth into the *Get* law by mandating that in deciding maintenance and property division, the courts must consider the effect of a barrier to remarriage. DRL §§ 236(5)(h) and 236(6)(d).

DRAFTING THE COMPLAINT

Paralegals are sometimes expected to draft simple divorce complaints. Computer software, such as Drafting Libraries, is available to generate divorce complaints as well as the many other documents and pleadings required in a divorce action. The program contains options that allow the drafter to allege the specifics which are required. A word of caution about software: it cannot think. If the statute has been amended since the program was written, the software will go right on doing what it was programmed to do before the amendment. Although not all firms now own or choose to use drafting software, most have word processing capacity and have standard pleadings and documents stored. Here again, you cannot simply change names and dates. No two cases are identical, and you want to do the very best for each individual client. While computers are almost miraculously useful, they are no substitute for your own knowledge and judgment. Form 5-5 is an example of a divorce complaint containing two causes of action, the first for cruel and inhuman treatment and the second for constructive abandonment based on refusal to engage in sexual relations.

📁 FORM 5-5

SUPREME COURT OF THE STATE OF NEW YORK
COUNTY OF ROCKLAND

--X   Index No.

JOSEPH A. QUINN

                         Plaintiff,   **VERIFIED COMPLAINT**

        against   ACTION FOR

                                               DIVORCE

RAMONA G. QUINN

                         Defendant.

--X

        The Plaintiff, by his attorney David R. Rogers, Esq., complaining of the Defendant, alleges the following:

FIRST: The Plaintiff and the Defendant were both over 18 years of age at the time of the commencement of this action.

SECOND: The Plaintiff and the Defendant were residents of the State of New York for a continuous period of at least two years immediately preceding the commencement of this action.

THIRD: The Plaintiff and the Defendant were married in a religious ceremony on October 1, 1968 in the Town of Marietta, County of Cobb, State of Georgia.   Upon information and belief, no action has previously been commenced to dissolve the marriage.

FOURTH: There are three children as a result of this marriage, to wit: Farrah, born February 1, 1976; Jaclyn, born September 19, 1980; and Kate, born May 1, 1985. Farrah is emancipated. The unemancipated children of the marriage now reside with the Plaintiff and Defendant. There is no other child as a result of this marriage, and no other child is expected.

AS AND FOR A FIRST CAUSE OF ACTION

FIFTH: At the following times, none of which is more than five years before the date of the commencement of this action, the Defendant committed the following acts which were cruel and inhuman and endangered the Plaintiff's physical and mental well-being, rendering it unsafe and improper for the Plaintiff to continue to reside with the Defendant:

        a) On June 3, 1994 Defendant struck Plaintiff with a stick of fire wood, as a result of which Plaintiff sustained a large bruise to his left shoulder.

        b) On July 4, 1995 Defendant mocked, humiliated and verbally abused Plaintiff at a family gathering in the presence of several of his friends and relatives, calling him "a good-for-nothing bum who never earned an honest dime in his life."

        c) On December 24, 1995 Defendant, while in an intoxicated condition, publicly embarrassed Plaintiff at his company's holiday party, unfairly accusing him of "chasing after other women."   This disgraceful scene culminated in Defendant's throwing a glass of eggnog in Plaintiff's face.

FORM 5-5 continued

AS AND FOR A SECOND CAUSE OF ACTION

SIXTH: Since January 2, 1995, a period in excess of one year, Defendant has without cause or justification refused to engage in sexual relations with the Plaintiff. During this period, Plaintiff has frequently implored Defendant to engage in marital relations, and Defendant has on each occasion refused without explanation. Said conduct by the Defendant constitutes constructive abandonment of the Plaintiff.

SEVENTH: The marriage was performed by a clergyman of the Baptist religion. Plaintiff has taken all steps solely within the power of the Plaintiff to remove any barrier to Defendant's remarriage.

        WHEREFORE, the Plaintiff demands judgment against the Defendant, dissolving the marriage between the parties to this action, and granting the following relief:

        That the Plaintiff shall have custody of the unemancipated children of the marriage, Jaclyn, born on September 19, 1980, and Kate, born on May 1, 1985.

        That the Defendant shall pay 200/00 dollars ($200.00) every other week (bi-weekly) to the Plaintiff for child support.

        That the Defendant shall have reasonable rights of visitation.

        That the Family Court shall have concurrent jurisdiction with the Supreme Court with respect to any future issues of custody, visitation, maintenance and support.

        That the Plaintiff shall be entitled to exclusive possession of the marital residence, 10 Main Street, New City, New York.

        That the Defendant shall pay one-half ($\frac{1}{2}$) of all reasonable medical and dental expenses of the unemancipated children.

        That the Defendant shall continue to maintain for the benefit of the Plaintiff and the children the health, hospitalization and medical insurance currently maintained, or equivalent and suitable insurance.

        That the Defendant shall continue to maintain for the benefit of the Plaintiff the existing life insurance policies of which the Defendant is the owner or named benficiary, or equivalent and suitable insurance.

        That the Defendant shall pay to the Plaintiff the reasonable counsel fees incurred by the Plaintiff in this action.

        That the Defendant may resume use of her maiden name, Ramona Regal.

That the marital property be equitably distributed.

That the Court grant such other and further relief as the Court may deem just and proper.

Dated: February 8, 1996

David R. Rogers, Esq.
1313 Courthouse Road
New City, New York 34567
(000) 876-1234

VERIFICATION

STATE OF NEW YORK   )
)
COUNTY OF ROCKLAND)

JOSEPH A. QUINN, being duly sworn, deposes and says:

That he is the Plaintiff herein; that he has read the foregoing complaint and knows the contents thereof; that the same is true to his own knowledge except as to the matters therein stated to be alleged on information and belief, and as to those matters, he believes it to be true.

_____
JOSEPH A. QUINN

SWORN TO BEFORE ME
this   day of

_____
NOTARY PUBLIC

PRACTICE TIP: The complaint contains preliminary jurisdictional allegations before stating the grounds for divorce. The first paragraph establishes that both parties have reached the legal age of majority and, therefore, no *guardian ad litem* is required. The second allegation satisfies the DRL § 230 requirement that the plaintiff have a proper nexus with New York in order to be allowed to file for divorce in this state. Often several or all of the DRL § 230 alternatives are present, and it is not necessary to allege more than one unless some are subject to challenge. The third paragraph establishes the plaintiff's standing to bring the divorce action by alleging the existence of a valid marriage. You cannot get divorced if you were never married in the first place. The fourth paragraph sets forth the names and birth dates of each child of the marriage and specifies which are not yet emancipated. In some complaints the children are called "the issue" of the marriage, a perfectly acceptable term. If you choose to use the term "issue," however, remember that it is always singular, no matter how many children the parties have. Listing the names and ages of the children is crucial because the judge who renders the judgment of divorce *must* award custody of each minor child. Stating the actual date of birth is preferable to giving the child's age; since the case may be pending for a long time, it is easier for the judge to compute a child's age at some point in the future using the birth date. If the wife is pregnant at the time the complaint is filed, the complaint should state that another child is expected so that there will never be any question whether the expected child is the child of the husband. After the preliminaries are out of the way, the complaint turns to the grounds for divorce. Format is flexible, and different attorneys prefer different styles. The important point is that the facts supporting each grounds for divorce be grouped together in a logical way, so that the court does not have to become a mind reader to grasp the meaning. The headings, such as "as and for a first cause of action," are optional, but are particularly useful as reference points in a long complaint. Some complaints contain allegations (not shown in the example) that are preemptive strikes against defenses the plaintiff thinks the defendant might assert. The complaint may allege, for example, that the plaintiff has always been a dutiful spouse or that the plaintiff did not condone any wrongdoing by the plaintiff. After the grounds comes the *Get* law paragraph. This allegation is required in all cases where the spouses were married in a religious ceremony, regardless of their religion. Finally, the complaint sets forth the relief requested in the WHEREFORE clause. All forms of relief demanded should be specified, but the dollar amounts of maintenance and child support need not be stated at this point. Instead, the complaint may demand "reasonable maintenance" and "child support in accordance with the Child Support Standards Act." The final paragraph is the plaintiff's verification, without which the court clerk will not accept the complaint for filing.

RECOGNITION OF FOREIGN DIVORCES

Divorces rendered both by other states of the United States and by other nations are both considered **foreign divorces**. Divorce judgments issued by sister states are generally recognized in New York because the **full faith and credit clause** of the United States Constitution mandates that such orders be treated as if they had been issued here. When the divorce has been obtained in a foreign country, our courts may recognize it under principles of **comity**. Comity, however, is not a constitutional requirement, and our courts will recognize a foreign order only when the foreign court's procedures satisfy our notions of due process. Comity is routinely extended to other jurisdictions, such as Canada, which share our common law heritage. If a divorce has been obtained *ex parte* or by mail order or if both sides did not have adequate notice and opportunity to be heard, our courts may refuse to recognize it as a valid order or judgment. In such a situation, New York may grant a divorce to the spouse who was the defendant in the foreign divorce proceeding or may refuse to enforce the terms of the foreign judgment.

The area of law devoted to resolving such problems is called Conflict of Laws. Even within the legal profession it is a rather esoteric specialty, and it is certainly not a subject that a legal assistant is expected to master. Fortunately, the addition to New York divorce law of the "living apart pursuant to a written separation agreement" ground for divorce has greatly reduced the amount of litigation concerning foreign divorces. Should your preliminary interview with the client reveal the likelihood that a foreign order or judgment exists, however, it is important to obtain all available details about it.

EFFECTS OF JUDGMENT OF DIVORCE

ECONOMIC CONSEQUENCES

Before July, 1980, when the Equitable Distribution Law went into effect, it mattered greatly to which spouse the divorce was granted. Being the guilty party had the drastic effect of barring the wife from alimony. As Chapters 7 and 8 discuss, ordinary marital fault, the sort of conduct which would usually constitute the grounds for divorce, is no longer considered relevant in awarding maintenance or in property division. Thus, it rarely matters from an economic standpoint whether the divorce is awarded to one spouse or the other or to both. If the goal of both parties is to end the marriage, it may be smarter for the defendant to save his or her energy to fight the economic issues rather than to contest the grounds for divorce. Remember that if both parties succeed in proving adultery, the divorce will be denied to each of them, with the net effect that they remain in a marriage neither may wish to continue.

RIGHT TO REMARRY

The court must decide ancillary issues such as maintenance, custody, child support and property division at the same time it adjudicates the status of the marriage. It may not grant the divorce first and leave the other issues hanging fire. CPLR § 3212. The divorce is final upon the entry of judgment, and both spouses are then free to remarry. The court sends a notification to the Department of Health, which then issues a Certificate of Dissolution of Marriage. The Certificate of Dissolution can be presented whenever official proof of the divorce is required, thus sparing the parties the possible embarrassment of showing the Judgment of Divorce that states the grounds for the divorce.

NAME CHANGES

Domestic Relations Law § 240-a requires that a judgment of divorce or annulment contain a provision that the woman may resume the use of her maiden name. Either parent may petition under the Civil Rights Act to change the surname of the minor child(ren) of the marriage without the consent of the other parent. To grant such an application, the court must be satisfied that the change of name will substantially promote the interest of the minor. CRL § 63.

LEGITIMACY OF CHILDREN

A judgment of divorce does not affect the legitimacy of children born or conceived prior to the divorce. If the judgment of divorce does not specify that a child born during the marriage is not legitimate, the presumption of legitimacy becomes irrebuttable. DRL § 175. Even if blood tests later scientifically establish that another man is the biological father of the child, the biological father cannot be adjudicated the father of the child unless the judgment of divorce is resettled.

CONCLUSION

Divorce is one of the most common reasons that ordinary, law-abiding people seek out an attorney. Whether the client is a celebrity millionaire or an average, over-extended-on-the-credit-cards working person, important issues are at stake. Major decisions must be made at a point when the client may find it hard to decide to get out of bed in the morning. A legal assistant who is tactful, patient, thorough, and organized can play a crucial role by gathering all the necessary facts and by being available to the client when the attorney in charge of the case is in court or is tied up on other matters. The paralegal also plays an important role in keeping the cost of divorce litigation within reason by assisting in the drafting of simple pleadings and documents. By keeping track of the many deadlines involved in a divorce case, the paralegal helps to keep the case moving as expeditiously as possible.

CHAPTER REVIEW QUESTIONS

1.   Kenneth and Marilyn argue constantly. They disagree about everything except their shared desire to end their marriage. By mutual agreement, they ceased sexual relations a year and a half ago. To prevent their quarrels from exceeding the bounds of civility, they have withdrawn from each other; Kenneth stays in the den watching TV, while Marilyn spends most evenings at her mother's house. On what grounds, if any, can Kenneth and Marilyn obtain a divorce?

2.   If Kenneth and Marilyn execute a separation agreement one month from today, how soon can they file for divorce?

3.   Brenda and Bernard have a stormy marriage. They are verbally abusive to each other, and on three separate occasions Bernard has slapped and shoved Brenda during heated arguments. Brenda obtained a temporary order of protection *ex parte* after one of these incidents, but she never served the court papers on Bernard, and the case was, therefore, dismissed. Does either of these spouses have grounds to file for divorce? If so, what grounds?

4.   Maureen and Theodore had what Maureen thought was a pretty good marriage until October 2, 1996, when Theodore packed his bags and left. He calls occasionally, but has refused to return or to enter into marriage counseling. When can Maureen file for divorce on the ground of abandonment?

5.   Duane and Grace were married in South Carolina. After a honeymoon trip to Niagra Falls, Grace's only visit to New York, they returned to South Carolina, where Grace was born and raised. They lived together there for two years, until the day Grace locked Duane out of the marital home and refused to give him the keys to the new locks. Duane came to New York, where he has family. He has taken a job in New York and intends to stay here. How long does he have to reside in New York before suing in New York for divorce on the ground of constructive abandonment?

6.   What is the matrimonial domicile in Duane and Grace's case?

7   Of what state is Grace a domiciliary?

8   If the summons and complaint in Duane's divorce action are personally served on Grace in South Carolina, does the New York court acquire *in personam* jurisdiction or *in rem*

jurisdiction? Will the New York court be able to award maintenance to Duane if he establishes that he is financially entitled to it? Explain the reasons for your answers.

CHAPTER ASSIGNMENT

The following fact pattern, the case of Wilma and Hugh Bickering, will be used for this assignment and for the assignments following Chapters 6, 7 and 8. Incorporating all information you think relevant, draft a divorce complaint with at least two causes of action for your firm's client, Wilma Bickering.

THE BICKERINGS

Mrs. Wilma Bickering is your firm's client. She lives with her husband, Hugh Bickering, and their two children at 35 Clinton Avenue, Brooklyn, New York 11230. They were married on October 1, 1981 at Our Lady of Saints Roman Catholic Church in Brooklyn, New York. The children are Carolyn, born June 12, 1984, and Joseph, born December 5, 1989, and adopted in 1990 by the Bickerings.

Marital Home

The single-family house in Brooklyn is jointly owned by the Bickerings. The house was purchased on January 5, 1982, and was recently appraised as being worth $200,000. The house was originally purchased for $148,000 and carries a monthly mortgage payment of $1,411.00. The down payment of $20,000 came from Hugh's inheritance from his father, who died in 1979, and the Bickerings secured a mortgage of $128,000.00 from Best Bank. The unpaid balance remaining on the mortgage is $62,554.99. Last year the Bickerings paid $1,500.00 in real estate taxes.

Wilma's Education, Employment, Hobbies and Income

Wilma works as a New York City Transit Authority Conductor and has a Bachelor's degree in Social Work from Brooklyn College. Wilma enjoys bus rides to Atlantic City. Last year she won $500.00 gambling at Atlantic City casinos. Wilma intends to report the $500.00 on the couple's joint 1996 tax return. Wilma sews all of the children's clothing. She makes all the draperies, curtains and furniture covers for the entire house. Wilma does all of the cooking and cleaning at the Brooklyn residence.

Hugh's Education, Employment, Hobbies and Income

Hugh is an Accountant for the Internal Revenue Service. He also receives $600.00 a month from a trust fund established by his mother who died in 1977. In addition, Hugh has a Master's degree in accounting from Pace University and is a Certified Public Accountant. Last year Hugh grossed $45,872.00 from his

Federal Government job, and Wilma grossed $37,742.64 from her Transit job.

Expenses

Monthly basic household expenses include: Brooklyn Union Gas $40.00; Con Ed $90.00; telephone $75.00; homeowners' insurance $75.00; water bill $100.00; and fuel $150.00. Hugh spends $15.00 per week on gas for his 1996, fully loaded, Maxima. His car note is $400.00 per month and his car insurance (full coverage) is $300.00 per month. Wilma has a 1993 Honda Accord that she bought used from a dealership for $3,000.00 in 1995. She spends $45.00 a month on gas and oil. The car is paid for in full, and monthly insurance for this second family car is $100.00. She has accumulated $800.00 in telephone bills by calling the Psychic Network for marital advice

Assets

The Bickerings have a joint checking account at Best Bank, which they use for daily expenses. This account has a current balance of $4,852.96. In addition to the savings from Wilma's paycheck at the Municipal Credit Union and Trans America, the current balances for which are reflected on Wilma's pay stub (year to date), the Bickerings also own 250 shares of the Vanguard STAR Fund. Hugh purchased 150 STAR fund shares at $9.98 per share in their joint names on December 31, 1987 with funds drawn from the joint checking account. The additional 100 shares were acquired through reinvested dividends of the STAR fund.

Liabilities

The Bickerings have a MasterCard with a $5,000.00 limit on a joint account, which is the current balance owing. The minimum monthly payment is $200.00. Nearly all the purchases were made by Hugh for customizing and detailing his Maxima.

The Children

Both children are above-average students at schools in the neighborhood and have many friends, especially Carolyn, who is a member of her school basketball team. Joseph is very attached to Hugh, who spends a lot of time with him on weekends. When Joseph was adopted he was very sickly and weak. Because of the Bickerings' joint care for him, he has grown to be healthy and strong, but of late he has become withdrawn as tensions in the house have increased. Wilma's mother, who lives two blocks away, watches both children at her house after school until Hugh and Wilma get home from work. Hugh's parents are deceased, and the rest of his family live in South Carolina. Until recently both parents would help the children with their homework in the evenings. Lately Hugh has been staying away from home frequently, so Wilma has been carrying on as best she can.

Marital Discord

Wilma says that she and Hugh have grown apart ever since she returned home unexpectedly early from a trip to Atlantic City in June of 1996 and found Hugh in bed with her best friend. After that incident Wilma insisted they no longer share a bedroom. She says that her husband has not shown her affection in 15 months and states that when she asks him why, he laughs and calls her ugly, fat, stupid. He curses her violently. She says that he slapped her face in September of 1996 because she asked him where he was going one Saturday night. She called the police, but Hugh was not arrested because she did not have any marks. She says that he has been drinking heavily and staying out nights ever since.

Every time Hugh and Wilma sat down together to file a joint tax return for last year they began arguing over Wilma's phone calls to the psychic network. Hugh called Wilma a loony-toon and said that he could predict a lonely future for her for free. Wilma says that Hugh is the reason she calls the psychic network and he should contribute to the bill, stating that it was cheaper than a psychiatrist. Consequently, the couple failed to file a joint 1996 tax return and requested an extension to file. The extension was granted.

Wilma wants full custody of the children and is willing to allow Hugh to visit them. She feels that the house is rightfully hers because she has worked like a dog to make the house beautiful for the family.

The particulars of the various accounts are as follows:

* **Municipal Credit Union**
  222 Montague Street
  Brooklyn, N.Y. 11234
  Account # 1112340

* **Trans America**
  5 World Trade Center
  New York, N.Y. 10001

* **Best Bank**
  399 Park Avenue
  New York, N.Y. 10033
  Account # 9912356 (Checking)
  Account # 9912365 (MasterCard)
  Account # 5632199 (Mortgage)

* **Vanguard STAR Fund**
  Vanguard Financial Center
  P.O. Box 2600
  Valley Forge, P.A. 19482-2600
  Account # 54321

WILMA'S PAY STUB

NEWYORK CITY TRANSIT AUTHORITY Wilma Bickering							TAXES/DEDUCTIONS	YEAR TO DATE
NYCTA2LIVINGSTON PLAZA,RM#8029 TAW2					FED TAX (S,02)		9963	203929
BROOKLYN NY 11201					SOCIAL SEC TAX		4467	105629
DESCRIPTION	RATE	HOURS	EARNINGS	YEAR TO DATE	MEDICARE TAX		1044	24703
REGULAR EARNING	176425	4000	70570	98360	NEW YORK (S,02)		3835	74094
NIGHT DIFF 01	12572	1600	2012	2135	NY CITY (R)		2160	40352
ADJ-HOURS+ 01			00	5129	TWU HBT CONTR.		544	5030
COMP DIFFER*AL			00	1603095	MUNICCREDIT UN		15300	244800
PEN.GR:IF APPL			72582	1708719	WM.PENN INS(B)		2000	46000
					TRAVL. INS.(C)		2050	47150
					TRANS AMERICA		1300	29900
					GARNISHMENT		00	95323
					NYCERS LOAN 56		7607	148628
					PENS(TA) 401K		2177	51247
					PEN(TA) 25/55		1669	39304
					COPE		15	330
					UNION DUES		859	19261

	EARNINGS	TAXES	DEDUCTIONS	NET PAY	PAY PERIOD	CHECK NUMBER	AMOUNT OF CHECK
CURRENT	72582	21469	33521	17592	BEGIN	2187152	17592
YEAR TO DATE	1708719	468707	726973	533039	END 10-28-95		

EXPLANATION OF WILMA'S PAY STUB

TWU HBT CONTR. (Health Insurance)	$ 5.44
MUNICIPAL CREDIT UNION (Savings)	153.00
WILLIAM PENN (Life Insurance)	20.00
TRAVELERS INSURANCE (Disability Insurance)	20.50
TRANS AMERICA (Savings)	13.00
NYCERS LOAN 56 (Pension Loan)	76.07
401-K PLAN	21.77
PENSION 25/55	16.69
COPE (Union Dues)	.15
UNION DUES	8.59

HUGH'S PAY STUB

INTERNAL REVENUE SERVICE									11202	
Salary		Rate	Time	Tax Deductible This Statement	STATEMENT OF EARNINGS AND LEAVE					
45 872 00		PA	F/T	2 024 55						
EARNINGS AND DEDUCTIONS										
ITEM		HOURS			AMOUNT					
Code	Description	1st wk.	P/P	Yr to Date	1st Wk.		P/P		Yr to Date	
01	Regular Time	18 00	40 00	968 00	86 98		879 20		14 649 96	
50	Credit Hours			18 00					381 28	
81	Annual Leave	24 00	40 00	182 00	827 52		879 20		4 186 08	
82	Sick Leave			49 00					1 073 58	
90	Other Leave			25 00					701 13	
75 02	Retirement @ .80%						14 07		158 28	
75 15	Thrift Savers Tax Def.						175 84		2 103 20	
	*Amt Based on 1758.40									
	60& O 10% F 30% C									
76	Social Security						108 02		1 803 28	
77	Federal Tax Exempts						195 67		2 342 72	
	Extra Federal Tax						20 00		240 00	
78	St Tax NY Exempts 301						82 55		107 06	
79	City Tax Exempts						52 71		629 88	
	New York NY									
81	FEGLI - Coverage $48000						7 92		94 72	
82	OPT FEGLI - Age Bracket 2						5 41		54 72	
83	FEMBRA ENROLL COD HU1								68 78	
87	Union Dues 10 LOCAL 0047						10 48		123 12	
88	Savings Acct. 3020						50 00		800 00	
97	Med. Hosp. Ins. (HITS)						25 50		308 00	
** **	GROSS PAY					1	788 40		21 032 00	
** **	NET PAY						998 12		11 880 78	

EXPLANATION OF HUGH'S PAY STUB

RETIREMENT @ .80% (not tax deferred)	14.07
THRIFT SAVERS (Tax deferred)	175.84
Amt based on $1756.40, weekly salary	
SOCIAL SECURITY (OASDI)	108.02
FEDERAL TAX (4 exemptions)	195.67
STATE TAX (1 exemption)	82.55
CITY TAX (0 exemptions)	52.71
FEGLI (life insurance)	7.92
OPT FEGLI (additional life insurance)	5.41
FEMBA ENROLL (Enrollment code)	
UNION DUES (Local 0047)	10.48
SAVINGS ACCT 3020 (Not tax deferred)	50.00
MED HOSP INS (HITS)	
(second part of social security)	25.50

6 CUSTODY AND VISITATION

"The only absolute in the law governing custody of children is that there are no absolutes." *Friederwitzer v. Friederwitzer*, 55 N.Y.2d 89, 447 N.Y.S.2d 893 (1982).

CUSTODY

The best custody case is the one that does not happen. Contested custody cases are ruinously expensive, time-consuming, and enormously stressful to the parents and children involved. All legal practitioners should initially approach every custody dispute with the idea that it will be resolved. While the paralegal conducting an initial interview will want to be sympathetic and reassuring to the client, every effort should be made to avoid adding fuel to the flames of animosity. In the long run, those flames will scar the child most of all.

In Chapter 4 we discussed the ways a married couple who are separating can arrive at an agreement concerning custody and visitation issues. Mediation is equally available to parents who never married and to married parents who are separating or divorcing. If a couple has never been married, they cannot use a separation agreement to resolve custody and visitation questions, but they may nevertheless enter into another type of agreement concerning these issues. If they desire to have their agreement incorporated into a court order, which is advisable, they may appear together in the Family Court with the agreement, file a custody petition, and ask the court to "so order" their **stipulation**.

Unfortunately, even with the most professional assistance, some custody and visitation disputes cannot be settled and will have to be litigated. One parent may be unreasonable or may pose a real threat to the child or to the other parent. Obviously, a parent should never bargain away the child's safety for money or for a "truce" that will not be lasting. Even if a case must go to court, however, it does not have to turn into a battle royal. If there is agreement about some of the issues, the parties may enter into a **trial stipulation** in which they limit the issues the court must decide. If, for example, the parents agree that the mother should have custody and the father should have visitation, but they disagree about the scope or length of the visitation, they should let the court know just what has been agreed and what is still in dispute. They may also agree upon one set of experts to perform home studies and mental health evaluations, rather than retaining competing experts.

Historical Background

Custody cases reflect society's values about family life and child-rearing in subtle and often unspoken ways. Custody decisions require a court to make predictions about a child's future welfare and happiness. Since no one can really know what a particular child's future holds, the court must make an educated guess based upon evidence that is often skimpy or contradictory and upon "expert" opinions that may be unconvincing to the court. Assumptions creep into the decision-making process that may seem to be self-evident truths at the time, but to later generations may appear to have been half-baked foolishness or outright prejudice. Thus, custody cases offer an intriguing window through which to glimpse the "family values" prevailing at various points throughout history.

If a couple divorced two hundred and fifty years ago, which parent was most likely to get custody? Students are usually surprised to learn that it was the father. To the judges of that time, however, it was not only not surprising, it was obvious. Divorces were extremely rare and were all but nonexistent among poor and middle-class people. Among the aristocracy, "custody" meant primarily decision-making power over one's children and the supervision of servants who provided the actual care and feeding of the children until they reached the age to go to boarding school. Women at the time were legally infants themselves. They were not allowed to own property or enter into binding contracts. How could such a legal non-person be entrusted with the sole custody of a child? Paternal preference was the common-law rule.

By the nineteenth century, the tide was turning. Women, although still perceived as weak and in need of masculine guidance and protection, came to be seen as possessing a special gift for raising children. Their "softness" and "gentleness" were particularly valued for the care of young children, those of "tender years." Thus, the courts sailed into the maternal preference era, awash in Victorian sentimentality about the silken cords of motherhood. As one opinion phrased it, "There is but a twilight zone between a mother's love and the atmosphere of heaven, and all things being equal, no child should be deprived of that maternal influence unless it be shown that there are special or extraordinary reasons for so doing." *Tuter v. Tuter*, 120 S.W.2d 203 (Mo. Ct. App. 1938). Many states, including New York, passed laws to revoke the common-law preference for the father. Some gave preference to the mother, some awarded the child to the "innocent spouse," and some, like New York in 1896, decreed that the custody determination should be based solely on the best interest of the child.

The existence of a gender-neutral statute did not guarantee a gender-neutral judicial outcome, however, since many courts continued to rule that the best interest of a child of "tender years" lay with the mother. As recently as the 1980's courts often awarded custody to the "non-working" parent, a slightly less blatant way of saying a young child should be with a stay-at-home mother. In *Pawelski v. Buchholtz*, 91 A.D.2d 1200, 459 N.Y.S.2d 190 (4 Dept. 1983), for example, the court found that the mother's availability to provide full-time child care outweighed her "moral laxity" in becoming pregnant with her present husband's child while she was still married to the father of the first child, whose custody was in dispute.

The most significant development in the law of custody over the past two centuries has been the increasing awareness of the child as a person rather than as a piece of property, or "chattel" of the parents. Unlike other trends in custody law, which have sometimes been as fleeting as the latest diet fad, this progression in the law has been consistent and enduring. In deciding custody a court is not primarily concerned with vindicating the rights of either parent, but rather exercises its *parens patriae* authority to protect the welfare of the child. The *parens patriae* doctrine comes to us through our common law tradition. In England the king was seen as the "father of the country," possessing both the authority and the responsibility to care for those who were helpless. When the United States overthrew the king and became a republic, the *parens patriae* authority was transferred to various organs of government, including the courts. In 1925 the great New York jurist Benjamin Cardozo stated this principle: "The chancellor in exercising his jurisdiction upon petition does not proceed upon the theory that the petitioner, whether father or mother, has a cause of action against the other or indeed against any one. He acts as parens patriae to do what is best for the interest of the child. He is to put himself in the position of a 'wise and affectionate, and careful parent.'" *Finlay v. Finlay*, 240 N.Y. 429, 148 N.E. 624 (1925).

After enacting what is now section 70 of the Domestic Relations Law, directing courts to "determine solely what is for the best interest of the child, and what will best promote its welfare and happiness, and make award [of custody] accordingly," the legislature resisted all further efforts to statutorily define "best interest of the child" until 1996, when the Domestic Relations Law was amended to make domestic violence a factor courts are mandated to consider in custody and visitation cases. DRL § 240 (1), FCA §§ 447, 467, 549(a), 651. New York has declined to adopt the Uniform Marriage and Divorce Act, and numerous bills which would have codified guidelines for the exercise of judicial discretion in custody cases have been voted down in the legislature. Thus, custody law remains overwhelmingly judge-made law.

A judicial opinion serves as precedent for a future case only if the later case is substantially similar to the earlier case. If there are significant factual differences between the two cases, the later case will be said to be **distinguishable** from the prior case and thus not controlled by its holding. No two custody cases are alike. Each combination of parental strengths and weaknesses and needs of the children is unique to the case at hand. For this reason, reported custody decisions offer little assistance in predicting the outcome of a particular case before the court.

BASICS BOX

Subject matter jurisdiction: Supreme Court and Family Court have concurrent original jurisdiction. Supreme Court also has ancillary jurisdiction in conjunction with a matrimonial action. Family Court also has jurisdiction in matrimonial actions on referral from Supreme Court.

Venue: If both parents and child are within New York, county of residence of either party or child. Court may decline jurisdiction if another locality has more significant connection. If one parent is out of state, child's "home state" as defined in UCCJA, unless New York exercises "emergency jurisdiction."

Standing: Any person except a foster parent may petition for custody. Parents, and, in some circumstances, grandparents and siblings may petition for visitation.

Grounds: When the two parents dispute custody the decision will be based upon the best interest of the child. When a non-parent litigates against a parent, the non-parent must show parental abandonment, unfitness, persisting neglect, or other extraordinary circumstances *plus* best interest.

Statute of Limitations: No statute of limitations. Custody may be litigated until the child reaches the age of 18 years.

Applicable statutes: DRL Art. 5; DRL § 240; FCA §§ 651-656.

Parent Versus Parent Custody Disputes

When two parents dispute the custody of their child, the court applies the "best interest of the child" standard to decide the case. There is no prima facie right to custody of the child in either parent. DRL § 70. The court may award **sole custody** to one parent, usually with visitation to the other parent, or may award **joint custody** to the two parents with a plan whereby the child's physical custody will be shared. "Joint custody" under New York law means that the parents will share major decision-making responsibility for the child, with each having the right to make minor, day-to-day decisions while the child is in their physical custody. "Joint physical custody" generally means that the child will reside approximately 50% of the time with each parent. Parents may share "joint custody," however, even if the child spends most of the time in one parent's residence.

Joint custody is a concept that has obvious popular appeal in that it accords the parents equal legal authority in their child's upbringing and is genuinely gender-neutral. The courts have held that it is appropriate, however, only when the parties are "relatively stable, amicable parents behaving in a mature, civilized fashion." *Braiman v. Braiman*, 44 N.Y.2d 584, 407 N.Y.S.2d 449 (1978). Since most parents who litigate custody do not fit this description, awards of joint custody in New York have been rare. Another argument against joint custody is that in families where there has been spousal abuse, joint custody permits the abusive spouse continued contact with and control over the abused parent. In *Drummond v. Drummond*, 205 A.D.2d 847, 613 N.Y.S.2d 717 (3 Dept. 1994), the court terminated a joint custody agreement and awarded sole custody to the mother, in part because the father had violated an order of protection. A bill that would have created a statutory presumption in favor of joint custody failed to pass the legislature in 1995.

In rendering its decision in a custody case, the court spells out the factors it thought significant in the particular case. In the absence of statutory criteria, the trial court has wide latitude to emphasize certain factors and to minimize or ignore others. Because custody cases are so fact-specific, comparatively few are appealed and even fewer reversed. Compared to the number of custody cases litigated, therefore, there are relatively few appellate decisions. Nevertheless, some trends are apparent and certain factors can be identified as particularly significant in judicial determinations of "best interest of the child."

"BEST INTEREST" FACTORS

Physical and Mental Health of Parents

It may seem harsh even to think of depriving a parent of custody because the parent suffers from an illness, for which he or she is certainly not to blame. Since the focus is on the child's welfare rather than on the rights of the parents, however, the court must consider the matter from the child's point of view. If a parent's mobility is severely limited or the parent must be hospitalized frequently, the court may find that the other parent is the more suitable custodian. Faced with a situation where the mother was an invalid who had been hospitalized eighty times in the past ten years, one court awarded custody to a father, who, the evidence showed, was better able to care for and discipline his son. Although the father was a homosexual, the court noted that he did not "flaunt" his homosexuality and that it had no deleterious effect on the 12-year-old son. *M.A.B. v. R.B.*, 134 Misc.2d 317, 510 N.Y.S.2d 960 (N.Y. Sup. Ct. 1986).

Physical illness or disability does not always result in an award of custody to the healthy parent, however. The fact that a mother was infected with HIV, the virus that causes AIDS, has been held to be insufficient basis for a change of custody to the father, for example. The court stated that although the mother sometimes felt weak, she was not incapacitated by her condition and that there was no risk of communicating the virus through close personal contact. *Matter of Steven L.*, 148 Misc.2d 779, 561 N.Y.S.2d 322 (Fam. Ct. Kings County 1990).

Morality and Lifestyle of Parents

As a general rule New York courts are reluctant to deny custody to a parent on the basis of the parent's sexual conduct or lifestyle unless it has been demonstrated that the parent's conduct is having, or is likely to have, a negative impact on the child. Since appellate opinions rarely discuss such evidence in detail, it is difficult to ascertain how such a showing has been made. In *DiStefano v. DiStefano*, 60 A.D.2d 976, 401 N.Y.S.2d 636 (4 Dept. 1978), for example, the Appellate Division, Fourth Department, affirmed a trial judge who had found, based on evidence from several clergymen, two psychiatrists, two psychologists, an anthropologist, a probation officer and a psychiatric social worker, that the mother's "failure to keep her lesbian relationship separate from her role as a mother" had a detrimental effect upon the children. Neither the testimony of the witnesses nor the nature of the harm to the children is detailed in the opinion, however, and one is left to wonder what an anthropologist might have had to say on the subject.

 CASE 6-1

ALLEN v. FARROW
197 A.D.2d 327, 611 N.Y.S.2d 859 (1 Dept. 1994)

Ross, J.

In this special proceeding commenced by petitioner to obtain custody of, or increased visitation with, the infant children Moses Amadeus Farrow, Dylan O'Sullivan Farrow and Satchel Farrow, we are called upon to review the IAS Court's decision which, *inter alia*, awarded custody of the three children to the respondent [mother], denied the petitioner's [father's] requests regarding visitation and awarded counsel fees to the respondent. Upon such review we conclude, for the reasons set forth below, that the determination of the IAS Court was in accordance with the best interests of these children, and accordingly, we affirm.

The petitioner and the respondent have brought themselves to this unhappy juncture primarily as a result of two recent events. These are, Mr. Allen's affair with Soon-Yi Previn and the alleged sexual abuse of Dylan O'Sullivan Farrow by Mr. Allen. While the parties had difficulties which grew during Ms. Farrow's pregnancy with Satchel, it was the discovery of the relationship between Mr. Allen and Ms. Previn that intensified Ms. Farrow's concerns about Mr. Allen's behavior toward Dylan, and resulted in the retention of counsel by both parties. While various aspects of this matter remain unclear, it is evident that each party assigns the blame for the current state of affairs to the other.

CASE 6-1 continued

The parties' respective arguments are very clear. The petitioner maintains that he was forced to commence this proceeding in order to preserve his parental rights to the three infant children, because the respondent commenced and continues to engage in a campaign to alienate him from his children and to ultimately defeat his legal rights to them. The petitioner contends, *inter alia*, that the respondent seeks to accomplish her goals primarily through manipulation of the children's perceptions of him. He wishes to obtain custody, ostensibly to counteract the detrimental psychological effects the respondent's actions have had on his children, and to provide them with a more stable atmosphere in which to develop. Mr. Allen specifically denies the allegations that he sexually abused Dylan and characterizes them as part of Ms. Farrow's extreme overreaction to his admitted relationship with Ms. Previn.

The respondent maintains that the petitioner has shown no genuine parental interest in, nor any regard for, the children's welfare and that any interest he has shown has been inappropriate and even harmful. Respondent cites the fact that the petitioner has commenced and maintained an intimate sexual relationship with her daughter Soon-Yi Previn, which he has refused to curtail, despite the obvious ill effects it has had on all of the children and the especially profound effect it has had on Moses. It is also contended that petitioner has at best, an inappropriately intense interest in, and at worst, an abusive relationship with, the parties' daughter Dylan. Further, the respondent maintains that petitioner's contact with the parties' biological son, Satchel, is harmful to the child in that petitioner represents an emotional threat and has on at least one occasion threatened physical harm. Respondent contends that the petitioner's only motive in commencing this proceeding was to retaliate against the allegations of child sexual abuse made against him by Ms. Farrow.

Certain salient facts concerning both Mr. Allen's and Ms. Farrow's relationships to their children and to each other are not disputed. Review of these facts in an objective manner and the conclusions that flow from them, demonstrate that the determination of the IAS Court as to both custody and visitation is amply supported by the record before this Court.

From the inception of Mr. Allen's relationship with Ms. Farrow in 1980, until a few months after the adoption of Dylan O'Sullivan Farrow on June 11, 1985, Mr. Allen wanted nothing to do with Ms. Farrow's children. Although Mr. Allen and Ms. Farrow attempted for approximately six months to have a child of their own, Mr. Allen did so apparently only after Ms. Farrow promised to assume full responsibility for the child. Following the adoption however, Mr. Allen became interested in developing a relationship with the newly adopted Dylan. While previously he rarely spent time in the respondent's apartment, after the adoption of Dylan he went to the respondent's Manhattan apartment more often, visited Ms. Farrow's Connecticut home and

📖 **CASE 6-1 continued**

even accompanied the Farrow family on vacations to Europe. Allen also developed a relationship with Moses Farrow, who had been adopted by the respondent in 1980 and was seven years old at the time of Dylan's adoption. However, Allen remained distant from Farrow's other six children.

In 1986 Ms. Farrow expressed a desire to adopt another child. Mr. Allen, while not enthusiastic at the prospect of the adoption of Dylan in 1985, was much more amenable to the idea in 1986. Before the adoption could be completed Ms. Farrow became pregnant with the parties' son Satchel. While the petitioner testified that he was happy at the idea of becoming a father, the record supports the finding that Mr. Allen showed little or no interest in the pregnancy. It is not disputed that Ms. Farrow began to withdraw from Mr. Allen during the pregnancy and that afterwards she did not wish Satchel to become attached to Mr. Allen.

According to Mr. Allen, Ms. Farrow became inordinately attached to the newborn Satchel to the exclusion of the other children. He viewed this as especially harmful to Dylan and began spending more time with her, ostensibly to make up for the lack of attention shown her by Ms. Farrow after the birth of Satchel. Mr. Allen maintains that his interest in and affection for Dylan always has been paternal in nature and never sexual. The various psychiatric experts who testified or otherwise provided reports did not conclude that Allen's behavior toward Dylan prior to August of 1992 was explicitly sexual in nature. However, the clear consensus was that his interest in Dylan was abnormally intense in that he made inordinate demands on her time and focused on her to the exclusion of Satchel and Moses even when they were present.

The record demonstrates that Ms. Farrow expressed concern to Allen about his relationship with Dylan, and that Allen expressed his concern to Ms. Farrow about her relationship with Satchel. In 1990 both Dylan and Satchel were evaluated by clinical psychologists. Dr. Coates began treatment of Satchel in 1990. In April of 1991 Dylan was referred to Dr. Schultz, a clinical psychologist specializing in the treatment of young children with serious emotional problems.

In 1990 at about the same time that the parties were growing distant from each other and expressing their concerns about the other's relationship with their youngest children, Mr. Allen began acknowledging Farrow's daughter Soon-Yi Previn. Previously he treated Ms. Previn in the same way he treated Ms. Farrow's other children from her prior marriage, rarely even speaking to them. In September of 1991 Ms. Previn began to attend Drew College in New Jersey. In December 1991 two events coincided. Mr. Allen's adoptions of Dylan and Moses were finalized and Mr. Allen began his sexual relationship with their sister Soon-Yi Previn.

In January of 1992, Mr. Allen took the photographs of Ms. Previn, which were discovered on the mantelpiece in his apartment by

📖 **CASE 6-1 continued**

Ms. Farrow and were introduced into evidence at the IAS proceeding. Mr. Allen in his trial testimony stated that he took the photos at Ms. Previn's suggestion and that he considered them erotic and not pornographic. We have viewed the photographs and do not share Mr. Allen's characterization of them. We find the fact that Mr. Allen took them at a time when he was formally assuming a legal responsibility for two of Ms. Previn's siblings to be totally unacceptable. The distinction Mr. Allen makes between Ms. Farrow's other children and Dylan, Satchel and Moses is lost on this Court. The children themselves do not draw the same distinction that Mr. Allen does. This is sadly demonstrated by the profound effect his relationship with Ms. Previn has had on the entire family. Allen's testimony that the photographs of Ms. Previn "were taken, as I said before, between two consenting adults wanting to do this" demonstrates a chosen ignorance of his and Ms. Previn's relationships to Ms. Farrow, his three children and Ms. Previn's other siblings. His continuation of the relationship, viewed in the best possible light, shows a distinct absence of judgment. It demonstrates to this court Mr. Allen's tendency to place inappropriate emphasis on his own wants and needs and to minimize and even ignore those of his children. At the very minimum, it demonstrates an absence of any parenting skills.

We recognize Mr. Allen's acknowledgment of the pain his relationship with Ms. Previn has caused the family. We also note his testimony that he tried to insulate the rest of the family from the "dispute" that resulted, and tried to "de-escalate the situation" by attempting to "placate" Ms. Farrow. It is true that Ms. Farrow's failure to conceal her feelings from the rest of the family and the acting out of her feelings of betrayal and anger toward Mr. Allen enhanced the effect of the situation on the rest of her family. We note though that the reasons for her behavior, however prolonged and extreme, are clearly visible in the record. On the other hand the record contains no acceptable explanation for Allen's commencement of the sexual relationship with Ms. Previn at the time he was adopting Moses and Satchel [*sic*], or for the continuation of that relationship at the time he was supposedly experiencing the joys of fatherhood.

While the petitioner's testimony regarding his attempts to de-escalate the dispute and to insulate the family from it, displays a measure of concern for his three children, it is clear that he should have realized the inevitable consequences of his actions well before his relationship with Ms. Previn became intimate. Allen's various inconsistent statements to Farrow of his intentions regarding Ms. Previn and his attempt to exonerate himself from any wrong doing, make it difficult for this Court to find that his expressed concern for the welfare of the family is genuine.

***

Therefore, we hold that in view of the totality of the circumstances, the best interests of these children would be served by

📖 **CASE 6-1 continued**

remaining together in the custody of Ms. Farrow, with the parties abiding by the [supervised] visitation schedule established by the trial court.

DISCUSSION TOPIC

The decision in the custody dispute between Woody Allen and Mia Farrow turned upon what the court calls "a distinct absence of judgment." What assumptions about family life underlie the opinion? Does the court articulate the values it believes significant? In this case the trial court did not receive testimony from an anthropologist, but it did hear from several psychiatrists. On what sort of evidence, if any, do you think the court's conclusions about the absence of judgment was based? Do you think the court was shocked by Mr. Allen's conduct? Were you? Do you think the court correctly weighed the weaknesses of each parent, Mr. Allen's poor judgment against Ms. Farrow's exacerbation of the situation?

Continuity

One of the assumptions courts often rely upon in custody cases is the belief that children need stability and continuity in their lives. This is one of the "self-evident truths" that most of us would agree with. Surprisingly, it was not a strong judicial consideration until about the middle of this century, when "experts" began to document what lay people had known all along -- the adverse effects children suffer when abruptly separated from familiar surroundings and loved caretakers. Even now, the principle is sometimes stated only to be overridden. In *Louise E.S. v. W. Stephen S.*, 64 N.Y.2d 946, 488 N.Y.S.2d 637 (1985), for example, the Court of Appeals held that stability was an important consideration, but not as important as the ability to provide for the child's emotional and intellectual development and the quality of the home environment and the parental guidance provided. In that case, the court switched custody to the father because the mother "paid insufficient attention to the child's development, with the result that he had few peers with whom to interact, was excessively absent from school, spent little, if any, time elsewhere than on petitioner's farm or at school, and had developed a behavioral problem in relation to his classmates."

Religion

When religion is a factor in a custody dispute, the courts are squeezed between constitutional amendments. The court cannot prefer one religion over another, or even one religion over no religion, because that would constitute an establishment of religion in violation of the Establishment Clause of the First Amendment. Neither can it interfere with a parent's right to expose the child to religion or to involve the child in worship, except in cases where such exposure is presenting a clear harm or risk of harm to the child. That would be an interference with the free exercise of religion and with the parent's right to raise the child without governmental interference. If, as discussed in Chapters 3 and 4, the parents have agreed that the child will be raised in a particular religion, the courts will gladly enforce the agreement, absent a showing that the child is being endangered by such exposure. In *Spring v. Glawon*, 89 A.D.2d 980, 454 N.Y.S.2d 140 (2 Dept. 1982), for example, the parents had agreed that the child was to have no religious upbringing without the express permission of both parents. The mother after the divorce enrolled the child in a Catholic school where he was receiving religious instruction. The court enforced the stipulation in the divorce judgment and directed the mother to remove the child from parochial school and enroll him in a public school.

If the parents have not reached an agreement, the general rule is that it is the right of the custodial parent to determine the child's religious educational program. *Weiss v. Weiss*, 52 N.Y.2d 170, 436 N.Y.S.2d 862 (1981). Even if the custodial parent changes to a different religion after the divorce than that practiced during the marriage, the courts are reluctant to interfere in the absence of an express agreement between the parents concerning the child's religious upbringing. In *De Luca v. De Luca*, 202 A.D.2d 580, 609 N.Y.S.2d 80 (2 Dept. 1994), both parents had been at least nominally Roman Catholics before and during their marriage. After their divorce, however, the mother, who was the custodial parent, became a Jehovah's Witness. The father petitioned for custody, claiming he was concerned that the Jehovah's Witness religion would not allow his children to receive proper medical attention and that the religion's prohibition against celebrating birthdays and holidays, including Christmas and Halloween, would have an adverse effect on the children. The Second Department refused to restrict the mother's right to expose the children to the Jehovah's Witness practices, stating, "Only when moral, mental, and physical conditions are so bad that they seriously affect the health or morals of the children should the court be called upon to act with respect to the disagreement between parents over the internal arrangements of family life."

Keeping Siblings Together

Courts often state that it is desirable to keep siblings together. Sometimes this is offered as a reason to disregard a child's expressed preference to reside with the parent to whom the court is *not* awarding custody, as in *Friederwitzer* (Case 4-2). At other times it seems to be used as a make-weight argument in a case where the court senses it is on thin ice. In *Fountain v. Fountain*, 83 A.D.2d 694, 442 N.Y.S.2d 604 (3 Dept. 1981), aff'd 55 N.Y.2d 838, 447 N.Y.S.2d 703, the court in awarding custody to the father stressed the advantages in continuity and noted a "strong policy" of keeping siblings together. Reading the dissent, however, one learns that nine months earlier the father "had violently assaulted [the mother], threatened to kill himself with a gun then in his immediate possession, and threatened either his wife or harm to himself with a knife in his immediate possession -- all in the presence or hearing of his children." The dissent also notes that the father had abducted the children from the mother after she had requested child support from him.

Willingness to Promote Relationship with Non-Custodial Parent

Situations in which one parent has alienated the children from the other parent present an uncomfortable dilemma to courts. On the one hand, the parent's conduct in interfering with visitation, making up false charges against the other parent, or speaking ill of the other parent in front of the children, is repugnant to the court. No judge wants to condone or reward such conduct. On the other hand, the parent has often been so successful in brainwashing the children that they are thoroughly estranged from or even afraid of the other parent. What remedies can a court employ to correct such a situation? The court may punish the parent for contempt for refusal to obey existing orders, as is discussed in the section on enforcement below. Sometimes, however, the parent is so obsessed with continuing the battle that even the threat of incarceration will not end the campaign of alienation, and sometimes the parent is sufficiently indirect in manipulating the children so that it is difficult even to prove a violation. Usually in such cases the parent against whom the campaign is being waged asks the court for custody of the child in order to reduce the influence of the alienating parent.

At first glance, the notion of awarding custody to the beleaguered parent has much appeal. It is decisive. It seems just. Remember, though, that the court's duty is to protect the *child's* interest, not to vindicate the rights of either parent. If the child perceives the "innocent" parent as a stranger or as a monster, an award of custody to that parent may be deeply upsetting to the child. Also, the "innocent" parent may not, on balance, be the better parent. He or she may not have as suitable a home or may have less time to spend with the child or may live a great distance from the child's extended family and playmates. The "bad" parent may be an outstanding parent in all respects but for the obsessive desire to obliterate the other parent from the child's life.

Faced with such hard choices, the courts try to look at the big picture, what the courts call "the totality of the circumstances." In *Betancourt v. Boughton*, 204 A.D.2d 804, 611 N.Y.S.2d 941 (3 Dept. 1994), the court awarded custody to the father after the mother repeatedly interfered with his visitation rights. The court noted that the mother "simply fails to recognize and appreciate respondent's role as the children's father and/or her obligation to encourage the children to develop a meaningful relationship with him." Similarly, the Fourth Department affirmed a Family Court judge's decision to switch custody to a father after the mother filed numerous false reports against him of physical and sexual abuse of the children. *Beyer v. Tranelli-Ashe*, 195 A.D.2d 972, 600 N.Y.S.2d 598 (4 Dept. 1993). In *Gloria S. v. Richard B.*, 80 A.D.2d 72, 437 N.Y.S.2d 411 (2 Dept. 1981) the Second Department awarded custody to the mother after the father, who had custody during the pendency of the litigation, frustrated the mother's visitation and secretly moved the child to Florida while the case was pending. Justice Weinstein's opinion in this matter movingly expresses the frustration courts experience in such cases: "This appeal places before the court another of those unfortunate child custody disputes in which parents, in vying with each other for the privilege of having custody over the object of their mutual affections, engage in conduct which inevitably harms all parties, but most of all the innocent child. We are called upon to determine that course which will further the law's well-settled mandate that the best interests of the child must always be paramount, as well as the equally well-established aversion to allowing a party to benefit from his own wrongful acts."

On the other hand, in a case where both parents were concerned and loving parents, but the father's work schedule made him less available to the child, the Second Department reversed a Family Court judge's transfer of custody to the father. The mother in that case had not waged a sustained campaign of alienation, but had moved to a new school district, which caused the child to have to leave the school where she had been doing very well. *Sullivan v. Sullivan,* 190 A.D.2d 852, 594 N.Y.S.2d 276 (2 Dept. 1993). Admittedly, it is difficult to predict the outcome of such a case. What is clear, however, is that interference with the other parent's relationship with the child is never a sound legal strategy. If a client can be helped through counseling or mediation to behave cooperatively and respectfully toward the other parent, psychological damage to the child and possibly dire legal consequences may be avoided.

Race As a Factor in Custody Disputes

Flexible though it is, the concept of "best interest of the child" cannot be used to condone or legitimize racial prejudice in violation of the Equal Protection Clause of the Constitution, as Case 6-2 demonstrates.

CASE 6-2

PALMORE v. SIDOTI
466 U.S. 429, 104 S.Ct. 1879 (1984)

CHIEF JUSTICE BURGER delivered the opinion of the Court.

    We granted certiorari to review a judgment of a state court divesting a natural mother of the custody of her infant child because of her remarriage to a person of a different race.

I

    When petitioner Linda Sidoti-Palmore and respondent Anthony J. Sidoti, both Caucasians, were divorced in May 1980 in Florida, the mother was awarded custody of their three-year-old daughter.

    In September 1981 the father sought custody of the child by filing a petition to modify the prior judgment because of charged conditions. The change was that the child's mother was then

📖 **CASE 6-2 continued**

cohabiting with a Negro, Clarence Palmore, Jr., whom she married two months later. Additionally, the father made several allegations of instances in which the mother had not properly cared for the child.

After hearing testimony from both parties and considering a court counselor's investigative report, the court noted that the father had made allegations about the child's care, but the court made no findings with respect to these allegations. On the contrary, the court made a finding that "there is no issue as to either party's devotion to the child, adequacy of housing facilities, or respectability of the new spouse of either parent."...

The court then addressed the recommendations of the court counselor, who had made an earlier report "in [another] case coming out of this circuit also involving the social consequences of an interracial marriage."...From this vague reference to that earlier case, the court turned to the present case and noted the recommendation for a change in custody because "the wife [petitioner] has chosen for herself and for her child, a life-style unacceptable to her father *and to society*....The child...is, or at school age will be, subject to environmental pressures not of choice."...

The court then concluded that the best interests of the child would be served by awarding custody to the father. The court's rationale is contained in the following:

> "The father's evident resentment of the mother's choice of a black partner is not sufficient to wrest custody from the mother. It is of some significance, however, that the mother did see fit to bring a man into her home and carry on a sexual relationship with him without being married to him. Such action tended to place gratification of her own desires ahead of her concern for the child's future welfare. *This Court feels that despite the strides that have been made in bettering relations between the races in this country, it is inevitable that Melanie will, if allowed to remain in her present situation and attains school age and thus more vulnerable to peer pressures, suffer from the social stigmatization that is sure to come."* ...

The Second District Court of Appeal affirmed without opinion, thus denying the Florida Supreme Court jurisdiction to review the case.

II

The judgment of a state court determining or reviewing a child custody decision is not ordinarily a likely candidate for review by this Court. However, the court's opinion, after stating that the "father's evident resentment of the mother's choice of a black partner is not sufficient" to deprive her of custody, then turns to what it regarded as the

📖 **CASE 6-2 continued**

damaging impact on the child from remaining in a racially-mixed household....This raises important federal concerns arising from the Constitution's commitment to eradicating discrimination based on race.

The Florida court did not focus directly on the parental qualifications of the natural mother or her present husband, or indeed on the father's qualifications to have custody of the child. The court found that "there is no issue as to either party's devotion to the child, adequacy of housing facilities, or respectability of the new spouse of either parent." This, taken with the absence of any negative finding as to the quality of the care provided by the mother, constitutes a rejection of any claim of petitioner's unfitness to continue the custody of her child.

The court correctly stated that the child's welfare was the controlling factor. But that court was entirely candid and made no effort to place its holding on any ground other than race. Taking the court's findings and rationale at face value, it is clear that the outcome would have been different had petitioner married a Caucasian male of similar respectability. A core purpose of the Fourteenth Amendment was to do away with all governmentally-imposed discrimination based on race. ...Such classifications are subject to the most exacting scrutiny; to pass constitutional muster, they must be justified by a compelling governmental interest and must be "necessary...to the accomplishment" of its legitimate purpose....

The State, of course, has a duty of the highest order to protect the interests of minor children, particularly those of tender years. In common with most states, Florida law mandates that custody determinations be made in the best interests of the children involved. ...The goal of granting custody based on the best interests of the child is indisputably a substantial governmental interest for purposes of the Equal Protection Clause.

It would ignore reality to suggest that racial and ethnic prejudices do not exist or that all manifestations of those prejudices have been eliminated. There is a risk that a child living with a step-parent of a different race may be subject to a variety of pressures and stresses not present if the child were living with parents of the same racial or ethnic origin.

The question, however, is whether the reality of private biases and the possible injury they might inflict are permissible considerations for removal of an infant child from the custody of its natural mother. We have little difficulty concluding that they are not. The Constitution cannot control such prejudices but neither can it tolerate them. Private biases may be outside the reach of the law, but the law cannot, directly or indirectly, give them effect.

***

Whatever problems racially-mixed households may pose for children in 1984 can no more support a denial of constitutional rights than could the stresses that residential integration was thought to entail in 1917.

📖 **CASE 6-2 continued**

The effects of racial prejudice, however real, cannot justify a racial classification removing an infant child from the custody of its natural mother found to be an appropriate person to have such custody.

    The judgment of the District Court of Appeal is reversed.

    It is so ordered.

DISCUSSION TOPIC

Three years before the U.S. Supreme Court's decision in *Palmore v. Sidoti*, a New York trial court judge was faced with a bitter custody dispute involving the interracial child of a mixed-race marriage. The father, who was black, argued that the child's best interest would be achieved by awarding custody to him, the parent with whom the child would be racially identified by a racially conscious society. After reviewing nationwide opinions in custody cases where race was a factor, the court concluded that race "is simply one of many factors which may be considered in a contest between biological parents for custody of an interracial child." Considering all the factors in the case, the court felt that the mother was the more suitable custodian and awarded custody to her. *Farmer v. Farmer*, 109 Misc.2d 137, 439 N.Y.S.2d 584 (N.Y. Sup. Ct.. 1981). Subsequent to the *Palmore* decision, race has virtually ceased to be mentioned as a factor in custody cases between parents. In light of the *Palmore* decision, do you think the *Farmer* court should have held that race is not a factor to be considered at all?

Child's Wishes

In keeping with the modern trend toward treating the child as a person in his or her own right rather than as the property of the parents, courts now consider the child's wishes in determining custody. Courts use several methods, usually in combination, to insure that the child's point of view is made known to the court including:

- Appointment of a law guardian and/or guardian ad litem to represent the child in the litigation;
- Interview of the child by a social worker and/or mental health professional;
- Interview of the child by the judge.

How much weight the court accords the child's wishes depends on the age and maturity of the child. *Eschbach v. Eschbach*, 56 N.Y.2d 167, 451 N.Y.S.2d 658 (1982). The court will also be sensitive to any signs that the child has been coached, bribed or otherwise influenced by one of the parents and will give less weight to the child's expressed preferences when the child has been influenced. See *Spetter v. Spetter*, 133 A.D.2d 750, 520 N.Y.S.2d 39 (2 Dept. 1987). When the "child" is a headstrong teenager, the old joke may come to mind:

"Where does a six hundred pound gorilla sleep? Anywhere he chooses." The court is not obliged to follow the child's wishes, however, but weighs them along with the many other factors bearing on the question of best interest.

Legal Representation for the Child

Although appointment of a legal representative for a child who is the subject of a custody dispute is not mandatory, it is highly preferred, especially when the child in question is old enough to be verbal and to have a point of view to communicate. See *Ladizhensky v. Ladizhensky,* 184 A.D.2d 756, 585 N.Y.S.2d 771 (2 Dept. 1992); *Hall v. Keats*, 184 A.D.2d 825, 584 N.Y.S.2d 212 (3 Dept. 1992). Both section 202.16(f) of the Uniform Civil Rules for the Supreme Court and Family Court Act section 249 authorize the court to appoint a law guardian for the child. The term **law guardian** is defined in FCA § 241 as "counsel" who "helps protect" a child's interest. Long before the Family Court Act was enacted, courts appointed **guardians ad litem** to protect the interests of persons suffering from a legal disability, a category which includes children as well as adults incapacitated by mental illness or mental retardation. Under the Family Court Act a law guardian must be an attorney [FCA § 242], whereas the guardian ad litem need only be a mature adult of sound and independent judgment. The function of the child's representative, by whatever name, is to make the child's wishes known to the court, to advocate for the child's point of view, and to make sure that the case is thoroughly investigated and all information relevant to the child's best interest is presented to the court. The child's legal representative also has standing to appeal the custody decision. FCA § 1120(b).

The child has a legal right to chose his or her own law guardian, but in most cases the court selects the law guardian or guardian ad litem from a variety of sources, depending on what resources are available in a particular community. Within New York City, for example, a law guardian might be an attorney employed by the Juvenile Rights Division of the Legal Aid Society or might be a member of one of the Appellate Division's Law Guardian panels or might come from a child advocacy organization such as Lawyers for Children. A guardian ad litem might be assigned from the New York Society for the Prevention of Cruelty to Children, which also provides legal representation, or from a social work organization which is providing services to the child. Usually the law guardian is compensated through public or charitable funds, although in some cases the courts have ordered parents to pay all or part of the law guardian's fee. See *Anonymous v. Anonymous,* 222 A.D.2d 295, 636 N.Y.S.2d 14 (1 Dept. 1995).

Forensic Evaluations

Evaluations and reports of investigations performed by social workers, probation officers and mental health professionals are often used in custody cases. These evaluations are referred to by the shorthand term "**forensics**," meaning that they are evaluations performed for the purposes of litigation. Courts rely on forensic evaluators to provide unbiased factual information and expert opinion. The court will pay particular attention to the evaluator's presentation of the child's wishes, since the evaluator will be someone trained in interviewing children. The forensic evaluation usually uncovers not only what the child *says* he wants, which may have been coached by a parent, but what the child's behavior, body language, facial expressions and mood reveal about his or her true feelings for each parent.

If the adequacy of the child's home environment is disputed, the court is likely to order a home investigation by a probation officer or social worker. If the psychological condition of the child or either parent is questioned, the court may order a psychological or mental health evaluation. In many cases, the court orders both home studies and psychological evaluations. In cases where money is no object, the parties may each retain their own set of evaluators. Since each set of evaluators usually makes recommendations favoring the party who retained them, this leads to a "battle of the experts." Multiple evaluations are expensive for the parents and hard on the child. To avoid such waste, the court may order the parties to agree upon one set of evaluators or to submit to examination by a neutral expert appointed by the court.

Social workers, psychologists, psychiatrists and other similar professionals who perform evaluations in custody cases are **expert witnesses**. An expert witness is one who by reason of his or her education, training, or professional experience or professional licensing is allowed to state an opinion on an issue within the scope of his or her expertise. Whoever calls the professional as a witness must satisfy the court as to the witness' credentials before asking the witness to state an opinion. If a professional has been recognized as an expert by any court, a later court is more likely also to deem him or her expert on the same subject. Of course, experts testify in all sorts of cases, not just family law matters. All America heard the testimony of the experts on blood analysis who testified about DNA in the televised criminal trial of O.J. Simpson, for example.

Lay witnesses, those who are not qualified as experts, are allowed to testify only about what they know through their own senses. With limited exceptions, lay witnesses are not permitted to state an opinion; they may state only what they saw, heard, touched, tasted, or smelled. The few exceptions to the lay witness rule pertain to matters within the ordinary experience of all people. Thus, a lay witness is allowed to testify that a person appeared drunk, but would not be allowed to state that the person is an alcoholic. This distinction presents particular complications in custody trials, since almost everyone thinks they are "expert" in child-rearing.

If the parties are involved in the selection of the forensic evaluators, the legal assistant may be called upon to help locate an available evaluator and to schedule the appointments for the firm's client. Attorneys often maintain a "little black book" of experts who are available to perform such evaluations.

They rely on word-of-mouth from other attorneys who have used a particular evaluator and on their own experiences with that professional. If the firm in which you are employed does not already have such a reference, offer to begin one. Be sure to include feedback from your firm's lawyers about each experience with the evaluator. Did the court accept the opinion of this evaluator? Did the witness testify in a professional and convincing manner? What precisely is the scope of this professional's expertise? Did the evaluator appear to have any bias or preconceived ideas that might present difficulties in a particular case? (For all their supposed neutrality, some expert witnesses are reputed to be "pro-mother" or "pro-father," for example.) Was the evaluator courteous to the litigants? How much time did the evaluator spend with each party? If the attorney in charge of the case is stumped in finding an expert, a good place to begin looking is through the Appellate Division of the department in which the custody case will be tried. Each department maintains a list of experts suggested by attorneys on the Law Guardian and Assigned Indigent Counsel Panels.

If you are asked to contact an expert who may be asked to perform a forensic evaluation, use a checklist such as Form 6-1 to make sure you obtain all the required information.

FORM 6-1

CHECKLIST FOR PRELIMINARY CONTACT WITH A FORENSIC EVALUATOR

1. Identify yourself and state whom your firm represents and the name of the attorney handling the case.

2. State the purpose of your call; for example, "Mr. Jones has asked me to inquire whether you would be available to perform a psychological evaluation of both parents and the child in a pending custody case." If the case involves unusual issues, such as allegations of sexual abuse of the children or domestic violence between the parents, be sure to inform the prospective evaluator, as such issues may require specialized expertise.

3. State the name(s) of the other parties to the case and the name(s) of the attorneys representing those parties.

4. Ask the expert whether he or she has ever previously treated or evaluated any party or family member of a party to the case.

5. Ask whether the expert has any other social or professional connection with any party or with the judge to whom the case is assigned.

6. Ask the expert how many similar evaluations he or she has

📁 **FORM 6-1   continued**

performed and whether he or she has ever been qualified as an expert in a court of law.

7. If the expert has previously been qualified in a court, how many times, in what courts, and in what field of expertise?

8. Ask what hourly fee the expert charges for such evaluations. If the maximum hourly rate has been predetermined, as is the case when the expert will be paid through the Law Guardian or Assigned Counsel Panel, ask the expert if he or she would accept the assignment at that rate of compensation.

9. Ask what the fee will be for the preparation of a written report and for testifying in court, if necessary. (This may be an hourly rate or a flat fee or a half-day or daily rate.)

10. Ask how many interviews the expert will require with each party and what length each interview will be.

11. Ask the expert how soon he or she would be able to begin the evaluation and when it could be completed. If the court has already ruled that the evaluation must be completed by a certain date, ask the expert if he or she could comply with that schedule.

12. Ask the expert to fax or mail an up-to-date resume or curriculum vitae (CV) to the attorney handing the case.

13. Thank the expert for taking the time to speak with you and say that you will pass all the information on to the attorney handling the case.

Interview of Child by the Judge

It is well settled that the judge trying a custody case may interview the child to ascertain the child's wishes. To make the child feel as relaxed as possible, the interview usually takes place in the judge's chambers or robing room rather than in the courtroom. Thus, the judge's discussion with the child is called an *in camera* **interview**, a Latin term which means "in chambers." This term has nothing to do with photography; do not confuse this procedure with the entirely different process by which a child's testimony in criminal proceedings is shown to the defendant through closed-circuit video.

The judge has wide discretion in setting the ground rules for the interview with the child. Depending on how old and how nervous or frightened the child is, the court may speak to the child alone or may permit the attorneys to be present. *Lincoln v. Lincoln*, 24 N.Y.2d 270, 299 N.Y.S.2d 842 (1969). The judge may do all the questioning of the child or may allow the attorneys to question so long as they do not badger or intimidate the child. The court reporter must record the interview. FCA § 664(a). If the transcript is ordered for appeal, the reporter transcribes the interview separately and sends that portion of the transcript directly to the Appellate Division, thus preserving the confidentiality of the child's statements. FCA § 664(b).

Parent Versus Non-Parent Custody Disputes

An important legacy of our common law tradition is the presumption that a child's best interest lies in being in the custody of a natural parent. This presumption embodies the fundamental public policy that the government should not intrude upon the sanctity of the family without very good reason. A court should not take a child away from its natural parent and give the child to a non-parent, even to a relative, just because the court may think the non-parent may do a "better" job of raising the child. The distinction here is between parents and all others. Relatives do not have any greater rights than a total stranger to take a child from the custody of the parents.

As with the other presumptions we have discussed, the effect of the presumption in favor of the natural parent is that the burden is put on the non-parent to overcome the presumption. Until 1976, courts had held that the presumption could be rebutted only by proof that the parent was unfit or had abandoned or surrendered the child. In that year, however, the Court of Appeals ruled in *Bennett v. Jeffreys* (Case 6-3) that the non-parent might also show "extraordinary circumstances" to rebut the presumption. Only if the non-parent can show unfitness, surrender, abandonment, persisting neglect, or other extraordinary circumstances does the court move on to a full best interest inquiry in which the parent and the non-parent stand on equal footing. *Bennett v. Jeffreys* is one of the most frequently cited cases in New York law.

📖 CASE 6-3

BENNETT v. JEFFREYS
40 N.Y.2d 543, 387 N.Y.S.2d 821 (1976)

BREITEL, Chief Judge.

     Petitioner is the natural mother of Gina Marie Bennett, now an eight-year-old girl. The mother in this proceeding seeks custody of her daughter from respondent, to whom the child had been entrusted since just after birth. Family Court ruled that, although the mother had not surrendered or abandoned the child and was not unfit, the child should remain with the present custodian, a former schoolmate of the child's grandmother. The Appellate Division reversed, one Justice dissenting, and awarded custody to the mother. Respondent custodian appeals.

CASE 6-3   continued

The issue is whether the natural mother, who has not surrendered, abandoned, or persistently neglected her child, may, nevertheless, be deprived of the custody of her child because of a prolonged separation from the child for most of its life.

There should be a reversal and a new hearing before the Family Court. The State may not deprive a parent of the custody of a child absent surrender, abandonment, persisting neglect, unfitness or other like extraordinary circumstances. If any of such extraordinary circumstances are present, the disposition of custody is influenced or controlled by what is in the best interest of the child. In the instant case extraordinary circumstances, namely, the prolonged separation of mother and child for most of the child's life, require inquiry into the best interest of the child. Neither court below examined sufficiently into the qualifications and backgrounds of the mother and the custodian to determine the best interest of the child. Consequently a new hearing should be held.

Some eight years ago, the mother, then 15 years old, unwed, and living with her parents, gave birth to the child. Under pressure from her mother, she reluctantly acquiesced in the transfer of the newborn infant to an older woman, Mrs. Jeffreys, a former classmate of the child's grandmother. The quality and quantity of the mother's later contacts with the child were disputed. The Family Court found, however, that there was no statutory surrender or abandonment. Pointedly, the Family Court found that the mother was not unfit. The Appellate Division agreed with this finding.

There was evidence that Mrs. Jeffreys intended to adopt the child at an early date. She testified, however, that she could not afford to do so and admitted that she never took formal steps to adopt.

The natural mother is now 23 and will soon graduate from college. She still lives with her family, in a private home with quarters available for herself and the child. The attitude of the mother's parents, however, is changed and they are now anxious that their daughter keep her child.

Mrs. Jeffreys, on the other hand, is now separated from her husband, is employed as a domestic, and, on occasion, has kept the child in a motel. It is significant that Mrs. Jeffreys once said that she was willing to surrender the child to the parent upon demand when the child reached the age of 12 or 13 years.

* * *

Absent extraordinary circumstance, narrowly categorized, it is not within the power of a court, or, by delegation of the Legislature or court, a social agency, to make significant decisions concerning the custody of children, merely because it could make a better decision or disposition. The State is *parens patriae* and always has been, but it has not displaced the parent in right or responsibility. Indeed, the courts and the law would, under existing constitutional principles, be powerless to supplant parents except for grievous cause or necessity.

📖 **CASE 6-3   continued**

...Examples of cause or necessity permitting displacement of or intrusion on parental control would be fault or omission by the parent seriously affecting the welfare of a child, the preservation of the child's freedom from serious physical harm, illness or death, or the child's right to an education, and the like....

The parent has a "right" to rear its child, and the child has a "right" to be reared by its parent. However, there are exceptions created by extraordinary circumstances, illustratively, surrender, abandonment, persisting neglect, unfitness and unfortunate or involuntary disruption of custody over an extended period of time. It is these exceptions which have engendered confusion, sometimes in thought but most often only in language.

The day is long past in this State, if it had ever been, when the right of a parent to the custody of his or her child, where the extraordinary circumstances are present, would be enforced inexorably, contrary to the best interest of the child, on the theory solely of an absolute legal right. Instead, in the extraordinary circumstances, when there is a conflict, the best interest of the child had always been regarded as superior to the right of parental custody. Indeed, analysis of the cases reveals a shifting of emphasis rather than a remaking of substance. This shifting reflects more the modern principle that a child is a person, and not a subperson over whom the parent has an absolute possessory interest. A child has rights too, some of which are of a constitutional magnitude....

***

To recapitulate: intervention by the State in the right and responsibility of a natural parent to custody of her or his child is warranted if there is first a judicial finding of surrender, abandonment, unfitness, persistent neglect, unfortunate or involuntary extended disruption of custody, or other equivalent but rare extraordinary circumstance which would drastically affect the welfare of the child. It is only on such a premise that the courts may then proceed to inquire into the best interest of the child and to order a custodial disposition on that ground.

In custody matters parties and courts may be very dependent on the auxiliary services of psychiatrists, psychologists, and trained social workers. This is good. But it may be an evil when the dependence is too obsequious or routine or the experts too casual. Particularly important is this caution where one or both parties may not have the means to retain their own experts and where publicly compensated experts or experts compensated by only one side have uncurbed leave to express opinions which may be subjective or are not narrowly controlled by the underlying facts.

***

Moreover, the child may be so long in the custody of the nonparent that, even though there had been no abandonment or persisting neglect by the parent, the psychological trauma of removal

📖 CASE 6-3 continued

is grave enough to threaten destruction of the child. Of course, such a situation would offer no opportunity for the court, under the guise of determining the best interest of the child, to weigh the material advantages offered by the adverse parties. As noted earlier, such considerations do not determine the best interest of the child....

***

In this case, there were extraordinary circumstances present, namely, the protracted separation of mother from child, combined with the mother's lack of an established household of her own, her unwed state, and the attachment of the child to the custodian. Thus, application of the principles discussed required an examination by the court into the best interest of the child.

***

In all of this troublesome and troubled area there is a fundamental principle. Neither law, nor policy, nor the tenets of our society would allow a child to be separated by officials of the State from its parent unless the circumstances are compelling. Neither the lawyers nor Judges in the judicial system nor the experts in psychology or social welfare may displace the primary responsibility of child-raising that naturally and legally falls to those who conceive and bear children. Again, this is not so much because it is their "right", but because it is their responsibility. The nature of human relationships suggests overall the natural workings of the child-rearing process as the most, desirable alternative. But absolute generalizations do not fulfill themselves and multifold exceptions give rise to cases where the natural workings of the process fail, not so much because a legal right had been lost, but because the best interest of the child dictates a finding of failure.

Accordingly, the order of the Appellate Division should be reversed, without costs, and the proceeding remitted to Family Court for a new hearing.

***

DISCUSSION TOPIC

In expanding the grounds upon which the presumption in favor of the natural parent could be rebutted to include protracted separation of the child from the natural parent, the court was influenced by the "psychological parent" theory then in vogue among mental health professionals. This theory stressed the psychological damage to the child incurred as a result of separation from the person to whom the child was "bonded," that is, whom the child perceived as his or her parent regardless of a biological connection. You can see that the court was wary of the potential for abuse of this concept, however, and the opinion cautions against over-reliance on "experts." How much weight do you think a court should give to the opinion of social workers, psychologists and psychiatrists in reaching a determination about custody?

The phrase "other extraordinary circumstances" cried out for judicial construction, and in the years since *Bennett v. Jeffreys* countless opinions have defined what circumstances are sufficiently extraordinary to meet the test. In *Lake v. Van Wormer*, 216 A.D.2d 735, 628 N.Y.S.2d 440 (3 Dept. 1995), extraordinary circumstances were found and custody awarded to an adult sibling based on proof that the relationship between the child and parent was contentious and characterized by repeated use of abusive language and that the parent drank. In *Commissioner of Social Services v. Sarah P.*, 216 A.D.2d 387, 629 N.Y.S.2d 47 (2 Dept. 1995), the fact that the children had sparse contact with the father while living with their grandmother all their lives, that the children had special medical needs, and that they would be separated from their step-brother if custody were awarded to the father, combined to make out extraordinary circumstances. The traumatic effect of separation from siblings was also held sufficient in *Curry v. Ashby*, 129 A.D.2d 310, 517 N.Y.S.2d 990 (1 Dept. 1987). A father's history of domestic violence and spousal abuse has also been held to constitute extraordinary circumstances that justified a best interest inquiry and award of custody to the maternal grandparents. *Antoinette M. v. Paul Seth G.*, 202 A.D.2d 429, 608 N.Y.S.2d 703 (2 Dept. 1994).

On the other hand, the fact that a father was suffering from post-traumatic stress disorder from his combat in Vietnam has been held not to constitute extraordinary circumstances, [*Anderson v. Mott*, 199 A.D.2d 961, 606 N.Y.S.2d 463 (4 Dept. 1993)], as was the fact that a parent used cocaine on a recreational basis prior to the birth of the child, [*Alfredo S. v. Nassau County Dept. of Social Services*, 172 A.D.2d 528, 568 N.Y.S.2d 123 (2 Dept. 1991)]. A prolonged, voluntary period of separation of the parent from the child remains the most commonly found extraordinary circumstance, but the Court of Appeals has made it clear that a period of separation is entitled to little weight if it is attributable to the parent's efforts to regain custody of the child by lawful means. *Dickson v. Lascaris*, 53 N.Y.2d 204, 440 N.Y.S.2d 884 (1981). For obvious reasons, courts do not wish to encourage the person who has physical possession of a child to draw out the litigation in order to create the lengthy separation that might make out extraordinary circumstances, and neither do they want the parent to use "self-help" to regain possession of the child to avoid such a result.

Foster Parents

When a child is in foster care, the custody of the child is vested in the agency, not in the foster parents. SSL § 383(2). Foster parents do not have standing to initiate custody proceedings for a foster child in their care. *Ninesling v. Nassau County Department of Social Services*, 46 N.Y.2d 382, 413 N.Y.S.2d 626 (1978). They do have a statutory right, however, to **intervene** in any proceeding involving the custody of a child who has been in their care for a year or more. SSL § 383(3). This provision includes several types of proceedings in addition to those filed as "custody" cases, including termination of parental rights proceedings and proceedings for the revocation of an adoption surrender.

The right to intervene, that is to become a party to the case, not only allows the foster parent to present evidence concerning the child's best interest, but also confers the right to appeal the decision, a valuable right indeed.

Procedures

If both parties are New York residents, a custody case can be brought by one of three methods. If the custody issue is part of a matrimonial action in Supreme Court, the request for custody should be included in the matrimonial action summons and complaint, as discussed in Chapter 5. If the custody is to be litigated in a separate case, however, it can be brought on in Supreme Court or Family Court by a **writ of habeas corpus** [DRL § 70; FCA § 651(b)] or in Family Court by an order to show cause with a custody petition. FCA § 651(a). With either a writ of habeas corpus or an order to show cause, notice to the respondent may be as short as the judge thinks comports with due process.

The availability of the two parallel procedures is largely a historical fluke. The writ of habeas corpus (Form 6-2) is an ancient document that requires someone who is allegedly illegally detaining another person to produce the person before the court. You may be more familiar with this writ through its use in criminal cases. Since the issuance of the writ is premised upon the supposed illegality of the detention, there was some question whether it could be used in cases where the person holding the child was doing so under color of law. If a non-parent was seeking custody from a parent, for example, the parent had the presumptive right to custody, and the suitability of proceeding by way of writ of habeas corpus was questionable. Thus, the custody petition brought on by order to show cause (Form 6-3) was devised as an alternative. Courts no longer anguish over such technicalities, and the "illegality" of the detention is understood to lie in the fact that it is alleged to be contrary to the best interest of the child. Still, the writ is the preferred device where a person who has superior legal rights seeks the return of a child from someone who has no legal rights to the child. If, for example, a non-parent took a child for a visit with the parent's permission and then refused to return the child at the agreed-upon time, the writ of habeas corpus would be the proper vehicle, since the parent has custody by operation of law and does not have to petition for it.

FORM 6-2

Secs. 115, 651 F.C.A.; 384–a S.S.L.; 71 D.R.L.   Gen. Form 22 (Petition–Habeas Corpus) 3/92

FAMILY COURT OF THE STATE OF NEW YORK COUNTY OF

....

In the Matter of a Proceeding under Article 6
of the Family Court Act

<table>
<tr><td>   **Petitioner(s),**</td><td>**Docket No.**
PETITION FOR WRIT OF</td></tr>
<tr><td>   –against–</td><td>**HABEAS CORPUS**</td></tr>
<tr><td>   **Respondent(s),**</td><td></td></tr>
</table>

....

TO THE FAMILY COURT:

      The undersigned Petitioner(s), respectfully show that:

      1. Petitioner(s), (resides) (has offices) at
and (is) (are) the   of [insert name, date of birth]
                                             who (is)(are) the subject(s) of this application.

      2. Respondent(s) (resides) (has offices) at
, and (is) (are) the   of said minor(s).

      3. (Upon information and belief,) (T) (t)he aforesaid minor(s) (is) (are) in the possession and control of the Respondent(s) and (has) (have) been since   . (Respondent(s) wrongfully and unlawfully (removed) (held) said minor(s) from the custody of the Petitioner(s) in that (s)he (they) (it)) (Respondent(s) wrongfully prevented or interfered with Petitioner('(s)(') visitation rights with said minor(s) in that (s)he (they) (it))

      4. (That Petitioner(s) (has) (have) requested the return of said minor(s) from Respondent(s) and Respondent(s) (has) (have) failed and refused to return said minor(s) to the custody of the Petitioner(s).)

      5. Said minor(s) (is) (are) not the subject(s) of any order, mandate, judgment or decree of any court of competent jurisdiction nor has any appeal been taken from any such order, mandate, judgment or decree except   , nor does any court or judge of the United States have exclusive jurisdiction to order said minor(s) released.

      6. (The custody of the minor(s) should be returned to the Petitioner(s),) (Visitation rights should be granted to Petitioner(s),) in that

).

      WHEREFORE, Petitioner(s) pray for a Writ of Habeas Corpus directed to the Respondent(s), commanding said Respondent(s) to produce the minor(s) in this Court, in order that (s)he (they) (it) may be given (custody) (possession and control) (of) (visitation rights to) said minor(s).

                                         _____
                                             Petitioner(s)

VERIFICATION

STATE OF NEW YORK)
COUNTY OF   ) ss.:

                                                              being duly sworn,
says that (he) (she) (they) (is) (are) Petitioner(s) in the above–named proceeding and that the foregoing petition is true to (his) (her) their own knowledge, except as to matters therein stated to be alleged on information and belief, and as to those matters (he) (she) (they) believes it to be true.

Subscribed and sworn to before me this
      day of   ,19   .   _____
                                               Petitioner(s)

_____
(Deputy) Clerk of the Court
      Notary Public

FORM 6-3

General Form 1   1/81
(Order to Show Cause)

FAMILY COURT OF THE STATE OF NEW YORK
COUNTY OF

In the Matter of a Proceeding Under
Article   of the Family Court Act

Petitioner,

- against -

Respondent.

Docket No.

ORDER TO SHOW CAUSE

Upon the petition of
verified the   . day of   , 19   , annexed hereto, it
is

ORDERED that
show cause before this Court at
New York, on the   day of   , 19   , at   o'clock
in the   noon of that day, or as soon thereafter as the parties can
be heard, why an order should not be made

and why such other and further relief should not be granted as the Court
may determine, and it is further

ORDERED that service by   of a copy of this Order
together with the papers upon which it is granted upon

on or before the   day of   , 19   , be deemed
sufficient service.

Dated: , 19   .

ENTER

J. F. C.

📁 **FORM 6-3 continued**

`Secs. 467, 549, 651, 652, 654 F.C.A

General Form 17
(Petition–Custody Visitation) 3/92

FAMILY COURT OF THE STATE OF NEW YORK COUNTY OF

....

In the Matter of a Proceeding for (Custody) (Visitation)
under Article Six of the Family Court Act

      Docket No.

               Petitioner,

                                PETITION
                                   for
     –against–   **(CUSTODY) (VISITATION)**

                   Respondent.

....

TO THE FAMILY COURT:

       The undersigned Petitioner respectfully shows that:

1. Petitioner,   , (resides at) (is located at)

2. Petitioner is *

3. (Upon information and belief) Respondent (resides at) (is located at)

4. (Upon information and belief) Respondent is *

5. This proceeding is commenced pursuant to section(s)   of the Family Court Act (in that
an order of referral was made and entered on   , 19   , by the
Supreme Court   County, referring the issue of (custody) (visitation) to
the Family Court of the State of New York in and for the County of   ).

6. The name, present address, age and date of birth of each child affected by this proceeding are as
follows:

NAME	**ADDRESS**	**AGE**	**DATE OF BIRTH**

* State relationship to child. If unrelated to the child (e.g. foster parent, agency or institution) so
state.

📁 **FORM 6-3 continued**

General form 17 page 2

**7. (Petitioner was married to the Respondent on   ,19   , at
           (and on   ,19   .(was legally separated)
(divorced) (the marriage was annulled) by order of   , County of
         .) A true copy of the (judgment) (separation agreement) is annexed hereto).

**8. (An order of filiation was made) (A paternity agreement or compromise was approved) by the
Family Court of   County on   , 19   , concerning the
(Petitioner) (Respondent) and the child(ren) who (is) (are) the subject of this proceeding. A true copy
of said (order) (agreement of compromise) is annexed hereto.

**9. (Upon information and belief) (Petitioner) (Respondent) (obtained custody of the child(ren) on
        , 19   , as follows:

).

**10. There has been a change of circumstances since entry of the (order) (judgment) awarding
(custody) (visitation) in that:

11. It would be in the best interest of the child(ren) to have (custody) (visitation) awarded to the
Petitioner for the following reasons:

12. No previous application has been made to any court or judge for the relief herein requested
(except:

).

     WHEREFORE, Petitioner prays for an order awarding (custody) (visitation) of the child(ren) named
herein to (the Petitioner) (   ) and for such other and further
relief as the Court may determine.

DATED: , 19   .

                                               _____

Petitioner   **VERIFICATION**

STATE OF NEW YORK   )
                        : ss.:
COUNTY OF   )

being duly sworn, says that (s)he is the Petitioner in the above–named proceeding and that the
foregoing petition is true to (his) (her) own knowledge, except as to matters therein stated to be alleged
on information and belief and as to those matters (s)he believes it to be true.

                                               _____
                                                  Petitioner

Sworn to before me this
day of   ,19   .

_____
(Deputy) Clerk of the Court
     Notary Public

** Delete if inapplicable

GUARDIANSHIP

The distinction between custody and **guardianship of the person** of a child is much less clear now than it once was. Historically, custody meant the day-to-day responsibility for the child, whereas guardianship of the person conferred decision-making authority over the child. Nowadays, legal custody carries with it full decision-making authority, and courts conversely assume that guardians will generally also have physical custody of the child. The distinctions that remain are largely procedural. Family Court and Surrogate's Court share concurrent original jurisdiction over guardianship, and both use Surrogate's Court procedures in guardianship cases. FCA § 661. Thus, **citation** is the form of process issued, instead of a summons, and the proceeding results in **letters of guardianship** instead of an order of custody. Interestingly, courts are required to obtain a clearance of the proposed guardian from the State Central Register of Child Abuse and Maltreatment, whereas such clearances are not mandatory in custody cases.

Parents can also name a **testamentary guardian** for their child in their will. A testamentary guardian assumes authority only in the event of the death of the parents. New York also has a new **Standby Guardianship** procedure, whereby a parent can designate someone to be responsible for the child in the event the parents dies or becomes incapacitated. SCPA § 1726. This law, which was enacted in 1994 in response to the AIDS epidemic, allows a parent who suffers from a debilitating or terminal illness to plan for the child's future without naming a testamentary guardian by will. Some such parents own little or no property, and for them the standby guardianship procedure is simpler and faster than probating a will. Because of guardianship's historical association with decision-making authority, some medical providers prefer that a non-parent who is signing a consent for major medical treatment of a child be designated as guardian rather than custodian, and some government agencies prefer to see an order of guardianship before making a non-parent the payee of benefits to which the child is entitled.

UNIFORM CHILD CUSTODY JURISDICTION ACT

Custody cases used to present nightmarish jurisdictional problems, since every state could assume jurisdiction if the child was physically present within the state. If the parents resided in two different states, the courts of each state might have custody cases pending concerning the same child, and all too often they made contradictory orders enforceable only in the state where the order was made. Sometimes one parent even abducted the child from the state where a custody case was pending in order to bring the child to another jurisdiction where that parent hoped to get an order more to his or her liking. To bring some order into this chaos, every state of the United States, the District of Columbia and the Virgin Islands have now enacted the Uniform Child Custody Jurisdiction Act (UCCJA), which is incorporated into our laws as Article 5-A of the Domestic Relations Law.

The purposes of the UCCJA are:

- To avoid jurisdictional competition among states which could result in shifting children from state to state;

- To promote cooperation among courts so that a custody decree is rendered in the state which is most able to make a best interest determination;

- To make sure that custody litigation takes place in the state with which the child and his family have the closest connection and where the most significant evidence is available concerning the child;

- To discourage continuing custody controversies so that the child can have greater security and stability;

- To deter abductions of children so as to obtain custody awards;

- To avoid re-litigation of custody decisions;

- To facilitate the enforcement of custody decrees of other states;

- To promote the exchange of information between various courts concerned with the same child. DRL § 75-b.

Under the UCCJA a New York court should assume jurisdiction of a custody case in only four situations: 1) New York is the child's home state or had been the home state within six months before the child was removed from New York by someone claiming the child's custody; *or* 2) it is in the best interest of the child for New York to assume jurisdiction because the child and at least one contestant for custody have a significant connection with this state *and* there is in New York substantial evidence concerning the child's present or future care, protection, training, and personal relationships; *or* 3) the child is physically present in New York *and* the child has been abandoned, *or* it is necessary in an emergency to protect the child; *or* 4) it appears that no other state would have jurisdiction *or* another state has declined to exercise jurisdiction on the ground that New York is the more appropriate forum to determine custody *and* it is in the best interest of the child for New York to assume jurisdiction. DRL § 75-d.

The critical term **"home state"** is defined in the UCCJA as the state in which the child, at the time of the commencement of the custody proceeding, has resided with his parent(s) or a person acting as parent for at least six consecutive months. If the child is less than six months old, the home state is the state in which the child has resided for a majority of the time since birth. DRL § 75-c (5).

In spite of all the "and's" and "or's" the UCCJA works surprisingly well. Most cases where New York should not assume jurisdiction can be weeded out quickly. Consider the following example:

> Raoul was born in New York. When he was one year old, his parents moved with him to Idaho, where they have lived ever since. Raoul is now a five-year-old kindergartner at his neighborhood school in Idaho. When Raoul's father informed his mother that he wanted a divorce and planned to seek custody of Raoul, the mother fled with Raoul to New York, where she is staying with Raoul's maternal grandparents. After being in New York for three weeks, she files for custody in a New York Family Court. Her custody petition alleges that she has always been the child's primary care giver, that the child is deeply attached to her, and that it is in Raoul's best interest that custody be awarded to the mother.

Applying the criteria of the UCCJA, it is readily apparent that New York should decline jurisdiction. 1) Raoul, although physically present in New York, has not resided in New York for six consecutive months at the time the custody petition was filed. His residence here for the first year of his life does not count for the purpose of establishing which state is his "home state." Idaho is Raoul's "home state." 2) Raoul's mother probably has a significant connection with New York, since she has family here. It may also be argued that Raoul has a significant connection, since he was born in New York. However, all the witnesses and evidence about Raoul's present care, such as his pediatrician and medical records and his school teachers and school records, are in Idaho. To satisfy the this subsection of the statute, the court must find *both* significant connection and evidence available in New York about the present or future care of the child. 3) Raoul has not been abandoned, and the allegations of the mother's petition do not spell out any sort of emergency, such as abuse or neglect of the child. Rather, they are perfectly routine "best interest" allegations. Remember, the issue at this point is not which parent should receive custody, but rather which court should make the custody decision. 4) Idaho would appear to have jurisdiction as the child's "home state," and Idaho has not declined jurisdiction.

Whenever either the petitioner or respondent in a custody case is a resident of a state other than New York, the custody case should be brought on by a UCCJA petition (Form 6-4), regardless of whether the child is physically present in the state. Because the court will have to determine whether New York is the child's home state, the UCCJA petition requires a careful recital in paragraph 7 of all the places the child has resided for the past five years. Note that the petitioner is also required to state in paragraph 9 whether custody proceedings are pending in any other jurisdiction.

▱ **FORM 6-4**

Article 5–A D.R.L.   General Form 19
Secs. 467, 549, 651, 652, 654 F.C.A   (Petition–Custody Visitation) (UCCJA) 3/92

FAMILY COURT OF THE STATE OF NEW YORK COUNTY OF _____

....

In the Matter of a Proceeding for (Custody) (Visitation)
under Article Six of the Family Court Act

                                        Petitioner,   **Docket No.**

        –against–

                                                        PETITION for (CUSTODY)
                                                        (VISITATION)(UNIFORM CHILD
                                        Respondent.   **CUSTODY JURISDICTION ACT)**

....

TO THE FAMILY COURT:
        The undersigned Petitioner respectfully shows that:

1. Petitioner,   , (resides at) (is located at)

2. Petitioner is *

3. (Upon information and belief) Respondent (resides at) (is located at)

4. (Upon information and belief) Respondent is *

5. This proceeding is commenced pursuant to section(s) of the Family Court Act (in that an order
of referral was made and entered on   , 19   , by the Supreme Court
County, referring the issue of (custody) (visitation) to the Family Court of the State of New York in and
for the County of   .) (and
of the Domestic Relations Law).

6. The name, present address, age and date of birth of each child affected by this proceeding are as
follows:
        NAME   **ADDRESS**   **AGE**   **DATE OF BIRTH**

7. (Upon information and belief) During the last five years each child affected by this proceeding lived
at:
        NAME   **ADDRESS**   **DURATION**
                                                                from   to

8. (Upon information and belief) The name and present address of the person(s) with whom each
child lived during the past five years are as follows:
        NAME   **ADDRESS**   **DURATION**
                                                                from   to

9. Petitioner has (not) participated as a (party)(witness) (   )
[specify other capacity] in other litigation concerning the custody of the same child(ren) in (New York
State) (   ) [specify other state] (or any other state).

* State relationship to child(ren). If unrelated to the child(ren) (e.g. foster parent, agency or
  institution), so state.

⬜ FORM 6-4 continued

General Form 19 page 2

10. (Upon information and belief (A) (No) custody proceeding concerning the custody of the same child(ren) is pending in (New York State) (   ) [specify other state] (or any other state) (which has (not) been stayed by order of the court).

**11. (Petitioner was married to the Respondent on   ,19   , at
                     (.) (and on   , 19   , (was) (legally separated) (divorced) (the marriage was annulled) by order of   , County of   .
A true copy of the (judgment) (separation agreement) is annexed hereto.)

**12. (An order of filiation was made) (A paternity agreement or compromise was approved) by the Family Court of   County on   , 19   , concerning the (Petitioner) (Respondent) and the child(ren) who (is)(are) the subject of this proceeding. A true copy of said (order) (agreement of compromise) is annexed hereto.

13. (Upon information and belief) (Petitioner) (Respondent) obtained custody of the child(ren) on   , 19   , as follows:

**14. There has been a change of circumstances since entry of the (order) (judgment) awarding (custody) (visitation) in that:

15. It would be in the best interest of the child(ren) to have (custody) (visitation) awarded to the Petitioner for the following reasons:

16. No previous application has been made to any court or judge for the relief herein requested, (except:).

WHEREFORE, Petitioner prays for an order awarding (custody) (visitation) of the child(ren) named herein to (the Petitioner) (   ) and for such other and further relief as the Court may determine.

DATED: , 19   .

                                                              ——————————————
                                                             Petitioner

STATE OF NEW YORK   )
                           :   ss.:
COUNTY OF   )

being duly sworn, says that (s)he is the Petitioner in the above–named proceeding and that the foregoing petition is true to (his) (her) own knowledge, except as to matters therein stated to be alleged on information and belief and as to those matters (s)he believes it to be true.

                                                              ——————————————
                                                              Petitioner

Sworn to before me this
day of   ,19   .

——————————————————
(Deputy) Clerk of the Court
    Notary Public
** Delete if inapplicable

In a UCCJA case the document which is the equivalent of a summons or order to show cause is called simply a "Notice." Service of the notice may be made by 1) personal delivery to the respondent outside the state, 2) by any form of mail for which a receipt can be obtained (certified or registered mail), or 3) in any other manner the court directs, including publication, if service by personal delivery or mail is "impracticable." Service by whatever means must be made at least 20 days before the hearing date. DRL § 75-f.

If a judge learns at any point during a UCCJA case that custody proceedings are pending in another state, the judge communicates with the judge in the other state to decide which court should proceed. Usually, the two judges simply speak by telephone, and in the vast majority of cases they agree. The judge who is declining jurisdiction then dismisses that custody case and the other court proceeds. The rare cases in which there is disagreement usually involve the "emergency jurisdiction" prong of the UCCJA. If both courts proceed, the matter may ultimately be resolved by application of a Federal statute, the Parental Kidnapping Prevention Act of 1980 (PKPA) (Pub. L. No.96-611, 94 Stat. 3568-73). Because the PKPA is a Federal law, it **preempts** any state statute, including the UCCJA, that is in conflict with it. This means that the Federal statute prevails, and any statute or judicial decision which conflicts with it will not be enforced. The interface between the UCCJA and the PKPA is a subject for specialists, but as a general proposition the PKPA emphasizes the home state concept over the other possible bases of jurisdiction provided in the UCCJA.

Whenever a legal assistant conducting a preliminary interview learns that either the child or one of the parties vying for custody is not in the State of New York, the legal assistant should obtain detailed information about the location and length of stay at all prior addresses throughout the child's life. Information must also be gathered about the connection of each party and the child with New York and the circumstances under which the child was removed from or to New York.

Enforcement

Interference with an order of custody is a serious offense; in fact, it is a felony under the PKPA. Even if criminal charges are not brought, a court may punish the offender for **contempt of court**, which can result in a fine or incarceration for up to six months in jail. At the very least a person who has interfered with a valid order of custody can expect to find his or her future contact with the child severely curtailed.

When a child is wrongfully removed from its custodian, the abductor often takes the child to another state or country. Since the adoption of the UCCJA this strategy is of no benefit to the wrongdoer. Under the UCCJA every state must enforce a valid custody order of a sister state. The procedure is for the clerk of the court that entered the order to provide a certified copy of the order, which should then be filed with the court in the enforcing state. The Department of

Criminal Justice Services in Albany provides information and assistance in cases of child abduction.

If a child under the age of 16 years has been wrongfully removed to another country, the International Child Abduction Remedies Act (ICARA), 42 U.S.C. § 11601, may require the child's return. The ICARA was enacted by Congress in 1980 to implement the Hague Convention treaty on the Civil Aspect of International Child Abduction. The treaty applies only among countries which have ratified it. These countries include most of the nations of Western Europe, as well as Argentina, Mexico, Ecuador, and Israel. Unfortunately, several countries from which New York has a significant number of immigrants, such as the Caribbean and Middle Eastern countries (other than Israel), have not yet ratified the Hague Convention treaty. To find out whether a country is a Hague Convention ratifier, consult the current pocket part of any standard treatise on custody or contact the Department of State in Washington, D.C., which publishes a handbook called International Parental Child Abduction.

Modification

Custody orders may be modified on a showing of changed circumstances, but courts will uproot a child only when it is quite clear that the child's best interests require the change. Thus, courts have held that an improvement in the condition of the non-custodial parent does not in itself constitute changed circumstances. *Wout v. Wout*, 32 A.D.2d 709, 300 N.Y.S.2d 24 (3 Dept. 1969). If a parent has overcome a problem, such as a drug problem, that led to the award of custody to the other parent or even to a non-parent, the court will not automatically transfer custody to the rehabilitated parent. Rather, the court will consider all the best interest factors that are relevant to any custody inquiry, including the child's wishes. If the child is doing well, the present custodian is fit, and the child prefers to remain with the present custodian, the court is unlikely to modify the custody order. Custody orders made after a full best interest hearing are more difficult to modify than those made by agreement of the parties, as you read in the *Friederwitzer* case (Case 4-2).

Unless the Supreme Court order or judgment in a matrimonial proceeding specifies that the Supreme Court retains jurisdiction of the issues of custody and visitation, the Family Court may enforce or modify the Supreme Court order upon a showing of changed circumstances. FCA § 652(b). Thus, if the Supreme Court order is silent on the point, the Family Court can exercise jurisdiction and in such cases possesses all the powers of the Supreme Court. Prior to 1981, Family Court could exercise jurisdiction only if the Supreme Court order contained language authorizing it to do so. Because of this historical background, matrimonial attorneys routinely include in matrimonial orders language conferring jurisdiction on the Family Court. It is important to remember, however, that the absence of such language has the opposite effect in orders entered prior to 1981 from that in orders entered subsequent to the amendment.

VISITATION

Non-Custodial Parent Visitation

The law strongly favors visitation between a non-custodial parent and the child. Older cases described visitation as a "right" of the non-custodial parent, but in keeping with the modern concept of the child as an individual rather than a piece of property, visitation is now viewed as a joint right of the non-custodial parent and the child. *Weiss v. Weiss*, 52 N.Y.2d 170, 436 N.Y.S.2d 862 (1981). Visitation should be frequent and regular, and should be curtailed only if there is substantial evidence that visitation would be detrimental to the welfare of the child. *Janousek v. Janousek*, 108 A.D.2d 782, 485 N.Y.S.2d 305 (2 Dept. 1985); *Nacson v. Nacson*, 166 A.D.2d 510, 560 N.Y.S.2d 792 (2 Dept. 1990); *Matter of Farrugia Children*, 106 A.D.2d 293, 483 N.Y.S.2d 6 (1 Dept. 1984).

Even when a parent cannot be trusted with the unsupervised care of a child, courts attempt to permit visitation to occur by imposing conditions such as supervision of the visits or restriction of the visits to short periods or specified locations. In *James P.W. v. Eileen M.W.*, 136 A.D.2d 549, 523 N.Y.S.2d 169 (2 Dept. 1988), the court ordered supervision because the mother suffered from bipolar mental illness. In *Johnson v. Allen*, 122 A.D.2d 51, 504 N.Y.S.2d 209 (2 Dept. 1986), the father was awarded visitation on condition that he attend Alcoholics Anonymous for a prescribed period.

RELOCATION

One of the thorniest problems our modern, mobile society has presented to the courts is the relocation of a custodial parent far from the home of the non-custodial parent. In Chapter 4 we discussed how a separation agreement may be used to minimize such difficulties when the move of the custodial parent is contemplated at the time of the separation. If the parents have never been married, however, or when the custodial parent's desire to move arises after the parents are already separated or divorced, the issue often lands the parties in court.

The Court of Appeals has recently ruled that the predominant consideration in a relocation case must be the best interest of the child. *Tropea v. Tropea; Browner v. Kenward*, 87 N.Y.2d 727, 642 N.Y.S.2d 575 (1996). The court stated that the rights and needs of the children must outweigh the rights of the custodial and noncustodial parents because the children "are innocent victims of their parents' decision to divorce and are the least equipped to handle the stresses of the changing family situation." In deciding whether to grant the custodial parent permission to move with the child, the courts should consider the impact of the move on the relationship between the child and the non-custodial parent, the parent's reasons for wanting to relocate, and the benefits that the child may enjoy or the harm that may ensue if the move is or is not permitted. "Other considerations that may have a bearing in particular cases," the opinion states, "are the good faith of the parents in requesting or opposing the move, the child's respective attachments to the custodial and non-custodial parent, the possibility of devising a visitation schedule that will enable the non-custodial parent to maintain a meaningful parent-child relationship, the quality of the lifestyle that the child would have if the proposed move were permitted or denied, the negative impact, if any, from continued or exacerbated hostility between the custodial and non-custodial parents, and the effect that the move may have on any extended-family relationships."

In relocation cases the real deciding factor often seems to be what the court feels would be the likely outcome of denying permission to relocate. If permission is denied, will the custodial parent make the move anyway? If so, the court must be prepared to switch custody to the other parent. In such a situation, the court must weigh the impact of the disruption in the child's life that would result from the move against the disruption that a change in custody would cause. In making such decisions, courts consider all the best interest factors already discussed. This is a particularly daunting task, however, since the court must speculate about the child's probable adjustment to two possible new environments that both may be significantly different from the present one.

Non-Parent Visitation

Two categories of relatives, grandparents and siblings, have statutory rights to sue for visitation. The Court of Appeals has held (Case 6-4) that in all other cases, the decision of a fit parent about whom the child may visit is absolute and final. This decision has created a peculiar situation where a non-parent has a right to sue for custody, alleging extraordinary circumstances, but not for visitation.

 **CASE 6-4**

RONALD FF. v. CINDY GG.
70 N.Y.2d 141, 517 N.Y.S.2d 932 (1987)

BELLACOSA, J.

Visitation rights may not be granted on the authority of the *Matter of Bennett v. Jeffreys* (40 NY2d 543) extraordinary circumstances rule, to a biological stranger where the child, born out of wedlock, is properly in the custody of his mother. Petitioner was proven by blood test and admissions not to be the father of the child. Respondent is conceded to be a fit mother, a conclusion supported by the evidence before the lower courts, and she has chosen to resist the legal effort to judicially confer visitation rights on petitioner. Under these key premises, the *Bennett* rule is inapplicable and unavailable. Nothing in this record establishes any basis for interfering with the mother's full custodial rights, which include the right to determine who

CASE 6-4 continued

may or may not associate with her child.

The mother and petitioner began dating in October 1979 while they were in high school. Their relationship continued until the early fall of 1981. In October 1981, the mother and petitioner broke up and she began dating another man whom she planned to marry. That engagement lasted one month and, in January of 1982, the mother and petitioner resumed their relationship. After they reunited, the mother-to-be informed petitioner that she was four months pregnant and it was possible that he was the father. Throughout the pregnancy, they resided together. Petitioner participated in the mother's childbirth courses, was present at the child's birth, and agreed, after initial refusal and dispute, to be listed as the father on the child's birth certificate. Over the next year or so, the mother and petitioner lived together sporadically. During periods of estrangement, petitioner continued to see the child regularly and was held out to be and considered himself to be the child's father. After the parties separated, the mother initiated support proceedings against petitioner through the County Department of Social Services.

In October 1983, upon learning of the mother's intent to move to Texas with the child, petitioner started this proceeding seeking an order temporarily restraining the mother from removing her child from the jurisdiction and granting him visitation rights. Family Court granted a temporary restraining order prohibiting the mother from removing the child from the State, and a hearing was directed on the issue of paternity. The results of a blood-grouping test excluded petitioner as the biological father, but the court nevertheless ordered a hearing on the matter of visitation. After a two-day hearing, the Family Court concluded that "in the present circumstances, it is in [the child's] best interest to continue his relationship with [petitioner and his] family by means of regular visitation". The court, citing *Matter of Bennett v. Jeffreys* (40 NY2d 543, *supra*), found "the circumstances in the instant case sufficiently extraordinary to warrant consideration of petitioner's request for visitation in light of the child's best interests despite petitioner's lack of paternal ties". Thus, the court ordered bimonthly visits with the child by petitioner and his parents. The court also lifted its previous order restraining the mother from removing the child to another State, but ordered the mother to notify petitioner 30 days in advance of any move from the county so that he could seek modification of the order of visitation.

The mother appealed, and the Appellate Division modified the order of the Family Court eliminating the visitation rights to petitioner's parents and, as so modified, affirmed....

The mother further appeals to us with respect to the affirmed visitation right accorded to petitioner. The central issue is whether the *Bennett* standard, first enunciated and to date applied only to custody disputes between parents and third parties, is available to allow visitation rights to a non-parent against the wishes of the custodial

📖 **CASE 6-4 continued**

parent. We conclude that the lower courts erred as a matter of law in using the *Bennett* test.

To be sure, visitation is a subspecies of custody, but the differences in degree in these relational categories are so great and so fundamental that rules like the *Bennett* rule, which have been carefully crafted and made available only to custody disputes, should not be casually extended to the visitation field. Thus, we expressly decline to do so.

It has long been recognized that, as between a parent and a third person, parental custody of a child may not be displaced absent grievous cause or necessity....An underlying rationale for this rule is that it is presumptively in a child's best interest to be raised by at least one parent unless the parents are determined to be unfit....

In *Matter of Bennett v. Jeffreys*...we articulated the narrow exception in which a court may consider whether the best interest of a child permits termination of parental custody....

In this case, no one questions the mother's fitness to raise her child and no one seeks to change custody. Thus, the *Bennett* rule has no application to the situation before us, and our inquiry is directed solely to the State's power to interfere with the right of this mother to choose those with whom her child associates. The State may not interfere with that fundamental right unless it shows some compelling State purpose which furthers the child's best interest.... No such compelling purposes are present in this case.

Finally, there is no legal support whatsoever for the order requiring a custodial parent to notify a nonparent of an intention to move from a particular area of this State.

***

DISCUSSION TOPIC

What harms do you think the court foresaw if the "extraordinary circumstances" rule was applied in visitation cases? Do you think it significant that this case presented a potential relocation problem? Do you think this decision properly balances the parent's rights and the child's rights? You might want to reread Judge Kaye's dissent in *Alison D. v. Virginia M.* (Case 1-2).

GRANDPARENT AND SIBLING VISITATION

Grandparents have a statutory right to use a writ of habeas corpus to seek visitation with their grandchildren where either or both of the parents of the child is or are deceased, or "where circumstances show that conditions exist which equity would see fit to intervene." DRL § 72. Divorce is the most commonly alleged equitable circumstance, but in 1991 the Court of Appeals ruled that this section is available to grandparents even when the nuclear family is intact. *Emanuel S. v. Joseph E.*, 78 N.Y.2d 178, 573 N.Y.S.2d 36 (1991). The court cautioned, however, that standing for grandparents to seek visitation is not automatic, and stated that the grandparents must prove that they have established a sufficient existing relationship with their grandchild or, if that has been frustrated by the parents, a sufficient effort to establish one, so that the court sees the situation as one deserving the court's intervention. If the court finds that the grandparents do have standing to seek visitation, the court then goes on to conduct a full best interest inquiry, as in any other visitation dispute.

In 1989, the legislature extended the same right to seek visitation to siblings. DRL § 71. Although the statute says the right is available to siblings "of half or whole blood," we can safely assume that it would extend to siblings by adoption as well. If the petitioning sibling is a minor, the proceeding may be brought by a "proper person" on the minor's behalf. As with grandparent visitation, if the court finds equitable circumstances warranting standing, the court then proceeds to hear evidence concerning whether visitation is in the child's best interest.

CONCLUSION

New York law concerning custody and visitation presents some surprises. While you may have already been familiar with the "best interest of the child" doctrine, you may not have expected that it would have so many twists and turns. In information gathering and trial preparation, the legal assistant must keep these ground rules firmly in mind: 1) Parents stand on equal footing in a custody dispute with no preference to either parent. 2) The court's concern is with the welfare of the child. If your firm's client is preoccupied with the wrongs the other spouse has done to him or herself, you must work to keep the custody interview focused on the effects of each parent's conduct on the *child*. 3) Non-parents, even close relatives, who are seeking custody of a child must prove that the parent is unfit or has abandoned the child or that "other extraordinary circumstances" exist before the court will consider the child's best interest. If the non-parent can overcome that threshold question, the non-parent must still prove that the child's best interest will be served by an award of custody to him or herself. 4) The law strongly favors visitation between a child and the non-custodial parent. A parent who seeks to limit the other parent's right of visitation must present compelling proof that the child would be endangered by the visitation. 5) A fit parent's right to decide whether a child may visit with a non-parent, other than a grandparent or sibling, is absolute. The courts will not entertain a petition for visitation by a non-parent other than a grandparent or sibling. 6) Grandparents and siblings may petition for visitation, but must show circumstances in which equity would see fit to intervene. If they pass this threshold test, they still must prove that visitation would be in the best interest of the child. 7) Custody disputes should usually be litigated in the jurisdiction that has the most available evidence about the child. If the parties disputing the child's custody live in different states, the child's "home state" should generally hear the case. 8) Interference with a lawful order of custody is a serious offense that may subject the offender to criminal and civil penalties and may result in severe curtailment of the offender's future access to the child.

CHAPTER REVIEW QUESTIONS

1.   Which of the following would *not* be relevant to a best interest of the child inquiry? a) Change of custody would result in separation of child from siblings and school in which child is flourishing academically. b) Teenaged child strongly desires to live with his father. c) One parent earns a larger salary than the other parent. d) One parent suffers from intermittent bouts of mental illness.

2.   Beatrice and Sheldon were married and have a daughter, Betty. Sheldon left the marital home and took Betty to stay with him at his sister's house. The parents are not legally separated, and divorce proceedings have not begun. Both parents and child reside in New York. What pleadings might Beatrice use to try to regain custody of Betty?

3.   In what court(s) could the custody case described in Question 2 be brought?

4.   Mike and Jeanette were not married. They have a child, Emma, and Mike has been adjudicated the child's father. Jeanette always had physical custody of the child, and Mike visited frequently. Since the couple got along amicably, they never obtained a court order concerning custody or visitation. Following Jeanette's tragic death in a car accident two months ago, Emma's maternal grandmother took the child to the grandmother's home in Connecticut and refuses to let Mike bring her back to New York. Can Mike sue for Emma's custody in New York? What sort of petition should he file?

5.   What state is Emma's home state? Why?

6.   A court in New York has awarded temporary custody of Emma to Mike, and the child is now residing with him here. If Emma's maternal grandmother wishes to cross-petition in New York for Emma's custody, what will she have to allege?

7.   If Emma's maternal grandmother decides not to contest Mike's custody of Emma but prefers to ask for visitation instead, what will she have to allege?

8.   Gabe and Marilyn were divorced in 1989 when their child, Lenny, was one year old. Pursuant to a separation agreement incorporated into the divorce decree, Marilyn got custody of Lenny, and Gabe got visitation

rights every other weekend, alternate holidays, and two weeks in the summer, all of which he has consistently exercised. The agreement does not contain any restriction on either parent's right to move. Marilyn now wishes to move to Florida to be near her aging parents who need her help. She has been offered a job at a slightly higher salary than she makes in New York. Lenny is attached to both parents and told the forensic evaluator that he wishes they could all live together. Do you think the court is likely to permit Marilyn to move with Lenny to Florida? Why or why not?

CHAPTER ASSIGNMENT

Using the fact pattern for the Bickerings at the end of Chapter 5, prepare a list of facts that support Wilma's application for custody of the children. You will use this list when you prepare the paragraphs pertaining to custody in Wilma's *pendente lite* motion, which is the assignment following Chapter 8. To assess the weaknesses of Wilma's case, also prepare a list of facts that would support Hugh's bid for custody, if he also seeks custody.

7 SUPPORT

> "For most of us, working with the Child Support
> Standards Act (CSSA) is a frightening prospect....For this
> reason and more, when certainty approaches us in
> handling some aspect of the CSSA, it is more welcome than
> a cool breeze on a hot summer's day." Joel R. Brandes
> and Carole L. Weidman, "Law and the Family: Social
> Security Disability Benefits and Child Support," *New York
> Law Journal*, July 25, 1995, p.3, col. 3.

The future has arrived in New York support law. Probably no other
development in Family Law has had so great an impact on the average person
as the revolution in the law of support. Both the spousal and child support
obligations have been drastically altered in less than a generation. When New
York's laws were made gender-neutral in 1980, as discussed in Chapter 1,
women for the first time became obligated to pay spousal support, and their
child support obligations were also expanded. More recently, the 1989 shift
from a needs-based method of calculating child support to a formula based on
a percentage of parental income evoked satisfaction in some quarters and
outrage in others. Spousal support and child support are now calculated by
entirely different methods. Beneficial as it may ultimately be, the rapid and total
change in this area has not only outstripped the ability of lay people to adjust to
the law's evolution, but has also engendered widespread confusion among legal
practitioners as well.

The sweeping changes New York has made in its law of child support have
come in response to Federal mandates designed to expand and streamline the
collection of child support. In the past two decades, assuring adequate support
for children has become a high national priority. In the late 1970's, national

studies identified three pervasive problems that had to be corrected in order to improve the level at which children are supported: child support awards were inadequate; enforcement of child support orders was woefully ineffective; and the process, at all stages, was too cumbersome, slow and inefficient. The Federal government enacted a series of laws that use funding as a "carrot and stick" to bring state governments in line with Federal policies. The Federal government reimburses the state for a percentage of the funds it expends in the collection of child support, but only if the state enacts laws that comply with Federal guidelines. 42 USCS §§ 651-667; Federal Family Support Act of 1988 (PL 100-485).

BASICS BOX

Subject matter jurisdiction: Family Court has exclusive original jurisdiction. Supreme Court has ancillary jurisdiction in conjunction with a matrimonial proceeding.

Venue: County where one of the parties resides or is domiciled.

Standing: Either spouse (maintenance), custodian of the child or the child (child support), and the Commissioner of Social Services (if either the child or the spouse is, or is likely to become, a public charge) all may sue for support.

Grounds: The petition must allege that the petitioner is in need of support and that the respondent is legally obligated to support petitioner and has the means to do so.

Statute of Limitations: Until the child reaches 21 years of age (original orders). 20 years for enforcement proceedings.

Applicable Statutes: FCA art. 4, §§ 545, 546, 561, art. 5-A; DRL §§ 3-A, 32, 236, 240; CPLR §§ 5241, 5242; SSL art. 3 (titles 6, 6-A, 6-B).

SUBJECT MATTER JURISDICTION

The Family Court has exclusive original jurisdiction over proceedings for support and maintenance, while the Supreme Court has ancillary jurisdiction in conjunction with pending matrimonial proceedings. Family Court also has referral jurisdiction when the Supreme Court sends it support and maintenance issues. Family Court does *not* have jurisdiction to enforce a separation agreement unless the agreement has been incorporated or merged into a judgment or court order. *Brescia v. Fitts*, 56 N.Y.2d 132, 451 N.Y.S.2d 68 (1982). If the separation agreement contains a waiver of support, however, the Family Court may nevertheless take jurisdiction and make an order of support, if the Family Court finds that the waiver of support was invalid. *Krochalis v. Krochalis*, 53 A.D.2d 1010, 386 N.Y.S.2d 266 (4 Dept. 1976) Because it is so common for proceedings in the two courts to overlap, it is worthwhile to take a moment to sort out the order of play:

- If a matrimonial action with a request for maintenance or child support is filed in Supreme Court first, then the Family Court is divested of jurisdiction over those issues. *Poliandro v. Poliandro*, 119 A.D.2d 577, 500 N.Y.S.2d 744 (2 Dept. 1986), *appeal dismissed*, 68 N.Y.2d 908, 508 N.Y.S.2d 948.

- If the Family Court support proceeding is filed first, the subsequent filing of a matrimonial proceeding does not divest the Family Court of jurisdiction over the case already before it. *Roy v. Roy*, 109 A.D.2d 150, 491 N.Y.S.2d 202 (3 Dept. 1985).

- If the Family Court has already made an order of support and the Supreme Court subsequently makes a different order of maintenance or child support, the Supreme Court order supersedes the Family Court order.

- If the Family Court has made an order of support and the Supreme Court has not yet made such an order, the Family Court continues to have jurisdiction to enforce its own order, despite a pending matrimonial proceeding in Supreme Court. *Rubenstein v. Yosef*, 198 A.D.2d 359, 603 N.Y.S.2d 336 (2 Dept. 1993).

- Family Court has jurisdiction to modify or enforce an order of support made either in Family or Supreme Court, unless the Supreme Court reserves exclusive jurisdiction to itself, which is very rarely done. If the judgment in the matrimonial proceeding is silent on the issue of jurisdiction, Family Court may exercise jurisdiction. FCA §§ 422(b), 445(b), 451, 461(b)(ii), 571(3)(b).

REFEREES AND HEARING EXAMINERS

In Supreme Court, the maintenance and child support aspects of a matrimonial proceeding are sometimes referred to a **referee**. Referees are attorneys designated to conduct trials of these issues. They are not judicial officers, however, and their decisions must be confirmed by the Supreme Court justice to whom the matrimonial case is assigned. The Supreme Court justice is the person who actually signs the judgment in the matrimonial proceeding, and an appeal from such a judgment is taken to the appropriate appellate division, as from any other Supreme Court order.

When a support case is filed in Family Court, the matter is immediately assigned to a **hearing examiner**. Hearing examiners are a key component in the system to expedite support cases. They are experts in this highly technical area of law, and their caseloads consist entirely of support cases. Thus, support cases do not get lost in the shuffle, as they sometimes did when they were mixed into a Family Court judge's calendar filled with other pressing matters such as abuse and juvenile delinquency cases. Although hearing examiners are not judges, they are statutorily empowered in support matters to exercise most of the powers of a judge. In addition, they may make orders adjudicating paternity in uncontested cases. They are not permitted to make orders concerning custody or visitation, however, and may not order incarceration of a respondent who has violated a support order. Hearing examiners "hear and determine" support cases, meaning that the orders they enter are fully binding on the parties. FCA § 439(a)(f). Appeals from Hearing Examiners' orders are taken by filing **objections,** as discussed below.

SPOUSAL SUPPORT

Each spouse is obligated to support the other if he or she is able and the other spouse lacks the ability to provide for his or her own reasonable needs. DRL § 236; FCA § 412. Spousal support, which is now called **maintenance**, may be ordered during the course of an ongoing marriage, if the parties are living apart, or in connection with an action for separation or divorce. In 1980, the New York legislature enacted the **equitable distribution** law [Chapter 281 of the Laws of 1980] which pertains to both spousal support and property division through matrimonial actions. As Chapters 1 and 8 discuss, the equitable distribution system is based upon the premise that marriage is an economic partnership in which the contributions, whether monetary or non-monetary, of both spouses are recognized. Before the equitable distribution law was passed, women were often awarded **alimony** when a marriage dissolved, but the term "maintenance" was substituted in the new law, to reflect important philosophical differences from the old concept of "alimony."

"OPTING OUT" OF THE EQUITABLE DISTRIBUTION LAW

As discussed in Chapters 3 and 4, a prenuptial or separation agreement may be used to avoid the application of the equitable distribution law. It is fairly easy to use such an agreement to "**opt out,**" that is, to waive all or part of the spousal support obligation as imposed by the equitable distribution law. So long as the agreement is not unconscionable, that is, it is fair in its totality, the spousal support waiver will usually be upheld. Opting out of the child support obligation, which is controlled by the Child Support Standards Act rather than the equitable distribution law, is a much more complicated business, as discussed below.

DURATION OF MAINTENANCE

Not only is "maintenance" gender-neutral, it is also meant to be a short-term obligation, unlike alimony, which often continued until the woman died or remarried or the former husband died. "Maintenance" is supposed to last only long enough for the less monied spouse to re-enter the job market and become self-supporting. In the 15 years since the passage of the equitable distribution law, however, it has become apparent that in many marriages, the primary asset is one spouse's earning power. Some spouses will never be able to support themselves at the standard of living the couple enjoyed as a married couple.

Thus, there has been a gradual trend back to long-term or lifetime maintenance awards. In *Chew v. Chew*, 157 Misc.2d 322, 596 N.Y.S.2d 950 (N.Y. Sup. Ct. 1992), for example, the wife was considerably younger than the husband and had an income of $180,000 a year. Although the husband had worked during the course of the parties' 17-year marriage, at the time of the divorce he had only a small income from a business he had recently started. The parties did not own much property to distribute. The court awarded the husband lifetime maintenance and ordered the wife to maintain life insurance to secure the payments.

Maintenance always terminates when the obligor dies. The obligor's estate is not required to continue the payments, even if the estate has sufficient funds. Thus, it is important that the obligor be required to maintain life insurance for the benefit of the former spouse if there are not enough other assets available to provide for the recipient in the event of the obligor's death. The Court of Appeals has upheld the authority of trial courts to order a spouse to obtain life insurance in conjunction with an award of maintenance. *Hartog v. Hartog*, 85 N.Y.2d 36, 623 N.Y.S.2d 537 (1995). Maintenance also terminates upon the remarriage of the recipient spouse, [DRL § 248] unless a separation agreement executed by the parties specifies to the contrary, in which case it continues and is enforceable as a contractual obligation. Maintenance continues even if the recipient is cohabiting with a non-marital partner, unless the recipient is holding herself out as the wife of the new domestic partner. *Bliss v. Bliss*, 66 N.Y.2d 382, 497 N.Y.S.2d 344 (1985). A separation agreement may, of course, specify that mere cohabitation will terminate the maintenance obligation.

STANDARDS FOR MAINTENANCE

To the extent possible, maintenance should provide for the less monied spouse to live at the standard of living the couple maintained during their marriage. *Melnik v. Melnik*, 118 A.D.2d 902, 499 N.Y.S.2d 470 (3 Dept. 1986). The maintenance award is based upon the couple's actual standard of living, not on how a hypothetical "reasonable" couple of the same income might have lived. If there are not enough funds to maintain both spouses at the marital standard after their separation, a common problem, then both spouses should have to tighten their belts the same number of notches.

The amount of maintenance that will be needed can be calculated by computing each party's income and reasonable expenses. If one spouse lacks sufficient income to meet his or her reasonable expenses, while the other spouse has more than enough, the spouse who has the excess will be ordered to pay the other spouse enough to provide for his or her reasonable needs. In matrimonial proceedings information about each spouse's means and expenses is disclosed through the net worth statement, as discussed in Chapter 8. If the matter is being litigated in Family Court and the couple does not have substantial assets, they may complete a short-form income and expense statement (Form 7-1) instead.

📁 **FORM 7-1**

Secs. 413, 424–a F.C.A. 236 D.R.L.   Form 4–17 (Support 8/89)

FAMILY COURT OF THE STATE OF NEW YORK COUNTY OF
_____

In the Matter of a Proceeding for Support under Article 4
of the Family Court Act

_____Petitioner,   Docket No._____
_____SS #

    –against–   **FINANCIAL DISCLOSURE
                                                              AFFIDAVIT***

                                                              SHORT FORM

_____Respondent.
_____S.S. #
_____ H.E._____ Court Date:_____

STATE OF NEW YORK   )
                      : SS.

COUNTY OF   )

                  ,the (Petitioner) (Respondent) herein, being duly sworn, deposes and
says that the following is an accurate statement of my net worth (assets of whatsoever kind and nature
and wherever situated minus liabilities), statement of income from all sources and statement of assets
transferred of whatsoever kind and nature and wherever situated:

That I reside at_____

I. INCOME
  (a) Employer (state if self–employed)_____
  (b) Employer's address_____
  (c) No of Dependents Claimed_____ (d) No. of Members of Household_____
  (e) Hours worked per week_____ (f) Weekly Gross Salary _____
  (g) Weekly Deductions:
      1. Soc. Security   2. N.Y. State Tax   3. Fed Tax   4. Other Deductions 5. Total Deductions
      $_____ $_____ $_____ $_____ $_____
  (h) Weekly Net Salary or Wages $_____
  (i) Income from other sources: (specify)** _____ $_____
  (j) Total Gross Income last year $_____
  (k) Income of other Members of Household: (specify)_____
      1. Weekly Gross Salary or Wages $_____ 2. Weekly Net Salary or Wages $_____

II. ASSETS
  (a) Savings Account Balance at (**Name of Bank(s)**)_____ $_____
  (b) Checking Account Balance at (**Name of Bank(s)**)_____ $_____
  (c) Automobile(s) 1. Year and Make_____ 2. Value $_____
  (d) Residence Owned (address)_____
      1. Market Value $_____ 2. Mortgage Owed $_____
  (e) Other Real Estate Owned_____
      1. Market Value $_____ 2. Mortgage Owed $_____
  (f) Other Property (for example: stocks and bonds, trailer, boat, etc.) Value $_____

***YOU ARE REQUIRED TO ATTACHED A CURRENT AND REPRESENTATIVE PAYCHECK STUB AND
MOST RECENTLY FILED STATE AND FEDERAL INCOME TAX RETURNS TO THIS FORM. YOU
MAY BE REQUIRED TO FURNISH PAST AND PRESENT INCOME TAX RETURNS; EMPLOYER
STATEMENTS; PAY STUBS; CORPORATE, BUSINESS OR PARTNERSHIP BOOKS AND RECORDS;
CORPORATE AND BUSINESS TAX RETURNS; AND RECEIPTS FOR EXPENSES OR SUCH OTHER
MEANS OF VERIFICATION AS THE COURT DETERMINES APPROPRIATE.**

**For Example: part–time job, tips, rents, pensions, dividends, unemployment insurance,
disability, workers comp., social security, vet ben., fellowships, stipends, annuities, etc.

FORM 7-1 continued

Form 4–17 Page 2

LIST ALL ASSETS TRANSFERRED IN ANY MANNER DURING PRECEDING THREE YEARS, OR LENGTH OF MARRIAGE, WHICHEVER IS SHORTER:

Description of Property	To Whom Transferred	Date of Transfer	Value
_____	_____	_____	$_____
_____	_____	_____	$_____

III. EXPENSES

(You may elect to list all expenses on a weekly basis or all expenses on a monthly basis, however, you must be consistent. If any items are paid on a monthly basis, divide by 4.3 to obtain weekly payment; if any items are paid on a weekly basis, multiply by 4.3 to obtain monthly payment.)

Total Amount

(a) Rent or Mortgage Payment: House_____Apt.____Room____   _____
(b) Real Estates Taxes (if not included in mortgage)   _____
(c) Food: Self_____Children_____(include lunches, etc.)   _____
(d) Utilities: 1. Gas_____ 2. Electric _____ 3. Telephone _____
    4. Heating Fuel_____ 5. Water/Garbage Removal _____ Total _____
(e) Clothing: Self _____ Children _____ Total _____
(f) Laundry and Dry Cleaning: Self _____Children_____ Total _____
(g) Medical, Dental and Medication:Self_____ Children _____ Total _____
(h) Insurance: Life_____Auto_____Fire_____ Total _____
(i) Other Insurance:(Health and Accident,hosp)(if not deducted from pay) _____
(j) Transportation: Carfare_____ Auto Maint._____ Gas/Oil_____ Total _____
(k)Auto Payment: Total Balance due on Loan _____
(l) Union Dues (if not deducted from pay) _____
(m)Tuition (specify)_____ _____
(n) Alimony or maintenance _____
(o) Child support in connection with previous marriage _____
(p) Other (for example: baby–sitters, recreation, etc.)(Specify)_____ _____
_____ TOTAL (weekly)(monthly)EXPENSES $_____

IV LIABILITIES, LOANS & DEBITS   MONTHLY PAYMENTS

(a)Owed to whom_____1. Purpose _____
   2.Date Incurred_____ 3.Total Balance due _____
(b)Owed to whom_____1. Purpose _____
   2.Date Incurred_____ 3.Total Balance due _____

TOTAL MONTHLY PAYMENTS $_____

Other financial data that should be brought to attention of Court: (Include amount of public assistance, supplemental security income, NYC or Yonkers tax paid)

The foregoing statement has been carefully read by the undersigned who states that it is true and correct.

_____
(Petitioner)   (Respondent)

Sworn to before me this

day of   , 19

_____

Statutory Factors

The determination of a fair maintenance award obviously entails much more than a mathematical calculation. To attempt to bring some consistency to the exercise of judicial judgment on this issue, and to facilitate appellate review, the equitable distribution statute, DRL § 236B(6)(a), sets forth 11 factors courts are required to consider in awarding maintenance:

1. The income and property of the respective parties;
2. The duration of the marriage, and the age and health of both spouses;
3. The present and future earning capacity of both parties;
4. The ability of the party seeking support to become self-supporting, and the amount of time and training required to accomplish that goal;
5. Reduced or lost lifetime earning capacity of the party seeking support due to delayed or lost education or career opportunities as a result of the marriage;
6. Which party has custody of any children of the marriage;
7. The tax consequences to each party;
8. Contributions of the party seeking support to the earning capacity of the other party;
9. The wasteful dissipation of marital property by either spouse;
10. Any transfer of marital property made without fair consideration;
11. Any other factor the court finds just and proper.

Marital Fault

As discussed in Chapter 5, misconduct constituting grounds for separation or divorce formerly barred the guilty spouse from receiving support. Since the passage of the equitable distribution law, however, most courts have held that marital fault bars spousal support only when it is **egregious**, that is, particularly shocking or outrageous. The rule that marital fault will be considered only when it is egregious is less hard and fast in regard to maintenance than it is to property division, however, with the Third Department having shown more willingness to regard marital fault as relevant in awarding maintenance. Even those courts that consider fault relevant to the size of the award have not treated it as an absolute bar to maintenance, however. In *Stevens v. Stevens*, 107 A.D.2d 987, 484 N.Y.S.2d 708 (3 Dept. 1985), for example, the court *reduced* the maintenance award to a wife who had committed adultery, berated the husband in front of friends and co-workers, and wounded him twice with a kitchen knife while trying to break into his locked briefcase.

TAX CONSEQUENCES OF MAINTENANCE

The income tax on maintenance must be paid by the recipient. The recipient must declare the amount actually received (not necessarily the same as the amount owed) on his or her income tax return, while the payer subtracts the amount actually paid as an adjustment to income. If the amounts stated in the two tax returns do not match, either or both parties will in all likelihood be audited. Notice that Factor 7, above, mandates the court to take the tax consequences into consideration in determining how much maintenance to award. This calculation is crucial, because, depending on the recipient's tax bracket (15%, 28%, 31%, 36%, or 39%), the recipient may wind up after taxes with much less, while the obligor enjoys a tax break that augments his or her disposable income.

CHILD SUPPORT

OBLIGATION OF BOTH PARENTS

Both parents of a child born during the course of a marriage are chargeable with support of the child. DRL § 32(3); FCA § 413(1). (You will recall from Chapter 3 that the child is deemed an in-wedlock child even if the marriage is void or voidable.) The father of a child born out of wedlock is also chargeable with support, but only if there has been an adjudication of paternity or he has acknowledged the child, as discussed in Chapter 9. Adoptive parents are, of course, liable for the support of their adopted children [DRL § 110], and the birth parents are relieved of their support obligation when the adoption is finalized [DRL § 117(1)(a)]. A step-parent is not liable for the support of a step-child unless the child is a recipient of public assistance, and even then the step-parent's obligation extends only to the amount of the public assistance grant and is secondary to that of the parents. FCA § 415; *Monroe County Dept. of Social Services ex rel. Palermo v. Palermo*, 192 A.D.2d 1114, 596 N.Y.S.2d 252 (4 Dept. 1993) . The step-parent's obligation continues only so long as he or she is married to the parent of the child who is receiving public assistance. In all cases, the child support obligation terminates on the death of the obligor, except that the estate may be liable for arrears. Thus, it is essential to provide for the support of the child, usually through life insurance or trust funds, in the event the obligor dies before the child reaches the age of majority.

DURATION OF CHILD SUPPORT OBLIGATION

Unless a separation agreement specifies a later date or event, the child support obligation ends when the child reaches the age of 21 years. It may terminate sooner if the child becomes **emancipated**. A child may become emancipated by 1) marrying, 2) entering military service, 3) holding full-time gainful employment such that the child is self-supporting, or 4) refusing to obey the parents' reasonable parental commands. The latter two methods must be taken with a grain of salt. Many teenagers hold part-time jobs, and many, if not most, go through a rebellious stage when they do not graciously accept parental authority. Neither of these typical conditions is sufficient to terminate a parent's support obligation. In 1971, the Court of Appeals noted "the surge of adolescent independence, the breakdown in parental authority and the frustration attending both," and noted that courts absent any violation of law, generally prefer to "leave the parties where they find them, lest they undermine the integrity of the family." *Roe v. Doe*, 29 N.Y.2d 188, 324 N.Y.S.2d 71 (1971).

If, however, a child has finished school and has a permanent job that pays enough for the child to meet all of his or her own reasonable expenses, the child may be found emancipated. Also, if a child persists in a lifestyle of which the parent disapproves, particularly if the child is living apart from the parents, the court may also terminate the child support obligation. In *Parker v. Stage*, 43 N.Y.2d 128, 400 N.Y.S.2d 794 (1977), for example, the Court of Appeals decided that a father did not have to contribute toward the support of his daughter, who refused to finish school or find a job and who was being supported by public assistance while living with her paramour. Similarly, in *Roe v. Doe, supra*, the court terminated the support obligation of the father, whose 20-year-old daughter refused to live in a dormitory of the university she attended and further refused to live in her parent's home. The daughter was residing in an off-campus apartment with a female friend.

CHILD SUPPORT STANDARDS ACT OF 1989

To comply with the Federal Family Support Act of 1988, New York, along with many other states, made radical changes in the way child support is calculated. Prior to 1989, child support had been determined in much the same way as maintenance. The child's needs were calculated by adding the amounts normally expended for the child's food, clothing, shelter, education, medical care and recreation, and the non-custodial parent was ordered to contribute as much of his or her disposable income as the court thought fair, taking into account the means of the custodial parent. While this method appears reasonable on its face, child support awards varied from judge to judge and often were not only inconsistent, but inadequate. Numerous national studies showed that in the years immediately following the parents' separation or divorce, most children experienced a decline in their standard of living, while that of the non-custodial parents stayed the same or rose.

To prevent children from unfairly bearing the burden of their parents' separation, the Federal government mandated the states to pass uniform standards for the calculation of child support. The result, in New York, was the Child Support Standards Act, (CSSA) [DRL § 240; FCA § 413], with its formula by which both Supreme and Family Courts must calculate child support based upon a percentage of the parents' income. If the parents' income cannot be ascertained, the court can still make an award based on the needs of the children. FCA § 413(1)(k); DRL § 240(1-b)(k).

The Basic Child Support Obligation

The basic child support obligation is equal to the combined income of the parents, based upon their most recent tax returns, multiplied by a percentage based upon the number of children. The total child support obligation is then divided between the parents in proportion to their respective incomes. The non-custodial parent pays the custodial parent his or her prorated share. The percentages are:

-      1 child   = 17%
-      2 children   = 25%
-      3 children   = 29%
-      4 children   = 31%
-      5 or more children = 35%

     FCA § 413(1)(b)(3); DRL § 240(1-b)(b)(3)

Determining Parental Income

"Income" for the purposes of the CSSA is a broad term. It includes not only earned income and income from investments, but also income or compensation voluntarily deferred or received from all of the following as well:

- workers' compensation;
- disability benefits;
- unemployment insurance benefits;
- social security benefits;
- veterans' benefits;
- pensions and retirement benefits;
- fellowships and stipends;
- annuity payments.

     FCA § 413(1)(b)(5)(iii); DRL § 240(1-b)(b)(5)(iii)

Imputed Income

The hearing examiner or judge hearing a support case may attribute to a respondent income the respondent does not actually have. The discretion to impute income is sometimes exercised when the obligor has purposely diminished his or her income to avoid child support. In *Cardia v. Cardia*, 203 A.D.2d 650, 610 N.Y.S.2d 620 (3 Dept. 1994), the husband left a lucrative job in advertising to open a children's clothing store, from which he claimed to be making much less money. The court found that he had willfully reduced his income, and imputed to him the income he made at his old job.

At the court's discretion, "income" may include **imputed** income from:

- non-income producing assets;
- job perquisites used for personal benefit (such as a company car);
- fringe benefits of employment;
- money, goods, or services from relatives or friends.

     FCA § 413(1)(b)(5)(iv); DRL § 240(1-b)(b)(5)(iv)

Allowable Deductions

Only eight deductions from gross income are allowed for CSSA computations. Note that the list does *not* include federal or New York State taxes. New York City and Yonkers city income taxes are deductible because those are the only two cities in New York that have city income tax; the intent was to make the formula work uniformly throughout the state.

- Unreimbursed employee business expenses that do not reduce personal expenditures (union dues, for example)
- Alimony or maintenance *actually* paid to a non-party spouse *pursuant to a court order or written agreement*
- Alimony or maintenance paid to a party spouse pursuant to a written agreement or court order that calls for an adjustment of child support when alimony or maintenance terminates
- Child support actually paid to a non-party pursuant to a court order or written agreement
- Public assistance
- Supplemental securtiy income
- New York City or Yonkers city income or earnings taxes actually paid
- Social Security (FICA) contributions.
  FCA § 413(1)(b)(5)(vii); DRL § 240(1-b)(b)(5)(vii)

Computing the Support Obligation

After the total income of each party has been ascertained and the allowable deductions have been subtracted, the two incomes are added together. This figure is called the "**combined parental income**." The next step is to multiply the combined parental income by the percentage specified for the number of children the parties have. Then, each parent's income is divided into the combined parental income to determine each parent's proportion of the total. For example, if husband Larry makes $50,000 a year after allowable deductions and wife Annette makes $25,000, the combined parental income is $75,000. If the parties have one child, the basic child support obligation is ($75,000 x .17 = $12,750. Larry's **prorata share** is 2/3 and Annette's is 1/3. If the husband is the custodial parent, the wife must pay him $4,250 per year for the support of the child. If the wife is the custodial parent, the husband must pay her $8,500.

The basic amount covers shelter, food, clothing, and all the child's other expenses except 1) medical expenses not reimbursed by insurance and 2) child care, which is an allowable additional expense only if the custodial parent works, goes to school, or is looking for work. Child care costs and unreimbursed medical expenses are shared by the parents in the same proportion as the basic obligation. Larry would bear 2/3 of the child care costs if Annette is the custodial parent, while Annette would be responsible for 1/3 if Larry is the custodian. Thus, if Annette pays $120 a week for a babysitter to mind the child after school until she gets home from work, Larry would be obligated to pay an additional $80 per week or ($80 x 52) $4,160 per year.

Step by Step Computation

Using Larry and Annette's case, let us repeat the child support computation step by step:

Step 1: Determine each parent's gross income. Larry's gross is $65,000; Annette's is $35,000.

Step 2: Subtract the allowable deductions. Larry has FICA and New York City income tax totaling $15,000; Annette has FICA and union dues totaling $10,000.
$65,000 - $15,000 = $50,000 (Larry)
$35,000 - $10,000 = $25,000 (Annette)

Step 3: Add the two parents' adjusted incomes to arrive at the combined parental income.
$50,000 + $25,000 = $75,000

Step 4: Determine the combined parental support obligation.
$75,000 x .17 = $12,750

Step 5: Prorate the parents' child support obligation.
$50,000 ÷ $75,000 = .666 (Larry)
$25,000 ÷ $75,000 = .333 (Annette)

Step 6: Determine each parent's obligation. Multiply the combined child support obligation by each parent's prorata share.
$12,750 x .666 = $8,500 (Larry)
$12,750 x .333 = $4,250 (Annette)

Step 7: Determine child care costs. (Be sure to use the same increment you used for the incomes.)
$120 (per week) x 52 = $6,500 per year

Step 8: Prorate the child care expenses. (When you multiply by numbers that will never come out even, like .33 or .66, you will be off by a very slight amount, but that is not important.)
$6,240 x .666 = $4,160 (Larry)
$6,240 x .333 = $2,080 (Annette, if Larry has custody and pays the same amount for babysitting.)

Step 9: Add the child care obligation to the basic obligation.
$8,500 + $4,160 = $12,660 (Larry)
$4,250 + $2,080 = $ 6,330 (Annette)

> PRACTICE TIP: It is necessary to determine the parents' prorated share of the child support obligation in order to calculate the additional liability for child care and unreimbursed medical expenses, but you can use a shortcut to figure out the percentage that covers all the other expenses: Just multiply the non-custodial parent's income (after having subtracted the allowable deductions) by the percentage applicable to the number of children. Let's try it with Larry and Annette. Larry's income (after deductions) was $50,000. $50,000 x .17 = $8,500. Annette's income was $25,000. $25,000 x .17 = $4,250. It works!

Child Support Standards Chart

To insure that all unrepresented litigants in Family Court child support proceedings understand how much support their children are entitled to under CSSA, the New York State Department of Social Services Office of Child Support Enforcement publishes and distributes in the Family Court the Child Support Standards Chart, which makes it easy to see how much the basic obligation is. The Chart works much like the tax tables in income tax instruction booklets. Since prorating income is too complicated for many unrepresented litigants, the Chart utilizes the "shortcut" method of computation described in the Practice Tip above. Form 7-2 consists of two sample pages from the 1996 Chart that cover the income ranges of Larry and Annette.

Child Support Worksheets

All litigants in Supreme Court matrimonial proceedings and Family Court litigants who have legal representation are required to complete Child Support Worksheets (Form 7-3) that are more detailed than the Child Support Standards Chart.

Payment Schedule

Once the obligation has been computed, a payment schedule must be established. Payments can be made weekly, bi-weekly, monthly, or at any other interval that is convenient for the parties. If the obligor is salaried, payments normally correspond to the frequency of the obligor's paycheck. Thus, if Larry is paying child support and he is paid bi-weekly, the court will probably order him to make the child support payments in bi-weekly increments. To convert an annual figure to smaller increments, simply divide the yearly obligation by the appropriate figure – 12 for monthly increments, 52 for a weekly payment, 26 for bi-weekly payments. To convert a monthly figure to weekly increments, divide by 4.3. How much should Larry's bi-weekly child support payment be? $326.60 + $160 (child care) = $486.60.

FORM 7-2

4/1/96

THE CHILD SUPPORT STANDARDS CHART   INCOME RANGE 20,000 -29,999

ANNUAL INCOME	NUMBER OF CHILDREN 1	2	3	4	5+
	ANNUAL OBLIGATION AMOUNT				
20,000 -20,099	3,400	5,000	5,800	6,200	7,000
20,100 -20,199	3,417	5,025	5,829	6,231	7,035
20,200 -20,299	3,434	5,050	5,858	6,262	7,070
20,300 -20,399	3,451	5,075	5,887	6,293	7,105
20,400 -20,499	3,468	5,100	5,916	6,324	7,140
20,500 -20,599	3,485	5,125	5,945	6,355	7,175
20,600 -20,699	3,502	5,150	5,974	6,386	7,210
20,700 -20,799	3,519	5,175	6,003	6,417	7,245
20,800 -20,899	3,536	5,200	6,032	6,448	7,280
20,900 -20,999	3,553	5,225	6,061	6,479	7,315

ANNUAL INCOME	NUMBER OF CHILDREN 1	2	3	4	5+
	ANNUAL OBLIGATION AMOUNT				
25,000 -25,099	4,250	6,250	7,250	7,750	8,750
25,100 -25,199	4,267	6,275	7,279	7,781	8,785
25,200 -25,299	4,284	6,300	7,308	7,812	8,820
25,300 -25,399	4,301	6,325	7,337	7,843	8,855
25,400 -25,499	4,318	6,350	7,366	7,874	8,890
25,500 -25,599	4,335	6,375	7,395	7,905	8,925
25,600 -25,699	4,352	6,400	7,424	7,936	8,960
25,700 -25,799	4,369	6,425	7,453	7,967	8,995
25,800 -25,899	4,386	6,450	7,482	7,998	9,030
25,900 -25,999	4,403	6,475	7,511	8,029	9,065

ANNUAL INCOME	NUMBER OF CHILDREN 1	2	3	4	5+
	ANNUAL OBLIGATION AMOUNT				
21,000 -21,099	3,570	5,250	6,090	6,510	7,350
21,100 -21,199	3,587	5,275	6,119	6,541	7,385
21,200 -21,299	3,604	5,300	6,148	6,572	7,420
21,300 -21,399	3,621	5,325	6,177	6,603	7,455
21,400 -21,499	3,638	5,350	6,206	6,634	7,490
21,500 -21,599	3,655	5,375	6,235	6,665	7,525
21,600 -21,699	3,672	5,400	6,264	6,696	7,560
21,700 -21,799	3,689	5,425	6,293	6,727	7,595
21,800 -21,899	3,706	5,450	6,322	6,758	7,630
21,900 -21,999	3,723	5,475	6,351	6,789	7,665

ANNUAL INCOME	NUMBER OF CHILDREN 1	2	3	4	5+
	ANNUAL OBLIGATION AMOUNT				
26,000 -26,099	4,420	6,500	7,540	8,060	9,100
26,100 -26,199	4,437	6,525	7,569	8,091	9,135
26,200 -26,299	4,454	6,550	7,598	8,122	9,170
26,300 -26,399	4,471	6,575	7,627	8,153	9,205
26,400 -26,499	4,488	6,600	7,656	8,184	9,240
26,500 -26,599	4,505	6,625	7,685	8,215	9,275
26,600 -26,699	4,522	6,650	7,714	8,246	9,310
26,700 -26,799	4,539	6,675	7,743	8,277	9,345
26,800 -26,899	4,556	6,700	7,772	8,308	9,380
26,900 -26,999	4,573	6,725	7,801	8,339	9,415

ANNUAL INCOME	NUMBER OF CHILDREN 1	2	3	4	5+
	ANNUAL OBLIGATION AMOUNT				
22,000 -22,099	3,740	5,500	6,380	6,820	7,700
22,100 -22,199	3,757	5,525	6,409	6,851	7,735
22,200 -22,299	3,774	5,550	6,438	6,882	7,770
22,300 -22,399	3,791	5,575	6,467	6,913	7,805
22,400 -22,499	3,808	5,600	6,496	6,944	7,840
22,500 -22,599	3,825	5,625	6,525	6,975	7,875
22,600 -22,699	3,842	5,650	6,554	7,006	7,910
22,700 -22,799	3,859	5,675	6,583	7,037	7,945
22,800 -22,899	3,876	5,700	6,612	7,068	7,980
22,900 -22,999	3,893	5,725	6,641	7,099	8,015

ANNUAL INCOME	NUMBER OF CHILDREN 1	2	3	4	5+
	ANNUAL OBLIGATION AMOUNT				
27,000 -27,099	4,590	6,750	7,830	8,370	9,450
27,100 -27,199	4,607	6,775	7,859	8,401	9,485
27,200 -27,299	4,624	6,800	7,888	8,432	9,520
27,300 -27,399	4,641	6,825	7,917	8,463	9,555
27,400 -27,499	4,658	6,850	7,946	8,494	9,590
27,500 -27,599	4,675	6,875	7,975	8,525	9,625
27,600 -27,699	4,692	6,900	8,004	8,556	9,660
27,700 -27,799	4,709	6,925	8,033	8,587	9,695
27,800 -27,899	4,726	6,950	8,062	8,618	9,730
27,900 -27,999	4,743	6,975	8,091	8,649	9,765

ANNUAL INCOME	NUMBER OF CHILDREN 1	2	3	4	5+
	ANNUAL OBLIGATION AMOUNT				
23,000 -23,099	3,910	5,750	6,670	7,130	8,050
23,100 -23,199	3,927	5,775	6,699	7,161	8,085
23,200 -23,299	3,944	5,800	6,728	7,192	8,120
23,300 -23,399	3,961	5,825	6,757	7,223	8,155
23,400 -23,499	3,978	5,850	6,786	7,254	8,190
23,500 -23,599	3,995	5,875	6,815	7,285	8,225
23,600 -23,699	4,012	5,900	6,844	7,316	8,260
23,700 -23,799	4,029	5,925	6,873	7,347	8,295
23,800 -23,899	4,046	5,950	6,902	7,378	8,330
23,900 -23,999	4,063	5,975	6,931	7,409	8,365

ANNUAL INCOME	NUMBER OF CHILDREN 1	2	3	4	5+
	ANNUAL OBLIGATION AMOUNT				
28,000 -28,099	4,760	7,000	8,120	8,680	9,800
28,100 -28,199	4,777	7,025	8,149	8,711	9,835
28,200 -28,299	4,794	7,050	8,178	8,742	9,870
28,300 -28,399	4,811	7,075	8,207	8,773	9,905
28,400 -28,499	4,828	7,100	8,236	8,804	9,940
28,500 -28,599	4,845	7,125	8,265	8,835	9,975
28,600 -28,699	4,862	7,150	8,294	8,866	10,010
28,700 -28,799	4,879	7,175	8,323	8,897	10,045
28,800 -28,899	4,896	7,200	8,352	8,928	10,080
28,900 -28,999	4,913	7,225	8,381	8,959	10,115

ANNUAL INCOME	NUMBER OF CHILDREN 1	2	3	4	5+
	ANNUAL OBLIGATION AMOUNT				
24,000 -24,099	4,080	6,000	6,960	7,440	8,400
24,100 -24,199	4,097	6,025	6,989	7,471	8,435
24,200 -24,299	4,114	6,050	7,018	7,502	8,470
24,300 -24,399	4,131	6,075	7,047	7,533	8,505
24,400 -24,499	4,148	6,100	7,076	7,564	8,540
24,500 -24,599	4,165	6,125	7,105	7,595	8,575
24,600 -24,699	4,182	6,150	7,134	7,626	8,610
24,700 -24,799	4,199	6,175	7,163	7,657	8,645
24,800 -24,899	4,216	6,200	7,192	7,688	8,680
24,900 -24,999	4,233	6,225	7,221	7,719	8,715

ANNUAL INCOME	NUMBER OF CHILDREN 1	2	3	4	5+
	ANNUAL OBLIGATION AMOUNT				
29,000 -29,099	4,930	7,250	8,410	8,990	10,150
29,100 -29,199	4,947	7,275	8,439	9,021	10,185
29,200 -29,299	4,964	7,300	8,468	9,052	10,220
29,300 -29,399	4,981	7,325	8,497	9,083	10,255
29,400 -29,499	4,998	7,350	8,526	9,114	10,290
29,500 -29,599	5,015	7,375	8,555	9,145	10,325
29,600 -29,699	5,032	7,400	8,584	9,176	10,360
29,700 -29,799	5,049	7,425	8,613	9,207	10,395
29,800 -29,899	5,066	7,450	8,642	9,238	10,430
29,900 -29,999	5,083	7,475	8,671	9,269	10,465

FORM 7-2 continued

4/1/96

THE CHILD SUPPORT STANDARDS CHART

INCOME RANGE
50,000 -59,999

NUMBER OF CHILDREN — ANNUAL OBLIGATION AMOUNT

ANNUAL INCOME	1	2	3	4	5+
50,000 -50,099	8,500	12,500	14,500	15,500	17,500
50,100 -50,199	8,517	12,525	14,529	15,531	17,535
50,200 -50,299	8,534	12,550	14,558	15,562	17,570
50,300 -50,399	8,551	12,575	14,587	15,593	17,605
50,400 -50,499	8,568	12,600	14,616	15,624	17,640
50,500 -50,599	8,585	12,625	14,645	15,655	17,675
50,600 -50,699	8,602	12,650	14,674	15,686	17,710
50,700 -50,799	8,619	12,675	14,703	15,717	17,745
50,800 -50,899	8,636	12,700	14,732	15,748	17,780
50,900 -50,999	8,653	12,725	14,761	15,779	17,815
51,000 -51,099	8,670	12,750	14,790	15,810	17,850
51,100 -51,199	8,687	12,775	14,819	15,841	17,885
51,200 -51,299	8,704	12,800	14,848	15,872	17,920
51,300 -51,399	8,721	12,825	14,877	15,903	17,955
51,400 -51,499	8,738	12,850	14,906	15,934	17,990
51,500 -51,599	8,755	12,875	14,935	15,965	18,025
51,600 -51,699	8,772	12,900	14,964	15,996	18,060
51,700 -51,799	8,789	12,925	14,993	16,027	18,095
51,800 -51,899	8,806	12,950	15,022	16,058	18,130
51,900 -51,999	8,823	12,975	15,051	16,089	18,165
52,000 -52,099	8,840	13,000	15,080	16,120	18,200
52,100 -52,199	8,857	13,025	15,109	16,151	18,235
52,200 -52,299	8,874	13,050	15,138	16,182	18,270
52,300 -52,399	8,891	13,075	15,167	16,213	18,305
52,400 -52,499	8,908	13,100	15,196	16,244	18,340
52,500 -52,599	8,925	13,125	15,225	16,275	18,375
52,600 -52,699	8,942	13,150	15,254	16,306	18,410
52,700 -52,799	8,959	13,175	15,283	16,337	18,445
52,800 -52,899	8,976	13,200	15,312	16,368	18,480
52,900 -52,999	8,993	13,225	15,341	16,399	18,515
53,000 -53,099	9,010	13,250	15,370	16,430	18,550
53,100 -53,199	9,027	13,275	15,399	16,461	18,585
53,200 -53,299	9,044	13,300	15,428	16,492	18,620
53,300 -53,399	9,061	13,325	15,457	16,523	18,655
53,400 -53,499	9,078	13,350	15,486	16,554	18,690
53,500 -53,599	9,095	13,375	15,515	16,585	18,725
53,600 -53,699	9,112	13,400	15,544	16,616	18,760
53,700 -53,799	9,129	13,425	15,573	16,647	18,795
53,800 -53,899	9,146	13,450	15,602	16,678	18,830
53,900 -53,999	9,163	13,475	15,631	16,709	18,865
54,000 -54,099	9,180	13,500	15,660	16,740	18,900
54,100 -54,199	9,197	13,525	15,689	16,771	18,935
54,200 -54,299	9,214	13,550	15,718	16,802	18,970
54,300 -54,399	9,231	13,575	15,747	16,833	19,005
54,400 -54,499	9,248	13,600	15,776	16,864	19,040
54,500 -54,599	9,265	13,625	15,805	16,895	19,075
54,600 -54,699	9,282	13,650	15,834	16,926	19,110
54,700 -54,799	9,299	13,675	15,863	16,957	19,145
54,800 -54,899	9,316	13,700	15,892	16,988	19,180
54,900 -54,999	9,333	13,725	15,921	17,019	19,215
55,000 -55,099	9,350	13,750	15,950	17,050	19,250
55,100 -55,199	9,367	13,775	15,979	17,081	19,285
55,200 -55,299	9,384	13,800	16,008	17,112	19,320
55,300 -55,399	9,401	13,825	16,037	17,143	19,355
55,400 -55,499	9,418	13,850	16,066	17,174	19,390
55,500 -55,599	9,435	13,875	16,095	17,205	19,425
55,600 -55,699	9,452	13,900	16,124	17,236	19,460
55,700 -55,799	9,469	13,925	16,153	17,267	19,495
55,800 -55,899	9,486	13,950	16,182	17,298	19,530
55,900 -55,999	9,503	13,975	16,211	17,329	19,565
56,000 -56,099	9,520	14,000	16,240	17,360	19,600
56,100 -56,199	9,537	14,025	16,269	17,391	19,635
56,200 -56,299	9,554	14,050	16,298	17,422	19,670
56,300 -56,399	9,571	14,075	16,327	17,453	19,705
56,400 -56,499	9,588	14,100	16,356	17,484	19,740
56,500 -56,599	9,605	14,125	16,385	17,515	19,775
56,600 -56,699	9,622	14,150	16,414	17,546	19,810
56,700 -56,799	9,639	14,175	16,443	17,577	19,845
56,800 -56,899	9,656	14,200	16,472	17,608	19,880
56,900 -56,999	9,673	14,225	16,501	17,639	19,915
57,000 -57,099	9,690	14,250	16,530	17,670	19,950
57,100 -57,199	9,707	14,275	16,559	17,701	19,985
57,200 -57,299	9,724	14,300	16,588	17,732	20,020
57,300 -57,399	9,741	14,325	16,617	17,763	20,055
57,400 -57,499	9,758	14,350	16,646	17,794	20,090
57,500 -57,599	9,775	14,375	16,675	17,825	20,125
57,600 -57,699	9,792	14,400	16,704	17,856	20,160
57,700 -57,799	9,809	14,425	16,733	17,887	20,195
57,800 -57,899	9,826	14,450	16,762	17,918	20,230
57,900 -57,999	9,843	14,475	16,791	17,949	20,265
58,000 -58,099	9,860	14,500	16,820	17,980	20,300
58,100 -58,199	9,877	14,525	16,849	18,011	20,335
58,200 -58,299	9,894	14,550	16,878	18,042	20,370
58,300 -58,399	9,911	14,575	16,907	18,073	20,405
58,400 -58,499	9,928	14,600	16,936	18,104	20,440
58,500 -58,599	9,945	14,625	16,965	18,135	20,475
58,600 -58,699	9,962	14,650	16,994	18,166	20,510
58,700 -58,799	9,979	14,675	17,023	18,197	20,545
58,800 -58,899	9,996	14,700	17,052	18,228	20,580
58,900 -58,999	10,013	14,725	17,081	18,259	20,615
59,000 -59,099	10,030	14,750	17,110	18,290	20,650
59,100 -59,199	10,047	14,775	17,139	18,321	20,685
59,200 -59,299	10,064	14,800	17,168	18,352	20,720
59,300 -59,399	10,081	14,825	17,197	18,383	20,755
59,400 -59,499	10,098	14,850	17,226	18,414	20,790
59,500 -59,599	10,115	14,875	17,255	18,445	20,825
59,600 -59,699	10,132	14,900	17,284	18,476	20,860
59,700 -59,799	10,149	14,925	17,313	18,507	20,895
59,800 -59,899	10,166	14,950	17,342	18,538	20,930
59,900 -59,999	10,183	14,975	17,371	18,569	20,965

📁 FORM 7-3

A 189—Child support worksheet, DRL §240(1-b), FCA §413(1), 5-95

COURT

COUNTY OF   Index/Docket No.

against   Plaintiff, Petitioner

Defendant, Respondent

CHILD SUPPORT WORKSHEETS

References are to DRL §240(1-b) and FCA §413(1)

Prepared by ....

Submitted by ☐ Plaintiff ☐ Defendant ☐ Petitioner ☐ Respondent

(All numbers used in these worksheets are YEARLY figures. Convert weekly or monthly figures to annualized numbers.)

		FATHER	MOTHER
STEP 1 MANDATORY PARENTAL INCOME *(b)(5)*			
1. Gross (total) income (as reported on most recent Federal tax return, or as computed in accordance with Internal Revenue Code and regulations): *(b)(5)(i)*			
The following items **MUST** *be added if not already included in Line 1:*			
2. Investment income: *(b)(5)(ii)*			
3. Workers' compensation: *(b)(5)(iii)(A)*			
4. Disability benefits: *(b)(5)(iii)(B)*			
5. Unemployment insurance benefits: *(b)(5)(iii)(C)*			
6. Social Security benefits: *(b)(5)(iii)(D)*			
7. Veterans benefits: *(b)(5)(iii)(E)*			
8. Pension/retirement income: *(b)(5)(iii)(F)*			
9. Fellowships and stipends: *(b)(5)(iii)(G)*			
10. Annuity payments: *(b)(5)(iii)(H)*			
11. If self-employed, depreciation greater than straight-line depreciation used in determining business income or investment credit: *(b)(5)(vi)(A)*			
12. If self-employed, entertainment and travel allowances deducted from business income to the extent the allowances reduce personal expenditures: *(b)(5)(vi)(B)*			
13. Former income voluntarily reduced to avoid child support: *(b)(5)(v)*			
14. Income voluntarily deferred: *(b)(5)(iii)*			
A. TOTAL MANDATORY INCOME:			

STEP 2   NON—MANDATORY PARENTAL INCOME

These items must be disclosed here. Their inclusion in the final calculations, however, is discretionary. In contested cases, the Court determines whether or not they are included. In uncontested cases, the parents and their attorneys or mediators must determine which should be included.

	FATHER	MOTHER
15. Income attributable to non-income producing assets: *(b)(5)(iv)(A)*		
16. Employment benefits that confer personal economic benefits: *(b)(5)(iv)(B)* (Such as meals, lodging, memberships, automobiles, other)		
17. Fringe benefits of employment: *(b)(5)(iv)(C)*		
18. Money, goods and services provided by relatives and friends: *(b)(5)(iv)(D)*		
B. TOTAL NON-MANDATORY INCOME:		
C. TOTAL INCOME *(add Line A + Line B)*		

📁 **FORM 7-3 continued**

STEP 3 DEDUCTIONS

19. Expenses of investment income listed on line 2: (b)(5)(ii) ....
20. Unreimbursed business expenses that do not reduce personal expenditures: (b)(5)(vii)(A) ....
21. Alimony or maintenance actually paid to a former spouse: (b)(5)(vii)(B) ....
22. Alimony or maintenance paid to the other parent but only if child support will increase when alimony stops: (b)(5)(vii)(C) ....
23. Child support actually paid to other children the parent is legally obligated to support: (b)(5)(vii)(D) ....
24. Public assistance: (b)(5)(vii)(E)...
25. Supplemental security income: (b)(5)(vii)(F)..
26. New York City or Yonkers income or earnings taxes actually paid: (b)(5)(vii)(G) ...
27. Social Security taxes (FICA) actually paid: (b)(5)(vii)(H)...........................

D. TOTAL DEDUCTIONS:...

E. FATHER'S INCOME (Line C minus Line D) .... $

F. MOTHER'S INCOME (Line C minus Line D).. $

STEP 4 (b)(4) **G. COMBINED PARENTAL INCOME:** (Line E plus Line F)....................... $

STEP 5 (b)(3) and (c)(2)

MULTIPLY Line G (up to $80,000) by the proper percentage (insert in Line H):
For 1 child ....17%   For 3 children ....29%   For 5 or more children .... 35% (minimum)
For 2 children ....25%   For 4 children 31%

H. COMBINED CHILD SUPPORT: ....

STEP 6 (c)(2)

DIVIDE the non-custodial parent's amount on Line E or Line F...
by the amount of Line G ....
to obtain the percentage allocated
I. to the non-custodial parent:.. %

STEP 7 (c)(2)   **J. MULTIPLY line H by Line I:**

STEP 8 (c)(3)

K. DECIDE the amount of child support to be paid on any combined parental income exceeding $80,000 per year using the percentages in Step 5 or the factors in Step 11-C or both: ....

L. ADD Line J and Line K...
    This is the amount of child support to be paid by the non-custodial parent to the custodial parent for all costs of the children, except for child care expenses, health care expenses, and college, post-secondary, private, special or enriched education.

STEP 9 SPECIAL NUMERICAL FACTORS

CHILD CARE EXPENSES

M. Cost of child care resulting from custodial parent's
    ☐ seeking work (c)(6) [discretionary]   ☐ working   ☐ attending elementary education
    ☐ attending secondary education   ☐ attending higher education
    ☐ attending vocational training leading to employment: (c)(4)...

N. MULTIPLY Line M by Line I: ....
    This is the amount the non-custodial parent must contribute to the custodial parent for child care.

📁 **FORM 7-3 continued**

HEALTH EXPENSES *(c)(5)*

O. Reasonable future health care expenses not covered by insurance: ....

P. MULTIPLY Line O by Line I: ....
   This is the amount the non-custodial parent must contribute to the custodial parent for health care or pay directly to the health care provider.

Q. EDUCATIONAL EXPENSE, if appropriate, see Step 11 (b) *(c)(7)* ....

STEP 10   LOW INCOME EXEMPTIONS *(d)*

R. Insert amount of non-custodial parent's income from Line E or Line F: ....

S. Add amounts on Line L, Line N, Line P and Line Q (This total is "basic child support"): .... ─────────────

T. SUBTRACT Line S from Line R: .... ═════════════

   If Line T is more than $10,084, then the low income exemptions do not apply and child support remains as determined in Steps 8 and 9. If so, go to Step 11.

   If Line T is less than $7,470†, than

U. Insert amount of non custodial parent's income from Line E or Line F: ....

V. Self-support reserve: .... ($10,084)*

W. Subtract Line V from Line U: .... ═════════════

          If Line W is more than $300 per year, then Line W is the amount of basic child support. If Line
          W is less than $300 per year, then basic child support must be a minimum of $300 per year.

   If Line T is less than $10,084* but more than $7,470†, then

X. Insert amount of non-custodial parent's income from Line E or Line F: ....

Y. Self-support reserve: .... ($10,084)*

Z. SUBTRACT Line Y from Line X : .... ═════════════

          If Line Z is more than $600 per year, then Line Z is the amount of basic child support. If
          Line Z is less than $600 per year, then basic child support must be a minimum of $600 per year.

STEP 11   NON-NUMERICAL FACTORS

   (a) NON-RECURRING INCOME *(e)*

      A portion of non-recurring income, such as life insurance proceeds, gifts and inheritances or lottery winnings, may be allocated to child support. The law does not mention a specific percentage for such non-recurring income. Such support is not modified by the low income exemptions.

   (b) EDUCATIONAL EXPENSES *(c)(7)*

      New York's child support law does not contain a specific percentage method to determine how parents should share the cost of education of their children. Traditionally, the courts have considered both parents' complete financial circumstances in deciding who pays how much. The most important elements of financial circumstances are income, reasonable expenses, and financial resources such as savings and investments.

───────

* $10,084 is the self-support reserve as of April 1, 1995. This figure changes on April 1 of each year. In future years, use the current self-support reserve which is 135% of the official Federal poverty level for a single person household as promulgated by the U.S. Department of Health and Human Services.

†$7,470 is the Federal poverty level as of April 1, 1995. This figure changes on April 1 of each year. In future years, use the current Federal poverty level for a single person household as promulgated by the U.S. Department of Health and Human Services.

FORM 7-3 continued

(c) ADDITIONAL FACTORS *(f)*

The child support guidelines law lists 10 factors that should be considered in deciding on the amount of child support for
- combined incomes of more than $80,000 per year or
- to vary the numerical result of these steps because the result is "unjust or inappropriate." However, any court order deviating from the guidelines must set forth the amount of "basic child support" (line S) resulting from the Guidelines and the reason for the deviation.

These factors are:
1. The financial resources of the parents and the child.
2. The physical and emotional health of the child and his her special needs and aptitudes
3. The standard of living the child would have enjoyed if the marriage or household was not dissolved.
4. The tax consequences to the parents.
5. The non-monetary contributions the parents will make toward the care and well-being of the child.
6. The educational needs of the parents.
7. The fact that the gross income of one parent is substantially less than the gross income of the other parent.
8. The needs of the other children of the non-custodial parent for whom the non-custodial parent is providing support, but only (a) if Line 23 is not deducted; (b) after considering the financial resources of any other person obligated to support the other children; and (c) if the resources available to support the other children are less then the resources available to support the children involved in this matter.
9. If a child is not on public assistance, the amount of extraordinary costs of visitation (such as out-of-state travel) or extended visits (other than the usual two to four week summer visits), but only if the custodial parent's expenses are substantially reduced by the visitation involved.
10. Any other factor the court decides is relevant.

NON JUDICIAL DETERMINATION OF CHILD SUPPORT *(h)*

Outside of court, parents are free to agree to any amount of support, so long as they sign a statement that they have been advised of the provisions of the child support guidelines law, the amount of "basic child support" (line S) resulting from the Guidelines and the reason for any deviation. Further, the Court must approve any deviation, and the court cannot approve agreements of less than $300 per year. This minimum is not per child, meaning that the minimum for 3 children is $300 per year, not $900 per year. In addition, the courts retain discretion over child support.

Verification *(h)(5)(i)*   *Required if married person files joint income tax return.*

STATE OF NEW YORK. COUNTY OF   ss.:

                                           being duly sworn, deposes and says: I am the
                                           in this case; I have read
these Child Support Worksheets and I know their contents; they are true to my own knowledge, except as to the matters stated to be on information and belief, and as to those I believe it to be true.

Sworn to before me on

                                                       The name signed must be printed beneath.

CERTIFICATION BY ATTORNEY

STATE OF NEW YORK, COUNTY OF

     I, the undersigned attorney, am admitted to practice law in the State of New York, and am an officer of the court. As counsel for the party on whose behalf the above paper is submitted, I HEREBY CERTIFY TO THE COURT UNDER PENALTIES OF PERJURY THAT I have no knowledge that the substance of the submission therein is false.

Dated:

                                                 Print name beneath signature.

Health Insurance

When a court makes a support order, the court must at the same time order that the dependent immediately be added to the obligor's employer-subsidized health insurance. FCA § 416; DRL § 240(1). Such an order is called a Qualified Medical Child Support Order (QMCSO) and is similar to a Qualified Domestic Relations Order (QDRO) discussed in Chapter 8. If the obligor fails to comply, the obligation may be enforced by an execution for medical support, which may require the employer to purchase, on behalf of the obligor, the insurance benefits required by the order. CPLR § 5241(b)(2). The employer is not obligated to provide any coverage to which the employee would not otherwise be entitled, however. Any support order that does not provide for medical insurance coverage is automatically modifiable.

Education

If the child attends public school, the basic child support obligation covers all peripheral expenses associated with public schooling, such as school trip fees and gym or sports team uniforms. Private school education (including parochial schools) is a more complicated question. The pre-CSSA rule was that a parent would be compelled to pay for private schooling only when there was an express or implied agreement to do so. An express agreement would generally be contained in a prenuptial or separation agreement. An implied agreement could be found where a child was already attending private school at the time of the parents' separation or where private education had been a part of the parents' family tradition. *Connolly v. Connolly*, 83 A.D.2d 136, 443 N.Y.S.2d 661 (1 Dept. 1981).

The post-CSSA rule is that courts may award educational expenses for private, special or enriched education or college, in the absence of an agreement, based on the circumstances of the case and the parties, the child's best interests, and the interests of justice. FCA § 413(1)(c)(7); DRL § 240(1-b)(c)(7). Courts have become noticeably more liberal in awarding funds for private school. Private schooling is becoming much more common among middle class people than it was a generation ago, and the courts have responded to this trend. Still, the award must be justified; courts will not presume that public school is inferior to private school. *Cohen v. Cohen*, 203 A.D.2d 411, 610 N.Y.S.2d 313 (2 Dept. 1994).

Whether a parent will be compelled to contribute towards the cost of a college education, or any sort of post- high school education for a child depends on three factors: 1) whether the parent has the means to finance the higher education, 2) the educational level of both parents, and 3) the academic ability of the child. If the child is a conscientious student and the parent has the financial ability to subsidize the child's education, the courts generally order the parent to contribute toward the cost of study at a public school. Private education at the post-high school level is subject to the same test as private elementary and high school education. Remember, however, that the support obligation terminates by operation of law when the child reaches the age of 21 years. If the custodial parent wishes the non-custodial parent to contribute towards the child's support and/or educational costs until the child completes college or graduate school, this provision *must* be included in an agreement, as discussed in Chapter 4.

Minimum Child Support Awards

All non-custodial parents must pay child support. The CSSA requires a minimum award of $25 per month, even if the non-custodial parent is on public assistance or has no income at all. FCA § 413 (1)(d); DRL § 240(1-b)(d). The obligor is permitted to rebut the presumption in favor of a minimum award, however, by showing that it would be unjust. *Rose v. Moody*, 83 N.Y.2d 65, 607 N.Y.S.2d 906 (1996), *cert. denied* 114 S.Ct. 1837 (1994). For low-income obligors an extra step is required in the calculation. Parents are allowed to retain a **self-support reserve** for their own needs. The self-support reserve is defined as 135% of the poverty income set by the Federal Department of Health and Human Services for a single person. In 1996, the poverty income was $7,740, and the self-support reserve figure was $10,449. You can always find out what the current numbers are by obtaining the Child Support Standards Chart from Family Court. If the support obligation computed using the steps above would reduce the parent's income below the self-support reserve, but not below the poverty line, the parent must pay $50 a month, or the difference between the parent's income and the self-support reserve, whichever is greater. FCA § 413(1)(d); DRL § 240(1-b)(d).

DEVIATING FROM CSSA GUIDELINES

When the combined parental income does not exceed $80,000, the court must apply the CSSA guidelines, unless the result would be unjust or inappropriate. FCA § 413(1)(f); DRL § 240(1-b)(f). The CSSA lists 10 factors a court or Hearing Examiner must consider and include in its decision if the court decides to make a child support order either larger or smaller than called for by the CSSA formula:

1.   financial resources of both parents and child;
2.   physical and emotional health, special needs, and aptitudes of the child;
3.   pre-separation standard of living for the child;
4.   tax consequences;
5.   non-monetary contributions of parents for the support of the child;
6.   educational needs of either parent;
7.   large discrepancy between the gross incomes of the parents;
8.   needs of non-subject children of non-custodial parent (children for whom support payments have not been deducted from income), and financial resources of any person obligated to support those non-subject children;
9.   extraordinary expenses associated with visitation;
10.   any other factors the court thinks relevant.
       FCA § 413(1)(f); DRL § 240(1-b)(f)

Multiple Families

One of the most vexing problems courts have faced in the application of the CSSA is how to be fair to all the children a parent may have in two or more households. The statute makes no distinction between in-wedlock and out-of-wedlock children, nor is the order of birth of the children relevant. Since child support payments made pursuant to a court order or written agreement are deducted from the respondent's gross income, however, it is obvious that the first child for whom support is ordered will receive a larger child support award than those for whom support is subsequently ordered. Actually, since the support order is **retroactive** to the date of the filing of the petition, what really counts is the date the petition was filed, rather than the date of the order. The result has been called "the race to the courthouse door."

Trial courts confronted with this issue had devised various "solutions" such as treating the children as a unit and dividing the percentage applicable to the total number of children among the several households. These attempts to find equitable solutions in difficult cases all involved deviating from the CSSA formula. The Appellate Division rejected these strategies in the decisions collectively reported as *Commissioner of Social Services on Behalf of Patricia H. v. Raymond S.*, 180 A.D.2d 510, 581 N.Y.S.2d 1 (1 Dept. 1992). The decision in that case noted that the percentages in the CSSA (17% for one child, 25% for two children, etc.) are based upon the premise that there are economies of scale in raising several children *in the same household*. This is a point that is intuitively obvious to every parent. When the children do not reside in the same household, however, those economies do not occur; the children do not play with the same toys, watch the same television, eat from the same giant economy size box of cereal, or use the same set of encyclopedias to do their homework. Thus, the Appellate Division reversed the trial courts and sent the cases back for child support to be calculated in accordance with the CSSA guidelines.

A different issue arises when a parent is both a custodial and a non-custodial parent. What if a married man, living with his wife and the children of the marriage, fathers a child with another woman, for example? In such a situation, the "paragraph (f)" factors permit the court some leeway. Factor 8, above, allows the court to consider the needs of the children with whom the respondent lives; at the same time, however, the court must consider the resources of the other parent of those children (in our example, the wife) that are available for the support of the children. Remember, however, that consideration can be given only to children to whom the respondent owes a legal duty of support. Thus, if the respondent is supporting out-of-wedlock children whose paternity has not been acknowledged or adjudicated, no allowances can be made for that support.

Combined Parental Income Above $80,000

When the combined parental income is greater than $80,000, CSSA says that the guidelines are not mandatory, although the court may exercise its discretion to apply them, considering the 10 paragraph (f) factors listed above. FCA § 413(1)(c)(1-3); DRL § 240(1-b)(c)(1-3). This statutory language had been widely interpreted as allowing courts to depart freely from the guidelines in dealing with income in excess of $80,000. Some courts had applied the CSSA formula to that portion of the combined parental income up to $80,000 and then disregarded whatever was left over. In other words, the statute was treated as if it created a rebuttable presumption against applying the formula to combined parental income in excess of $80,000. In *Cassano v. Cassano*, Case 7-1, the Court of Appeals made it clear that the CSSA guidelines may be applied to the total combined parental income.

 **CASE 7-1**

CASSANO v. CASSANO
85 N.Y.2d 649, 628 N.Y.S.2d 10 (1995)

KAYE, CHIEF JUDGE

The focus of this appeal is the Child Support Standard Act (Family Ct Act § 413; Domestic Relations Law § 240), which includes a numeric formula for calculating the award of child support, prescribing criteria as to combined parental income under $80,000 and criteria as to income above that amount. We are asked to review an award determined by application of the statutory formula to combined parental income exceeding $80,000. We conclude that the award was proper and affirm the Appellate Division order so holding.

The parties here were divorced in 1986, with two children, one of whom is now emancipated. Plaintiff mother was awarded custody of the children and defendant father was ordered to pay $125 per week in child support. In 1989 plaintiff petitioned for an upward modification of the support award for the nonemancipated child pursuant to the newly enacted child support statute, and defendant cross-petitioned for a downward modification.

After taking evidence in a two-day hearing relating to the family's income and expenses, the Hearing Examiner found a substantial increase in the parties' financial circumstances warranting increased child support. On combined parental income of $99,944 (64.4% of it attributable to the father), the Hearing Examiner ordered defendant to pay $218 per week. That amount was determined by multiplying the parents' total income by the statutory percentage (17%) and then allocating 64.4% of that amount to the father. The Hearing Examiner further ordered defendant to pay his pro rata share of the child's private school costs and unreimbursed medical expenses.

Before Family Court, the father contended that the Hearing

📖 **CASE 7-1 continued**

Examiner erred in applying the statutory percentage to income over $80,000 without setting forth reasons for that particular award. Family Court concluded that the statute permitted that and, absent good cause, refused to interfere with the Hearing Examiner's exercise of discretion to apply the percentage. The Appellate Division agreed with the father that Family Court was required to state reasons for the award of child support on combined parental income over $80,000 but found that requirement satisfied by the Hearing Examiner's in-depth consideration of the parties' circumstances. The Appellate Division additionally affirmed the award of unreimbursed medical expenses. We now affirm.

The Child Support Standards Act, effective September 15, 1989, replaced a needs-based discretionary system with a precisely articulated, three-step method for determining child support. Enactment of this statute after long efforts signaled a new era in calculating child support awards...

The Act had among its objectives the assurance that both parents would contribute to the support of the children, and that the children would not "unfairly bear the economic burden of parental separation"...Emphasis was to shift "from a balancing of the expressed needs of the child and the income available to the parents after expenses to the total income available to the parents and the standard of living that should be shared with the child"....

Further, the Legislature perceived that the existing system produced inconsistent, unpredictable and often seemingly arbitrary results, which undermined the parties' confidence in the fairness of the process.... Consequently, the new statute sought to create greater uniformity, predictability and equity in fixing child support awards, while at the same time maintaining the degree of judicial discretion necessary to address unique circumstances....

As the statute directs, step one of the three-step method is the court's calculation of "combined parental income" in accordance with Family Ct Act § 413(1)(b)(4)-(5) (See Domestic Relations Law § 240 for analogous provisions). Second, the court multiplies that figure, up to $80,000, by a specified percentage based upon the number of children in the household -- 17 % for one child -- and then allocates that amount between the parents according to their share of the total income....

Third, where combined parental income exceeds $80,000 -- the situation at issue in this case -- the statute provides that "the court shall determine the amount of child support for the amount of the combined parental income in excess of such dollar amount through consideration of the factors set forth in paragraph (f) of this subdivision and/or the child support percentage" (Family Ct Act § 413[1][c][3]). The "paragraph (f)" factors include the financial resources of the parents and child, the health of the child and any special needs, the standard of living the child would have had if the marriage had not ended, tax consequences, non-monetary contributions of the parents toward the child, the educational

CASE 7-1 continued

needs of the parents, the disparity in the parents' incomes, the needs of other nonparty children receiving support from one of the parents, extraordinary expenses incurred in exercising visitation and any other factors the court determines are relevant (Family Ct Act § 413[1][f]).

Whenever the basic child support obligation derived by application of the formula would be "unjust or inappropriate," the court must consider the "paragraph (f)" factors. That is so whether parental income is above or below $80,000 (Family Ct Act § § 413[1][b][1]; [c][2], [3]). If the formula is rejected, the statute directs that the court "set forth, in a written order, the factors it considered" -- an unbending requirement that cannot be waived by either party or counsel (Family Ct Act § 413[1][g]).

The question now before us is whether the court must articulate a reason for its award of child support on parental income exceeding $80,000 when it chooses simply to apply the statutory percentage. Defendant urges not only that there must be a stated reason but also that the stated reason must relate to the needs of the child, much as under prior law.

That question has generated uncertainty. Some courts have calculated child support awards simply by applying the statutory percentages to parental income over $80,000.... Others have rejected a "blind application" of the child support percentage to income over $80,000, requiring express findings as to the child's actual needs.... The case law has even been read to limit the application of the percentages to income below $80,000....

Obviously, determining what the Child Support Standards Act requires begins with the statute itself.

***

As to combined parental income over $80,000, the statute explicitly affords an option: the court may apply the factors set forth in section 413(1)(f) "*and/or* the child support percentage" (Family Ct Act 413[1][c][3]).... Pertinent as well to income above $80,000 is the provision that the court may disregard the formula if "unjust and inappropriate" but in that event, must give its reasons in a formal written order, which cannot be waived by either party...

The parties' arguments for and against requiring an elaboration of reasons where the statutory percentage is applied to income exceeding $80,000 center on the term "and/or" -- a term that has long irked grammarians.... In that legislative purpose, not grammatical perfection guides our determination, we must seek to give meaning to the term "and/or" in the context of the statute's over-all objective.... In our view, "and/or" should be read to afford courts the discretion to apply the "paragraph (f)" factors, or to apply the statutory percentages, or to apply both in fixing the basic child support obligation on parental income over $80,000. That interpretation is consistent with the language of the section and with the objectives of the Child Support Standards Act.

📖 **CASE 7-1 continued**

That conclusion does not, however, end our analysis. Given that the statute explicitly vests discretion in the court and that the exercise of discretion is subject to review for abuse, some record articulation of the reasons for the court's choice to apply the percentage is necessary to facilitate that review....

In the present case, the Hearing Examiner conducted a two-day inquiry into the parties' circumstances and set forth her findings in detail. The Appellate Division was satisfied, as are we, that there was sufficient record indication that no extraordinary circumstances were present, and application of the statutory 17% to the $19,214 income above $80,000 was therefore justified and not an abuse of discretion.

Finally, we affirm as well the Appellate Divisions's conclusion that the father is required to pay his pro rata share of the child's unreimbursed medical expenses. The statute specifies that the court "shall prorate each parent's share of future reasonable health care expenses of the child not covered by insurance" (Family Ct Act § 413[1][c][5]). Defendant's insistence that this order constitutes an impermissible open-ended obligation, as the Second Department earlier held...is meritless in light of the Act.

Accordingly, the order of the Appellate Division, insofar as appealed from, should be affirmed, with costs.

DISCUSSION TOPIC

What situations can you think of in which it might be appropriate to limit the application of the guidelines to the first $80,000 of combined parental income? Are the "paragraph (f)" factors broad enough to permit deviation under those scenarios? The theory of CSSA is that the child should enjoy the standard of living of the higher-income parent. The custodial parent is not required to account for how the child support money is spent. How do you think this works out when the custodial parent is not entitled to maintenance (as when the parents were never married, for example), and the custodial parent cannot support him or herself at the non-custodial parent's standard of living? What impact do you think it has on the family when the custodial parent has other children in the home from other relationships, and those children receive less support from their non-custodial parents?

"OPTING OUT" OF CSSA GUIDELINES

To have any hope of enforceability, agreements entered into since the passage of CSSA that provide for below-guidelines child support must contain four special provisions:

1.   a statement that the parties have been advised of the guidelines;
2.   a statement that an order of support entered pursuant to the guidelines would be presumptively correct;

3.   if the agreement deviates from the guidelines, the amount that would have been awarded under the guidelines;

4.   the reasons the agreement provides for a different amount from that which would have been awarded pursuant to the guidelines.

      FCA § 413(1)(h); DRL § 240(1-b)(h)

Even when the combined parental income is below $80,000, opting out of the guidelines is extremely difficult. The court must be entirely satisfied that the needs of the child have been fully considered and have not been subordinated to the parents' desires to negotiate an agreement to their own advantage. Where the parties have combined parental income in excess of $80,000, satisfying the opting out requirements has been greatly complicated by the *Cassano* decision.

To satisfy the first and third requirements, the child support worksheet is usually annexed as an exhibit to the separation agreement. Suppose the non-custodial parent of two children has an annual income (after allowable deductions) of $100,000, while the custodial parent makes $25,000 a year (after allowable deductions). If the formula applies to the portion of the income above $80,000, the annual child support obligation of the non-custodial parent would be $25,000. (Shortcut method: $100,000 x .25 = $25,000; Long method: N-CP's prorata share is 80% ∴ $125,000 x .8 = $100,000 ⇒$100,000 x .25 = $25,000.) If, on the other hand, it applies only up to $80,000 of the combined parental income, the non-custodial parent would be obligated to pay only $16,000 a year for child support. (N-CP's prorata share is 80% ∴ $80,000 x .8 = $64,000 ⇒$64,000 x .25 = $16,000.)

Obviously, this is a substantial disparity in the child support obligation resulting from even a modest amount of income above $80,000. Since *Cassano* establishes that there is no presumption either for or against applying the formula to the entire parental income, an agreement between parties having a combined income above $80,000 probably should contain worksheets showing the calculation both ways. That is the easy part, however. A far more difficult hurdle is to satisfy the second requirement by stating that an award calculated by the guidelines would be presumptively correct. Since the parties cannot know whether a court would exercise its discretion to apply the formula to the entire income or only to the first $80,000, which amount would be "correct"? The final Herculean task is to comply with the fourth requirement to articulate satisfactory reasons to deviate, not only from the amount which would have been awarded on the first $80,000, but also on the many thousands that may lie above that figure.

CHILDREN RECEIVING PUBLIC SUPPORT

When a child is receiving public assistance (Aid to Dependent Children), the Commissioner of Social Services may initiate proceedings to recoup from the non-custodial parent the amount of public money expended for the child's support. FCA §§ 422(a), 522; SSL § 102(1). If necessary, the Commissioner may first initiate a paternity proceeding (Chapter 9) to establish the father's duty to support. Furthermore, when a child is in foster care, the Commissioner should seek support from the child's parents. SSL § 398(6)(d). In addition to the Commissioner's own statutory standing to sue for support, the custodial parent of a child receiving public assistance is required as a precondition for receiving assistance to assign to the Commissioner the parent's right to seek support. SSL § 348. When the parent's rights have been assigned to the Commissioner, the Commissioner may seek support in accordance with the CSSA guidelines, and the support award is not limited by the amount of the public assistance grant. The excess is paid to the custodial parent. *Commissioner of Social Services on Behalf of Wandel v. Segarra*, 78 N.Y.2d 220, 573 N.Y.S.2d 56 (1991). In New York City, all proceedings to collect support for children receiving public assistance are heard in the citywide Child Support Enforcement Term (CSET) located in the Manhattan Family Court.

In one respect, support for a child receiving public assistance differs significantly from support for a child who is not publicly supported. In proceedings pending as of April 2, 1992 and thereafter, support is retroactive to the date the child became eligible for public assistance rather than from the date the support petition was filed. Retroactive support is calculated as **arrears** (money owed) at the time the order of support is entered. Thus, if the child has been receiving public assistance for a long while before the support petition is filed, the obligor may owe months or years worth of back support at the time the order is entered. If the obligor is also on public assistance, however, the arrears cannot exceed $500.

METHODS OF PAYMENT

Income Deduction Order

All orders for child support must be paid through **income deduction** unless the parties agree otherwise or the court finds good cause not to order income deduction. FCA § 440(b)(2). When the order of support is for a child in receipt of public assistance, the parties are not permitted to agree to any other method of payment, although the court can still find good cause not to require income withholding. FCA § 440(b)(1). "Good cause" is defined as "substantial harm to the debtor," and the statute specifies that the absence of arrears does not constitute good cause. In other words, income deduction of the child support obligation is now automatic in most cases from the time a child support order is made.

An **income deduction order (IDO)** (Form 7-4), also called a **payroll deduction order (PDO)**, is a form of garnishment, whereby child support payments are deducted directly from the obligor's paycheck, pension payment or almost any other income except public assistance. The money deducted from the obligor's income may be paid to the custodial parent through a support collection unit, discussed below, through the new statewide centralized support collection unit in Albany, or directly to the custodial parent.

📂 FORM 7-4

§ 25:48G   Income Deduction Order by Hearing Examiner With Payment to Support Collection Unit, Based on Official Form [Form— Family Court Act 439, 448; CPLR 5241, 5242(b)]

At a term of the Family Court of the State of New York, held in and for the County of _____, at _____, New York, on _____, 19___.

Present: Hearing Examiner
_____

In the Matter of a Proceeding for) Support Under Article _____) of the Family Court Act) _____,) Petitioner,) —against—) _____,) Respondent.))	INCOME DEDUCTION ORDER (Support Collection Unit) Docket No. _____ [Name of Assigned Judge]

SPECIFIC WRITTEN OBJECTIONS TO THIS ORDER MAY BE FILED WITH THIS COURT WITHIN 30 DAYS AFTER ENTRY OF THIS ORDER.

WHEREAS an order of support, dated _____, 19___, having been made by the _____ Court of _____ County, State of _____ whereby the above-named Respondent was directed to pay the sum of $_____ (bi-) (weekly) (semi) (monthly) (quarterly) to the Support Collection Unit of _____ County for support of _____; and

WHEREAS said payments have not been made and there is due and owing said creditor the amount of $_____; and

Said Respondent now being entitled to receive income as defined as CPLR Section 5241(a) from _____, an (income payor) (employer) as defined in CPLR Section 5241(a), whose address is _____; and good cause having been shown therefor,

Now therefore, it is

ORDERED that pursuant to sections 5241 and 5242 of the Civil Practice Law and Rules, said (employer) (income payor) is directed to deduct from all income as defined in CPLR Section 5241(a), due or payable to the Respondent by said (employer) (income payor) the sum of $_____ (bi-) (weekly) (semi) (monthly) (quarterly) to be applied to insure compliance with the direction in said order of support, and a further sum of $_____ to be applied to the reduction of arrears until the amount of $_____ in arrears is paid in full; and to remit the amount so deducted to the following address: _____ within ten days of the date that Respondent is paid.

Attached hereto is a NOTICE TO EMPLOYER OR INCOME PAYOR which is incorporated by reference and enforceable as if contained herein.

TO: _____

Dated: _____, 19___

ENTER:

_____
Hearing Examiner

ATTEST: A TRUE COPY

_____
Clerk of the Court

FORM 7-4 continued

Notice to Employer or Income Payor

Pursuant to CPLR § 5241 you must commence deductions no later than the first pay period that occurs 14 days following the service of the Income Execution upon you, and payment must be remitted within 10 days of the date that the debtor is paid. Each payment shall include the identity and social security number of the debtor and the date and amount of each withholding of the debtor's income included in the payment. "Date of withholding" means the date on which the income would otherwise have been paid or made available to the debtor were it not withheld by the employer or income payor.

Pursuant to the provisions of CPLR § 5252, discrimination against employees and prospective employees based upon wage assignment or income execution is prohibited. A violation thereof is punishable as a CONTEMPT OF COURT by fine or imprisonment or both.

Deductions from income shall not exceed the following: Where a debtor IS currently supporting a spouse or dependent child other than the creditor, the amount of the deductions to be withheld shall not exceed fifty percent of the earnings of the debtor remaining after the deduction therefrom of any amounts required by law to be withheld ("disposable earnings"), except that if any part of such deduction is to be applied to the reduction of arrears which shall have accrued more than twelve weeks prior to the beginning of the week for which such earnings are payable, the amount of such deduction shall not exceed fifty-five percent of disposable earnings.

Where a debtor IS NOT currently supporting a spouse or dependent child other than the creditor, the amount of the deductions to be withheld shall not exceed sixty percent of the earnings of the debtor remaining after the deductions therefrom of any amounts required by law to be withheld ("disposable earnings"), except that if any part of such deduction is to be applied to the reduction of arrears which shall have accrued more than twelve weeks prior to the beginning of the week for which such earnings are payable, the amount of such deduction shall not exceed sixty-five percent of disposable earnings. CPLR § 5241(g).

Support Collection Units

Support Collection Units, which are administered by the Department of Social Services Bureau of Child Support Services, collect and disburse child support payments and keep records of the amounts paid. All child support payments for children in receipt of public assistance must be paid through a Support Collection Unit (SCU). Even where public assistance is not involved, however, a court may order that payments for child support or combined orders of child and spousal support be made through SCU. This option is particularly useful where the custodial parent has difficulty keeping track of payments or where the payor frequently makes partial or late payments or pays with checks that bounce. Payments to SCU must be made by money order or cashier's or certified check. In addition to their collection, disbursement and accounting functions, Support Collection Units also have extensive modification and enforcement authority, discussed in the Modification and Enforcement sections below.

Direct Payment

If the court does not make an income deduction order or order payment through SCU, the support obligor will be expected to make payments directly to the recipient. This method imposes a heavy burden of record keeping on both sides, particularly the payor. In any future enforcement proceedings, the payor will be expected to produce proof of payment. Since the statute of limitations for support enforcement proceedings is 20 years from the date of default [CPLR § 211(e)], the payor must be prepared to keep canceled checks or receipts for a very long time. Support payments should never be made directly to a recipient in cash unless the payor is confident that the recipient will sign a receipt for the payment. Moreover, child support payments should never be made "in kind," that is the payor should not buy clothing or other items for the child in the expectation that these purchases will be offset against the support obligation. In all probability, the court will treat such purchases as gifts to the child over and above the support obligation.

PROCEDURAL CONSIDERATIONS

Service

Service of the summons in a Family Court support case may be made by personal service only eight days before the court date, a provision that reflects the urgent need petitioners may have for the support they are seeking. FCA § 427(a). If personal service cannot be accomplished after reasonable effort, the court may order substituted service. FCA § 427(b). Mail service to the respondent's last known address, also on eight days notice, is permitted even when personal or substituted service has not been attempted. No default may be taken after mail service, however, unless the court is satisfied that the respondent had actual notice of the proceeding. FCA § 427(c).

Long Arm Jurisdiction

The CPLR provides that in a support case a New York court may exercise long arm personal jurisdiction (discussed in Chapter 5) over a person who has a duty to support a New York resident or domiciliary, even though the obligor is no longer a New York resident or domiciliary, if 1) New York was the matrimonial domicile of the parties before their separation, or 2) the obligor abandoned the obligee in New York, or 3) the claim for support accrued under New York law or under an agreement executed in New York. CPLR § 302(b). Service may be made outside the state [CPLR § 314] or outside the United States.

Expedited Process

To make sure that children do not go hungry while their parents wrangle in protracted court proceedings, an expedited process was enacted [FCA § 117(c)], which applies to all Family Court support proceedings. Temporary or permanent support must be ordered on the court date when the summons is returnable. A temporary order of support is made without a full hearing based upon the court's or hearing examiner's "guesstimate" of the obligor's resources as revealed by the financial disclosure available at the time. Since the support order is retroactive to the date of the filing of the petition, there are almost always **retroactive arrears** when the permanent order is entered. Retroactive arrears are calculated by multiplying the permanent order by the number of payments that would have been due from the filing date. For example, if the permanent order is for $100 a week, and 20 weeks have elapsed between the filing of the petition and the entry of the permanent order of support, the retroactive arrears would be $2,000. If the permanent order of support turns out to be less than the temporary order, the overpayment may be credited to the obligor as an offset against retroactive arrears. If, on the other hand, it is smaller than the permanent order, the discrepancy will be reflected in the retroactive arrears. Even if the temporary order is the same as the permanent order and has been fully paid, there will still be some retroactive arrears covering the period between the filing date and the entry of the temporary order on the first return of process date.

Another feature of the expedited process is the requirement that all applications to modify or vacate an order of support must be accompanied by affidavits or other evidentiary materials that make out a prima facie case. These provisions together make it difficult for a litigant to misuse the court process as a way of wearing out the other party in an attempt to achieve an unfair advantage.

Objections to Hearing Examiners' Orders

Appeals from orders made by Hearing Examiners follow a different route from appeals of other Family Court orders. Generally, Family Court orders are appealable directly to the Appellate Division of the Department in which the case was decided. Appeals from Hearing Examiners' orders have an extra, interim step, the filing of objections. FCA § 439. The procedure is designed to be accessible to *pro se* litigants, and a minimum of procedural formality is required. Either party who is dissatisfied with the order may within 30 days of the entry of the order, or 30 days of the date of mailing if the party was not in court, complete a written statement of the reasons he or she thinks the order is unfair and serve a copy of the objections on the other party. The other party then has 13 days to submit a rebuttal to the objections, and the matter is assigned to a Family Court judge for review. The judge may require the preparation of a transcript, or may listen to the tape recording of the hearing. (Proceedings before Hearing Examiners are mechanically recorded.) The judge may 1) deny the objections, thus affirming the Hearing Examiner's order, or 2) make new findings of fact, with or without conducting a new hearing, or 3) send one or more issues in the case back to the Hearing Examiner for further proceedings. Once the judge issues an order, the case may then be appealed to the Appellate Division pursuant to Article 11 of the Family Court Act.

UNIFORM SUPPORT OF DEPENDENTS LAW

The Uniform Support of Dependents Law (USDL), DRL Article 3-A, is designed to secure support for dependent spouses and children across county and state lines and even some national borders. All the states of the United States except Texas, the District of Columbia, Guam, Puerto Rico, and the Virgin Islands have adopted the USDL. Reciprocity is also exercised with the provinces and territories of Canada, Australia, Bermuda, Fiji, France, Germany, Great Britain, New Zealand, Northern Ireland, Scotland, and South Africa. The list of subscribers changes as new jurisdictions sign on; the most current listing can always be found by checking Article 3-A of the Domestic Relations Law.

The USDL applies when a party charged with support lives in New York and the dependent lives in another county, state or country with reciprocal laws, or the other way around, the dependent lives in New York and the obligor lives in another jurisdiction with reciprocal laws. The jurisdiction in which the petitioner resides or is domiciled is called the **initiating jurisdiction**, while the place where the respondent lives is called the **responding jurisdiction**. Family Court has exclusive original jurisdiction, and Supreme Court has ancillary jurisdiction with matrimonial proceedings. Both public agencies and private petitioners may utilize the USDL.

The amount of the support obligation is the same under a USDL proceeding as in a regular support case. The differences are procedural. A USDL case begins with the filing of a verified petition in the petitioner's county of residence or domicile. A Family Court judge in that jurisdiction then orders the petition to be forwarded to the responding jurisdiction. Service is made in accordance with the laws of the responding jurisdiction, and a hearing is then held in the responding jurisdiction, with a public officer acting as the petitioner's attorney. Petitioners in USDL proceedings initiated in New York are represented by the Corporation Counsel in the City of New York and by the County Attorneys elsewhere in the state. Neither the petitioner nor the petitioner's witnesses have to appear. Instead, both direct and cross examination are in the form of depositions and/or written interrogatories. When an order of support is issued, the respondent must pay under the responding court's supervision, in New York through the Support Collection Unit.

REGISTRATION OF FOREIGN SUPPORT ORDER

In addition to, or instead of, the remedies available under the USDL, a person who has an order of support from another state may register it with the Clerk of Court for filing in the Registry of Foreign Child Support Orders. Once registered the order will be enforced as if it were a New York support order. DRL § 37-a(6)(a). Foreign orders cannot be modified in New York, however, unless both parties have severed all connection with the jurisdiction that made the order. To register a **foreign support order** the following must be submitted:

- a certified copy of the order;
- a copy of the reciprocal support act of the jurisdiction where the order was made;
- a verified statement setting forth the respondent's address, the amount of support due, other states of registration, respondent's employer and property subject to execution.
  DRL § 37-a(5)(a).

TAX CONSEQUENCES OF CHILD SUPPORT

The income tax on child support is handled exactly the reverse of maintenance; that is, the income tax on child support is the obligation of the payor, not the recipient. The amount paid in child support is *not* declared as income by the recipient, and is *not* deducted from the declared income of the obligor. Naturally, this leads some payors to the temptation to try to disguise child support as maintenance. If the payor is in a higher income tax bracket than the recipient, the payor may urge the recipient to agree to accept a larger award of maintenance in exchange for a smaller amount of child support, pointing out that they could then split the tax savings.

Up to a point, this may be wise tax planning, but the IRS is alert to these strategies and has adopted counter-measures to restrict them. First, if the award is **unallocated**, that is, if it does not specify how much is for maintenance and how much for child support, the entire award will be treated as child support for income tax purposes. Second, the award will be treated as child support if the support obligation terminates or drops upon an event usually associated with the end of the child support obligation, such as the death, marriage or emancipation of a child. Even if the parties try to disguise the emancipation provision, for example, by stipulating that the "maintenance" will cease on a particular date (which just happens to be the child's 21st birthday), the IRS computers will immediately spot the "coincidence" and redistribute the tax liability.

Whichever parent contributes more than half of the child's support is entitled to claim the dependent exemption, currently $2,500, for each child. Since the support obligation is now prorated, it is generally easy to see who is entitled to the exemption. In the case of Larry and Annette, for example, Larry would be the parent to claim the exemption, whether or not he is the custodial parent, since he is responsible for ⅔ of the child support obligation. The exemption goes to the parent who *actually* contributes more than half of the child's support in the year for which the tax return is filed, however, so if Annette has custody and Larry fails to keep up his child support payments, he may lose his claim to the exemption.

MODIFICATION OF SUPPORT

Modification of support awards is a difficult area of the law, rivaled only by custody litigation for its unpredictability. An application to modify an order of support may be made by petition, counterclaim, motion or cross-motion. Either party to a support case may apply for modification if circumstances have changed in a way not anticipated by the parties. The payor may move for **downward modification** on the grounds that the recipient no longer needs the support money or that the payor is no longer able to pay. The recipient may request **upward modification** on the grounds that the recipient's needs have increased or, if the original award was a minimal award that did not fully satisfy the existing needs, that the payor is now financially able to meet the recipient's needs. Full financial disclosure is required from both parties in a modification proceeding, as it is in an original support case. Modification orders are effective as of the date the application for modification was filed. Arrears cannot be "forgiven" for the period prior to the filing of the modification application, even if the obligor was truly unable to pay. FCA § 451. *Commissioner of Social Services of the City of New York v. Gomez*, 221 A.D.2d 39, 645 N.Y.S.2d 776 (1 Dept. 1996).

For an applicant to prove either increased needs or decreased ability to pay the existing support award, the applicant must establish the financial circumstances that existed at the time of the award or most recent modification. This is the baseline upon which the alleged change is premised. The court hearing the modification application will not allow the parties to re-litigate either the propriety of the original award or the adjudicated facts upon which it was based. Any information known to the parties at the time they entered into an agreement pertaining to support, or which should have been made known to the court hearing the original support case, is off limits in a modification case. Only events that have occurred subsequent to the prior award are relevant. If the modification application is made in the same court that made the last award, the court will be able to pull its own file and review the decision and the financial disclosure documents upon which it was based. Since Family Court has jurisdiction to modify Supreme Court support awards, however, and parties often change their counties of residence after divorce, the modification application is often brought in a court other than the one that made the original support order. If the application is made to a different court, the legal assistant may be called upon to obtain the record of the prior court. This can be accomplished by obtaining a "so ordered" subpoena (one signed by a judge) and serving it on the Clerk of Court of whatever court made the last support award. Be sure to include the docket or index number of the prior proceeding and the full names of both parties.

Standards for modification vary according to whether the underlying award was for maintenance or child support and whether it was originally arrived at through agreement or was decided by a judge or hearing examiner after hearing. Moreover, the standards for modification of child support depend upon whether the order sought to be modified was made before or after the enactment of the Child Support Standards Act.

MODIFICATION OF MAINTENANCE

Modifying Maintenance Fixed by Agreement

If maintenance (or alimony) was incorporated into a separation agreement or stipulation of settlement incorporated into a judgment or court order, it is extremely difficult to modify. The *McMains* rule, discussed in Chapter 4, was codified in the Equitable Distribution Law, which provides that maintenance based on an underlying agreement can only be modified, either upward or downward, upon a showing of "extreme hardship." DRL § 236(b)(9)(b). The courts have interpreted the "extreme hardship" standard very strictly, denying applications for downward modification whenever the former spouse's financial difficulties may prove temporary or where the payor's financial circumstances have not greatly deteriorated. In *Pintus v. Pintus*, 104 A.D.2d 866, 480 N.Y.S.2d 501 (2 Dept. 1984), for example, downward modification was denied although the payor-husband had been unemployed for almost six months. Since the passage of the Equitable Distribution Law, a court-ordered downward modification supersedes the underlying agreement, even if the agreement was not merged into the judgment in the matrimonial action. Thus, a recipient of maintenance can no longer sue to enforce a post-1980 separation agreement as a contract once a court has granted downward modification.

Modifying Judicially Determined Maintenance

Modification of spousal support or maintenance not based upon an agreement can be granted upon a showing of "changed circumstances." Where an upward modification is sought, the applicant must show both that the applicant's needs have increased in a way not contemplated in the original judicial proceeding and also that the payor has sufficient means to meet those increased needs. An upward modification application by a recipient of maintenance was denied, for example, where the application alleged a medical condition that had existed at the time of the original award and failed to allege that the condition had worsened and further failed to adequately set forth facts indicating that the recipient lacked the financial resources to meet her own needs. *Trainor v.*

Trainor, 188 A.D.2d 461, 590 N.Y.S.2d 910 (2 Dept. 1992). Similarly, applications for downward modification must aver not only that the payor has suffered some financial downturn, but also that the payor currently lacks the means to pay the support award. An application by a physician that he was no longer able to practice medicine was found facially insufficient, that is, it did not even warrant a hearing, because the doctor failed to disclose his other assets and sources of income, which might have been adequate to meet his support obligations. *Praeger v. Praeger*, 162 A.D.2d 671, 557 N.Y.S.2d 394 (2 Dept. 1990). Inflation, by itself, is not a sufficient basis for modification, since inflation affects both parties equally.

MODIFICATION OF CHILD SUPPORT

Modifying Child Support Fixed By Agreement

Child support based upon a separation agreement or stipulation of settlement is easier to modify than maintenance based upon an agreement, but that does not mean that the agreement will be lightly disregarded. If the agreement was entered into *before the passage of CSSA*, modification is controlled by the Court of Appeals decisions in the *Boden* and *Brescia v. Fitts* cases discussed in Chapter 4. The net effect of these decisions is that child support is always modifiable when the child's best interest requires it, but that the custodial parent has the burden of showing that she or he cannot meet the child's needs. Modification will not be allowed merely because the child would be entitled to a larger support award under CSSA than pursuant to the agreement. If modification is permitted, however, the CSSA guidelines will be applied to the new order, even though CSSA did not exist at the time the parents entered into their agreement.

If the agreement was made *after CSSA became effective*, it will specify the parties' reasons for deviating from the CSSA guidelines. (See, "'OPTING OUT' OF CSSA GUIDELINES," above.) In deciding whether to modify an agreement that opted out of CSSA, the judge or hearing examiner must first determine whether the reasons for deviation stated by the parties in the agreement are still valid. Perhaps, for example, the custodial parent agreed to accept an award below the guidelines in exchange for the non-custodial parent's agreement to pay all of the child's private school tuition. Subsequently, the custodial parent and the child moved into an excellent school district with superior public schools, which the child now attends. Since the non-custodial parent is now relieved of the burden of paying the private school tuition, it may be reasonable to require him or her to pay a full guidelines award, which would help the custodial parent to meet the probably higher shelter costs in the new residence.

A question as yet unanswered is what standards the courts will use to modify a post-CSSA agreement that deviated from the guidelines, when the reasons stated for deviation have not changed. Given the strong public policy in favor of adequate child support, it seems likely that in such situations the courts will fall back on the *Brescia v. Fitts* analysis and modify when the child's best interest requires an increase and the custodial parent is unable to meet the child's needs. Perhaps a student currently using this textbook will go on to work on a case that will clarify the law on this point.

Modifying Judicially Determined Child Support

When the child support award was judicially determined the applicant need only establish that circumstances have changed substantially in a way not provided for in the original award. If the original order did not fully provide for the child's needs or was below guidelines because of the non-custodial parent's self-support reserve, it is only necessary to show that the non-custodial parent is now able to pay his or her prorata share. While modification of a pre-CSSA order will not be granted merely on a showing that the child would be entitled under CSSA to more than was initially awarded, the CSSA guidelines will be applied once changed circumstances have been proved justifying modification.

In deciding whether to grant upward modification of child support, courts have considered increased needs of the child, resulting from age-related activities or special circumstances, increases in the cost of living, the child's current and former lifestyle, and changes in the financial circumstances of the parents. The fact that the non-custodial parent's income has increased has been held by itself not sufficient to justify modification; rather, the applicant must also demonstrate that the child's needs are not being met. In light of the income-based adjustment process for support orders payable through SCU, discussed below, it is unclear whether this line of cases is still good law.

Sometimes an application for upward modification is based on financial reverses of one parent rather than increased needs of the child. A parent's job loss is usually considered a change of circumstances warranting modification, so long as the parent who lost the job is making a good faith effort to find a new job. The parent who lost the job may be the custodial parent seeking upward modification or the non-custodial parent seeking downward modification. Remember, however, that if the parent has quit his or her job or has deliberately provoked his or her firing, the court may impute the income that parent is no longer earning and refuse to lower the child support obligation. (This is a codification of a judge-made doctrine called "voluntary relinquishment." If you are doing research in this area, you might try using that term as a keyword.) Even if the parent was laid off through no fault of his or her own, the court may refuse to lower the child support award right away, but rather may wait to see if the job will soon be replaced.

An issue that frequently arises in modification proceedings is what consideration should be given to the fact that a non-custodial parent has a new family to support. The expenses associated with a second family are not a basis for downward modification. *Windwer v. Windwer*, 39 A.D.2d 927, 333 N.Y.S.2d 205 (2 Dept. 1972), aff'd 33 N.Y.2d 599, 347 N.Y.S.2d 458(1973). If the custodial parent applies for upward modification, however, some courts have held that the expenses of the new family may be considered. See, *Cream v. Brace*, 124 Misc.2d 647, 476 N.Y.S.2d 739 (Fam. Ct. Queens County 1984).

Adjustment of Orders Payable Through SCU

All support orders for children receiving public assistance are reviewed every three years for adjustment without further application of any party. All other orders paid through SCU will be reviewed for upward adjustment every three years if requested by a party. FCA § 413(3); SSL § 111-g. If the current support order deviates at least 10 percent from the correct amount as calculated pursuant to the provisions of CSSA, a new order must be issued. Upon being notified of a proposed adjustment, the payor has 35 days to object in writing, and a hearing may be scheduled on the objection before a hearing examiner. The proposed order is based upon income information supplied by the payor and the payor's employer. If the objector fails to complete a net worth statement or provide current financial data, the Support Collection Bureau can obtain that information without the consent of the payor from the New York State Taxation Department, the wage reporting system, and credit bureaus. If the non-custodial parent fails to provide information and such information cannot be obtained elsewhere, the order will be adjusted in accordance with the consumer price index, a national index of inflation.

The existence of this parallel modification process, whereby support orders can be upwardly modified without the necessity of filing a modification petition or proving changed circumstances, calls into question the continuing validity of the judicial decisions that require a showing of changed circumstances other than an increase in the income of the obligor to warrant upward modification. It seems probable that an equal protection challenge will be mounted.

SUPPORT ENFORCEMENT

Effective enforcement of support orders is the final, crucial, and most challenging step in achieving meaningful support for dependent spouses, former-spouses and children. The amount of unpaid support in the United States has become not just a national concern but a national scandal. According to statistics relied upon by the Federal District Court for the Southern District of New York, of the $48 billion in child support owed nationally in 1992, almost 73 percent was never paid. *United States v. Nichols*, 928 F.Supp. 302 (1996).

When a support obligor misses a support payment or pays only part of what is owed, the obligor is said to have defaulted on the obligation. The term "**default**" as used here has a slightly different meaning from the usage you may be familiar with, although it is related. A person who fails to appear in court when summoned to do so is said to be in default. Here, the meaning is that a person has failed in another legal obligation, the obligation to make court-ordered support payments. A person who fails to fulfill the terms of a contract or agreement is also said to be in default. Each instance when the obligor fails to fully perform the obligation imposed by the court order or contract is treated as a separate "default." Even if a support obligor accidentally failed to make the payment or was unable at the time to pay, the missed payment is nevertheless a default. If the obligor knowingly, consciously and voluntarily chose to disregard the court order, although possessed of sufficient means to pay, the default is a **willful default**.

Orders of support may be enforced either in Supreme or Family Court, and either court *must* 1) enter a money judgment, and 2) award legal fees, and *may* 3) issue an income deduction order, 4) require the obligor to provide an undertaking, 5) sequester property, 6) place a defaulting obligor on probation, 7) suspend the driving license or business or professional license of the defaulting parent, or 8) incarcerate a parent who has willfully defaulted on the support obligation. FCA § 454; DRL § 236(9). Orders of support may also be enforced without judicial intervention. A Support Collection Unit may intercept the tax refund of a defaulting parent, [SSL § 111-b(7),(8), (13)(a)], and may also intercept lottery winnings and unemployment benefits [SSL §§ 111-b(10), 111-j]. Remember that Family Court cannot enforce support due pursuant to an agreement unless the agreement has been incorporated into a court order.

ENFORCEMENT REMEDIES

Entry of Money Judgment

A **money judgment** is a judgment directing the payment of a sum of money. When a court finds that a support order has been violated, it must direct the entry of a money judgment for the full amount of the arrears. FCA § 454(2)(a). If the default was willful, interest on the arrears may be added into the judgment. FCA § 460(1)(e); DRL § 244. Interest is calculated from the date when the payment was due, at the prevailing rate of interest on judgments provided in the CPLR. When support arrears have been reduced to a money judgment, a support creditor has all the remedies of any other creditor, including **seizure** and sale of both personal and real property, and issuance of **restraining notices**, which bar the recipient of the notice (such as a bank at which the debtor has an account) from transferring or releasing the debtor's property. CPLR Art. 52. These remedies may be exercised by the support creditor in addition to any other enforcement remedies the court may order. The entry of a money judgment has a practical effect that is particularly useful when the support debtor is self-employed or is the owner of a business: the entry of the money judgment ruins the debtor's credit rating, thus making it difficult to borrow money or obtain a mortgage. Deprived of access to credit, the debtor may become motivated to satisfy the judgment in order to remove the cloud from his or her credit rating.

Award of Legal Fees

Upon finding a willful violation, the court must order payment of petitioner's counsel fees. FCA § 454(3). Whenever a court awards counsel fees, however, the court expects more than the presentation of a bill for services rendered. The attorney seeking payment must present an attorney's affirmation in support of the application. An **affirmation** is the same as an affidavit except that it is affirmed upon the penalties of perjury and is not notarized. Attorneys, as "officers of the court," are allowed to swear on their own honor rather than having to appear before a notary. The affirmation must detail the amount of time spent on the case, state the hourly rate the attorney charged for his or her services, and indicate what payment the attorney has already received. The affirmation also sets forth the attorney's experience and qualifications, as justification for the fee charged. This information may be included in the body of the affirmation or in a CV annexed as an exhibit to the affidavit.

Income Withholding

If an income deduction order was not made at the time the original support order was entered, such an order can be issued later as a method of enforcement. This is the most widely used child enforcement tool, and it is usually highly effective when the obligor has any regular source of income. In an enforcement proceeding, the amount of past due child support is totaled and divided into increments, which are tacked onto the regular child support payments. If, for example the arrears total $2,000, and the normal child support payment is $100 a week, the hearing examiner might issue an income deduction order for $100 per week plus an additional $50 per week until the arrears have been paid up. Once the $2,000 debt has been paid, the deduction reverts to $100 a week, unless it has been upwardly modified in the meantime.

Income withholding can also be accomplished without judicial intervention. A Support Collection Unit, a creditor's attorney, a sheriff or a court clerk may issue an **income execution** when a support obligor has failed three times to make full payment of support due. CPLR § 5241. An income execution works the same way as an income deduction order.

When an income execution has been issued by a Support Collection Unit, the debtor has 15 days to file an objection with the Unit. The SCU then evaluates the objection and notifies the debtor of its decision within 45 days. It then serves the execution. CPLR § 5241(d). A debtor who wishes to appeal the matter further may then file an Article 78 proceeding in Supreme Court to overturn the SCU's findings. Since it is not easy for an unrepresented debtor to file an Article 78 proceeding, this procedure is a great advantage to support recipients who receive payment through SCU.

When an income deduction has been issued by a creditor's attorney, a sheriff or a court clerk, it must first be served on the debtor, who has 15 days to move to challenge it, either in Family or Supreme Court, if the debtor believes it is based upon a mistake of fact. CPLR § 5241(a)(8), (d). The alleged mistake of fact might be that the money has been paid or that the agreement has been modified.

If a debtor is supporting a dependent other than the beneficiary of the support order, the maximum that can be deducted is 50 percent of the debtor's net pay.

If the arrears are 12 weeks old or more, however, the percentage increases to 55 percent. If the obligor has no other dependents, 60 percent may be deducted, and the percentage rises to 65 percent if the obligor has no dependents and the arrears are at least 12 weeks old. CPLR § 5241(g)(1). Income executions are not subject to the self-support reserve limitations of the CSSA. FCA § 413(1)(d); DRL § 240(1-b)(d). Income withholding orders for support take priority over any other levy or garnishment, even if the other garnishment was imposed prior to the support order.

Undertaking

An **undertaking** is a bond or cash deposit posted by the support debtor with the clerk of court to insure future compliance with an order of support. FCA § 471; DRL § 241. The undertaking may be required for up to three years, which period can be extended for good cause. If the support obligor misses a payment or makes partial payment, the amount owed is deducted from the undertaking. Thus, the undertaking may be viewed as a form of prospective enforcement that is appropriate when the obligor has a bad track record. For as long as the undertaking lasts, the recipient is relieved of the burden of incessant enforcement proceedings.

Sequestration

Sequestration is the taking of a debtor's property as security for payment of the debt. It is permitted when a support order has been violated and 1) the debtor leaves the state or threatens to leave, or 2) where the debtor cannot be found within the state (but the property is within New York), or 3) where the debtor is hiding to avoid the service of process. FCA §§ 429, 457; DRL § 241; SSL § 103.

Probation

Probation is a rarely used enforcement tool. Family Court Act section 454(3) authorizes the court to place the support debtor under the supervision of the Department of Probation, which can monitor the obligor's employment and support payments. While it is safe to say that the Support Collection Units are better equipped than the Department of Probation to monitor support payments, courts occasionally order a respondent to report to Probation concerning his or her efforts to seek employment. Probation may be appropriate, for example, where a support order has been suspended or downwardly modified because the payor's lost his or her job.

Suspension of Licenses

In 1996, the legislature passed additional laws designed to put teeth into the enforcement of support. When child support arrears total four or more months of support, not counting retroactive arrears, the debtor's driving license may be suspended. FCA § 458-a; DRL § 244-b; SSL § 111-b; Vehicle and Traffic Law

§§ 510(4-e), 511(7), 530(5), 530(5-a). Obligors who are recipients of public assistance or supplemental security income or whose income falls below the self-support reserve are excluded from the application of these provisions.

Similarly, if an obligor is four or more months behind on child support, the obligor's state-issued business or professional license may also be suspended. FCA § 458-b; DRL § 244-c. If the respondent is an attorney, the matter is referred to the Appellate Division in its capacity as licenser of attorneys. The debtor attorney has a right to a hearing before the Appellate Division, but the only issue at the hearing is whether the arrears have been paid in full. The propriety of the support award or the ability of the respondent to pay are not issues that can be raised in the hearing. Judiciary Law § 90.

Incarceration

If a judge (not a hearing examiner) finds that a respondent willfully violated a support order, the respondent may be punished for contempt by fine or incarceration. The respondent may be committed to jail for up to six months. FCA § 454(3). A finding of willfulness requires proof both of ability to pay and failure to do so. A respondent is presumed to have the means to support his or her dependents. FCA § 437. The petitioner, to make out a prima facie case, need only show that payment was not made. The respondent then has to attempt to rebut the presumption with proof of inability to pay. *Powers v. Powers*, 86 N.Y.2d 63, 629 N.Y.S.2d 984 (1995). If the defaulting obligor is employed, the court may order that the sentence be served on weekends.

Criminal Sanctions

In New York "nonsupport of a child" is a misdemeanor. Penal Law § 260.05. In 1992, when Congress enacted the Child Support Recovery Act of 1992 [18 U.S.C. § 228(a)], it became a federal crime to willfully fail to make a past due support payment for a child residing in another state. The constitutionality of this statute is subject to challenge. One-third of the dozen courts that have ruled on the question have held that it violates the Interstate Commerce clause of the United States Constitution. Eventually the issue will make its way to the Supreme Court.

VISITATION AND SUPPORT ENFORCEMENT

In considering the impact of deprivation of visitation on the non-custodial parent's support obligation, it is necessary to distinguish child support from maintenance, and agreed-upon support from that which was judicially determined. For over 100 years, courts construed visitation and support provisions in separation agreements as "dependent covenants," meaning that if one provision was violated, the other would not be enforced. In 1978, this line of cases was statutorily modified when the Domestic Relations Law was amended to provide that child support arrears may not be canceled due to interference with visitation. DRL § 241. Section 241 does provide that maintenance may be suspended, and maintenance arrears canceled, where the recipient has interfered with the payor's visitation rights. These issues must be heard by a judge; hearing examiners are not authorized to decide visitation and custody questions, even when they arise in the context of a support hearing. FCA § 439.

The statute leaves open the questions of whether, and under what circumstances, child support may be *prospectively* suspended due to the custodial parents interference with visitation or the child's refusal to visit. Although there are many decisions on this subject, the law in this area is highly unsettled. One clear rule is that child support will not be suspended where the child is a recipient of public support. Beyond that, the practitioner can only look at general trends. Many of the cases in which child support has been suspended were relocation cases. Since the rules for relocation have been considerably liberalized by the Court of Appeals decision in *Tropea*, discussed in Chapter 6, courts will presumably have less occasion to suspend support due to wrongful relocation by the custodial parent. Further, in view of the strong public policy favoring collection of child support, courts are unlikely to condone such a drastic step as cutting off support except in the most egregious circumstances.

CONCLUSION

New York's recent sweeping legislative overhaul of support law attempts to transform the collection of support from a blood sport into a dispassionate accounting exercise. In ironing out the inevitable wrinkles in the new legislation, the courts have been ill served by a substantial body of hoary case law precedents that, literally, do not fill the new bills. While this mismatch has engendered confusion, and more than a little frustration, among legal practitioners, it also provides an unparalleled challenge to participate in the dawning of a new legal era. Collection of meaningful support is truly a public service, but dealing with clients in support cases requires extraordinary diplomacy. The legal assistant, in the preliminary interview, may be the first to begin breaking the news to the client that the law is not even remotely what the client thought it was. Hang on to your calculator and your sense of humor.

CHAPTER REVIEW QUESTIONS

1.   Brenda and Roger have physically separated, but have not yet begun divorce proceedings. Brenda has not worked since the couple's son was born two years ago. She is unable to pay the bills since Roger moved out. In what court can she seek support for herself and the child? How soon will she get a temporary order of support?

2.   If Brenda petitions for support in Family Court, who will hear the case? If Roger, upon being served with the summons in the support case, files a petition for visitation with his son, will both cases be heard together? Why or why not?

3.   After Brenda obtains an order of support in Family Court, she files a divorce proceeding with a request for equitable distribution and child support. Before any orders have been made in the matrimonial case, however, Roger falls behind in making the support payments ordered by the Family Court. Can Brenda petition in Family Court to enforce the Family Court support order?

4.   If after filing her support case Brenda decides to take a job that pays exactly enough to pay the rent, can she still seek support for herself? Why or why not?

5.   Charlotte and Dean had no children and hardly any property when they separated. They married young and soon realized they were not right for each other. Both are employed, but since Dean has a better job, he agreed to pay Charlotte $100 a week maintenance for two years while she took a course to become a paralegal. Their separation agreement to this effect was incorporated into their conversion divorce judgment. A month after the divorce became final, and three months before the maintenance was to end, Dean won the lottery and is now a millionaire. Charlotte still has her old job and is almost finished with the paralegal training. If Charlotte moves for upward modification or extension of the maintenance, is her application likely to be granted? What arguments might be made on each party's behalf?

6.   Vivian and Jack have been married for 23 years and have lived life in the fast lane. Vivian is a highly paid advertising executive, while Jack has held a series of modestly compensated jobs in publishing. Jack has always been a very involved father for the couple's two daughters, who are now away at college. After the youngest child left home, so did Jack. He told Vivian he was sick of the social demands her job made and tired of keeping up pretenses in a loveless marriage. He refuses to return to the marital home. If Vivian sues Jack for divorce on the ground of abandonment, can Jack demand maintenance? Is it relevant that he is the defendant in the divorce? Do you think the court is likely to award Jack no maintenance, short-term maintenance, or lifetime maintenance? If he does receive maintenance, will he have to pay income tax on it?

7.   Molly and Peter divorced when their only son was 13. Since the boy preferred to live with his father, Molly agreed to Peter's custody of the child. Molly makes $35,000 a year, while Peter makes $135,000. Can Molly be ordered to pay child support to Peter? How much, if anything, would she be expected to pay under the CSSA guidelines?

8.   After being ordered to pay child support, Molly is so incensed that she quits her job and goes into freelance work. She now claims to make under $20,000 a year. She makes no further application to the court until Peter petitions for enforcement of the child support order, at which

time she cross-petitions for downward modification. The arrears at the time Molly filed her modification petition totaled $1,500. If Molly proves that she was no longer earning her previous salary at the time the arrears accrued, will the arrears be canceled? Why or why not? Is her modification petition likely to be successful? What doctrine do you think the court is likely to invoke?

9. If the court fixes Molly's arrears at $2,000 (because she has fallen further behind while the case was pending), what enforcement remedies might be appropriate? Molly owns an automobile and has bank accounts with balances totaling $40,000. Do you think Peter should ask the court to order that future support payments be made through SCU? What advantages would this procedure provide?

10. Elizabeth and Bruce have two young children. They are negotiating a separation agreement. Elizabeth is in a lower tax bracket than Bruce, and she is willing to agree to accept less child support than the CSSA guidelines would provide, in exchange for higher maintenance. What provisions must the separation agreement include in order to be enforceable? Do you think that the agreement should provide for the child support to increase if Elizabeth remarries or otherwise becomes ineligible to receive maintenance? Do you think it is a good idea for Elizabeth to agree to this proposal? Will the couple be able to articulate convincing reasons for deviating from the guidelines? If after a couple of years Elizabeth's income increases so that her tax bracket is as high as Bruce's, will she have grounds for modification of the child support? Why or why not? If the agreement provides that maintenance ceases when the child becomes 21 years of age, will the payments be treated as child support or maintenance for income tax purposes?

CHAPTER ASSIGNMENT

Using the fact pattern at the end of Chapter 5 and the Child Support Worksheets (Form 7-2), determine the child support obligation of both Wilma and Hugh Bickering.

8 PROPERTY DIVISION

"Although plaintiff's contributions as a homemaker are indeed worthy of full consideration, there is no requirement that the distribution of each item of marital property be on an equal or 50 - 50 basis." *Arvantides v. Arvantides*, 64 N.Y.2d 1033, 489 N.Y.S.2d 58 (1985).

In 1980, New York adopted the equitable distribution system of dividing marital property when a marriage is terminated. Under the equitable distribution system, marital property is divided *fairly*, but not necessarily equally. Before adopting the equitable distribution statute in its present form, the legislature voted down a proposal which would have created a rebuttable presumption that the marital property should be split 50-50. New York's system is, therefore, significantly different from the **community property** system in effect in states such as Texas, California and Louisiana, in which all marital property is jointly owned and presumptively will be evenly divided upon divorce. Prior to adopting the equitable distribution system, New York had followed the **title** theory, under which an asset would presumptively be distributed to the spouse who held title to that asset.

Either party to a divorce or an annulment may ask the court for equitable distribution as ancillary relief in the matrimonial action, but parties to a judicial separation action cannot demand equitable distribution because the spouses remain married to each other after a decree of separation. As discussed in Chapters 3 and 4, spouses are allowed to "opt out" of equitable distribution by using a prenuptial, postnuptial or separation agreement to specify some other method of dividing their property in the event of a divorce. They might agree, for example, that all property acquired after marriage will be split equally or that each asset will be the sole property of the spouse who holds title to it, or they might provide that some assets be split, while other specified assets remain undivided.

ECONOMIC PARTNERSHIP

The principle underlying the equitable distribution system is that marriage is an economic partnership in which the contributions of each spouse should be recognized, whether they were the financial contributions of a wage earner or the intangible contributions of a homemaker. While the principle is laudable, the equitable distribution statute has proved difficult to apply. It is questionable whether non-working or lower wage earning spouses are actually faring any better now than they did under the old system. One study, reported in *The New York Law Journal* on October 15, 1991, found that the percentage of a couple's assets awarded to wives under equitable distribution in 1984 was actually 2 percent less than they received in 1978 under the title system. What is certain is that the equitable distribution process is extremely expensive and labor-intensive. Matrimonial lawyers jokingly refer to the equitable distribution statute as The Full-Employment Act for Accountants, Actuaries and Appraisers, and, they might add, for paralegals.

To limit judges' discretion in making equitable distribution decisions (and to keep old prejudices from creeping in), the equitable distribution statute, Domestic Relations Law §236 Part B, sets forth 12 factors judges are required to consider in determining equitable distribution of property:

1.   the income and property of each party at the time of the marriage, and at the time of the commencement of the action;

2.   the duration of the marriage and the age and health of both parties;

3.   the need of a custodial parent to occupy or own the marital residence and to use or own its household effects;

4.   the loss of inheritance and pension rights upon dissolution of the marriage as of the date of dissolution;

5.   any award of maintenance;

6.   any equitable claim to, interest in, or direct or indirect contribution made to acquisition of such marital property by the party not having title, including joint efforts or expenditures and contributions and services as a spouse, parent, wage earner and homemaker, and to the career or career potential of the other party;

7.   the liquid or non-liquid character of all marital property;

8.   the probable future financial circumstances of each party;

9.   the impossibility or difficulty of evaluating any component asset or any interest in a business, corporation, or profession and the economic desirability of retaining such asset or interest intact and free from any claim or interference by the other party;

10.   the tax consequences to each party;

11.   wasteful dissipation of assets by either spouse;

12.   any transfer or encumbrance made in contemplation of a matrimonial action without fair consideration.

MARITAL FAULT

In addition to the 12 mandatory factors, the statute also contains a "catch all," factor 13, which allows the court to weigh in "any other factor which the court shall expressly find to be just and proper." Although factor 13 appears to be a broad grant of judicial discretion, it was actually the solution to a political impasse in the passage of the equitable distribution law. As we discussed in Chapter 5, matrimonial law reform in New York is always highly controversial, and the passage of the equitable distribution statute was surrounded by the same sort of emotionally charged debate which had accompanied changes in the grounds for divorce a decade earlier. One particularly contentious issue was the role of matrimonial fault in the asset division process. Under the old system, marital fault was very important. The courts commonly penalized the naughty and rewarded the nice, the so-called "innocent spouse." Since the legislature was unable to reach an agreement on a provision of the proposed bill which would have expressly prohibited consideration of marital fault, they substituted factor thirteen, with the understanding that the courts would resolve the question.

The Court of Appeals ultimately held that factor 13 *does not* permit courts to consider ordinary marital fault in equitable distribution decisions. Only "egregious fault," that is, misconduct which "shocks the conscience of the court," may be considered. One spouse's having hired a "hit man" to murder the other spouse (a plot which fortunately failed) has been found to constitute egregious fault, for example. *Brancoveanu v. Brancoveanu*, 145 A.D.2d 393, 535 N.Y.S.2d 86 (2 Dept. 1988), *appeal dismissed* 73 N.Y.2d 994, 540 N.Y.S.2d 1006, *cert. denied* 502 U.S. 854, 112 S.Ct. 165. A husband's reneging on an express promise to do all in his power to sire children with his wife has been held not egregious. *McCann v. McCann*, 156 Misc.2d 540, 593 N.Y.S.2d 917 (N.Y. Sup. Ct. 1993).

Equitable distribution proceeds through several stages. As each phase is discussed, consider which of the 12 mandatory factors are most relevant.

IDENTIFICATION

The first step is to inventory all the property the spouses own either separately or together. What is **property**? Is it real estate such as land and the marital home? Is it personal property such as a car or a bank account? For the purposes of equitable distribution, "property" is all that and much more. In addition to the obvious forms of real and personal property, the list must also include **intellectual property**, such as copyrights and patents, **contingent interests**, such as prospective inheritances, and **vested interests in trusts**, such as pension rights and deferred compensation plans. Virtually any tangible or intangible asset from which a profit can be made or income can be produced is a form of property. As you will see in *O'Brien* (Case 8-1), a professional license is a form of property, and even a career itself has been held to be an asset subject to equitable distribution, as *Elkus* (Case 8-2) illustrates.

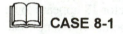 **CASE 8-1**

O'BRIEN v. O'BRIEN
66 N.Y.2d 576, 498 N.Y.S.2d 743 (1985)

SIMONS, J.

In this divorce action, the parties' only asset of any consequence is the husband's newly acquired license to practice medicine. The principal issue presented is whether that license, acquired during their marriage, is marital property subject to equitable distribution under Domestic Relations Law § 236(B)(5)....

I

Plaintiff [husband] and defendant [wife] married on April 3, 1971. At the time both were employed as teachers at the same private school. Defendant had a bachelor's degree and a temporary teaching certificate but required 18 months of postgraduate classes at an approximate cost of $3,000, excluding living expenses, to obtain permanent certification in New York. She claimed, and the trial court found, that she had relinquished the opportunity to obtain permanent certification while plaintiff pursued his education. At the time of the marriage, plaintiff had completed only three and one-half years of college but shortly afterward he returned to school at night to earn his bachelor's degree and to complete sufficient premedical courses to enter medical school. In September 1973 the parties moved to Guadalajara, Mexico, where plaintiff became a full-time medical student. While he pursued his studies, defendant held several teaching and tutorial positions and contributed her earnings to their joint expenses. The parties returned to New York in December 1976 so that plaintiff could complete the last

📖 **CASE 8-1 continued**

two semesters of medical school and internship training here. After they returned, defendant resumed her former teaching position and remained in it at the time this action was commenced. Plaintiff was licensed to practice medicine in October 1980. He commenced this action for divorce two months later. At the time of trial, he was a resident in general surgery.

***

Defendant presented expert testimony that the present value of plaintiff's medical license was $472,000.... [The expert] also gave his opinion that the present value of defendant's contribution to plaintiff's medical education was $103,390....

The [trial] court, after considering the life-style that plaintiff would enjoy from the enhanced earning potential his medical license would bring and defendant's contributions and efforts toward attainment of it, made a distributive award to her of $188,800, representing 40% of the value of the license, and ordered it paid in 11 annual installments of various amounts beginning November 1, 1982 and ending November 1, 1992....

II

The Equitable Distribution Law contemplates only two classes of property: marital property and separate property.... Plaintiff does not contend that his license is excluded from distribution because it is separate property; rather, he claims that it is not property at all but represents a personal attainment in acquiring knowledge. He rests his argument on decisions in similar cases from other jurisdictions and on his view that a license does not satisfy common-law concepts of property.

***

Section 236 provides that in making an equitable distribution of marital property "the court shall consider [factor 6]."...The words mean exactly what they say: that an interest in a profession or professional career potential is marital property which may be represented by direct or indirect contributions of the non-title-holding spouse, including financial contributions and nonfinancial contributions made by caring for the home and family.

The history which preceded enactment of the statute confirms this interpretation. Reform of section 236 was advocated because experience had proven that application of the traditional common-law title theory of property had caused inequalities upon dissolution of a marriage. The Legislature replaced the existing system with equitable distribution of marital property, an entirely new theory which considered all the circumstances of the case and of the respective parties to the marriage.

The determination that a professional license is marital property is also consistent with the conceptual base upon which the statute rests.

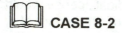 **CASE 8-1 continued**

As this case demonstrates, few undertakings during a marriage better qualify as the type of joint effort that the statute's economic partnership theory is intended to address than contributions toward one spouse's acquisition of a professional license. Working spouses are often required to contribute substantial income as wage earners, sacrifice their own educational or career goals and opportunities for child rearing, perform the bulk of household duties and responsibilities and forego the acquisition of marital assets that could have been accumulated if the professional spouse had been employed rather than occupied with the study and training necessary to acquire a professional license.

***

CASE 8-2

ELKUS v. ELKUS
169 A.D.2d 134, 572 N.Y.S.2d 901 (1 Dept. 1991)

ROSENBERGER, Justice

In this matrimonial action, the plaintiff, Frederica von Stade Elkus, moved for an order determining, prior to trial, whether her career and/or celebrity status constituted marital property subject to equitable distribution.... Contrary to the conclusion reached by the Supreme Court, we find that to the extent the defendant's contributions and efforts led to an increase in the value of the plaintiff's career, this appreciation was a product of the marital partnership, and therefore, marital property subject to equitable distribution.

At the time of her marriage to the defendant on February 9, 1973, the plaintiff had just embarked on her career, performing minor roles with the Metropolitan Opera Company. During the course of the marriage, the plaintiff's career succeeded dramatically and her income rose accordingly. In the first year of the marriage, she earned $2,250. In 1989, she earned $621,878. She is now a celebrated artist with the Metropolitan Opera, as well as an international recording artist, concert and television performer. She has garnered numerous awards, and has performed for the President of the United States.

During the marriage, the defendant traveled with the plaintiff throughout the world, attending and critiquing her performances and rehearsals, and photographed her for album covers and magazine articles. The defendant was also the plaintiff's voice coach and teacher for ten years of the marriage. He states that he sacrificed his own career as a singer and teacher to devote himself to the plaintiff's career and to the lives of their young children, and that his efforts enabled the plaintiff to become one of the most celebrated opera singers in the

📖 **CASE 8-2 continued**

world. Since the plaintiff's career and/or celebrity status increased in value during the marriage due in part to his contributions, the defendant contends that he is entitled to equitable distribution of this marital property.

***

In *Golub v. Golub,* 139 Misc.2d 440, 527 N.Y.S.2d 946 (Sup.Ct. New York Co.), the Supreme Court agreed with the defendant husband that the increase in value in the acting and modeling career of his wife, Marisa Berenson, was marital property subject to equitable distribution as a result of his contributions thereto. Like Ms. von Stade, Ms. Berenson claimed that since her celebrity status was neither "professional" nor a "license," and, since her show business career was subject to substantial fluctuation, it should not be considered "marital property.".... As the *Golub* court found, it is the enhanced earning capacity that a medical license affords its holder that the *O'Brien* court deemed valuable, not the document itself. There is no rational basis upon which to distinguish between a degree, a license, or any other special skill that generates substantial income.

***

Like the parties here, after Joe Piscopo and his wife married in 1973, they focused on one goal -- the facilitation of his rise to stardom (*Piscopo v. Piscopo,* 231 N.J. Super. 576, 555 A.2d 1190, aff'd., 232 N.J. Super. 559, 557 A.2d 1040, certification denied, 117 N.J. 156, 564 A.2d 875). The defendant wife claimed that her husband's celebrity goodwill was a distributable asset and that she was entitled to a share in his excess earning capacity to which she contributed as homemaker, caretaker of their child, and sounding board for his artistic ideas.

Rejecting Mr. Piscopo's argument that celebrity goodwill is distinguishable from professional goodwill since professional goodwill has educational and regulatory requirements while celebrity goodwill requires ineffable talent, the court held that "it is the person with particular and uncommon aptitude for some specialized discipline whether law, medicine or entertainment that transforms the average professional or entertainer into one with measurable goodwill.".... We agree with the courts that have considered the issue, that the enhanced skills of an artist such as the plaintiff, albeit growing from an innate talent, which have enabled her to become an exceptional earner, may be valued as marital property subject to equitable distribution.

***

DISCUSSION TOPIC

Most jurisdictions that have dealt with the *O'Brien* question have ruled differently. Many have held that such contributions as the O'Brien and Elkus spouses made should be considered in relation to maintenance rather than property distribution. What are the pros and cons of each approach? What is the difference between a "job" and a "career"? Can a career such as Ms. von Stade's or Ms. Berenson's be evaluated with a reasonable degree of certainty?

Financial Disclosure

Although a checklist may be used initially to gather information about a matrimonial client's assets, ultimately a Statement of Net Worth (Form 8-1), must be prepared, since the Uniform Rules for the Trial Courts require that it be filed by both parties in any contested action in which a judicial determination may be made with respect to alimony, counsel fees, maintenance, child support, or equitable distribution. 22 NYCRR § 202.16. The significance of this document is highlighted by a new court rule requiring that the net worth statement be accompanied by a certification, under penalties of perjury, that counsel has no knowledge that the substance of the papers is inaccurate. 22 NYCRR § 202.16(e).

Although the net worth statement appears rather intimidating because of its length and quantity of detail, it is actually quite straightforward. You do not have to be an accountant to complete a net worth statement, but you must master the terminology it requires. A **stock** is an **equity**, that is, an ownership interest, in the company issuing the stock. A **bond**, on the other hand, is a credit instrument, representing that the bond holder has lent money to the company or governmental agency that issued the bond. Stocks may pay a **dividend**, that is, a distribution to the stockholders of a portion of the company's profits. Bonds pay interest, which may be taxable if the issuer is a private company, or non-taxable if the issuer is a governmental agency.

There are no secrets in equitable distribution. Broad financial disclosure is the rule, and in addition to the compulsory net worth statement, all the other discovery devices provided in CPLR Article 31 are available. Discovery can cover the entire duration of the marriage, subject to the court's power to make a protective order in favor of the party from whom information is sought, if it appears that the party seeking discovery is on a "fishing expedition." The court will establish a timetable for discovery. It may be short if there are few assets, but may be as long as six months from the date the case was assigned to the judge, if the case is more complex. Form 8-2 is an example of a tracking form for discovery in divorce actions.

📁 **FORM 8-1**

Revised 6/10/96

COURT

COUNTY OF _____   Index No. _____

                      Plaintiff,   STATEMENT OF

      - against -   NET WORTH

                                           (DRL §236)

                     Defendant.

_____   Date of commencement of action _____

     Complete all items, marking "NONE," "INAPPLICABLE" and "UNKNOWN," if appropriate)

STATE OF _____   COUNTY OF _____   SS.:

          _____, the (Petitioner) (Respondent) (Plaintiff) (Defendant) herein, being duly sworn, deposes and says that the following is an accurate statement as of _____, of my net worth (assets of whatsoever kind and nature and wherever situated minus liabilities), statement of income from all sources and statement of assets transferred of whatsoever kind and nature and wherever situated:

I.   FAMILY DATA:
     (a) Husband's age _____
     (b) Wife's age _____
     (c) Date married _____
     (d) Date (separated)(divorced) _____
     (e) Number of dependent children under 21 years _____
     (f) Names and ages of children

               _____
               _____
               _____
               _____

     (g) Custody of Children _____Husband ____Wife
     (h) Minor children of prior marriage: ____Husband ____Wife
     (i) (Husband)(Wife) (paying)(receiving) $_____ as alimony (maintenance) and/or $_____ child support in connection with prior marriage
     (j) Custody of children of prior marriage:
          Name_____
          Address_____
     (k) Is marital residence occupied by Husband_____ Wife_____ Both_____
     (l) Husband's present address

          _____
          Wife's present address

          _____
     (m) Occupation of Husband _____ Occupation of Wife _____
     (n) Husband's employer

          _____
     (o) Wife's employer

          _____
     (p) Education, training and skills [Include dates of attainment of degrees, etc.]
             Husband _____
             Wife _____
     (q) Husband's health _____
     (r) Wife's health _____
     (s) Children's health _____

📁 FORM 8-1 continued

2.

II. EXPENSES: (You may elect to list all expenses on a weekly basis or all expenses on
     a monthly basis, however, you must be consistent. If any items are paid on a
     monthly basis, divide by 4.3 to obtain weekly payments; if any items are paid on a
     weekly basis, multiply by 4.3 to obtain monthly payment. Attach additional sheet,
     if needed. Items included under "Other" should be listed separately with separate
     dollar amounts.)

                    Expenses listed [] weekly   [] monthly

(a) Housing
     1. Rent   _____   4. Condominium charges   _____
     2. Mortgage and   5. Cooperative apartment
        amortization   _____   maintenance   _____
     3. Real estate taxes _____
                                        Total: Housing $_____
(b) Utilities
     1. Fuel oil   _____   4. Telephone   _____
     2. Gas   _____   5. Water   _____
     3. Electricity   _____
                                        Total: Utilities $_____
(c) Food
     1. Groceries   _____   5. Liquor/alcohol   _____
     2. School lunches   _____   6. Home entertainment   _____
     3. Lunches at work _____   7. Other _____   _____
     4. Dining Out   _____
                                        Total: Food $_____
(d) Clothing
     1. Husband   _____   3. Children   _____
     2. Wife   _____   4. Other _____   _____
                                        Total: Clothing $_____
(e) Laundry
     1. Laundry at home _____   3. Other _____   _____
     2. Dry cleaning   _____
                                        Total: Laundry $_____
(f) Insurance
     1. Life   _____   6. Medical plan   _____
     2. Homeowner's/tenant's_____   7. Dental plan   _____
     3. Fire, theft and   8. Optical plan   _____
        liability   _____   9. Disability   _____
     4. Automotive   _____   10. Worker's Compensation _____
     5. Umbrella policy _____   11. Other _____   _____
                                        Total: Insurance $_____
(g) Unreimbursed medical
     1. Medical   _____   5. Surgical, nursing,
     2. Dental   _____   hospital   _____
     3. Optical   _____   6. Other _____   _____
     4. Pharmaceutical   _____
                                        Total: Unreimbursed medical $_____
(h) Household maintenance
     1. Repairs   _____   5. Painting   _____
     2. Furniture, furnishings   6. Sanitation/carting   _____
        housewares   _____   7. Gardening/landscaping _____
     3. Cleaning supplies _____   8. Snow removal   _____
     4. Appliances, including   9. Extermination   _____
        maintenance   _____   10. Other _____   _____

                                        Total: Household maintenance $_____

📁 FORM 8-1 continued

3.

(i) Household help
  1. Babysitter _____   3. Other _____ _____
  2. Domestic (housekeeper, maid, etc.) _____
                          Total: Household help $_____

(j) Automotive
  Year:_____ Make:_____ Personal: ___ Business: ___
  Year:_____ Make:_____ Personal: ___ Business: ___
  Year:_____ Make:_____ Personal: ___ Business: ___
  1. Payments   _____   4. Car wash   _____
  2. Gas and oil   _____   5. Registration and license_____
  3. Repairs   _____   6. Parking and tolls   _____
              7. Other _____
                          Total: Automotive $_____

(k) Educational
  1. Nursery and pre-school _____   6. School transportation _____
  2. Primary and secondary _____   7. School supplies/books _____
  3. College   _____   8. Tutoring   _____
  4. Post-graduate   _____   9. School events   _____
  5. Religious instruction _____ 10. Other _____   _____
                          Total: Educational $_____

(l) Recreational
  1. Summer camp   _____   9. Country club/pool club _____
  2. Vacations   _____ 10. Health club   _____
  3. Movies   _____ 11. Sporting goods   _____
  4. Theatre, ballet, etc. _____ 12. Hobbies   _____
  5. Video rentals   _____ 13. Music/dance lessons   _____
  6. Tapes, CD's, etc.   _____ 14. Sports lessons   _____
  7. Cable television   _____ 15. Birthday parties   _____
  8. Team sports   _____ 16. Other _____   _____
                          Total: Recreational $_____

(m) Income taxes
  1. Federal   _____   3. City   _____
  2. State   _____   4. Social Security and   _____
                                        Medicare
                          Total: Income taxes $_____

(n) Miscellaneous
  1. Beauty parlor/barber _____   9. Union and organi-
  2. Beauty aids/cosmetics,   zation dues   _____
       drug items   _____ 10. Commutation and
                                        transportation   _____
  3. Cigarettes/tobacco   _____ 11. Veterinarian/pet expenses_____
  4. Books, magazines,   12. Child support payments
       newspapers   _____   (prior marriage)   _____
  5. Children's allowances _____ 13. Alimony and maintenance payments
  6. Gifts   _____   (prior marriage)   _____
  7. Charitable contributions_____ 14. Loan payments   _____
  8. Religious organization   15. Unreimbursed business
       dues   _____   expenses   _____
                          Total: Miscellaneous $_____

(o) Other
  1. _____ _____   3. _____ _____
  2. _____ _____   4. _____ _____
                          Total: Other $_____

              TOTAL EXPENSES: $_____

FORM 8-1 continued

4.

III. GROSS INCOME: (State source of income and annual amount. Attach additional sheet, if needed).

(a) Salary or wages: (State whether income has changed during the year preceding date of this affidavit ____. If so, set. forth name and address of all employers during preceding year and average weekly wage paid by each. Indicate overtime earnings separately. Attach previous year's W-2 or income tax return.)

_____   _____
_____   _____

(b) Weekly deductions:
     1. Federal tax ....   _____
     2. New York State tax........................   _____
     3. Local tax.................................   _____
     4. Social Security...........................   _____
     5. Medicare..................................   _____
     6. Other payroll deductions (specify)........   _____
(c) Social Security number _____
(d) Number and names of dependents claimed: _____
(e) Bonus, commissions, fringe benefits (use of auto,
       memberships, etc.)........................   _____
(f) Partnership, royalties, sale of assets
       (income and installment payments)..........   _____
(g) Dividends and interest (state whether taxable
       or not)....................................   _____
(h) Real estate (income only)....................   _____
(i) Trust, profit sharing and annuities
       (principal distribution and income)........   _____
(j) Pension (income only)........................   _____
(k) Awards, prizes, grants (state whether taxable)   _____
(l) Bequests, legacies and gifts.................   _____
(m) Income from all other sources................   _____
       (including alimony, maintenance or child support
       from prior marriage)
(n) Tax preference items:
     1. Long term capital gain deduction..........
     2. Depreciation, amortization or depletion....   _____
     3. Stock options -- excess of fair market
          value over amount paid....................   _____
(o) If any child or other member of your household
       is employed, set forth name and that person's
       annual income
(p) Social Security..............................   _____
(q) Disability benefits..........................   _____
(r) Public assistance............................   _____
(s) Other..   _____

                                    TOTAL INCOME: _____

📁 FORM 8-1 continued

5.

IV. ASSETS: (If any asset is held jointly with spouse or another, so state, and set forth your respective shares. Attach additional sheets, if needed.)

A. Cash Accounts
    Cash
        1.1 a. Location _____
            b. Source of funds _____
            c. Amount _____ $_____
                                   Total: Cash $_____

    Checking Accounts
        2.1 a. Financial institution _____
            b. Account number _____
            c. Title holder _____
            d. Date opened _____
            e. Source of Funds _____
            f. Balance _____ $_____

        2.2 a. Financial institution _____
            b. Account number _____
             c. Title Holder _____
            d. Date opened _____
            e. Source of Funds _____
            f. Balance _____ $_____
                            Total: Checking $_____

    Savings accounts (including individual, joint, totten trust, certificates of deposit, treasury notes)
        3.1 a. Financial institution _____
            b. Account number _____
             c. Title holder _____
             d. Type of account _____
            e. Date opened _____
            f. Source of funds _____
            g. Balance _____ $_____

        3.2 a. Financial institution _____
            b. Account number _____
             c. Title holder _____
             d. Type of account _____
            e. Date opened _____
            f. Source of funds _____
            g. Balance _____ $_____
                            Total: Savings $_____

    Security deposits, earnest money, etc.
        4.1 a. Location _____
            b. Title owner _____
             c. Type of deposit _____
            e. Source of funds _____
            f. Date of deposit _____
            g. Amount _____ $_____
                            Total: Security
                            Deposits, etc. $_____

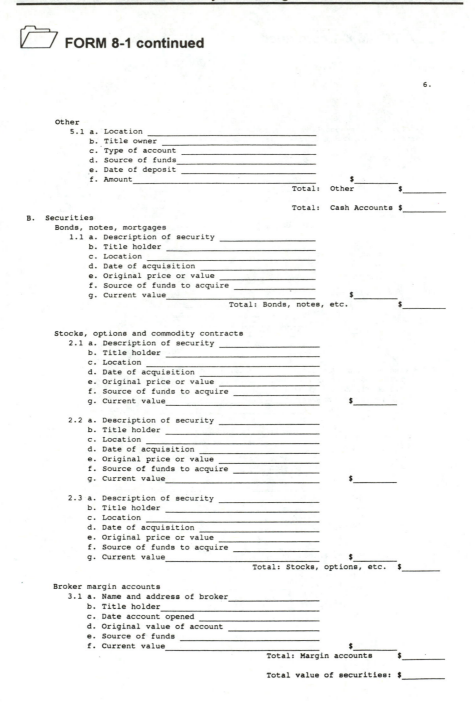 **FORM 8-1 continued**

6.

```
Other
   5.1 a. Location _____
       b. Title owner _____
       c. Type of account _____
       d. Source of funds_____
       e. Date of deposit _____
       f. Amount_____         $_____
                                    Total:  Other          $_____

                                    Total:  Cash Accounts  $_____
B.  Securities
    Bonds, notes, mortgages
       1.1 a. Description of security _____
           b. Title holder _____
           c. Location _____
           d. Date of acquisition _____
           e. Original price or value _____
           f. Source of funds to acquire _____
           g. Current value_____   $_____
                                 Total: Bonds, notes, etc.          $_____


    Stocks, options and commodity contracts
       2.1 a. Description of security _____
           b. Title holder _____
           c. Location _____
           d. Date of acquisition _____
           e. Original price or value _____
           f. Source of funds to acquire _____
           g. Current value_____   $_____

       2.2 a. Description of security _____
           b. Title holder _____
           c. Location _____
           d. Date of acquisition _____
           e. Original price or value _____
           f. Source of funds to acquire _____
           g. Current value_____   $_____

       2.3 a. Description of security _____
           b. Title holder _____
           c. Location _____
           d. Date of acquisition _____
           e. Original price or value _____
           f. Source of funds to acquire _____
           g. Current value_____   $_____
                                 Total: Stocks, options, etc.  $_____

    Broker margin accounts
       3.1 a. Name and address of broker_____
           b. Title holder_____
           c. Date account opened _____
           d. Original value of account _____
           e. Source of funds _____
           f. Current value_____  $_____
                                 Total: Margin accounts     $_____

                                 Total value of securities: $_____
```

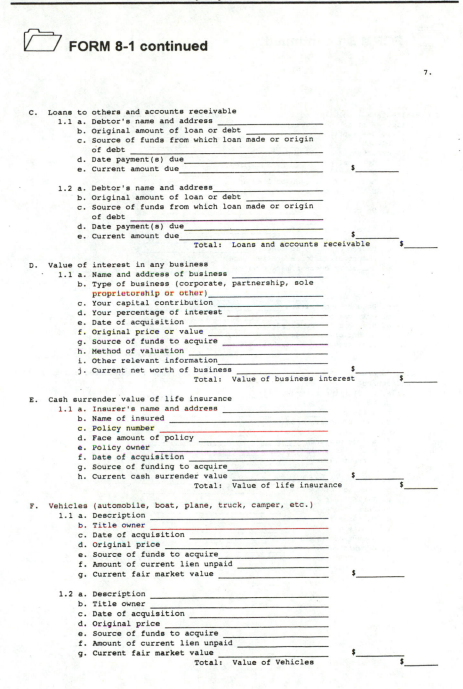

FORM 8-1 continued

7.

C. Loans to others and accounts receivable
   1.1 a. Debtor's name and address _____
       b. Original amount of loan or debt _____
       c. Source of funds from which loan made or origin
          of debt _____
       d. Date payment(s) due_____
       e. Current amount due_____ $_____

   1.2 a. Debtor's name and address_____
       b. Original amount of loan or debt _____
       c. Source of funds from which loan made or origin
          of debt _____
       d. Date payment(s) due_____
       e. Current amount due_____ $_____
                  Total: Loans and accounts receivable $_____

D. Value of interest in any business
   1.1 a. Name and address of business _____
       b. Type of business (corporate, partnership, sole
          proprietorship or other)_____
       c. Your capital contribution _____
       d. Your percentage of interest _____
       e. Date of acquisition _____
       f. Original price or value _____
       g. Source of funds to acquire _____
       h. Method of valuation _____
       i. Other relevant information_____
       j. Current net worth of business _____ $_____
                  Total: Value of business interest $_____

E. Cash surrender value of life insurance
   1.1 a. Insurer's name and address _____
       b. Name of insured _____
       c. Policy number _____
       d. Face amount of policy _____
       e. Policy owner _____
       f. Date of acquisition _____
       g. Source of funding to acquire_____
       h. Current cash surrender value _____ $_____
                  Total: Value of life insurance $_____

F. Vehicles (automobile, boat, plane, truck, camper, etc.)
   1.1 a. Description _____
       b. Title owner _____
       c. Date of acquisition _____
       d. Original price _____
       e. Source of funds to acquire_____
       f. Amount of current lien unpaid _____
       g. Current fair market value _____ $_____

   1.2 a. Description _____
       b. Title owner _____
       c. Date of acquisition _____
       d. Original price _____
       e. Source of funds to acquire _____
       f. Amount of current lien unpaid _____
       g. Current fair market value _____ $_____
                  Total: Value of Vehicles $_____

⬁ FORM 8-1 continued

8.

G. Real estate (including real property, leaseholds, life estates, etc. at market
   value -- do not deduct any mortgage)
   1.1 a. Description _____
       b. Title owner _____
       c. Date of acquisition _____
       d. Original price _____
       e. Source of funds to acquire _____
       f. Amount of mortgage or lien unpaid _____
       g. Estimated current market value _____ $_____

   1.2 a. Description _____
       b. Title owner _____
       c. Date of acquisition _____
       d. Original price _____
       e. Source of funds to acquire _____
       f. Amount of mortgage or lien unpaid _____
       g. Estimated current market value _____ $_____

   1.3 a. Description _____
       b. Title owner _____
       c. Date of acquisition _____
       d. Original price _____
       e. Source of funds to acquire _____
       f. Amount of mortgage or lien unpaid _____
       g. Estimated current market value _____ $_____
                              Total: Value of real estate $_____

H. Vested interests in trusts (pension, profit sharing, legacies, deferred compensation
   and others)
   1.1 a. Description of trust _____
       b. Location of assets _____
       c. Title owner _____
       d. Date of acquisition _____
       e. Original investment _____
       f. Source of funds _____
       g. Amount of unpaid liens _____
       h. Current value _____ $_____

   1.2 a. Description of trust _____
       b. Location of assets _____
       c. Title owner _____
       d. Date of acquisition _____
       e. Original investment _____
       f. Source of funds _____
       g. Amount of unpaid liens _____
       h. Current value _____ $_____
                              Total: Vested interest in trusts $_____

📁 **FORM 8-1 continued**

9.

I. Contingent interests (stock options, interests subject to life estates, prospective inheritances, etc.)
    1.1 a. Description _____
         b. Location _____
         c. Date of vesting _____
         d. Title owner _____
         e. Date of acquisition _____
         f. Original price or value _____
         g. Source of funds to acquire _____
         h. Method of valuation _____
         i. Current value _____ $_____
                                       Total: Contingent interests $_____

J. Household furnishings
    1.1 a. Description _____
         b. Location _____
         c. Title owner _____
         d. Original price _____
         e. Source of funds to acquire _____
         f. Amount of lien unpaid _____
         g. Current value _____ $_____
                                         Total: Household furnishings $_____

K. Jewelry, art, antiques, precious objects, gold and precious metals (only if valued at more than $500)
    1.1 a. Description _____
         b. Title owner _____
         c. Location _____
         d. Original price or value _____
         e. Source of funds to acquire _____
         f. Amount of lien unpaid _____
         g. Current value _____ $_____

    1.2 a. Description _____
         b. Title owner _____
         c. Location _____
         d. Original price or value _____
         e. Source of funds to acquire _____
         f. Amount of lien unpaid _____
         g. Current value _____ $_____
                                       Total: Jewelry, art, etc.: $_____

L. Other (e.g., tax shelter investments, collections, judgments, causes of action, patents, trademarks, copyrights, and any other asset not hereinabove itemized)
    1.1 a. Description _____
         b. Title owner _____
         c. Location _____
         d. Original price or value _____
         e. Source of funds to acquire _____
         f. Amount of lien unpaid _____
         g. Current value _____ $_____

📁 **FORM 8-1 continued**

10.

1.2 a. Description _____
    b. Title owner _____
    c. Location _____
    d. Original price or value _____
    e. Source of funds to acquire _____
    f. Amount of lien unpaid _____
    g. Current value _____ $_____

                              Total: Other $_____

                   TOTAL: ASSETS $_____

V. LIABILITIES

A. Accounts payable
    1.1 a. Name and address of creditor_____
       b. Debtor_____
       c. Amount of original debt _____
       d. Date of incurring debt _____
       e. Purpose _____
       f. Monthly or other periodic payment _____
       g. Amount of current debt_____ $_____

    1.2 a. Name and address of creditor_____
       b. Debtor_____
       c. Amount of original debt _____
       d. Date of incurring debt _____
       e. Purpose _____
       f. Monthly or other periodic payment _____
       g. Amount of current debt_____ $_____

    1.3 a. Name and address of creditor_____
       b. Debtor_____ _____
       c. Amount of original debt _____
       d. Date of incurring debt _____
       e. Purpose _____
       f. Monthly or other periodic payment _____
       g. Amount of current debt_____ $_____

    1.4 a. Name and address of creditor_____
       b. Debtor_____
       c. Amount of original debt _____
       d. Date of incurring debt _____
       e. Purpose _____
       f. Monthly or other periodic payment _____
       g. Amount of current debt_____ $_____

    1.5 a. Name and address of creditor_____
       b. Debtor_____
       c. Amount of original debt _____
       d. Date of incurring debt _____
       e. Purpose _____
       f. Monthly or other periodic payment _____
       g. Amount of current debt_____ $_____

                   Total: Accounts payable $_____

📁 **FORM 8-1 continued**

11.

B. Notes payable
    1.1 a. Name and address of note holder_____
        b. Debtor_____
        c. Amount of original debt _____
        d. Date of incurring debt _____
        e. Purpose _____
        f. Monthly or other periodic payment_____
        g. Amount of current debt_____ $_____

    1.2 a. Name and address of note holder_____
        b. Debtor_____
        c. Amount of original debt _____
        d. Date of incurring debt _____
        e. Purpose _____
        f. Monthly or other periodic payment _____
        g. Amount of current debt_____ $_____
                            Total: Notes payable $_____

C. Installment accounts payable (security agreements, chattel mortgages)
    1.1 a. Name and address of creditor _____
        b. Debtor_____
        c. Amount of original debt _____
        d. Date of incurring debt _____
        e. Purpose _____
        f. Monthly or other periodic payment_____
        g. Amount of current debt_____ $_____

    1.2 a. Name and address of creditor _____
        b. Debtor_____
        c. Amount of original debt _____
        d. Date of incurring debt _____
        e. Purpose _____
        f. Monthly or other periodic payment _____
        g. Amount of current debt_____ $_____
                  Total: Installment accounts $_____

D. Brokers' margin accounts
    1.1 a. Name and address of broker _____
        b. Amount of original debt _____
        c. Date of incurring debt _____
        d. Purpose _____
        e. Monthly or other periodic payment_____
        f. Amount of current debt_____ $_____
                  Total: Brokers' margin accounts $_____

E. Mortgages payable on real estate
    1.1 a. Name and address of mortgagee _____
        b. Address of property mortgaged _____
        c. Mortgagor(s) _____
        d. Original debt _____
        e. Date of incurring debt _____
        f. Monthly or other periodic payment _____
        g. Maturity Date _____
        h. Amount of current debt_____ $_____

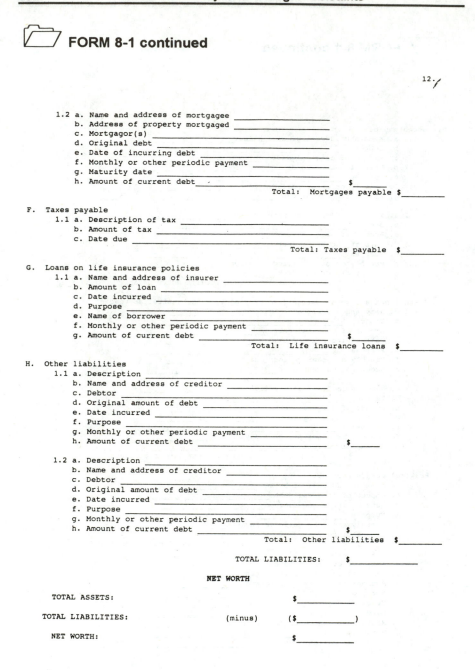

FORM 8-1 continued

12.

```
  1.2 a. Name and address of mortgagee _____
      b. Address of property mortgaged _____
      c. Mortgagor(s) _____
      d. Original debt _____
      e. Date of incurring debt _____
      f. Monthly or other periodic payment _____
      g. Maturity date _____
      h. Amount of current debt _____  $_____
                              Total:  Mortgages payable  $_____

F.  Taxes payable
  1.1 a. Description of tax _____
      b. Amount of tax _____
      c. Date due _____
                              Total: Taxes payable  $_____

G.  Loans on life insurance policies
  1.1 a. Name and address of insurer _____
      b. Amount of loan _____
      c. Date incurred _____
      d. Purpose _____
      e. Name of borrower _____
      f. Monthly or other periodic payment _____
      g. Amount of current debt _____  $_____
                              Total:  Life insurance loans  $_____

H.  Other liabilities
  1.1 a. Description _____
      b. Name and address of creditor _____
      c. Debtor _____
      d. Original amount of debt _____
      e. Date incurred _____
      f. Purpose _____
      g. Monthly or other periodic payment _____
      h. Amount of current debt _____  $_____

  1.2 a. Description _____
      b. Name and address of creditor _____
      c. Debtor _____
      d. Original amount of debt _____
      e. Date incurred _____
      f. Purpose _____
      g. Monthly or other periodic payment _____
      h. Amount of current debt _____  $_____
                              Total:  Other liabilities  $_____
                     TOTAL LIABILITIES:    $_____
```

NET WORTH

```
   TOTAL ASSETS:                      $_____

   TOTAL LIABILITIES:      (minus)    ($_____)

   NET WORTH:                         $_____
```

📁 FORM 8-1 continued

13.

VI. ASSETS TRANSFERRED: (List all assets transferred in any manner during the preceding three years, or length of the marriage, whichever is shorter [transfers in the routine course of business which resulted in an exchange of assets of substantially equivalent value need not be specifically disclosed where such assets are otherwise identified in the statement of net worth]).

Description of Property	To Whom Transferred and Relationship to Transferee	Date of Transfer	Value
_____	_____	_____	_____
_____	_____	_____	_____
_____	_____	_____	_____

VII. SUPPORT REQUIREMENTS:

(a) Deponent is at present (paying)(receiving) $_____ per (week)(month), and prior to separation (paid)(received) $_____ per (week)(month) to cover expenses for _____

    These payments are being made (voluntarily)(pursuant to court order or judgment)(pursuant to separation agreement), and there are (no) arrears outstanding (in the sum of $_____ to date).

(b) Deponent requests for support of each child $_____ per (week)(month). Total for children $_____.

(c) Deponent requests for support of self $_____ per (week)(month).

(d) The day of the (week)(month) on which payment should be made is _____.

VIII. COUNSEL FEE REQUIREMENTS:

(a) Deponent requests for counsel fee and disbursements the sum of _____.

(b) Deponent has paid counsel the sum of $_____ and has agreed with counsel concerning fees as follows:

    _____

    _____

    _____

(c) There is (not) a retainer agreement or written agreement relating to payment of legal fees. (A copy of any such agreement must be annexed.)

IX. ACCOUNTANT AND APPRAISAL FEES REQUIREMENTS:

(a) Deponent requests for accountants' fees and disbursements the sum of $_____. (Include basis for fee, e.g., hourly rate, flat rate)

(b) Deponent requests for appraisal fees and disbursements the sum of $_____. (Include basis for fee, e.g., hourly rate, flat rate)

(c) Deponent requires the services of an accountant for the following reasons:

    _____

    _____

(d) Deponent requires the services of an appraiser for the following reasons:

    _____

    _____

📁 FORM 8-1 continued

14.

X. Other data concerning the financial circumstances of the parties that should be brought to the attention of the Court are:

_____ _____ _____ _____ _____ _____

The foregoing statements and a rider consisting of _____ page(s) annexed hereto and made part hereof, have been carefully read by the undersigned who states that they are true and correct.

_____
(Petitioner)   (Respondent)
(Plaintiff)   (Defendant)

Sworn to before me this
   day of   , 19

CERTIFICATION OF ATTORNEY

   I hereby certify under penalty of perjury and as an officer of the court that I have no knowledge that the substance of any of the factual submissions contained in this document is false.

_____
(The name signed must be printed beneath)

Dated:

📁 FORM 8-2

CASE TRACKING FORM

FILE:_____

**DATE SERVED
AND/OR RECEIVED**

SUMMONS_____

NOTICE OF APPEARANCE_____

COMPLAINT_____

ANSWER AND COUNTERCLAIMS_____

REPLY_____

OUR DEMAND FOR NET WORTH STATEMENT_____

ADVERSARY'S DEMAND FOR NET WORTH STATEMENT_____

OUR NET WORTH STATEMENT_____

ADVERSARY'S NET WORTH STATEMENT_____

OUR DEMAND FOR INTERROGATORIES_____

ADVERSARY'S DEMAND FOR INTERROGATORIES_____

OUR RESPONSE_____

ADVERSARY'S RESPONSE_____

OUR DEMAND FOR PENSION/PAYROLL AUTHORIZATION_____

ADVERSARY'S DEMAND FOR PENSION/PAYROLL AUTHORIZATION_____

OUR PENSION/PAYROLL AUTHORIZATION_____

ADVERSARY'S PENSION/PAYROLL AUTHORIZATION_____

OUR NOTICE TO DEPOSE_____

ADVERSARY'S NOTICE TO DEPOSE_____

DEPOSITIONS HELD ON_____

OUR REAL ESTATE APPRAISAL_____

OUR PENSION APPRAISAL_____

OUR BUSINESS APPRAISAL_____

MISCELLANEOUS APPRAISALS_____

PRELIMINARY CONFERENCE REQUESTED_____

PRESERVATION

As soon as the assets have been identified, prompt action must be taken to preserve them. A contested divorce case can take months, or even years, and if the titled spouse were permitted unfettered control of assets during that time, there might be nothing left to distribute at the end of the case. A *pendente lite* **motion** is often used to insure that assets are not transferred or dissipated during the pendency of the matrimonial action. You recall that a motion is an application to the court for relief within an action. A *pendente lite* motion asks the court to order certain things that a party to the case needs while the litigation is going on. In a divorce case the *pendente lite* motion typically requests interim orders of custody and child support, if there are children of the marriage, and may also ask for temporary maintenance, interim counsel fees, accountants' and appraisers' fees and for exclusive possession or use and occupancy of the marital residence.

If there are *any* assets that might be distributed, the *pendente lite* motion should demand that the court "**enjoin** the [opposing party] from removing any items of personal property located in the marital residence (other than clothing and personal effects), and enjoin the transfer of any personal property, real property or any interest in personal property or real property acquired by the parties during the time of the marriage until further order of the court." If time is of the essence, the *pendente lite* application should be brought on by an order to show cause containing an immediate injunction, so that no transfers can occur before the motion is heard in court. An example of an affidavit in support of such a motion is included as Form 8-3.

CHARACTERIZATION

Once all property has been identified and preserved for distribution, the next step is to figure out which of the assets are subject to equitable distribution. Only marital property will be distributed. Separate property continues to belong to its owner. **Marital property** includes all property acquired by either or both spouses during the marriage and before the execution of a separation agreement or the commencement of a matrimonial action, without regard to the form in which the title is held, except for that which meets the definition of separate property. DRL § 236(B)(c). Note that what counts is *when* the property was acquired, not whose paycheck paid for it. Even lottery winnings from a lottery ticket purchased by one spouse during the marriage are marital property, although the other spouse had nothing to do with buying the ticket or picking the winning numbers.

⊟ FORM 8-3

SUPREME COURT OF THE STATE OF NEW YORK
COUNTY OF RICHMOND
---X

JANE DOE,

Plaintiff,	**AFFIDAVIT OF PLAINTIFF**
	IN SUPPORT OF MOTION
	FOR
	PENDENTE LITE RELIEF

    -- against --

JOHN DOE,

                 Defendant.

---X

STATE OF NEW YORK   )
) ss.:
COUNTY OF RICHMOND)

        I, Jane Doe, being duly sworn, depose and say that:

        1.   I am the Plaintiff in the above captioned action, which is an action for a divorce based upon the grounds of the adultery of the Defendant. I make this affidavit in support of my application for *pendente lite* relief.

        2.   The Plaintiff and the Defendant were married in the City of Buffalo, County of Erie, State of New York, on June 2, 1980.

        3.   The parties have two children born during this marriage, to wit: Mack, born on April 15, 1985, and Molly, born on May 7, 1988. Neither child is emancipated.

        4.   This action was commenced on September 12, 1995, by service upon the Defendant of the Summons With Notice and Verified Complaint attached hereto and made a part hereof as Exhibit A. A copy of the Affidavit of Service is attached hereto and made a part hereof as Exhibit B.

        5.   I reside at 33 Magnolia Drive, Staten Island, New York, and Defendant resides at the same address.

        6.   My current employment status, approximate annual income and approximate net worth are as stated in the Net Worth Statement of the Plaintiff annexed hereto and made a part hereof as Exhibit C.

        7.   Upon information and belief, the Defendant is currently employed as a Systems Analyst at Major Corporation, Inc., 42 Bond Street, New York, New York, at an annual salary of approximately $65,000. His net worth is not known to me, as he has not yet filed his Net Worth Statement.

📁 FORM 8-3 continued

8.   I am dependent upon the Defendant for my support. As his income far exceeds mine, I cannot possibly maintain the standard of living the Defendant and I have enjoyed during our marriage without support from the Defendant.

9.   The children are dependent upon the Defendant for support and are entitled to support from the Defendant. The amount of child support being sought is the basic child support obligation determined pursuant to Section 240 (1-b) of the Domestic Relations Law.

10.   The best interest of the children will be promoted by awarding their custody to me. Defendant spends little time with the children, whereas I am home when they return from school and I provide appropriate supervision and affection for them.

11.   I have retained Susan Smart, Esq. as my attorney in this action. In light of the respective financial abilities of Defendant and myself, it is necessary that the Defendant pay a reasonable amount as and for the fees of my attorney during the pendency of this action.

WHEREFORE, it is respectfully requested that the Court grant the aforesaid relief, and such other and further relief as the court may deem just and proper.

_____
                                 Jane Doe

Subscribed and sworn to before me
on

_____
        Notary Public

My commission expires on

[Notary's stamp with county
admitted and certification #]

> PRACTICE TIP: An affidavit consists of several parts. At the top appear the name of the court and county of venue in which the underlying action is pending. Next comes the caption, which contains the names of the parties. The caption must be exactly the same in every paper filed in the action. Do not insert any middle initials or names that did not appear in the original caption. To the right of the caption is the title of the document, which should be specific. Before the case is over, the court file will be bulging with affidavits; in order to find this particular affidavit quickly the court will need to know whose affidavit it is and for what purpose it was submitted. Just below the caption of the action is the "caption of venue" followed by "ss," an abbreviation of the Latin word *scilicet*, which means "to wit" or "namely." Do *not* insert anyone's social security number there. The county, not borough, which is inserted at this point is the county where the affidavit is executed, which may not be the same as the county in which the action is pending. The body of the affidavit comes next. It must contain a concise statement in support of each type of relief requested in the motion. There is no one "right" form for the body of the affidavit, but consistency and organization are key. Stick to the same voice; if your client is referring to herself as "I" in paragraph 1, do not switch to "the Plaintiff" in paragraph 5. Keep the statements in support of each form of relief in separate paragraphs. The WHEREFORE clause contains the prayer for relief. The *jurat*, oath, comes last. The affirmant's signature must be taken in front of a notary, as an affidavit is a sworn statement subject to the penalties of perjury. Never have the client sign first and then take the document to a notary later. Wait until the notary is actually present to administer the oath.

Separate property is that which was acquired before marriage and property acquired through inheritance or gift from someone other than the spouse. Wedding gifts, however, are marital property. Separate property also includes income from separate property, such as interest on a bank account. Any increase in the value of separate property remains separate property, except when appreciation results from the contributions or efforts of the other spouse. Property acquired in exchange for separate property is also considered separate property. DRL § 236(B)(1)(d). There is a rebuttable presumption that property acquired during the marriage is marital property. Since the party seeking to rebut the presumption has the burden of presenting proof to convince the court that the presumed fact is *not* true, the spouse claiming that a particular asset acquired during marriage is separate property will always have to present evidence to substantiate that claim.

Tracing

Ironing out the wrinkles in these definitions has produced a large volume of litigation since the equitable distribution statute became effective. What happens if an item of separate property has changed form? Suppose, for example, the wife at the time of her marriage had a savings account of $2,000, but five years into the marriage grew dissatisfied with the interest rate she was receiving on the account and decided to invest her money in a mutual fund. Assume the accrued interest has increased the balance in the account to $2,500 at that point. Applying the definition above of separate property, you readily see that the entire $2,500 is her separate property, because the interest is **passive appreciation**, not due to the efforts of either spouse. When she buys into the mutual fund, however, she is already married, and the mutual fund, therefore, will be presumed to be marital property since it was acquired during the marriage. Five years later the couple divorces. The stock market has done well, and wife's initial investment of $2,500 has doubled. Are the mutual fund shares, now worth $5,000, separate property or marital property?

The answer is that the fund shares will be considered separate property only if the wife can prove that they were acquired "in exchange for" her savings bank account. The process by which property is followed through its various forms over time is called **tracing**, and it is prime work for paralegals. In deciding whether a particular asset was acquired "in exchange" for another, the court considers how closely the price of the subsequent investment or asset matches the sale price of the previous one, how close in time the subsequent purchase was to the sale or liquidation of the previous asset, whether there was any other obvious source of the funds used to purchase the asset, and in whose name the subsequent asset is held.

Here, title comes back into the picture, but keep it in its place. The only relevance of title to equitable distribution is in tracing separate property. If a spouse puts a previously separate asset into both spouses' names, the court may find that the spouse meant to make the previously separate property a gift to the marriage, that is, to convert it into marital property. This is particularly so when previously separate funds are deposited into a joint bank account, since Banking Law section 675 creates a rebuttable presumption that title to such an account is vested jointly in the persons named on the account.

Using our previous example, if the wife invested the same amount in the mutual fund that she withdrew from the savings bank account, and if she invested the money in the mutual fund shortly after withdrawing it from the bank, she will probably succeed in proving that it is still separate property if she has held the mutual fund shares in her sole name. Obtaining and assembling the documentation needed to prove these facts -- such as bank statements, brokerage statements, and purchase confirmation slips -- is the legal assistant's job. If your firm's client has destroyed or misplaced these records, duplicates can be obtained by subpoena from the bank or broker or by having the client submit a written request for duplicates to the bank, fund or broker, a service for which a fee is usually charged.

> PRACTICE TIP: Look closely at the Net Worth Statement (Form 8-1). You will notice in ASSETS (Section IV) that information must be provided about the assets as they existed at the time of acquisition and in their current condition. (In some larger format versions of the Net Worth Statement, these columns appear on separate pages, so that at first glance you may think there are two duplicate pages.) By comparing the original purchase price with the current fair market value, the court will know whether the asset has appreciated or depreciated. The "source of funds to acquire" line generally shows whether the party preparing the Net Worth Statement is claiming an asset acquired during marriage as separate property. If the husband's statement says that a particular asset was purchased with money he received from an inheritance, while the wife's statement says it was purchased from general income, the court will know that there is a dispute of fact as to whether that asset is separate property or marital property. The terms used in Section IV appear in the Glossary.

Commingling

Commingling, mixing separate and marital assets, does not automatically wipe out the separate interest of the spouse who originally owned the property. A common situation in which commingling occurs is when one spouse owns a business before the marriage which prospers during the course of the marriage. The increase in the value of the business is considered **active appreciation**, meaning that the business flourished because of the efforts of at least one of the spouses. In such a case the original owner of the business is credited with the value of the business as it existed at the time of the marriage, but the appreciation is considered marital property subject to distribution. Even if one spouse has never worked in or participated in the business during the marriage, the "non-working" spouse may be awarded a share of the value of the business in recognition of his or her contributions as a homemaker or social asset to the "working" spouse's career or earning potential. *Price v. Price*, 69 N.Y.2d 8, 511 N.Y.S.2d 219 (1986).

Marital Residence

Another common commingling problem concerns the marital residence. In one version of this scenario an individual purchases the house or apartment *before* marriage by making a downpayment and taking a mortgage, and then marries before the mortgage is fully paid. During the marriage, mortgage payments are made from marital earnings, which are, as you now know, marital property. Assume that the house at the time of the divorce is worth considerably more than it was at the time of marriage and that the couple has made no significant additions or renovations to the house. Further assume that the couple did not have the foresight to address this issue in a prenuptial or post-nuptial agreement. Is the spouse of the title holder entitled to receive any portion of the value of the house through equitable distribution?

This is a question to which the Court of Appeals has not yet given a definitive answer. Since the appreciation in our example is due to market forces, such as a general rise in the value of real estate and inflation, it is passive appreciation, which under a strict reading of the statute should be considered separate property. Under this theory, the non-titled spouse would receive no portion of the appreciation. This does not seem entirely fair, however, and the courts have struggled to find a way to recognize the contributions of the non-titled spouse in maintaining the home and keeping up the mortgage payments.

One avenue is to treat "passive appreciation" on a marital home somewhat differently from "passive appreciation" on other assets, such as an investment property or a bank account. Maintaining a home in livable condition requires constant cleaning and many small repairs of which no records are likely to be kept. While recognizing that such contributions are indeed valuable, the courts have been reluctant to assign a random value to them. In *Josan v. Josan,* 134 A.D.2d 486, 521 N.Y.S.2d 270 (2 Dept. 1987), the Appellate Division, Second Department, sent the case back to the trial court to take expert testimony on the value of such contributions. In *Denholz v. Denholz*, 147 A.D.2d 522, 537 N.Y.S.2d 607 (2 Dept. 1989), however, the same Appellate Division affirmed an award to the wife of two-thirds of the appreciated value of the marital residence which the husband had purchased *outright* prior to marriage. The Appellate Division of the Third Department has taken a slightly different approach. In *Dietz v. Dietz,* 203 A.D.2d 879, 610 N.Y.S.2d 981 (2 Dept. 1994), the marital residence, which was purchased by the wife prior to marriage and had always been in her sole name, was deemed separate property. Instead of getting into the issue of active versus passive appreciation, the court awarded the husband a credit of $25,000, "representing repayment for contributions made in the form of down payments, repairs and mortgage payments."

Another marital home scenario occurs when separate property has been contributed towards the purchase of the marital home *after* marriage. Suppose, for example, that the down payment was made from the wife's inheritance and thereafter the mortgage payments were made out of general income. What credit in equitable distribution is the wife entitled to for the house? In this scenario the marital home is presumptively marital property, since it was acquired during the marriage. If she can prove that her inheritance was applied to the down payment, however, the wife will receive credit for that contribution "off the top" plus whatever portion of the balance of the fair market value of the house the court decides her contributions warrant. *Lolli-Ghetti v. Lolli-Ghetti,* 165 A.D.2d 426, 568 N.Y.S.2d 29 (1 Dept. 1991). There is some divergence of opinion concerning whether the credit for the contribution of separate property should be a dollar for dollar credit as the *Lolli-Ghetti* court calculated, or some percentage of the total value of the house. In *McAlpine v. McAlpine*, 143 Misc.2d 30, 539 N.Y.S.2d 680 (N.Y. Sup. Ct. 1989), the husband had contributed one quarter of the purchase price and was credited with his original contribution plus one quarter of the appreciation as separate property. Deciding which of these formulas to advocate in a particular case is, of course, the job of the attorney. The significance of these cases for the legal assistant is that they underscore the importance of assembling the records and documents supporting your firm's client's contributions in a thorough and orderly fashion, so that the attorney in charge of the case can readily ascertain which theory will result in the largest award to the client.

EVALUATION

By far the most unwieldy part of the equitable distribution process is the proof of value of each marital asset. Not only are some forms of property extremely difficult to evaluate, but the legislature failed to specify the applicable valuation date. You recall that marital property is acquired only until "the execution of a separation agreement or the commencement of a matrimonial action." DRL § 236(B)(1)(c). Although the term "matrimonial actions" under the Domestic Relations Law includes judicial separation as well as annulment and divorce, the Court of Appeals has ruled that the commencement of an action for judicial separation does not necessarily act as a cut-off to the acquisition of marital property, but rather may be considered, along with other relevant factors in determining whether an asset is separate or marital property. *Anglin v. Anglin,* 80 N.Y.2d 553, 592 N.Y.S.2d 630 (1992).

Even if the cut-off date is clear, it is not necessarily the same as the valuation date. Obviously, the valuation date cannot be later than the trial, but it may be as early as the commencement of the divorce proceeding or some date between the commencement of the divorce action and the trial. To further complicate matters, different assets may have different valuation dates. The parties may agree upon the valuation dates, but if they cannot agree, the court will fix the dates. A consensus seems to be developing among the four departments to use the date of the commencement of the action as the valuation date for assets which are actively appreciating, such as a business in which one spouse is actively involved, absent a showing that using that date would result in a clear inequity to one party. For assets which have grown passively through market forces, a bank account which has accrued interest for example, the valuation date will usually be the date of trial. The value of pension rights is determined as of the date of the commencement of the action. *Majauskas v. Majauskas*, 61 N.Y.2d 481, 474 N.Y.S.2d 699 (1984).

No Merger Doctrine

Since New York recognizes educational degrees, professional licenses, and professional practices each as a form of property, a predictable issue arose concerning the spouse who attained all three during the course of a marriage. If the wife earned her M.D. degree during the marriage, then received her medical license and then went into practice as a pediatrician, will the court evaluate the degree, the license and the practice as three distinct items of marital property? The answer is yes. In 1995 the Court of Appeals rejected the doctrine of merger, which all four judicial departments had been applying for seven years. The courts had held that as each new level is achieved, the previous one merged into it for evaluation purposes. In *McSparron v. McSparron*, 87 N.Y.2d 275, 639 N.Y.S.2d 265 (1995), Judge Vito Titone wrote that the merger doctrine is inconsistent with the letter and the spirit of *O'Brien*. "The merger doctrine should be discarded in favor of a common-sense approach that recognizes the ongoing independent vitality that a professional license may have and focuses solely on the problem of valuing that asset in a way that avoids duplicative awards."

Before distributing marital property, the court *must* evaluate every asset. If the parties agree upon the value of a particular asset, they can enter a **stipulation** as to the worth of that particular asset. If they do not agree, expert testimony must be presented from an accountant or appraiser stating the value of each asset. Legal assistants are rarely called upon to select these experts; usually the attorney chooses someone with whom he or she has had prior dealings or who is well recommended. The legal assistant is often expected to correspond with the experts, however, and it is essential to be clear concerning the valuation dates to be used and the date by which the expert's report must be received. Since the reports will be exchanged as part of the discovery process, failure to turn over the report to opposing counsel by a fixed date may result in **preclusion** of that evidence, that is the court may refuse to receive the report in evidence or to allow the expert to testify. A good tickler system, which warns you of approaching deadlines, is crucial. If your firm has a tickler system in place, be sure you are using it effectively. If such a system has not been established in the office in which you are employed, do yourself a favor (and maybe earn a raise) by devising one. If you are computer-literate, you will find it easy and fun to use the computer for this purpose.

DISTRIBUTION

Finally, the court will actually divide the marital property. After fixing a percentage to which each spouse is entitled, using the 13 factors, the court will establish a method for the division of each asset. In addition to factor 6, which was discussed extensively in the *O'Brien* and *Elkus* cases, factor 11, "wasteful dissipation of assets by either spouse," receives special attention at this point. Although, as discussed above, "ordinary marital fault" is irrelevant in equitable distribution, *economic fault* is important. This is consistent with the equitable distribution theory of marriage as an economic partnership. Thus, if one spouse has gambled away the couple's assets or has invested in harebrained schemes or otherwise frittered away valuable property, the court may award much of what is left to the other spouse. The *Gastineau* case (Case 8-3) is an example of such a situation.

 **CASE 8-3**

GASTINEAU v. GASTINEAU
151 Misc.2d 813, 573 N.Y.S.2d 819 (N.Y. Sup. Ct. 1991)

H. PATRICK LEIS, III, J.

***

The parties were married in December of 1979. This action was commenced in September 1986. Consequently, this is a marriage of short duration. The plaintiff [wife] is 31 years old and the defendant is 34. The parties have one child, Brittany, born on November 6, 1982.

***

The parties married just after Marc Gastineau had been drafted by the New York Jets to play professional football. The plaintiff, at that time, was a sophomore at the University of Alabama. The plaintiff never completed her college education, nor did she work during the course of the marriage.

***

According to the uncontroverted testimony of the plaintiff, in 1979 (the defendant's first year in professional football) the defendant earned a salary of $55,000. In his second year, 1980, the defendant's salary was approximately $75,000. In 1981 it was approximately $95,000 and in 1982 he earned approximately $250,000. The defendant's tax returns...indicate that the defendant earned $423,291 in 1983, $488,994 in 1984, $858,035 in 1985, $595,127 in 1986, $953,531 in 1987 and in 1988, his last year with the New York Jets, his contract salary was $775,000 plus $50,000 in bonuses. It must be noted that in most years the defendant earned moneys in excess of his contract salary as a result of promotions, advertisements and bonuses.

...During the course of the parties' marriage, plaintiff and defendant acquired many luxury items including a power boat, a BMW,

📖 **CASE 8-3 continued**

a Corvette, a Rolls Royce, a Porsche, a Mercedes and two motorcycles. They continually had a housekeeper who not only cleaned the house but prepared the parties' meals. In addition, the parties frequently dined out at expensive restaurants. The plaintiff testified that as a result of this life-style she has become accustomed to buying only the most expensive clothes and going to the best of restaurants.

In 1988 the defendant began an illicit relationship with Brigitte Nielsen. When Ms. Nielsen was diagnosed as having cancer the defendant testified that he could no longer concentrate on playing football. At that time the defendant was under contract with the New York Jets at a salary of $775,000. He left professional football in October 1988 (breaking his contract) after the sixth game of the 1988 season. The defendant went to Arizona and remained with Ms. Nielsen while she underwent treatment for cancer.

Regardless of whether the defendant wanted to be with his girlfriend while she underwent treatment for cancer, he had a responsibility to support his wife and child. The court cannot condone Mr. Gastineau's walking away from a lucrative football contract when the result is that his wife and child are deprived of adequate support.

***

This is not a long-term marriage, and there has been minimal testimony elicited concerning the plaintiff's direct or indirect contributions to the defendant's acquisition of marital assets. Although it was the defendant's own athletic abilities and disciplined training which make it possible for him to obtain and retain his position as a professional football player, equity dictates, under the facts of this case, that the plaintiff receive *one third of the marital assets*. The defendant's decision to voluntarily terminate his contract with the New York Jets, depriving plaintiff and the parties' child of the standard of living to which they had become accustomed, his failure to obtain meaningful employment thereafter and the indirect contributions made by the plaintiff during the course of the marriage warrant an award to the plaintiff of one third of the parties' marital assets....

***

DISCUSSION TOPIC
Which factors besides factor 11 did the court consider significant in the *Gastineau* case? How did the court arrive at the one-third percentage for the wife? Do you think the award was fair? What does this decision show about the amount of discretion trial judges retain under the equitable distribution statute?

Liquidity

An asset such as a bank account can easily be divided. Some assets, however, are not so liquid and some, such as pension rights, may not be available for distribution at the time of the divorce. Suppose, for example, the court, applying factor 3, decides that the custodial parent should have the marital residence, and suppose further that it is the only "big ticket" asset the couple owns. If the court finds that the custodial parent's fair share in equitable distribution is 40 percent, how does the non-custodial parent get the 60 percent to which he or she is entitled?

The court has several options in such a situation. Of course, the court could direct that the residence be sold, but that might work a hardship on the children, who would be uprooted at a time when they probably need all the stability they can get. More likely, the court will direct the custodial parent to pay the non-custodial parent the 60 percent share of the value of the house at some point in the future. If the children are almost grown and will be leaving home in a few years, the court may order that the house be sold at some fixed future date, perhaps six months after the youngest child reaches the age of 18. Another possibility is that the court might order the custodial parent to pay the non-custodial parent's share in "installments" over a period of years, or might give the custodial parent a lower award of maintenance than he or she would otherwise be entitled to.

Pension and Retirement Benefits

Pension rights are among the most commonly held assets, and often they are a family's only significant asset. Unfortunately, they are difficult to deal with in the equitable distribution process, as both their evaluation and distribution pose special challenges. If a spouse has already retired at the time of the divorce, the court can simply direct that the other spouse receive a specified percentage of each payment of the pension. In such a case it is not essential to have the worth of the entire pension evaluated.

If the spouse has not yet reached retirement, however, the pension rights which accrued during the marriage should still be evaluated and distributed just like any other form of marital property. The Court of Appeals has recently held that even non-vested pension rights, those which will be lost if the pension plan participant leaves his or her employment, may be distributed. *Burns v. Burns*, 84 N.Y.2d 369, 618 N.Y.S.2d 761 (1994). This will require the services of an expert, as the value of even a vested pension depends on many variables such as the life expectancy of the spouse who will receive the pension and projections of future inflation. Once the expert has put a dollar value on the pension, the problem becomes how to distribute it. If enough marital assets are available at the time of the divorce, by far the easiest and most reliable form of distribution is to have the pension-holder spouse make a lump-sum payment to the other spouse of his or her share or to make an "in-kind award" of some other asset of comparable value instead of the pension.

Often the other assets are insufficient to compensate for the hefty value of the pension. In such a situation, distribution of the pension must await the actual payment of the pension upon the retirement of the pensioned spouse. Although the court could order the recipient to pay the other spouse a specified percentage of each pension payment, such an order would put a burden on the other spouse to keep track of the spouse who will receive the pension over a potentially extended period of years until retirement. The alternative is to order the employer who will be paying the pension to make payments directly to the former spouse of a specified amount or a specified percentage of the pension.

QDRO

Prior to 1984, such orders were prohibited by Federal law, but the Retirement Equity Act of 1984 made it possible to distribute all or part of a spouse's pension benefits under a private pension plan if the distribution is pursuant to a **"qualified domestic relations order."** A "qualified" order is a judgment, decree or order (including those based on a settlement agreement) made pursuant to state domestic relations law covering issues such as support, maintenance and property distribution. 29 U.S.C.A. § 1056. A QDRO, called "quadro" among matrimonial lawyers, must contain the last known name and address of both the pension plan participant and the alternate payee, the amount or percentage awarded to the alternate payee, the period to which the order applies, and the name of the plan to which the order relates. An example of a QDRO is included as Form 8-4, but since many plan administrators impose their own additional requirements, it is wise to check with the plan administrator before drafting the QDRO.

After the QDRO is signed by the judge handling the equitable distribution, the order is submitted to the administrator of the pension plan, who must promptly notify both the plan participant and the alternate payee of the administrator's receipt of the order. The administrator must then notify the participant and the alternate payee within a reasonable time whether the administrator deems the order "qualified." If the administrator challenges the order and no action is taken within 18 months, then the benefits will be paid as if the order had never been made. Thus, the submission of the QDRO to the plan administrator, the receipt of the confirmation of receipt by the administrator, and the notification of approval or challenge from the plan administrator are all important dates to include in your tickler system.

📂 FORM 8-4

At I.A.S. Term, Part VII of the Supreme Court of the State of New York, held in and for the County of Richmond, at the Courthouse, 18 Richmond Terrace, Staten Island, New York, on the 24th day of July, 1996.

PRESENT:

     HON. JANE MILLER
            Justice.

--X

Katherine Morgan,

                Plaintiff,   QUALIFIED DOMESTIC

     against   RELATIONS ORDER

Michael Morgan,   Index No.

               Defendant.

--X

The parties having stipulated in writing on May 22, 1996 with respect to the defendant's pension with the United Food and Commercial Workers Local No. 50, and

Now, on the reading and filing of said stipulation agreed and consented to by both parties,

Now on motion of Nicholas Johnson, Esq., attorney for the plaintiff herein, it is

ORDERED, that with respect to retirement benefits of defendant, Michael Morgan (hereinafter referred to as "participant"), in the United Food and Commercial Workers Local No. 50 Pension Plan, (hereinafter referred to as the "Pension Plan"), plaintiff, Katherine Morgan (hereinafter referred to as the "Alternate Payee"), shall receive, directly from the Pension Plan, payments from the Participant's retirement benefits under said Pension Plan, as follows:

1. The Participant in the Pension Plan is Michael Morgan, pension number 8630090, who resides at 651 Island Boulevard, Staten Island, New York. The Alternate Payee is Katherine Morgan, who resides at 81592 Victory Boulevard, Staten Island, New York.

2. The name of the Pension Plan is the United Food and Commercial Workers Local No. 50 Pension Plan. The Pension Plan is located at 4268 Sutpin Boulevard, Queens, New York.

3. That by written Stipulation of Settlement entered into on May 22, 1996, the parties have agreed that the Alternate Payee is entitled to 50% of the Participant's pension retirement allowance.

4. That the Pension Plan shall pay the Alternate Payee directly, at her current address, set forth above, or at any subsequent address she may designate in writing, 50% of the Participant's retirement allowance computed without optional modification of the Participant. The payments shall be effective as of

🗁 FORM 8-4 continued

the date of service of this QDRO.

       5. That this order is issued pursuant to Section 236, Part B of the Domestic Relations Law of the State of New York, which relates to the determination of marital property rights as defined therein between spouses and former spouses in actions for divorce; and it is further

       Ordered, that this Court retains jurisdiction of this action and the parties thereto for the purpose of making whatever changes may be required to effectuate this order or any amendment thereto.

ENTER,

_____

J.S.C.

TAX CONSIDERATIONS IN PROPERTY DIVISION

CAPITAL GAINS

In Chapter 7 we discussed the income tax consequences of maintenance and child support. To understand the tax consequences of equitable distribution, we must consider not only ordinary income tax but capital gains taxes as well. A **capital gain** is realized when an asset is sold at a profit. If, for example, you own a house which you lease to a tenant, the rent you receive is income, but if you sell the house itself at a profit, you realize a capital gain, and the Internal Revenue Service will levy a tax on the profit. Capital gains taxes are reported at the same time as ordinary income taxes, but they are reported on a separate schedule.

Equitable distribution is not, in itself, a taxable event. Monies paid in a distributive award, even if paid in installments, are not "income" to the recipient, because they are, after all, only a return to the spouse of his or her own property, albeit in the form of cash. For capital gains tax purposes any transfer of title from one spouse to the other, or from joint names to one spouse's sole name at the time of equitable distribution, does not trigger any capital gains tax, even though the asset may be worth more at the time of the equitable distribution than it was at the time it was purchased. Why then, does factor 10 of the equitable distribution statute mandate the court to consider the tax consequences to each party?

To answer this question you only have to remember the old saying that nothing is certain but death and taxes. Somewhere down the line, there is every likelihood that someone is going to pay a tax on that asset. Considering the possible tax consequences of the transfer of a particular asset is called "tax impacting" the asset. Let us return to our example of the house that is rented out, and assume that the husband is awarded sole title to that house in the equitable distribution order. A few years after the divorce, he decides to sell the house. *Now* he has to pay a capital gains tax. What is his profit? It is the difference between the "basis" (usually the original purchase price) during the marriage, and the sale price, minus any costs he may have incurred in maintaining or improving the house since the original purchase. Since 1984, when the tax code was amended, the transfer of the house incident to the equitable distribution does not count. The fair market value of the house at the time of the divorce is not the "basis." Thus, if the capital gains tax rate at the time the husband sells is 28%, the house is actually worth 28% less to him than it looked like it was worth on paper at the time the equitable distribution judge was putting the assets into "his" and "hers" columns.

Is this fair? Maybe not, but it is unavoidable in some cases. How could the court know at the time of equitable distribution whether the husband would ever sell that house, or whether he would make a profit from the sale, or what the capital gains tax rate would be when he sells? The courts have dealt with these imponderables by devising a rule that an asset will only be "tax impacted" if its sale is imminent; otherwise the consequences would be too speculative. Even if the sale is "imminent," the courts will generally refuse to consider tax consequences unless expert testimony is offered on the issue. The Court of Appeals has affirmed a "tax impacted" award in the absence of expert testimony, however, based only on the husband's testimony that he would have to sell certain assets to satisfy the distributive equitable distribution award. *Hartog v. Hartog*, 85 N.Y.2d 36, 623 N.Y.S.2d 537 (1995).

RECAPTURE

In Chapter 7 we discussed the ways in which spouses sometimes try to disguise maintenance as child support in order to pay a lower rate of income tax on it. Similar strategies are employed with equitable distribution awards, but here again the IRS has laws on its side to limit such ploys. As you know, the income tax on maintenance is paid by the recipient; the payor subtracts the payments from income as an "adjustment" on the tax return. If one spouse is in a higher tax bracket than the other spouse, the higher bracket spouse might have a lower tax bill if periodic payments were treated as maintenance rather than as a distributive property division.

Suppose, for example, that Fast Track and Getting Started are getting divorced. Fast Track is in the 30% tax bracket, while Getting Started is in the 15% bracket. Fast Track must pay Getting Started $15,000 a year for the next two years as compensation for Getting Started's interest in a piece of marital property. In addition, Fast Track's attorney has advised that Getting Started will be entitled to maintenance for four years in order to complete college. It occurs to Fast Track that if the payout for the property were tacked onto the maintenance, Fast Track could save on income tax. This is called "front loading." Fast Track offers to give Getting Started an extra 15% on the two property payments to cover the income tax in the lower bracket if the payments are called "maintenance." Fast Track would then have a net savings of 15%, or $2,250, on the equitable distribution payout. As an inducement, Fast Track sweetens some other terms of the last settlement offer that was on the negotiation table.

There are two important reasons why Getting Started might not want to agree to such an arrangement. First, maintenance payments cease, at the latest, upon the death or remarriage of the recipient, whereas an equitable distribution award must be paid after the spouse remarries and must be paid to the recipient's estate in the event of death. Second, maintenance payments also cease upon the death of the payor, whereas the estate of the payor is liable for an unpaid equitable distribution award. Perhaps the couple are young and healthy, however, and Getting Started is willing to take that chance. To minimize the extent to which spouses can collude in this fashion, all equitable distribution property transfers must occur within six years of the dissolution of the marriage.

In addition, the IRS is allowed to **recapture**, that is to recover, a tax deduction previously taken by a taxpayer. The recapture formula is based on the disparity between the amount of "maintenance" paid in the first, second, and third "post-separation" years. The current recapture formula is: 1) Add $15,000, called the "floor," to the amount of maintenance paid in the third year. 2) Subtract the total from the amount paid in the second year. The answer is called the "adjusted second year." 3) Add the adjusted second year to the actual third year and divide the total by two. 4) Add $15,000. 5) Subtract that figure from the amount of maintenance actually paid in the first year. This is the excess which will be "recaptured" by having the payor report it as income and the recipient deduct it on his or her 1040 forms. Although the formula looks gruesome, it is actually not hard to work out with the step-by-step worksheet which is included in IRS Publication 504. Be sure to use the current year's worksheet, because the "floor" changes from time to time.

CONCLUSION

Equitable distribution is a time-consuming process which requires meticulous attention to detail. Obtaining such a quantity of precise information from a client who is probably under stress and possibly unsophisticated in financial matters makes heavy demands on the legal assistant. Although the client's thoughts may be scattered, the legal assistant must stay focused. Data sheets and interview protocols will help, but knowing when to ask a follow-up question requires an understanding of how the data will be used. Keep the blueprint of the equitable distribution system firmly in mind. The steps in the process are 1) identifying all property, 2) preserving it for possible distribution, 3) determining whether it is separate or marital property, 4) evaluating each asset, and 5) arriving at a scheme for distribution of the marital property which is fair and workable.

CHAPTER REVIEW QUESTIONS

1.   How does New York's equitable distribution system differ from the community property system of property division and from the former title-based system?

2.   Bob and Sue marry in 1975, and at that time neither has any assets. For the first two years of their marriage both are employed, and Sue saves her entire salary in an account in her own name while they live off of Bob's salary. Sue then leaves her job to stay home with their newborn son. Bob and Sue then buy a marital residence in their joint names, using the entire balance of the savings account for the downpayment. For the next five years the mortgage is paid from Bob's salary, while Sue stays home as a full-time mother and homemaker. They divorce. The marital residence is now worth $15,000 more than at time of purchase. Is the home separate property, marital property, or some of both? Why?

3.   Your firm's client participates in a deferred compensation plan at work. On what line(s) of his net worth statement (Form 8-1) do you declare it?

4.   David and Donna purchase a piece of property outright during the marriage, using $10,000 of David's inheritance and $40,00 of general income for the $50,000 purchase price. At the time of their divorce three years later, the fair market value of the land is $60,000. They have made no improvements to the property. The court decides that marital property should be divided 50-50. If the land is sold at the time of the divorce, how much does David get if the court uses the dollar-for-dollar method of crediting separate property and how much if it uses the percentage-of-the-whole method?

5.   As a part of the equitable distribution award, your firm's client took title to shares of stock which had been purchased during the marriage. The stock originally cost $5,000 and at the time of the divorce had a fair market value of $10,000. If she sells the stock four years after the divorce for $15,000, how much is her capital gain?

6.   At the preliminary interview your firm's client mentions that his wife is a doctor in practice with her father. Of late she has been talking about needing a long vacation and possibly a change of career. Would you ignore this information because it is not the next question on your interview protocol? If not, what would you do?

CHAPTER ASSIGNMENT

As in Chapter 5, you are a paralegal in the firm representing Wilma Bickering in her divorce from her husband Hugh. The attorney in charge of the case asks you to assist in drafting a motion for *pendente lite* relief for Mrs. Bickering. Using the fact pattern in Chapter 5, draft: 1) the notice of motion, 2) Wilma's affidavit in support of the motion (using Form 8-3 as a model), and 3) Wilma's net worth statement (Form 8-1). For the paragraphs in support of her application for custody, use the facts you listed for the Chapter 6 assignment. In the sections of the net worth statement concerning maintenance and child support requirements, insert the amounts you computed in the assignment following Chapter 7.

The motion is a collection of documents together in one blueback: the notice of motion goes on top, followed by Mrs. Bickering's affidavit in support. Underneath come the exhibits, which should include copies of the summons with notice and the verified complaint, which you drafted for Mrs. Bickering in Chapter 5, and Mrs. Bickering's net worth statement, which you will prepare now. (Although in actual practice an attorney's affirmation should also be included in support of any counsel fees application, you may omit that for the purposes of this assignment.)

9 NON-MARITAL CHILDREN

"It is true that paternity jurisdiction was originally created solely as a vehicle to identify persons liable for the support of children born out of wedlock and not to decide parental status.... However, more recent developments, notably the enactment giving putative fathers the right to initiate paternity proceedings...and numerous other laws conferring rights and benefits flowing from an order of filiation, have largely eroded the general proposition that a paternity proceeding may not be brought to determine status...." *Sharon GG. v. Duane HH.*, 95 A.D.2d 466, 467 N.Y.S.2d 941 (3 Dept. 1983).

VOLUNTARY ACKNOWLEDGMENT OF PATERNITY

The father of a child born out of wedlock may acknowledge paternity of his child in a variety of ways. If both parents agree that a particular man is the father, they may execute a **voluntary acknowledgment of paternity** at the hospital immediately preceding or following the birth of the child. Public Health Law § 4135-b. Such an acknowledgment has the same force and effect as an adjudication of paternity made by a court and establishes the obligation of both parents to provide for the support of the child. If filed with the registrar of the district in which the birth certificate has been filed and with the **putative father register**, the acknowledgment also establishes the child's right to inherit from the father and his paternal kin under the laws of intestacy. Estates, Powers and Trusts Law § 4-1.2(B). The terms "putative" and "alleged" father are used to describe a man who is said to be the father. When the father has executed an acknowledgment of paternity, he should be called the "acknowledged" father, and after paternity has been decided by a court, the father should be referred to as the "adjudicated" father.

The same type of acknowledgment (Form 9-1) may also be executed later at the Department of Health where the birth certificate is on file or in an office of the Social Services Department. SSL § 111-k. Such an acknowledgment also establishes the father's liability to contribute to the support of the child. DRL § 33(5); FCA § 516-a. When a voluntary acknowledgment of paternity is executed, the name of the acknowledged father will appear on the child's birth certificate. The child's surname may be changed, however, only upon the consent of both parents. A copy of the acknowledgment is forwarded to the Putative Father Register in Albany. Because the parents executing such an acknowledgment are giving up the many procedural rights they would be accorded if paternity were adjudicated in court, the signing of the acknowledgment must be preceded by a written explanation of their rights and the consequences of signing the voluntary acknowledgment.

A putative father may also claim paternity -- without the cooperation of the mother -- by filing, before or after the birth of the child, a notice of intent to claim paternity with the Putative Father Register maintained by the State Department of Social Services at 10 North Pearl Street in Albany. In addition to the names of putative fathers who have filed claims of paternity, the Register also contains the names of adjudicated fathers and those who have signed voluntary acknowledgments. A father whose name appears on the Register is entitled to notice of certain court proceedings concerning the child, most significantly adoption proceedings, as discussed in Chapter 13. The filing of a claim of paternity does not obligate the putative father to pay support, however, and, thus, is not the equivalent of a voluntary acknowledgment or adjudication of paternity. A notice of intent to claim paternity may be revoked at any time, another significant difference from a voluntary acknowledgment or adjudication of paternity.

Informal acknowledgment of paternity by a father may also be legally significant. If a man has "openly and notoriously acknowledged" a child as his own, the child may inherit from him, even though paternity was not established in court or formally acknowledged prior to his death. EPTL § 4-1.2(a)(2)(C). A paternity proceeding may also be maintained in Family Court after the death of the alleged father if 1) he has openly and notoriously acknowledged the child during his lifetime or 2) the father was the petitioner in the proceeding or 3) a blood genetic marker test has been administered to the putative father prior to his death or 4) the putative father acknowledged paternity of the child in open court. FCA § 519. A paternity proceeding may also be maintained after the death of the mother. No threshold showing is required that the mother named or acknowledged the alleged father as the father of the child during her lifetime in order to initiate the proceeding, although such proof may, of course, be offered in support of the case. FCA § 518.

📁 **FORM 9-1**

PRINT ALL INFORMATION

STATE OF
COUNTY OF ⎬ ss.:

_____ and _____
Father's Full Name (Print)   Mother's Full Name (Print)

being duly sworn depose and state that they are respectively _____ and _____ years of age and that they reside at

_____ and _____
Father's Residence   Mother's Residence

Applicants are the parents of a child who was born at _____ on _____
                                                      Hospital   Date of Child's Birth

and whose certificate is on file in the name of _____
                                              Name of Child as it appears on Birth Certificate (Print)

Certificate # _____ of the year _____ Borough of _____

Applicant (father) _____ states that he is the natural father of the
of the above-named child and that he desires and consents to the filing of a new birth certificate for the child, giving
the applicant's name as the father and naming the child, so that the child will be known as

_____
CHILD'S FULL NEW NAME   FIRST   MIDDLE   LAST

Applicant (mother) _____ states that she is the natural mother of the
above-named child and that she was single and free to marry at the time of the conception of this child and that she
joins the father in requesting the filing of a new certificate of birth for the child.

Applicants jointly state there has never been any court action in connection with the paternity of this child.

Wherefore, Applicants respectfully request the Honorable Commissioner of Health to file a new certificate of birth in
lieu of the original record on file with the Department of Health.

INFORMATION TO BE ADDED OR CORRECTED	AS IT APPEARS ON BIRTH CERTIFICATE	AS IT SHOULD BE (PRINT CLEARLY)	
FATHER'S NAME	NOT SHOWN		
FATHER'S PLACE OF BIRTH	NOT SHOWN		
FATHER'S DATE OF BIRTH AND AGE AT TIME OF CHILD'S BIRTH	NOT SHOWN	Date of Birth	Age

FORM 9-1 continued

NOTE: Signature of paternal grandparent is required if father of child is under 18. Signature of maternal grandparent is required if mother of child is under 18.

ALL FOREIGN LANGUAGE DOCUMENTS MUST HAVE CERTIFIED ENGLISH TRANSLATION.

Subscribed and sworn before me

FATHER'S SIGNATURE AND SOCIAL SECURITY NUMBER	DATE	NOTARY PUBLIC OR COMMISSIONER OF DEEDS

NOTARY LIST IDENTIFICATION SHOWN

County or
State: _____ Lic.# _____

MOTHER'S SIGNATURE AND SOCIAL SECURITY NUMBER	DATE	NOTARY PUBLIC OR COMMISSIONER OF DEEDS

NOTARY LIST IDENTIFICATION SHOWN

County or
State: _____ Lic.# _____

PATERNAL GRANDPARENT (Only if Required)	DATE	NOTARY PUBLIC OR COMMISSIONER OF DEEDS

NOTARY LIST IDENTIFICATION SHOWN

County or
State: _____ Lic.# _____

MATERNAL GRANDPARENT (Only if Required)	DATE	NOTARY PUBLIC OR COMMISSIONER OF DEEDS

NOTARY LIST IDENTIFICATION SHOWN

County or
State: _____ Lic # _____

VR56 (2/93)   DIVISION OF VITAL RECORDS · DEPARTMENT OF HEALTH · CITY OF NEW YORK

Evidence of "open and notorious" acknowledgment may include statements by witnesses that the putative father directly told them he was the father of the child or that he indirectly acknowledged the child by introducing the child as "my son" or "my daughter." It might also include proof that the alleged father performed fatherly duties, such as providing support for the child or attending school meetings to which parents were invited. Documentary evidence can also be important proof of "open and notorious" acknowledgment. If the alleged father listed the child as a dependent on his tax return or on his health insurance, the petitioner's case will be very strong. Even less formal documents, such as a report card of the child signed by the putative father, can be persuasive evidence.

PATERNITY PROCEEDINGS

If both parents are not prepared to voluntarily acknowledge that a particular man is the father of a child born out of wedlock, it will be necessary to file a **paternity proceeding** so that the court can adjudicate the child's parentage. Even if paternity has already been voluntarily acknowledged, it is still a good idea to obtain an **order of filiation**, the document which legally establishes the child's paternity. Every state in the union will accord the court order full faith and credit, whereas different jurisdictions may give less weight to an acknowledgment of paternity.

BASICS BOX

Subject matter jurisdiction: Family Court has exclusive original jurisdiction. Surrogate's Court has ancillary jurisdiction.

Venue: County where the mother, the child, or the father resides or is found.

Standing: The mother, the child, a person claiming to be the father, the child's guardian or next of kin, a representative of a charitable society, and the Commissioner of Social Services (if the child is, or is likely to become, a public charge) all may bring suit to establish paternity.

Grounds: The petition must allege that the child was born out of wedlock and that the petitioner or respondent is the father of the child.

Statute of Limitations: Until the child reaches 21 years of age. Proceedings may be brought after the child reaches 21 if the father has acknowledged paternity in writing or by furnishing support.

Applicable Statutes: Family Court Act article 5; EPTL § 4-1.2.

Paternity proceedings have been revolutionized in the past generation by a combination of scientific developments and radically changed social mores. In the past, paternity cases were ugly spectacles in which the reputation of the petitioner-mother was often besmirched by testimony that men other than the respondent had what the law euphemistically calls "access" to the petitioner. The development of reliable blood tests to prove as well as disprove paternity has greatly reduced both the number of false allegations and false denials of paternity. If either party has genuine doubts about the child's paternity, a blood test is ordered, after which the case usually is either withdrawn or paternity is admitted. Very few cases nowadays go through a full trial.

In the past, paternity proceedings were viewed primarily as a means to establish the out-of-wedlock father's obligation for child support. There were even some cases holding that a paternity proceeding could not be maintained if support was not an issue. Courts now recognize that there are many advantages, apart from financial matters, to establishing paternity. At about the same time that reliable scientific proof of paternity became available, the social stigma of illegitimacy began to wane, making both parties more willing to acknowledge the biological realities of their child's parentage. Out-of-wedlock births have become more commonplace. In 1992, almost 100,000 children were born to unmarried mothers in New York State, 35% of all live births in that year. *Vital Statistics of New York State*. A strong fathers' rights movement has also encouraged many men to come forward to claim their offspring and to assert the right to play an active role in the upbringing of their children. Today, the father is as likely as the mother to be the one who seeks an order of filiation.

AGREEMENT OR COMPROMISE

Because paternity cases used to be so unpleasant, the Family Court Act permits the parties to enter into an agreement or compromise concerning the support of the child. Such agreements are binding on the mother and child only when the Family Court determines that the agreement provides adequate support and is fully secured. FCA § 516. Once such an agreement is judicially approved and has been completely performed, it bars other remedies of the mother or child for the support and education of the child. Compromise agreements are rarely used today, since the primary motivation for their use was to avoid a messy trial, which the availability of reliable blood tests has rendered unnecessary. Courts today are reluctant to approve a compromise that does not include the entry of an order of filiation, as there are so many benefits for which a child becomes eligible after paternity has been established. Compromise agreements became less attractive from the putative father's point of view as well, when the Court of Appeals ruled in 1992 that they do not bar the Commissioner of Social Services from pursuing a claim for increased support from the putative father when the child is receiving public assistance. *Commissioner of Social Services of City of New York v. Ruben O.*, 80 N.Y.2d 409, 590 N.Y.S.2d 847 (1992).

BLOOD TESTS

Three types of blood tests are used in paternity proceedings: blood typing, HLA, and DNA. When the parties and subject child are tested in a paternity case, blood samples are taken at a certified laboratory. All three blood tests can be performed on each blood specimen, so that it is not necessary for blood to be drawn more than once from each individual. As only a small quantity of blood is required for testing, the procedure is not very painful, nor does it jeopardize the health of the individuals from whom the blood is drawn. The cost of the test, which can be substantial, must be born initially by the party who requests the test. If the person requesting the test is financially unable to bear the cost, the court may direct payment by the local social services district. At the end of the case, however, the court may direct that the cost of the blood test be apportioned between the parties according to their respective means or be assessed against the party who does not prevail on the issue of paternity. The court is required to order blood tests on the request of either party and may also order them on the court's own motion.

If the results of an HLA or DNA test establish a **probability of paternity** of 95% or greater, the laboratory report creates a rebuttable presumption of paternity. FCA § 532(a). A certified report of the results of an HLA or DNA test may be received into evidence in the same manner as a hospital record pursuant to CPLR § 4518. FCA § 532(b). The certification and delegation of authority forms required to make a hospital record admissible in evidence under CPLR § 4518 are discussed more fully in Chapter 12. All four Appellate Divisions have held that in a contested proceeding the petitioner's case cannot consist exclusively of the blood test results, but rather must be based as well on evidence that petitioner and respondent engaged in sexual intercourse around the probable time of the conception of the child.

Blood Typing Test

The oldest type of blood grouping test, which is only admissible in evidence to *disprove* paternity, is based upon blood typing. If you have ever donated blood or received a transfusion, you probably know that human blood is typed as A, B, AB or O, positive or negative. If the child's blood is of a type that could not have resulted from the mother and the alleged father -- if, for example the child's blood is positive (a dominant genetic trait), whereas the petitioner and respondent both have negative blood types (a recessive trait) -- the alleged father is **excluded** by the blood test. Because the exclusion is definitive, this test result is admissible to show that the alleged father is *not* the biological father of the subject child. If he is not excluded, however, the result cannot be used to prove paternity, because millions of other men would also not be excluded. If the alleged father is not excluded by this test, the laboratory will go on to the HLA test.

HLA Test

The **Human Leukocyte Antigen test** is based upon the matching of genetic markers, called antigens, which are found on the surface of the white cells of the blood, called leukocytes. Because these genetic markers are much more specific than blood types, fewer people are likely to have the same antigens. Comparing the antigens of the mother, the alleged father, and the child to a broad sample of the population, it is possible to establish a **combined paternity index (CPI)**, which is a ratio of the genetic probability that the alleged father and the mother could produce a child with the observed markers compared to the likelihood of the mother and a random man producing the child. Thus, if the CPI is 100 to 1, it means that the alleged father is 100 times more likely to be the father than a random man. The probability of paternity is computed by multiplying the combined paternity index by a figure called the **prior probability**. The prior probability reflects the strength of all the non-genetic evidence for or against paternity. Usually the prior probability is set at .5, meaning that it is assumed that there is a 50/50 chance that the alleged father is the biological father of the child, but the court can select a higher or lower prior probability. The following probability of paternity table shows the relationship between the CPI and the prior probability:

CPI	PRIOR PROBABILITY		
	0.1	0.5	0.9
100	91.7%	99.0%	99.9%
500	98.2%	99.8%	99.9%
1000	99.1%	99.9%	99.9%

Prior to 1981, blood test results had been admissible in evidence only to disprove paternity. The amendment that allowed their use as affirmative evidence of paternity sparked an interesting constitutional challenge, as you see in Case 9-1.

CASE 9-1

DEPARTMENT OF SOCIAL SERVICES on BEHALF of SANDRA C. v. THOMAS J.S.
100 A.D.2d 119, 474 N.Y.S.2d 322 (2 Dept. 1984)

BRACKEN, J.

In June of 1981, the Suffolk County Department of Social Services instituted a paternity proceeding pursuant to article 5 of the Family Court Act, on behalf of Sandra C., a recipient of public assistance, to adjudicate appellant Thomas J. S. to be the father of a female child born out of wedlock to Sandra C. on October 29, 1976.

After refusing to attend an appointment to undergo blood-grouping tests, scheduled for December 10, 1981, appellant [alleged father] moved, *inter alia*, to vacate a demand that he submit to a human leucocyte antigen (HLA) test. Appellant's motion was premised on the ground that section 532 of the Family Court Act (as amd by L 1981, ch 9, § 2), to the extent that it authorizes the results of HLA testing to be used as affirmative proof of paternity, deprives a putative father of his Fourteenth Amendment right to due process of law and equal protection of the laws and his Fifth Amendment privilege against self incrimination.

📖 **CASE 9-1 continued**

***

Appellant contends that because the results of HLA testing may provide only a 90% chance of exclusion, the 1981 amendment, which allows the affirmative use of test results as evidence of paternity, will deprive 10% of the tested putative fathers of their constitutional right to due process of law. Furthermore, appellant maintains that, in the past, blood-grouping tests could be used solely for exclusionary purposes, thereby protecting the alleged father from fraudulent claims, and that this amendment violates such long-standing policy by authorizing the results to be used as direct evidence of paternity.

Initially, we note that prior to the 1981 amendment, section 532, which by its provisions precluded blood test results from being admitted in evidence as affirmative proof of paternity, was not an expression of an evidentiary rule that blood tests could be used only as a shield for the putative father's protection. Rather, the section was reflective of the fact that the only blood test available at the time of the original enactment of section 532 in 1962...was the Landsteiner blood-grouping test, a test involving only the red blood cells. While the test was a reliable and accepted scientific procedure, it was and still is not sophisticated enough to exclude more than 60% of random males because such red blood cell testing involves only a limited number of variables.... The Landsteiner test, therefore, could establish the fact of nonpaternity in a case where the putative father was excluded by the results; conversely, if a putative father was not so excluded, the test was not sufficiently reliable to establish the fact of paternity because there existed a 40% chance, more or less, that based upon untested genetic variables, the putative father might still be excluded. Thus the Landsteiner procedure simply was not precise enough to have probative value as affirmative proof of paternity....

In contrast to previously employed blood-grouping tests, however, the HLA test is far more comprehensive because it is based upon tissue typing of the white blood cells and involves a much greater number of variables.

***

Like other blood-grouping tests, the HLA test is an exclusionary one, the purpose and effect of which is to establish nonpaternity. However, utilization of the HLA and associated sophisticated tests can increase the probability of exclusion to such a high degree as to affirmatively prove paternity where a putative father is not excluded by the test results. When all tests are utilized, including all blood-typing tests, and no exclusion results, the average theoretical degree of probability of actual paternity or actual nonpaternity will be 99.999999999%.... The difference in the percentage depends upon the blood type of the particular individuals tested and the number of related blood-group systems which are used in addition to the HLA test....

It is clear then that HLA test interpretations are not based upon arbitrarily assigned numerical probability values or upon a statistical

📖 **CASE 9-1 continued**

theory unsupported by the evidence, but are based upon objectively ascertainable data and a statistical theory based upon research and experiment.

***

Moreover, since section 532 of the Family Court Act does not accord HLA results the status of definitive or conclusive proof of paternity, such test results are only evidence which the trier of fact has at its disposal to aid in its determination, and the results are to be given such weight as the trier of fact deems appropriate. We therefore conclude that the probative value of an HLA test result outweighs the danger of any undue prejudice. Accordingly, we hold that section 532 of the Family Court Act, as amended to authorize the use of HLA test results as inclusionary evidence of paternity, does not violate a putative father's Fourteenth Amendment right to due process of law.

***

Appellant next contends that section 532 of the Family Court Act violates his Fifth Amendment privilege against self incrimination. Additionally, he argues that section 532, which authorizes the court to compel a putative father to submit to blood tests, the results of which would be admissible at trial to establish paternity, conflicts with section 531 of that act. Section 531 states, in pertinent part, that: "The mother or the alleged father shall be competent to testify *but the respondent shall not be compelled to testify"* (emphasis supplied).

It has long been established that an accused's privilege against self incrimination under the Fifth and Fourteenth Amendments is not implicated where he is subjected to a blood test to determine if he was driving while intoxicated (*Schmerber v. California*, 384 U.S. 757). The rationale of such a determination is that blood test evidence obtained for use in a criminal case is neither testimony nor evidence relating to some communicative act or writing, and, therefore, does not involve the privilege.

The courts of this State have applied the *Schmerber* rationale to conclude that compulsory blood testing in paternity proceedings does not implicate the privilege....

With respect to the alleged conflict between sections 531 and 532 of the Family Court Act, the Court of Appeals has construed section 531 as giving the respondent in a paternity proceeding complete protection against being compelled to testify or produce communicative evidence, not only at the hearing, but also at the pretrial discovery stage of the proceeding.... When the Legislature amended section 532 in 1981, it presumably was aware of the privilege created by section 531, as well as the judicial construction of the latter enactment. The clear implication is that the Legislature viewed the amendment to section 532 either as creating an exception to the privilege that had been previously created by section 531, or, more likely, as falling completely outside the scope of the prohibition against

📖 **CASE 9-1 continued**

testimonial compulsion as contained in section 531 and defined in *Schmerber v. California (supra)*....

***

DNA Test

The DNA test, like the HLA, is a genetic marker test, and the results are admissible to prove as well as disprove paternity. The greater accuracy of DNA testing lies in the fact that the material tested is Deoxyribonucleic Acid, a compound found in every cell of the body that carries all genetic information. Normal human beings have 23 pairs of chromosomes, which are comprised of DNA. One chromosome of each pair is inherited from each parent. Thus, one of each pair of a child's chromosomes comes from the mother, and the other one must come from the father. If the alleged father does not have a chromosome which matches one of the child's chromosomes, he cannot be the biological father, and he is, accordingly, excluded. Since identical twins have identical DNA, genetic marker testing cannot differentiate which twin is the father.

There are at present two types of DNA tests: RFLP (Restriction Fragment Length Polymorphism) and PCR (Polymerase Chain Reaction). In RFLP testing, parts of sections between the genes of three to five chromosomes are examined. If there is a match, paternity is all but established, with a 99% degree of certainty. In PCR testing, the actual genes themselves are examined. There are several PCR tests, which examine different genes. If all the tests match the father and child, paternity is established with a 99% degree of scientific confidence. If any one of the PCR tests does not match the alleged father, he is definitely excluded. Of course, for the results to be reliable, the samples of genetic material must be protected from contamination, and the results must be properly interpreted, tasks which require scrupulous laboratory standards. Form 9-2 lists the laboratories approved for various types of paternity testing by the New York State Department of Health.

SPECIAL PROCEDURAL AND EVIDENTIARY RULES

Clear and Convincing Evidence

As you know, most civil cases must be proved by a preponderance of the evidence, whereas criminal cases must be proved beyond a reasonable doubt. There is a third standard of proof, **clear and convincing evidence**, which is applicable to certain types of civil proceedings, including paternity cases. The "clear and convincing evidence" standard is higher than "fair preponderance" but lower than "beyond a reasonable doubt." It is applied in civil cases involving loss of liberty, such as involuntary hospital confinement of mentally ill persons, or cases of a particularly momentous, and usually irreversible,

📖 **FORM 9-2**

NEW YORK STATE PERMIT - PATERNITY TESTING LABORATORIES

Laboratory Name	PFI & Code	RBC Antigens	Blood Proteins	HLA Serology	HLA DNA	DNA PCR	DNA RFLP
Bender Hygienic Laboratory Inc. 9 Samaritan Drive Albany, NY 12208 518-472-9124	1888 0101A010	X		X			
CBR Laboratories Inc. 800 Huntington Avenue Boston, MA 02115 617-731-6470	4027 822007A4	X					
Clinical Testing and Research Inc. 20 Wilsey Square Ridgewood, NJ 07450 201-652-2088	3180 831121A0	X		X	X	X	
Gen-Biotech, Inc. Executive Park North Albany, NY 12203 518-437-1507	4117 0101A310	X		X			X
Genetic Design, Inc. 7017 Albert Pick Road Greensboro, NC 27409 919-668-3210	3955 834014A0	X	X	X	X	X	X
GENETRIX Immunogenetics Laboratory 1410 North 3rd Street Phoenix, AZ 85004 602-945-4363	4367 803007A1			X			
Lifecodes Corporation 550 West Avenue Stamford, CT 06902 203-320-9500	4908 807028A0				X	X	X
Maryland Medical Metpath 1901 Sulphur Spring Road Baltimore, MD 21227 410-247-9100	4029 921003A0	X	X	X			X
Roche Biomedical Laboratories Inc. 1447 York Court Burlington, NC 27215 919-584-5171	2502 834004A0	X	X	X	X	X	X
SUNY Health Science Center at Syracuse Clinical Pathology Lab. 750 East Adams Street Syracuse, NY 13210 315-464-4460	2220 3301M070	X		X			

Effective Date: 3/20/95

nature. Paternity cases fall into the latter category, because a whole host of life-long reciprocal rights and obligations are established by an order of filiation. The Court of Appeals has described "clear and convincing evidence" as proof which is " 'entirely satisfactory' and creates a genuine belief that respondent is the father of the child." *Commissioner of Social Services v. Philip De G.*, 59 N.Y.2d 137, 463 N.Y.S.2d 761 (1983). Borderline HLA results coupled with credible testimony that the mother engaged in sexual relations with several men at the time of conception have been held not to satisfy the clear and convincing evidence requirement. *Jackson v. Ricks*, 186 A.D.2d 1032, 588 N.Y.S.2d 676 (4 Dept. 1992).

Right to Remain Silent

The respondent in a paternity proceeding, whether mother or alleged father, may not be compelled to testify. FCA § 531. This statutory privilege should not be confused with the constitutional right to remain silent in a criminal case, however. In a criminal case, the defendant's right to remain silent is absolute. The prosecutor cannot comment upon the defendant's failure to testify, and the trier of fact, whether judge or jury, may not draw any inference of guilt from it. In an ordinary civil proceeding, as you know, the opposite is true: everything that is not denied is deemed admitted. In a paternity case the rule is different; the respondent's silence does not constitute an admission, but the court may draw from it "the strongest inference against [the respondent] that the opposing evidence in the record permits." *Commissioner of Social Services v. Philip De G., supra.* Of course, an unfavorable inference can be drawn only as to those matters of which the respondent is expected to have knowledge. If the petitioner is the mother, for example, the respondent would probably not be expected to know whether she had sexual relations with another man at the time of conception. He would know whether he himself had sexual relations with her at the relevant time, however, so that his failure to deny that such relations occurred would enhance the credibility of petitioner's testimony that such relations did take place.

Discovery

Because of the testimonial privilege, the petitioner in a paternity proceeding cannot compel the respondent to submit to an examination before trial (EBT) nor to answer interrogatories. The respondent can employ these discovery devices to obtain information from the petitioner, however. If the respondent is the alleged father, he may be in genuine ignorance, not only concerning the petitioner's sexual activities at the time of conception, but also of such details of the child's birth as whether the infant was born at full-term or prematurely. In such situations, the discovery process is essential. Form 9-3 is an example of interrogatories that might be submitted by a respondent alleged father on the issue of paternity.

📖 **FORM 9-3**

DEMAND FOR INTERROGATORIES

The Respondent, John Doe, requests the Petitioner, Jane Roe, to answer under oath, in accordance with Article 31 of the CPLR, the following interrogatories:

1.   Set forth the date or dates when you and respondent allegedly had sexual intercourse.

2.   For each date listed above set forth the following information:

       a)   The place;

       b)   Approximate time of day;

       c)   Names of any witnesses to these acts or witnesses you intend to call to establish access.

       d)   Whether either you or respondent used birth control medication or devices on any of these occasions.

3.   What is the date of birth of the child?

4.   What is the alleged date of conception of this child?

5.   What were the dates your last menstrual period commenced and ended before the alleged date of conception?

6.   From the date of your last menstrual period before conception to the alleged date of conception, set forth the following information:

       a)   Whether you had sexual intercourse with any other person besides respondent;

       b)   If yes, set forth the name, address of the person, the date of the act, the place of the act, the approximate time of the act.

7.   Set forth the name or names and addresses of any person, besides the respondent, with whom you had sexual intercourse one month prior to and one month after the alleged date of conception.

8.   Set forth the name and address of the obstetrician who delivered this child.

       <u>Please attach complete copies of the obstetrician's medical records and medical records from the hospital or facility from which the child was delivered</u>

9.   Set forth the name, address and telephone number of the

📖 FORM 9-3 continued

pediatrician or pediatricians who have attended to or treated the child.

<u>Please attach complete copies of the pediatrician's or pediatricians' medical records.</u>

10. Have you ever used birth control prior to having sexual intercourse. If yes, please state:

     a)   The name or type of birth control medication or device;
     b)   If prescribed by a physician, the name and address of the physician;
     c)   The frequency with which you took or used birth control.

Proof of Resemblance Inadmissible

It is well settled that evidence purporting to show a physical resemblance between an alleged father and child is not admissible in a paternity proceeding. The child is not supposed to be brought into the courtroom during the proceeding, and photographs may not be offered to show resemblance. *Commissioner of Welfare of City of New York v. Leroy C.*, 45 A.D.2d 963, 359 N.Y.S.2d 341 (2 Dept. 1974). Although physical resemblance is neither accurate nor reliable proof of paternity, it can be powerfully persuasive. The New York rule is designed to prevent results such as the famous (or infamous) case in which Charlie Chaplin was held to be the father of a child because of physical resemblance, although the blood test had excluded him. *Berry v. Chaplin*, 74 Cal.App.2d 442, 169 P.2d 442 (1946).

Service

The preferred method of service in a paternity case, as in all civil proceedings, is personal delivery of the summons, together with the *verified* petition, to the respondent or to a person of suitable age and discretion at respondent's place of abode or business. The summons must be served at least eight days before the hearing date. FCA § 525. Mail service is also allowed, but no default may be taken after mail service unless there is proof that the respondent had actual notice of the hearing date, which requirement may be satisfied by submitting a receipt for certified mail signed by the respondent. FCA § 525(c). If personal service cannot be effectuated after "reasonable effort," service may be made by delivery to an agent designated for service or by nail and mail as provided in CPLR § 308. FCA § 525(b).

The Family Court also has power to issue a warrant for the respondent when it appears that 1) the summons cannot be served or 2) the respondent has failed to obey the summons or 3) the respondent is likely to leave the jurisdiction or 4) the safety of the petitioner is endangered or 5) a respondent on bail or on parole has failed to appear. FCA § 526.

Other Proceedings in which Paternity May Be Established

Although the Family Court has exclusive original jurisdiction to entertain a paternity petition, the issue of paternity may arise in other courts. In the context of a divorce case brought by the husband, the Supreme Court may determine the legitimacy of any child born or begotten after the ground for divorce arose. DRL § 175(2). In addition, the Supreme Court, as the court of general jurisdiction, may hear a **declaratory judgment** proceeding to determine paternity. The Supreme Court may also determine paternity in habeas corpus proceedings in which a man claiming to be the father seeks custody of a child. The issue of who is the father of a child also arises in Surrogate's Court in connection with adoption and probate proceedings, and Surrogate's Court has ancillary jurisdiction to determine paternity when the issue is presented in such cases. FCA § 511.

In Family Court as well, the issue of paternity sometimes comes up in cases other than those filed as paternity proceedings. In a neglect proceeding, custody proceeding, family offense proceeding, a termination of parental rights case or adoption, the issue of who is the father of the child may be presented. To offer a speedy resolution of the issue, the Family Court Act provides that in any proceeding in Family Court, the court may make an order of filiation if 1) both parents are before the court, and 2) the father waives both the filing of a petition and the right to a hearing, and 3) the court is satisfied as to the paternity of the child from the sworn statements of the parents. FCA § 564.

EFFECTS OF ORDER OF FILIATION

When the court makes an order of filiation establishing who is the father of a child born out of wedlock, the clerk of the court transmits a notification of the order to the Commissioner of Health of the City of New York, if the child was born in New York City, or to the State Commissioner of Health, if the child was born elsewhere in New York State (Form 9-4). The name of the father is then included on the child's birth certificate. Notification is also submitted to the Putative Father Registry.

Once an order of filiation has been made, the child and the father have all the reciprocal rights and obligations of parenthood discussed throughout this textbook. A child whose paternity has been adjudicated has, at least in New York, virtually all the same rights as a legitimate child and is in no legal sense inferior to other children who may be born in wedlock to either parent. The adjudicated father's obligation to support the mother of the child is limited to contribution toward the expenses of her pregnancy, confinement and recovery. His obligation to support the child, however, is exactly the same as toward any in-wedlock children he may have. Once paternity has been established, the

📖 **FORM 9-4**

New York State Department of Health
Vital Records Section/Birth Amendment Unit

Notification Concerning
an Order of Filiation

TO: Commissioner of Health, New York State Department of Health, Albany, New York 12237-0023

SUBJECT (check one): ☐ Order of Filiation   ☐ Abrogation of Filiation Order

1. Information on Original Certificate

Infant	1. Name First Middle Last			
	2. Sex Male ☐ Female ☐	3. Date of Birth M D Y	4a. County (NYS)	4b. Town	4c. City or Village
Mother	5a. First Middle Last Maiden Name			5b. Social Security #

2. Corrected Maiden Name of Mother (If in error on original certificate)

Mother	6a. First Middle Last Maiden Name	6b. Social Security #

3. Information Submitted for Amended Certificate

Father	7a. Name First Middle Last	7b. Age	7c. State of Birth (Country if not USA)	7d. Social Security #

4. Name and Address Mother is Currently Using

Mother	8. Name: First Middle Last
	9. Mailing Address (Include Zip Code)

5. Attorney

Attorney	10. Name: First Middle Last	11. Firm
	12. Mailing Address (Include Zip Code)	

6. Certification

SEAL OF THE COURT

Pursuant to Section 543/544 of the Family Court Act,

I, _____,Clerk of the Family

Court of _____ County, do hereby notify you that an

order of filiation/abrogation of filiation order was made by the said

court on the _____ day of _____,

19____ in the case of _____,

complainant, vs. _____,defendant,

adjudging _____ to be/not to be father

of the above-named child.

_____
Signed: Clerk of the Court   Date

DOH-1524 (11/91)

support order will be retroactive to the date of the filing of the paternity petition. If the child is receiving public assistance, support will be owed from the date the child became eligible for public assistance, if that date is earlier than the filing date. FCA § 545(1). The court even has discretion to order the father to make payments to reimburse the mother for money spent on the child from the child's birth to the date of the filing of the paternity petition. FCA § 545(2). If blood tests have been performed and the alleged father is not excluded, the court can go ahead and enter a temporary order of support even before the order of filiation is made, if the alleged father wilfully fails to appear in court. FCA § 542(b). As you can see, these sections are designed to remove all temptation for the respondent to stall or drag out the paternity proceeding.

The fact that the child was conceived contrary to the wishes of the father in no was diminishes the support obligation, as Case 9-2 illustrates.

CASE 9-2

L. PAMELA P. v. FRANK S.
59 N.Y.2d 1, 462 N.Y.S.2d 819 (1983)

WACHTLER, J.

The issue on this appeal is whether a father, whose paternity of a child has been established, may assert, as a defense to his support obligation the deliberate misrepresentation of the mother concerning her use of contraception. We agree with the Appellate Division that the mother's alleged deceit has no bearing upon a father's obligation to support his child or upon the manner in which the parents' respective support obligations are determined. The order of the Appellate Division should therefore be affirmed.

Following a hearing on the paternity petition, Family Court made an order of filiation, having found by clear and convincing evidence that respondent is the father of petitioner's child. Thereafter respondent endeavored to establish that petitioner, intending to have respondent's child regardless of his wishes, misrepresented to him that she was using contraception. Although petitioner conceded that she was not, at the time of conception, using any form of birth control, she denied that any conversation concerning contraception took place.

***

Although at one time the objective of paternity proceedings was merely to prevent a child born out of wedlock from becoming a public charge, it is now well established that the appropriate emphasis must be upon the welfare of the child.... The primary purpose of establishing paternity is to ensure that adequate provision will be made for the child's needs, in accordance with the means of the parents.

📖 **CASE 9-2 continued**

***

Respondent argues, however, that petitioner's intentional misrepresentation that she was practicing birth control deprived him of his constitutional right to decide whether to father a child. Recognizing that petitioner herself engaged in no State action by her conduct, respondent urges that imposition of a support obligation upon him under these circumstances constitutes State involvement sufficient to give vitality to his constitutional claim.

Assuming, without deciding, that sufficient State action is present in this case we conclude that respondent's contentions fall short of stating any recognized aspect of the constitutional right of privacy.

Clearly, respondent has a constitutionally protected right to decide for himself whether to father a child.... This right is deemed so fundamental that governmental interference in this area of decision-making may be justified only by compelling State interests.... Yet, the interest protected has always been stated in terms of governmental restrictions on the individual's access to contraceptive devices.... It involves the freedom to decide for oneself, without unreasonable governmental interference, whether to avoid procreation through the use of contraception. This aspect of the right of privacy has never been extended so far as to regulate the conduct of private actors as between themselves. Indeed, as the Appellate Division recognized, judicial inquiry into so fundamentally private and intimate conduct as is required to determine the validity of respondent's assertions may itself involve impermissible State interference with the privacy of these individuals....

The interest asserted by the father on this appeal is not, strictly speaking, his freedom to choose to avoid procreation, because the mother's conduct in no way limited his right to use contraception. Rather, he seeks to have his choice regarding procreation fully respected by other individuals and effectuated to the extent that he should be relieved of his obligation to support a child that he did not voluntarily choose to have. But respondent's constitutional entitlement to avoid procreation does not encompass a right to avoid a child support obligation simply because another private person has not fully respected his desires in this regard. However unfairly respondent may have been treated by petitioner's failure to allow him an equal voice in the decision to conceive a child, such a wrong does not rise to the level of a constitutional violation.

***

An order of filiation, although it adjudicates parentage, does not "legitimize" the child. A child is made legitimate only by the marriage of its parents, either before or after the child's birth. DRL § 24. Correct terminology is important, since a legitimate child can claim all his or her rights without presenting any proof of paternity, whereas an out-of-wedlock child will have to present a copy of the acknowledgment or order of filiation. Oddly, although we still use the term "legitimate" to refer to the in-wedlock child, the terms "illegitimate child" and "bastard" were banished from the statute books and from all public and judicial proceedings in 1925. General Construction Law § 59. The proper legal term for a non-marital child is "child born out of wedlock."

Presumption of Legitimacy and Equitable Estoppel

Under common law, a child conceived or born during the course of a marriage is presumed to be the child of the mother's husband. This ancient **presumption of legitimacy** is still in effect in New York and, although rebuttable, is often described as one of the strongest legal presumptions. Since paternity proceedings are now viewed as an adjudication of status, and not just as a means of establishing the alleged father's support obligation, it is necessary to add the husband of the mother as a party to a paternity proceeding when a man other than the husband is alleged to be the father of a child conceived or born during the course of a marriage. *Matter of Richard W. v. Roberta Y.*, 212 A.D.2d 89, 629 N.Y.S.2d 512 (3 Dept. 1995). The husband of the mother is called the "presumed" father or "legal" father in court proceedings.

When the legitimacy of an in-wedlock child is challenged, the courts often use the doctrine of **equitable estoppel** to prevent the issue from being litigated. The doctrine of equitable estoppel is judge-made law that prevents an old issue from being litigated after everyone involved has relied on the status quo for a long time and harm would result from forcing them to accept a different version of the truth. For example, where a husband has known for years that a child born to his wife might actually have been fathered by another man, but the husband has treated the child as his own and has allowed the child to think of him as father, the courts probably will not permit the husband suddenly to raise the issue of the child's paternity at the point when the court is about to make an award of child support. It is easy for the courts to apply the doctrine of estoppel when the child would lose valuable support rights and there is no competing claim to the child, but what about when the biological father wants to assert his paternity and establish a relationship with the child? Such triangles are obviously much more complicated, as Case 9-3 illustrates.

📖 **CASE 9-3**

ETTORE I. v. ANGELA D.
127 A.D.2d 6, 513 N.Y.S.2d 733 (2 Dept.1987)

Eiber, J.

We are asked in the context of this contested paternity proceeding to determine whether the doctrine of equitable estoppel may properly be invoked to prevent the petitioner [alleged father] from securing an order of filiation which would effectively divest a child of

CASE 9-3 continued

her status as the legitimate daughter of the appellants [mother and her husband] herein.

Erin D., the child whose parentage is at stake in this dispute, was born on August 24, 1981. On or about June 1, 1984, when Erin was approximately two years and nine months of age, the petitioner commenced the instant paternity proceeding contending that he was, in fact, Erin's biological father and that Erin had been conceived during the course of his adulterous affair with the child's mother, the appellant Angela D.

The appellant, Robert D., the husband of the child's mother, steadfastly maintains that Erin is his child. The appellants jointly oppose this paternity proceeding, notwithstanding their legal separation in later 1984. The appellants also have another child, a son, who was born on September 3, 1983.

***

Although the issue of the availability of the doctrine of equitable estoppel as a defense to the petitioner's claim of paternity was first alluded to by the appellant husband, it was Erin's Law Guardian who actively pursued and effectively injected this issue into the proceeding. The essence of her argument was that the petitioner should be precluded from asserting any claim of paternity because he had allowed a protracted period of time to elapse before instituting this proceeding and, in the interim, had indirectly promoted or at the very least acquiesced "in the establishment and growth of the parent-child bond" between Erin and the appellant husband. Moreover, although the petitioner alleged that he was first made aware of his status as Erin's biological parent shortly after she was conceived, the Law Guardian noted that he nevertheless permitted the appellant husband to assume and accept all the "financial and emotional burdens of child rearing". Therefore, the Law Guardian urged that the court conduct a full hearing to determine whether the petitioner should be estopped from proving paternity by virtue of his delay in commencing this proceeding.

***

The petitioner, who was 42 years of age at the time of the hearing, testified that he met the appellant mother in 1980, at her place of employment. Although Mrs. D. was married and was cohabiting with her husband, she and the petitioner nevertheless engaged in sexual relations. They remained intimate until December of 1980 which encompassed the time of probable conception. The petitioner claimed that on one occasion, the appellant mother informed him that she had conceived his child. The petitioner perceived this information to be true, in view of his belief that the marital relationship between appellants had been progressively deteriorating. At no time, however, did Mrs. D. indicate to the petitioner that she had abstained from engaging in sexual relations with her husband during the time of their affair.

CASE 9-3 continued

So far as the evidence indicates, the petitioner conveyed his desire to be acknowledged as Erin's father; however, the appellant mother refused to allow him visitation. Instead of endeavoring to act upon his rights, the petitioner permitted the appellant husband to assume all parental responsibilities for the child. He attempted to justify his inaction by asserting that he did not wish to upset or otherwise disrupt the family unit. When asked whether he was concerned that the child was forming strong emotional bonds with appellant husband, the petitioner unhesitatingly declared: "there was nothing I could do about it".

It is also relevant to this case that the petitioner admitted that he had fortuitously encountered Erin on only two occasions since her birth: once when she was 15 months old, and again, when she was 2½ years old. On neither of these occasions was there any contact between the petitioner and the child.

The petitioner never attempted to communicate with the appellant husband regarding Erin's paternal origins. Nor did he ever object to the fact that the appellant husband has assumed all parental responsibilities and was designated Erin's father on her birth certificate and when baptismal rites were administered. The petitioner neither paid for nor offered to pay for the medical or hospital expenses incurred in connection with the child's birth. Notwithstanding the foregoing, the petitioner, in an effort to substantiate his asserted concern for the child, referred in his hearing testimony to three checks which he had given to the appellant mother in the aggregate sum of $324.75. It was subsequently established, however, that of these three checks, only one, in the amount of $25, had been specifically designated for Erin.

***

The appellant husband, during the course of his testimony, confirmed his love for Erin. He maintains a close relationship with the child, and she has always referred to him as "Daddy". The results of the HLA test in no way altered his commitment to the child, and he evinced a willingness to continue to support the child both emotionally and financially.

***

We note that, in general, the doctrine of equitable estoppel may successfully be invoked, in the interest of fairness, to prevent the enforcement of rights which would ultimately work fraud or injustice upon the person against whom enforcement is sought.... An estoppel defense may also be invoked where the failure to promptly assert a right has given rise to circumstances rendering it inequitable to permit the exercise of the right after a lapse of time.... Because of the same qualitative considerations which support the invocation of estoppel in other areas of law, the courts, in more recent years, have recognized the availability of this doctrine as a viable defense in various forms of proceedings involving domestic disputes.

***

CASE 9-3 continued

There can be no doubt, on the record before us, that a reversal of the Family Court's order would best serve Erin's interests. When we reflect upon the emotional fragility of a child of such tender age, and the child's need for continuity, we would be remiss if we failed to note that the inevitable effect of destroying the child's image of her family would be catastrophic and fraught with lasting trauma. Moreover, as the child's Law Guardian aptly recognizes in her brief, there is an additional concern -- one which is highly pertinent to the case at bar -- and that is "an appreciation of the extreme difficulty, if not impossibility, of substituting a stranger for someone, who, as a consequence of years of concern and love for a child, has become the 'psychological' parent". Therefore, to meet the need for a just and pragmatic result, the petitioner's efforts to vindicate his rights must give way to the child's emotional well-being as well as the societal interests in shielding the child from the grave repercussions of being branded illegitimate.

Such a conclusion, in concept and in fact is particularly warranted under the circumstances here extant since the petitioner failed to promptly pursue any legal rights he might otherwise have had during the child's formative years. Throughout the period of the petitioner's inaction, Erin was exposed to and nurtured by the love of the appellant husband. This relationship continues to flourish as a direct consequence of the petitioner's silence and his acquiescence. Although the petitioner testified that he did not attempt to secure an order of filiation at an earlier date, despite his unyielding belief that Erin was his child, because he did not wish to disrupt the harmony of the family, we find the petitioner's assertions to be particularly unconvincing, given his conceded awareness of the marital difficulties which the appellants were experiencing at the time of Erin's conception and throughout the period of time thereafter. Moreover, the veracity of his excuse is further undermined by the fact that he had apparently engaged in a lengthy campaign to persuade the appellant mother to leave her husband. The petitioner also candidly admitted that he never thought the appellants' marriage would survive. He finally commenced this proceeding only after his proposal of marriage was rejected by the appellant mother. Based on the foregoing, we cannot help but wonder if the petitioner is truly attempting to vindicate his rights as biological father or if he is merely attempting to be vindictive. We do know that the reality of what the petitioner seeks to do is to deprive Erin of the only father she has ever known and to place a stranger in his stead. We conclude, however, that the petitioner has not made a showing "sufficient to overcome the undisputed equities in the husband's favor nor the benefits to the child accruing by preserving its legitimacy"....Acceptance of such a self-serving excuse would be fundamentally inconsistent with the purpose of estoppel, which is to protect innocent children from an irreparable loss of legal rights and status and to protect the rights of unsuspecting persons who have developed strong bonds with the child during the period of inaction.

📖 **CASE 9-3 continued**

Moreover, were we to sanction the petitioner's conduct, the defense of estoppel would be rendered substantially meaningless and the innocent victims of belated challenges to paternity would be deprived of any protection under the law. In accordance with this analysis, the order appealed from must be reversed and the proceeding dismissed.

***

DISCUSSION TOPIC

Do you agree with the result in this case? Is the decision designed to protect the child or the husband of the mother? Note that it was the law guardian who urged the doctrine of equitable estoppel. Do you think the result would have been different if the husband were already subject to a support order and had not been diligent in making payments? What if the husband had been ambivalent or neutral about the outcome? Do you think the holding reflects the court's disapproval of the adulterous relationship between the petitioner and the mother of the child? How does the court's emphasis on "bonding" square with the holdings in *Matter of Ronald FF. v. Cindy GG.* (Case 6-4) and *Matter of Alison D. v. Virginia M.* (Case 1-2)?

Children Conceived by Artificial Insemination

A child born to a married woman as a result of artificial insemination is deemed the legitimate child of the husband if 1) the insemination was performed by a person authorized to practice medicine, 2) with the written consent of the woman *and* her husband, and 3) the physician who performed the procedure certifies that he rendered the service. The case of *Anonymous v. Anonymous*, 151 A.D.2d 330, 542 N.Y.S.2d 586 (1 Dept. 1989) concerned a child born as a result of artificial insemination to a married woman whose husband had *not* executed a written consent to the procedure. The court ruled that the requirements of the statute must be strictly complied with. Since the husband had not executed a written consent, the child was not considered legitimate.

When a child is born to an unmarried woman as a result of artificial insemination, can the biological father bring a paternity action? In *Thomas S. v. Robin Y.*, 209 A.D.2d 298, 618 N.Y.S.2d 356 (1 Dept. 1994), the First Department held that a sperm donor who is known to his child as her father and who has had considerable contact with her at the instance of her mother is entitled to an order of filiation. The decision is carefully limited to its facts, and it is not clear how wide the court meant to open the door to such suits. Nevertheless, the opinion at the very least highlights the importance of the participants in such a procedure entering into a written agreement spelling out their intentions regarding the child's future involvement, if any, with the sperm donor.

CONCLUSION

Paternity proceedings today are conducted in a businesslike manner, with primary concern focused on assuring to the child all the benefits to which he or she may be entitled. Paternity should be established as early in the child's life as possible, preferably through voluntary acknowledgment at the hospital at the time of birth. Procrastination rarely benefits either parent, and may result in complicating what should have been a simple legal matter. Although the legal assistant working on such a matter may sometimes personally disapprove of the conduct of the parents, it is essential that the legal assistant maintain a professional, non-judgmental demeanor if the client is to share personal and often embarrassing information willingly.

CHAPTER REVIEW QUESTIONS

1. Lisa is a 17-year-old woman who has approached your firm about representing her in a paternity proceeding against her putative father. Lisa's mother died many years ago without having legally established Lisa's paternity. Since that time, Lisa has been raised by her putative father's sister. Lisa is an outstanding student, and she wishes to go to college. Her putative father, although proud of her good grades, thinks college is a waste of time for a girl, and he has stated that he will not support her after she graduates from high school and will not contribute toward the cost of her college education. Lisa would like the court to compel her father to contribute towards her support while she is in college. Does Lisa have standing to file a paternity case against her alleged father? Has the statute of limitations run to file such a case? In what court would Lisa's petition be filed? Does the fact that Lisa's mother is deceased make it impossible for Lisa to bring the paternity case?

2. Marvin and Sonia, although never married, had lived together for five years until last August when Sonia left Marvin to live with another man. At the time Sonia and Marvin began living together, Sonia was pregnant with Dion. Sonia told Marvin that he is Dion's father, and Marvin is listed as father on Dion's birth certificate. Marvin loves Dion dearly and supported him and assisted in his care while the parties were living together. Dion calls Marvin "Daddy" and worships the ground Marvin walks on. After the breakup, your firm filed a visitation petition on Marvin's behalf, as Sonia was not allowing him to see the child. Sonia's lawyer filed an answer claiming that Marvin is not entitled to visitation because he is not Dion's biological father. Sonia states that she is sure that blood tests will prove Marvin is not Dion's father. The attorney from your firm who is handling Marvin's case tells you that Marvin will not have standing to sue for visitation if he is not Dion's father. He asks you to research the matter and see if there is any way to prevent the court from ordering the blood tests. What doctrine

would you research? What are the points in Marvin's favor under that doctrine? Would you suggest to the attorney in charge of the case that he might ask the court to appoint a law guardian for Dion?

3.   Jackson and Martine signed a voluntary acknowledgment of paternity in the hospital at the time of the birth of Jackson Jr. in 1995. Can Martine, who has custody of the child, file a support proceeding against Jackson without first having to file a paternity case?

4.   Assume that Jackson Jr. is one year old at the time Martine files for support. When Jackson was six months old he had a hernia repair operation that was not fully paid for by Martine's health insurance. Can Martine ask the court to order Jackson to reimburse her for the money she paid for the operation?

5.   James has filed a paternity petition claiming to be the father of Jonathan, a child born to Jennifer. At the time of Jonathan's birth, Jennifer was legally married to Douglas, although she had not had sexual relations with Douglas or even seen him for three years before Jonathan's birth. Jonathan's birth certificate contains no father's name. Who is entitled to notice of the paternity proceeding? Why?

CHAPTER ASSIGNMENT

Prepare an interview checklist of questions to ask the mother of an out-of-wedlock child who wishes to file a paternity proceeding. At the next session of class, you may be asked to interview a fellow student, using your checklist. Rehearse the phrasing of your questions and the demeanor you will display while asking questions about such intimate matters.

10 FAMILY OFFENSES

> "The legislature hereby finds that there are few more
> prevalent or more serious problems confronting the
> families and households of New York than domestic
> violence. It is a crime which destroys the household as a
> place of safety, sanctuary, freedom and nurturing for all
> household members." Family Protection and Domestic
> Violence Intervention Act of 1994, Laws of 1994, ch. 222,
> § 1.

If to name a thing is to know it, we have hardly begun to understand the problem variously called domestic violence, spousal abuse, violence between intimates, family violence, woman battering, wife beating and husband abuse. In New York, assault, menacing, reckless endangerment, harassment, and disorderly conduct are referred to as **family offenses** when the victim is related to the perpetrator by consanguinity or affinity or is a former spouse or has a child in common with the perpetrator. The choice of terms is not an academic quibble. Often, it determines to whom social services will be available and who will be brought under the umbrella of legal protection. Always, it reflects a way of conceptualizing the issue -- as a couple's problem, a family problem, a social problem, a political problem, or the psychological or behavioral problem of an individual, either the victim or the perpetrator.

"Domestic violence" was defined by the American Medical Association in 1992 as "an ongoing, debilitating experience of physical, psychological and/or sexual abuse in the home, associated with increased isolation from the outside world and limited personal freedom and accessibility to resources. Whenever a woman is placed in physical danger or controlled by the threat or use of physical force, she has been abused." *American Medical Association Diagnostic and*

313

Treatment Guidelines on Domestic Violence.

Because statistics are gathered under so many different definitions for a variety of medical, social service and law enforcement purposes, it is difficult even to determine the true scope of the problem. The limited data available are sufficient, however, to demonstrate that domestic violence is a national problem that cuts across regional, ethnic, religious, and socio-economic boundaries. The U.S. Department of Justice reported that "violence between intimates," defined as murders, rapes, robberies, and assaults committed by spouses, ex-spouses, boyfriends or girlfriends, averaged over 600,000 annually between 1987 and 1991, with assault being by far the most common. While race, ethnicity and location of residence were insignificant variables, gender was crucial; women were more than 10 times as likely as men to be the victims of violence by an intimate, although women are much less likely than men to become victims of violent crime in general. As New York Assemblywoman Helene Weinstein noted in supporting recent domestic violence legislation, "The home is actually a more dangerous place for American women than are city streets."

In New York in 1993, almost 85,000 family offenses (a definition much broader than "violence between intimates") were reported, an increase of 14% from 1992. Since family violence was certainly underreported in the past, and may still be, we cannot be sure whether the increase represents more violence or better reporting. In New York State, where the Criminal and Family Courts have concurrent original jurisdiction over family offenses, almost 51,000 new family offense petitions were filed in Family Courts in 1995, half of which were filed in New York City. Even more troubling is the fact that almost 8,000 violation of order of protection petitions were filed throughout the state, which underscores the importance of vigorous and meaningful enforcement efforts. In 1993, the most recent year for which breakdowns by relationship are available, women filed 18,444 petitions against their husbands, 1,234 against former husbands, and 8,154 against men with whom they had a child in common, while men filed less than 4,000 in total against their wives, former wives, and women with whom they had a child in common. Thus, women filing petitions against men with whom they had intimate relationships constituted well over half of the almost 40,000 family offense petitions filed in 1993.

THEORIES ABOUT DOMESTIC VIOLENCE

Logically, one would expect the search for understanding of domestic violence to begin with studies of the batterers. In practice, however, it is the battered women who have been studied. Two explanations are often advanced for the disparate amount of research devoted to the female victims of domestic violence. One possibility is that violence against women is so pervasive in so many societies that it seems "normal" and, thus, unworthy of study. Certainly in our own society and in our common law tradition, as discussed in Chapter 1, wife beating was condoned for centuries. The assumption has been widespread, therefore, that violence is "natural" to men, either because of their physical makeup or as a result of social conditioning. The few studies of batterers that do exist lend some credence to this belief. They have found no statistically significant demographic characteristics in common among perpetrators of domestic violence. Neither class, race, religion, age, employment status, nor prior criminal record stood out as particularly associated with a tendency toward domestic violence. A large number of batterers, however, had either witnessed or experienced violence in childhood, lending support to the premise that domestic violence is learned behavior.

The second explanation for the greater amount of attention paid to the victims than the victimizers is that it is the woman's behavior that is of more concern to the helping professions. It is invariably the battered woman, rather than the offender, who reaches out for help. Having had contact with the victim and offered whatever they had to give by way of assistance, social workers, psychologists, physicians, police and judges are often frustrated when the abused woman returns to or elects to remain with her abuser. The consuming question for such professionals, therefore, is "Why does she stay?" Most of the existing research attempts to answer this question.

"BATTERED WOMAN'S SYNDROME"

The term "**battered woman's syndrome**" (BWS) was coined by Dr. Lenore E. Walker in a ground-breaking book, *The Battered Woman*, published in 1979. After studying a large number of women who had been victims of domestic violence, Dr. Walker postulated that many (but not all) battered women develop a constellation of psychological symptoms, in medical terms a "syndrome," which affect the battered woman's behavior and response to abuse in ways that would not be readily apparent to a lay person. Although Dr. Walker's theories have been challenged by other scholars, as discussed below, and have been modified to some extent by Dr. Walker herself, legal practitioners should be familiar with the theory because it has been accepted as valid for a variety of purposes in courts of law.

Dr. Walker observed that domestic violence follows a three-stage cycle: tension building, acute battering, and contrition by the batterer (often referred to as the "honeymoon phase"). The repeated cycles of violence produce in the abused woman a condition of "learned helplessness." As the cycles recur, the woman's motivation to respond decreases, and she becomes passive and depressed and loses her self-confidence. As her own self-esteem erodes, the battered woman blames herself for the abuse and attributes an inordinate amount of power to her abuser. Ultimately, the battered woman is unable to recognize or avail herself of avenues of escape from the abusive situation.

Walker's theory is related to other research in the field of psychology, such as studies of Vietnam War veterans and victims of child abuse, who often show similar symptoms after prolonged exposure to erratic and episodic violence. The psychological diagnosis "**Post-traumatic Stress Disorder**" was formulated to describe the condition, and "battered woman's syndrome" is sometimes referred to as a subcategory of Post-traumatic Stress Disorder. You will encounter Post-traumatic Stress Disorder again in the next chapter of this textbook, where it is discussed in connection with sexual abuse of children.

Dr. Walker's work developed several important points that the legal system has responded to both in legislative changes and through case law. She noted, for example, that domestic violence often escalates over time. Although in some relationships physical violence may begin early in the relationship, in many cases it is proceeded or accompanied by other forms of abuse that are equally damaging to the victim. These may include insults, rejection, threats and accusations, emotional blackmail, distortion of reality, possessiveness, unrealistic expectations, threats to harm or to take away the children, financial blackmail, and sexual abuse. Recognizing that allegations concerning a single instance of abuse would not give the court a true picture of the victim's situation, the New York legislature in 1981 amended the Family Court Act to require that a petition clerk who drafts a petition for a *pro se* litigant must include all the allegations presented, rather than alleging only the most recent event or a past event that appears particularly egregious. FCA § 216-c(1). Because Walker's work stressed that the victim of domestic violence may feel isolated and unsure of herself when she attempts to seek help, the Family Court Act provides that either party to a family offense proceeding may have a non-witness friend, relative, or social worker present in the court room to provide moral support. FCA § 838.

Expert testimony that a woman is suffering from battered woman's syndrome may be offered in court for a variety of purposes. If a battered woman ultimately prosecutes her abuser either in Criminal or Family Court, battered woman's syndrome testimony may be relevant to her credibility as a witness. It may be offered to explain why she failed to seek help or to prosecute earlier instances of abuse or to explain why she gave innocuous explanations of her injuries to friends, relatives, police or medical personnel that are inconsistent with her present testimony. If the battered woman is being criminally prosecuted herself, because she has killed or injured the abuser, BWS testimony may be offered in support of a self-defense claim. In New York, this defense is called "justification," and it is only available if the defendant did not use "excessive force" to ward off the attack. Thus, testimony about BWS might be offered to demonstrate that the force used was a reasonable response to the threat as the woman perceived it. BWS testimony may also be relevant in a child protective proceeding to explain why a battered woman was unable to take appropriate steps to protect her children from abuse by the man who was also abusing her. BWS testimony has been held admissible in New York for all of these purposes. See *People v. Emick*, 103 A.D.2d 643, 481 N.Y.S.2d 552 (4 Dept. 1984); *People v. Ciervo*, 123 A.D.2d 393, 506 N.Y.S.2d 462 (2 Dept. 1986); *People v. Barrett*, 189 A.D.2d 879, 592 N.Y.S.2d 766 (2 Dept. 1993); *People v. Torres*, 128 Misc.2d 129, 488 N.Y.S.2d 358 (N.Y. Sup. Ct. 1985); *Matter of Glenn G.*, 154 Misc.2d 677, 587 N.Y.S.2d 464 (Fam.Ct. Kings County 1992).

Despite its enormous influence, Walker's work has not gone unchallenged. The theory has been criticized for failing to recognize and account for the substantial number of women who do remove themselves from abusive situations, for characterizing "learned helplessness" as the final stage in a pattern of deterioration, rather than a phase from which some women spontaneously move on to help-seeking, and for its formulation of BWS as a psychological disorder of the victim. Those who believe that BWS should not be seen as a disorder of the victim point out that such a characterization plays into stereotypes of women as hysterical, masochistic, and weak-willed. They argue that in our culture, women are encouraged to be nurturing and accommodating and that they are viewed as responsible for the success of relationships. To describe as disordered a woman who has actually perfectly conformed to the expectations of her society ignores the political and social reality of women's lives. These critics note that in a society which still underpays women for their work and regards an "unattached" woman as a social oddity, financial and social pressures to remain in an abusive relationship may be unfairly discounted. Further, they contend that the services offered to abused women are often too uncoordinated and short-term to deal with the task of rebuilding entire lives. Worst of all, the stigmatization of the battered woman as psychologically disturbed cuts her off from other women, whose community and support she desperately needs to reconstitute her life. Many of these commentators are proponents of long-term, resident-managed shelters rather than psychotherapy as the best form of assistance for battered women.

FAMILY OFFENSE PROCEEDINGS

BASICS BOX

Subject matter jurisdiction: Family and criminal courts (which include city, town, or village courts, County Courts and Criminal Court in New York City) and criminal term of Supreme Court have concurrent original jurisdiction. Supreme Court (civil term) has ancillary jurisdiction to issue an Order of Protection where a matrimonial or custody case is pending

Venue: County of residence of either party (including a shelter where a party may be staying) or county where the charged acts occurred.

Standing: In Family Court, persons related by consanguinity or affinity, ex-spouses, persons who have a child in common; in a criminal court, any person who has been the victim of a crime.

Grounds: Assault in the 2nd and 3rd degrees, Attempted Assault, Menacing in the 2nd and 3rd degrees, Reckless Endangerment, Harassment in the 1st and 2nd degrees, Aggravated Harassment, and Disorderly Conduct, including Disorderly Conduct in the home.

Statute of Limitations: None in Family Court; varies by degree of offense in criminal courts.

Applicable statutes: FCA Art. 8; DRL §§ 252, 240(3); various sections of the Penal Law and Criminal Procedure Law.

On January 1, 1995, the Family Protection and Domestic Violence Intervention Act of 1994 went into effect. This legislation significantly changed the judicial handling of family offense cases in criminal and family courts, as well as requests for orders of protection in matrimonial proceedings. In the following discussion, these recent amendments will be highlighted.

CONCURRENT JURISDICTION

Pursuant to the new Domestic Violence Intervention Act, Family Court and various criminal courts have concurrent original jurisdiction over family offenses. FCA §§ 115(e), 813(3); Criminal Procedure Law § 100.07. The petitioner may proceed in *either or both* courts. Although it is unusual in law for a plaintiff to be allowed to utilize two courts at the same time, the theory here is similar to that which underlies the simultaneous prosecution of child abuse in criminal and family courts. The purposes of the two proceedings are somewhat different, although they overlap; the purposes of the Family Court proceeding are to stop the violence, to protect the victim, and to offer rehabilitative services if desired, while the primary purpose of the Criminal Court proceeding is to punish the offender. The two courts do share the authority to issue orders of protection, however, and the potential for inconsistent or contradictory judicial outcomes does exist. One court might issue an order allowing the batterer to remain in the home under certain conditions, whereas the other court might exclude him. This is a problem the courts are likely to be called upon to resolve at some point. Whenever the Family Court is not in session (nights and weekends), the appropriate local criminal court has the power to modify or expand a temporary order of protection already issued by the Family Court. The Act does preclude one possible abuse of concurrent jurisdiction by providing that admissions made by, or testimony taken from, either party in Family Court in the absence of counsel or a valid waiver of counsel cannot be used in Criminal Court proceedings, although criminal court testimony is admissible in the Family Court proceedings. Criminal Procedure Law § 60.46.

In deciding which court(s) to utilize, the petitioner should consider what relief besides the order of protection she or he seeks. The Criminal Court has the power to put the offender in jail, whereas the Family Court can only incarcerate the offender for the violation of an existing order of protection. On the other hand, the Family Court has the power to issue an order of support on an emergency basis, provide for the temporary custody of the children, and make a referral for counseling. Petitioners also have different degrees of control over the proceedings in the two courts; in Family Court, the petitioner has the exclusive option to decide whether to proceed, while in Criminal Court it is the District Attorney who decides whether to prosecute and whether to accept a plea bargain. The District Attorney, however, is now required to notify the victim of the decision not to prosecute a family offense, to dismiss charges, or to enter into a plea bargain with the offender. If the victim and the offender are domestic partners, but do not have a child in common, the victim will not have a choice.

In such a situation, a criminal court is the only allowable forum. The appropriate criminal court can issue an Order of Protection to an unrelated complainant or witness in any criminal prosecution. Criminal Procedure Law §§ 530.11, 530.12, 530.13.

The Domestic Violence Intervention Act requires that a victim of domestic violence be given notice, in English and Spanish, by law enforcement agencies, prosecutors, hospital emergency rooms and the courts, advising the petitioner of certain rights, including the right to pursue the case in both courts. Form 10-1 is the English version of the notice given to petitioners in the New York County Family Court. On the actual court form, the Spanish version is on the other side of the page.

FORM 10-1

INFORMATION FOR VICTIMS OF DOMESTIC VIOLENCE

If you are the victim of domestic violence and a police officer has responded, you may request that the officer assist in providing for your safety and that of your children, including providing information on how to obtain a temporary order of protection. You also may request that the officer assist you in obtaining your essential personal effects and in locating and taking you and your children, or assist in making arrangements to take you and your children, to a safe place within such officer's jurisdiction, including but not limited to a domestic violence program, a family member's or a friend's residence, or a similar place of safety. When the officer's jurisdiction is more than a single county, you may ask the officer to take you and your children, or make arrangements to take you and your children, to a place of safety in the county where the incident occurred. If you or your children are in need of medical treatment, you have the right to request that the officer assist you in obtaining such medical treatment. You may request a copy of any incident reports at no cost from the law enforcement agency.

You may ask the district attorney or law enforcement officer to file a criminal complaint. You also have the right to file a petition in the Family Court when a family offense has been committed against you. You have the right to have your petition and request for an order of protection filed on the same day you appear in court, and such request must be heard that same day or the next day court is in session. Either court may issue an order of protection from conduct constituting a family offense which could include, among other provisions, an order for the respondent or defendant to stay away from you and your children. The Family Court also may order the payment of temporary child support and award you temporary custody of your children. If the Family Court is not in session, you may seek immediate assistance from a criminal court in obtaining an order of protection.

You have the right to seek legal counsel of your own choosing and if you proceed in Family Court and if it is determined that you cannot afford an attorney, one must be appointed to represent you without cost to you.

The forms you need to obtain an order of protection are available from the Family Court and the local criminal court:

📁 **FORM 10-1 continued**

Family Court	Local Criminal Court
New York County Family Court	New York County Criminal Court
60 Lafayette Street	100 Centre Street
New York, New York 10013	New York, New York 10013

The resources available in this community for information relating to domestic violence, treatment of injuries, and places of safety and shelters can be accessed by calling the following toll-free numbers for the New York State Coalition Against Domestic Violence Hotline:

(English): 1-800-942-6906
(Spanish): 1-800-942-6908

You also may call the domestic violence hotline near you:

Filing a criminal complaint or a family court petition containing allegations that are knowingly false is a crime.

Orders of Protection in Other Proceedings

In addition to criminal complaints and Family Offense proceedings pursuant to Article 8 of the Family Court Act, Orders of Protection may be obtained in several other types of proceedings. The Supreme Court has the authority to issue Orders of Protection in conjunction with pending matrimonial proceedings. DRL §§ 252, 240(3). Moreover, the Family Court may issue them in paternity, support, custody/visitation, child protective, juvenile delinquency, PINS, and foster care review proceedings. As Chapter 11 discusses, the terms and length of the various orders differ from one type of case to another, as well as who may apply for the order and against whom it may run. In some cases, it may be more convenient for the domestic violence victim to ask for the order in an already pending case rather than to file a new petition under Article 8, but in other instances the court may not be able to issue the sort of order the victim really needs in the pending case.

GROUNDS

Family offenses include Assault in the 2nd and 3rd degrees, Attempted Assault, Menacing in the 2nd and 3rd degrees, Reckless Endangerment, Harassment in the 1st and 2nd degrees, Aggravated Harassment, and Disorderly Conduct, including disorderly conduct in the home. FCA § 812(1). These terms are defined in the Penal Law. Assault is the intentional or reckless infliction of physical injury [Penal Law § 120.00] or serious physical injury [Penal Law § 120.05]; Menacing is conduct that instills in the victim the fear of physical injury by displaying a weapon or stalking [Penal Law § 120.14] or causes fear of immediate physical injury by any other means [Penal Law § 120.15]; and

Reckless Endangerment is reckless conduct that places the victim in danger of serious physical injury [Penal Law § 120.20]. Harassment takes several forms. Blows, punches and slaps that do not cause physical injury to the victim are one form of Harassment. Penal Law § 240.30(3). Annoying or alarming telephone calls or mail are another form of Harassment [Penal Law § 240.30(2)], and stalking is another [Penal Law § 240.25]. Although in the Penal Law these offenses range from violations to misdemeanors to felonies, they are all equally valid grounds for a Family Court petition. The court's decision concerning the disposition of the case, what terms to include in an order of protection, for example, is based on the court's assessment of the danger to the petitioner and not on whether the offense is a violation or a felony.

PRELIMINARY PROCEDURES

Petitioner's Initial Court Appearance

Most petitioners in family offense cases appear *pro se*. In Family Court, the case begins when the prospective petitioner is interviewed by a petition clerk, who drafts the petition on a court form (Form 10-2) based upon information supplied by the petitioner. In some counties outside New York City, a probation officer may screen the cases first, and in some counties, the probation officer drafts the petition.

After the petition is drafted, the petitioner appears before a judge, who must advise the petitioner of the right to retain legal representation or, if indigent, to have counsel appointed. The court then issues either a summons or a warrant for the respondent. Although the summons is the standard form of process, the court may issue a warrant if 1) the summons cannot be served, or 2) the respondent has failed to obey the summons, or 3) the respondent is likely to leave the jurisdiction, or 4) a summons would be ineffectual, or 5) the safety of the petitioner is endangered, or 6) the safety of a child is endangered, or 7) aggravating circumstances exist. "Aggravating circumstances," a term added to the statute by the Domestic Violence Intervention Act of 1994, may include physical injury to the petitioner, use of a dangerous instrument against the petitioner, or respondent's history of repeated violations of orders of protection or prior convictions for crimes against the petitioner. FCA § 827

In conjunction with the summons or warrant, the court may issue a temporary order of protection and may include in it any of the terms permissible in a final order of protection discussed below. In deciding what terms to include, the court considers what provisions are necessary for the petitioner's safety, prior incidents of abuse, the respondent's compliance with prior orders of protection, the extent of the petitioner's injury, threats, drug and alcohol abuse by the respondent, and the respondent's access to weapons. FCA § 828(1)(a).

 **FORM 10-2**

Secs. 812, 818, 821, F.C.A   Form 8-2 (Family Offense) 10/95

FAMILY COURT OF THE STATE OF NEW YORK
COUNTY OF
....

                                          Petitioner,   **Docket No.**

          –against–

                                                       PETITION

                                   Respondent.
....

TO THE FAMILY COURT:

The undersigned Petitioner respectfully shows that:

1.   Petitioner resides at _____ ,
     County of _____ , State of New York:
     (a) and is the (spouse) (former spouse) (parent) (step–parent) (child) (step–child) of Respondent;
     (b) and has a child in common with Respondent;
     (c) and is the _____
                                                (specify)

2.   Respondent resides at _____ ,
     County of _____ , State of New York.

3.   [Upon information and belief], (O)on or about the _____ day of _____ ,
     19 , at _____ , the Respondent committed
     an act or acts which constitute (disorderly conduct) (aggravated harassment in the second
     degree) (harassment in the first degree) (harassment in the second degree) (menacing in the
     second degree) (menacing in the third degree) (reckless endangerment) (assault in the second
     degree) (assault in the third degree) (attempted assault), in that the Respondent

*3a.   (Upon information and belief) The following aggravating circumstances,** are present in this
       case in that:

*If inapplicable write N/A

**"Aggravating circumstances" shall mean physical injury or serious physical injury to the petitioner caused by the respondent, the use of a dangerous instrument against petitioner by the respondent, a history of repeated violations of orders of protection by the respondent, prior convictions for crimes against the petitioner by the respondent or the exposure of any family or household member to physical injury by the respondent and like incidents, behavior and occurrences which constitute an immediate and ongoing danger to the petitioner or any member of the petitioner's family or household.

📁 **FORM 10-2 continued**

Form 8–2
Page 2

*4. The following are the names, ages and relationships to the Petitioner and/or Respondent of each and every child in the family household:

NAME   RELATIONSHIP TO   AGE OF
         PETITIONER/RESPONDENT   CHILD

_____   _____   _____

_____   _____   _____

_____   _____   _____

_____   _____   _____

*5. (Upon information and belief) The following criminal, matrimonial or Family Court proceeding(s) involving the respondent (has) (have) been filed [indicate the court, date and status]:

*6. Indicate whether a previous application has been made to any court or judge for the relief requested herein and, if so, the relief, if any granted and the date of such relief.

*7. (Upon information and belief) Respondent is licensed to carry, possess, repair and dispose of firearms and is in possession of the following licensed or unlicensed firearms [indicate the number and type of any firearms]:

WHEREFORE, Petitioner prays

(a) that the Respondent be adjudged to have committed the family offense alleged;

(b) that the Court enter an order of protection, specifying conditions of behavior to be observed by the Respondent in accordance with Section 842 of the Family Court Act; and for such other and further relief as to the Court seems just and proper.

Dated: , 19   .

_____
Petitioner

*If inapplicable write N/A.

📁 FORM 10-2 continued

FORM – GENERAL VERIFICATION

VERIFICATION

STATE OF NEW YORK   )
)   ss.:
COUNTY OF   )

, above named being duly sworn, deposes and says: I am the Petitioner in the within action; that I have read and know the contents of the foregoing Petition; that the same is true to my own knowledge, except as to matters therein stated to be alleged on information and belief, and that as to those matters, I believe it to be true.

_____
                                    Petitioner

Sworn to before me this
day of   ,19   .

_____
   Court Assistant
   Notary Public

**VERIFICATION IN PROCEEDING
BY GOVERNMENTAL AGENCY**

STATE OF NEW YORK   )
)   ss.:
COUNTY OF   )

, being duly sworn, deposes and says: That I am   ,and am acquainted with the facts and circumstances of the above–entitled proceeding; that I have read the foregoing petition and know the contents thereof; that the same is true to my own knowledge except as to those matters herein stated to be alleged upon information and belief, and that as to those matters I believe them to be true.

_____
                                    Petitioner

Sworn to before me this
day of   ,19   .

_____
   Court Assistant
   Notary Public

PRACTICE TIPS: Paragraph 1 establishes one possible basis of venue, the residence of the petitioner. Remember that residence is defined in Family Court Act section 818 to include a battered women's shelter. If the petitioner is staying in a battered women's shelter, *the address of the shelter must be kept confidential* for the protection of the residents and staff. DRL § 75(1), (4), (5). Paragraph 1 also establishes petitioner's standing to file a Family Offense petition based upon the petitioner's relationship to the respondent. Paragraph 2, respondent's residence, is another possible basis of venue. Paragraph 3 is a recitation of the events complained of, the grounds for the petition. The date and place of the most recent occurrence are included in the blanks at the beginning of the paragraph, but remember that the petition clerk must include all prior incidents related by the petitioner. If the space provided is insufficient, this paragraph may be continued on another sheet of paper. The place where the incident occurred is a third alternative basis of venue. Paragraph 3 should contain enough detail to give the flavor of the incident. Avoid conclusory language; do not say "Respondent injured petitioner," but instead write, for example, "Respondent hit the Petitioner in the mouth with his fist, splitting her lip and loosening her front teeth." If children witnessed the incident or were present in the home when it occurred, that fact should be noted, as should any allegation that respondent was under the influence of alcohol or drugs. Use or threatened use of a weapon should always be mentioned. Paragraph 3(a) alleges "aggravating circumstances," as explained by the asterisks at the bottom of the page. Aggravating circumstances may be considered by the court in deciding whether to issue a warrant and also in determining the length of any final Order of Protection that may be entered after the hearing. Paragraph 4 lists every child who resides in the household. This information is mandatory. The court has authority to direct the filing of an abuse or neglect proceeding on behalf of the children or to direct the local child protective agency to conduct an investigation into the children's welfare, and this information will help the court decide whether the children are in any danger. Paragraph 5 alerts the court to the possibility that other courts may have already issued Orders of Protection for or against the petitioner. Paragraph 6 is the standard disclosure required whenever an *ex parte* application is made. (Here the *ex parte* relief would be the temporary Order of Protection.) Paragraph 7 is relevant because, as discussed below, the court can order that a respondent's firearms permit be suspended or revoked. The WHEREFORE clause is, as in every complaint, the prayer for relief. The petition must be verified. Family Court petition clerks are court assistants and have the same power as a notary public to take the petitioner's oath. The second verification is used only if the petition is filed by a police officer or other official.

When a respondent is arrested pursuant to a Family Court warrant, the Family Court, after providing the respondent with a copy of the petition and advising the respondent of the right to counsel, including the right to have an attorney appointed if the respondent is indigent, will then direct release, bail or commitment. A respondent who is committed to jail has the right to a preliminary hearing within 120 hours, or 144 hours of the arrest if a weekend or legal holiday intervenes. FCA § 821-a. These time frames were added by the Domestic Violence Intervention Act.

Service of Summons

As befits the emergency nature of Family Offense proceedings, service may be as short as 24 hours before the court date specified in the summons. FCA § 826. (In Family Court jargon the date specified in the summons for the respondent's appearance is called the **"return of process" date**.) Note, however, that the court may set whatever court date it deems appropriate in the circumstances, and is not required to set a date within a particular number of days of the initial appearance of the petitioner. Thus, the Article 8 procedure differs from the requirement, discussed in Chapter 11, that in child protective proceedings the process must be made returnable within three court days. If the respondent in a Family Offense case has had less than three days notice, although the service is valid, the respondent may request an adjournment of the hearing to three days from the date of service.

Service of the summons may be made, as in any civil case, by any person over the age of 18 other than the petitioner. Since the petitioner may not be able to hire a professional process server, and friends and family members may be reluctant to get involved, the Family Court Act provides that a peace officer or police officer may serve the court papers if an Order of Protection has been issued. FCA § 153-b. This section applies in any proceeding where an Order of Protection has been issued, by the way, not only in Article 8 cases. The court gives a copy of the papers to the petitioner to serve if she or he chooses, but also, if a temporary Order of Protection has been entered, sends a copy directly to the police or sheriff's department for service. FCA § 153-b(c). When a police officer makes service, the officer fills out and signs a special affidavit of service that is affirmed (signed under the penalty of perjury) but does not require notarization.

The court supplies blank affidavit of service forms of both types (civilian's and police officer's) to the petitioner at the time the summons is issued, together with an instruction sheet. It is important that the petitioner remember to have the appropriate affidavit of service completed and to bring the affidavit to court on the return of process date, as the court will not be able to issue a final Order of Protection without proof of service. If the petitioner is not present when service is made by a police officer, the police department will send the affidavit to court, and in some counties this is the routine method, regardless of whether the petitioner is on the scene when service is made. In New York City, however, it is preferable for the petitioner to bring the affidavit if possible, because the affidavits submitted through the police department often do not arrive in court until after the return of process date.

HEARING

On the date process is returnable, the court will proceed to factfinding if the petitioner is present with a valid affidavit of service and the respondent has defaulted. Usually the court conducts a brief, informal inquest in which the judge asks the petitioner a few questions about the incidents alleged in the petition and clarifies what provisions the petitioner wants in the final Order of Protection. If the respondent appears, the court advises both parties of the right to counsel. If the respondent requests counsel, the court adjourns the matter for the respondent to retain counsel or assigns an 18-b attorney to either or both parties if they are financially eligible. If the respondent wishes to have a hearing, the matter is tried in Family Court as a civil proceeding by a preponderance of the evidence standard. FCA § 832. In Criminal Court, proof beyond a reasonable doubt is, of course, required.

SETTLEMENT

Most Family Offense cases in Family Court do not actually proceed to trial. If the respondent has counsel, the attorney will advise him or her, and if the respondent has waived counsel, the court will inform the respondent, that the respondent may consent to the entry of an Order of Protection without any admission of wrongdoing. Many respondents elect this option rather than to go through a hearing, the outcome of which might have a negative impact on subsequent divorce or custody proceedings. The petitioner is usually satisfied with this option, because the petitioner obtains the Order of Protection without the stress of a hearing.

Sometimes a respondent will offer to consent to an Order of Protection for the petitioner if the respondent also gets an Order of Protection against the petitioner. The court cannot grant **mutual Orders of Protection** unless a cross-petition or counter-claim has been filed. FCA § 154-b. Even if a cross-petition has been filed, mutual Orders of Protection are rarely a good settlement idea. If the parties, each holding an Order of Protection, have a dispute and the police are called to the scene, the police are, as discussed below, required to arrest both parties on each other's complaint of a violation of their respective Orders of Protection. Usually this defeats the peacekeeping purpose of an Order of Protection and may leave the parties' children without a parent at home to care for them.

DISPOSITION

Technically, the court is supposed to conduct a separate dispositional hearing in any contested Family Offense case, but in actual practice the factfinding and dispositional hearings are often rolled into one. If a respondent has participated in rehabilitative services such as counseling subsequent to the filing of the petition, however, the court should definitely conduct a dispositional hearing, because this is the sort of evidence that would be admissible in a dispositional hearing, but not at the factfinding stage. Hearsay evidence and evidence of prior uncharged acts are admissible at the dispositional hearing. FCA § 834. The purpose of the dispositional hearing is to determine the terms of the order of protection and any additional relief or services the court may order.

Possible dispositions in an Article 8 case include:

- dismissing the petition if the allegations are not proved;

- suspending judgment for up to six months;

- placing the respondent on probation for up to one year, and requiring the respondent to participate in a batterer's education program designed to help end violent behavior and, if appropriate, drug and alcohol counseling, and to order the respondent to pay for this treatment if respondent has the means;

- directing respondent to pay restitution to the petitioner in an amount not to exceed $10,000, which may be ordered in conjunction with any other dispositional order except dismissal of the petition;

- entering an order of temporary child support sufficient to meet the child's needs, even though information about the respondent's income and assets may be unavailable;

- awarding custody of the parties' child to either parent or to an appropriate relative during the term of an Order of Protection;

- entering an Order of Protection, which may be made in conjunction with any other disposition except dismissal of the petition. FCA § 841.

The provisions for restitution, batterer's programs, and temporary child support are new additions from the Domestic Violence Intervention Act.

ORDER OF PROTECTION

Nothing is more closely associated in the public mind with Family Court than the Order of Protection (Form 10-3). Among legal instruments, its potency is exceeded only by an arrest warrant. Unless it is served and enforced, however, the Order of Protection is just a piece of paper, and even if properly served and vigorously enforced, the Order of Protection may not be sufficient to protect the victim of domestic violence. It is the best the legal system has to offer the victim, however, since preventive detention of potential lawbreakers is prohibited by the Constitution.

FORM 10-3

F.C.A. 430, 550, 655, 828 & 1029   Form GF5a 10/96

ORI NO: NY 023023J

ORDER NO: 1996–K_____

PRESENT: Hon.

_____

In the Matter of a Proceeding under
Article _____ of the Family Court Act

_____

Petitioner
Date of Birth:

      v.

_____

Respondent
Date of Birth:

At a Term of the Family Court
County of Kings, State of New York
283 Adams Street
Brooklyn, New York 11201

ORDER OF PROTECTION

Docket No. _____

☐ After Inquest

NOTICE: YOUR WILLFUL FAILURE TO OBEY THIS ORDER MAY SUBJECT YOU TO MANDATORY ARREST AND CRIMINAL PROSECUTION, WHICH MAY RESULT IN YOUR INCARCERATION FOR UP TO SEVEN YEARS FOR CONTEMPT, AND/OR MAY SUBJECT YOU TO FAMILY COURT PROSECUTION AND INCARCERATION FOR UP TO SIX MONTHS FOR CONTEMPT OF COURT.

Whereas a determination has been made in accordance with Article _____ of the Family Court Act, (after hearing) (on consent) that an Order of Protection is necessary and desirable in this proceeding, therefore;

It is hereby ordered:

That the respondent observe the following conditions of behavior:

[01] ☐ Stay away from   a. ☐ [name(s) of protected persons]_____
                       And from the:
                  b. ☐ home of_____
                  c. ☐ school of_____
                  d. ☐ business of_____
                  e. ☐ place of employment of_____ ;
                  f. ☐ other [specify]_____ ;

[02] ☐ That the respondent refrain from assault, harassment, menacing, reckless endangerment, disorderly conduct, intimidation, threats or any criminal offense against [specify victim(s) or members of victim's family or household]_____

_____

_____ ;

[11] ☐ That [specify individual] _____ be permitted to enter the residence during [specify date/time]_____ to remove personal belongings not in issue in litigation;

[04] ☐ That the respondent refrain from (indicate acts)_____ that create an unreasonable risk to the health, safety or welfare of [specify child(ren)]_____

[05] ☐ That [specify individual]_____ who is entitled to visitation by court order or separation agreement be permitted to visit with the [specify child(ren)_____ , during the following periods of time [specify]_____ under the following terms and conditions [specify]_____

[07] ☐ That the Custody of [specify child(ren)]_____ shall be awarded to [specify]_____ under the following terms and conditions [specify]_____ ;

FORM 10-3 continued

[12]□ Surrender any and all firearms owned or possessed, including, but not limited to, the following: _____. Such surrender shall take place on or before [specify day/time]:_____ at:_____.
That the above respondent's license to carry, possess, repair, sell or otherwise dispose of firearms pursuant to PL §400, is hereby:

[13A] □ Suspended or

[13B] □ revoked and/or

[13C] □ the respondent shall remain ineligible to receive a firearm license during the period of this order.

[99] □ Specify other condition(s)_____
_____
_____;

FINDINGS OF AGGRAVATED CIRCUMSTANCES
The court has made a finding on the record of the existence of the following AGGRAVATING CIRCUMSTANCES:
_____
_____

It is further ordered that this order of protection remain in effect until_____.

DATED:_____   _____
                                    JUDGE FAMILY COURT

___ Service Executed   Date:_____   Time: _____

___ **Party Against Whom Order Issued Received Copy Of Order In Court**
The Family Court Act provides that presentation of a copy of this order of protection to any police officer or peace officer acting pursuant to his or her special duties shall authorize, and in some situations may require, such officer to arrest a person who has violated its terms and to bring him or her before the court to face whatever penalties may be imposed therefore.
Federal law provides that this order must be honored and enforced by state and tribal courts, including courts of a state, the District of Columbia, a commonwealth, territory or possession of the United States, if it is established that the person against whom the order is sought has or will be afforded reasonable notice and opportunity to be heard in accordance with state law sufficient to protect that person's rights (18 U.S.C. 2265).

DURATION OF ORDERS OF PROTECTION

Unless the court finds aggravating circumstances, the maximum duration of an Article 8 Order of Protection is one year. If aggravating circumstances are found, the order may run for three years. The court must state on the record the basis upon which it found aggravating circumstances, and the order must state on its face that it is based upon aggravating circumstances.

Orders of Protection entered in support, paternity, and custody cases (whether in Supreme or Family Court) may remain in effect for the minority of the child or the duration of the related order of support or custody.

STATEWIDE ORDER OF PROTECTION REGISTRY

You have no doubt noted that at several points in a Family Offense case, the court is required to know about and take into consideration the respondent's compliance with other Orders of Protection. The determination of aggravating circumstances is such an instance. The court must have accurate information upon which to base such a determination, and the Statewide Registry of Orders of Protection was created by the Domestic Violence Intervention Act of 1994 to facilitate access to such information by the judiciary and law enforcement. The registry is attached to the New York State Police Information Network and contains Orders of Protection issued in criminal, matrimonial, and Family Court cases. It contains information regarding the pendency, history, service and conditions of Orders of Protection, as well as the status of warrants. Executive Law § 21-a. To assure compatibility with the Statewide Registry, all Orders of Protection, regardless of which court issues them, must be on official uniform forms.

TERMS OF ORDER OF PROTECTION

The court has wide discretion under Article 8 to fashion an Order of Protection to fit the needs of the victim of domestic violence. Under Family Court Act section 842, permissible provisions include that the respondent:

- not assault, attempt to assault, menace, recklessly endanger, or harass the petitioner and cease all offensive conduct towards the petitioner;

- stay away from the home, school, business or place of employment of the petitioner or a child of the petitioner, or from any other designated place the court determines after considering whether the Order of Protection will serve its purpose without such a condition, taking into account the respondent's compliance with prior Orders of Protection, prior incidents of abuse, extent of petitioner's injuries, threats, respondent's drug or alcohol abuse, and respondent's access to weapons;

- may visit with his or her child, or a child for whom the respondent has a court order of visitation, at stated periods;

- refrain from committing a family offense or criminal offense against the child of petitioner or against the custodian of the child;

- may enter the residence during a specified period of time to remove personal belongings not in issue in the Family Offense case or in a pending matrimonial proceeding;

- refrain from acts of commission or omission that create an unreasonable risk to the health, safety, or welfare of a child;

- pay reasonable counsel fees incurred in obtaining or enforcing the Order of Protection;

- attend a batterer's education program and pay the costs of such program, if possessed of sufficient means;

- provide directly, or by means of health insurance, for expenses incurred for medical care and treatment arising from the incidents forming the basis for the issuance of the order;

- observe any other conditions the court finds necessary for the protection of the petitioner.

If the finding was to Assault or Attempted Assault, Menacing or Reckless Endangerment, the court may also revoke or suspend the respondent's license to carry or possess a firearm. Penal Law § 400.00. The court *may not* put any term into the Order of Protection that runs against the petitioner unless a cross-petition or counterclaim has been filed.

A copy of the Order of Protection must be given to each party. FCA § 168(1). The clerk of court also sends a copy to the police or sheriff's department in the county where the petitioner resides. Copies should also be given to the petitioner to file with the police or sheriff's department in the county where the petitioner or the child shops, attends school or religious services, receives medical care or visits relatives. FCA § 168(2).

EFFECTS OF ORDER OF PROTECTION

MANDATORY ARREST

Advocates for victims of domestic violence have long complained that law enforcement personnel did not take family violence seriously. Police responding to a domestic dispute would sometimes try to calm everyone down and then leave without arresting the perpetrator. An important addition of the Domestic

Violence Intervention Act is the requirement that police must make an arrest if they have reasonable cause to believe a felony has been committed against a family member. If the offense is a misdemeanor, an arrest must be made unless the victim requests that the perpetrator not be arrested. Arrest is also mandatory where an Order of Protection of which the respondent has actual knowledge has been violated, either by the commission of a Family Offense (including those defined in the penal law as violations and misdemeanors), or by violation of a "stay-away" provision in an Order of Protection. Criminal Procedure Law § 140.10.

VIOLATION PROCEEDINGS

A petitioner may file a violation petition in Family Court, whether or not the respondent has been arrested, in the same manner as an initial Family Offense petition. A summons may be issued, which must be served personally on the respondent together with the petition. In the alternative, the court may issue a warrant for the respondent's arrest. If an arrest has been made at the time the police respond to the scene, the police will bring the respondent to court, and the police or sheriff may file the violation petition. No summons is required, since the respondent is already present in court.

Here again, there is concurrent jurisdiction. The petitioner may file both a Family Court violation petition and a complaint in a criminal court. FCA § 847. In addition to its own original jurisdiction, a criminal court also has referral jurisdiction when a Family Court transfers a case to it. When a petition alleging a violation of an order of protection is filed in Family Court, the Family Court may either hear the violation and determine if the violation constitutes contempt of court, or may hear the violation and transfer the underlying criminal charge to the Criminal Court, or may transfer the entire proceeding to the Criminal Court. FCA § 846. Since the respondent would be subject to incarceration in both courts, this provision appears to present potential double jeopardy problems, which the courts may be called upon to resolve in the future.

Criminal Sanctions for Violation of Order of Protection

In 1996, the legislature upgraded the criminal penalties applicable in cases of violations of orders of protection. Where the violation involved the intentional or reckless infliction of physical injury, it now constitutes Aggravated Criminal Contempt, a class D felony. Penal Law § 215.52. Violations involving the display of (or threat to display) a deadly weapon, dangerous instrument, or what appears to be a firearm constitute the class E felony of Criminal Contempt. Penal Law § 215.51. Violations involving stalking and threats or harassment by telephone or mail, and those in which the offender intentionally or recklessly causes damage to the property of the victim in an amount exceeding $250 also constitute class E felonies.

Family Court Orders After Finding of Violation

If the Family Court finds that a respondent has willfully violated an Order of Protection it may:

- make a new Order of Protection;

- modify an existing Order of Protection;

- revoke or order forfeiture of the respondent's bail;

- order the respondent to pay the petitioner's counsel fees;

- commit the respondent to jail for as long as six months. FCA § 846-a.

If the respondent is committed to jail, the court may order that the period of incarceration be served on weekends and overnight with work release time. At any time during the period of commitment, the court can suspend the sentence or revoke the work release and order the respondent to serve the balance of the period full time.

Multiple Violations

A respondent can be committed to jail for up to six months for each violation of an Order of Protection. Sometimes a respondent repeatedly violates an order within a short span of time, and in such cases, the violation petitions may be consolidated and tried at the same time. The question was presented whether a respondent who in a single trial was found to have committed multiple violations could receive consecutive sentences of six months in jail for each violation or only six months in total. In the *Walker* case, Case 10-1, the Court of Appeals held that a respondent who has committed repeated violations can receive consecutive terms of commitment.

📖 **CASE 10-1**

Emma Walker v. Fred Walker
86 N.Y.2d 624, 635 N.Y.S.2d 152 (1995)

BELLACOSA, Judge.

The sole issue in this case is the discretionary authority of the Family Court to impose consecutive six-month incarcerations for three separate violations of an order of protection. The respondent former husband in the Family Court proceeding is the appellant before this Court on an appeal as of right taken on the dissent of two Justices at the Appellate Division.

📖 **CASE 10-1 continued**

By a dispositional order in 1993, Family Court committed appellant to jail for multiple violations of a Family Court order of protection secured by his former wife. In the same order, the court suspended an additional nine-month commitment for other discrete violations. The court then issued a new order of protection, essentially directing Fred Walker to refrain from any contact whatsoever with Emma Walker. While jailed, he nevertheless sent three separate written communications to her. As the protected and aggrieved party, she filed two further petitions alleging these three new, willful failures to obey the latest order of protection and seeking appropriate relief. After a hearing, Family Court found that appellant disobeyed the new order by the three separate acts of communication.

In adjudicating the latest round of violations, Family Court issued a dispositional order revoking the suspension of the prior commitment and, pursuant to Family Court Act § 846-a, also ordered defendant jailed for six months for each of the new violations. The combined period of incarceration accumulated to 27 months. Only the consecutive six-month jail commitments imposed by Family Court for these three violations are at issue here. The dispositive legal question on this appeal emanated from the commitment authorization in Family Court Act § 846-a and particularizes to whether Family Court is authorized to impose consecutive commitments for separate, multiple violations of one order of protection.

The Appellate Division, with two Justices dissenting in part, affirmed Family Court's dispositional order, holding that consecutive periods of incarceration are authorized. In affirming, we hold that the Family Court is not generally precluded from imposing, in the exercise of prudent and appropriate discretion, a maximum six-month jail commitment for each separate and distinct violation of an order of protection, to be served consecutively.

***

Sections 841 and 842 of the Family Court Act authorize the inclusion of orders of protection as part of dispositional orders in family offense proceedings. Family Court Act § 846-a prescribes the procedure and penalty for failure to obey such an order:

> "If a respondent is brought before the court for failure to obey any lawful order issued under this article and if, after hearing, the court is satisfied by competent proof that the respondent has willfully failed to obey any such order, the court may...commit the respondent to jail for a term not to exceed six months."

Appellant claims that the statute allows a maximum of six months' incarceration only, regardless of the number of willful acts of disobedience against the same order. That limitation finds no support, however, in the statute or its purpose.

📖 **CASE 10-1 continued**

Under appellant's argument, a violator already penalized for willfully failing to obey an order of protection would garner immunity from further official sanction for persistent, separate violations.... Such an approach is in no way compelled or warranted by the governing statutes, sentencing principles or reasonable statutory analysis. Its incongruous and untenable result would also constitute an invitation to violate and no incentive to obey.

That appellant disobeyed the court's order from jail serves only to underscore the need for an effective judicial option for appropriate punishment and deterrence. To disallow consecutive penalties under these circumstances would also elevate form over substance and frustrate the core purpose of Family Court Act article 8, which is designed to provide reasonable means and methods of protection and enforcement for victims of domestic violence. We thus reject this construction and constriction of the statutory authority of Family Court Judges in dealing with such situations and agree with the resolution of this matter by both courts below.

In 1980, the Legislature amended the Family Court Act to provide new focus and direction for more aggressive measures that would protect victims of domestic violence.... The statute unequivocally and firmly declares that a proceeding under article 8 "is for the purpose of attempting to stop violence, end the family disruption and obtain protection.".... Stricter enforcement of orders of protection thus became the statutory order of the day and continues as the prevailing policy today. Importantly, no restriction on consecutive punishment for separate acts is statutorily expressed. We conclude also that no such limitation may be reasonably inferred from the diametrically opposite thrust of the legislative intent.

***

Instead of appellant's inverted focus – that section 846-a does not specifically authorize consecutive sentences – we advert to Chief Judge Cardozo's teaching that "[n]othing short of obvious compulsion will lead us to a reading of the statute whereby the pains and penalties of crimes are shorn of all terrors more poignant than a form of words.".... That reasoning and eloquent expression apply with equal force to the Family Court's enforcement and punishment authority with respect to orders of protection pursuant to section 846-a. The three consecutive penalties imposed on appellant for his willful flouting (from jail, while serving time for prior violations of an earlier order of protection) of the most recent order of protection fit within the authorization of Family Court Act § 846-a. That also helps to insure that the statute and order are not "shorn of all terrors" and relegated to merely "a form of words."....

Accordingly, the order of the Appellate Division should be affirmed, without costs.

DISCUSSION TOPIC

Do you think the punishment the court imposed in this case was fair, or do you think six months of incarceration for each of the written communications the respondent sent from jail was excessive? Do you think the petitioner will be safe when the respondent is released from jail? Will she be safer than she would have been if the court had made a milder disposition?

CONCLUSION

Domestic violence is an issue about which the law has made a complete reversal. Having begun with the notion that a man should discipline his wife, physically if necessary, lest she become a nuisance to the community, the law then shifted to the idea that domestic violence was a private matter in which the law should intervene only when the violence itself became a public nuisance. As women gained enhanced legal recognition, the law could no longer turn a blind eye to their abuse within the family, and family offenses were formally banned. Still, domestic violence was not regarded as a serious matter, and the response of law enforcement agencies and the legal system was haphazard and often ineffectual. Recently, the legal system has recognized that family violence is a serious social problem that takes a heavy toll in human suffering and spawns further violence, which spills over into the larger society outside the home. Through education programs, better coordination among courts and law enforcement agencies, stiffer penalties, and vigorous enforcement, the legal system is now sending a clear message that family violence will no longer be tolerated.

CHAPTER REVIEW QUESTIONS

1. After several incidents of physical and verbal abuse by her husband David, Nadine takes the two children of the marriage and goes to stay at her parents' house. She retains an attorney, who serves David with a summons and complaint for divorce on the grounds of cruel and inhuman treatment. After receiving the court papers, David calls Nadine and suggests that she come by the marital residence to pick up some of the children's clothing and to discuss support and property division terms. Nadine accepts this invitation, and the discussion proceeds calmly for half an hour, after which David becomes enraged and throws their wedding photo at Nadine. The glass in the picture frame breaks and cuts Nadine's cheek. Nadine escapes from the house and calls the police. In what court(s) could Nadine seek help? What relief could she ask for in each court?

2. If Nadine wishes to make a criminal complaint, with what crimes might David be charged?

3. Are the police obligated to arrest David on Nadine's complaint? Why?

4.   Tom and Marjory are not married, but they have a child together. After Tom broke off the relationship with Marjory and got involved with a new girlfriend, Marjory followed him from place to place and came to his office where she made huge, profanity-laden scenes in front of his co-workers. From which court(s) might Tom seek an Order of Protection? What terms are likely to be included in the order?

5.   Tom obtains a temporary Order of Protection that specifies, among other things, that Marjory is to stay away form his place of work. If Marjory, after having been duly served with the order, comes to Tom's job and creates another scene, what legal remedies does Tom have?

6.   If the police are called to the scene of the incident that occurs after Marjory has been served with the order, do they have to arrest Marjory? (Assume that there is no property damage or personal injury involved in the incident.)

7.   If the court finds that Marjory willfully violated the temporary Order of Protection, what penalty could Marjory receive if Tom has proceeded in Family Court and what if he has proceeded in a criminal court?

8.   When Marjory appears in court to answer the violation charge, she requests the court to assign an attorney because she is indigent. If she is indigent, does the court have to assign an attorney? Tom then asks for an attorney also, but the court finds that his income is too high to qualify for 18-b counsel. Must the court offer to adjourn the case so that Tom can retain an attorney?

CHAPTER ASSIGNMENT

You are a petition clerk in the Brooklyn Family Court. Using Form 10-2 as a model, draft a family offense petition for Mary Jones. Ms. Jones would like to use the Brooklyn court; she has waited 3 hours to get to your desk. If you think this litigant cannot file in Brooklyn, draft the petition anyway, using the venue you think proper. Mary Jones relates the following information to you:

I live at 678 Parkside Avenue, Manhattan, but I'm staying in a battered women's shelter at 37 Hope Avenue, Brooklyn. I don't want my boyfriend to know where I am now. Night before last, my boyfriend, John Jones, came home late. He stays sometimes with me and sometimes with his mother, who lives at 80-91 53rd Street in Queens. He had been drinking, and he started throwing things around the house and yelling. The baby woke up and started crying. He said, "Bitch, you better get out of that bed and fix me something to eat." I was trying to get Becky quieted down. She's only 15 months old, and she always starts screaming when John gets loud. He grabbed me and pulled me away from the crib. I started yelling that he should be ashamed to scare his daughter that way. He pushed me against the wall, and I tried to get to the telephone. He pulled the phone cord out of the wall and hit me in the mouth with the receiver.

Somebody in the hall yelled, "I've called the police," and John ran into the bedroom. I grabbed the baby and ran out. I went to a neighbor's house and called the police, but when they got there, John had already left. I'm afraid to stay there because John has keys, and he always says if I don't shape up he's going to kill me with a gun he has hidden somewhere. I saw a doctor at the shelter, and she said the bruise on my mouth doesn't need stitches. One of my teeth is a little loose, so I can't bite on that side of my mouth for a while.

11 CHILD PROTECTION

"This article is designed to establish procedures to help protect children from injury or mistreatment and to help safeguard their physical, mental, and emotional well-being. It is designed to provide a due process of law for determining when the state, through its family court, may intervene against the wishes of a parent on behalf of a child so that his needs are properly met." FCA § 1011.

We like to believe we live in a society that dotes on children and makes their care and protection its highest priority, but the facts about child abuse and neglect should cause us to take a hard look at ourselves. In 1994, there were 3.1 million reports of child maltreatment in the United States, about a third of which were substantiated. Across the nation in that year 1,300 children died of maltreatment by their custodians, 74 in New York City alone. In New York City, 43,000 children are in foster care, most as a result of abuse or neglect. In 1995, approximately 1,400 abuse petitions and 6,600 neglect petitions were filed in Family Courts across New York State.

In Chapter 6 we discussed the presumption that a child's best interest will be served by allowing the child to be reared by at least one of its natural parents. So long as there is a fit parent, the State will not intervene, even if a non-parent caretaker might do a better job of raising the child. In this chapter we will learn how the State, through its child protective agencies and Family Court, steps in when it must to protect children who are in danger. Child abuse and neglect are prosecuted in Family Court primarily through proceedings pursuant to Article 10 of the Family Court Act, and this chapter focuses on those proceedings. Such allegations also arise in other types of cases, however.

OTHER PROCEEDINGS CONCERNING CHILD MALTREATMENT

Criminal Prosecutions

You probably are aware that child abuse cases often result in criminal proceedings as well as child protective proceedings in Family Court. These are entirely distinct legal proceedings. The purposes of the criminal prosecution are to punish the perpetrator and to set an example to deter others who might be tempted to abuse children. The goals of the Family Court proceedings, on the other hand, are to protect the children from further harm; to rehabilitate the abuser and the abused children; to try to reunite the family if that can be safely accomplished; and if not, to make sure that the children find a suitable home with the best available caretakers. Criminal and Family Court proceedings often occur within the same span of time, and the respondent in a Family Court proceeding may also be the defendant in a pending criminal case. These are not "concurrent" proceedings, however. Each court has exclusive original jurisdiction over the matter pending in that court.

Custody Cases

Child abuse allegations also arise in custody proceedings, and child abuse and custody proceedings, either in Supreme or Family Court, may be going on at the same time. When a custody case is pending in Family Court at the same time as a child protective proceeding, the two cases are assigned to the same judge, who usually combines the custody case with the dispositional phase of the child protective case. If the custody case is in Supreme Court, the Supreme Court Justice may postpone the custody case until the Family Court has finished the child protective proceeding or may proceed to try the custody case, perhaps hearing testimony from the same witnesses who will also be called in the Family Court matter.

Family Offense Proceedings

Family Offense petitions often contain allegations of child maltreatment. The petition may be filed by a parent on behalf of a child, alleging that a respondent to whom the child is related by consanguinity or affinity harmed the child in a way that constitutes a family offense. Often, however, the petition states that the respondent struck the child inadvertently when he or she attempted to hit the other parent or that the child was hurt when the child intervened to try to stop the fight between the parents. Usually in such cases the court will order an investigation by the local child protective agency. Depending on what the investigation reveals, the court may either allow the case to proceed as a Family Offense proceeding or may direct the child protective agency to file an Article 10 proceeding on behalf of the child. In many instances, the child protective agency files the Article 10 case on its own initiative without awaiting a directive from the court to do so.

If substantial harm or risk of harm to a child exists, it is generally preferable that the matter be dealt with as an Article 10 case. Attorneys representing child protective agencies have expertise in presenting such cases, which is usually superior to that possessed by counsel who might be assigned to represent the petitioner in a Family Offense proceeding. Moreover, the petitioner in a Family Offense proceeding may be ambivalent about prosecuting the other parent, and if the petitioner fails to follow through with the case, the child's safety may be compromised. Finally, the appointment of a law guardian for the child is mandatory in an Article 10 case, thus insuring that the child's point of view will be fully represented.

PHASES OF A CHILD PROTECTIVE CASE

Child protective cases have four distinct phases, each of which is governed by its own legal mandates: 1) investigation, 2) filing of petition to factfinding hearing, 3) fact-finding hearing, and 4) disposition. If the child protective process results in the child's placement in foster care, there is a fifth phase, permanency planning, which is discussed in Chapter 13.

Investigative Phase

A child protective investigation usually begins either with a report to the police or a call to the child abuse Hotline at the State Central Register of Child Abuse and Maltreatment. The statewide toll free Hotline number is 1-800-342-3720. If the police arrive on the scene first, they will phone in a report to the Register, and they may also make an emergency removal of the child from the home. Anyone who has reasonable suspicion of child maltreatment may make a report to the Register, but certain people are *required* to report suspected child abuse or maltreatment. These **mandated** reporters (SSL § 413) include:

- Physicians (including residents and interns and physician assistants)
- Dentists and dental hygienists
- Optometrists
- Osteopaths, chiropractors, and podiatrists
- Christian Science practitioners
- Nurses
- Psychologists
- Hospital personnel engaged in admission, examination, care or treatment of patients
- Medical examiners and coroners
- Social Workers, foster care workers, and day care workers
- Police and peace officers
- District attorneys and investigators employed by district attorneys

When the State Central Register receives a report of suspected maltreatment, referred to as an **Oral Report Transmittal (ORT)** or by its form number as a "2221," the report is faxed to the local social services district office and assigned to an investigative case worker. Within 24 hours the case worker commences the investigation, usually by calling the source of the report and visiting the case address. The case worker discusses the allegations of the 2221 with the adults in the home and talks privately with the children, if they are verbal. The case worker also physically examines the children for observable signs of abuse, such as bruises and scars. If the investigator believes the children are in imminent danger, they may be removed from the home at that time and taken to a hospital or child care facility. SSL § 417; FCA § 1024. If emergency removal is not required, the case worker will offer the family services such as casework supervision, drug or alcohol rehabilitation, parenting skills training, psychotherapy or family counseling, and homemaker assistance.

Article 10 Petition

BASICS BOX

Subject matter jurisdiction: Family Court has exclusive original jurisdiction.
Venue: County where the child or the person having custody of the child resides or is domiciled. "Residence" includes homeless or emergency shelter.
Standing: Child protective agency or a person on the court's direction.
Grounds: The petition must allege that the child was neglected or physically, mentally, emotionally or sexually abused.
Statute of Limitations: Until the child reaches 18 years of age.
Applicable Statutes: FCA article 10; SSL title 6.

If a child has been removed from the home, or if the child's caretakers prove uncooperative with the services offered to the family, it will be necessary for the child protective agency to file a petition pursuant to Article 10 of the Family Court Act. Only an authorized **child protective agency** or a person designated by the court may file an Article 10 case. A child protective agency is a society for the prevention of cruelty to children or the local Department of Social Services. If the child has already been removed, the petition must be filed "forthwith" and in any event no later than three court days after the removal. FCA § 1026.

WHO MAY BE CHARGED WITH CHILD ABUSE OR NEGLECT

Although the possible petitioners are limited in an Article 10 case, the list of possible respondents is long. Parents, guardians, custodians and any other **person legally responsible** for the child's care at the relevant time may be charged. The term "person legally responsible" includes any person continually or at regular intervals found in the household of the child when the person's conduct causes or contributes to the abuse or neglect of the child. FCA § 1012(g). If a child is abused by a stranger or by a caretaker who does not live in the home, such as a school bus driver or day care worker, the matter is prosecuted in a criminal court rather than Family Court. Although the term "person legally responsible" is designed to be broad enough to cover mistreatment by the paramour of a parent or by another family member who is living with the child or is a frequent visitor to the household, its precise scope depends on numerous factors, as Case 11-1 illustrates.

 **CASE 11-1**

IN THE MATTER OF YOLANDA D.
1996 WL 603701 (N.Y.)

SMITH, J. -- The issue presented on this appeal is whether Family Court properly exercised jurisdiction over the appellant uncle of the abused child as a person legally responsible for his niece's care (see Family Ct. Act § 1012[a], [g]. Concluding that appellant was a proper respondent in the child protective proceeding pursuant to section 1012(a) of the Family Court Act, we affirm the order of the Appellate Division.

The respondent on this appeal, the Orange County Department of Social Services (DSS), brought this Family Court Act article 10 proceeding alleging that appellant sexually abused his niece, Yolanda D., during the summer of 1991. The petition alleged that the abuse occurred on numerous occasions at appellant's Pennsylvania home. After a hearing, Family Court found that appellant had sexually abused his 12-year-old niece during the summer of 1991, and that he had been a person legally responsible for her care during that time. Family Court also found that Yolanda had been sexually abused by the appellant when she was 10 and 11 years old. Yolanda was adjudged an abused child and a dispositional order was entered placing appellant under the supervision of DSS and requiring him to attend a sex offender therapy program. Family Court also directed the entry of an order of protection requiring the appellant to stay 1,000 feet away from Yolanda and the other children named in the petition.

Appellant appealed the factfinding and dispositional orders arguing in part that he had not been a proper respondent in the Family Court proceeding because he was not a person legally responsible for Yolanda's care. The Appellate Division rejected appellant's jurisdictional challenge, determined that appellant's role was the "functional equivalent of a parent" and affirmed Family Court's finding that appellant was a proper respondent under section 1012(a) of the Family Court Act. We granted appellant's motion for leave to appeal to this Court.

The sole issue raised by the appellant on this appeal is whether he met the statutory definition of a "person legally responsible" for Yolanda's care during the summer of 1991. A child protective proceeding is brought against a "respondent," a term defined by article 10 as "any parent or other person legally responsible for a child's care who is alleged to have abused or neglected such child" (Fam. Ct. Act § 1012[a]. Section 1012(g) further defines "person legally responsible" as

📖 **CASE 11-1 continued**

"The child's custodian, guardian [sic], any other person responsible for the child's care at the relevant time. Custodian may include any person continually or at regular intervals found in the same household as the child when the conduct of such person causes or contributes to the abuse or neglect of the child."

Appellant argues that he did not fit within any of the statutory categories of legally responsible person at the time the abuse occurred. Initially, appellant contends that he was not a custodian because he was not a regular or continuous member of his niece's household or the functional equivalent of a parent. As to the catchall provision in the statute, "any other person responsible for the child's care at the relevant time," appellant would limit this category to individuals acting in loco parentis or assuming a parental role toward the child, who are also regular or continuous members of the child's household. DSS, the respondent on this appeal, contends that the record supports the Appellate Division's affirmance of the finding that appellant was a person legally responsible for Yolanda's care.

***

Appellant's narrow interpretation of "other person responsible for the child's care" is ... unsupported by the terms of the statute. By seeking to limit the application of this provision to those persons who may be found in the child's household on a regular or continuous basis, appellant renders it coextensive with "custodian," making it superfluous. Since courts must, where possible, give effect to every word of a statute, and "other person legally responsible" exists side by side with "custodian" in section 1012(g), a person may be a proper respondent in a child protective proceeding even if that person is not a custodian of the child.

***

Since section 1011 of the Family Court Act casts intervention by a Family Court as an event likely to occur against the wishes of a parent, article 10 proceedings are geared toward protecting the child from injury or mistreatment which may result from abusive or deficient parenting. Subsections (a) and (g) of section 1012 embody legislative recognition of the reality that parenting functions are not always performed by a parent but may be discharged by other persons including custodians, guardians and paramours who perform caretaking duties commonly associated with parents. Thus, the common thread running through the various categories of person legally responsible for a child's care is that these persons serve as the functional equivalent of parents.

***

A person acting in loco parentis intends to assume the responsibility to support and care for the child on a permanent basis.... In contrast, a person may act as the functional equivalent of a

📖 **CASE 11-1 continued**

parent even though that person assumes temporary care or custody of a child (for example, a paramour may be subject to child protective proceedings as a respondent even if the paramour has no intention of caring for the child on a permanent basis). We therefore reject the argument that article 10 should be applied only to those persons who intend to support and care for a child on a permanent basis. However, the care given the child must be analogous to parenting and occur in a household or "family" setting.

Determining whether a particular person has acted as the functional equivalent of a parent is a discretionary, fact-intensive inquiry which will vary according to the particular circumstances of each case. Factors such as the frequency and nature of the contact between the child and respondent, the nature and extent of the control exercised by the respondent over the child's environment, the duration of the respondent's contact with the child, and the respondent's relationship to the child's parent(s) are some of the variables which should be considered and weighed by a court in determining whether a respondent fits within the catchall category of section 1012(g). The factors listed here are not meant to be exhaustive, but merely illustrate some of the salient considerations in making an appropriate determination. The weight to be accorded each factor will, of course, be dependent on the circumstances of the particular case but the purpose of the inquiry will remain constant.

A person is a proper respondent in an article 10 proceeding as an "other person legally responsible for the child's care" if that person acts as the functional equivalent of a parent in a familial or household setting. Finally, article 10 should not be construed to include persons who assume fleeting or temporary care of a child such as a supervisor of a play-date or an overnight visitor or to those persons who provide extended daily care of children in institutional settings, such as teachers.

We are satisfied that the record here supports the finding that appellant was a person legally responsible for Yolanda's care during the summer of 1991. Appellant, the brother of Yolanda's mother, characterized his relationship with his niece during the summer of 1991 as "pretty close, you know, as family." Appellant testified that his niece visited him at his apartment in Pennsylvania six or seven times (approximately every other week) throughout the summer of 1991, and slept overnight at his home on three or four occasions. Appellant's girlfriend, who lived with the appellant during the relevant time period, testified that the niece visited two weekends a month during the summer of 1991. These visits occurred with the consent of Yolanda's mother who did not accompany Yolanda when she went to see her uncle in Pennsylvania or when she stayed overnight at appellant's apartment. Appellant also regularly visited Yolanda's home in order to attend birthday parties and to visit his mother.

📖 **CASE 11-1 continued**

The record supports the finding that appellant was a person legally responsible for Yolanda either as her custodian or as an "other person legally responsible" for her care. Yolanda, already familiar with her uncle as a regular visitor in her own home, was a regular visitor at appellant's Pennsylvania apartment during the summer of 1991 while appellant resided there. Thus, appellant was regularly in the same household as Yolanda during the relevant time, an environment he controlled, and he regarded his relationship with Yolanda as close and familial. Moreover, by permitting Yolanda to stay overnight in his home, appellant provided shelter, a traditional parental function, in an area geographically distant from the child's own household. The confluence of all these facts indicates that the Appellate Division had an adequate record basis for affirming the finding that appellant was a person responsible for Yolanda's care during the summer of 1991.

Accordingly, the order of the Appellate Division should be affirmed, with costs.

DEFINITIONS OF CHILD ABUSE AND NEGLECT

Abuse

The popular press uses the terms child abuse and child neglect interchangeably, but they have distinct legal definitions. **Child abuse** encompasses both physical and sexual abuse of children under 18 years of age. **Physical abuse** is the intentional infliction of physical injury by other than accidental means which causes or creates 1) a substantial risk of death, 2) serious or protracted disfigurement, 3) protracted impairment of physical or emotional health, or 4) protracted loss or impairment of the function of any bodily organ.

Sexual abuse is the commission of a sex offense against the child as defined in the Penal Law or use of the child in a pornographic performance, film, or photograph. The Penal Law's catalogue of sex offenses includes all the obvious sex crimes, such as rape, as well as fondling. Note that sexual abuse need not involve any physical injury of the child. A person who allows a child to be either physically or sexually abused is also guilty of abuse.

Neglect

Neglect, the failure of the parent or person legally responsible to provide minimally adequate care to a child under 18 years of age, covers a wide variety of situations. Failure to provide adequate food, clothing, shelter, medical care or education constitutes neglect, as does inadequate supervision. Excessive corporal punishment, parental drug or alcohol abuse to the extent that the caretaker loses self-control, and abandonment are also forms of child neglect.

Courts have repeatedly held that neither cultural differences nor parents' religious beliefs justify conduct that seriously injures or endangers a child. *Matter of M.*, 91 A.D.2d 612, 456 N.Y.S.2d 413 (2 Dept. 1982) states the prevailing view: "As *parens patriae*, this court must require that such uniform humane standards concerning the care and treatment of children are applied in every case, including the one at bar. Clearly, subdivision 1 of section 35.10 of the Penal Law [allowing reasonable corporal punishment as a form of discipline], relied upon by appellant, was in no way intended to permit the cruel beating of children, nor were the freedoms guaranteed to us by the First Amendment intended to embrace such behavior in the name of religion."

Neglect may also be charged when a parent's mental illness or mental retardation renders the parent unable to provide minimally adequate care. A petition based on imminent risk may be filed before a mentally ill parent has even taken a newborn baby home from the hospital. Although this may seem harsh, bear in mind that the focus of Article 10 is the protection of the child, not punishment of the parent. To make out a case of neglect, the petitioning agency must prove that the parent's failure to exercise a minimum degree of care has resulted in impairment or presents imminent risk of impairment of the child's physical or emotional condition. Thus, if a parent's mental illness or retardation does not interfere with parenting ability, a neglect petition cannot be sustained.

Sometimes the line between abuse and neglect is blurry. If a parent spanks a child so hard that the child sustains multiple bruises and welts, that constitutes excessive corporal punishment, a form of neglect. On the other hand, if the beating results in a serious injury such as fractured bone or a ruptured internal organ, it is abuse. Similarly, a parent's failure to provide adequate food for a child may be neglect, but if the child becomes so malnourished that the child's life or growth potential is threatened, the parent will be charged with abuse. Some cases are harder to call. If a parent strikes a child with an implement such as a belt or an electrical cord, for example, and the blow lands near the child's eye, the parent may be charged with abuse, even though the injury was minor, because of the imminent risk of damage to the child's eye. When a child is burned by other than accidental means, abuse is charged even if the burn was not severe, since burning a child is not an appropriate form of punishment under any circumstances.

CONFIDENTIALITY

Section 1043 of the Family Court Act authorizes the court to exclude the public and the press from child protective proceedings. The Appellate Divisions of both the First and Second Departments have indicated a preference for closed courtrooms in such cases. *Matter of Katherine B.*, 189 A.D.2d 443, 596 N.Y.S.2d 847 (2 Dept.1993); *Matter of Ruben R. et al.*, 219 A.D.2d 117, 641 N.Y.S.2d 621 (1996). In addition, reports to the Statewide Central Register of Child Abuse and Maltreatment and the case records maintained by child protective and child care agencies are also confidential pursuant to various sections of the Social Services Law. Attorneys, as officers of the court, and legal assistants employed by attorneys engaged in child protective proceedings are fully bound by these confidentiality provisions. Under no circumstances should a legal assistant reveal information that a court has deemed confidential.

PRELIMINARY HEARINGS

If a child has already been removed from the home at the time the petition is filed, the court will immediately conduct a hearing pursuant to section 1027 of the Family Court Act to determine whether the child should be **paroled** to a parent or **remanded** to the Commissioner of Social Services for foster care pending the final disposition of the case. The summons must be made returnable within three court days. The short service time is a procedural protection afforded the respondents to balance the agency's right to remove the child before service is made. When the respondents appear in court, they are assigned an attorney if they cannot afford to hire one. If the parent or other person legally responsible was not present at the 1027 hearing, or if a 1027 hearing was not held, the parent or law guardian may request a hearing pursuant to 1028 of the Family Court Act to determine whether the child should be returned home. **Hearsay evidence** is admissible at such preliminary hearings, and the issue before the court at that time is whether return to the home would pose an "imminent danger to the child's life or health."

If the court finds that the child could safely be in the care of the parent with certain services provided in the home, the court may order the child protective agency to provide the services and supervision. If one parent was not the perpetrator of the abuse, the court may release the child to that parent and make a Temporary Order of Protection excluding the perpetrator from the home or restricting the perpetrator's contact with the child. FCA § 1029. If release to a parent is not possible, the court will inquire whether there is a relative available to care for the child. Only if both parents are unsuitable and no relative can be found to provide care does the child go into foster care with strangers. If foster care is the only alternative, every effort is made to locate a foster home within a reasonable geographic distance of the parent's home, so that visitation will be convenient. Siblings must be placed together unless their health, safety or welfare would be endangered. FCA § 1027-a. Sometimes when older children have difficulty adjusting to a foster home, a group home setting may be used. As soon as the court determines where the child should stay while the case is pending, a date is set for the fact-finding hearing, and the attorneys begin to prepare for trial.

DISCOVERY

Article 10 contains its own discovery sections, 1038 and 1038-a, which were added to the article to end years of conflict and uncertainty about the scope of discovery in child protective proceedings. Of course, the controversy has not entirely abated, but the ground rules are clearer. Broad discovery is generally preferred in civil proceedings. A trial is a search for the truth, and knowing in advance what evidence will be presented equips each side to cross examine witnesses effectively and to present witnesses who may rebut or clarify the evidence offered by the other side. Surprises are best left for reruns of Perry Mason. In child protective cases, however, statutory confidentiality of certain information and concerns for protection of vulnerable child witnesses limit the scope of pretrial discovery. Sections 1038 and 1038-a of the Family Court Act attempt to resolve the competing policies of disclosure and confidentiality in child protective proceedings.

As you recall from Chapter 2, when the Family Court Act sets out specific procedures, the Family Court Act procedures take precedence over the general procedures in the CPLR. Family Court Act sections 1038 and 1038-a cover discovery of hospital records, case records and photographs; examinations of the child by physicians, psychologists, and social workers; videotaping of examinations; depositions of parties and non-party witnesses; and compelling respondents to provide non-testimonial evidence such as samples of hair or urine. These sections accord the child's law guardian the same powers of discovery as the petitioner and respondent have. Any party may subpoena hospital and public or private agency records, but the petitioner is allowed to delete the identity of the person who made the report of suspected child abuse or maltreatment.

A respondent or law guardian is also permitted to make a motion to have the child examined by a physician, psychologist or social worker selected by the moving party. The Court of Appeals had held, however, that such applications are not to be routinely granted. In *Matter of Jessica R.*, 78 N.Y.2d 1031, 576 N.Y.S.2d 77 (1991), the court wrote, "The statute places the burden on the court to exercise sound judgment after weighing all the factors bearing on the potential benefit to the applicant and the truth-finding process, if both sides are able to present experts who have examined the child, and the potential harm to the child which may result from the additional exam."

Other forms of discovery provided in the CPLR but not mentioned in the Family Court Act are still available. One such provision that is important in child protective cases is the Demand for Expert Witness Disclosure pursuant to CPLR 3101(d)(1)(i). Chapter 6 discussed how a witness may be qualified as an expert. Expert witnesses play a vital role in child abuse cases, as the proof of abuse often depends upon an expert's testimony that the injury the child sustained could not have been caused by accidental means. Hospital emergency room personnel and the investigating case worker ask the parent or person legally responsible to provide an account of how the child was injured. If the history provided by the parent does not medically account for the child's injuries, there is a strong suspicion of abuse. Suppose, for example, that the child has rib fractures on both right and left ribs. The mother claims that the baby rolled off the bed while she went to answer a telephone call. The doctor may testify that the child could not have fractured ribs on both sides in a single fall and may also render an opinion that a fall from such a low height could not have caused even a single broken bone. If the child is a newborn infant, the doctor might also testify that such a young baby cannot turn himself over and could not have rolled off the bed.

A legal assistant providing litigation support may be asked to draft the Demand for Expert Disclosure or the response to such a demand. Forms 11-1 and 11-2 are a Demand and Response for Expert Witness Disclosure such as might be used in a child abuse case where the subject child is severely malnourished.

FORM 11-1

Demand for Expert Witness Disclosure

FAMILY COURT OF THE STATE OF NEW YORK
COUNTY OF NEW YORK

---X

In the Matter of
   TEDDY LITTLE

A Child under the age of Eighteen Years Alleged to be Abused
and Neglected by
   PAUL PICCARD and
   AILEEN PICCARD,

              Respondents

---X

Docket number
N98877/97

PLEASE TAKE NOTICE that pursuant to CPLR 3101(d)(1)(i), the Respondent requests that Petitioner, Commissioner of Social Services, identify each person whom petitioner expects to call as an expert witness at the fact-finding hearing of the above-captioned matter, and for any subsequent hearings in this matter held before a Court of competent jurisdiction, and that you disclose in reasonable detail and specificity:

The subject matter on which each such expert is expected to testify; the substance of the facts and opinions on which each expert is expected to testify; the qualifications of each expert expected to testify; and a summary of the grounds for each expert's opinion.

Dated: New York, New York
     April 3, 1997

                    Jeremiah N. James, Esq.
                    Attorney for Respondent, Paul Piccard
                    3456 Court Street, Suite 93
                    New York, N.Y. 10133

To: Patricia X. Carbono, Esq.
Office of Legal Affairs
300 Centre Street
New York, N.Y. 10010

📁 **FORM 11-2**

RESPONSE TO DEMAND FOR DISCLOSURE OF EXPERT WITNESS TESTIMONY

FAMILY COURT OF THE STATE OF NEW YORK
COUNTY OF NEW YORK

---X

In the Matter of
       TEDDY LITTLE   **Docket number**
                                                      N98877/97

A Child under the age of Eighteen Years Alleged to be Abused
and Neglected by

       PAUL PICCARD and
       AILEEN PICCARD,

                           Respondents

---X

      Patricia X. Carbono, an attorney licensed and admitted to practice before the courts of this state, affirms the following to be true upon penalty of perjury pursuant to Section 2106 of the New York Civil Practice Law and Rules:

      I am the attorney for the petitioner in the above-titled action. As such, I am fully familiar with all papers and proceedings herein.

1. The above-mentioned matter is scheduled for fact-finding hearing before the Honorable Judith Judge on May 5, 1997.

2. The petitioner in this matter intends to call Dr. Charles Lew as an expert witness in this matter. Dr. Lew is an attending pediatrician at New York West Side Hospital. He is licensed to practice medicine in the state of New York and is Board Certified in Pediatrics. Dr. Lew's testimony is expected to address the allegations of failure to thrive contained in the petition.

3. Dr. Lew is expected to state that he diagnosed Teddy Little with malnutrition and failure to thrive with an inorganic etiology. Dr. Lew's diagnosis was based upon charting the child's height and weight on charts which are standard in the medical profession and finding them to be in extremely low percentiles. During his hospital stay, the child gained weight readily with no unusual feeding, which indicated to Dr. Lew within a reasonable degree of medical certainty that the cause of the child's low weight and height was food deprivation prior to his hospitalization.

New York, New York
April 13, 1997

                                                                       —————————————
                                                        Patricia X. Carbono, Esq.

PRE-TRIAL RESOLUTION

Child protective cases are sometimes resolved before trial. Although the settlement options are available at any point after the filing of an Article 10 petition, they are most commonly utilized after counsel have used the discovery process to assess the strengths and weaknesses of the opposing side's case.

Withdrawal of Petition

If after the filing of an Article 10 petition the child protective agency becomes convinced that the respondent is prepared to cooperate with services without court supervision or that the respondent is no longer in need of services, the petition may be withdrawn without prejudice. The effect of a **withdrawal without prejudice** is that the petitioner may re-file a petition containing the same allegations as the withdrawn petition if respondent should cease to be cooperative. By contrast, allegations in a petition that has been withdrawn with prejudice or dismissed with prejudice after trial can never be asserted again, although, of course, new allegations may be made if the child is subsequently re-abused or neglected. To leave a clear record, petitioner may specifically condition the withdrawal on the respondent's cooperation with certain services or observing certain conditions of behavior, such as abstaining from drug use.

Adjournment in Contemplation of Dismissal

If all parties (including the law guardian) consent, a case may be adjourned in contemplation of dismissal for up to one year. FCA § 1039(a). An **adjournment in contemplation of dismissal**, commonly called an **ACD**, is an adjournment of the case for a period of up to one year with a view to ultimate dismissal of the petition in furtherance of justice if the respondent fulfills the conditions of the ACD order. FCA § 1039(b). Conditions may include supervision by a child protective agency and acceptance of referrals for services such as drug rehabilitation or parenting skills training. If during the ACD period the respondent is not living up to the conditions, the case may be restored to the court calendar by either the petitioner or the law guardian, and the matter is then scheduled for factfinding hearing within 60 days.

Finding on Consent

Article 10 provides a method whereby the respondent in a child protective proceeding may consent to a finding of abuse or neglect without either admitting wrongdoing or going to trial. This type of disposition, commonly referred to by its section number, 1051(a), can only be made on consent of all parties, including the law guardian. Note that a consent to jurisdiction under 1051(a) results in an actual finding of abuse or neglect, unlike an ACD where the petition is ultimately dismissed if the respondent fulfills the conditions. It is similar to a "no contest" plea in that it spares the respondent the stress of a trial when the prospects for the respondent's case may be dim, but does not require the respondent to make an admission under oath that might be used against the respondent in any other proceedings, such as a criminal case. Submissions to jurisdiction pursuant to section 1051(a) are usually made when the petitioner, respondent and law guardian have negotiated an agreed-upon disposition of the case.

Admissions

A respondent may choose to admit to certain allegations of an Article 10 petition. Such admissions are usually made in exchange for petitioner's agreement to withdraw other allegations. The respondent might admit to having left the child alone and unsupervised for a period of time, for example, without admitting that he or she abuses drugs. Admissions to abuse are rare, since they might be used against the respondent in pending or future criminal proceedings. Petitioner may agree to accept a partial admission when the proof of certain allegations is weak, when a necessary witness is unavailable, or to spare one family member from having to testify against another. Usually when an admission is offered, the petitioner, respondent, and law guardian have agreed upon a disposition of the case, subject to the court's approval. The court must agree to accept such an admission, and in deciding whether to do so, the court will consider the impact of a limited admission on the long-term future of the family. As Chapter 12 discusses, a finding of abuse or neglect is often the beginning of a process in which the agencies involved with the family try to rehabilitate the respondents and reunite the family. Since the service plan for the family will be based in part upon the court's findings in the Article 10 case, the findings should reasonably reflect the problems that actually exist in the family. An admission to educational neglect is of little value if the primary problem in the family is severe domestic violence or sex abuse.

Whenever the Family Court intends to accept an admission by a respondent, the respondent must be fully advised of the consequences of such an admission. Before hearing the admission, the court will **allocute** the respondent concerning the dispositional alternatives, including the possibility that the child may be placed in foster care, and will advise the respondent that following an admission to abuse or neglect the report on the State Central Register will not be expunged. FCA § 1051(f).

Factfinding Hearing

Proof of child abuse or neglect poses special challenges. The acts charged almost always occurred behind closed doors, and the victims may be too young to testify in their own behalf. Even an older child who could tell what happened to himself or to a sibling may be unwilling to do so, out of fear or dependence or love for the perpetrator. When the abuse has been administered as a form of "discipline," the child may blame herself and believe that she has been placed in foster care because she misbehaved. In its procedures and evidentiary rules, Article 10 attempts to provide due process to the accused, but at the same time to accommodate the special problems of proof present in a child protective case.

As a general rule, child abuse or neglect must be proved by a preponderance of "competent," that is, non-hearsay, evidence. Section 1046 of the Family Court Act creates several evidentiary exceptions, however, which bring the prosecutor's difficult job within the realm of possibility.

SPECIAL PROCEDURAL AND EVIDENTIARY RULES

Proof of Abuse or Neglect of Another Child of the Respondent

The statute specifies that proof of abuse or neglect of another child who is the responsibility of the Respondent is admissible to prove that the child named in the petition before the court is likely to be abused or neglected. Thus, if only one "target child" in the family has been mistreated, the court can nevertheless make a finding of neglect or abuse of all the children in the family. This is called a **derivative finding**. Even if the mistreatment occurred in the past and the child now before the court was born later, the court may still consider what happened to the other child. In such a case, a finding of abuse or neglect of the afterborn child is not automatic, however. If the parent has cooperated with rehabilitative services, or if the circumstances of the prior mistreatment were unique, the court may not believe that the parent poses any danger to the new baby. Were it not for this statutory exception, however, a court might rule that what happened to the other child is not relevant to the present case. The exception arises from the common experience that parents who mistreat one child often repeat the pattern with other children in their care.

Shifting Burden of Proof

Proof that a child has sustained injuries of a sort that would not ordinarily be sustained but for the acts or omissions of the parent or person legally responsible makes out a prima facie case of abuse or neglect. The effect of this rule of evidence is that once the petitioner has proved that a child is in a condition that ordinarily would not come about accidentally, the Respondent must then come forward with proof to explain the child's injuries. This rule is similar to the *res ipsa loquitur* rule ("the thing speaks for itself") with which you may be familiar from torts cases. Remember that since Article 10 cases are civil proceedings, the Fifth Amendment privilege against self-incrimination does not apply.

Thus, the petitioner does not have to establish precisely how the child was injured, but only that the injury was unlikely to have been accidental. Children suffer many routine childhood bumps and bruises, but certain types of injury raise strong suspicions of abuse. Many children break an arm or leg, for example, but medical experts are able to tell whether the nature of the fracture matches the parent's version of the incident. Spiral fractures, caused by a twisting force, are not often sustained accidentally. Similarly, if a child was burned by pulling a pot of boiling water on herself, the burn will be irregular in shape and will probably be accompanied by splash burns around the major burn area. On the other hand, if the child's hand or foot has been deliberately immersed in hot water, the burn area will often look like a glove or sock, with a sharp demarcation between the burned skin and the unaffected area of the arm or leg. If a parent offers no explanation, or an unconvincing explanation, for such an injury, a finding of abuse or neglect will be made.

Parental Substance Abuse

As discussed above, the petitioner in an Article 10 case usually has to prove that a parent's conduct has harmed the child or poses an imminent risk of harm. When a parent repeatedly misuses drugs or alcoholic beverages to the extent that would ordinarily produce a state of intoxication or substantial impairment of judgment, the burden of proof then shifts to the parent to prove that the child is not likely to be harmed. If the parent is regularly participating in a recognized rehabilitative program, however, the petitioner must prove actual harm or threat of harm. This is an important evidentiary exception, since many neglect cases contain an allegation of substance abuse.

More controversial is the question whether proof of prenatal drug use by a parent should be sufficient to sustain a finding of neglect. Since drugs consumed by a pregnant woman cross the placenta and enter the system of the fetus, the parent's use of a drug during pregnancy is often revealed when the baby has a **positive toxicology report**, that is, the drug is detected in the urine of the newborn infant. In *Matter of Dante M.*, 87 N.Y.2d 73, 637 N.Y.S.2d 666 (1995) the Court of Appeals ruled that a positive toxicology report by itself is insufficient to sustain a neglect finding, but a positive toxicology report in conjunction with other evidence, such as a history of prior drug abuse or neglect of other children, is sufficient. In the continuing give and take between the courts and the legislature that has been mentioned so often throughout this textbook, a bill is before the legislature to amend Article 10 to make the positive toxicology report by itself prima facie proof of neglect.

Business Record Exception

Family Court Act section 1046(a)(iv) essentially duplicates CPLR § 4518 in allowing a business record, which would otherwise be considered hearsay evidence, to be admitted for the proof of the statements in the record. A business record may be a hospital record, child protective agency record, or any other writing, record or photograph that contains information concerning the abuse or neglect of a child. To qualify as a business record, a record must have been made in the ordinary course of business, and it must be within the ordinary course of business to make such a record. The record must also have been maintained under the control of the record-keeping organization, and the entries in the record must have been made contemporaneously with or shortly after the events described in the record. Although this may sound like gobbledygook, it makes sense when you understand the underlying purpose of the business record exception to the hearsay rule.

Let's say the record in question is a hospital record that contains the diagnosis in the hypothetical malnutrition case of Teddy Little, the "case" Forms 11-1 and 11-2 pertained to. The hospital record contains notations by many doctors nurses, dietitians, laboratory technicians and other medical personnel who examined or treated Teddy or participated in his care from the moment he arrived in the emergency room until he was discharged from the hospital. It is obviously not feasible for the petitioner to call as witnesses all the dozens of medical workers who played some role in Teddy's care. Nevertheless, their notations in the record concerning Teddy's diet and weight gain in the course of his stay in the hospital are important elements of proof. The business record exception permits the record to come into evidence instead of the live testimony of so many witnesses. The record cannot be cross examined, but its reliability comes from the fact that the record is maintained by the hospital for its own use in providing good medical care to Teddy. It was not created to be used in the present court case, and thus the various medical providers who made notations in the record had no motive to falsify the information they wrote in the record.

In order to be admitted into evidence, a business record must be accompanied by a **certification** from the head of the hospital, agency or business that 1) it is the full and complete record of the act, transaction or event, 2) it was made within a reasonable time of the events described in the record, 3) it was made in the ordinary course of business, and 4) it was in the ordinary course of the business of that particular hospital, agency or institution to keep such records.

Naturally, the head of a hospital has many important duties and cannot be expected to spend the day reviewing the many records subpoenaed to court. Therefore, the head of the hospital or agency or business is allowed to delegate that responsibility to a staff member. If the certification is signed by someone other than the head of the institution, the record must also be accompanied by a **delegation** form signed by the head of the institution and the delegated employee.

Many large hospitals keep their own supply of certification and delegation forms, since they receive hundreds of subpoenas every year. Smaller laboratories and clinics, however, may be unfamiliar with the procedure. In any case, the safest way to make sure that the subpoenaed record will arrive in court with the proper certification and delegation forms is to send blank forms with the subpoena. Form 11-3 is an example of a Certification, while 11-4 is a Delegation form.

📁 **FORM 11-3**

CERTIFICATION

I,_____, the _____
                NAME   TITLE

of_____
                              INSTITUTION

hereby certify that the record attached is in the custody of and is the full and complete record of the condition, act, transaction, occurrence or event of this Institution concerning

_____of_____
     NAME OF PATIENT   ADDRESS

I further certify that this record was made in the regular course of business of this institution and it is in the regular course of business of this institution to make such record, and such record was made at the time of the condition, act, transaction, occurrence or event, or within a reasonable time thereafter.

Date:_____

                                        _____
                                              Signature

FORM 11-4

DELEGATION OF AUTHORITY

I,_____, the head of
NAME

_____certify
INSTITUTION

that_____	_____
NAME OF EMPLOYEE		TITLE

whose signature appears below, is a responsible employee of this institution. I hereby authorize him/her to certify records of this institution as the full and complete record of the condition, act, transaction, occurrence, or event, which has been made in the regular course of business of this institution to make such records, at the time of the condition, act, transaction, occurrence or event, or within a reasonable time thereafter.

Date:_____

_____
Signature of Head of Institution

_____
Signature of Authorized Employee

Child Abuse Register Reports Admissible

Reports made to the Statewide Central Register of Child Abuse and Maltreatment are admissible in evidence only if they were made by a mandated reporter. Often, several reports are filed with the Register concerning the same incident. One may have been called in by a neighbor who heard the child screaming (a non-mandated reporter), one by police officers who arrived on the scene, and one by the doctor who examined the child in the emergency room (all mandated reporters). Other people who were involved in the incident may also have made additional reports. When the legal assistant assembles the documents that will be offered in evidence, therefore, each 2221 must be scrutinized to determine whether or not it was made by a mandated reporter.

Testimonial Privileges Do Not Apply

Most of the testimonial privileges that are generally applicable in legal proceedings are not recognized in Article 10 cases. All of the following are waived:

- Husband – Wife
- Physician – Patient
- Psychologist – Client
- Social Worker – Client
- Rape Crisis Counselor – Client

Can you think of two that have *not* been eliminated? That's right, the privileges for confidential communications to clergy and to attorneys continue to attach in Article 10 cases as they do in all other legal proceedings.

Child's Out-of-Court Statements

In terms of its actual impact on the proof of child protective cases, by far the most significant evidentiary exception in Article 10 is the admissibility of the child's out-of-court statements relating to an allegation of abuse or neglect. Suppose a child comes to school with a black eye. An alert teacher asks the child how he got hurt. The child says, "Mommy punched me." Under Article 10 the teacher is permitted to testify to what the child said. Without this exception to the hearsay rule, the child would have to take the witness stand and be subject to cross examination in order for the court to hear the child's version of the event. The Article 10 rule is designed to spare the child the traumatic experience of testifying against the parent and to insure that the court will hear the child's statement even if the child is later too frightened or confused to testify. Since this exception creates a huge loophole in the hearsay rule, however, the statute attempts to balance the scales somewhat by providing that a child's out-of court statement by itself cannot sustain a finding of abuse or neglect. To sustain a finding, the child's statement must be **corroborated** by additional evidence. Corroborating evidence is evidence of a different type that confirms or supports other evidence.

The corroboration requirement has been a continuing source of controversy in child protective cases, particularly in sex abuse cases, where the child's statement is often the primary evidence against the perpetrator. In 1985, in response to a series of court decisions the legislature thought interpreted the corroboration requirement too strictly, FCA § 1046(a)(vi) was amended to specify that any other evidence admissible under Article 10 that tends to support the child's statements is sufficient corroboration. The Article 10 standard is thus considerably less stringent than the corroboration requirement applicable in criminal proceedings. When corroboration is required in a criminal proceeding, for example when a defendant is testifying against his partners in crime, every material element of the crime must be corroborated. In an Article 10 case, by contrast, the corroborating evidence need only be something that generally tends to support the reliability of the child's statement.

In sexual abuse cases, medical evidence may be used to corroborate a child's statement. A preadolescent child's infection with a sexually transmitted disease is obviously powerful corroboration. Medical testimony about the condition of a female child's internal anatomy may also be offered, although this is not as simple as laymen may think. The absence of a hymen is not conclusive proof of abuse, as some baby girls are born with little or no hymen. Pediatric gynecology is a specialty within a specialty, and if you are called upon to assist in selecting an expert to perform a gynecological examination of a young child, you may have to look beyond your local community. Call the nearest teaching hospital, that is, a hospital affiliated with a medical school, get connected to the pediatrics department and ask for a referral.

In many sex abuse cases, there is no medical evidence at all. Remember that in the definitions section above you learned that some forms of sex abuse do not involve penetration of the child. In such cases, where is corroboration to be found? If a witness is available who saw any portion of the events, that testimony may be sufficient corroboration. It is not necessary that the witness have observed the actual sexual acts. Suppose that a child states that her father came into her bed at night and fondled her inappropriately. Another child who shared the bedroom may testify that the father was in fact in the subject child's bed in the middle of the night, and even if the child was unable to see what actually occurred in the bed, the confirmation that he was there might provide sufficient corroboration.

If there is neither medical evidence nor a witness to any portion of the event, corroboration may be offered in the form of expert testimony that the child shows the psychological symptoms of a child who has been sexually abused. This so-called **validation** testimony was first accepted as corroboration by the Court of Appeals in *Matter of Nicole V.*, 71 N.Y.2d 112, 524 N.Y.S.2d 19 (1987). The validation evidence in that case consisted of the testimony of Nicole's therapist. The therapist explained that children who have been sexually abused often manifest symptoms such as age-inappropriate knowledge of sexual behavior, enuresis (bed wetting), regressive behavior, withdrawal, severe temper tantrums, or depression. Nicole exhibited an uncommunicative, withdrawn demeanor and knowledge of sexual activity far beyond the norm for a child of 3½. She also had severe temper tantrums and nightmares. She had consistently reported her claims of sexual abuse over a long period of time to various people.

In the decade since *Nicole V.* was decided, the controversy surrounding validation testimony has intensified. Some of the experts whose research papers were relied upon in the early acceptance of validation testimony have now "clarified" their positions and contend that some of the symptoms Nicole displayed, such as nightmares and enuresis, are non-specific symptoms of anxiety in a young child that could be caused by a variety of tensions. The qualifications and expertise of some of the "validators" are also questionable. These issues are addressed in the majority and dissenting opinions in *Matter of Jaclyn P.*, Case 11-2.

CASE 11-2

MATTER OF JACLYN P.
86 N.Y.2d 875, 635 N.Y.S.2d 169 (1995)

MEMORANDUM -- The judgment appealed from and the order of the Appellate Division brought up for review should be affirmed with costs.

In this child protective proceeding, petitioner Department of Social Services commenced proceedings against respondent-father alleging that he had sexually abused and neglected his two young daughters, Melissa and Jaclyn. At a hearing before Family Court, the children's mother testified that her daughter Melissa had described repeated incidents of respondent's abuse of both children. Several medical doctors and mental health professionals who had examined one or more of the family members testified that there were no physical signs of abuse and that they were unable to confirm or refute the allegation that Melissa had been abused by her father.

The "validation" testimony (see, Matter of Nicole V., 71 N.Y.2d 122) was provided by Yael Layish, a certified social worker who had interviewed Melissa extensively using anatomically correct dolls and a technique called the "Sue White protocol." Layish ultimately obtained detailed descriptions from Melissa of incidents of abuse that had been directed against her and her sister. Based on her professional judgment, Layish concluded that these descriptions were accurate and reliable.

Respondent testified on his own behalf and denied sexually abusing his daughters. His mother, who had supervised the children's visits with their father, testified that Melissa never complained to her of any problems with respondent. A psychologist and family therapist hired by respondent testified from two observations of the children and their father that the allegations of abuse were unfounded.

Family Court dismissed the abuse and neglect petition, declaring simply that "the evidence was absolutely even." On appeal, however, Family Court's order was reversed by the Appellate Division which, after evaluating the testimony of each witness, concluded that Layish's testimony, along with the other evidence, provided a sufficient ground for a finding of abuse. The court found Layish's testimony "highly reliable" and respondent's evidence "unpersuasive," and determined that the evidence preponderated in favor of the presentment agency .... After a dispositional hearing, respondent took the present appeal by permission of this Court.

On the central legal question presented by this appeal, we conclude that the weight of the evidence more closely comports with the Appellate Division's determination.... Layish's testimony corroborated the child's out-of-court statements of abuse and, along with the other evidence presented, provided sufficient support for a finding of abuse against respondent even though the acts charged by their nature did not result in physical injury such as that found in Nicole V....

📖 **CASE 11-2 continued**

SMITH, J. (dissenting) – Because I believe the majority has not adequately addressed the issues raised in this proceeding, I dissent.

The Nassau County Department of Social Services commenced this child protective proceeding alleging that appellant, Robert P., sexually abused his two daughters, Jaclyn P., (age 2 at the time of the incidents alleged here) and Melissa P. (age 3 at the time of the incidents alleged here). A preliminary evaluation was conducted of Melissa by Yael Layish, a certified social worker. After three visits, Layish was unable to conclude that Melissa was abused. Layish continued as Melissa's therapist and after approximately seven or eight visits following the initial evaluation, Melissa stated that she had been sexually abused by her father.

The first issue raised by appellant concerns the qualifications of the expert. Appellant contends that the qualifications of Layish to give expert corroborative testimony were never established. Specifically, the appellant argued that Layish could give testimony about Melissa's out-of-court statements but was not qualified to give an opinion as to whether or not the child had been sexually abused, in part because she was a social worker and not a psychiatrist or psychologist. The Family Court ruled only "that she is an expert in the area of child sexual abuse." It did not specifically address the issue of her expertise in a case involving corroboration of alleged sexual abuse where there were no physical findings of sexual abuse.

This case is different from that of *Matter of Nicole V.* ...There, the expert's qualifications to give corroborative opinion testimony were not challenged and she "was qualified, without objection, simply as an expert in counseling sexually abused children".... This Court found that the out-of-court statements of the child, Nicole V., were corroborated both by the testimony of the expert and by physical evidence. Where, as here, an expert's qualifications are challenged, the appropriate course is for the expert's prior contact with similarly situated children to be considered. In this case such testimony should include the expert's prior treatment of children of similar age, alleged to have been sexually abused, where there was no physical evidence of sexual abuse. Additionally, testimony should include the expert's level of specialized training, the procedures utilized and the rationale for using them. Knowledge of methodologies generally accepted in the field is also relevant

The second issue here involves the procedures used by an expert to determine whether or not a child has been sexually abused. Here appellant challenges the use of dolls by the expert in trying to determine if the child Melissa had been sexually abused....

The literature indicates that the use of dolls with pronounced genitalia may or may not influence a child's reaction to the dolls and may affect the credibility of the determination that a child has been abused. For these and other reasons, some courts do not permit the use of anatomical dolls in determining sexual abuse. Here, there was no evidence of the acceptance or nonacceptance by the scientific

📖   **CASE 11-2 continued**

community of the use of dolls in determining sexual abuse of children. The use of these dolls in the determination of sexual abuse is a controversial subject which has been clearly raised in this case and requires this Court's approval or disapproval after it appropriately weighs the opinions of the scientific community.

> For these reasons, I would reverse the order of the Appellate Division and require a reopened hearing at which these issues are specifically addressed.

DISCUSSION TOPIC

Do you think Article 10, with its special procedures and rules of evidence, strikes a fair balance between the rights of the accused and the need of the child for protection? What are the risks of error on either side? You might want to read *Matter of Tammie Z.*, 66 N.Y.2d 1, 494 N.Y.S.2d 686 (1985), which discusses these questions.

Dispositional Phase

If the court finds that the allegations of the petition have not been proved by a fair preponderance of the credible evidence or that the aid of the court is not required, the petition will be dismissed and the case is then over. If, on the other hand, the court finds neglect or abuse or both, the case then moves into the dispositional phase. Regardless of whether the finding is to abuse or neglect, the dispositional alternatives are the same, although the court will, naturally, take into account the nature of the harm to the child in deciding the appropriate disposition.

The purpose of the dispositional hearing is to consider the current circumstances of the family and to make whatever orders are necessary for the safety of the child, the rehabilitation of the respondents, and the restoration of the child to physical and psychological health. At the factfinding hearing the court is limited to hearing evidence about the allegations of the petition. Any changes that may have occurred in the family's situation subsequent to the filing of the petition cannot be brought out at the factfinding. At the dispositional hearing, however, the court will find out what has been going on in the weeks or months that have passed since the petition was filed. At the conclusion of the factfinding hearing the court usually orders an **investigation and report**, commonly called an **I&R**, to be prepared by the child protective agency or the probation department. The court may also order a mental health evaluation of the respondent(s), and may also order additional reports from agencies providing services to the respondents and the child. Hearsay evidence is admissible at the dispositional hearing, so that these reports may come into evidence without the necessity of calling the preparers of the reports as witnesses.

While the court case has been pending, the child protective agency will have continued to offer to the respondent whatever services the court has ordered in the preliminary hearings and any additional services the respondent has requested or agreed to accept. At the dispositional hearing the court will hear whether those services have been effective. If the child had been remanded for foster care, it may be possible to release the child to the parent if the parent has been regularly attending a drug rehabilitation program or participating in psychotherapy or parenting skills training since the preliminary hearing. On the other hand the respondent's situation may not have improved or may have even worsened.

DISPOSITIONS

With up-to-the-minute information in hand, the court will choose among several possible dispositions:

- suspended judgment;
- release to the parent or other person legally responsible;
- release with supervision of the respondent;
- issuance of an order of protection;
- placement of the child in foster care, either under the auspices of the Commissioner of Social Services or directly with a relative or other suitable person.

Suspended Judgment

A suspended judgment may last up to one year and may be extended for another year if the court finds that exceptional circumstances require an extension. The court will specify certain conditions the respondent must observe during the period of the suspended judgment, and if those conditions are fulfilled, the petition will be dismissed at the end of the suspended judgment period. By successfully completing the suspended judgment period, the respondent avoids the stigma of a neglect or abuse finding. The conditions of such an order usually include cooperation with certain services, such as counseling or substance abuse treatment. The suspended judgment is a rarely used disposition that is appropriate only when the court believes that the harm to the child was an isolated incident or when the court has great confidence in the respondent's motivation to overcome the problem that led to the abuse or neglect of the child.

Release to Parent or Other Person Legally Responsible

An outright release to a respondent parent is also a rare disposition, but far more common is a release to a non-respondent parent. Sometimes when the parents do not live together, the non-custodial parent may have been unaware that the child was being mistreated. Once informed of the situation, the non-respondent parent may act appropriately to assume custody and assure the safety of the child. If the court is confident that the non-respondent parent will take all the right measures to protect the child in the future, further court involvement may be unnecessary.

Release Under Supervision

Release to a parent or other person legally responsible under supervision is the disposition most often utilized in cases where a parent has cooperated fully with services following the filing of the Article 10 petition. The supervision is generally provided by the child welfare component of the Department of Social Services, with progress reports provided to the court and the law guardian. The dispositional order will specify services the agency is required to provide and the respondent to accept, and it may contain other conditions, such as that the parent insure the child's regular school attendance or enforce an order of protection prohibiting or limiting contact between the child and the abuser. Both release with supervision and unconditional release are available dispositions regardless of whether the child was ever in foster care. The "release" in question is the release of the child from the court process, not from foster care.

Placement

If the evidence at the dispositional hearing indicates that the child cannot safely be released to the parent or person legally responsible, even with supervision or services, the child will have to be placed in foster care. The maximum initial period of placement is one year, but the placement may thereafter be extended from year to year as discussed in Chapter 12. Most placements are with the Commissioner of Social Services, but this does not necessarily mean that the child will reside with strangers. Often a relative will be licensed as a **kinship foster parent**. A child may also be placed directly with a relative or other suitable person, in which case the relative does not receive foster care payments. A direct placement is similar to an award of custody to the relative, but it is time-limited (a maximum of one year) and is accompanied by a service plan that aims to reunite the parent with the child within the placement period.

Order of Protection

An order of protection in an Article 10 case is not a disposition by itself, but rather serves to assist or strengthen another disposition with which it runs concurrently. The Family Court Act authorizes the court to issue orders of protection in several types of cases, including family offense proceedings, custody, termination of parental rights, juvenile delinquency, PINS, paternity, and support cases, as well as child protective proceedings. The various types of orders of protection, although they look much the same, differ in their permissible conditions, period of valid length, and persons against whom the order of protection may be made. Look for the "Order of Protection" section in the Article of the Family Court Act that applies to the case type you are dealing with, therefore, to be sure of the permissible scope of the order. For child protective cases, the relevant section is FCA § 1056, which permits the court to issue an Order of Protection against a parent or other person legally responsible for the child *or* against the spouse of the parent or other person legally responsible.

An Order of Protection in an Article 10 case may include any reasonable conditions of behavior to be observed by the person the order runs against, including:

- requiring the person to stay away from the child or the other spouse or parent of the subject child, and from their home, school, or place of business;
- specifying when the parent or other person entitled to visitation may visit the child;
- ordering the person to refrain from committing a family offense as defined in Article 8 of the Family Court Act or any criminal offense against the child or parent or custodian of the child;
- permitting a designated party to enter the home at a specified time to remove personal belongings;
- ordering the person to refrain from any acts that create an unreasonable risk to the health, safety, or welfare of the child;
- requiring the person to pay for medical care or treatment arising from the incidents which formed the basis of the child protective proceeding.

The maximum length of an Article 10 Order of Protection depends upon against whom the order runs. If the Order is made against a parent, it can last no longer than the period of supervision or placement of which it is an adjunct. If it is made against another member of the household or person legally responsible, such as a paramour of the parent, it may last until the child's 18th birthday.

PROVIDING LITIGATION SUPPORT

OPENING A FILE

Legal assistants provide support at every stage of child protective proceedings. The legal assistant's first function usually is to open the file. A legal file is not a random hodgepodge of documents, but rather an orderly assemblage of materials. Every law office has a file maintenance protocol, the specifics of which may vary according to the type of case involved. In child protective cases, the legal assistant must take care in the very first step -- naming the file; some offices maintain files in the mother's name, while others use the names of the subject children. Typically, the first documents to go into the file are a referral from the client agency, a copy of the 2221 report(s), and a running court action sheet on which the attorney handling the case will note what transpires each time the case goes before a judge. When a court case will be lengthy or involve multiple parties or many documents, the "file" may actually be many files, broken down by party or by date or by the phase of the case. Discovery files, for example, may be in a separate folder. Keeping litigation files orderly and up-to-date is crucial, because the file may be an attorney's only source of information in the courtroom. When the judge asks a question, the attorney will not be able to rummage around his desk or file cabinet to find the answer.

PREPARING THE DISCOVERY PACKAGE

The attorneys for the respondents and the law guardian will typically demand disclosure of the child protective agency's Uniform Case Record; police incident reports; Central Register reports (2221's); hospital records; physicians' and psychologists' reports; CV's of expert witnesses; video and audio tapes, if any, of examinations of the subject child(ren); any photographs that were taken of the child's injuries; and toxicology reports, if substance abuse is alleged. In anticipation of the routine discovery demand, the legal assistant is expected to gather these documents into a discovery packet. No material should be sent out, however, until the attorney in charge of the case expressly so instructs the paralegal.

CONTACTING POTENTIAL WITNESSES

A legal assistant may be asked to contact potential witnesses to ascertain the dates they are available to testify, and, in some cases, to find out what they will say if called as witnesses. Any conversation that goes beyond scheduling issues should be undertaken only on the express instructions of the attorney handling the case and should be limited in scope. Do not be drawn into discussion about the merits of the case, and do not attempt to feed answers to the witness or in any fashion influence the testimony the witness will give. Since the case may be adjourned once or twice before the trial commences, and the trial, once started, may extend over several court dates, the scheduling process may have to be repeated several times. Explain this to the witness at the outset, and ask the time and method most convenient to the witness for you to contact him or her in the future.

No matter how willing, or even eager, a witness may sound initially, a subpoena should be prepared and served for every witness who will be called to testify. The subpoena should be made returnable for the first trial date, but if it is unlikely that the witness will actually testify on that date, arrange to have the witness "on call," that is, the witness will remain at home or in his or her office but agrees to come to court immediately when notified by phone. Be sure to find out precisely the length of the trip from the witness's location to the courthouse, and make sure you obtain a direct phone number to the witness's location. Witnesses are generally appreciative of the "on call" procedure, and they usually cooperate when you explain that you are showing them this consideration because you know they are busy people. Even cooperative witnesses need reminders, however, so do not forget to call a day in advance to confirm.

PREPARING A TRIAL NOTEBOOK

In complex cases involving many witnesses and **exhibits** (documentary or physical evidence, such as hospital records), the legal assistant may be asked to prepare a trial notebook. The trial notebook consists of a trial outline, a witness sheet for each witness, and a list of exhibits. A **trial outline** is an overview of the elements of the case arranged in a logical and effective manner. It is the master plan of the case and includes the allegations to be proved in the order in which the case will be presented, specifying which witnesses and exhibits will be used to establish each fact.

A **witness sheet** is prepared for each proposed witness, listing the direct examination questions and the anticipated answers. If the witness will be required to lay a foundation for the introduction of any exhibit, the exhibit number should be highlighted on that witness's sheet. If objections are anticipated to any portion of a witness's testimony, the authority relied upon for its admissibility should be summarized on the witness sheet. Problems that may crop up during cross examination should also be noted on the witness sheet, along with strategies for damage control.

The **exhibits list** serves the obvious purpose of reminding the trial attorney of all the physical and documentary evidence that must be offered in a particular case. In the stress of trial, it is easier than you might think to forget to put in an exhibit. If only a few exhibits are to be offered, they are usually marked in evidence by the court reporter or court clerk as they are offered. If there are numerous exhibits, however, it is preferable to pre-mark them, so that the flow of the trial is not interrupted each time an exhibit is offered.

ASSISTING AT THE TRIAL

In a complex trial, the trial attorney may ask the legal assistant to sit in at the trial to take notes and follow the trial outline to make sure nothing is omitted. Although the legal assistant will not speak or "appear" on the record, the attorney will identify the legal assistant to the court. Space permitting, the legal assistant is seated at the counsel table or right behind the attorney, so that the two can communicate without moving around. The legal assistant should dress appropriately and observe all the formalities of courtroom decorum.

VOLUNTARY PLACEMENT

Not all children in foster care are there as a result of abuse or neglect proceedings. Some are placed voluntarily by parents who recognize that they need assistance. Many voluntary placements begin with reports of suspected maltreatment and proceed through the same early investigative phase as cases which go to court. If the parent recognizes the need for placement, however, it may not be necessary to file an Article 10 petition. If, for example, a parent realizes that he or she has a drug problem requiring residential treatment, that parent may sign a **voluntary placement agreement** so the child can be cared for while the parent is in a drug treatment facility.

Some parents seek help before a report of suspected maltreatment has been filed. They may request assistance with a problem that has not yet resulted in neglect but is likely to do so if untreated, or the child may need residential treatment for behavioral difficulties. If the problem can be treated without removing the child from the home, **preventive services** such as family counseling or parenting skills training may be offered to avert placement. If the child has to be removed from the home, the agency must first try to locate a suitable relative to care for the child. Siblings should be placed together unless it would be contrary to the best interest of the children. SSL 384-a(1).

Voluntary Placement Agreements are contracts between the Commissioner of Social Services and the parent, and as such they may contain whatever terms the Commissioner and the parent agree upon. SSL 384-a(2). By definition, however, they are agreements for *temporary* foster care placement, and should not be confused with surrenders for adoption, which are discussed in Chapter 12. The right of the parent to demand the return of the child depends upon whether or not the agreement specifies a definite date or event by which the child must be returned. If the agreement is a definite date instrument, the agency must return the child before or within 10 days after the event unless a court order to the contrary has been obtained in a child protective or termination of parental rights or custody or foster care review proceeding. If the instrument is an indefinite date agreement, the agency must return the child within 20 days of the parent's demand for return, unless a contrary order has been made within the 20 days. SSL 384-a(2).

Court Approval of Voluntary Placement Agreements

When a parent signs a voluntary placement agreement, the Commissioner must file a petition within 30 days pursuant to Social Services Law section 358-a for the Family Court to approve the placement instrument. The court must be satisfied that the parent executed the instrument knowingly and voluntarily, that is, that the parent fully understood the terms of the placement agreement and was not in any way misled or coerced into signing it. To approve the placement, the court must also find that placement serves the child's best interest and that reasonable efforts were made prior to the placement to eliminate the need for the child's removal from home. If preventive efforts were not made, the petitioner must show why such efforts would have been futile or harmful to the child. In the 358-a hearing the court may also set up a visitation schedule and should also make sure that siblings have been placed in the same home whenever possible.

CONCLUSION

Article 10 of the Family Court Act provides a vehicle for the court to intervene when necessary to protect children under the age of 18 who are abused or neglected. Because our society places great value on the integrity of the family, the statute is an intricate web of procedural and evidentiary provisions designed to balance the rights of the family members involved. The respondents' interests are protected by the right to counsel, including assigned counsel if the respondent cannot afford to hire an attorney, the short time for service of the summons, the right to preliminary hearings in which the petitioner must prove imminent danger if the child is removed from the home, by the discovery provisions, and by the narrow definitions of neglect and abuse. The child's need for protection is recognized in the sections of the statute that permit the child to be removed from the home even before a petition is filed, by the immediate assignment of a law guardian as soon as a petition is filed, and by the numerous evidentiary exceptions applicable to Article 10 cases.

Legal assistants are utilized in child protective proceedings primarily to provide litigation support. Because of the short time for service of the summons and the scheduling of preliminary hearings within three court days, child protective proceedings often seem hectic and pressured, especially in the early stages. Even in the comparatively leisurely factfinding stage, preparation may be impeded by witnesses who are hard to reach or reluctant to testify and by the delay in receiving subpoenaed records. Good checklists, a well-constructed tickler system, and persistence are the legal assistant's greatest assets in the face of such obstacles. Solid preparation is a much-appreciated anchor in the storm of fast-paced litigation.

CHAPTER REVIEW QUESTIONS

Vernon is the father and custodial parent of David, age 18 months, and Alice, age 4 years. Vernon and the children and Vernon's girlfriend, Claire, have lived together for a year since Michelle, the children's mother asked him to assume custody. Michelle felt at that time that her recreational drug use was getting out of hand and she needed to seek treatment. She entered an outpatient program and has been attending regularly, although she has had a few relapses during the year. She spends every Saturday with the children, but Vernon does not permit the children to sleep at her house. On several of the visits Alice has told Michelle that Claire is "mean." Since Alice is very attached to Michelle, Michelle assumed that Alice was saying that she would prefer to live with Michelle. Feeling guilty and afraid to stir up trouble, Michelle did not pursue the matter. She simply reassured the child that soon she would be able to come back home to live with Mommy.

On the last visit, however, Michelle noticed that Alice was wincing when she sat down. Michelle removed Alice's jeans and observed numerous linear bruises and welts on the child's buttocks and thighs. Alice told Michelle that Claire had beaten her with a belt because she spilled grape juice on the living room rug and that Claire had hit her before, "a lot." Alice said Vernon was at work at the time of the recent incident, but on previous occasions he had been home when Claire hit her. Alice also mentioned that Claire doesn't hit so hard when Daddy is home. Michelle phoned in a report to the Hotline. When the caseworker arrived, Michelle learned that Alice's nursery school teacher had phoned in a report the day before and that a caseworker had already been out to Vernon's house. Alice had refused to tell the teacher how she got hurt, and Vernon claimed to know nothing of the incident.

The caseworker, Michelle and the children go to the emergency room of the local hospital, where both children are examined. Alice's bruises and welts are noted in the hospital record and photographed. Alice also tells the doctor and the caseworker about the beating by Claire, and Alice's statements are recorded in the agency case record and in the hospital record. A mild painkiller is prescribed for Alice, and she is released to the case worker. No injuries are noted on David. Alice tells her mother and the case worker that David never gets hit because he's just a baby.

1. Can Claire be charged as a respondent in a neglect case concerning Alice? What is her legal relationship to the child?

2. If Claire can be named as a respondent, what would the allegation against her be?

3. Can Vernon be charged? If so, what would the allegation against him be?

4. Can Michelle be charged with neglect although the children do not live with her? If so, what would the allegation(s) be?

5. Can a neglect petition be filed on David's behalf, based on the mistreatment of Alice?

6. At the initial court appearance, if all parties agree to the parole of both children to Michelle under the supervision of the child protective agency, what services might the court order in conjunction with the parole?

7. Is the hospital record of the emergency room visit admissible in evidence at the factfinding hearing? What forms would have to be attached to the record to make it admissible? Can the photographs taken at the hospital come into evidence?

8. Is the 2221 called in by Alice's teacher admissible in evidence at the factfinding hearing? What about the one called in by Michelle? What is the difference in the two reports?

9. Can the case worker testify as to what Alice told her about the incident? Can Michelle?

10. Can the court consider the evidence about what happened to Alice in deciding whether David is neglected? Do you think the court is likely to find David neglected? Why or why not?

11. Assume that Vernon, Claire and Michelle were all named as respondents and that the court has made findings of neglect against all three. Further assume that the I&R shows that Michelle has not used drugs since the children were paroled to her. What disposition do you think would be appropriate in this case and why?

CHAPTER ASSIGNMENT

You are a legal assistant in the office of the attorney for the child protective agency that will be presenting the neglect petition on behalf of Alice and David. Draft a concise trial preparation outline for the case, subject to revision after conference with the attorney.

You are a legal assistant in the office of an attorney who is representing a respondent in an Article 10 physical abuse proceeding in Family Court. The client is also being criminally prosecuted on charges arising from the incidents that are the basis of the Family Court case. The attorney asks you to research the following questions: 1) Should the Family Court case be dismissed as violating the respondent's privilege against double jeopardy? 2) Must the Family Court case be adjourned until after the criminal case has concluded so that the respondent can exercise his right to testify in the Family Court proceeding without sacrificing his Fifth Amendment privilege against self-incrimination? 3) If the Family Court case is not adjourned and the respondent elects not to testify in the Family Court proceeding, can the Family Court judge find that the respondent has failed to provide an adequate explanation for the child's injuries, which are of a sort that would not ordinarily have occurred but for the acts or omissions of the parent? Prepare an interoffice memorandum addressing these questions.

12 PERMANENCY PLANNING

> "Appellee foster parents as well as natural parents question the accuracy of the idealized picture portrayed by New York. They note that children often stay in 'temporary' foster care for much longer than contemplated by the theory of the system.... Indeed, many children apparently remain in this 'limbo' indefinitely.... The District Court also found that the longer a child remains in foster care, the more likely it is that he will never leave." *Smith v. Organization Of Foster Families*, 431 U.S. 816, 97 S.Ct. 2094 (1977).

CASE PLANNING

As soon as a child comes into foster care, efforts begin to get him out. Not only is foster care a disposition of last resort, but it is a temporary condition intended to be as brief as possible. An elaborate statutory and regulatory scheme mandates the steps that should be undertaken to facilitate the child's discharge from foster care. Many components of this scheme were enacted in 1979 as the Child Welfare Reform Act (CWRA), a comprehensive set of amendments to the Social Services Law designed both to prevent and to shorten foster care. Pursuant to this legislation, every child in foster care is assigned a **permanency goal** which the foster care agency works to achieve.

Unless both parents have decided at the outset to give the child up for adoption, the initial permanency goal will be "discharge to parent." Pursuant to Social Services Law § 409-e, the foster care agency and the parents should consult to formulate a family services plan with short-term, intermediate, and long-term goals, and actions to be taken to achieve each goal. The plan should identify immediate problems requiring intervention and specify the services appropriate to assist the family and should estimate the time necessary to ameliorate the problems. After the first 90 days, then six months later and every six months thereafter, the family services plan must be reviewed and modified as necessary.

Part 439 of the New York Code of Rules and Regulations (NYCRR) sets time frames within which the chosen permanency goal must be accomplished. If the goal is discharge to a parent, the child must be returned home within 24 months of placement, unless an extension is approved by the State Department of Social Services. If the goal of discharge to a parent cannot be accomplished within the approved time, the goal must be changed to adoption or independent living. When the goal is adoption, the child must be freed for adoption within 12 months of the setting of the adoption goal and placed in an adoptive home within 6 months of being freed. Adoption should take place within 12 months of the adoptive placement.

The goal of independent living can be assigned to a child 14 years or older who is not expected to be returned home or adopted, or to a child of any age who is living with a certified or approved kinship foster parent if neither return to a parent nor adoption would be in the child's best interest. When the goal is independent living, the agency should offer education and practical training to prepare the child to live on his own. A court order that is inconsistent with the agency-determined goal automatically overrides the agency's choice of goal. Thus, if the agency has "discharge to parent" as the goal, and the court orders that the child be freed for adoption, the goal is immediately changed to "adoption" without any further exchange of paperwork between the voluntary agency and the local or State Department of Social Services.

Uniform Case Record

For every child in foster care, as well as those receiving preventive services designed to prevent foster care placement, the agency must maintain a **Uniform Case Record**. SSL § 409-f. Regulations setting forth in detail the information to be included and the manner in which the case record is to be maintained are in Part 428 of 18 NYCRR. From the beginning, the record must contain **progress notes,** the case workers' chronological account of all contacts with the family. The record should also contain a legal documents section, which contains copies of all court orders pertaining to the family, such as the order of disposition in the Article 10 case or the Approval of Foster Care from the 358-a proceeding, discussed in Chapter 11. The agency's efforts to involve the parent(s) in the planning process must be thoroughly documented.

Besides being a legal requirement, a well-maintained case record is a practical necessity. The case worker assigned to a family may leave the agency's employ after working for months with the family, and it is essential that the new worker have a complete case record in order to maintain the continuity of permanency planning. In addition, the case record is admissible in evidence as a business record, as discussed in Chapter 11, and it may be crucial evidence in the legal proceedings discussed below.

Diligent Search

It is not unusual for the whereabouts of the parents of children in foster care to become unknown to the agency. Sometimes the parents are **undomiciled**, that is they have no legal residence, at the time the children enter foster care, while others lose their homes or change addresses while the children are in placement. Sometimes this instability results from the same problems that led to the placement of the children, problems such as drug addiction and mental illness, for example. Other parents may deliberately conceal their whereabouts because they are being sought on criminal charges or are living in circumstances they fear may make a negative impression on the case worker.

When an agency loses track of a parent, the agency is required to make a **diligent search** for the parent. If the parent is located, the planning process can continue. If the parent is not found, the diligent search is used as the basis for an application in future legal proceedings for alternative service, since personal service will not be possible. Responsibility for the search is often delegated to a legal assistant.

The object of a diligent search is to actually find the parent. The diligent search is not a hocus pocus designed to satisfy the court that the person cannot be found, but rather a good faith attempt to locate the missing parent. Thus, the search should begin with a careful review of the case record to identify family members and friends of the parent who might provide meaningful leads to the parent's current whereabouts. At the same time those leads are being pursued, the person carrying out the search should send out inquires to hospitals and governmental agencies with which the missing parent may have had contact.

The search should concentrate on the locality or region where the parent is believed to be residing or was last known to reside. It is important that all avenues of search be pursued simultaneously, because if the search is done in a piecemeal fashion, the responses obtained at the beginning will be stale before the search is complete. As each response is received, it should be reviewed, and if it offers any new leads, further inquiries should be pursued immediately. The progress of the search must be monitored regularly, and if responses from some agencies do not arrive within a reasonable time, a new inquiry should be submitted. A diligent search takes time. It is a good idea to begin the search about three months before it will be needed for court. When the search is complete, the results are compiled in an affidavit, which is submitted to the court, together with a request for some form of alternative service, such as publication, at the next court proceeding. Form 12-1 is a checklist for a diligent search. Remember that the search must be tailored to the individual sought, and additional inquiries may be required beyond those reflected in Form 12-1.

📁 **FORM 12-1**

DILIGENT SEARCH CHECKLIST

INQUIRY	DATE	RESULT
Dept. of Probation		
Local Corrections Dept.		
State Corrections Dept.		
City Morgue		
Public Assistance Dept.		
Post Office serving client's last known address		
Missing Persons Bureau		
N.Y.S. Parole Board		
N.Y.S. Mental Health Dept.		
Local homeless shelter		
Hospital (name) serving client's neighborhood		
Board of Elections		
County/citywide telephone book search		
Relative (name) by phone/ letter/ in person		
Relative (name) by phone/ letter/ in person		
Friend (name) by phone/ letter/ in person		
Friend (name) by phone/ letter/ in person		
Telegram to client at last known address		

FOSTER CARE REVIEW PROCEEDINGS

When a child is in foster care, the child's status must be reviewed periodically by a judge. If the child has been placed voluntarily, the agency must petition for a review pursuant to Section 392 of the Social Services Law no later than 18 months after the child's placement. If the placement resulted from an Article 10 case, an extension of placement proceeding must be initiated at the end of the placement period, which, you will recall, cannot exceed one year.

SSL § 392 REVIEWS

Procedures

The petition for foster care review should be filed in the county where the agency has its principal office or where the child resides. In New York City, however, all foster care review proceedings are heard in Citywide Central Foster Care Review Term situated in the Manhattan Family Court, which is deemed to be the county of venue. Since many of the foster care agencies in New York City have an office in Manhattan and the petitions are usually filed by the New York City Commissioner of Social Services, this arrangement is administratively convenient. Although both the voluntary foster care agencies providing care under contract with the Commissioner and the foster parents also have standing to file foster care review petitions, they do not often do so.

The petition must be filed no later than 60 days before the expiration of the child's 18th month in care. The names and addresses of the foster parents and the biological parents may be omitted from the petition, but the petition must then be accompanied by a verified schedule setting forth this information for the court's use. Notice of the hearing, including a statement of the possible dispositions, must be given to the agency, the foster parents, the parent or guardian who signed the voluntary placement agreement, and the prospective adoptive parent of a child freed for adoption if the child has been in that home for 12 months. Service of the notice must be made at least 20 days before the hearing date in the manner the court directs. If service is by mail, as is common in 392 proceedings, the mail must be sent registered or certified.

392 Hearing

The primary purpose of a 392 hearing is for the court to review the adequacy of the permanency planning for the child in foster care. Although the statute specifies that the disposition shall be made "in accordance with the best interest of the child," the Court of Appeals has clarified that a 392 hearing is not a pure "best interest" hearing in which the biological parents and the foster parents stand on equal footing. *Matter of Michael B.*, 80 N.Y.2d 299, 590 N.Y.S.2d 60 (1992). Rather, the court must begin by weighing past and continued foster care against discharge to the biological parent or other relative or suitable person. Having thus weighed the evidence, the court chooses among the following dispositional alternatives:

•   Continuing foster care for up to one year, with the option of directing the agency to have the child reside in a specific foster home;

•   Returning a child who has not been freed for adoption to the parent, guardian or relative who signed the voluntary placement agreement;

•   Placing the child in the custody of another relative or other suitable person;

•   Directing the agency to legally free the child for adoption, if the court finds reasonable cause to believe that grounds for a termination of parental rights proceeding exist.

Even after a child is freed for adoption, foster care review proceedings must be conducted until the adoption of the child is finalized. In the case of a child freed for adoption, the court has several special dispositional alternatives:

•   Directing that the child be placed for adoption in the foster family home where he resides or has resided or with any other person.

•   If the child has been freed for six months but not placed for adoption, the court may order various measures, such as photolisting, to expedite the child's adoptive placement. If the child has been placed in an adoptive home, but no adoption petition has been filed within 12 months, the court may order services to expedite the adoption by the family with whom the child is placed. If the agency fails to comply with the court's order, the court may at the next hearing direct that the custody and guardianship of the child be transferred to another agency.

The foster care review court may make an order of protection as a condition of or in assistance of any other dispositional order. The allowable terms of such an order are broad; it may set forth "reasonable conditions of behavior" to be observed by any person or agency who is before the court.

EXTENSION OF PLACEMENT PROCEEDINGS

Where a child has been placed pursuant to an Article 10 abuse or neglect proceeding, the agency must petition for extension of placement at least 60 days before the expiration of the placement period. If the child has returned to the parent on **trial discharge**, a period usually lasting 90 days during which the agency intensively supervises the transition from foster care to the natural parent's home, the agency should petition to extend placement until the time when the discharge to the parent will be final. Once placement has **lapsed**, that is it has not been extended, the child can be taken back into foster care only if a new neglect petition is filed and the court finds imminent danger, as is required for remand under any other Article 10 case.

Despite the advances in computerized case tracking, far too many placements are still allowed to lapse. A legal assistant charged with the responsibility of filing extension petitions should be mindful that failing to file in a timely fashion may compromise the welfare of the foster child and will certainly result in the filing of a new neglect proceeding, with its panoply of preliminary, fact-finding and dispositional hearings, rather than the single hearing called for in an extension of placement proceeding.

Procedures

Service is made by mail at least eight days before the court date or in whatever other manner the court may direct. The natural parents, the child's law guardian, the agency supervising the placement, and the foster parents must all be served. The most recent UCR should be annexed to the petition, and in some cases may comprise the proof at the hearing, as hearsay evidence is admissible. If the information in the UCR is stale, however, which is often the case due to the 60-day advance filing requirement, the court will require a more current report or testimony concerning the present situation.

Extension of Placement Hearing

In the extension hearing, the court considers whether the conditions that led to the placement have changed, whether the services plan requires modification, and whether the parents and the agency have complied with the plan. The court must decide whether extending placement would be consistent with the permanency goal and whether the child would be at risk of abuse or neglect if returned to the parent. Placement may be extended for up to one year, and the court may also order the agency to undertake efforts to strengthen the parental relationship, such as encouraging visitation and assisting the parent in finding appropriate housing, employment, counseling, medical care or psychiatric treatment. The court may also order the agency to initiate termination of parental rights proceedings if the court finds reasonable grounds to believe that grounds for such a proceeding exist, and may set a date by which the petition is to be filed. When the child reaches the age of 18, the child's consent to extend placement is required. Placement cannot under any circumstances be extended past the child's 21st birthday.

FCA § 1055-a REVIEWS

Foster care reviews for a court-placed child continue after the child is freed for adoption until the child reaches the age of 18 or the adoption is finalized. The statute is confusing as to the timing of § 1055-a reviews. If the freed child has not been placed in an adoptive home, the petition must be filed six months after the child was freed; if the child has been placed in an adoptive home but no petition for adoption has been filed, then the petition must be filed 12 months after the placement in the adoptive home. In any event, however, a petition must be filed no later than 60 days before the end of the child's 18th month in foster care. The following example may clarify:

> Lyle is placed in foster care as a result of an Article 10 neglect proceeding on January 2, 1996. His parents have no contact whatsoever with him or with the agency, and a proceeding to terminate parental rights on the ground of abandonment results in an order dated October 2, 1996, committing his custody and guardianship to the agency. On December 2, 1996, his foster home placement is officially converted into an adoptive placement, as the foster parents are approved and eager to adopt. The prospective adoptive parents file their adoption petition on March 2, 1997. The 1055-a petition for foster care review must be filed no later than April 3, 1997, unless the adoption has been finalized before that date, as that date is 60 days prior to June 2, 1997, the end of Lyle's 18th month in foster care. Neither Lyle's placement in an adoptive home nor the filing of the adoption petition extends the time for review past the expiration of the 18th month in foster care.

FREEING A CHILD FOR ADOPTION

Once the goal has been changed to adoption, the agency must undertake to sever the legal bond between the birth parents and the child so that the child is legally free for adoption. This may be accomplished by the parent's voluntary act of surrendering the child for adoption, or, if the parent is unavailable or is opposed to the plan of adoption, by a court proceeding to terminate parental rights.

SURRENDER FOR ADOPTION

A parent of a child in foster care may give the child up for adoption by executing a **surrender** for adoption. The term surrender is reserved for adoption and should not be confused with a voluntary placement agreement discussed in Chapter 11. Surrenders may be taken either out-of-court, **extra-judicial surrenders**, or in court, **judicial surrenders**. Because it is complex and highly vulnerable to challenge, the extra-judicial surrender is seldom used. Since an extra-judicial surrender must subsequently be judicially approved in a court proceeding of which the parent is notified, it is generally preferable to have the surrender executed before a judge or surrogate in the first place.

Surrender Instrument

The surrender instrument may contain any terms that the parent and the agency agree upon. Pursuant to SSL § 383-c(5), however, it must contain the following information in plain English:

- That the parent is giving up all rights to have custody, to visit with, to speak with, to write to or to learn about the child forever, unless the parties have agreed to different terms;

- That the child will be adopted without the parent's consent, without further notice to the parent, and will be adopted by any person the agency chooses, unless the surrender paper contains the name of the person(s) who will be adopting the child;

- That the parent cannot be forced to sign the surrender paper and cannot be punished for refusing to sign the surrender;

- That the parent has the right before signing the surrender to speak to an attorney of his or her own choosing or any other person the parent may wish to speak to;

- That the parent has the right to have that lawyer or other person present at the time of the execution of the surrender;

- That the parent has the right to ask the court to appoint an attorney free of charge if the parent cannot afford to hire one;

- That the parent has the right to supportive counseling.

The portion of the statute that permits a parent to specify in the surrender instrument who is to adopt the child and to include provisions for post-adoption visitation or contact with the child became effective October 1, 1989. While such surrenders, commonly called **conditional surrenders**, are now widely used, important issues remain unresolved. First, the legal status of a child who has been surrendered for adoption by a specified person who is subsequently unable to complete the adoption is unclear. Suppose the person named as the adoptive resource in the surrender dies before the adoption is finalized, for example. If the parent who signed the surrender demands the return of the child at that point, does the agency have the right to retain custody? If the biological parent has disappeared, can the conditional surrender be used in the adoption of the child by another person? Since the agency ceases to work with the biological parent following the surrender, the agency is unlikely to have current information about the condition of the parent and almost certainly will not have grounds to terminate parental rights.

The second important, as yet unanswered, question concerns the enforceability of provisions for visitation or contact with the child after the adoption is finalized. As discussed in Chapter 13, the Domestic Relations Law makes no provision for conditional orders of adoption. Subsequent to the adoption, the biological parent is no longer the child's parent in the eyes of the law, and, as you learned in Chapter 6, a non-parent (other than a grandparent or sibling) does not have standing to sue for visitation. Thus, the visitation terms of an adoption surrender are of dubious enforceability.

One appellate court has ruled that at most such provisions confer standing upon the biological parent to sue for visitation after the adoption. *Matter of Gerald*, 211 A.D.2d 17, 625 N.Y.S.2d 509 (1 Dept. 1995). On the other hand, the Court of Appeals has suggested that it may be prepared to recognize "open adoption." In the context of a discussion of the changing nature of adoption in *Matter of Jacob and Matter of Dana*, 86 N.Y.2d 651, 636 N.Y.S.2d 716 (1995), (the case, discussed in Chapter 13, which permitted adoption by unmarried domestic partners), Chief Judge Judith Kaye wrote that by passing the conditional surrender statute, the legislature must have meant to reject the idea that adoption terminates all of the natural parents' rights to the child. Until this issue is definitively resolved by the Court of Appeals, attorneys will continue to advise their clients that the law is unsettled on the issue of post-adoption visitation by birth parents.

Extra-judicial Surrenders

A surrender taken out of court must be executed before a notary in the presence of at least two witnesses. One witness must be an employee of the child care agency who is specially trained to receive surrenders, and at least one must be a certified social worker or an attorney who is *not* an employee, volunteer, consultant, or agent for the agency. SSL § 383-c(4)(a). When such a surrender is taken, an application for judicial approval must be filed within 15 days. SSL § 383-c(4)(b).

Judicial Surrenders

Before a judicial surrender is executed, the judge must allocute the parent concerning: the right to counsel, including the right to assigned counsel if the parent cannot afford to hire an attorney; the right to supportive counseling; the consequences of signing the surrender, including losing the right to custody of and visitation with the child; and the fact that the surrender is irrevocable immediately upon its execution. Often the judge asks the parent a few questions to make sure that the parent fully understands the nature of adoption and the terms of the instrument and may also offer to answer any question the parent may have before signing the document. If the court is satisfied that the parent has made a fully informed and voluntary choice to surrender the child, the parent then signs the document in front of the judge, and the judge signs an order approving the surrender. The surrender must be filed in the office of the County Clerk, where it is kept in a special book not open to inspection by the general public.

TERMINATION OF PARENTAL RIGHTS

Foster care is intended to be a temporary situation. If a parent of a child in foster care fails to cooperate with the services the child care agency offers, or if the parent drops out altogether, the agency must find another way to provide the child with a permanent home. Often adoption is the best avenue to permanency for such a child, but if the parent is unavailable to sign a surrender or is unwilling to surrender, the agency will have to initiate court action to terminate the parent's rights before placing the child for adoption. The legislative intent that children should be provided with permanent homes is expressed in the preamble to the termination of parental rights statute, section 384-b of the Social Services Law: "[W]hen it is clear that the natural parent cannot or will not provide a normal family home for the child and when continued foster care is not an appropriate plan for the child, then a permanent alternative home should be sought for the child." SSL § 384-b(1)(a)(iv).

BASICS BOX

Subject matter jurisdiction: Family Court and Surrogate's Court share concurrent original jurisdiction. Surrogate's jurisdiction limited as to grounds.

Venue: County where either parent resides or agency has its principal place of business, unless child placed under FCA Art. 10, in which case county where the Art. 10 case was heard.

Standing: Foster care agency; in some circumstances, foster parents and law guardian.

Grounds: Abandonment; permanent neglect; mental illness of parent; mental retardation of parent; severe or repeated abuse; parent(s) deceased.

Statute of Limitations: Until the child reaches 18 years of age.

Applicable Statutes: SSL § 384-b; FCA §§ 611-634; SCPA Article 17.

STANDING

An authorized child care agency or relative with whom the child is directly placed may initiate proceedings for the commitment of the guardianship and custody of a foster child at any point when grounds exist. As a practical matter, the soonest such a petition can be filed is when the child has been in care six months, including the time the child was remanded prior to final disposition of the child protective proceedings, since even total abandonment must persist for at least six months before a petition to terminate parental rights can be filed. The court in an extension of placement proceeding or foster care review may also authorize the foster parent to file a petition, but this provision is rarely used because of the awkwardness of the foster parent attempting to prove the agency's diligent efforts to work with the birth parents. If the court has ordered the agency to file the petition, and the agency has not done so, the child's law guardian or guardian ad litem may file. SSL § 384-b(3)(b).

VENUE

The venue provisions for termination of parental rights are tricky. If the child was placed as a result of Article 10 proceedings, the petition to terminate parental rights should be filed in the county where the Article 10 proceeding was heard and should, "wherever practicable," be assigned to the same judge who heard the Article 10 case. SSL § 384-b(3)(c). This requirement was added to the statute in an attempt to reduce delay in freeing children for adoption by making one judge responsible for the child throughout his or her placement. Sometimes, however, siblings have been placed through proceedings heard by different judges, occasionally in different counties. In such a situation, the agency may petition to free all the siblings for adoption at the same time, and may file before any judge who heard any one of the Article 10 cases. If the child was placed by some means other than an Article 10 case, the termination of parental rights case should be initiated in the county where either of the parents reside, or if their residence is not known, in the county where the agency has a business office or the child resides. SSL § 384-b(3)(c).

SUBJECT MATTER JURISDICTION

The subject matter jurisdiction for termination of parental rights cases is also peculiar. Family Court and Surrogate's Court have concurrent original jurisdiction, but while Family Court has jurisdiction on all the possible grounds, Surrogate's Court can only hear petitions alleging abandonment. SSL § 384-b(3)(d). This is a historical anomaly for which there is no longer rhyme or reason, so it must simply be accepted and remembered. When a case is filed in the Family Court, the procedures of the Family Court Act apply unless they conflict with Social Services Law section 384-b. When it is filed in the Surrogate's Court, the Surrogate's Court Procedure Act applies, unless in conflict with section 384-b.

GROUNDS

Although there are five grounds pursuant to which the custody and guardianship of a child under the age of 18 may be committed to an agency, foster parent, or relative-caretaker, only four are now used. The statute provides that a commitment petition may be filed when both parents (whose consent to the adoption of the child would have been required) are dead, but subsequent amendments to the adoption statute allow the agency to consent to the adoption of the child in such a situation without first obtaining a commitment order. Thus, that ground for commitment is obsolete.

A firm grasp of the grounds upon which a termination of parental rights case may be based is essential for the legal assistant employed by a child care agency, as one task commonly delegated to a legal assistant is to read and digest or summarize the uniform case record for use in such litigation. The summary may be used in the trial outline as a basis for the attorney's questioning of the case worker, or the case record itself, as a business record, may be offered in evidence if the proof covers a period prior to the current case worker's assignment to the case. If the record is to be offered into evidence, the attorney may want the paralegal to mark relevant portions of the record with a paper clip or tab marker, so that the court will be able to find them easily.

Alternative pleading is common in termination of parental rights cases. As you read about the various grounds, you will see that they are so specific and complex that the proof may be insufficient for one or more of the possible grounds. Regardless of which theory is most likely, therefore, the paralegal will probably be asked to summarize all contacts between the agency and the parent under headings such as "Visits," "Referrals for Services," "Planning Conferences," and "Correspondence."

Abandonment

A child is **abandoned** when the parent evinces an intent to forego his or her parental rights and obligations by failing to visit or communicate with the child or agency, although able to do so, for a period of six months immediately preceding the filing of the termination of parental rights petition. SSL § 384-b(5)(a). Note that, like abandonment as a grounds for divorce, the conduct must be voluntary. If the parent cannot maintain contact because of circumstances over which the parent has no control, or if the agency has prevented or discouraged contact with the child, abandonment will not be found. The termination statute has a couple of twists that are absent in the divorce law, however. First, in the absence of evidence to the contrary, the parent's ability to maintain contact is presumed. Second, the parent's subjective intent, expressed or not, does not preclude a finding of abandonment if the parent has not in fact visited, communicated with, or supported the child. The fact that the parent was incarcerated during the six-month period does not preclude a finding of abandonment. Although an incarcerated parent cannot visit the child unless the child is brought to the prison, the parent can nevertheless maintain contact with the child and with the agency by telephone or letter. *Matter of Ulysses T.*, 66 N.Y.2d 773, 497 N.Y.S.2d 368 (1985).

Although the words of the abandonment statute, "failure to visit and to communicate with the child or agency," might be taken to mean that abandonment can only be found where there is a total absence of contact by the parent, the courts have developed the judicial doctrine of "insubstantial contact." Thus, the courts have held that insignificant contacts during the six-month period, such as a parent making a single telephone call or scheduling an appointment or visit that is not kept, do not vitiate the period of abandonment. *Matter of Cecelia A.*, 199 A.D.2d 582, 604 N.Y.S.2d 327 (3 Dept. 1993); *Matter of Michael W.*, 191 A.D.2d 287, 595 N.Y.S.2d 30 (1 Dept. 1993).

The agency is not required in abandonment cases to prove that it has made diligent efforts to encourage the parent to maintain contact. At the same time, however, an agency may not ignore, "write off," or discourage either parent. *"Baby Boy" D.*, Case 12-1, is an interesting illustration of the difficulty of striking the proper balance between the need for expeditious permanency planning and the necessity of offering each parent an opportunity to plan for the child. In Chapter 2, the complexity of New York's multi-level child care system was discussed. Note that in this case, the Appellate Division did not fault the foster care agency for its lack of efforts, but rather found that the father was discouraged by "a confusing bureaucracy."

📖 **CASE 12-1**

IN THE MATTER OF THE GUARDIANSHIP OF "BABY BOY" D., a/k/a SONIE D.
196 A.D.2d 773, 602 N.Y.S.2d 102 (1 Dept. 1993)

MEMORANDUM DECISION.

Order, Family Court, Bronx County (Gloria Sosa-Lintner, J.), entered December 22, 1992, which, insofar as appealed from, denied petitioner Agency's application to terminate respondent putative father's parental rights on the ground of abandonment, unanimously affirmed, without costs.

Once petitioner had shown no contact between respondent and the child for the six months immediately preceding commencement of the proceeding, an inference of abandonment arose, rebuttable by proof that respondent was unable to maintain contact or was discouraged from doing so by petitioner.... Although Family Court improperly based its ruling in large part upon petitioner's failure to show that it attempted to contact respondent..., there is ample evidence in the record to find that repeated efforts by respondent to locate the child were thwarted by a confusing bureaucracy, and that he attempted to follow instructions to locate the child's mother as well.

Permanent Neglect

If, despite the agency's diligent efforts to assist, develop and encourage a meaningful parent-child relationship, a parent fails for a period of more than one year following a child's placement in foster care to plan for the discharge of the child from care or fails to maintain contact with the child or fails to visit the child regularly, the parent's rights to the child may be terminated on the ground of **permanent neglect**. SSL § 384-b(7). The definition of permanent neglect is the product of a delicate balancing of the rights of the child, the parent and the child care agency. The fact that the agency must work with the natural parent(s) for a year before seeking to terminate parental rights reflects obvious concern for the parents' rights. The agency's efforts must be "diligent," which countless judicial opinions have interpreted to mean good faith efforts that are tailored to the needs and capacities of the parent. *Matter of Star A.*, 55 N.Y.2d 560, 450 N.Y.S.2d 465 (1982). Proof of diligent efforts is a threshold requirement to a finding of permanent neglect. Even if the parent has made no improvement at all, parental rights will not be terminated unless the agency has made affirmative, repeated, and meaningful efforts to help the parent. *Matter of Sheila G.*, 61 N.Y.2d 368, 474 N.Y.S.2d 421 (1984). The statute specifies that diligent efforts include, but are not limited to:

- consultation with the parents to develop a service plan for the family;
- making suitable arrangements for the parents to visit the child, including taking the child to a facility in which the parent is incarcerated, if such visitation is in the child's best interest;
- assistance to the parents so that problems preventing the discharge of the child from care may be resolved;
- informing the parents of the child's progress, development, and health.

The stringent diligent efforts requirement is balanced by the fact that the efforts need not have been made in the year immediately preceding the filing of the termination of parental rights petition and by the fact that the agency is excused from diligent efforts if the parent fails to keep the agency informed of his or her whereabouts for a period of six months or more. *In re Crystal K.*, 204 A.D.2d 105, 611 N.Y.S.2d 528 (1 Dept. 1994). The agency is also excused from diligent efforts when such efforts would be detrimental to the interests of the child. Judicial decisions have sharply limited the use of this exception, however. The fact-finding stage of a termination of parental rights proceeding is not a "best interest hearing" like a custody case, and the agency may not unilaterally determine to withhold efforts because it perceives that the child would be better off with the foster parents. *Matter of Sheila G., supra.*

The statute specifies that the plan formulated by the parent must be "realistic and feasible," and good faith efforts do not preclude a finding of permanent neglect. SSL § 384-b(7)(c). In recent years a developing body of case law has stressed that the parents must actually benefit from the services in which they participate, and not merely go through the motions of attending a program. In *Commitment of Custody and Guardianship of William J.*, --A.D.2d--, 644 N.Y.S.2d 226 (1 Dept. 1996), the First Department Appellate Division held that where domestic violence was the primary obstacle preventing reunification of the family, the respondent's "denial of abusive behavior and failure to utilize rehabilitative services" justified a finding of permanent neglect.

The fact that a parent is incarcerated also does not preclude a finding of permanent neglect. The period of time a parent is hospitalized or institutionalized, however, tolls the statute. The time cannot be counted against the parent for the purposes of permanent neglect, but the periods before and after the parent's hospitalization or institutionalization can be added together to make up the required year of efforts. SSL § 384-b(7)(d)(ii).

Mental Illness of Parent

Parental rights may be terminated if a child has been in foster care for a year and the parent is unable to provide proper and adequate care for the child because the parent suffers from a mental illness. SSL § 384-b(4)(c). This ground for termination of parental rights was the subject of much controversy in the 1970's when section 384-b was enacted, and some students may feel uncomfortable with it. The statute contains several hurdles, however, that were included specifically to prevent agencies from using it indiscriminately. First, note that the child must be in foster care for a year before the petition can be filed. This provision applies regardless of how long the parent has been mentally ill prior to the child's entry into foster care.

Second, mental illness is carefully defined as "a disease or mental condition which is manifested by a disorder or disturbance in behavior, feeling, thinking or judgment to such an extent that if [the foster child] were placed in or returned to the custody of the parent, the child would be in danger of becoming a neglected child as defined in the family court act." SSL § 384-b(6)(a). This definition is sufficiently stringent to rule out all but major mental disorders, and significantly, the symptoms of the illness must pose an imminent risk of harm to the child.

Third, the statue requires proof that the parent is mentally ill "presently and for the foreseeable future." Thus, the petitioning agency must establish not only that the parent is ill, but also that the prognosis is poor. If the parent has not had access to appropriate medication and psychotherapy, the parent's rights cannot be terminated until a medically recognized course of treatment has been attempted. *Matter of Hime Y.*, 52 N.Y.2d 242, 437 N.Y.S.2d 286 (1981).

Fourth, the testimony of a psychiatrist or psychologist is required. SSL § 384-b(6)(c) The court is not permitted to make a finding on this ground based only on the assessment of a social worker or the judge's own opinion of whether the respondent's symptoms manifest a mental disorder. The parent's attorney has the right to observe the examination of the respondent by the court-appointed psychiatrist or psychologist. *Matter of Guardianship and Custody of Alexander L.*, 60 N.Y.2d 329, 469 N.Y.S.2d 626 (1983). An adjudication pursuant to SSL § 384-b that a parent is mentally ill does not impair any other legal rights the parent may have. SSL § 384-b(6)(d). Thus, the parent is not subject to involuntary hospitalization or the appointment of a conservator, for example.

Mental Retardation of Parent

As with the mental illness ground for termination of parental rights, the mental retardation ground is circumscribed. The primary danger the opponents of the legislation foresaw in the mental retardation ground for termination was the potential to misdiagnose cultural limitation as mental retardation. Thus, the legislature defined mental retardation in such a way as to prevent this abuse. "Mental retardation" means, "subaverage intellectual functioning which originates during the developmental period and is associated with impairment in adaptive behavior to such an extent that if [the foster child] were placed in or returned to the custody of the parent, the child would be in danger of becoming a neglected child as defined in the family court act." SSL § 384-b(6)(b). Note the requirement that the problem have begun during the developmental period, and, as in the mental illness ground, the linkage of the manifestations of the retardation to the protection of the child. As in the mental illness ground, the child must have been in foster care for a year before the termination of parental rights proceeding can be initiated, which gives the agency the opportunity to work with the parent to see if he or she can be trained in the skills essential to child rearing. The agency must also establish that the parent will continue to be mentally retarded in the foreseeable future.

Severe or Repeated Abuse

This ground for termination of parental rights was also highly controversial at its enactment in 1981. Several versions of the bill failed passage, and the present version is the product of many revisions. Unfortunately, in the attempt to get the bill passed, the end product was burdened with so many complexities that it is unworkable. Consequently, this ground for termination is virtually unused. Termination of the parental rights of abusive parents can be, and routinely is, accomplished using the permanent neglect ground, as the permanent neglect statute is a much more flexible and realistic tool.

The severe or repeated abuse statute presents four major problems. First, the agency is required in the termination of parental rights proceeding to prove the severe or repeated abuse by clear and convincing evidence, whereas in an Article 10 child abuse proceeding, you will recall, the fair preponderance of the evidence standard is sufficient. *Matter of Tammie Z.*, 66 N.Y.2d 1, 494 N.Y.S.2d 686 (1985). Thus, to proceed on this ground, the agency would have to re-prove the underlying abuse.

Second, the severe abuse must be of the child in foster care, rather than of a sibling. Even if a parent has fatally abused a sibling, that fact is insufficient for termination of parental rights under this statute. Third, the severe abuse statute contains a diligent efforts requirement that is even more stringent than the diligent efforts an agency must establish for the purposes of permanent neglect. Here, the agency must prove not only that the efforts were unsuccessful, but also that they are likely to be unsuccessful in the foreseeable future.

Finally, the agency is held to a higher standard in the dispositional phase of a severe or repeated abuse case. Hearsay evidence is not admissible in the dispositional hearing following a finding on this ground, whereas dispositional hearsay is allowed in every other cause of action for termination of parental rights. Recently, as a result of several highly publicized abuse cases, public interest in severe abuse as a ground for termination has revived, and a bill is pending in the Legislature that may remove some of these obstacles from the statute.

SPECIAL PROCEDURAL AND EVIDENTIARY RULES

Like Article 10 child protective proceedings, proceedings to terminate parental rights are governed by special procedures and rules of evidence. Most of the special rules of evidence are in section 384-b itself, while the procedures to be followed when the case is brought in Family Court are in sections 611 through 634 of the Family Court Act.

Service of Process

Service of the summons, if the case is brought in Family Court, or citation, if brought in Surrogate's Court, must be made at least 20 days before the court date in the manner provided in SCPA § 307. Personal service is preferred, but if after reasonable effort personal service cannot be accomplished, the judge may authorize service by publication as provided in CPLR § 316. Only one publication is required, however. If the summons is personally served, it must be accompanied by the petition. If service is made by publication, however, the petition is not published, but the summons must contain a special notice stating 1) the date, time, place, and purpose of the proceeding, 2) that if the respondent fails to appear, all of his or her parental rights may be terminated, 3) that a failure to appear constitutes a denial of the respondent's interest in the child, which may result, without further notice, in the transfer or commitment of the child's care, custody or guardianship or in the child's adoption in this or any subsequent proceeding in which custody or guardianship or adoption may be at issue.

Privileges Do Not Apply

As in Article 10 cases, the privileges usually attaching to confidential communications between husband and wife, physician and patient, psychologist and client, and social worker and client are inapplicable. Note that confidential communications to clergy and attorneys remain privileged.

Clear and Convincing Evidence Required

In Chapter 9 the "clear and convincing" standard of proof was introduced and its role in paternity proceedings discussed. Termination of parental rights proceedings may be viewed as the flip side of paternity proceedings. Each is an adjudication of the status of parenthood; one creates a parental relation, the other ends it. Because of the grave and irrevocable nature of the proceedings, termination of parental rights also requires clear and convincing proof. SSL § 384-b(3)(g). When the case involves an Indian child, the Indian Child Welfare Act, 25 U.S.C.A. § 1911(a), preempts because it is a Federal statute, and proof beyond a reasonable doubt is required. In its original form, the New York termination statute required only proof by a preponderance of the evidence, but the statute was amended when the United States Supreme Court held, in Case 12-2, that due process mandates clear and convincing proof.

📖 **CASE 12-2**

SANTOSKY v. KRAMER
455 U.S. 745, 102 S.Ct. 1388 (1982)

Justice BLACKMUN delivered the opinion of the Court.
***

Petitioners John Santosky II and Annie Santosky are the natural parents of Tina and John III. In November 1973, after incidents reflecting parental neglect, respondent Kramer, Commissioner of the Ulster County Department of Social Services, initiated a neglect proceeding under Fam.Ct.Act § 1022 and removed Tina from her natural home. About 10 months later, he removed John III and placed him with foster parents. On the day John was taken, Annie Santosky gave birth to a third child, Jed. When Jed was only three days old, respondent transferred him to a foster home on the ground that immediate removal was necessary to avoid imminent danger to his life or health.

In October 1978, respondent petitioned the Ulster County Family Court to terminate petitioners' parental rights in the three children. Petitioners challenged the constitutionality of the "fair preponderance of the evidence" standard specified in Fam.Ct.Act § 622. The Family Court Judge rejected this constitutional challenge, and weighed the evidence under the statutory standard. While acknowledging that the Santoskys had maintained contact with their children, the judge found those visits "at best superficial and devoid of any real emotional content." After deciding that the agency had made "'diligent efforts' to encourage and strengthen the parental relationship," he concluded that the Santoskys were incapable, even with public assistance, of planning for the future of their children. The judge later held a dispositional hearing and ruled that the best interests of the three children required permanent termination of the Santoskys' custody.

Petitioners appealed, again contesting the constitutionality of § 622's standard of proof. The New York Supreme Court, Appellate Division, affirmed, holding application of the preponderance-of-the-evidence standard "proper and constitutional." That standard, the court reasoned, "recognizes and seeks to balance rights possessed by the child...with those of the natural parents...."

The New York Court of Appeals then dismissed petitioners' appeal to that court "upon the ground that no substantial constitutional question is directly involved." We granted certiorari to consider petitioners' constitutional claim.

II

Last Term in *Lassiter v. Department of Social Services*, 452 U.S. 18, 101 S.Ct. 2153, 68 L.Ed.2d 640 (1981), this Court, by a 5-4 vote, held that the Fourteenth Amendment's Due Process Clause does not require the appointment of counsel for indigent parents in every parental status termination proceeding. The case casts light, however,

📖 **CASE 12-2 continued**

on the two central questions here -- whether process is constitutionally due a natural parent at a State's parental rights termination proceeding, and, if so, what process is due.

In *Lassiter,* it was "not disputed that state intervention to terminate the relationship between [a parent] and [the] child must be accomplished by procedures meeting the requisites of the Due Process Clause."... The absence of dispute reflected this Court's historical recognition that freedom of personal choice in matters of family life is a fundamental liberty interest protected by the Fourteenth Amendment....

The fundamental liberty interest of natural parents in the care, custody, and management of their child does not evaporate simply because they have not been model parents or have lost temporary custody of their child to the State. Even when blood relationships are strained, parents retain a vital interest in preventing the irretrievable destruction of their family life. If anything, persons faced with forced dissolution of their parental rights have a more critical need for procedural protections than do those resisting state intervention into ongoing family affairs. When the State moves to destroy weakened familial bonds, it must provide the parents with fundamentally fair procedures.

In *Lassiter,* the Court and three dissenters agreed that the nature of the process due in parental rights termination proceedings turns on a balancing of the "three distinct factors" specified in *Mathews v. Eldridge,* 424 U.S. 319, 335, 96 S.Ct. 893, 903, 47 L.Ed.2d 18 (1976): the private interests affected by the proceeding; the risk of error created by the State's chosen procedure; and the countervailing governmental interest supporting use of the challenged procedure.

***

In *Addington v. Texas,* 441 U.S. 418, 99 S.Ct. 1804, 60 L.Ed.2d 323 (1979), the Court, by a unanimous vote of the participating Justices, declared: "The function of a standard of proof, as that concept is embodied in the Due Process Clause and in the realm of factfinding, is to 'instruct the factfinder concerning the degree of confidence our society thinks he should have in the correctness of factual conclusions for a particular type of adjudication.'"... *Addington* teaches that, in any given proceeding, the minimum standard of proof tolerated by the due process requirement reflects not only the weight of the private and public interests affected, but also a societal judgment about how the risk of error should be distributed between the litigants.

***

This Court has mandated an intermediate standard of proof -- "clear and convincing evidence" -- when the individual interests at stake in a state proceeding are both "particularly important" and "more substantial than mere loss of money." Notwithstanding "the state's 'civil labels and good intentions,'"...the Court has deemed this level of certainty necessary to preserve fundamental fairness in a variety of

📖 CASE 12-2 continued

government-initiated proceedings that threaten the individual involved with "a significant deprivation of liberty" or "stigma."

***

III

In parental rights termination proceedings, the private interest affected is commanding; the risk of error from using a preponderance standard is substantial; and the countervailing governmental interest favoring that standard is comparatively slight. Evaluation of the three *Eldridge* factors compels the conclusion that use of a "fair preponderance of the evidence" standard in such proceedings is inconsistent with due process.

A

***

Lassiter declared it "plain beyond the need for multiple citation" that a natural parent's "desire for and right to 'the companionship, care, custody, and management of his or her children'" is an interest far more precious than any property right....When the State initiates a parental rights termination proceeding, it seeks not merely to infringe that fundamental liberty interest, but to end it. "If the State prevails, it will have worked a unique kind of deprivation.... A parent's interest in the accuracy and justice of the decision to terminate his or her parental status is, therefore, a commanding one."

***

Thus, the first Eldridge factor -- the private interest affected -- weighs heavily against use of the preponderance standard at a state-initiated permanent neglect proceeding. We do not deny that the child and his foster parents are also deeply interested in the outcome of that contest. But at the factfinding stage of the New York proceeding, the focus emphatically is not on them.

The factfinding does not purport -- and is not intended -- to balance the child's interest in a normal family home against the parents' interest in raising the child. Nor does it purport to determine whether the natural parents or the foster parents would provide the better home. Rather, the factfinding hearing pits the State directly against the parents. The State alleges that the natural parents are at fault. Fam.Ct.Act § 614.1.(d). The questions disputed and decided are what the State did -- "made diligent efforts," § 614.1.(c) -- and what the natural parents did not do -- "maintain contact with or plan for the future of the child." § 614.1.(d). The State marshals an array of public resources to prove its case and disprove the parents' case. Victory by the State not only makes termination of parental rights possible; it entails a judicial determination that the parents are unfit to raise their own children.

At the factfinding, the State cannot presume that a child and his parents are adversaries. After the State has established parental unfitness at that initial proceeding, the court may assume at the *dispositional* stage that the interests of the child and the natural

📖 **CASE 12-2 continued**

parents do diverge. See Fam.Ct.Act § 631 (judge shall make his order "solely on the basis of the best interests of the child," and thus has no obligation to consider the natural parents' rights in selecting dispositional alternatives). But until the State proves parental unfitness, the child and his parents share a vital interest in preventing erroneous termination of their natural relationship. Thus, at the factfinding, the interests of the child and his natural parents coincide to favor use of error-reducing procedures.

***

B

Under *Mathews v. Eldridge*, we next must consider both the risk of erroneous deprivation of private interests resulting from use of a "fair preponderance" standard and the likelihood that a higher evidentiary standard would reduce that risk.... Since the factfinding phase of a permanent neglect proceeding is an adversary contest between the State and the natural parents, the relevant question is whether a preponderance standard fairly allocates the risk of an erroneous factfinding between these two parties.

In New York, the factfinding stage of a state-initiated permanent neglect proceeding bears many of the indicia of a criminal trial.... The State seeks to establish a series of historical facts about the intensity of its agency's efforts to reunite the family, the infrequency and insubstantiality of the parents' contacts with their child, and the parents' inability or unwillingness to formulate a plan for the child's future. The attorneys submit documentary evidence, and call witnesses who are subject to cross-examination. Based on all the evidence, the judge then determines whether the State has proved the statutory elements of permanent neglect by a fair preponderance of the evidence. § 622.

At such a proceeding, numerous factors combine to magnify the risk of erroneous factfinding. Permanent neglect proceedings employ imprecise substantive standards that leave determinations unusually open to the subjective values of the judge.... In appraising the nature and quality of a complex series of encounters among the agency, the parents, and the child, the court possesses unusual discretion to underweigh probative facts that might favor the parent. Because parents subject to termination proceedings are often poor, uneducated, or members of minority groups,...such proceedings are often vulnerable to judgments based on cultural or class bias.

The State's ability to assemble its case almost inevitably dwarfs the parents' ability to mount a defense. No predetermined limits restrict the sums an agency may spend in prosecuting a given termination proceeding. The State's attorney usually will be expert on the issues contested and the procedures employed at the factfinding hearing, and enjoys full access to all public records concerning the family. The State may call on experts in family relations, psychology, and medicine to bolster its case. Furthermore, the primary witnesses at the hearing will be the agency's own professional caseworkers whom the State has

CASE 12-2 continued

empowered both to investigate the family situation and to testify against the parents. Indeed, because the child is already in agency custody, the State even has the power to shape the historical events that form the basis for termination.

The disparity between the adversaries' litigation resources is matched by a striking asymmetry in their litigation options. Unlike criminal defendants, natural parents have no "double jeopardy" defense against repeated state termination efforts. If the State initially fails to win termination, as New York did here, ...it always can try once again to cut off the parents' rights after gathering more or better evidence. Yet even when the parents have attained the level of fitness required by the State, they have no similar means by which they can forestall future termination efforts.

***

Raising the standard of proof would have both practical and symbolic consequences.... "Increasing the burden of proof is one way to impress the factfinder with the importance of the decision and thereby perhaps to reduce the chances that inappropriate" terminations will be ordered.

***

For the child, the likely consequence of an erroneous failure to terminate is preservation of an uneasy status quo. For the natural parents, however, the consequence of an erroneous termination is the unnecessary destruction of their natural family. A standard that allocates the risk of error nearly equally between those two outcomes does not reflect properly their relative severity.

C

Two state interests are at stake in parental rights termination proceedings -- a *parens patriae* interest in preserving and promoting the welfare of the child and a fiscal and administrative interest in reducing the cost and burden of such proceedings. A standard of proof more strict than preponderance of the evidence is consistent with both interests.

***

The State's interest in finding the child an alternative permanent home arises only "when it is *clear* that the natural parent cannot or will not provide a normal family home for the child." Soc.Serv.Law § 384-b.1.(a)(iv) (emphasis added). At the factfinding, that goal is served by procedures that promote an accurate determination of whether the natural parents can and will provide a normal home.

***

A majority of the States have concluded that a "clear and convincing evidence" standard of proof strikes a fair balance between the rights of the natural parents and the State's legitimate concerns.... We hold that such a standard adequately conveys to the factfinder the level of subjective certainty about his factual conclusions necessary to satisfy due process. We further hold that determination of the precise

📖 CASE 12-2 continued

burden equal to or greater than that standard is a matter of state law properly left to state legislatures and state courts.

***

Justice REHNQUIST, with whom THE CHIEF JUSTICE, Justice WHITE, and Justice O'CONNOR join, dissenting.

***

State intervention in domestic relations has always been an unhappy but necessary feature of life in our organized society. For all of our experience in this area, we have found no fully satisfactory solutions to the painful problem of child abuse and neglect. We have found, however, that leaving the States free to experiment with various remedies has produced novel approaches and promising progress.

Throughout this experience the Court has scrupulously refrained from interfering with state answers to domestic relations questions.... This is not to say that the Court should blink at clear constitutional violations in state statutes, but rather that in this area, of all areas, "substantial weight must be given to the good-faith judgments of the individuals [administering a program]...that the procedures they have provided assure fair consideration of the...claims of individuals."...

***

When, in the context of a permanent neglect termination proceeding, the interests of the child and the State in a stable, nurturing homelife are balanced against the interests of the parents in the rearing of their child, it cannot be said that either set of interests is so clearly paramount as to require that the risk of error be allocated to one side or the other. Accordingly, a State constitutionally may conclude that the risk of error should be borne in roughly equal fashion by use of the preponderance-of-the-evidence standard of proof.

***

For the reasons heretofore stated, I believe that the Court today errs in concluding that the New York standard of proof in parental-rights termination proceedings violates due process of law. The decision disregards New York's earnest efforts to *aid* parents in regaining the custody of their children and a host of procedural protections placed around parental rights and interests. The Court finds a constitutional violation only by a tunnel-vision application of due process principles that altogether loses sight of the unmistakable fairness of the New York procedure.

Even more worrisome, today's decision cavalierly rejects the considered judgment of the New York Legislature in an area traditionally entrusted to state care. The Court thereby begins, I fear, a trend of federal intervention in state family law matters which surely will stifle creative responses to vexing problems. Accordingly, I dissent.

DISCUSSION TOPIC

Do you believe that use of the preponderance-of-the-evidence standard was a "clear constitutional violation," or do you agree with Justice Rehnquist that the states should be given more leeway to experiment with procedures in such cases? The issue of Federal versus local decision making in child welfare matters is currently a hot topic, as the Federal government moves toward block grants and relinquishes some of the control it has exercised in such matters for the past two decades.

Dispositional Phase

A dispositional hearing is required only when the finding is to permanent neglect or severe or repeated abuse. Although the court can terminate parental rights after a finding of abandonment, mental illness, or mental retardation without conducting a dispositional hearing, the court may exercise its discretion to hold one, and most trial courts prefer to do so unless the evidence would substantially duplicate what the court has already heard at the factfinding hearing. Hearsay evidence is admissible at any dispositional hearing, except, as noted above, where the finding is to severe or repeated abuse. Sometimes the court orders reports to be prepared specially for the dispositional hearing, such as a mental health study of the parent, but usually the child care agency has enough current information on hand.

In the dispositional hearing, the judge will hear and consider evidence concerning the bonding between the child and the parents and between the child and the foster parents, along with evidence concerning the respondent parent's current functioning. If the child is over 14, the court is expressly authorized to consider the child's wishes. SSL § 384-b(3)(k). The age of 14 is significant here because that is the age when a child must consent to his or her adoption. As a practical matter, however, most courts consider the wishes of any child old enough to express them, as in custody cases, according the preferences of an older child more weight. To insure that the child's point of view is fully represented at every stage of the proceeding, the appointment of a law guardian is mandatory.

The dispositional hearing is a straight best interest hearing, as the factfinding has overcome the presumption in favor of the biological parents. The agency is not required to prove that the child is likely to be adopted. SSL § 384-b(3)(i). This may seem odd, since the primary purpose of the proceeding is to free the child for adoption, but the intent is to make sure that handicapped and older children have the same opportunity as other children to be adopted. After they are freed for adoption, such children are "photolisted" in a book available in all adoption agencies. If their current foster parents do not choose to adopt, every effort is made to find adoptive homes. In fact, some adoption agencies specialize in finding homes for "hard to place" children.

DISPOSITIONS

Technically, after a finding of abandonment, mental illness or mental retardation, the disposition of commitment of custody and guardianship to the agency is automatic, since no dispositional hearing is required and the statute provides for no other disposition. As discussed above, however, many Family Court judges believe they retain discretion to dismiss a petition even after a finding on one of those grounds if termination of parental rights would be contrary to the best interest of the child.

The statute provides a wider choice of dispositional alternatives where the court has made a finding of permanent neglect. The court may 1) dismiss the petition, 2) suspend judgment, or 3) commit the guardianship and custody of the child to the agency. FCA § 631. In addition, if the petition is dismissed, the court can reconsider the underlying order of placement and order the child returned to the parent.

Dismissal

Dismissal usually occurs only if the agency fails to prove its case by clear and convincing evidence. Outright dismissals based on best interest considerations are rare, although they have occasionally been granted where the child has turned 14 during the course of the proceeding and does not wish to be adopted.

Suspended Judgment

If a child is bonded to the natural parent and the parent has made substantial progress toward rehabilitation, the court may choose to suspend judgment in the matter to see whether discharge to the parent can take place. Although a suspended judgment may be entered after fully contested factfinding and dispositional hearings, it is more often a negotiated disposition offered when a respondent has made an admission to permanent neglect. A suspended judgment gives the parent one last opportunity to make use of the services offered to overcome the problems that are preventing discharge of the child. The suspended judgment period may be for up to one year initially, and the court may extend it for an additional year if exceptional circumstances require. The allowable terms and conditions of a suspended judgment are specified in Rule 205.50 of the Uniform Rules of the Family Court. A suspended judgment *must* contain at least one of the following conditions to be observed by the respondent:

- Maintain communication with the child by letter or telephone at specified intervals;
- Maintain consistent contact with the child and visit regularly;
- Cooperate with the foster care agency in developing and bringing to fruition a plan for the child's future;
- Cooperate with a court-approved plan to encourage and strengthen the parent-child relationship;

- Contribute towards the support of the child, if financially able to do so;
- Seek proper housing for the child;
- Cooperate with referrals for medical or psychiatric diagnosis or treatment, substance abuse treatment, employment, or family counseling, and sign releases so that the agency can obtain information about the respondent's progress in any such program;
- Any other reasonable condition that may ameliorate the conditions that gave rise to the filing of the petition.

A copy of the order suspending judgment, with all the terms and conditions spelled out, must be served upon the respondent, and the order must state that a failure to obey the order may lead to the commitment of guardianship and custody of the child to the agency.

Commitment of Custody and Guardianship

If the court finds that the child's best interest will be promoted by terminating the parents' rights, the court will enter an order committing the custody and guardianship of the child to the agency. If a voluntary agency has brought the petition, custody and guardianship are usually committed "jointly and severally" to the voluntary agency and the Commissioner of Social Services. This is done in case the voluntary agency should go out of business or the child should be transferred to another agency before adoption. In such a situation, the Commissioner would be authorized to consent to the child's adoption without having to resettle the commitment order.

The order of commitment terminates the parents' rights to custody, visitation and contact with the child, and it authorizes the agency to consent to the adoption of the child without further notice to the respondent parents. It does not terminate the child's right to support from the natural parents, however, nor does it cut off the child's right to inherit from or through the natural parents. SSL § 384-b(9). Those rights are terminated only when the child is adopted, at which time the child acquires support and inheritance right from the adoptive parents, as discussed in Chapter 13.

Notice of entry of the order of commitment must also be served on all parties who appeared in the litigation and on the foster parents if they have been approved as the child's adoptive parents. SSL § 384-b(10). Service of the notice of entry, Form 12-2, insures that all parties who did not default in the proceeding receive a conformed copy of the order as it was signed by the judge, and it starts the clock running on the time to appeal the order. Approved adoptive parents must also be notified that they may now file a petition to adopt and must be informed of the procedure required to finalize the adoption. If any foster parents, relatives, or other persons interested in adopting the child do file adoption petitions, the judge who heard the termination of parental rights proceeding keeps the adoption cases. SSL § 384-b(11).

◿ **FORM 12-2**

FAMILY COURT OF THE STATE OF NEW YORK
COUNTY OF KINGS

....

In the Matter of the Guardianship of the Person   Docket No. B-9876/97
and Custody of

NOTICE OF ENTRY

RONALD JAMES PRINCE,

A Minor

....

　　　TAKE NOTICE, that Findings of Fact, Conclusions of Law and Order of Disposition, true copies of which are annexed hereto, were signed by the Honorable Jose Rodriguez, Judge of the Family Court of the State of New York, and entered by the Clerk of Kings County Family Court, 283 Adams Street, Brooklyn, New York 11201 on March 5, 1997.

Dated: Brooklyn, New York
　　　 March 6, 1997

　　　　　　　　　　　　　　　　Michael Y. Nesbitt, P. C.
　　　　　　　　　　　　　　　　Attorney for Petitioner
　　　　　　　　　　　　　　　　21 Court Street, Suite 1313
　　　　　　　　　　　　　　　　Brooklyn, New York 11201
　　　　　　　　　　　　　　　　Tel. No. (718) 558-2129

To: Lily McIntyre, Esq.
　　　Law Guardian for the Child
　　　Legal Aid Society
　　　175 Remsen Street
　　　Brooklyn, New York 11201

　　　Warren P. Carter, Esq.
　　　Attorney for Respondent Mary Prince
　　　115 Fifth Avenue, 28 Floor
　　　New York, New York 10175

A **certified copy** of the order of commitment must be recorded in the office of the county clerk in the same manner as a surrender. The originals of all pleadings and orders in a litigation remain with the court. A certified copy of any document in a court file is obtained by taking a **conformed copy** to the clerk of the court where the original is filed. A conformed copy is a copy on which all of the changes the court has made appear on the copy. Judges do not always sign an order or judgment exactly as it is presented. Sometimes the judge adds or strikes out certain provisions. Of course, the judge's signature and the date of signing always have to be conformed. On the signature line, the conformed copy should show "/s/" and the printed name of the judge as signed. After reviewing the conformed copy to make sure that it reflects all the changes the judge has made, the clerk stamps the document with a rubber stamp that says, "This is to certify that this is a true copy of [here the clerk writes in the name of the document, such as 'Order of Commitment'] made in the matter designated in such copy and shown by the records of the [Family] Court of the State of New York, within the City of [New York] for the County of [Kings]". The clerk then signs and dates the certification.

CONCLUSION

Permanency planning, the process of finding a permanent home for a child outside of the foster care system, requires careful attention to many time limits imposed by statutes, regulations and court orders. Legal assistants are utilized to track these deadlines and to prepare the petitions and documentation needed for the foster care review, extension of placement and surrender or termination of parental rights proceedings that may be take place before permanency for the child is achieved. A legal assistant engaged in such work must thoroughly master the details of the agency's record keeping and tracking procedures. Accurate entry of data is crucial. The legal assistant should not assume, for example, that placement has been extended for a year merely because that is the maximum the statute permits. Instead, the paralegal should consult the extension of placement order to obtain the actual expiration date of the extension and to note any other deadlines the court may have imposed for delivery of services or initiation of termination of parental rights proceedings. Although permanency planning may lack the drama of child protective litigation, it has at least as great an impact on the child's welfare.

CHAPTER REVIEW QUESTIONS

1.   Timothy is remanded to the Commissioner of Social Services for foster care on March 18, 1997 as a result of his mother's crack addiction. His father was never identified. The mother defaulted after personal service in the neglect proceeding, and a finding of neglect and order of disposition placing Timothy with the Commissioner for up to one year were entered on May 20, 1997. No family member has visited Timothy since he first came into foster care, and the mother's whereabouts cannot be ascertained. What is the earliest date a petition to terminate parental rights could be filed? If parental rights have not been terminated, by what date must the petition to extend placement be filed? If parental rights are terminated on June 5, 1997, and Timothy's placement is converted into an adoptive placement the next day, by when must the 1055-a review petition be filed, assuming the adoption has not been finalized sooner?

2.   If the agency elects to file the termination petition when Timothy has been in care for less that one year, what ground(s) for termination should it plead? If more than a year has elapsed since Timothy came into care, what additional ground(s) might be plead? Has the agency made "diligent efforts" to assist Timothy's mother? Does this case fall into one of the exceptions to the "diligent efforts" requirement?

3.   Tamara entered foster care on the same date as Timothy and was placed with the Commissioner on the same date, also through a neglect petition based on the mother's drug abuse and the father's violence against the mother in the presence of the child. The father has since died, and the mother is also suffering from a terminal illness. The child is placed in a kinship foster home with the mother's sister, and the mother wishes to have the child adopted by the maternal aunt so that the child will have a secure home after the mother's death. What legal steps must be taken to achieve the mother's goal for the child? Can the mother specify that the aunt (foster mother) be the person to adopt Tamara? If the mother wishes to visit Tamara so long as she is physically able, can her visitation rights be legally assured? If Tamara has not been freed for adoption by March 18, 1997, what sort of petition must be filed?

4.   Malcolm is a 10-year-old with many emotional and behavioral problems. He is truant from school, he shoplifts, and his mother suspects he is using drugs and alcohol. His mother knows she cannot control him and wants him placed in a facility where he can receive treatment and supervision. What sort of document will she be asked to sign to put Malcolm in the custody of the Commissioner of Social Services? What legal proceedings must be initiated soon after this document is signed, and when? What other steps will Malcolm's mother and the foster care agency be required to take after he comes into foster care?

5.   If Malcolm is still in care 16 months after his placement, what type of petition must the agency file? What are the issues before the court in such a proceeding?

CHAPTER ASSIGNMENT

Find the office of the County Clerk in the county where your school is located.

Make arrangements through your Family Law instructor to visit a Family Court. Prepare a written report of what you saw and learned there. Remember to preserve the confidentiality of the litigants. Your professor may ask you to share your observations with the class.

13 ADOPTION

"Our adoption statute embodies the fundamental social concept that the relationship of parent and child may be established by operation of law.... Despite the absence of any blood ties, in the eyes of the law an adopted child becomes 'the natural child of the adoptive parent' with all the attendant personal and proprietary incidents to that relationship." *Matter of Robert Paul P.*, 63 N.Y.2d 233, 481 N.Y.S.2d 652 (1984).

Although the adoption of a child is generally a happy event, family law practitioners must be mindful that adoption involves a delicate balancing of the rights of the biological parents, the adoptive parents and the adoptive child. For every set of joyful adoptive parents, there are birth parents who have lost a child, and every adoptive child has lost not only its birth parents, but the opportunity to be adopted by parents other than those whom the court is approving as the adoptive parents. Since courts are understandably reluctant to disturb an adoption once it has been finalized, the steps preliminary to the finalization must be completed with the utmost care and attention to detail. Adoptive parents are usually eager to complete the process quickly so they can feel truly secure in their relationship with the adoptive child, but while unnecessary delay should always be avoided, it is equally important to take enough time to be precise and accurate and to be in full compliance with the law. The recent, highly-publicized cases of "Baby Jessica" (*DeBoer v. Schmidt [In re Baby Girl Clausen]*, 199 Mich. App. 10, 501 N.W.2d 193 [Mich. Sup. Ct.]) and "Baby Richard," (*Adoption Petition of Doe [Kirchner]*, 638 N.E. 2d 181 [Ill. Sup. Ct. 1994]), in which adoptive children were returned to their birth parents years after they were placed with the prospective adoptive parents, serve as a painful reminder that nothing is more heartbreaking than an adoption which is challenged after the adoptive parents and adoptive child have bonded with each other.

BASICS BOX

Subject matter jurisdiction: Family Court and Surrogate's Court have concurrent original jurisdiction.

Venue: County of residence of adoptive parent(s). If adoptive parents are not New York residents, then county where adoptive child resides (Private-Placement) or county where authorized agency has its principal office (Agency adoptions).

Standing: An adult unmarried person, an adult husband and wife together, and an adult married person living separate and apart from spouse pursuant to a decree or judgment of separation or a written separation agreement or an adult married person who has been living separate and apart from spouse for at least three years prior to commencing the adoption proceeding may adopt. (Child not deemed child or step-child of non-adopting spouse.)

Grounds: Petitioner(s) must satisfy the court that the child is legally free for adoption and that the adoption will promote the child's best interests.

Statute of Limitations: None. Adults can be adopted with their own consent.

Applicable statutes: Domestic Relations Law article VII; Family Court Act § 641; Surrogate's Court Procedure Act § 2402; N.Y. Constitution, article 6 § 13 (subd. b).

Adoption law in New York is particularly complicated, since New York is a jurisdiction which permits both agency and non-agency adoptions, called in the Domestic Relations Law **"private-placement" adoptions.** Some adoptive parents prefer the greater anonymity and skilled matching of parents and child that adoption from an authorized adoption agency offers, while others find the speed and personal involvement of an independent adoption more to their liking. Some adoptive parents pursue both avenues and settle on whichever route results soonest in the placement of an adoptive child into their custody. Both forms of adoption are completely legal in New York, but there are special requirements for each. In this chapter issues common to both types of adoption will be discussed first. The special requirements of each type of adoption are then considered separately.

ETHICAL CONSIDERATIONS

PAYMENTS TO BIRTH PARENTS

Adoption proceedings pose several special ethical considerations. First, to avoid "baby selling," the legislature has imposed restrictions on the money adoptive parents can pay in connection with an adoption. Adoptive parents are allowed to pay to the birth parents "fees, compensation and other remunerations" incidental to the birth or care of the adoptive child or to the pregnancy or care of the birth mother or the placement or adoption of the child or which are incurred in arranging for the placement or for the adoption of the child. DRL § 115(8). This may include reimbursing the birth parents for any legal fees they paid in connection with the adoption. Adoptive parents may not pay the birth parents any amount over their actual expenses, however. In other words, they are not permitted to buy the baby. Since there are many more parents seeking adoptive children than there are children available for adoption, the temptation always exists to inflate the "expenses" to induce the birth parents to give the baby to the adoptive parents who make the most generous offer. This is illegal because the child's best interests then become subordinate to financial considerations. To control this practice, adoptive parents are required to file an affidavit of financial disclosure (Form 13-1) stating exactly what moneys have been paid.

📁 FORM 13-1

FAMILY COURT OF THE STATE OF NEW YORK
COUNTY OF MONROE

....

In the Matter of the Adoption of
A Child Whose First Name Is

MARIA

Docket No. A-9876/96

AFFIDAVIT OF FINANCIAL
DISCLOSURE -- PARENTS
(Private-Placement)

....

STATE OF NEW YORK	)
	ss.:
COUNTY OF MONROE	)

George Bodden and Luisa Bodden being duly sworn, depose and say:

That deponents reside at 123 Maple Lane, Syracuse, New York and are the petitioning adoptive parents of the above-named adoptive child; and

That deponents have paid or given or caused to be paid or given or undertaken to pay or give the following expenses, contributions, compensation or thing of value, either directly or indirectly, to any person, agency, association, corporation, institution, society or organization, in connection with the placing out of said adoptive child with deponents or with the adoption of said adoptive child by deponents:

Medical
Tender Care Hospital..$1,394.85
Dr. James Johnson, pediatrician.........................$1,132.00

📁 **FORM 13-1 continued**

Personal

Maternity clothes	$ 40.00
Rent for 6 months at $200.00/month	$1,200.00
Harry Hunter, attorney for biological mother	$1,741.80
Attorney for adoptive parents -- fee	$3,500.00

Attorney for adoptive parents -- expenses

facsimile	$ 48.00
Federal Express	$ 95.25
original birth certificate	$ 18.00
photocopies	$ 82.65
postage	$ 33.57
telephone	$ 48.16
medical records	$ 109.06

That deponents have requested, received or accepted either directly or indirectly, the following compensation or thing of value from any person, agency, association, corporation, institution, society or other organization in connection with the placing out of said adoptive child with deponents or with the adoption of said child by deponents:

None.

_____
George Bodden,
Adoptive Father

_____
Luisa Bodden,
Adoptive Mother

Sworn to before me this
    day of   , 199

JUDGE OF THE FAMILY COURT
COUNTY OF MONROE

DUAL REPRESENTATION PROHIBITED

Because adoptions are not adversarial proceedings in the traditional sense, an ethical issue arises concerning the legal representation of the adoptive parents and the birth parents. Although it may seem that the adoptive parents and the birth parents share the same goal of having the child successfully adopted, a potential conflict exists between them, and if the birth parents should decide at any point to challenge the adoption, the conflict would become actual. For this reason, one attorney may not represent both an adoptive parent and a birth parent. Even though a birth parent's attorney's fee may be reimbursed by the adoptive parents, the birth parent's attorney is under an obligation only to the birth parent, regardless of who will ultimately pay the fee. Violation of this rule may result in disbarment or suspension from the practice of law, as Case 13-1 illustrates.

 **CASE 13-1**

Matter of Stanley B. Michelman, an attorney and counselor-at-law.

202 A.D.2d 87, 616 N.Y.S.2d 409 (2 Dept. 1994)

Before Mangano, P.J., and Thompson, Sullivan, Lawrence and J. O'Brien, JJ.

Disciplinary proceeding instituted by the Grievance Committee for the Ninth Judicial District....

Per Curiam -- In this proceeding, the respondent was charged with six allegations of professional misconduct....

Charge One of the petition alleged that the respondent engaged in an impermissible conflict of interest by representing and/or advising both adoptive parents and the biological mother in a private placement adoption in violation of Code of Professional Responsibility, DR 5-105. In or about 1987, a biological mother was referred to the respondent by a medical doctor and the respondent assisted the biological mother in selecting adoptive parents who were his clients. The respondent represented the adoptive parents in the private placement adoption in the Westchester County Surrogate's Court. The respondent discussed the nature and consequences of adoption with the biological mother, obtained background information from her, and prepared various documents to forward to the biological mother concerning her health, family history, and the history of the birth father. The respondent also prepared and forwarded to the biological mother documents she would be required to execute after the birth of her child. Upon the birth of the child, the respondent prepared the surrender papers for execution by the biological mother, obtained medical information and coordinated arrangements to obtain custody....

Charge Three alleged that the respondent engaged in an impermissible conflict of interest by representing and/or advising both the adoptive parents and the biological mother in a private placement adoption in violation of Code of Professional Responsibility, DR 5-105.

📖 CASE 13-1 continued

In or about December 1989, the biological mother in a private placement adoption, which was later finalized in the Nassau County Family Court, was referred to the respondent by a medical doctor. The respondent met with the biological mother on several occasions and reviewed the backgrounds of several prospective adoptive parents with her. According to testimony of the biological mother and her father, the respondent expressly stated that he would represent the biological mother in this adoption. The respondent arranged for telephone communications between the biological mother and the adoptive parents, who were his clients.

The respondent advised the biological mother regarding the nature and consequences of adoption, answered her questions, advised her regarding the potential availability of "open adoptions," and discussed with her various procedures that would occur depending upon whether she decided to give birth in New York or New Jersey. The respondent arranged for the biological mother's room and board. Disbursements on her behalf were made through the respondent's escrow account.

Upon learning that the biological mother had been admitted to a medical facility in New Jersey where she gave birth, the respondent coordinated arrangements for the adoptive parents to obtain physical custody of the child. On or about February 23, 1990, the day after the child's birth, the biological mother went to the respondent's office and signed an extra-judicial consent and other documents prepared by the respondent for her signature. The respondent answered any questions the biological mother and/or her parents had regarding these documents. According to the testimony of the biological mother and her father, the respondent stated for the first time that he was representing the adoptive parents and was not representing the biological mother.

***

Upon review of the evidence adduced, we conclude that the Special Referee properly sustained all six charges....

In determining an appropriate measure of discipline to impose, the respondent emphasizes that the underlying adoptions were completed successfully in that both adoptive parents and biological mothers were satisfied with the outcomes.... The respondent is nevertheless guilty of serious professional misconduct. He has been the subject of three Letters of Admonition from the petitioner and has received several other warnings as well.

***

Under the circumstances, the respondent is suspended from the practice of law for three years.

All concur.

BABY BROKERS

Only an **authorized child care agency** can place a child for adoption in New York. Although private-placement adoptions are legal, the birth parents and adoptive parents must select each other by themselves without an intermediary. SSL § 374(2). Moreover, it is illegal for anyone other than an authorized child care agency to accept or to pay a fee, directly or indirectly, in connection with the placement or adoption of a child who is born in New York or brought into New York for the purposes of adoption. Actual legal fees and reimbursement of the reasonable and necessary expenses incurred in connection with the birth of the child are excepted. SSL § 374(6). Any person who violates this law is guilty of a misdemeanor for the first offense and a felony for a subsequent offense. SSL § 389(2).

CONFIDENTIALITY

In addition to the general confidentiality considerations discussed in Chapter 2, adoption proceedings are cloaked in particular secrecy. Domestic Relations Law § 114(2) states:

> No person, including the attorney for the adoptive parents shall disclose the surname of the child directly or indirectly to the adoptive parents except upon order of the court. No person shall be allowed access to such sealed records and order and any index thereof except upon an order of a judge or surrogate of the court in which the order was made or of a justice of the supreme court. No order for disclosure or access and inspection shall be granted except on good cause shown and on due notice to the adoptive parents and to such additional persons as the court may direct.

In agency adoptions, neither the papers filed in the adoption proceeding nor any document which is required to be signed by the adoptive parents should contain the surname of the child. DRL § 112(4).

These provisions were enacted at a time when being born out-of-wedlock carried a much greater stigma than it does now, and, since most adoptive children were born out-of-wedlock, the intent was to spare both the child and the birth mother that shame. Adoptive parents also often did not want to disclose that the child was adopted, because infertility also carried a certain stigma. Today, the climate of public opinion is more sympathetic, and most adoptive parents tell the child that he or she is adopted. In private-placement adoptions the adoptive parents and birth parents often meet and sometimes form relationships, which they may plan to continue after the adoption is finalized. Nevertheless, the statute remains in effect to permit the two sets of parents to make that decision for themselves and to protect the privacy of any party who may choose to maintain it.

Adults who were adopted as children sometimes wonder about their birth parents and the circumstances surrounding their adoption, and some conduct extensive searches for this information. Because adoption records remain sealed permanently, and New York courts have been reluctant to find "good cause" to unseal them, some adult adoptees feel that they are being deprived of information about themselves long after the need for confidentiality has abated. In 1994, legislation was passed which makes it easier for adoptees to have their records opened when they need information for medical purposes. Under the new statute, a certification from a physician licensed in the state of New York that the information is needed to address a serious physical or mental illness constitutes prima facie evidence of good cause to unseal the records. DRL § 114(4).

To provide more non-identifying information about the birth parents to adoptive parents in agency adoptions, the statute was amended in 1989 to require that the agency provide to petitioners a schedule setting forth the child's medical history, heritage of the parents -- including nationality, ethnic background and race -- education of the parents at the time of the birth of the adoptive child, general physical appearance of the parents at the time of the birth of the child -- including height, weight, color of hair, eyes and skin -- occupation of the parents at the time of the birth of the child, health and medical history of the parents at the time of the birth of the child, including all available information concerning conditions believed to be hereditary, information about any drugs or medication taken during the pregnancy by the child's mother, any other information which may be a factor in influencing the child's health, and information about the birth parents' talents, hobbies and special interests. DRL § 114(1).

The New York State Department of Health also maintains an **adoption information registry** [Public Health Law § 4138-c], through which an adoptee over the age of 21 years, a biological parent whose consent to the adoption was required, or an adoptive parent may apply to obtain non-identifying information about the birth parents. If the adoptee, the birth parents whose consent was required and the adoptive parents have all registered, the Department may release identifying information. Authorized child care agencies may also establish mutual consent voluntary adoption registries, which function in a similar fashion. Public Health Law § 4138-d. Improper disclosure of registry information, however, constitutes a class A misdemeanor.

WHO MAY ADOPT

Any unmarried adult may adopt a child alone, and any married couple may adopt together. Step-parents may adopt their step-children, although it is important to remember that the requirements for obtaining the consent of the biological father are the same in step-parent adoptions as they are in any other adoption. In addition, to facilitate adoption by foster parents, the legislature in 1984 added the provision that a married adult who is legally separated by a written separation agreement or decree of separation may adopt. In 1991 the statute was further amended to permit adoption by an adult who has been living separate and apart from his or her spouse for at least three years. When a separated adult adopts, the non-adopting spouse does not become the parent or step-parent of the child and acquires no rights and incurs no obligations towards the child. DRL § 110.

Foster parents who have cared for a child continuously for 12 months may apply to have the foster care placement converted into an adoptive placement, and if the child is eligible for adoption, the agency must give first consideration and preference to their application over all other applications for adoptive placement. The final determination of the propriety of the adoption, however, is within the discretion of the court. SSL § 383(3).

Much controversy has of late surrounded the question whether an unmarried couple may adopt a child together. New York recently became the third state in the union whose highest court has allowed an unmarried petitioner to adopt the biological child of a life partner. *Matter of Dana,* 86 N.Y.2d 651, 636 N.Y.S.2d 716 (1995). The petitioner was the partner of the biological mother in a lesbian relationship. The mother had conceived the child as a result of artificial insemination with the sperm of an anonymous donor. The Appellate Division, Second Department, had denied the adoption, holding that this result was required by the plain meaning of the Domestic Relations Law. Their decision stated that Petitioner could not adopt as a single parent, because that would have required termination of the natural mother's rights. Neither could she adopt as a step-parent, because the couple was not, and could not be, married. The Appellate Division, Fourth Department, had come to the same conclusion by similar reasoning in a case concerning a heterosexual couple, *Matter of Jacob,* where the mother's domestic partner sought to adopt her two children from a previous relationship without terminating the mother's rights, and that decision was also reversed by the Court of Appeals in the same decision.

The Court of Appeals was split four to three in *Matter of Jacob* and *Matter of Dana.* Chief Judge Judith Kaye, writing for the majority, recognized that since adoption did not exist at common law and is wholly a creature of statute, the statute must be strictly construed. The opinion then continued, "What is to be construed strictly and applied rigorously in this sensitive area of the law, however, is legislative purpose as well as legislative language. Thus, the adoption statute must be applied in harmony with the humanitarian principle that adoption is a means of securing the best possible home for a child." The court found that adoption would serve the children's best interest in these cases in practical ways, by guaranteeing advantages such as social security and life insurance benefits, the right to sue for the wrongful death of a parent, the right to inherit under rules of intestacy, and eligibility for coverage under both parents' health insurance policies, and by making both adults legally responsible for the child's support. The court found even more important the emotional security for the child of knowing that in the event of the death or disability of the biological parent, the other parent would have presumptive custody and that the child's relationship with both adults would continue in the event that the adults should separate.

CONSENTS TO ADOPTION

WHOSE CONSENT IS REQUIRED

The consent of the birth mother is required for the adoption of a child, whether the child is born in or out of wedlock. The consent of an in-wedlock father is also always required. Because of the common-law presumption of legitimacy, the consent of a man to whom the mother was married at the time of the conception or birth of the child is required, even though he is not the biological father, unless the presumption has been rebutted in some earlier judicial proceeding. The presumption of legitimacy establishes that any child conceived or born during the course of a marriage is the child of the mother's husband. Although the presumption is rebuttable, it is one of the strongest presumptions existing in law, and courts will not override it based solely on the mother's statement that a man other than the husband is the father. The consent of the adoptive child is also required if the child is over the age of 14 years, unless the judge or Surrogate before whom the adoption is pending dispenses with the child's consent.

Of course, the consent of parents is not required if their parental rights have previously been terminated and custody and guardianship transferred to an authorized child care agency. Where an agency has obtained custody and guardianship prior to the commencement of the adoption proceeding, the agency consents to the adoption of the child in its custody. In a private-placement adoption, the court may dispense with a parent's consent if the parent is mentally ill or mentally retarded as defined in SSL § 384-b(6), and is presently and for the foreseeable future unable to provide proper care for the child. Consent to a private-placement adoption may also not be required of a parent who "evinces an intent to forego his or her parental or custodial rights and obligations as manifested by his or her failure for a period of six months to visit the child and communicate with the child or person having legal custody of the child, although able to do so." DRL § 111(2)(a). This provision is very similar, but not identical, to the abandonment grounds, discussed in Chapter 12, under which an authorized agency may bring termination of parental rights proceedings pursuant to SSL § 384-b. Note that the SSL definition of abandonment says "although not prevented or discouraged from doing so by the agency," whereas the DRL language is "although able to do so." Moreover, an agency is limited to proving abandonment for the six- month period immediately prior to the date on which the petition to terminate parental rights is filed [SSL § 384-b(4)(b)], while DRL § 111 contains no such limitation.

EQUITABLE ADOPTION

The agreement of the adoptive parents to the adoption is usually readily given. In rare cases, however, a prospective adoptive parent, after filing a petition to adopt, either dies or withdraws his or her agreement before the adoption is finalized. In such a situation, a court may, in the exercise of its equity powers, consider the child to be the adopted child of the person who agreed to adopt. This doctrine of **equitable adoption**, also called **adoption by estoppel**, is used only in the most exceptional cases in New York. *Matter of C. and O.*, 84 N.Y. 2d 91, 615 N.Y.S.2d 318 (1994), was a case in which in 1988 a couple had obtained custody of two children for adoption, one of whom had been brought into this country from the Philippines specifically for the purpose. The couple had filed petitions to adopt shortly thereafter. Before the adoptions were finalized, however, the couple became embroiled in what the court described as "a bitter public divorce action," and the prospective adoptive father refused to appear in court for the finalization of the adoption. Although the court recognized that the lives of the children had been irreversibly transformed and that they were being used as pawns in the divorce action, the court declined to "impose" the adoption. The opinion stated that the case did not present the "exceptional circumstances" which would justify such a drastic remedy. The court clearly contemplated that after the divorce the wife would be able to adopt as a single parent, however, and further indicated that the pre-adoptive father who reneged might be compelled to contribute towards the children's support.

CONSENT OF OUT-OF-WEDLOCK FATHER

No aspect of family law has evolved more dramatically in the past generation than the legal rights of out-of-wedlock fathers of prospective adoptive children. Prior to 1979, an out-of-wedlock father's consent to adoption was not required in any circumstance. The landmark case of *Caban v. Mohammed* (Case 13-2), generated a ferment in the law which continues to this day.

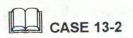 **CASE 13-2**

CABAN v. MOHAMMED
441 U.S. 388, 99 S.Ct. 1760 (1979)

Mr. Justice POWELL delivered the opinion of the Court.
***

Abdiel Caban and appellee Maria Mohammed lived together in New York City from September 1968 until the end of 1973. During this time Caban and Mohammed represented themselves as being husband and wife, although they never legally married. Indeed, until 1974 Caban was married to another woman, from whom he was separated. While living with the appellant, Mohammed gave birth to two children.... Abdiel Caban was identified as the father on each child's birth certificate, and lived with the children as their father until the end of 1973. Together with Mohammed, he contributed to the support of the family.

In December 1973, Mohammed took the two children and left the appellant to take up residence with appellee Kazim Mohammed,

📖 **CASE 13-2 continued**

whom she married on January 30, 1974.... Caban was able to see the children each week when they came to visit their grandmother.

***

In January 1976, appellees filed a petition under § 110 of the New York Domestic Relations Law to adopt David and Denise.

***

The Surrogate granted the Mohammeds' petition to adopt the children, thereby cutting off all of appellant's parental rights and obligations.

***

The New York Supreme Court, Appellate Division affirmed.... The New York Court of Appeals dismissed the appeal in a memorandum decision based on *In re Malpica-Orsini, supra.*

***

Gender-based distinctions "must serve important governmental objectives and must be substantially related to achievement of those objectives" in order to withstand judicial scrutiny under the Equal Protection Clause.... The question before us, therefore, is whether the distinction in [DRL] § 111 between unmarried mothers and unmarried fathers bears a substantial relation to some important state interest. Appellees assert that the distinction is justified by a fundamental difference between maternal and paternal relations -- that "a natural mother, absent special circumstances, bears a closer relationship with her child...than a father does."

Contrary to appellee's argument and to the apparent presumption underlying § 111, maternal and paternal roles are not invariably different in importance. Even if unwed mothers as a class were closer than unwed fathers to their newborn infants, this generalization concerning parent-child relations would become less acceptable as the age of the child increased. The present case demonstrates that an unwed father may have a relationship with his children fully comparable to that of the mother. Appellant Caban, appellee Maria Mohammed, and their two children lived together as a natural family for several years. As members of this family, both mother and father participated in the care and support of their children. There is no reason to believe that the Caban children -- aged 4 and 6 at the time of the adoption proceedings -- had a relationship with their mother unrivaled by the affection and concern of their father. We reject, therefore, the claim that the broad, gender-based distinction of § 111 is required by any universal difference between maternal and paternal relations at every phase of a child's development. As an alternative justification for § 111, appellees argue that the distinction between unwed fathers and unwed mothers is substantially related to the State's interest in promoting the adoption of illegitimate children. Although the legislative history of § 111 is sparse,...the New York Court of Appeals identified as the legislature's purpose in enacting § 111 the furthering of the interests of illegitimate children, for whom

CASE 13-2 continued

adoption often is the best course.... The court reasoned that people wishing to adopt a child born out of wedlock would be discouraged if the natural father could prevent the adoption by the mere withholding of his consent....

The State's interest in providing for the well-being of illegitimate children is an important one. We do not question that the best interests of such children often may require their adoption into new families who will give them the stability of a normal, two-parent home. Moreover, adoption will remove the stigma under which illegitimate children suffer. But the unquestioned right of the State to further these desirable ends by legislation is not in itself sufficient to justify the gender-based distinction of § 111....

The New York Court of Appeals...suggested that the requiring of unmarried fathers' consent for adoption would pose a strong impediment for adoption because often it is impossible to locate unwed fathers when adoption proceedings are brought, whereas mothers are more likely to remain with their children. Even if the special difficulties attendant upon locating and identifying unwed fathers at birth would justify a legislative distinction between mothers and fathers of newborns, these difficulties need not persist past infancy.... But in cases such as this, where the father has established a substantial relationship with the child and has admitted his paternity, a State should have no difficulty in identifying the father even of children born out of wedlock....

In sum, we believe that § 111 is another example of "overbroad generalizations" in gender-based classifications.... The effect of New York's classification is to discriminate against unwed fathers even when their identity is known and they have manifested a significant paternal interest in the child.... Section 111 both excludes some loving fathers from full participation in the decision whether their children will be adopted and, at the same time, enables some alienated mothers arbitrarily to cut off the paternal rights of fathers. We conclude that this undifferentiated distinction between unwed mothers and unwed fathers, applicable in all circumstances where adoption of a child of theirs is at issue, does not bear a substantial relationship to the State's asserted interests.

The judgment of the New York Court of Appeals is
Reversed.

Mr. Justice Stewart filed a dissenting opinion.
Mr. Justice Stevens filed a dissenting opinion in which Mr. Chief Justice Burger and Mr. Justice Rehnquist joined.

Following *Caban*, DRL § 111 was amended to specify what conduct on the part of out-of-wedlock fathers would constitute a manifestation of a "significant paternal interest" so as to require their consent to the adoption of their children.

DRL § 111(2)(e) specifies that the consent is *not required* of a parent who has executed an instrument denying paternity of the child or consenting to the other parent's surrender of the child or consent to the child's adoption. Concerning which fathers' consents *are required*, the legislators, taking their cue from the distinction in *Caban* between infants and older children, specified different conduct by the fathers of children placed for adoption over the age of six months than for those placed under the age of six months. Under DRL § 111(d), the consent of a father of a child placed out with adoptive parents *more than six months after birth* is required only if the father has maintained substantial and continuous or repeated contact with the child as manifested by payment of fair and reasonable support and either visiting the child at least monthly when able to do so or, if physically or financially unable to visit, by communicating regularly with the child or with the person or agency having the care or custody of the child. A father who openly lived with the child for a period of six months within the year immediately preceding the placement of the child for adoption and who openly held himself out to be the father is deemed to have maintained substantial and continuous contact with the child.

The consent of a father whose child was placed for adoption at *less than six months of age* was required only if he had lived with the child's mother for a continuous period of six months immediately preceding the placement of the child for adoption and openly held himself out as the father and paid a fair and reasonable amount in connection with the mother's pregnancy or for the birth of the child. DRL § 111(e). This subsection of the Domestic Relations Law was held unconstitutional in *Matter of Raquel Marie X.*, 76 N.Y.2d 387, 559 N.Y.S.2d 855, *cert. denied* 498 U.S. 984, 111 S.Ct. 517 (1990). Writing for a unanimous court, Judge Judith Kaye stated that "a father who has promptly taken every available avenue to demonstrate that he is willing and able to enter into the fullest possible relationship with his under-six-month-old child should have an equally fully protected interest in preventing termination of the relationship by strangers, even if he has not as yet actually been able to form that relationship." The court found that the "living together" requirement improperly focused on the relationship between the father and the mother, rather than on the relationship, or desire to form a relationship, between the father and the child.

The legislature has not yet responded to *Raquel Marie X.* by reformulating the criteria for requirement of consent by an out-of-wedlock father of an infant placed for adoption under the age of six months. In the interim, the courts are following the instruction of the decision to decide the issue on a case by case basis, based upon evidence showing whether a father has demonstrated "a willingness himself to assume full custody of the child -- not merely to block adoption by others." In *Matter of Raymond "AA" v. Jane Doe et al.*, 217 A.D.2d 757, 629 N.Y.S.2d 321 (3 Dept. 1995), for example, a family court judge's determination to dispense with the father's consent was affirmed where the father had lived with the mother during the pregnancy and had openly asserted his paternity and had petitioned for custody shortly after the birth of the child. While living with the mother, however, the father had abused alcohol, marijuana, crack cocaine, and LSD, under the influence of which he became so violent and physically abusive to the mother that she left their residence before the birth of the child. During the time the father lived with the mother-to-be, he used all of his own public assistance and part of her allotment to buy alcohol and drugs, and did not purchase anything for the mother or the baby except a $10 stroller, nor did he discuss with the mother any future plans for the baby other than where it would sleep.

DISCUSSION TOPIC

What criteria for the consent of a father of a child placed for adoption under the age of six months should be included when the Domestic Relations Law is amended? What conduct can be expected of a father when the mother places the child for adoption at birth? Should the mother of the child be required to reveal the identity of the father of the child if she knows it?

"Notice Only" Fathers

In addition to the out-of-wedlock fathers whose consent to adoption is required, the legislature also created a category of fathers who are entitled to receive notice of the adoption proceeding. DRL § 111-a. The "notice only" category is considerably broader than the "consent" category and includes:

- any person adjudicated by a New York court to be the father;

- any person adjudicated the father by a court of another state or territory of the United States when a certified copy of the order has been filed with the Putative Father Registry;

- any person who has timely filed an unrevoked notice of intent to claim paternity of the child with the Putative Father Registry;

- any person who is recorded on the child's birth certificate as father;

- any person who is openly living with the child and the child's mother at the time the proceeding is initiated;

- any person who has been identified as the child's father by the mother in a written, sworn statement;

- any person who was married to the child's mother within six months subsequent to the birth of the child and prior to the execution of a surrender for adoption or the initiation of a proceeding to terminate parental rights;

- any person who has filed with the Putative Father Registry an instrument acknowledging paternity of the child.

The Putative Father Registry, maintained by the New York State Department of Social Services at 10 North Pearl St., Albany, New York, 12243 is discussed in Chapter 9. Although DRL § 111-a specifies that notice to these fathers is for the sole purpose of enabling such a father to present evidence to the court relevant to the best interest of the child, it is likely that any father whose name appears on the Putative Father Registry clearance form (Form 13-2), or who otherwise is entitled to notice pursuant to DRL § 111-a, and whose child was placed for adoption under the age of six months would also be allowed to present evidence that he was a person whose consent to adoption is required pursuant to the decision in *Raquel Marie X.*

FORM 13-2

DSS-2725 (REV. 5/77)

**REQUEST/RESPONSE
FOR NAME AND/OR ADDRESS
OF FATHER OF CHILD
BORN OUT-OF-WEDLOCK**
(Print or Type All Information)

FORWARD ORIGINAL
AND 1 COPY TO:
NYS DSS
Putative Father Registry

REQUEST

		REQUEST DATE
CHILD'S NAME	CHILD'S BIRTHDATE	REQUESTING AGENCY (Name and Address)
FATHER'S NAME		
MOTHER'S NAME	AGENCY OFFICIAL	AGENCY TEL. NO

RESPONSE

		RESPONSE DATE
PUTATIVE FATHER'S NAME	ADDRESS	DATE REGISTERED
DATE CHANGE OF ADDRESS REGISTERED	STAFF REGISTRAR - PUTATIVE FATHER REGISTRY	REGISTRY TEL. NO.

COMMENTS:

INDIAN CHILDREN

When the child to be adopted is a Native American, called in the Federal law an **Indian child**, New York law is preempted by the Federal Indian Child Welfare Act of 1978 (25 USC § 1901 *et seq*.). The ICWA defines a child as Indian if the child is an unmarried person under the age of 18 years who is a member of an Indian tribe or is eligible for membership in an Indian tribe and is the biological child of a member of an Indian tribe. If a child to be adopted qualifies as an Indian child, notification of the proposed adoption is given to the tribe through the Bureau of Indian Affairs, and the tribe then informs the court whether it wishes to assume jurisdiction under tribal law. Unless the tribe declines jurisdiction, the state court is divested of jurisdiction.

FORM OF CONSENT

In an agency adoption, the parental rights of living biological parents will have been terminated and the custody and guardianship of the child committed to the authorized agency prior to the commencement of the adoption proceeding, either by surrender or by judicial termination of parental rights as discussed in Chapter 12. The agency then consents to the adoption in the adoption proceeding itself.

In a private-placement adoption, a biological parent may consent before any New York judge or Surrogate having jurisdiction over adoptions or before a court of another state, provided that the court in the other state is a **court of record** which has jurisdiction over adoption proceedings. Where the consent is taken in another state, a transcript of that proceeding is filed as part of the adoption proceeding. DRL § 115-b. A **judicial consent** becomes **irrevocable** immediately upon execution and acknowledgment. When a birth parent appears before a court to consent to adoption, the judge advises the parent of the right to be represented by independent counsel of his or her own choosing and of the right to supportive counseling. The judge then discusses adoption with the parent to be sure that the parent understands the consequences of the consent and that the parent has not been coerced or bribed in any fashion.

A birth parent of a child in a private-placement adoption may also legally execute the consent document out of court, unless the parent is in foster care, in which case only a judicial consent may be taken. An **extrajudicial consent** is revocable within 45 days of its execution upon written notice to the court in which the adoption proceeding has been or is to be commenced. After that time no action for revocation may be commenced. The consent document must so state in 18 point type and must contain the name and address of the court in which the adoption proceeding has been or will be commenced. DRL § 115-b(4). A consent to adoption must be given freely without any fraud or duress. Although extrajudicial consents are legal, and the legislature has voted down several bills which would have abolished them, they are not preferred because they are subject to challenge on grounds of fraud. Some judges and Surrogates are so uncomfortable with extrajudicial consents that they exercise their discretion to require the consenting parent to appear before them to ratify the consent. Although the Domestic Relations Law is silent concerning when an adoption consent may be executed, the Appellate Division, Third Department, has held that a consent executed before the birth of the child is voidable. *People ex rel. Anonymous v. Anonymous*, 139 A.D.2d 189, 530 N.Y.S.2d 613 (3 Dept. 1988).

INTERSTATE COMPACT APPROVAL

When New York residents plan to bring a child for the purposes of adoption into New York from another state which participates in the Interstate Compact on the Placement of Children, they must meet the requirements of this reciprocal legislation. SSL § 374-a, Art. III. With the exception of Nevada, every state in the union and the District of Columbia and the Virgin Islands all have complementary Interstate Compact legislation. An Interstate Compact Placement Request is submitted to the compact administrator in the state where the child resides, called under the compact the "sending state." If the sending state's administrator is satisfied that the procedures of that state have been complied with, the request is then forwarded to the New York compact administrator for permission to bring the child into New York, called the "receiving state." A home study of the adoptive parents, a Child Abuse Register Clearance, and a certified copy of the certification order must accompany the request.

BEST INTERESTS OF THE CHILD

To grant an order of adoption, the judge or Surrogate must be satisfied that the adoption will promote the best interests of the adoptive child. There are no hard and fast rules concerning the age, living conditions or financial situation of the adoptive parents. All sorts of people adopt, including senior citizens and recipients of public assistance. When an adoptive child is being well cared for and the child and the adoptive parent have bonded to each other at the time adverse information about the background of the adoptive parent comes to light, the courts are reluctant to disapprove the adoption unless the unfavorable information directly implicates the adoptive parent's ability to provide a safe home environment for the adoptive child. In *Matter of Baby Girl W.*, 151 A.D.2d 968, 542 N.Y.S.2d 415 (A.D. 4 Dept. 1989), for example, the Appellate Division, Fourth Department, reversed an Oneida County Surrogate who had refused to approve the adoption by adoptive parents who had misrepresented their educational backgrounds, employment histories, and financial condition and who had equivocated when asked to explain discrepancies during the court hearing.

Besides the basic information about the adoptive parents contained in the petition, additional background about the adoptive parents is presented to the court in the form of an **investigation report.** In an agency adoption, the investigation report is prepared by the agency caseworker, whereas in a private-placement adoption it is prepared by a "disinterested person" designated by the court. DRL § 116(3). The judge may designate the court's probation service or an authorized agency or a social worker the court deems qualified. The investigation report describes the relationship of each adoptive parent with their own family of origin and recounts the adoptive parents' educational and employment histories as well as their income. The marital relationship of the adoptive parents and their attitudes towards adoption are discussed. Of course, the quality of care they are providing the adoptive child and the bonding between the adoptive parents and the child are covered in detail. A clearance on each adoptive parent is obtained from the State Central Register of Child Abuse and Maltreatment maintained by the State Department of Social Services in Albany, and each adoptive parent must submit a current medical report detailing their current state of health. If the court is not satisfied with the investigation report, the judge or Surrogate may order a supplemental report or may order that the entire investigation be redone by another "disinterested person."

The adoptive parents must appear before the court at the finalization hearing, along with the adoptive child, unless the judge or Surrogate dispenses with the child's appearance. Testimony is rarely taken at the finalization hearing. The court usually will have satisfied itself in advance of the propriety of the adoption, although occasionally the court may ask the social worker or the adoptive parents questions to clarify some minor issue. Before the finalization is scheduled, the submitted papers are reviewed by several persons -- including the adoption clerk, the judge's court attorney or law assistant, and the judge or Surrogate. If the documents are incomplete or inconsistent, if, for example, the child's birth date is stated one way in the petition and another way in the agreement of adoption, the incorrect document will have to be withdrawn and resubmitted. Careful drafting and proofreading are, therefore, crucial to the expeditious scheduling of the finalization. Agency adoptions must be calendared for finalization within 60 days of the filing of the petition and supporting documents, but if the submissions are incomplete, the court will adjourn the matter. 22 NYCRR 205.59 At the finalization hearing the adoptive parents swear, or re-swear, to the truth of all information contained in the documents which have been submitted, and the judge or Surrogate signs the order of adoption (Form 13-3). The court then sends a notification of adoption to the department of health, which issues an amended birth certificate.

DISCUSSION TOPIC
What factors do you think a court should consider in determining whether a proposed adoption will promote the best interests of the adoptive child? Are they the same factors as in a custody case, or should different or additional factors be significant? Should the court consider how well the adoptive parents and the child match in physical appearance or in their talents and interests? Should the court consider whether more desirable adoptive parents might be available for the child?

📁 **FORM 13-3**

D.R.L. §§ 111, 112(b), 113, 114   Form 13-B
                                                    (Order of Adoption -
                                                      Private-Placement)
                                                           6/96

                              At a term of the Family Court
                              of the State of New York,
                              held in and for the
                              County of
                              at   , New York,
                              on   .
PRESENT:

        Hon.
              Judge
....

In the Matter of the Adoption of   (Docket) (File) No.
A Child Whose First Name Is

                                        ORDER OF ADOPTION
                                        (Private-Placement)
....

      The Petition of   (and
                          ), verified the   day of
                 , 19   , having been duly presented to this
Court, together with an agreement on the part of the petitioning adoptive
parent(s) to adopt and treat as (his)(her)(their) own lawful child
and whose birth day is   , 19   , and who was born at
                             as set forth in the petition
for adoption herein, said petition having been attached thereto and
made a part thereof a document setting forth all available information
comprising the adoptive child's medical history; together with the
affidavit(s) of

and the consent(s) of

                                                              ;

📁 FORM 13-3 continued

Form 13-B page 2

AND, although (his)(her)(their) consent(s) (is)(are) not required, the Court having given notice of the proposed adoption to

[recite facts relative thereto]

;

AND the aforesaid petitioning adoptive parents and the adoptive child and all other persons whose consents are required as aforesaid having personally appeared before this Court for examination, except

;

AND an investigation having been ordered and made and the written report of such investigation having been filed with the Court, as required by the Domestic Relations Law;

(AND the Court having (shortened)(dispensed with) the three month waiting period between its receiving the petition to adopt and this order of adoption, pursuant to section 116 of the Domestic Relations Law, because

;)

AND the adoptive child having resided with the petitioning adoptive parent(s) since   (and the judge having dispensed with the three-month period of residency with the adoptive parent(s), pursuant to section 112 and 116 of the Domestic Relations Law because

(AND the court having inquired of the statewide central register of child abuse and maltreatment and having been informed that the (child) (adoptive parent(s)) (is)(are)(not) a subject of or another person named in an indicated report filed with such register as such terms are defined in section 412 of the Social Services Law, (AND there being available to this Court findings of a court inquiry made within the preceding twelve months, of the statewide central register of child abuse and maltreatment that the (child) (adoptive parent(s)) (is)(are) (not) a subject of or another parson named in an indicated report filed with such register as such terms are defined in section 412 of the Social Services Law) and the Court having given due consideration to any information contained therein;

FORM 13-3 continued

Form 13-B page 3

AND this Court being satisfied that the best interests of the adoptive child will be promoted by the adoption and that there is no reasonable objection to the proposed change of the name of the adoptive child;

NOW, on motion of
Attorney for the petitioner(s) herein, and upon all the papers and proceedings herein, it is

ORDERED that the petition of
(and   ) for the adoption of
                                                    , a person born on
19   , at   , be and the same hereby is allowed
and approved; and it is further

ORDERED that the said adoptive child shall henceforth be regarded and treated in all respects as the lawful child of the said adoptive parent(s); and it is further

ORDERED that the name of the said adoptive child be and the same hereby is changed to   and that
the said adoptive child shall hereafter be known by that name; and it is further

(ORDERED that the Clerk prepare, certify and deliver to
                  a copy of this order; and it is further)

ORDERED that the child's medical history, heritage of the parents, which shall include nationality, ethnic background and race; education, which shall be the number of years of school completed by the parents at the time of the birth of the adoptive child; general physical appearance of the parents at the time of the birth of the adoptive child, including height, weight, color of hair, eyes, skin; occupation of the parents at the time of birth of the adoptive child; health and medical history of the parents at the time of birth of the adoptive child, including all available information setting forth conditions or diseases believed to be hereditary, any drugs or medication taken during pregnancy by the mother; and other information which may be a factor influencing the child's present or future well-being, talents, hobbies and special interests of the parents as contained in the petition shall be furnished to the adoptive parents; and it is

📂 **FORM 13-3 continued**

Form 13-B page 4

ORDERED that this order, together with all other papers pertaining to the adoption, shall be filed and kept as provided in the Domestic Relations Law and shall not be subject to access or inspections except as provided in said Law.

Dated:

ENTER

_____
(J.F.C.) (SURROGATE)

PRIVATE-PLACEMENT ADOPTIONS

Because the birth parents and adoptive parents in private-placement adoptions select each other without professional assistance and the period of placement before adoption is not monitored by an authorized child care agency, these adoptions are vulnerable to difficulties which might not arise if an agency were supervising. In 1988, in the wake of the tragic case of Lisa Steinberg, in which one child was killed and another neglected by an individual to whom the birth mothers had entrusted the children for adoption, the Domestic Relations Law was substantially revised to increase court supervision of private-placement adoptions. The amendments added two new stages to private-placement adoptions, pre-placement certification of the prospective adoptive parents [DRL § 115(1)(b)] and the issuance of a temporary order of guardianship to cover the period before the adoption is finalized [DRL § 115-c].

PRACTICE TIP:

TIMETABLE FOR PRIVATE-PLACEMENT ADOPTIONS

STEP	PERIOD
Petition for certification	
Certification investigation	Allow about 6 months
Certification of prospective adoptive parents	Valid 18 to 36 months
Interstate compact approval if required	Allow about 7 to 10 business days
Transfer of Physical Custody of Child	
Consents of birth parents	Within 10 days of transfer
Filing of petition to adopt or application for temporary guardianship	Within 10 days of transfer Valid 9 months, extendable until adoption finalized
Filing of petition to adopt	
Finalization investigation	Mandatory 3 months residency in adoptive home
All documents filed with court	except for step-parent adoptions, unless waived by court
Finalization hearing	
Order of adoption signed	

CERTIFICATION OF PROSPECTIVE ADOPTIVE PARENTS

Before taking physical custody of a child for the purposes of adoption, the prospective adoptive parents must file a petition for certification as "qualified adoptive parents." DRL § 115-d. A pre-placement investigation is then undertaken by a "disinterested person," whom the adoptive parents are allowed to choose themselves, but who must be a qualified social worker or probation officer who has no interest in the outcome of the investigation. Note that this procedure differs from the investigation at the finalization stage, where the court must designate the disinterested investigator. The investigation process also includes a clearance on the prospective adoptive parents from the Central Register of Child Abuse and Maltreatment and a fingerprint check to ascertain whether they have any criminal history in the state of New York. The certification order, if granted, is valid for 18 months, during which the prospective adoptive parents are free to search for an adoptive child. If necessary, the certification may be extended for an additional 18 months.

TEMPORARY ORDER OF GUARDIANSHIP

Once the prospective adoptive parents have taken physical custody of a child whom they intend to adopt and the birth parents have executed consents to the adoption of the child, the adoptive parents are required to file either a petition to adopt or an application for a temporary order of guardianship within ten court days. The petition to adopt in such cases is deemed to be an application for a temporary order of guardianship. The application for an order of guardianship must be accompanied by an affidavit of the adoptive parents describing any change of circumstances since their certification as qualified adoptive parents. An order of temporary guardianship is valid for nine months [SCPA § 1725(c)] and may be extended for successive three-month periods upon "good cause shown."

SURROGATE PARENTING

Surrogate parenting is an arrangement whereby a woman agrees to be artificially inseminated with the sperm of a man who is not her husband or to be impregnated with an embryo that is the product of an ovum fertilized with the sperm of a man who is not her husband, with the intent to consent to the adoption of the child so conceived by the wife of the genetic father. After much public debate, the legislature in 1992 declared surrogate parenting contracts to be against public policy. Such contracts are void and unenforceable in the state of New York. DRL § 122. A birth mother and her husband, a genetic father and his wife and the genetic mother and her husband (if different from the birth mother) who request, accept, receive, pay or give any fee in connection with any surrogate parenting contract are subject to civil penalties not to exceed $500. Anyone who induces, arranges or otherwise assists in the formation of such a contract is subject to forfeiture of the compensation and civil penalties for the first offense. Any subsequent offense constitutes a felony. DRL § 123.

AGENCY ADOPTIONS

Because of the statutory scheme to prevent birth parents and adoptive parents from obtaining identifying information about each other in agency adoptions, the paperwork in agency adoptions is divided between the petitioning adoptive parents and the agency. To assist practitioners, who are often confused about the division of responsibility, courts issue guidelines (Form 13-4) for submission of papers. As you see, in an agency adoption the agency submits a verified schedule and an affidavit of custody containing information about the birth parents which is unknown to the adoptive parents. The agency also submits its own consent form, the report of its investigation of the adoptive parents' home, and all the paperwork relevant to the subsidy approval, if the adoptive parents are to receive subsidy payments.

RELIGIOUS PREFERENCE

In the Guidelines (Form 13-4) you may have noticed that among the documents the agency files is the natural parent's religious preference form (Number 14 in the Guidelines). This document is required because the New York State Constitution [Article 6 § 32] and the Social Services Law [§ 373] and the Family Court Act [§ 116] all mandate that an agency placing a child for adoption respect the parents' religious preference "where practicable." The birth parent is allowed to specify that the child should be placed with adoptive parents of the same religion as the birth parent, of a different religion, without regard to religion, or with religion as a subordinate consideration. In *Dickens v. Ernesto*, 30 N.Y.2d 61, 330 N.Y.S.2d 346 (1972), the Court of Appeals held that these statutes did not violate the Establishment of Religion clause of the First Amendment of the United States Constitution, since religion is not the controlling factor. Rather, it is only one of many factors bearing on best interest of the child.

DISCUSSION TOPIC

Is religion actually a factor bearing on the best interest of a child? To what social concerns do the religious preference statutes relate? Do they discriminate against potential adoptive parents who practice religions that are not widely known or observed in our society? What legitimate state interest do these statutes promote? Do they facilitate adoption, or do they slow down the process?

📁   **FORM 13-4**

NEW YORK FAMILY COURT GUIDELINES FOR FILING IN AGENCY ADOPTIONS

Petitioner(s)' Attorney prepares and submits:

1. Petition
    a.   Must be signed and verified prior to filing
    b.   If over 18, adoptive child must sign
2. Agreement and Consent
    a.   Must be signed and acknowledged prior to filing

NOTE:

Adoptive child over 14 must submit separate consent pursuant to DRL §111 (1)
    a.   Must be signed and acknowledged prior to filing

3. Affidavit of Attorney [presenting natural or adoptive parent(s) to court]
4. SSL § 374(6)/ 22 NYCRR 205.53(b) (8) Affidavit
5. Adoptive Parent(s) Marital History Affidavit
    a.   List prior marriages of petitioner(s)
    b.   Attach certified copies of marriage certificate and divorce decrees or death certificates, if applicable
6. Proposed Order of Investigation
7.   Proposed Order of Adoption
    a.   One original and two copies
8. Certificate of Adoption
    a.   Submit 3 copies
    b.   Complete with new name of child
9. Supplemental Affidavit [signed by petitioner(s)]
    a.   Include any changes in circumstances since filing of petition
10. 22 NYCRR 603.23 and 691.23 ("OCA") Affidavit
    a.   After filing papers with court and obtaining docket number, submit original affidavit to OCA
    b.   File copy of affidavit, with original OCA receipt, with court

ALL FOREIGN DOCUMENTS SUBMITTED MUST BE PROVEN IN ACCORDANCE WITH CPLR § 4542. IF SUCH DOCUMENTS REQUIRE ENGLISH TRANSLATION, THE TRANSLATION MUST BE ACCOMPANIED BY THE TRANSLATOR'S NOTARIZED AFFIDAVIT ATTESTING TO HIS/HER QUALIFICATIONS AND TO THE ACCURACY OF THE TRANSLATION. CPLR § 2101 (B)

PLEASE SUBMIT 2 SELF-ADDRESSED, STAMPED ENVELOPES.

FORM 13-4 continued

Agency prepares and submits:

11. Certified Copy of Child's Birth Certificate
    a. Submit 2, if child is born in New York City
12. Verified Schedule
    a. Copy of subsidy agreement, if applicable
    b. Copy of child's medical history, [containing medical update within last year]
    c. SSL § 373-a Affidavit [stating that adoptive parents were provided with medical histories of child and natural parent(s), including psychological information, to the extent such histories are available]
    d. Attach copy of Interstate Compact Approval, if applicable
13. Agency Home Study
    a. Verified by appropriate official and dated
14. Proof that Child is Eligible for Adoption
    a. Surrender instruments of natural parent(s) or guardian [executed in compliance with SSL § 384 (3)]
    - Affidavit of natural parent(s) religious preference, if any
    - Affidavit of putative father acknowledging paternity and consenting to adoption, if relevant
    - Affidavit of natural parent(s)' marital history [including certified death certificate, if applicable]
    - Certified death certificate [when alleged that consent of notice is not required because of death]
    - DRL §§ 111 a and 111 affidavits, if applicable
    - Denial of paternity and waiver of notice, if applicable
    - Transfer of guardianship/custody, if applicable
    b. Certified orders terminating parental rights, including appellate disposition if any
    - DRL §§ 111 a and 111 affidavits, if applicable
    - Transfer of guardianship/custody, if applicable
    - Affidavit of no appeal [from agency or attorney of record in termination proceeding], if applicable
15. Child Abuse Clearance Form
    a. Submit current SCR clearance
    b. If adoptive parent(s) reside out of state, submit equivalent child abuse clearance from state of residence
16. Putative Father Registry Form
    a. Required in all cases where child is born ou -of wedlock
    b. Also required for in-wedlock child whose legal father denies paternity
17. Agency's Affidavit of Payment to Agency
    a. Required in all cases of surrender or termination where CSS is not involved
    b. State whether or not any fees were paid by adoptive parent(s) and, if so, set forth amounts and purposes of fees
18. New York City Notification of Order of Adoption [if child born in New York City]
19. Albany Report of Adoption [if child born outside New York City]
20. Medical Report of Adoptive Parent (s) [current, within last year]

RACE AS A FACTOR IN ADOPTIVE PLACEMENT

In Chapter 6 we learned that following *Palmore v. Sidoti* (Case 6-2) racial matching ceased to be an articulated consideration in custody disputes between parents. Race and ethnicity continue to be of concern in agency adoptions, however. Racial discrimination is outlawed by the U.S. and New York Constitutions and by Title VI of the Federal Civil Rights Act of 1964, which states that no person "shall, on ground of race, color, or national origin, be excluded from participation in, be denied the benefits of, or be subjected to discrimination under any program or activity receiving federal financial assistance." 42 U.S.C.A. § 2000d. Since all New York authorized child care agencies receive direct or indirect federal funding, they are bound by the Civil Rights Act and cannot refuse an applicant solely on the basis of race or ethnicity.

Transracial adoptions, those in which a child is placed with adoptive parents of a different race from the child, pose more complicated questions, however. Does placement with parents of the same race as the child promote a child's best interest? Do transracial adoptions cause a form of racial or ethnic genocide, by which the State contributes to the extermination of a race by giving its children to parents of another race? These issues have been hotly debated over the past generation, with the National Association of Black Social Workers taking a vocal position that Caucasian parents should not adopt African-American children.

The view that a child's ethnicity should be preserved has been incorporated into New York law in the Rules and Regulations governing adoption agencies. Agencies are mandated to make an effort to place each child in a home as similar to and compatible with his or her ethnic and racial background as possible. 18 NYCRR § 421.18. Adoption subsidies, discussed below, are also available to promote adoption of children whose ethnic background make them "hard to place." 18 NYCRR § 426.2. Priority for adoption is also based on a variety of characteristics, including race, shared by the largest number of children awaiting adoption. 18 NYCRR § 421.13.

The number of children in foster care awaiting adoption has grown exponentially in the past decade, in New York and across the nation. The national figure was said to be 500,000 in 1994. Out of concern that ethnic preference laws were contributing to the delay in placing these children for adoption, Congress passed the Multiethnic Placement Act of 1994. Under this act an agency receiving Federal funding may not deny any person the opportunity to become an adoptive parent solely on the basis of race, color, or national origin of the applicant or the adoptive child involved. Agencies are also required to develop plans for the diligent recruitment of potential adoptive families that reflect the ethnic diversity of children in the State for whom adoptive homes are needed. 42 U.S.C.A. § 622(9). At the same time, however, agencies may not delay or deny adoptive placement or otherwise discriminate in making a placement, solely on the basis of race, color, or national origin of the applicant or the child. 42 U.S.C.A. § 5115a(a)(1)(B). An agency is allowed to consider the cultural, ethnic, or racial background of the child and the capacity of the prospective foster or adoptive parents to meet the needs of a child of this background as one of a number of factors used to determine the best interests of a child.

SUBSIDY

When a child has been in foster care for a period of time before being freed for adoption, the foster parents may wish to adopt when the child becomes eligible for adoption. Usually adoption by the foster parents is in the child's best interests, because the child has bonded to the foster parents and is considered a part of the family. Some foster parents would be unable or unwilling to adopt unless they could receive a monthly payment equivalent to the foster care board rate. To encourage adoption of such children, an adoption subsidy may be provided to the adoptive parents if the child is "hard to place," "handicapped," or has special medical needs. SSL §§ 450-454. A "hard to place child" is one who has not been placed for adoption within six months from the date his guardianship and custody were committed to an authorized agency or who possesses any personal or familial attribute or problem which would be an obstacle to the child's adoption. The subsidy is paid by the New York State Department of Social Services and is equal to the monthly foster care board rate the foster parents have been receiving. In addition to the monthly subsidy, adoptive parents of such a child may be reimbursed for non-recurring adoption expenses, such as attorney fees, connected with the adoption.

EFFECTS OF ADOPTION

With limited exceptions, adoption severs all legal ties between the adoptive child and his or her birth parents. The birth parents are relieved of all parental duties toward the child, including the duty of support, but they also have no further rights with regard to the child. Adoption terminates the child's right to inherit from the birth parents, but the child acquires the right to inherit from the adoptive parents and their family members exactly as if he or she had been born into the adoptive family. Adoption does not terminate any right which may have accrued to the child prior to the adoption, however; for example, if the child's birth parent died prior to the adoption in a manner giving rise to a wrongful death claim, the child may pursue the claim after adoption.

Prior to 1991, it was well-settled law in New York that adoption severed all rights of the biological parents, including the right to visitation with the child. When the legislature amended the Social Services Law to permit conditional surrenders, discussed in Chapter 12, it did not amend the Domestic Relations Law to permit conditional orders of adoption, popularly called **"open adoptions."** The courts were then compelled to reconcile the apparent inconsistency in the two statutes. Although this problem has not yet been definitively resolved, the Appellate Division, First Department, has endorsed the reasoning of a family court judge in *Matter of Alexandra C.*, 157 Misc.2d 262, 596 N.Y.S.2d 958 (Fam.Ct. Queens County 1993) who held that the visitation provision of a conditional surrender did not create an automatic right of visitation, but rather that it conferred standing upon the biological parent to petition for post-adoption visitation. *Matter of Gerald*, 211 A.D.2d 17, 625 N.Y.S.2d 509 (1 Dept. 1995). As discussed in Chapter 12, however, the court of appeals has recently indicated that it may be prepared to reconsider this issue.

Although adoption generally cuts off the birth parents' right to have contact with the child, except that which the adoptive parents may in their discretion choose to permit, it has been held not to terminate the biological grandparents' right to petition for visitation pursuant to DRL § 72, *People ex rel. Sibley v. Sheppard*, 54 N.Y.2d 320, 445 N.Y.S.2d 420 (1981), and, similarly, of biological sibling to petition pursuant to DRL § 71, *Hatch on Behalf of Angela J v. Cortland County Dept. of Social Services*, 199 A.D.2d 765, 605 N.Y.S.2d 428 (3 Dept. 1993).

CONCLUSION

Adoption is the legal creation of a new family, and like birth itself, it entails both joy and pain. Legal practitioners who have the honor of attending at such an awe-inspiring event must assume a special duty of care to make sure the new family has a solid legal foundation. Although the labor may be long and tedious, most practitioners find it immensely satisfying. Save a corner in your office to display the photographs you will receive of the families you have helped to create.

CHAPTER REVIEW QUESTIONS

1.   The consent of which of the following would be required for the adoption of a child placed for adoption at seven months of age? Why or why not?

> A. The 16-year-old birth mother of a child born out of wedlock.
> B. The former husband of the mother, from whom she was divorced one month after the birth of the child and who is not the biological father of the child.
> C. A 15-year-old child who is being adopted by his aunt following the death of his parents.
> D. An out-of-wedlock father who lived with the mother and child and contributed to the support of the child in accordance with his means.
> E. An in-wedlock father who has filed for divorce from the mother.

F. An out-of-wedlock father who has executed a consent to the mother's surrender of the child for adoption.

2.   A young woman, whose private-placement adoption your firm handled when she was an infant, telephones the office on a day when you are assigned to field calls. She states that she has been having emotional problems and her therapist thinks it would be beneficial to her to know more about her background. She asks you to look into her old file and tell her about her birth parents and the circumstances of her adoption. What should you say?

3.   Your firm represents prospective adoptive parents of a child born out of wedlock. The mother has not identified the father of the child. What documents will you need to present to the court concerning the father?

4.   Your firm represents prospective adoptive parents of a child born in the state of Minnesota. What documents must be obtained before your firm's clients bring the child into the State of New York?

5.   A friend of your mother is caring for her grandchild, whose mother is gravely ill. The father is already deceased. She would like to adopt the child but fears that her age (62) and the fact that she receives public assistance would make an unfavorable impression on the court. She is worried that if she does not obtain proper legal rights to the child, however, another relative may try to obtain custody of the child. She asks your opinion. What should you say?

CHAPTER ASSIGNMENT

1. Draft an Order of Adoption for George and Luisa Bodden, who are adopting Maria del Angeles. In addition to the information contained in the Boddens' financial disclosure affidavit contained in the chapter, use the following facts: The Boddens' petition to adopt was verified on February 14 of last year and was filed with the court on February 18. Maria was 2 months old at the time, having been born on December 14 of the previous year in Mt. Vernon, Westchester County, New York. Both birth parents executed judicial consents on December 18, and the Boddens took Maria directly home from Tender Care Hospital on that day. The Boddens were described in glowing terms in the investigation report, and their names do not appear on the Statewide Register of Child Abuse or Maltreatment. They have named the child Jennifer Marie Bodden.

2. Prepare a checklist of personal documents a prospective adoptive parent needs to assemble. For which stages of the adoption will these documents be required?

GLOSSARY

Abandoned child: A child under the age of 18 years whose parents have not contacted, visited or supported the child for six months or more. Full legal definition SSL § 384-b(5).

Active appreciation: Increase in value of property due to the efforts of the owner or spouse of the owner.

Adjournment in contemplation of dismissal (ACD): Adjournment of a legal proceeding for a specified length of time and upon specified conditions. If the conditions are fulfilled, the proceeding is dismissed at the conclusion of the adjournment period.

Administrative hearing: A proceeding conducted before a hearing officer of a governmental agency, such as the Department of Social Services, to challenge an action or decision taken by the agency, such as the denial of an application to adopt.

Adoption by estoppel: Adoption of a child without formal statutory procedures based upon conduct or promises made that make it inequitable to deny the adoptee's claim to rights, such as support or inheritance.

Adoption information registry: A data bank maintained by the Department of Health containing the names of birth parents and adoptees who wish to get in contact with each other.

Affidavit: A written declaration of facts sworn to before a person authorized to administer an oath.

Affinity: Relationship established by law, through marriage or adoption.

Affirm: 1) Swear under the penalties of perjury. 2) Confirm, ratify or let stand the decision of a trial level court.

Affirmation: A statement of fact made under the penalties of perjury without being sworn to before a person authorized to administer an oath.

Alimony: Term in use before the equitable distribution law for support of spouse or former spouse.

Allocution: Explanation by judge to a litigant of the litigant's rights and obligations, given before an admission to charges or execution of a document such as a judicial surrender or consent to adoption.

Alternative pleading: Alleging two or more grounds for the relief requested in a complaint or petition.

Amortization: Repayment of a debt gradually through combined principal and interest payments. In the beginning most of the payment is for interest, but over time more and more is applied to principal, thus increasing the equity gradually.

Ancillary jurisdiction: Power of a court to hear certain issues only when those issues are related to other issues over which the court has original jurisdiction.

Annuity: A contract by which a person contributes a certain amount of money, after which the person is guaranteed to receive periodic payments for a specific period. Annuities are sold by insurance companies and are often used to provide the annuitant with retirement income.

Annulment: A judicial declaration that a marriage is invalid.

Antenuptial agreement: An agreement made before marriage that sets forth the rights and obligations, particularly the property and inheritance rights, of the spouses during the marriage and in the event of divorce. Requirements for enforceability in DRL § 236(B)(3).

Appellate jurisdiction: The authority of a court to decide an appeal from a trial court.

Appraised current market value: The price for which a professional appraiser has determined an asset would sell if it were offered for sale now.

Arrears: Unpaid debts, such a past-due support.

Artificial insemination: Impregnation of a woman using donated sperm which is introduced into the woman's body though a medical procedure rather than through sexual intercourse.

Authorized child care agency: An agency, association, corporation, institution, society or other organization incorporated under the laws of New York and empowered by law to care for, place out, or board children. Full legal definition SSL § 371(10).

Authorized officiant: A person, such as a judge or member of the clergy, empowered to perform a wedding ceremony.

Battered woman's syndrome: A constellation of psychological effects resulting from abuse by a spouse or domestic partner.

Bigamy: Entering into marriage while having a legal spouse still living.

Binding arbitration: Submission of a dispute to an impartial third party, rather than to a court, with the understanding that the parties will abide by the arbitrator's decision and not appeal the decision.

Bond: A debt security or IOU issued by a government agency or corporation that promises to pay a stated rate of interest and to return the face value on a specified maturity date.

Breach: Violation of a legal obligation; failure to fulfill the terms of a contract.

Broker's margin account: Securities bought on credit (margin) and left in the broker's name and possession for ease of trading.

Capital asset: Any form of property from which income can be produced

Capital gains: The increase in the value of a capital asset, usually the difference between the purchase price and the sale price.

Cash surrender value: The amount of money an insurance company will pay the holder of a life insurance policy if the policy holder terminates the policy before dying.

Cause of action: Each ground for relief alleged in a complaint or petition.

Certification: A statement by the head of a business or hospital or institution, or by a person to whom the authority has been delegated, that a business record is a true and complete record.

Certified copy: A copy of a court document that a court clerk has compared to the original and guarantees to be complete and accurate.

Chattel: A piece of personal property.

Child abuse: 1) Infliction of physical injury to a child by other than accidental means which causes or creates a substantial risk of death or serious or protracted disfigurement or impairment of physical or emotional health or losss or impairment of any bodily organ. 2) Sexual abuse of a person under 18 years of age. (See, "Sexual abuse" *infra*.) Full legal definition in FCA § 1012(e).

Child neglect: Failure to provide a child with minimally adequate food, shelter, education or supervision. Formal legal definition FCA § 1012(f).

Child protective agency: A social service agency authorized to investigate allegations of child maltreatment and to institute child protective proceedings in court.

Citation: A notice to appear in court on a specified date.

Clear and convincing evidence: A standard of proof intermediate between "fair preponderance of the evidence" and "proof beyond a reasonable doubt."

Cohabitation: Living together without benefit of marriage.

Collateral attack: An attempt to re-litigate an issue in a proceeding other than the one in which the issue was originally raised.

Combined parental income: Under the Child Support Standards Act, the income of both parents, minus statutorily allowed deductions, added together.

Combined paternity index (CPI): Ratio of genetic probability that a mother and alleged father could produce a child with certain blood characteristics compared to the likelihood of the mother and a random man producing the child.

Comity: The courts of one state or country giving effect to the laws and judicial decisions of another state or country as a matter of deference and respect, even though there is no obligation to do so.

Commodity contract: A contract to buy or sell a specific quantity and quality of a product (such as oil or wheat) in the future for an agreed-upon price. These contracts are speculative since the product may be scarce or non-existent at the agreed-upon time. The contracts themselves are traded like securities.

Community property: Property acquired during the course of a marriage in a community property jurisdiction, such as California, in which each spouse is presumed to have an undivided one-half interest.

Conclusory pleading: A complaint, petition, or answer to same that tracks the language of the statutory grounds without giving supporting details.

Concurrent jurisdiction: The equal power of two or more courts to hear the same type of case.

Conditional surrender: A surrender for adoption that contains provisions controlling behavior or rights of the agency or adoptive parents subsequent to the surrender, such as a restriction on who may adopt the child.

Confidence: Privileged information revealed by a client to an attorney in the course of the attorney-client relationship.

Conformed copy: A copy of a court document, such as an order, to which all the changes have been made so that it is exactly like the original in the court file.

Consanguinity: Relationship by blood.

Contempt: Wilful violation of a court order.

Contingent interest: An interest that may come into effect if an event occurs that is possible, but not assured.

Conversion divorce: A divorce granted upon the ground that the husband and wife have been living apart pursuant to a written separation agreement or judicial separation order for one year or more and have fully complied with the terms of the agreement or order.

Corroboration: Evidence that tends to confirm or support other evidence.

Coupon rate: The fixed rate of interest a bond pays.

Court of record: A court that is required to keep a record of its proceedings. Court proceedings may be recorded by a court reporter or mechanically recorded by a tape machine.

Creditor: One to whom a debt is owed.

Current equity: The present ownership interest in a piece of property, calculated by subtracting the total of debts or liens against the property (such a mortgage) from the current market value.

Debtor: One who owes money.

Declaratory judgment: A court order adjudicating a status or issue without giving any additional relief.

Default: 1) The failure to fulfill a legal obligation established by contract or court order. 2) Failure to appear in court when properly summoned to do so.

Deferred compensation: Salary or wages not paid to the earner at the usual time, but rather held by the employer for payment at a later time, usually upon the retirement of the employee. Taxes on deferred compensation are owed when the deferred compensation is actually paid.

Delegation: A form executed by the head of a business, hospital, or institution authorizing an employee to certify a business record.

Depreciation: An accounting device whereby a physical asset, such as a piece of land or business equipment, declines in value over its useful life. The tax consequences of depreciation are that the property owner can deduct the depreciation from income taxes each year, but must pay larger capital gains taxes when the asset is sold. When an asset has been depreciated, the basis for capital gains tax purposes is not the purchase price but the depreciated value. Thus, if an asset has been fully depreciated, capital gains tax will be owned on the entire sale price.

Derivative finding: A finding of abuse or neglect based upon likelihood of harm to the subject child premised upon proof of abuse or neglect of another child.

Diligent search: Thorough and painstaking efforts to locate a person named as a respondent or defendant in a court proceeding.

Distinguishable: Sufficiently different in essential legal characteristics so as to have no value as legal precedent.

Dividend: Distribution to stockholders of a prorata share of the earnings of the company. A dividend is income to the shareholder.

Domestic partner: A person of the same or opposite sex with whom one lives in a committed, long-term, intimate relationship.

Domicile: True, permanent abode.

Downward modification: In support law, a reduction of the support obligation.

Durational requirement: A threshold period during which certain conduct must have persisted in order to constitute a ground for court action.

Ecclesiastical: Related to the church; clerical.

Egregious fault: Odious, offensive conduct more repugnant than that which would merely provide grounds for court relief.

18-B attorney A lawyer from the Assigned Counsel Panel, paid with public funds to represent an indigent litigant.

Emancipated minor: A child who is no longer the responsibility of, nor under the control of, his or her parent.

Enjoin: Require that a person refrain or abstain from some act.

Equitable distribution: New York system by which marital property and income must be divided fairly, but not necessarily equally, upon dissolution of marriage.

Equitable estoppel: Doctrine that the conduct of a person will preclude him or her from asserting rights against another person who has justifiably relied on the conduct and who would suffer damage if the person were now allowed to assert such rights.

Equity: 1) Ownership interest. 2) A stock.

Estimated current market value: The amount for which the person completing a net worth statement thinks an asset could be sold at the time the net worth statement is being prepared usually determined by professional appraisal.

Exclusive original jurisdiction: The authority of only one court, to hear a certain type of case or rule on a particular issue.

Exhibit: 1) An item offered in evidence in a trial. 2) A document attached to a motion papers.

Exhibits list: A list of items that have been or will be offered in evidence in a trial.

Expert witness: A witness possessing knowledge about a subject not within the ken of the ordinary lay person.

Express contract: A formal contract created by the agreement of the parties.

Extrafamilial: Coming from outside the family.

Extra-judicial surrender: A surrender for adoption executed by the birth parent in a setting other than a court.

Family offense: Misconduct specified in FCA § 812 directed against a person to whom one is related by consanguinity or affinity, a former spouse, or a person with whom one has a spouse in common.

Fiduciary relationship: A legal relationship in which one party has the right to place great care and trust in the other, such as Guardian-Ward or Executor-Estate.

Foreign divorce: A divorce obtained in another state or country.

Foreign support order: An order of support obtained in another state or country.

Forensics: Medical, psychological or social evaluations performed for the purpose of litigation.

Fraud: 1) A knowing or deliberate misrepresentation about a matter that is material to the issue at hand (such as marriage) and upon which the complainant has relied to his or her detriment. 2) A failure to disclose vital information that should have been disclosed.

Full faith and credit clause: U.S. Constitution Art. IV, sec. 1; this clause requires the states to recognize the legislative acts, public records, and judicial decisions of other states.

General jurisdiction: The power of a court to hear any type of case or issue that is presented to it.

Get law: Provisions of the Domestic Relations Law that require a plaintiff in a divorce case to swear that he or she has done everything in his or her power to enable the defendant to obtain a religious divorce and that further authorize courts to take the failure to do so into account in deciding equitable distribution issues.

Good faith basis: The requirement that a complainant have some genuine reason to believe that scandalous allegations are true.

Grounds: The elements of a cause of action; the conduct of a defendant or respondent justifying judicial relief.

Guardian *ad litem*: A person appointed to represent the interest of a party to a court case when the party is under a disability such as infancy or mental incompetence.

Guardianship of the person: The legal authority to make decisions concerning the care or upbringing of a minor.

Hearing examiner: A person who is statutorily empowered to hear and decide support cases.

Hearsay evidence: Evidence obtained through some source other than the sense impressions of the witness.

Home state: The state under the Uniform Child Custody Jurisdiction Act that generally should hear a custody case, usually the state in which the child has resided for the six months immediately preceding the filing of the petition.

Human leukocyte antigen test (HLA): A type of blood test used to determine paternity.

IAS: A trial court to which a case is assigned pursuant to the Individual Assignment System.

Implied contract: A contract inferred from the conduct of the parties and the surrounding circumstances, rather than from the explicit agreement of the parties.

Imputed income: A value or monetary worth assigned for income tax or child support purposes to certain gifts or non-monetary benefits of the obligor.

In camera interview: Interview of a child by a judge in the judge's chambers or robing room.

Incest: Sexual relations between persons so closely related that the law would not permit them to marry. Full legal definition Penal Law § 255.25.

Income: Money obtained from employment, benefits, winnings, maintenance, or investments, including but not limited to salary, wages, commissions, bonuses, interest, dividends, and rental income.

Income deduction order: An order that support payment be taken directly out of the obligor's paycheck or benefits check and paid to the dependent or to a Support Collection Unit.

Income execution: A legal document requiring that a debt, such as child support, be deducted directly from the debtor's income.

Incorporated: In matrimonial proceedings, a provision that a separation agreement becomes a part of the divorce decree.

Indian child: An unmarried person under the age of 18 years who is a member of an Indian tribe or is eligible for membership in an Indian tribe and is the biological child of a member of an Indian tribe.

Initiating jurisdiction: The place where the petitioner in a Uniform Support of Dependants case lives.

In personam jurisdiction: Power of the court over the person (as opposed to the property) of a litigant.

In rem jurisdiction: Power of the court over the property, of a litigant; power to adjudicate the status of a marriage.

In vitro fertilization: Conception of a child by mixing sperm and egg in a laboratory setting, in a test tube or similar laboratory device .

Intellectual property: Rights, such as copyrights, patents, and trademarks, to obtain income from the products of one's intellectual or artistic efforts.

Intervene: To become a party to a litigation by request because the outcome of the litigation will affect on the intervenor.

Intrafamilial: Within the family.

Investigation and report (I&R): An assessment and report of the results, performed pursuant to court order, often by the Department of Social Services or Probation.

Irrebuttable: Final; not subject to challenge.

Irrevocable: Not reversible; not subject to being set aside.

Joint custody: Equally shared decision making authority over a child.

Judicial consent: Consent of a birth parent to the adoption of a child in a private adoption, executed before a judge.

Judicial separation: Legal separation granted by a judge as a result of a separation action upon grounds specified in the Domestic Relations Law.

Judicial surrender: Surrender of a child to an agency for adoption executed by a birth parent before a judge.

Kinship foster parent: A relative of a child in foster care approved to care for the child and receive foster care payments.

Lapsed placement: A court-ordered foster care placement that has not been extended before the expiration of the order of placement.

Law guardian: An attorney who represents a child as the child's lawyer. Full legal definition FCA § 242.

Lay witness: An ordinary person possessing no special knowledge about the issue in question, who is not allowed to state an opinion.

Legal presumption A statement, allegation, or averment that a court will accept as true without any proof.

Letters of guardianship: Legal papers authorizing an individual to act as guardian of a child.

Lien: An encumbrance on property for the payment of a debt.

Limited jurisdiction: The authority of a court to hear only specified types of cases.

Maintenance: Support for a spouse or former spouse. Full legal definition DRL § 236(B)(1)(a).

Mandated reporter: One who by virtue of his or her profession or occupation is required by the Social Services Law to report suspected child abuse or maltreatment to the State Central Register of Child Abuse and Maltreatment.

Marital property: Property subject to equitable distribution, presumptively including all property acquired between the date of the wedding and the filing of a matrimonial action or execution of a separation agreement, unless the property otherwise falls within the definition of separate property. Full legal definition DRL § 236(B)(1)(c).

Market value: The amount for which an asset could be sold.

Marriage: 1) Wedding ceremony. 2) The status of being legally married.

Material misrepresentation: A deliberate falsehood that goes to the heart of the matter at hand, such as the decision to marry.

Matrimonial domicile: The place where the spouses most recently lived as husband and wife.

Maturity: The specified date upon which the principal (face or par value) of a bond will be repaid.

Merged: Combined in such a way as to lose separate legal identity and enforceability.

Miscegenation: Marriage by persons of separate races.

Money judgment: A court order specifying an amount owed and permitting the creditor to collect the money using various legal remedies.

Monogamy: Having only one legal spouse at a time.

Mortgage: Legal agreement between the purchaser of a property and a financial institution or individual who lends the purchaser the money, using the property as security or collateral for the loan.

Mutual fund: A pool of money from a number of investors that is invested by a professional fund manager. The investor who purchases shares in a mutual fund becomes a part owner of the fund, but not of the securities held by the fund.

Mutual Orders of Protection: Orders of Protection issued to parties who are cross petitioners/respondents in a family offense case.

Net average value (NAV): The market value or price of a mutual fund share calculated daily by adding the value of all the securities in the fund's portfolio, subtracting liabilities, and dividing that by the number of shares outstanding. To learn the price of a share of a mutual fund, check the NAV column by the fund's name in the financial pages of a newspaper or on the Internet.

Net worth statement: An affidavit, required in most litigation concerning support or property division, showing the litigant's income, assets, and debts. The individual's net worth is the excess of his or her assets over liabilities. *Nisi prius* **court:** Original or trial-level court.

Note: A short term credit security that is like a bond except that it is generally payable in one month to three years.

Notice of entry: Legal document, usually served by the winning party in a law suit, informing the other parties that the final court order has been signed.

Nuclear family: Mother, father and their children

Objection: Document by which a party to a support case decided by a hearing examiner requests that a judge review the hearing examiner's order.

Open Adoption: An adoption in which it is contemplated that the birth parent may continue to have some form of contact, perhaps including visitation, with the child after the adoption.

"Opt out": Waiver of the provisions of the equitable distribution law or the Child Support Standard Act by agreement, such as in an antenuptial or separation agreement.

Oral report transmittal (ORT) A report of suspected child abuse or maltreatment; also called a "2221."

Order of filiation: An order adjudicating who is the father of a child born out of wedlock.

Original jurisdiction: Authority of a court to hear and decide a case.

Parens patriae: The authority of a court or other governmental agency acting in a protective or benevolent capacity.

Paroled: Released under the supervision of the court pending further orders of the court.

Par value: The principal or face value of a bond.

Passive appreciation: Increase in value of an asset that occurs due to market forces or inflation, without the efforts of the property owner.

Paternity: Fatherhood.

Payroll deduction order: An income deduction order specifically pertaining to deductions from the support obligor's paycheck.

Pendente lite **motion:** An application to the court for relief such as temporary support and temporary custody of children pending the final outcome of the litigation.

Permanency goal: The child care agency's long-term objective for getting a child out of foster care.

Permanent neglect: Failure of the parent of a child in foster care to plan for the discharge of the child from foster care or to visit the child regularly while in foster care. Full legal definition SSL § 384-b(7).

Person legally responsible: A person who may be charged with child abuse or neglect by virtue of being found regularly or at continuous intervals in the child's home or having acted as the functional equivalent of a parent to the child, and having contributed to the abuse or neglect of the child. Full legal definition FCA § 1012(g).

Personal jurisdiction: Power of the court over a defendant or respondent in a court proceeding.

Personal knowledge: Information acquired directly through one's own senses.

Physical abuse: Inflicting or allowing to be inflicted serious physical injury or risk of same on a child under the age of 18 years. Full legal definition FCA § 1012(e)(I); (ii).

Polygamous: Having more than one wife at a time.

Positive toxicology report: Report by a medical laboratory, based upon testing of blood or urine, indicating the presence of drugs in a person's system.

Postnuptial agreement: Agreement entered into after marriage.

Post-traumatic stress disorder: A constellation of symptoms resulting from exposure to an extremely frightening or painful experience.

Preclusion: Making something impossible.

Prenuptial agreement: See "Antenuptial agreement" *infra*.

Presumption: A statement, allegation or averment that a court will accept as true without any evidence being presented.

Presumption of legitimacy: The legal presumption that a child conceived or born during the course of a marriage is the child of the mother's husband.

Preventive services: Social services intended to forestall or shorten foster care placement.

Primary source: Statute or published judicial opinion.

Private-placement adoption: Adoption of a child arranged directly between the birth parents and the adoptive parents without agency intervention.

Probability of paternity: The likelihood that a particular man is the father of a child as compared to a random man of the same ethnic background.

Profit sharing: A form of compensation based upon an employee's receipt of a percentage of the profits of the business.

Progress notes: Chronological entries in the case record of a child protective agency or child care agency summarizing the caseworkers' contacts with persons involved in the case.

Property: Anything that can be owned or possessed.

Prorata share: Each parent's percentage of the child support obligation.

Putative father registry: Data bank maintained by the New York State Department of Social Services containing the names of men adjudicated or acknowledged to be the fathers of out-of-wedlock children, as well as those men who have claimed paternity of a child by filing with the registry.

Qualified domestic relations order: A court order directing that a former spouse is to receive a portion of the other spouse's pension directly from the pension plan.

Rebuttable: Subject to being challenged or disproved.

Recital: A formal statement of the facts relied upon by the parties in entering into an agreement.

Referee: A person to whom a judge refers a case to take testimony and to file a report with the court.

Referral jurisdiction: The power of a court to hear a certain type of case or issue in a case if another court sends the case or issue to it.

Remand: 1) Temporary court placement of a child in foster care before the final disposition of the case. 2) Action of an appellate court in sending a case back to the lower court for further proceedings.

Residence: The place where a person is living.

Responding jurisdiction: The place where the respondent in a USDL proceeding lives.

Restraining notice: A legal document prohibiting an organization, such as a bank, from disbursing funds held for a debtor against whom a judgment has been entered.

Retroactive arrears: Money owed for support from a specified point prior to the entry of the final order of support.

Return of process date: The date specified in a summons or citation for the defendant or respondent to appear in court.

Reverse: Overturn the decision of a trial court.

Royalties: Payment to the author or composer of a percentage of the sales price of each copy sold of a book or musical composition.

Secondary source: Any book or article about law other than a statute or judicial decision, such as a treatise or law review article.

Secret: Private information about a client, acquired by an attorney in the course of the attorney's representation of the client, which the client would not want to have publicly disclosed.

Security: Any financial instrument that signifies an ownership or debt interest, such as a stock or bond.

Security deposit: The sum of money a renter pays to the landlord to guarantee future payment of the rent.

Seizure: To take possession of property through confiscation or impoundment.

Self-support reserve: The amount of money a low-income child support obligor is allowed to keep for his or her own needs.

Separate property: Property acquired before marriage or through gift or inheritance and property acquired in exchange for separate property or through passive appreciation of separate property. Full legal definition DRL § 236(B)(1)(d).

Separation agreement: A formal agreement entered into when spouses plan to live apart and possibly to divorce, setting forth the rights and obligations of each spouse during the period of separation and in the event of divorce. Requirements for enforceability DRL § 236(B)(3).

Sequestration: Attachment of property or funds pending the outcome of a litigation.

Severability clause: A clause in a contract or agreement stating that if one portion of the contract is declared invalid, the remaining portions shall continue to be effective.

Sexual abuse: Committing or allowing to be committed upon a child under the age of 18 years a sex offense as defined in the Penal Law. Full legal definition FCA § 1012(e)(iii).

Share: A unit of stock representing ownership in a corporation.

Sole custody: The right of one individual to make all decisions concerning a child and to provide care for the child.

Specific performance: A remedy for breach of contract whereby the defaulting party is ordered to perform the contract according to its precise terms.

Specific pleading: Alleging details in a complaint or petition concerning the wrongful conduct of the defendant or respondent.

Standby guardian: A person who is authorized to take over as a child's guardian if the parent should die or become incapacitated.

Standing: The right to bring a particular type of legal proceeding or to raise a particular issue within a proceeding.

Status: A person's legal relation to the rest of the community.

Statute of limitations: The period of time after which a legal proceeding cannot be initiated based upon a particular event.

Stipulation: A voluntary agreement between parties to a litigation concerning some matter relevant to the litigation, so that evidence does not have to be introduced about that matter.

Stock: A unit of ownership in a company. The value of a share of stock in a publically traded company can be ascertained by consulting the financial pages of a newspaper or on the Internet. To find it, however, you must know the company's abreviation and on which stock exchange it is traded.

Stock option: The right, but not the obligation, to buy or sell a specified number of shares of stock at a specified time and price. Like commmodieties contracts, stock options are themselves traded independently of the stocks to which the option relates.

Subject matter jurisdiction: The authority of a court to decide a certain type of case or issue within a case.

Summons: A notice to appear in court on a specified date.

Summons with notice: A summons in a matrimonial procceding accompanied by a statement of all the forms of relief the plaintiff will seek in the proceeding.
Support Collection Unit: Offices operated by the Department of Social Services for the collection, disbursement, and accounting of support payments.

Surrender: Legal document signed by a birth parent committing the care and custody of a child to an authorized child care agency for the purposes of adoption.

Tax exempt: Not subject to income tax.

Tax shelter: An investment whose primary benefit to the owner is the tax deductions it provides.

Testamentary guardian: A guardian of a child appointed by will.

Title: Right of ownership as evidenced by a deed or certificate of title.

Tracing: The process by which separate property is followed in its various forms throughout the course of a marriage.

Trial discharge: Conditional release of a child from foster care under the supervision of a child care agency for a period which is generally three months. During the trial period, the agency can take the child back into foster care without having to initiate a new court proceeding or obtain a new voluntary placement agreement.

Trial outline: A written summary of the witnesses and evidence to be presented in a litigation.

Trial stipulation: An agreement that certain issues will not be litigated in a trial.

Trust fund: An arrangement whereby money is given to one person -- a trustee -- to manage and pay out income for the benefit of specified beneficiaries.

Unallocated support: Child support and maintenance added together without specification of how much of the payment is for child support and how much for maintenance.

Unconscionable: So oppressive, one-sided, or unfair as to be dishonorable and legally unenforceable.

Undertaking: Money deposited as security against possible future default in support payments.

Undomiciled: Homeless.

Uniform case record: A record maintained by a child care or child protective agency documenting all contacts the agency's employees have with, or on behalf of, the family to whom services are being rendered.

Upon information and belief: Based upon reasonably reliable hearsay information.

Upward modification: Increase in support payments.

Validation: An evaluation by a mental health professional to ascertain whether a child is suffering from psychological symptoms consistent with having been sexually abused.

Venue: The county or geographical location in which a court having subject matter jurisdiction should hear a case.

Verified: Sworn to by the petitioner or plaintiff.

Vested interest: A benefit to which a person has an assured right, although the benefit may not be paid until some future time.

Void: Having no legal force or effect.

Voidable: Subject to cancellation; nullifiable.

Voluntary acknowledgment of paternity: A sworn statement by the father of an out-of-wedlock child that he is the father of the child.

Voluntary placement agreement: A written agreement executed by the custodian of a child placing the child in foster care.

Willful default: 1) Failure to appear in court after having been duly served with process. 2) Deliberate failure to perform a legal obligation.

Withdrawal without prejudice: Removing a case from a court's docket without a determination on the merits, so that the case may be restored to the calendar in the future if necessary.

Without prejudice: The issue is not judicially decided and may be litigated in the future.

Witness sheet: A list of persons who will testify in a court proceeding with a summary of each persons expected testimony.

Yield: The rate at which an investment pays out interest or dividend income. Yield is calculated by dividing the amount actually paid for the investment (such as a share of stock or a bond) by the amount paid in dividends or interest.

INDEX

A

G

Gains, Capital, 282
Gains, Capital, Tax on, 282-283
Garnishment, 225
Gender Neutralization,
    of Sexual Offenses, 20
    of Support, 15-16, 197
General Jurisdiction, 44
Genetic Marker Tests, 197
Georgia, 10
Gestational Mother, 10
Get, 139
Get Law, 139, 143
Gift, 271
Goal, Permanency, 375, 381
Goals of Client, 50
Good Faith Basis, 137
Governing Law Clause, 97
Grandparent Visitation, 2, 193-
    194, 435
Gross Income, Adjusted, 204, 283
Grounds, 42, 43, 63
Grounds, Fault, 113, 123
Grounds for Annulment, 72-75
Grounds for Divorce, 122-133,
    144
Grounds for Family Offense,
    320-321
Grounds for Judicial Separation,
    109
Grounds for Termination of
    Parental Rights, 386-391
Grounds, No-Fault, 113, 130,
    132
Guardian,
    Law, 40, 42, 122, 168,
    169, 171, 350, 351, 354,
    399
    Standby, 183
    Testamentary 183,
Guardian *ad Litem*, 143, 168
Guardian of the Person, 183
Guardianship, 51, 58, 183
    Commitment of,
    Letters of, 183
    Temporary Order of,

428, 429
Guidelines, Agency Adoptions,
    430, 431
Guidelines, Child Support, 207,
    234
Guidelines, Matrimonial Part,
    123, 124
Guilty Spouse, 144

H

H.L.A., 293-297, 299
Habeas Corpus, Writ of, 178,
    302
    Form, 179
Hague Convention, 189
Harassment, 320, 331, 333
Health, 204
Health Insurance, 217, 332, 413
Hearing, 59
Hearing Examiner, 199, 241
Hearsay Evidence, 328, 350,
    356, 357, 361, 365, 399
Heart Balm, 65
Heir, 44
Historical Notes, 51
Home Environment, 170
Home, Foster, 350
Home State, 184
Homemaker, 246
Homosexuality, 68
Human Leukocyte Antigen Test,
    293-297
Husband Abuse, 313
Husband-Wife Privilege, 5, 361,
    392

I

I&R, 59, 365
I.A.S., 44
I.D.O., 225
I.R.S., 231, 283
Identification of Marital
    Property, 248-251
Illegitimacy, 31, 306
Illicit Sexual Relations, 66

No-Fault Divorce, 113, 130, 132
Nonage, 72
Nondisclosure, Financial, 52
Non-marital Partners, 66-67, 201
Nonmolestation Clause, 97
Nonsupport, 109
Nonsupport, Criminal, 240
Non-Traditional Families, 4-9
Non-Vested Pension Rights, 279
Notarization, 142, 238, 271, 384
Notebook, Trial, 369-370
Notes of Decisions, 51
Not-for-Profit Agencies, 40, 41
Not-for-Profit Sector, 40, 41
Notice of Entry, 401
Notice of Intent to Claim
        Paternity, 420
Notice of Issue, 122,
Notice Only Fathers, 419
Notice, Summons with, 136
Notice, UCCJA, 188
Notification Concerning an Order
        of Filiation, 302
Notification of Order of
        Adoption, 423
Nuclear Family, 4
Nurses, 343

O

Objections to Hearing
        Examiner's Order 200,
        229-230
Objections, 44, 49
Obligation, Ethical, 50
Occupational License, 237
Offense, Family, 2, 51, 58
Officiant, Authorized, 67
Oklahoma, 10
Open Adoption, 384, 434
Operation of Law, 66, 76
Opting Out
        of Child Support, 91,
        200, 223
        of Equitable Distribution,
        76, 81, 200, 245
Oral Report Transmittal, 343

Order of Adoption, 423, 424
Order of Filiation, 31, 291, 292,
        302, 304, 305
Order of Protection, 157, 318,
        327, 328-333
Order of Protection, Form, 329-
        330
Order to Show Cause, 178
Order, Void, 44
Orders of Protection Registry,
        Statewide, 331
Original Jurisdiction, 44, 45
Out-of-Court Statements,
        of Child, 361-365
Out-of-Wedlock Children, 31,
        287, 302, 306
Out-of-Wedlock Fathers, 415-420
Outline, Trial, 369, 386
Overreaching, 81,82, 113

P

P.D.O., 225
PINS, 32, 58, 320, 367
PKPA, 188
PLI, 54
Page, Copyright, ii
Paralegal Associations, National
        Federation of, 54
Paralegal Ethics, 56-57
Paralegal Tasks and Skills, 42-56
Paralegal Supervision, 56
Paramour, 345
Parens Patriae, 30, 72, 91, 92,
        155
Parent, Psychological, 176
Parents, Foster, 177, 401, 412,
        413, 434
Parental Consent to Marriage,
        68, 72
Parental Fitness, 30, 73
Parental Kidnapping Prevention
        Act, 188
Parental Rights, Termination of,
        40, 42, 58, 59, 177, 302,
        367, 380, 381, 384-403

Stipulation, 153, 154, 276
Stock, 252
Structure of N.Y. Child Welfare
    System, 60
Subject Matter Jurisdiction, 42,
    43-48, 198
Subpoena, 233
Subsidy, Adoption, 434
Substance Abuse, 357, 369
Substituted Service, 136
Suffrage, Women's, 26-27
Summons with Notice, 136
Supervised Visitation, 190
Supervision by Agency, 354,
    366, 367
Supervision of Paralegal, 56
Support, 50, 51, 58, 134, 197-
    241, 320, 367
Support, Child, 29, 31, 32, 205-
    232
Support Collections Unit, 225,
    228, 231, 236, 238
Support, Direct Payment of, 228
Support, Duty to, 2, 90, 200,
    205, 219, 288, 302, 434
Support Enforcement, 237-241
Support Guidelines, Child, 207
Support, Modification of, 90,
    232-236
Support Procedures, 228-230
Support, Spousal, 90-91, 200-
    205
Support, Unallocated, 231
Support, Waiver of, 81, 90 198
Supreme Court, New York, 44
    86, 189, 199, 206
Supreme Court Terminology, 59
Supreme Court, United States, 55
Surnames, Change of, 145, 288
Surrender for Adoption, 51, 173,
    177, 382-384
        Conditional, 383, 434
Surrogacy Agreement, 429
Surrogacy Brokers, 429
Surrogate Parenting, 429
Surrogate's Court, 45, 46, 183
Surrogate's Court Procedure Act,

    45, 52, 183, 386
Suspended Judgment, 328, 366,
    400
Suspension of Firearms Permit,
    325, 332
Suspension of Licenses, 237,
    239-240
Syndrome, Battered Woman's,
    315-317
Syndrome, Post-traumatic Stress,
    315, 316
System, N.Y. Child Welfare, 60
System, N.Y. Court, 41, 44, 45

T

392 Reviews, 379
1055-a Reviews, 381
Table, Terminology, 59
Table, Terms, Shorthand, 59
Tax Basis, 283
Tax Brackets, 205, 231
Tax Consequences of Child
    Support, 231-232
Tax Consequences of Equitable
    Distribution, 282-284
Tax Consequences of
    Maintenance, 204-205
Tax Exemption, 232
Tax Impacting, 283
Tax Refund Intercept, 237
Tax Return, 204
Tax Returns, Preparation of, 57
Taxable Gain, 282, 283
Technologies, Reproductive, 9-10
Temporary Custody, 318
Temporary Order
    of Guardianship, 428,
    429
    of Protection, 321
    of Support, 229, 268,
    328
Tender Years Doctrine, 154
Tennessee, 10
Termination of Parental Rights,
    40, 42, 58, 59, 177, 302,
    367, 380, 381, 384-403